ECSCW 2007

Liam J. Bannon • Ina Wagner • Carl Gutwin •
Richard H.R. Harper • Kjeld Schmidt
Editors

ECSCW 2007

Proceedings of the 10th European Conference on
Computer-Supported Cooperative Work, Limerick,
Ireland, 24-28 September 2007

 Springer

Liam J. Bannon
University of Limerick, Ireland

Ina Wagner
Technical University of Vienna, Austria

Carl Gutwin
University of Saskatchewan, Canada

Richard H.R. Harper
Microsoft Research Cambridge, UK

Kjeld Schmidt
IT University of Copenhagen, Denmark

British Library Cataloguing in Publication Data
A catalogue record for this book is available from the British Library

ISBN-13: 978-1-84996-707-5   e-ISBN-13: 978-1-84800-031-5

Printed on acid-free paper

9 8 7 6 5 4 3 2 1

Springer Science+Business Media
springer.com

Table of Contents

Table of Contents

Table of Contents

From the editors

This volume represents the proceedings of ECSCW'07, the 10th European Conference on Computer Supported Cooperative Work, held in Limerick, Ireland. This is a significant milestone for our field, an multidisciplinary research community focusing on the understanding and technical augmentation of cooperative work practices embracing the social, technical, and design sciences. With the emergence of ubiquitous and mobile computing, new challenges have been presented to the research community in terms of how we conceptualize and investigate augmented work practices, but the issues of communication, coordination and collaboration within our working lives remain as core concerns for our field, as can be seen in the papers presented here.

The full papers presented in this volume have been selected from a pool of 123 full length paper submissions of excellent quality, making for a difficult, and lengthy, reviewing process. The relatively small number of paper acceptances demonstrates a commitment to high quality and to maintaining a single-track conference programme format, as a way of ensuring a shared awareness among the community of the latest research activity in the field. We are sure that you will find the papers of interest, and a significant contribution to the general CSCW field.

Many people have worked hard to ensure the success of this event, and we wish to briefly acknowledge them here:

All the authors who submitted high-quality papers to the Conference, thus ensuring the overall quality of the event.

All of those who contributed to the conference through taking part in workshops, master-classes, panels, demonstrations, posters, etc.

The Programme Committee and the external reviewers, who gave of their time and energy to perform a selfless task to a very high standard.

The Organizing Committee, who did trojan work behind the scenes to make everything work smoothly, on time and within budget.

The student volunteers who provide support throughout the event.

The many sponsors and supporters of ECSCW'07 for their contributions to the conference and the community more generally.

Liam Bannon, Ina Wagner,
Carl Gutwin, Richard Harper, and Kjeld Schmidt

ECSCW 2007 Conference Committee

Conference Co-chairs:

Liam Bannon, University of Limerick, Ireland
Ina Wagner, Technical University of Vienna, Austria

Program Co-chairs:

Richard Harper, Microsoft Research Cambridge, UK
Carl Gutwin, University of Saskatchewan, Canada

Conference Committee:

Workshops:
Mark Rouncefield, Lancaster University, UK
Demos & Videos:
Annette Aboulafia, University of Limerick, Ireland
Posters:
David Pinelle, University of Nevada Las Vegas, USA
Doctoral Colloquium:
Alex Taylor, Microsoft Research Cambridge, UK
Susanne Bødker, University of Aarhus, Denmark

Organizing Committee:

Local Arrangements:
Gabriela Avram, University of Limerick, Ireland
Luigina Ciolfi, University of Limerick, Ireland
Anne Murphy, University of Limerick, Ireland
Student Volunteers:
Michael Cooke, University of Limerick, Ireland
Emanuela Mazzone, University of Central Lancashire, UK
Anders Sigfridsson, University of Limerick, Ireland

ECSCW 2007 Program Committee

Liam Bannon, University of Limerick, Ireland

Susanne Bødker, University of Aarhus, Denmark

Barry Brown, Glasgow University, UK

Peter Carstensen, IT University of Copenhagen, Denmark

Monica Divitini, NTNU Trondheim, Norway

Geraldine Fitzpatrick, University of Sussex, UK

Connor Graham, University of Melbourne, Australia

Nicholas Graham, Queen's University, Canada

Christine Halverson, IBM, USA

Jon Hindmarsh, King's College London, UK

Shahram Izadi, Microsoft Research Cambridge, UK

Oskar Juhlin, Interactive Institute, Sweden

Dave Kirk, University of Nottingham, UK

Kari Kuutti, University of Oulu, Finland

Hideaki Kuzuoka, University of Tsukuba, Japan

Du Li, Texas A&M, USA

Paul Luff, King's College London, UK

David Macdonald, University of Washington, USA

Gary Marsden, University of Cape Town, South Africa

Andrew Monk, University of York, UK

Michael Muller, IBM, USA

Kenton O'Hara, HP Labs, UK

Mark Perry, Brunel University, UK

Volkmar Pipek, University of Siegen, Germany

Wolfgang Prinz. Fraunhofer, FIT, Germany

Dave Randall, Manchester Metropolitan University, UK

Mark Rouncefield, Lancaster University, UK

Nicolas Roussel, Université Paris-Sud (LRI) & INRIA Futurs, France

Colston Sanger, London South Bank University, UK

Albrecht Schmidt, Ludwig-Maximilians-University Munich, Germany

Kjeld Schmidt, IT University of Copenhagen, Denmark

Carla Simone University of Milano-Bicocca, Italy

Danae Stanton Fraser, University of Bath, UK

John Tang, IBM, USA

Alex Taylor, Microsoft Research Cambridge, UK

Ina Wagner Technical University of Vienna, Austria

Leon Watts, University of Bath, UK

Volker Wulf, University of Siegen, Germany

External reviewers

Sandrine Balbo

Richard Banks

Peter Benda

Giorgio de Michelis

Mattias Esbjörnsson

Beki Grinter

Pamela Hinds

Claudia Ignat

Anab Jain

Anders Mørch

Leysia Palen

Wally Smith

David Sun

Bettina Törpel

Alexandra Weilenmann

L. Bannon, I. Wagner, C. Gutwin, R. Harper, and K. Schmidt (eds.).
ECSCW'07: Proceedings of the Tenth European Conference on Computer Supported Cooperative Work, 24-28 September 2007, Limerick, Ireland
© Springer 2007

What Did I Miss? Visualizing the Past through Video Traces

Michael Nunes[1], Saul Greenberg[1], Sheelagh Carpendale[1] and Carl Gutwin[2]

[1]University of Calgary, Calgary, AB, T2N 1N4 Canada
[2]University of Saskatchewan, Saskatoon, SK, S7N 5C9 Canada
{saul, nunes, sheelagh}@cpsc.ucalgary.ca, gutwin@cs.ususk.ca

Abstract. Always-on media spaces broadcast video between collaborators to provide mutual awareness and to encourage casual interaction. This video can be easily recorded on the fly as a *video trace*. Ostensibly, people can review this video history to gain a better idea of the activities and availability of their collaborators. Such systems are obviously highly contentious, as they raise significant privacy concerns. However, the ease of capturing video means that video trace systems will appear in the near future.

To push the boundaries and encourage debate about video trace technologies within the CSCW community, we created TIMELINE, a highly effective visualization system that combines ideas in *slit scanning* as used in interactive art to allow people to easily and rapidly explore a video history in detail. We describe its design and implementation, and begin the debate by offering preliminary reflections on how it can be used and misused. To encourage this debate, TIMELINE is freely available for others to try.

Introduction

Video media spaces (VMS) are always-on video channels that connect people and places (e.g., Bly 1993; McEwan 2005). Their primary purpose is to provide collaborators with awareness that leads to casual interaction. Once the subject of esoteric research requiring specialized equipment and networks (Bly 1993), the wide availability of inexpensive web cameras combined with the Internet and powerful home computers now let people easily create their own media spaces.

Researchers have argued that VMS are valuable for distributed groups with a real need or desire to recreate the kinds of interactions that normally happen when they physically work close to one another (e.g., Kraut, Egido and Galegher 1990; Whittaker, Frolich, and Daly-Jones 1994). The video acts as a surrogate for inter-personal proximity by bringing distant people closer together: one can see other people's presence and activity over the video channel. This interpersonal aware-ness creates opportunities for people to engage in light-weight casual interactions through the video channel at (hopefully) appropriate times and in an appropriate manner. While such always-on video raises an Orwellian specter of Big Brother, VMS are increasingly accepted by everyday computer users, e.g., when friends stay connected with one another for long periods of the day through the free digi-tal video capabilities of some Instant Messengers, or when small communities share a collective *n*-way media space through experimental systems such as the COMMUNITY BAR (McEwan and Greenberg 2005).

Video is quite good at providing rich 'at-a-glance' awareness of activities of others, which in turn lets people estimate availability for conversation. The prob-lem is that video still misses much when compared to everyday situations where people co-habit a space (Hudson and Smith 1996). Most importantly, video de-mands *foreground attention*, while in everyday life people notice the activities of others in the *background periphery of attention*: for example, people see others as they walk by and their comings and goings, and they hear the sounds they make. That is, VMS only works if people are looking at their computer screen. The re-sult is that people who use VMS do not get as good a sense of others' activities over time, which in turn affects how they can interpret what others are doing and how available they are for conversation.

To partially solve the problems of current VMS, Hudson and Smith (1996) suggest that media spaces could be augmented by giving people a visualization that displays the recent patterns of activities – the *activity history* – of others, which also reveals rhythms in people's behaviors over time (Begole et. al. 2002).

One way to reveal this activity history is through a *video trace* – a video his-tory visualization that reveals important media space events over time, and that also allows easy inspection of those events. Using video is powerful, as the raw images potentially provide a more expressive record of past activity when com-pared to abstracted activity information (see §Related Work). Video is captured as it arrives (a simple matter with current computer technologies), and is recon-structed as an interactive visualization that reveals an overview of the video his-tory. The idea is that people can infer relevant patterns in the visualization, and even explore it in detail to acquire a better idea of the past activities of their col-laborators and what it suggests about their current availability.

Video trace systems are obviously highly contentious, as they raise significant privacy concerns. Brief embarrassing or private actions are now captured, easily found and replayed at full fidelity. Previously hidden time-based work patterns are revealed, such as how many hours someone is actually working over a day. While some would argue that we should not encourage research in this area, we strongly believe that the simplicity of the idea along with the ease of capturing video means that – useful or not – video trace systems will appear in the near future, e.g., created and disseminated by grass roots developers, or included in commercial products such as Instant Messaging systems, or marketed for domestic surveillance. The real problem is that there has been little debate about such systems. Part of this problem is that prior video trace prototypes do not provide the richness necessary to really explore their expected uses (see §Related Work). Consequently, they do not incite detailed debate about their expected uses, and the tradeoffs between awareness-gathering needs and privacy.

To push the boundaries and encourage debate about video trace technologies within CSCW and other communities, we created TIMELINE: a highly revealing visualization system that allows people to easily and rapidly explore a video history in detail. As we will see, TIMELINE applies the overview and detail approach from information visualization to *slit scanning* as used in interactive arts. In subsequent sections, we describe TIMELINE's design and implementation so others can replicate it, and how it relates to prior work. We then begin the debate by offering preliminary reflections, people's reactions to it, as well as potential uses and abuses. To encourage further debate, TIMELINE is available for others to try: http://grouplab.cpsc.ucalgary.ca/cookbook/ (select TimeLine in the sidebar).

Finally, while our own motivation was to see how TIMELINE provides additional awareness cues in a media space (something not yet proven), it is not constrained to this domain. Indeed, the debate has ramifications to other domains that could find video trace technology valuable.

TimeLine

The TIMELINE visualization of a video history trace lets people do the following:
a) immediately see patterns of activity within a video history via a technique called slit-scanning;
b) use minute, hour, day and week visualizations to present longitudinal overviews views of the history at different time granularities;
c) explore patterns across different parts of the scene by moving the slit;
d) rapidly explore event details within a large video stream by scrubbing;
e) retrieve further details of the far past by selecting times of interest.

This section describes these features. We stress that the static images in this paper are a poor substitute for actually using the system. We highly recommend that viewers either try our download or watch our on-line companion video (Nunes, et. al., 2006, also at http://grouplab.cpsc.ucalgary.ca/papers/). As well, we recommend viewing the paper's images in color (electronic PDF or color printing) *vs.* as a grey-scale printout.

Slit scanning

TIMELINE uses an existing technique based on *slit scanning* (Levin 2006, Davidhazy 2007) to create a composite image of video activities over time. Slit scanning, originally developed in photography (see   §Related

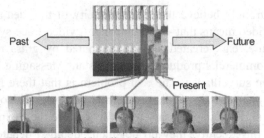

Figure 1. How video slices implement slit scanning.

Work), exposes film to only a narrow slit from a scene; while panning the camera smoothly captures a normal scene, interesting images are created by irregular panning (spatially distorted scenes), or when objects moving in the scene are seen as motion over space. The same approach is realized in video by *video slicing*.

Video slicing first extracts a scan line from a video frame, and then adds that line to a composite image over time. Figure 1 illustrates this process over 5 frame sequences. To exaggerate the effect, we illustrate a slice that is several pixels wide and ~1 second intervals between sequences. The same area in each frame is extracted from the captured video frames (red boxes, bottom), and added to the right side of the composite image (top). Thus the top image portrays a pattern showing an empty room (first 7 slices), and then the person arriving in the room and sitting down behind the camera. Slices need not be vertical.

TIMELINE, illustrated in Figure 2, implements video slicing using 1 pixel wide vertical slices captured at 17 frames per second (fps) to give a smooth scanning effect. The full-sized real-time video stream, shown at the bottom left of the Figure 2, is displayed within a floating window. The vertical red line within that window is the *slit focus bar*, and specifies which pixel column slice is being extracted from the video frame. The slice is added to the right side of the top row. In this case the face is 'blurred' as the person is moving back and forth across the scan line during capture.

Minute, Hour, Day and Week Visualizations

Somewhat similar to the Last Clock (Angesleva and Cooper 2005), a week-long timepiece is created by selectively adding slices at different time intervals to other rows. In this way, TIMELINE shows the last minute (1st row), hour (2nd row), day (3rd row), and week (4th row) of captured video. This process is done continuously. Thus the visualization itself, in combination with the dynamics of how new frames are added to it over time, gives viewers an overview of the short- and long-terms rhythms of activity across the composite image.

Each row captures different granularities of video frames, which means a single slice (especially in the week row) can actually represent many frames collected in a large interval of time. In these cases, and as described in

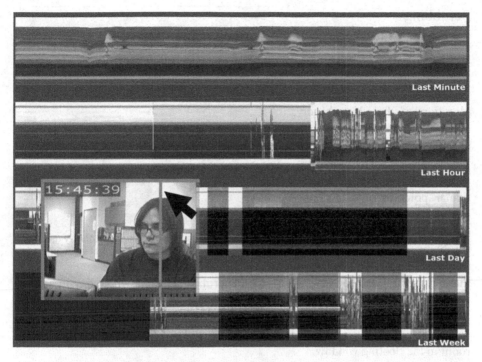

Figure 2. TIMELINE in action. The video history shows a personal workspace over several days.

§Implementation, TIMELINE uses an image differencing method that chooses the most information-rich frame to display from the many available frames.

Adjusting the Slit

One way in which TIMELINE extends on previous systems such as the Last Clock (Angesleva and Cooper 2005) is by allowing viewers to adjust the focus area of the slit. As mentioned above, the red line is the slit focus bar, which indicates the column from which the video slices are taken. Viewers can interactively focus the visualization on a different area of the scene by moving the slit focus bar over a new column in the video frame. As the bar is being moved, the entire visualization is updated immediately and smoothly. Thus one can 'scan' the scene, where interesting patterns emerge within the minute, hour, day and week rows as the bar is moved. For example, Figure 3 illustrates the same overview as Figure 2. Here, the viewer has moved the slit focus bar over the doorway in order to see people as they come and go. The visualization clearly shows this activity, where slow scans of moving people are seen as they enter and leave in the minute row. The hour row shows the same activity around the doorway, except that the movement is compacted into single columns of activity. That is, they are seen as 'disturbances' in the hour timeline.

Scrubbing

Another significant difference between TIMELINE and other systems is that TIMELINE allows for very rapid and detailed exploration of the video history. When a person drags the mouse to move the cursor across any of the visualization rows, the corresponding video taken at that particular point in time is rapidly displayed in the floating window. For example, quickly scrubbing over the entire day row will replay the events of

Figure 3. Moving the slit focus bar immediately updates the visualization. The cursor is also scrubbing a time.

that day at the same speed, i.e., a 1 second scrub replays the whole day in a second. Scrubbing is illustrated in Figure 3, where the viewer is scrubbing back and forth over an image of a person in the minute row (under the cursor and as indicated by the translucent band) to see replay details of that person entering the room in the floating window.

This scrubbing capability of TIMELINE is important, and distinguishes it as an awareness system. The constructed visualization lets people notice activities, variations and disturbances in the scene over different time scales, as represented in the minute, hour, day and week rows. Quickly scrubbing over an area of interest reveals the actual activity that produced that visual. That is, the visualization provides an overview of activity during the week, while scrubbing lets people quickly investigate details of possible interest.

Retrieving Details of the Far Past

Scrubbing the minute view always shows all stored frames, which were captured at 17 fps. To see beyond the last minute, one must move to the hour/day/week rows. However, the video sampling rate and thus the granularity of the playback detail in these rows is much coarser than in the minute row, as more time elapses between selectable frames. In TIMELINE, for example, each slice in the hour row actually represents about 3.3 seconds of activity. In other words, while 56 frames were seen by the system in these 3.3 seconds, only 1 is stored in the hour view. Similarly, each day slice represents 1 1/3 minutes (1344 frames), and each week slice about 9 1/3 minutes (9408 frames). Scrubbing will show the frame represented by that slice, but not the others within that interval. Yet those other frames could be important for understanding what is going on.

To remedy this, TIMELINE provides detailed exploration of the distant past by allowing a person to select an area of interest by right clicking in one of the coarser-grained rows, illustrated in Figure 4. TIMELINE then retrieves the detailed video around that time period, populates the more detailed rows with that video, and freezes the visualization to show how it would have

Figure 4. Regions in coarser grained rows can be selected for detailed exploration in the finer grained rows.

appeared during that moment in time. Figure 4 shows a person selecting a time of interest in the day row (cursor, far left). The detailed frames around that time period are retrieved and used to populate the hour and minute rows. Feedback to show the relationships between these time periods are indicated by the green braces between these rows. Right clicking returns to the 'live' view.

Reading the TimeLine Visualization

Previous researchers have suggested that knowing others' activities over time could help the viewer identify opportune moments to make contact with them, i.e., not only when others are reachable, but when they are likely amenable to being contacted (e.g., Begole et. al. 2002; Fogarty et. al. 2005). Begole et. al. (2002) observe that many activities often recur over days and weeks as long-term patterns, or 'work rhythms'. Patterns typically indicate: when remote colleagues arrive and depart for the day or when they take breaks; whether they are working; how visitors enter and leave the area and how long they stay; the ebb and flow of meetings and phone calls over the day; and differences in activities between work days. Fogarty et. al. (2005) and Johnson and Greenberg (1999) further argue that details of activities are highly correlated with non-interruptibility. These include knowing things such as: whether they are talking on the phone and/or to guests; the number of guests, if a person is just leaving or entering, and so on.

Many of these activities are hinted at in the overview visualization, and are easily seen during scrubbing (as long as they are in the camera's field of view). At first, images produced by the visualization may appear difficult to understand. Yet viewers quickly learn to read them. The full-sized frame in the floating window also serves as a good point of reference to help people understand what different patterns mean as they are being generated (indeed, our experiences are that people enjoy moving in front of the camera to create these patterns).

For example, consider some of the prior figures. In Figure 2, we clearly see that the person is sitting in front of their computer. The partial scans of that person's

Figure 5. The visualization reveals a brief visit.

face suggest they are moving their head only slightly, i.e., they are concentrating intently on the screen. Glancing at the hour row, we see that this person has been there for about 20 minutes. Earlier in that hour, the constant pattern suggests that the person was away. Yet there are several visual disturbances (the vertical white and grey lines), which are likely people walking by in the background. The day and week rows give a broader overview. The day row shows (from left to right), the previous afternoon, lights going off for about an hour but back on again (someone has likely left and reentered the room later), and then off again over the nighttime until the person returns in the morning. The week shows almost 5 days of day and night activity: we clearly see (going left to right) that this person has worked two partial days (the weekend) and then two full days.

As another example Figure 3 shows the TIMELINE with the focus column set on the distant doorway, revealing people as they enter and exit the room. The minute line visualization shows a recognizable person as they pass through the doorway, while the hour shows these changes as single column perturbations.

Figure 4 is somewhat similar the Figure 2, except in this case we see more 'coming and going' activity by the person. We know it is the same person because the colors and patterns of his shirt are the same (indeed, looking at the week view we see that he has worn the same shirt for several days).

Figure 5 extracts a portion of an Hour row from a home telecommuter. Here we see a more or less regular pattern of the person working at the computer over this hour. However, a tall red line at the left of the row differs from other colors and patterns in the scene (i.e., the telecommuter is wearing an orange shirt, not a red one). This disturbance suggests that a 2nd person has briefly entered the scene. Scrubbing over that area reveals that it is the tele-commuter's wife coming to give him a quick kiss on the cheek (as seen in the focus window).

Figure 6a+b shows how camera angles can reveal quite different information. As evident in the focus window of Figure 6a, the worker has positioned his camera to capture a side view of his desk: the telephone, keyboard and partial view of a seated person are all visible. The annotated minute view in Figure 6b reveals activity around the desk as interesting patterns. From left to right, we see an arriving person (blue jeans and shirt are visible), then fingers as he types on the keyboard. The person then picks up his phone, as indicated by the black bar (the phone pattern) changing to tan desk color and the fingers disappearing from the keyboard. We then see the phone returning and the person resume typing for a few moments. The following solid pattern suggests that the person is still there but no longer typing (because there is no 'leaving body' pattern).

Implementation

TIMELINE is developed in C# .NET and uses two home-grown toolkits. EASYIMAGES provides a camera class that makes it very easy to retrieve frames from a webcam video stream attached to a particular computer. .NETWORKING is a notification server that lets people publish multimedia data to a shared diction-ary data structure; the system automatically takes data posted by one client, and propagates it to other clients that have subscribed to that data (Boyle and Green-berg 2005a). The TIMELINE CAPTURE client captures the webcam video stream from a person's computer. It then publishes each video frame to the TIMELINE VIEWER, which processes and displays it as described below.

TIMELINE is extremely responsive. To achieve this, the TIMELINE VIEWER stores in memory all relevant video frames that have a 1:1 correspondence with the currently displayed slices. This makes it possible to instantly regenerate the visualization as people moved the slit focus bar (by quickly extracting the rele-vant pixel slices from all frames), or to immediately display the appropriate frame in the floating window while scrubbing.

Internally, each row is represented by an object that independently samples the video input stream at a sampling rate appropriate for its time frame, and only stores the ones that are represented as a slice on the display in an array as an un-compressed frame. For pragmatic reasons, we chose a constant frame array size of 1020 for each row, and a frame size of 320 * 240 pixels in dimension – a common format for webcam streams. This provides a 'reasonable' balance between frame rate for the minute row (17 fps * 60 seconds = 1020 frames / minute) and memory use (1020 frames * 320 * 240 pixels/frame * 24 color bits/pixel ~= 225 MB / row or 900

Figure 6a. The scene

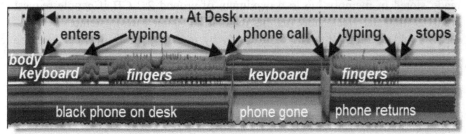

Figure 6b. The minute row captured by the camera angle of Figure 6a.

MB across all rows). In addition to the currently visible frames, each line also stores a single 1020 * 240 pixel image that represents the currently visible video slice visualization itself. TIMELINE then resizes this image to fit a window, regardless of that window's resolution.

Next, recall that each row has a different sampling rate: only the slices in the minute row shows a real time sampling of the video, whereas each slice in the minute, hour and month rows represent increasingly longer interval containing many frames. As we go from the hour to the day and the week rows, the interval between sampling successive frames lengthens, and we increase the chance of not capturing significant though brief events occurring within the omitted frames. Thus TIMELINE uses a *change detection algorithm* to select the 'best' frame from a series of frames in an interval as the most likely to contain a significant event: this is the frame whose pixels differ the most from the previously displayed frame. When the sampling interval elapses, the row adds that frame to its frame array, and that row's video slice image is updated by shifting it left one pixel and drawing the appropriate column from the new frame in the rightmost column.

Each row also keeps an archive of video frames on disk; this archive allows previously seen frames to be selectively displayed when a person wants to retrieve details from the distant past (it is far too expensive to keep these in memory). All frames are stored as a series of MPEG4 v2 compressed video files that are in 1020 frame numbered segments, i.e., that match a unit of frames that can fit in a particular row. As new incoming frames replace old ones in a row, the row object removes them both from the display and from memory and writes them to disk. We keep separate archives for each row rather than a single monolithic archive; this speeds up the process of retrieving and displaying region details in the distant past. When a person selects a past point in time to review, the archives comprising the rows at that particular moment of time are retrieved. Still, the operation is expensive: there is a noticeable delay (typically a few seconds) to rebuild all retrieved row images from disc. As a side note, we are careful to retain a copy of incoming video even when people are reviewing sequences from the distant past, which means that a person can switch back to the live visualization with no loss of information.

TIMELINE is memory intensive. It requires about 900 MB for the basic fully populated display. When it reads in from the archive, it is adding to what is already stored in memory: up to a maximum of around 2.2 GB if people request archives from the week view (as this reads in all other rows). Memory requirements could be brought down significantly by reducing the frames per line, the frame resolution, or frame bit depth.

 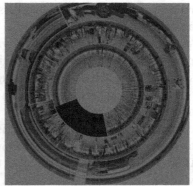

Figure 7. Hammer thrower by George Silk. Reproduced from National Gallery of Australia gallery of Silk's work: www.nga.gov.au/Silk/Gallery.htm

Figure 8. LAST CLOCK. Reproduced from Angesleva and Cooper (2005).

Related Work

Photography and Interactive Art

The idea of using slit-scans to capture people's activity evolved as a method in photography, film and interactive art installations. There are far too many examples of its use to cover here: Levin (2006) has an excellent compilation.

Slit-scan methods were historically used for creating photographic distortions: a fine slit was moved past the film as the picture was being exposed (Davidhazy, 2007). An example photo is shown in Figure 7: Silk's Hammer Thrower from the U.S. track team Olympic tryouts, published in Life magazine on July 18, 1960.

Various art projects extend this idea to live digital video. For example, Romy Achituf's Pixel Present (1998) used slit-scan to capture and display live digital video of audience members walking by a large screen. The closest visualization to our work is Angesleva and Coopers' (2005) LAST CLOCK (Figure 8). As with other artists, they use video to capture slit-scan images of people moving around an area. However, they stretch the idea of time by fashioning the visualization as a series of concentric rings – a clock – that shows 12 hours of footage. There are three rings: the outer one is the composite image of the last 60 seconds, the middle the last 60 minutes, and the inner ring is the last 12 hours. The regions where new slit scans replace the old become the second, minute and hour hand of a clock, e.g., the white lines in Figure 8 gives the time 5:45:55.

Unlike TIMELINE, most approaches to slit-scan art (including LAST CLOCK) create a static image that cannot be explored further. To quote: "Slit-Scan imaging techniques are used to create *static images* of time-based phenomena" (Levin 2006, emphasis added). Sitll, a few artists allow rudimentary navigation. ARTIFACTS OF THE PRESENCE ERA (Viegas et. al. 2004) used a rock formation metaphor as the visualization. Rows of slices taken over time are layered atop one another, where older layers were visually flattened and compressed to mimic strata. Visitors could crudely navigate between layers: turning a knob would display a single video frame representing an entire layer. This is equivalent to a person only being able to retrieve a single frame for an entire TIMELINE row.

Other researchers used the idea of representing captured video as a volume, and then exploring this volume by passing a plane through it. That is, instead of capturing images by a slit-scan, it is the slicing of the volume with the plane that creates a slit scan visualization showing portions of successive frames over time. Elliot's (1993) VIDEOSTREAMER transformed video into a variety of unusual viewing streams and shapes (e.g., a 3d cube). One could see the edges of the cube (which creates a slit-scan of the sides and tops of each frame), and then navigate the shape by mousing over it. Fels, Lee and Mass (2000) let people slice through the volume at any angle and position. Again, their purpose was art: None of these systems have the level of interactivity provided by TIMELINE.

Video Media Spaces

A handful of researchers in Computer Supported Cooperative Work have experimented with the notion of somehow capturing people's activity over time, and using this information to augment a media space. Hudson and Smith motivated this in 1996 "to provide a more general idea of recent patterns of activity without requiring the constant attention of the receiving user" (p. 255).

One approach uses activity graphs: video frames are analyzed for differences, and a graph visually portrays the amount of change in the video over time. For example, an empty office will be seen mostly as a flat line, a person entering or leaving will be seen as a spike, while a seated person will be seen as a wavy line reflecting that person's small motions. Hudson and Smith (1996) introduced such activity graphs as a way to augment a media space, while Lee, Girgensohn and Schlueter (1997) recommend using such graphs *instead* of video transmission as a way to include people who refused to use video due to privacy concerns.

Hudson and Smith's (1996) WHEN DID KEITH LEAVE? uses multiple video frames to show activities over time as well as an activity graph. The system collects a small series of still images over time that characterize the flow of activity in the space. Their algorithm selects and displays a small number of frames (e.g., five) from a video stream, where the chosen frames are those that show significant visual differences in activity. Whenever a new frame is captured, it adds it to the series (while removing the oldest one) when at least 20% of the new image had changed. Thus the series of images need not be linear with time. Gutwin (2002) provides an alternative to this visualization, where he suggested (but did not implement) a short-term video trace where several video snapshots taken in the recent past are alpha-blended onto the current video frame. Hudson and Smith (1996) advocated a somewhat similar technique except that changes were shown

a) Playback   b) Alpha blending   c) Random pixel blending

d) Displaying past frames as storyboard miniatures.

Figure 9. Other earlier approaches tried by the authors on visualization a video trace

as shadows, thus showing some activity (darkness = movement) while masking its details. In all these works, the concept of video traces was a side issue that was not explored in depth: Gutwin (2002) was investigating traces as a way to mitigate network issues in telepointer tracking, while Hudson and Smith 1996 were primarily focused on privacy in VMS. In other related work, Terry (2004) explains a method for simultaneously showing multiple points of time from the same scene in a single image. More generally, Roussel introduces the notion of *multiscale communication* as a communication system that supports variable degrees of engagement.

In parallel with video traces, a variety of other researchers try to extract and visually portray patterns collected from computer usage logs and from physical sensors. For example, Begole et. al. (2002) describe how they generate rhythms of personal activities as actograms by analyzing and modeling a person's computer activity, their mail, phone and instant messaging use, and their online calendar appointments. Fogarty, Hudson, et. al. (2004) argue that sensor data can be used to generate models that differentiate between interruptible and non-interruptible situations. While their purpose is to use this data mostly for automating whether a person is interruptible at a particular instance in time, the same data could easily be used to generate temporal patterns of activity.

Our Early Investigations

Our investigations prior to building TIMELINE led to other visualizations of activity history. First is *rapid playback*, inspired by Dietz and Yerazunis's (1991). When a person moves and then returns the cell phone back to the ear, the phone replays the missed conversational passage as high-speed pitch-preserved audio. Similarly, our video-based approach, illustrated in Figure 9a, displays the current image while automatically capturing the last n video frames (we used 100 frames captured at 1 frame every two seconds, or 2 1/3 minutes of past activity). The viewer can play back this captured video stream at 20x or 40x normal speed (i.e., as a 10 second or 5 second movie) by pressing a particular speed replay button (Figure 9a, buttons on bottom left – this screen capture is in the middle of rapidly replaying the sequence). This effect works quite well for quickly reviewing the very recent past, and can be extended to include longer time periods and different frame rates. It is limited because no overview is given of past activities, and the person has to actively decide to review the video.

We then realized Gutwin's (2002) unimplemented idea of *frame alpha-blending,* that composites several past frames onto a single video frame, as illustrated in Figure 9b (this varies Hudson and Smith's 1996 Shadow method). The further into the past, the more faded a change appeared. As before, a person could set the frame rate. While this did give a sense of activity, it did not satisfy. It did not scale well beyond a modest number of frames (as the changes in the alpha blended images proved too translucent). If the frame rate was high, so was the glimpse into the past (i.e., activity was usually realized as motion blur). If the frame rate was low, then the composite images were disjoint and hard to interpret.

With *random pixel blending*, we overlaid a percentage of randomly chosen pixels from the just-taken video frame onto the displayed image (Figure 9c). The actual percentage is specified via the slider. If the percentage is small (e.g., 15%), then motions are realized as a pixel scatter blur effect. If a person remains somewhat still, details are slowly filled in. Because backgrounds change rarely, they come in at full view. For example, Figure 9c shows the same image as in Figure 5a. The telecommuter is sitting fairly still behind his computer – thus his image (as well as the room background) is more or less complete. His wife just walked in and gave him a kiss on the cheek; because she is moving, this is seen as scattered pixels as she came through the doorway (top left). A hint of her clothes color is just visible (red shirt and blue jeans) at the bottom left, as is the top of her head as she leans over to kiss him (middle left). Thus privacy is somewhat protected: people are aware of stable events, but details and rapidly done actions are obscured. As with alpha blending this works only with the very recent past.

Figure 9d illustrates our *storyboard display*, a variation of Hudson and Smith's "When did Keith leave" approach (1996). An end user sets a sample rate for extracting frames from the video stream, and the last n samples are displayed as miniatures in a visual storyboard. For example, Figure 9d has a sample rate of 1 per second; thus the 45 miniatures in the storyboard reveal the last 45 seconds of activity. If it was set at (say) 1 sample per minute, the storyboard would reveal the last 45 minutes of activity. As with TIMELINE, it displays the frame that differs the most from the last storyboard sample. New samples also over-write old ones in the wrap-around sequence (the latest sample is outlined in red, i.e., the 3rd image in the top row in Figure 9d). Compared to "When did Keith leave", this approach conserves time as a true linear stream, and the smaller low resolution images adds some privacy protection. Yet our own impressions of this storyboard technique were not favorable. Because of the many images, it was hard to tell 'at a glance' what was going on. As well, setting a high sample rate (e.g., 1 sample per second) proved distracting and did not provide a long enough history window to justify the screen space. Yet setting a low frame rate (e.g., 1 sample per minute) omits multiple key events that could happen within the sampling period, e.g., 2 visitors arriving and leaving within a few moments of each other.

Reflection

This paper described TIMELINE as a very efficient method for seeing and reviewing past events. We placed TIMELINE within the context of prior work, provided enough details of its implementation so that others can replicate it, and also make it freely available for others to try.

Yet our motivation is not to provide TIMELINE as a solution. Rather, we want to use it as a case study that pushes the extremes of what is possible, and to provoke debate about video trace technologies. In this spirit we re-ignite the debate, started by Hudson and Smith (1996) and Begole et. al. (2002), by offering a preliminary reflection on TIMELINE's use. We base our reflections on the reactions of many people (including ourselves) to the Timeline system during numerous live demonstrations and through self-trials. First, we ran TIMELINE as a video mirror within a public interactive installation. The installation was located in a highly visible public part of our research laboratory on a 60" touch-sensitive plasma display (using a webcam attached to this display), and hundreds of visitors saw and tried it as part of several open-house days. Second, we used TIMELINE ourselves, on personal workstations within our laboratory as well as at home.

People's Positive Reactions and Suggested Uses.

Readability. The live installation verified that the visualization is easily readable. With only a brief introduction to how it works, visitors could comprehend and read the visualization display, especially because they could see how their actions were immediately represented within it. They were able to spot themselves in the visualization, pick out events such as the arrival of a crowd for a demonstration session, and see the rhythms of activity between night and day. People found it easy to reason about what the display was showing. They could fine odd events of interest, such as a brief period of light in the middle of the night. Scrubbing and moving the slice focus bar let people determine how patterns in the visualization were created, enhancing their understanding as well as their ability to read other parts of it. While static images produced using slit-scanning techniques can appear to be distorted and strange, augmenting them with this level of interactivity brings them into comprehension.

Self-Reflection and Playfulness. People were intrigued to see themselves within Timeline. This replicates prior experience in slit-scan art installations. People made patterns within the visualization by waving arms or colourful items, or even slowly turning around in front of the camera to produce a flat scan of their head all the way around. Visitors would often pose in front of the installation to leave their mark in the visualization (also noted by Viegas et. al. 2004).

Voyeurism occurs when people get pleasure observing other people, and this certainly occurs within Timeline use. People were often fascinated by TIMELINE'S ability to see what others were doing in the past, where they found scrubbing and cyclic replay of a scene compelling.

Rhythms. People commented on the aesthetics of the TIMELINE visualization as a history mirror: it clearly showed the cyclic rhythms of activity and how changes occur over time within a space.

Surveillance. While the public demonstrations were set up as an interactive installation, people also suggested practical uses for it. Many said that TIMELINE had great potential as a surveillance system used for security purposes. Ideas ranged from its use by trained security personnel, to home monitoring (nanny cams), to property protection when away, and to equivalents of baby monitors.

Analysis Tool. People also suggested that TIMELINE could be useful as a research analysis tool for detecting patterns and counting key events in captured video streams collected for research TIMELINE.

Video editing. Could TIMELINE be used within a video editing context? We don't have the answer to this, for the constant motion of a camera would give quite a different visual effect than what has been shown in our paper. Still, as an alternate visualization TIMELINE may be useful to find scene changes, or moments when the camera's point of view have drifted off its central target to a new target in the scene.

A low-bandwidth ambient distributed awareness. TIMELINE may also work as a pure peripheral awareness display that doubles as an art installation. Instead of sending video frames, we could just send columns (the vertical slice) which is quite low bandwidth. This visualization could work as a 'long-distance relationship' awareness display that is less intrusive than full frame video, where its lower fidelity protects privacy better than full video.

Negative Reaction: The Privacy Issue.

Now we turn to the dark side. Privacy is an extremely serious issue, since TIMELINE sometimes does its job too well. Hudson and Smith (1996) believe systems such as these demonstrate how privacy issues might occur when providing awareness information through a video trace: transient activities of a person are no longer lost if the system records and displays significant events. Our own uses of the system reflect these concerns.

Reluctance and perception of risk. Even as creators we were reluctant to use it in broadcast mode for long periods of time. TIMELINE's power makes it invasive. Potentially embarrassing, private or inappropriate behaviors are not only captured, but easily found and replayed. A trade-off arises: while we and our collaborators could benefit by using the system to see each other's recent activities and events, it also serves as a (perhaps unintended) surveillance system (see Boyle and Greenberg 2005b discussion of privacy issues in VMS).

It captures more than you. We often used TIMELINE as a local mirror within our research laboratory, an open space that included other workers. Yet this immediately incited concerns from other inhabitants of the laboratory, for they were very uncomfortable with the idea of being permanently captured on video for others to see (even though all actions were in a public space). There were meetings and discussions about this, and eventually people were willing to have it run in very limited situations because they valued its use for research. Even so, we found that we inadvertently captured other people in embarrassing situations, e.g., a cleaner who went to sleep on a lab couch during a night work shift.

Similarly, one author telecommutes from his home, and regularly uses a traditional VMS. He was willing to use TIMELINE in work situations with his distant colleagues, but was concerned that other family members using the home office would be captured unintentionally. This would not only be embarrassing for a family member if caught in a compromising situation, but also for the distant viewer who could unintentionally see that situation in TIMELINE.

Tacit information becomes explicit. Another downfall is that TIMELINE also allows people to very easily compare their activity with others (if multiple instances are running), and in turn they may become overly self-critical of their own work habits, or of others. Tacit information becomes explicit. The system allows observations such as "did I work as many hours as my colleagues?" This could lead to undue stress on the workers' part, which would be magnified if the worker knew their video stream was being broadcast.

Distraction. There is also the issue of distraction with TIMELINE's full-screen view. This can be solved by embedding it into more traditional media spaces. For example, the inset figure shows it redesigned to fit within Community Bar (McEwan and Greenberg 2005). People see a traditional media space view in a side bar, but can raise a video trace by mousing over it for an overview of hourly activities. Clicking this trace then raises the full TIMELINE system.

Yet we can control what is captured. Adjusting the camera angle can make a large difference in what is captured, and consequently can reduce privacy invasion. For example, Figures 6a+b show how pointing the camera at a desk highlights when a person is at their computer and/or on the phone, but does not transmit head shots or surrounding areas. Similarly, positioning the camera outside an office doorway (as done by Buxton 1997) means that the remote viewer can only see what people walking by a hallway can see, and that closing the door protects oneself in both the physical and virtual space.

Next Steps

There is much that we have not done in this paper. We did not formally evaluate TIMELINE'S usability as a visualization, nor did we formally compare it to other time-based approaches. We speculated, but did not prove, that a video trace is actually useful as an availability tool. We argued that privacy is a problem but have not really deployed it to see how people would really adjust and/or negotiate its use in their real world context. Clearly, there are many future avenues of research (but this should not preclude debate). A few are described below.

Usefulness as an awareness tool. Our original motivation was that a video trace would be a good way to augment a media space, where it would provide people with addition cues to determine availability and interruptability. Yet the jury is still out on this. It could be that a glimpse into the past adds little, or that very simple techniques showing the last few moments and/ or key events would suffice. Indeed, there is active debate within CSCW concerning exactly what information suffices as a good predictor of interruptibility (Fogarty et. al. 2005).

Comparitive usefulness as a video history tool. We argued that TIMELINE is a good visualization tool that provides both an overview and query-in-depth. While our informal observations suggest that this is in fact the case, we have not compared it to other 'conventional' techniques. Perhaps TIMELINE offers insufficient fidelity of historical information (narrow field of view, image quality, lack of audio). Or perhaps other approaches for visualizing video-based activities over time may prove move effective, e.g., Terry (2004), Hudson and Smith (1996), Begole et. al. (2002). This comparison clearly needs to be done.

Art was the original motivation for slit scanning *vs.* purposeful applications. We believe that bringing high interaction capabilities to bear on slit-scanning could enhance overall artistic effect. However, we are not artists, so next steps could include involving artists in the project to see how they modify and repurpose TimeLine.

Novelty *vs.* Real Use. Is the attraction of TIMELINE due to a novelty effect, or does it have long-standing value? Once people learn the visualization, how do they use it to interpret a scene and to look back at history? What canonical tasks emerge over time, and how can we modify TIMELINE to suit these tasks? Obviously, these questions can only be answered through a long-term longitudinal study of TIMELINE's use in real world contexts by real people.

Privacy protection is obviously important, but the question remains of how one can balance privacy and awareness. Perhaps a good starting point is to embed and evaluate other privacy preservation image processing techniques within TIMELINE e.g., context-sensing for controlling when video is taken (Neustaedter and Greenberg 2003), image blurring in low-risk situations (Boyle and Greenberg 2005b), or novel techniques such as those proposed by Hudson and Smith (1996).

Conclusion

TIMELINE is best viewed as an investigation into the extreme, where it asks the question "what would it be like if we could easily see and explore a video trace of a distant person or scene? Currently, it is difficult to predict where it might be best used and the cultural practices that would evolve around it. Perhaps TIMELINE could be suited to areas that are largely accepted as public rather than private offices and workspaces. Perhaps it would work well between tight teams or social intimates with a strong desire to stay connected. Perhaps it can be used as a base reference to other approaches, e.g., to see if low fidelity actogram graphs (Begole et. al. 2002) provide comparatively sufficient awareness information while still safeguarding privacy. Or perhaps CSCW is the wrong venue; it may better serve as a security system, as art, or as video analysis. This is clearly an area for future – and perhaps controversial – research. Let the debate continue.

Acknowledgements

This research was partially funded by NSERC through its scholarship, Discovery Grant and NECTAR Networks grant program, and by Alberta Ingenuity and iCORE. We also thank our industrial sponsors: Microsoft Research and Smart Technologies, Inc.

Software. TIMELINE, EasyImages, and .Networking available at http://grouplab.cpsc.ucalgary.ca/cookbook/.

References

Achituf, R. (1998): *'Pixel present: A gestural scanner.'* Accessed March, 2007. http://www.gavaligai.com/main/sub/installation/PixelPresent/PixelPresent.html

Angesleva, J. and Cooper, R. (2005): 'Last Clock'. IEEE Comput. Graph. Appl. 25, 1, 20-23.

Begole, J., Tang, J. C., Smith, R. B., and Yankelovich, N. (2002): 'Work rhythms: analyzing visualizations of awareness histories of distributed groups'. *Proc ACM CSCW '02*. 334-343.

Bly, S. Harrison, S. and Irwin S. (1993): 'Media Spaces: Bringing people together in a video, audio, and computing environment', *Comm. ACM*, 3, 1, 28-47.

Boyle, M. and Greenberg, S. (2005a) 'Rapidly Prototyping Multimedia Groupware'. *Proc Distributed Multimedia Systems* (DMS'05), Knowledge Systems Institute, IL, USA.

Boyle, M. and Greenberg, S. (2005b): 'The language of privacy: Learning from video media space analysis and design'. *ACM Trans. Computer-Human Interaction* (TOCHI). 12 (2).

Buxton, W. (1997): 'Living in augmented reality: Ubiquitous media and reactive environments'. In K. Finn, A. Sellen & S. Wilber (Eds.). *Video Mediated Communication*. LEA Press.

Davidhazy, A. (accessed March, 2007) *Slit-scan photography*. School of Photographic Arts and Sciences, Rochester Institute of Technology. http://www.rit.edu/~andpph/text-slit-scan.html.

Dietz, P. H. and Yerazunis, W. (2001): 'Real-time audio buffering for telephone applications'. *Proc ACM UIST*. 193-194.

Elliot, E. (1993): '*Watch * Grab * Arrange * See: Thinking with motion images via streams and collages*'. MS Thesis, Master of Science in Visual Studies, January, MIT.

Fels S., Lee, E. and Mase, K. (2000): 'Techniques for Interactive Video Cubism'. *Proc ACM Multimedia*. 368-370.

Fogarty, J., Hudson, S. E., Atkeson, C. G., Avrahami, D., Forlizzi, J., Kiesler, S., Lee, J. C., and Yang, J. (2005): 'Predicting human interruptibility with sensors'. *ACM TOCHI* 12 (1).

Gutwin, C. (2002): 'Traces: Visualizing the immediate past to support group interaction'. *Proc Graphics Interface*. 43-50.

Hudson, S. E. and Smith, I. (1996): 'Techniques for addressing fundamental privacy and disruption tradeoffs in awareness support systems'. *Proc ACM CSCW*. 248-257.

Johnson, B. and Greenberg, S. (1999): 'Judging People's Availability for Interaction from Video Snapshots'. *Proc. HICSS Distributed Group Support Systems Minitrack*, Jan., IEEE Press.

Kraut, R., Egidio, C., Galegher, J. (1990): 'Patterns of contact and communication in scientific research collaboration'. *Intellectual Teamwork: Social and Technological Foundations of Cooperative Work*. LEA

Lee, A., Girgensohn, A., and Schlueter, K. (1997): 'NYNEX portholes: initial user reactions and redesign implications'. *Proc ACM GROUP*. ACM Press, 385-394.

Levin, G. (2006) 'An informal catalogue of slit-scan video artworks'. Last edited December 29, 2006. http://www.flong.com/writings/lists/list_slit_scan.html.

McEwan, G. and Greenberg, S. (2005): 'Supporting social worlds with the Community Bar', *Proc. ACM Group* 21-30.

Neustaedter, C. and Greenberg, S. (2003): 'The design of a context-aware home media space. *Proc UBICOMP'03*, 297-314, LNCS Vol 2864, Springer-Verlag.

Nunes, M., Greenberg, S., Carpendale, S. and Gutwin, C. (2006): 'Timeline: Video Traces for Awareness'. *Video Proc. ACM CSCW'06*, ACM Press. Viewable at http://grouplab.cpsc.ucalgary.ca/papers/

Roussel, N. (2006) 'Towards multiscale communications systems'. Rapport de Recherche 1439, LRI, Université Paris-Sud, France.

Terry, M. (2004) 'Making space for time in time-lapse photography'. *Siggraph Tech. Sketches*.

Viégas, F. B., Perry, E., Howe, E., and Donath, J. (2004): 'Artifacts of the Presence Era: Using Information Visualization to Create an Evocative Souvenir'. *Proc IEEE Infovis'04*. 105-111.

Whittaker, S., Frolich, D., and Daly-Jones, O. (1994): 'Informal workplace communication: What is it like and how might we support it?' *Proc ACM CSCW*, 131-138

L. Bannon, I. Wagner, C. Gutwin, R. Harper, and K. Schmidt (eds.).
ECSCW'07: Proceedings of the Tenth European Conference on Computer Supported Cooperative Work, 24-28 September 2007, Limerick, Ireland
© Springer 2007

Social bookmarking and exploratory search

David Millen, Meng Yang, Steven Whittaker*, Jonathan Feinberg

IBM Cambridge, MA, USA 02142, *Sheffield University, Sheffield, S1 4DP, UK

{david_r_millen,yangmeng,jdf@us.ibm.com}, s.whittaker@shef.ac.uk

ABSTRACT. In this paper, we explore various search tasks that are supported by a social bookmarking service. These bookmarking services hold great potential to powerfully combine personal tagging of information sources with interactive browsing, resulting in better social navigation. While there has been considerable interest in social tagging systems in recent years, little is known about their actual usage. In this paper, we present the results of a field study of a social bookmarking service that has been deployed in a large enterprise. We present new qualitative and quantitative data on how a corporate social tagging system was used, through both event logs (click level analysis) and interviews. We observed three types of search activities: community browsing, personal search, and explicit search. Community browsing was the most frequently used, and confirms the value of the social aspects of the system. We conclude that social bookmarking services support various kinds of exploratory search, and provide better personal bookmark management and enhance social navigation.

Introduction

In recent years, there has been tremendous growth in shared bookmarking applications. Introduced in 2003, the del.icio.us social bookmark website was one of the first of this kind of application, and has enjoyed an early and large base of committed users. A flurry of similar offerings has since been unveiled [see (Hammond, et al., 2005) for a recent review].

These internet oriented social bookmarking services have been adapted for use in large organizations. Examples include the *dogear* (Millen, et al., 2006) and *onomi* social bookmarking services (Damianos, et al., 2007). Both of these enterprise-ready bookmarking services support bookmarking of both internet and intranet information sources, and provide user authentication via corporate directories.

There are two distinguishing characteristics of social bookmarking systems. The first is the use of keywords, or tags, that a user enters to describe the links he or she saves. These tags allow users to organize and display their collection with labels that are meaningful to them. Furthermore, multiple tags allow bookmarks to belong to more than one category, a limitation of the traditional hierarchically organized folders found in most Web browsers. The second significant characteristic of these social bookmark applications is the social nature of their use. While bookmark collections are personally created and maintained, they are also typically visible to others. As a result, users benefit by getting pointers to new information from others while at the same time getting a general sense of other people's interests.

These new social bookmarking applications are a natural and powerful extension of existing social navigation tools and practices (see, for example, (Dieberger, 2003; Munro, 1999)). They provide a mix of both direct (intentional) navigational advice as well as indirect (inferred) advice based on collective public behavior. By definition – these social bookmarking systems provide "social filtering" on resources from the web and intranet. The act of bookmarking indicates to others that one is interested in a given resource. At the same time, tags provide semantic information about the way the resource can be viewed.

Social bookmarking systems arguably provide support for search activities that range from simple fact-finding to more exploratory or social forms of search. Fact-finding or what is called "known-item" retrieval is supported by traditional application *explicit search* capabilities. Users generate query terms and sift through lists of search results to find the appropriate bookmark (and associated web site). These known-item search tasks are usually characterized by a well understood search problem and reasonable understanding of the search domain.

Known-item retrieval is also supported in social bookmarking applications by *browsing* through collections of one's own (personal) bookmarks, which have been explicitly created, tagged and annotated by end-users. Social bookmarking applications typically allow personal bookmark browsing in one of two ways. The first is by sifting through scrollable pages of bookmarks, and the second is by or by performing a *tag query* of the collection by clicking on a tag.

Social bookmarking tools also support *exploratory* search activities. In exploratory search, the problem definition is less well structured and the emphasis may be on learning or analysis (Marchionini, 2006). One form of this less goal-oriented browsing found in social bookmarking applications is to browse bookmarks by *time*, enabling end-users to serendipitously follow recent bookmark that they find interesting. A second exploratory browsing strategy supported by social bookmarking applications is to explore *popular* bookmarks, where frequency of bookmarking a specific URL is a simple measure of popularity.

There are two other particularly interesting forms of exploratory search supported by social bookmarking services. The first is where end-users click on a visible name and the bookmarks for that person appear. The second is where collaborative tags are used to query the bookmark collection.

While there has been considerable interest in social tagging systems in recent years, little is known about their actual usage. Some work has been done to investigate tag growth and entropy (Golder and Huberman, 2006; Kittur, et al., 2007; Marlow, et al., 2006) and tag choice (Sen, et al., 2006). Little is known, however, about actual usage and the ways in which social bookmarking might help people find information.

In this paper, we present the results of a field study of a social bookmarking service that has been deployed in a large enterprise. We present new qualitative and quantitative data on how a corporate social tagging system was used, through both event logs (click level analysis) and interviews. We are generally interested in understanding the different ways that this social bookmarking service supports different kinds of search. In particular, we are interested in understanding how social bookmarking tools are used to find, refind and explore information resources.

These are important ideas to explore in the enterprise context. Enterprise search has been shown to be ineffective (see, for example, (Mukherjee and Mao, 2004)) and such social search tools may provide a significant alternative method for enterprise information access.

Dogear Social Bookmarking Service

The dogear social bookmarking service is a social bookmarking tool designed to support organizations and large corporations. Adapting social bookmarking to the corporate environment meant enhancing some of the technology's standard features. Rather than allow the use of pseudonyms, dogear requires the use of real names and authentication with a corporate directory. Real name identity allows dogear users to look-up additional information about other people in various corporate databases (e.g., corporate online directory and the enterprise Web). It also facilitates communication between users of dogear since most corporate collaboration tools (such as e-mail, and chat) use real name identities. For example, if someone is looking for a colleague who is knowledgeable about Java, he or she might look to see who has bookmarked articles on that topic and then send an e-mail to get more information. Finally, real name identity may also promote more responsible use of the system. A user who is required to identify himself or herself should be far less likely than a pseudonymous user to post and share links to questionable material.

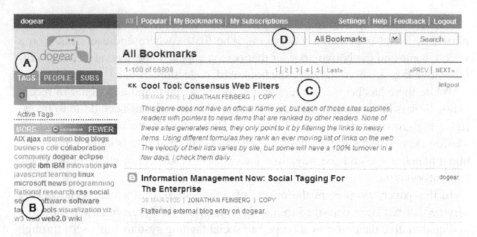

Figure 1. Screen shot of dogear social bookmarking service.

A second distinguishing characteristic of dogear is that it was designed to work behind corporate firewalls. This allows intranet resources to be bookmarked and shared among coworkers (e.g., human resource links, team or project resources, etc.) For example, if an employee wanted information on how to fill out expense report forms, he or she might search dogear using the tag "expense report" to find a list of intranet bookmarks that others in the company found useful.

Figure 1 shows the front page of dogear, featuring the bookmarks most recently added by a dogear user. The tabs at the top of the left-hand column (A) provide: a link to the user's tags; a list of people who have bookmarked the same URLs; and a list of the individual's bookmark subscriptions. The Active Tags (B) area shows an indexed tag cloud with a slider that can reduce the number of tags shown based on their frequency of appearance.

A list of bookmarks runs down the center of the screen (C). Each bookmark includes a title, optional descriptive text, tags, when the bookmark was made, and information about the author. Clicking on the title takes you to the bookmarked site. Clicking on a tag takes you to a list of the other bookmarks that the author has tagged with the same keyword. Clicking on the author's name takes you to a list of the author's bookmarks. Dogear's search (D) lets you search bookmarks by tag, person, or type of collection (all bookmarks/my bookmarks).

Social Tagging of Content

One of the major innovations in social bookmarking services has been the widespread adoption of user-generated keywords (or social tags) that are associated with the web content. In most social bookmarking services, the tag histories are revealed in the user interface in what have been popularly called *tag clouds* (see, for example Figure 2(a)). In the service we studied, a slider control allows the tag cloud to be expanded or contracted to reveal more or less of the tag index. Font darkness is used to show more frequently used tags, with a darker font indicating more use.

While human generated keywords as metadata have been available in many applications for a long time, we think that the ability to browse the bookmark collection via tags is critically important, as *pivot browsing* provides a real and immediate benefit to the end-user for having provided the tags in the first place.

Tag clouds are either system-wide, or specific to one user, depending on the current view. System-wide tag clouds quickly grow to an unmanageable size. In the social bookmarking service studied in this research, the enterprise tag cloud was truncated to include only the most active or popular tags.

In the system studied here, personal tag clouds were also provided and visible to other users of the bookmarking service. The personal tag clouds allowed other viewers to get a sense of the current interests of the other coworkers. The individual tag collections also provide important navigational support as another person's bookmark collection could be browsed by simply clicking on tags.

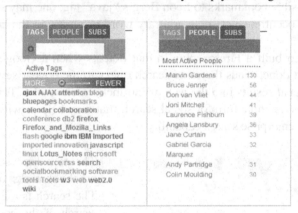

Figure 2(a) tag cloud   Figure 2 (b) People links

The bookmarking service under study also supported direct navigation to bookmarks that are tagged with two or more tags in combination. As the user selects additional associated tags, a new list of tags that co-occur with the previous ones is presented. This allows individuals to easily navigate the bookmark collection via tag clusters.

Social Navigation via People

In addition to browsing with end-user generated tags, it is also possible to navigate the bookmark collection through direct navigation of people links. These links are created using the *author* metadata that is associated with each bookmark. As can be seen in Figure 2(b), the navigation interface presents a separate tab, labeled "people." In the social bookmarking service home page, a list of the most active users is shown, with a number indicating the number of bookmarks recently created by each user. These "live names" may be clicked and the bookmark collection for that individual is presented.

This navigation by person allows for casual, or intentional, browsing of the bookmark collections of people of interest. End-users who see names of people who they know to be strong information seekers or brokers can navigate directly to see their bookmark collection.

dogear search

The search box in *dogear* works as expected; the user types in a free text query, and a list of bookmarks is returned, in order of relevance. The drop down options allow the user to search by user name ("People"), by tag ("All Tags"), by all fields within the user's bookmarks ("My Bookmarks"), or within the currently displayed set of bookmarks ("These Bookmarks"). For example, having restricted the currently visible bookmarks to Leon Berg's "java" tag, one may search within that set for the occurrence of some arbitrary word or phrase in the description or title.

We have also built a Firefox plug-in that detects when a Google or intranet search has been done, sends the same search query to the dogear service, and integrates the dogear results into the web or intranet search results. This *search insertion* provides a simple form of social search that may help provide a more robust and useful enterprise search capability

The top three search results are bookmarks from dogear. The search is a Lucene-based search of the bookmark contents (annotations, title, and tags).

The lower portion of the screen contains search results from the enterprise search engine, which is based on Omnifind search technology.

Figure 3. Example of search results.

A screen shot of the integrated search results for an enterprise search can be seen in Figure 3. At the top of the screen, labeled "injected results," are the results from the *dogear* query, which have been dynamically inserted into the enterprise search results. The top three *dogear* results are presented. Below the *dogear* results, are the traditional results from the enterprise search.

Every time a search query is initiated, a log event (search) is recorded, and every time one of the dogear bookmarks is clicked (from the integrated search results) a log event (click) is created. We are able, therefore, to determine both the number of external searches initiated, and also the click-through rates for the dogear bookmarks.

Field Study Results

To answer our research questions, we performed a field study of an enterprise bookmarking service deployed in a large multi-national company. Our general understanding of the use of the enterprise bookmarking service was based on many sources of user data, including log files, the primary bookmark data files, and in-depth interviews with 15 end-users of the service. Included in the log files are user actions (e.g., create, delete, edit a bookmark, bookmark "clicks"), user and bookmark owner identifiers, and a time and date stamp.

After a short friendly trial (~3 months), the system was introduced in mid-2005. By mid 2006, the system contains over 100,000 bookmarks and 250,000 tags created by over 1600 active end-users The activity analysis presented here is based on log files covering a 12 month period from July, 2005 to July, 2006 (~450K records). The sampling period, therefore, can be considered the first year of system use or adoption.

While the individuals using the *dogear* bookmarking service all worked in a high-tech industry for a large enterprise, they are reasonably diverse in the kind of work that they did the organizations and geography in which they worked. Table 1 show the breakdown of users by organization and geography. Users were distributed across eight major organizations, with more than a quarter coming from the software development organization. While the user base is significantly based in the US, over half of the system users were from other countries.

Organization	Total	%		Geography	Total	%
Software	1701	28%		USA	2564	45%
Consulting	1043	17%		United Kingdom	506	9%
Sales	865	14%		Germany	415	7%
Tech Delivery	613	10%		Canada	356	6%
Systems	392	6%		Japan	311	6%
Services	387	6%		India	259	5%
Research	233	4%		Australia	173	3%
Headquarters	203	3%		China	94	2%
Other	702	11%		Other	966	18%

Table 1. Demographics of bookmarking service users.

Supporting various search activities

In this paper we are particularly interested in understanding how the bookmarking service supports various kind of exploratory search activities We examined the logfiles for a 12 month sample (June 2005 - July 2006) to get a sense of how often end-users navigated through the bookmark collection using tags, names, and explicit search features. To better understand the results of the end-user actions, we have considered three general kinds of search, which are described in Table 2. These three kinds of search represent different user motivations and strategies. We will attempt to understand these end-user behaviors through a combination of logfile analysis and end-user interviews.

Community browsing	Examining bookmarks created by the community by time (*recent* bookmarks,), by frequency (most *popular* sites bookmarked), by *people,* and by *tags*.
Personal search	Looking for bookmarks from one's own personal collection of bookmarks.
Explicit search	Using a traditional search box to enter a set of search terms

Table 2 Different kinds of search supported.

The results of our logfile analysis are presented in Table 3. We group the results by the different kinds of search that we described above. We show the number of times that a particular navigation path resulted in a page view, i.e., a click-through to the original information resource that was bookmarked. Finally, we present the percentage of navigation events that resulted in a page view.

Action	# events	# clicks	% clicked
Community browsing			
Recent	77,132	15,621	20%
Popular	9,724	3,408	35%
People	26,535	5,074	25%
People x tag(s)	6,320	1,499	24%
Community Tag(s)	15,941	3,767	24%
Total	135,652	29,369	22%
Personal search			
Mybookmarks	57,236	9,949	17%
My tag(s)	20,980	6,387	30%
Total	78,216	16,336	21%
Explicit search			
Search- Internal dogear	29,961	11,667	39%
Search–plug-in enterprise	70,706	22,861	32%
Total	100,667	34,528	34%

Table 3 Logfile results for various search activities.

The page view percentage might be considered a search "completion" rate, and may be suggestive of different kinds of search strategies. For example, larger click-through percentages might indicate a more goal-oriented search. At minimum, the click-though percentages provide an estimate of the usefulness of the search results that were presented via each of the various search pathways.

Community browsing

The most frequent way to view information is using one of the community browsing mechanisms supported in dogear. The large total for community –related views (135K) confirms the value of the social aspects of the system. At the same time, the generally modest number of click-throughs (~22% of occasions on average) suggests that community browsing is used more for profiling information and other people than for known item retrieval.

Community Browsing: Recent and Popular Bookmarks

As can be seen in Table 3, the single most common way to view the dogear bookmark collection is to look at a listing of the most recently added bookmarks [Recent − 77132 above]. In some respects, this is not very surprising as there is a main dogear menu link labeled "all" and it is recommended in the application "help" to add a browser toolbar link to this dogear page.

Several dogear users that we interviewed indicated that they scan this list of newly created bookmarks with some regularity, much like they would scan news of blog feeds, exploiting the fact that dogear users form a shared community of interest within this organization. For example, one informant said:

> The first thing I normally go to in Dogear is *All* because I'm interested in finding out what everyone is doing. And I equate Dogear to basically Slashdot for IBM plus everything else on the Internet. ... I think it's better than Slashdot. Before when Dogear was starting, Slashdot was ... a little superior because there was still a lot of people, more and more people out there finding a lot of interesting feeds. And now that Dogear has achieved critical mass, there are a lot of people within IBM who I know and I respect, they've been picking up lots of interesting things that Slashdot folks haven't been picking up on.

This same informant indicated that he had changed his scanning the *all* list over time as the volume and variability of the bookmark content changed.

> I would scan through probably maybe three or four pages a day if I have time. ...when I started with Dogear, I would actually scan maybe more, but the volume was less. And it was a lot easier to pick -- sift through things. But now that there's more bookmarks today, and there's a lot of people from the other parts organization that I don't necessarily care about, I reduced the amount of pages I look at.

There were fewer reports from informants about the use if the "popular" or most active bookmarks, although one person indicated that he was aware of the top three bookmarked sites. There appear to be a relatively large percentage of page views on the popular bookmarks, indicating significant interest in what other people have already found. The click through results (35%) also suggests that, compared with recency, popularity is an effective recommendation about which resources might be worth reading.

Community Browsing: People Search

Of greater interest, perhaps, we note that there is considerable interest in browsing other peoples' bookmark collections. As can be seen in Table 3, the most frequent way to browse another user's bookmarks is by clicking on that person's name (26535). Once again, we also examined the number of times that end-users clicked through on a URL that had been bookmarked by another. The click-through results in Table 3 show that browsing someone else's bookmarks often results in following the URL to the original information source (25 percent of the time). This confirms the utility of social navigation in identifying useful informational resources.

These results suggest widespread curiosity about what others are bookmarking and provide evidence of the kind of explicit social navigation that is taking place within the bookmarking service. These results are significant as they represent a novel form of information browsing within the enterprise. Comments from end-user interviews confirm that the bookmarking service is supporting social navigation. One respondent indicated that she browsed the links of others for different reasons. In one case, it was to infer the currents topics of interest for an organization thought leader:

> It's usually I'm just looking at the people I know ... thought leaders and trying to get at ..., what is their thinking... And that might come up just through their tags or just through their content, or a combination.

This same kind of people browsing can be used to informally learn about the interest of coworkers. One dogear user said:

> "the most value to me is finding people --- who have specific expertise, or experience, or interest ... more than anything it's helped me become familiar with people. "

Another respondent indicated that navigating tags was a good way to informally find people with interest or expertise on various topics.

> And it just seems like a fabulous way of either finding people who either might know about something or might have bookmarked something that I would be interested in...

This same respondent indicated that another significant benefit is being able to trust the information sources based on knowledge of the people in the group.

> ...there would be words that I would be thinking in my head, like key words. And if I saw them in a tag cloud, then I would click on them and ... all these things would show up that have potential of being what I'm looking for. And I would do that as opposed to going to Google because in some way, it's a somewhat trusted community already. ... I respect the people in this community and they probably know things that I would be interested in. And I would trust their sources.

Another respondent indicated that she was especially interested in what others with similar job roles were bookmarking.

> "And generally, ..., on technical sales, a lot of the things that I'm looking for are going to be things that are other people that do what I do what I too am looking for. And so if I see a search that somebody else has done and somebody has bookmarked something, there's probably a better chance that that's been useful to me as well."

Community Browsing: Topic Search

Another popular way to browse other users' bookmarks is by selecting a specific tag from the system-wide tag cloud (Community browsing by tags – 15491). One respondent indicated that tag browsing was an efficient way to keep up-to-date on a particular subject.

> And sometimes when I'm searching by topic, like if I'm working on – if I have a thought or an idea, or I'm writing something, let's say about attention management, I might want to see what's new on attention, and I'll just search that tag to see what's new, rather than searching my subscriptions or on social networking or task management.

Another informant described different using social searching to do learn about new topics.

> So, an example is ...somebody that I work with was telling me that they have suddenly gotten interested in Second Life. Second Life is a virtual reality environment, and I knew that there was a bunch of people in [company] who were tracking it. So, I thought ... let me look and see what other people have found about Second Life because that is something that people who use Dogear are likely to have found.

The same informant described looking through other bookmarks tagged with "second life" until she can " get an idea of what is this thing? What is this category?" She continues to search until she finds a reasonable description.

> Now, in this particular case ... here is something that is a reasonable description. It gives you some idea and, oh, look, it's Business Week. Well, I can click on that because that is going to tell me in plain English what Second Life is.

> So, there is some serendipity that occurs within that, but it is really because I am looking for the beginnings of information about something. I am not looking for deep research.

The most popular tags used for topic browsing include specific technologies (e.g., ajax, linux, javascript, and websphere) or emerging topic of interest (e.g., web2.0, wiki, blog). Other popular tag queries seem to be around general terms or broad categories of information (e.g., social-software, programming, architecture, and design). Of some interest is the fact that the tag *dogear* was the fifth most frequently browsed, which may have assisted in adoption and information diffusion about the new social bookmarking tool.

Personal Search

Overall, personal search is the least frequent way for people to access the system – accounting for many fewer accesses than community browsing or explicit search. This is an interesting finding because previous literature has suggested that a primary motivation for social tagging systems is that they provide users with ways to manage and browse their own information, whereas our data show that for dogear at least, personal search is less frequent than other forms of access. In particular this argues for the utility of the social/community features of the system.

As can be seen in Table 3, end-users also browse the bookmark space by looking at their own collection (mybookmarks - 57,236) and navigating through their collection using personal tags (my tags - 20,980). The use of personal tag browsing suggests that tags are serving as a useful way to filter bookmarks once users build up larger collections of bookmarks.

In Table 3, there is also evidence that end-users actually use the bookmarking service to "revisit" information sources that they have previously bookmarked. In fact, when end-users navigate their bookmarks using their personal tags, they click through 30% of the time. This finding is contrary to early research suggesting that classic single-user web bookmarking is ineffective as users seldom turn to bookmarks they have created (Jones, et al., 2003).

Several of the end-users that we interviewed indicated that this support of personal bookmark management was an important characteristic of the service. One end-user highlighted the ability to centrally store bookmarks:

> And I find a lot of personal value, or at least personal comfort, in realizing that I saved this stuff somewhere, and it's refreshable, and it's in that location.

Another end-user said that social tags were very helpful in managing the overload of blog content:

> Because I have a lot of blogs that I read and I have found that this (bookmarking service) is just a better way, a quicker way for me to organize them. I will click the word blog, the tag, and then I'll see all the blogs.

The specific need to re-find information was highlighted by another informant

> I bookmark anything that I think I am going to want to go back to. I think that's the general reason for bookmarks, and often I will, as I am browsing stuff, not bookmark it because I say, oh, I will be able to find it, and then I realize that I am looking for it one day, and I can't find it, so then I will go and bookmark it.

The most popular tags used by individuals to browse their personal bookmark collection were quite similar to those used to browse the community collection described above. Examples of tags used more often for personal bookmark search include: mine, education, learning, career and travel. These tags appear to categorize information resources of personal interest for career planning, training, or personal travel.

Explicit search of dogear bookmarks

Explicit search is overall used more frequently than personal search but less than community browsing. As described above, there is a general search capability provided within the dogear service. As can be seen in Table 3, the internal dogear search capability is the fourth most used way to "explore" the dogear collection (29,961 times). There is also an ability to search the *dogear* bookmarks as part of a more general enterprise search. The number of external search events shows that the external search plug-in is the second most used way to find bookmarks (70,706). Of particular note, is the high click-through rate (39% and 32%) for search actions, which indicates a more purposeful searching of the collection than for either personal or community browsing.

Several dogear users commented on the value of the dogear search that was integrated into the more general search tools (i.e. Google and enterprise search). One benefit was simply being reminded (inline) that related content has been bookmarked on dogear.

Another thing that happens is that even though the Google results are more specific generally, because it's more of a general search than dog ear, I may, depending who the person was that created the bookmark, I may tend to go look at it

Another informant indicated that she frequently did enterprise searches and then decided to redo the search in dogear.

Because a lot of times, I mean especially if it's an internal [enterprise] search, ..., you search for something and you're like, "Man, I can't find it." And then you just jump over to Dogear and you get it.

Other dogear end-users have indicated that an important reason for preferring the dogear results over generic search results was the fact that very inclusion in the dogear collection meant that the search had been actively pre-filtered by a community of interest or trusted IBM colleagues.

Patterns of Search

We were also interested in how patterns of search/browsing differed for different groups of end-users. In order to see whether there were differences in social bookmarking use as a function of bookmarking experience, we looked at the distribution of community versus personal search activities. We compared the distributions for experienced (or heavy) bookmarkers, which we defined as individuals having more than 100 bookmarks, with medium bookmarkers, which we defined as having between 10 and 100 bookmarks). The results can be seen in Figure 4.

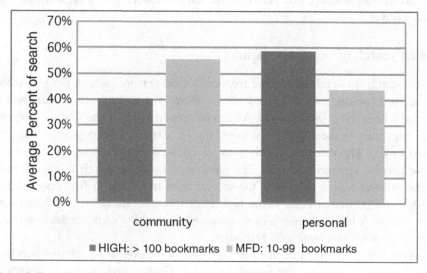

Figure 4. Type of navigation as a function of number of bookmarks.

The interesting result is that individuals with more bookmarks (>100 bookmarks) spend a significantly larger percentage of their browsing time looking at their own collection of bookmarks. This is consistent with a view that prolific bookmarkers spend time, and presumably derive more value, refinding things that they have previously found. The medium bookmarkers (10-99 bookmarks) spend a larger portion of their time exploring other people's collections. This suggests that less experienced bookmarkers spend more of their search time in learning or discovery search activities.

We would expect to see a change in searching behavior to occur over time as individuals add more and more bookmarks to their personal collection. In particular, we expect that bookmark organization and management will become increasingly important user activities for heavy bookmarkers, which is consistent with earlier reported research on browser-based bookmarks (Abrams, et al., 1998).

Looking for Patterns using Cluster Analysis

As with studies of general web browsing and search ((Heer and Chi, 2002; Sellen, et al., 2002) we expected to observe different search patterns emerge in the use of a social bookmarking service. To better see the patterns of use, we performed a cluster analysis (K-means) for the different types of search activities. We first normalized the use data for each end-user by computing the percentage of each search type (i.e., community, person, topic, personal, and explicit search). The K-means cluster analysis is then performed, which finds related groups of users with similar distributions of the five search activities. The resulting cluster solution, shown in Table 4, shows the average percentage of item type for each of four easily interpretable clusters. To help understand these clusters, we have also provided for each cluster: the number of individuals in the cluster (N), the average number of bookmarks, and the average number of browsing events.

Cluster 1 is comprised of end-users with the largest percentage of *personal* browsing activity (60 %), coupled with the largest average number of bookmarks (155). This cluster is comprised of the kinds of informants cited above who claim to use a social bookmarking service heavily to store a personal bookmark collection and then to refind things that were already found. The individual who indicated that she used dogear to manage a collection of blogs would be a good exemplar of this cluster.

Cluster 2 has the largest number of members (851) and appears to be made up of individuals who are heavy browsers of the community collection (49 %) as well as individuals who spend the largest percentage of time using *explicit search* (23%). This group is an interesting mix. They spend a fair amount of time performing social (community) browsing as well as explicit searching to find information that has already been found and bookmarked. The interview respondent who scans the recent bookmark list, or individuals who user explicit search to locate bookmarks would be exemplars of this cluster.

Clusters 3 and 4 are made up of individuals with less experience using the bookmarking service, as indicated by the lower average number of log events for these two groups (43 and 66 respectively), and fewer bookmarks (5 and 17 respectively). Cluster 3 has a heavy weighting on topic searches (46%) which is consistent with the informant above who described looking for information about "second life." Cluster 4, with a heavy weighting on people queries (42%) is suggestive of the informants above who describe looking for information from known experts or organization leaders.

The small number of average bookmarks for clusters 3 and 4 suggests that the initial use of a social bookmarking application is spent performing more exploratory search tasks like learning what has been bookmarked for a topic (e.g., Ajax or Web 2.0) or looking at what a particular colleague has been bookmarking.

	Cluster			
	1	2	3	4
Community	.20	**.49**	**.28**	**.26**
People	.08	.08	.08	**.42**
Topic	.04	.06	**.46**	.07
Personal	**.60**	.13	.07	.13
Explicit Search	.07	**.23**	.10	.13
N	466	851	238	317
Avg. bookmarks	155	34	5	17
Avg. # events	190	124	43	66

Table 4. Results of cluster analysis.

Discussion

In this paper we have investigated the use of a social bookmarking application within a large enterprise. We have described and examined the design elements that support different kinds of browsing or search activities, including social tags, people browsing, and multiple search interfaces (i.e. both internal dogear search and through the Firefox plug-in). The results of our log file analysis confirm that these navigational elements are used by end-users of the social bookmarking service, while interview comments provide support that both personal and social navigation benefits are being realized. The quantitative and qualitative results presented in this paper show that social bookmarking systems support a variety of exploratory search activities, which help satisfy end-users' learning and investigative information needs.

The results above show that community browsing is the most frequent way to search/browse for information. Community browsing includes looking at the community collection, looking at co-worker's collections and browsing by topics defined by social tags. This kind of social browsing may be due, in large part, to one of the unique characteristics of enterprise social bookmarking services. End-users of these kinds of services are required to use corporate identities (i.e. no pseudonyms allowed). This enables others in the enterprise to easily recognize a coworker in a list of people tags (see Fig 2(b)) or as a creator of a specific book-mark. Once recognized, it is easy to learn from organizational thought leaders or to learn about the interest of new team members. Furthermore, coworkers provide an important selection and filtering function for information content.

The interview comments indicated that a large portion of this community browsing is in support of what Marchionini would call *learning* and *investigative* search activities (Marchionini, 2006). For example, individuals mentioned following the name links in dogear to learn more about someone and to find out what others are interested in. Interviews also revealed cases in which dogear users followed a tag (or multiple tags) to learn about a particular technology. This is important because it helps promote informal discovery of information and learning about people. This exploration of other people's bookmarks is a very promising way to support lightweight information sharing or knowledge management within an organization.

The second most frequent form of search that we observed was explicit search. The relatively high proportion of click-throughs for search tasks, combined with interview comments, suggest that social bookmarking services provide a good way to capture high value pointers to information sources. This suggests that social bookmarking services, integrated with traditional search engines, have the potential to solve the tough enterprise search problem (Mukherjee and Mao, 2004). The explicit search capabilities appear to be used for what Marchionini refers to as *look-up* and *learning* activities.

The results of this study suggest that social bookmarking services provide significant benefits for managing personal bookmarks. There is substantial browsing of personal bookmarks, which often result in revisits to the original content source, suggesting the superiority of our system over more traditional bookmarking methods. The interview comments suggest that much of the use of personal bookmarks is to refind information, which would support various *look-up* search activities, as described by Marchionini (2006). The cluster results show that personal browsing is most often associated with a larger collection of personal bookmarks.

The results presented here are part of a growing body of work underway to understand how various kinds of collaborative tools can help with exploratory search (White, et al., 2006). There are a number of challenges in finding ways to integrate social interaction with exploratory search. Furthermore, there are a

number of measurement and evaluation challenges that have been identified for
these kinds of exploratory search tools (White, et al., 2006).

Design implications and future work

Most social bookmarking services (e.g., del.icio.us) provide a set of common core
features. Most provide community browsing by bookmark frequency or most recent bookmarks, as well as pivot queries by tags and names. In addition, all provide application specific search of the bookmark database. We would argue that
similar results would be found in a usage level analysis of these systems.

An enterprise-grade social bookmarking service, such as *dogear*, requires the
use and authentication of a real name identity. As described above, this allows
easy integration of other corporate collaboration tools within the bookmarking
service. This is important in that community browsing can be automatically augmented by links to corporate directories, blogs and other information sources. It is
possible that community searching will be a richer experience in a corporate
bookmarking system.

An enterprise bookmarking service is also different from many bookmarking
services found on the web in that the user population comes from a trusted community, and is often bound by an explicit corporate code of conduct. This may
change the kinds of social interaction on the site, and very likely change the content of the bookmark collection.

There are a number of implications for the future design of *dogear* (or similar
bookmarking services). It seems that although people prefer to browse by recency
(i.e. view recent), they actually find more useful information using popularity (as
indicated by click-through results).). So the interface should be redesigned to respect this. Similarly, for refinding personal resources the "mybookmarks" user
interface could better support tag searching by providing a list of recent search
terms or most used tags for each individual. And finally, people browsing could
be enhanced with group or *friends* support in the user interface. It is easy to imagine articulated social networks supported in this kind of service. The social network could be used for general bookmark displays or bookmark and tag recommendations.

There remain several interesting research questions for social bookmarking
applications. First, it is important to better understand how collaborative tagging
and social bookmarking can be more tightly integrated with enterprise search.
Second, while initial work has been done to understand tag and folksonomy development, there are a number of interesting questions about how to optimize
these vocabularies to support various browsing tasks. And finally, there are a
number of questions about how these kinds of social software applications are
adopted and how communities develop. Social network analytic techniques have
been explored and show promise as a way to understand this phenomenon.

References

Abrams, D., Baecker, R. and Chignell, M. (1998): 'Information archiving with bookmarks: personal Web space construction and organization'. In *Proceedings of the SIGCHI Conference on Human Factors in Computing Systems* Los Angeles, California, USA, April, 1998, pp. 41-48.

Damianos, L. E., Cuomo, D., Griffith, J., Hirst, D. M. and Smallwood, J. (2007): 'Exploring the Adoption, Utility, and Social Influences of Social Bookmarking in a Corporate Environment'. In *40th Annual Hawaii International Conference on System Sciences* Waikoloa, HI, USA January, 2007, pp. 86-86.

Dieberger, A. a. G., M. (2003): 'CoWeb - experiences with collaborative Web spaces.' In C. a. F. Lueg, D. : *From Usenet to CoWebs: Interacting with Social Information Spaces.* Springer-Verlag, New York, 2003, 155--166.

Golder, S. A. and Huberman, B. A. (2006): 'Usage patterns of collaborative tagging systems', *Journal of Information Science*, 32, 2, 2006, pp. 198-208.

Hammond, T., Hannay, T., Lund, B. and Scott, J. (2005): 'Social bookmarking tools (I) A General Review', *D-Lib Magazine*, 2005, ISSN: 1082-9873.

Heer, J. and Chi, E. H. (2002): 'Separating the swarm: categorization methods for user sessions on the web'. In *Proceedings of the SIGCHI Conference on Human Factors in Computing Systems*. Minneapolis, Minnesota, USA, April, 2002, pp. 243--250.

Jones, W., Bruce, H. and Dumais, S. (2003): 'How do people get back to information on the web? How can they do it better'. In *9th IFIP TC13 International Conference on Human-Computer Interaction (INTERACT 2003)* Zurich, Switzerland, Sept, 2003, 793-796.

Kittur, A., Chi, E., Pendelton, B., Suh, B. and Mytkowicz, T. (2007): 'Power of the Few vs. Wisdom of the Crowd: Wikipedia and the Rise of the Bourgeoisie.' In *Proceedings of the SIGCHI Conference on Human Factors in Computing Systems* San Jose, CA, USA, April, 2007, pp. 453--462.

Marchionini, G. (2006): 'Exploratory search: from finding to understanding', *Communications of the ACM*, 49, 4, 41-46.

Marlow, C., Naaman, M., Boyd, D. and Davis, M. (2006): 'HT06, tagging paper, taxonomy, Flickr, academic article, to read'. In *Proceedings of the seventeenth conference on Hypertext and hypermedia* Odense, Denmark, August, 2006, pp. 31-39.

Millen, D. R., Feinberg, J. and Kerr, B. (2006): 'Dogear: Social bookmarking in the enterprise'. In *Proceedings of the SIGCHI Conference on Human Factors in Computing Systems* Montreal, Quebec, Canada, April, 2006, pp. 111-120.

Mukherjee, R. and Mao, J. (2004): 'Enterprise Search: Tough Stuff', *Queue*, 2, 2, April, 2004, 36-46.

Munro, A. J., Hook, K., and Benyon (1999): *Social Navigation of Information Space.* Springer, London, 1999.

Sellen, A. J., Murphy, R. and Shaw, K. L. (2002): 'How knowledge workers use the web'. In *Proceedings of the SIGCHI Conference on Human Factors in Computing Systems*. Minneapolis, Minnesota, USA, April, 2002, pp. 227-234.

Sen, S., Lam, S. K., Rashid, A. M., Cosley, D., Frankowski, D., Osterhouse, J., Harper, F. M. and Riedl, J. (2006): 'tagging, communities, vocabulary, evolution'. In *Proceedings of the 2006 20th Anniversary Conference on Computer Supported Cooperative Work* Banff, Alberta, Canada, November, 2006, pp. 181-190.

White, R. W., Kules, B., Drucker, S. M. and Schraefel, m. c. (2006): 'Introduction SPECIAL ISSUE: Supporting exploratory search ', *Communications of the ACM*, 49, 4, 36-39.

White, R. W., Muresan, G. and Marchionini, G. (2006): 'Report on ACM SIGIR 2006 workshop on evaluating exploratory search systems', *SIGIR Forum*, 40, 2, 52-60.

L. Bannon, I. Wagner, C. Gutwin, R. Harper, and K. Schmidt (eds.).
ECSCW'07: Proceedings of the Tenth European Conference on Computer Supported Cooperative
Work, 24-28 September 2007, Limerick, Ireland
© Springer 2007   41

Instrumental action: the timely exchange of implements during surgical operations

Marcus Sanchez Svensson, Christian Heath and Paul Luff

Blekinge Insitute of Technology, Sweden and King's College London, UK

Marcus.sanchezsvensson@bth.se, Christian.Heath@kcl.ac.uk, Paul.Luff@kcl.ac.uk

Abstract. In this paper we analyse an apparently simple collaborative activity, that of passing an implement from one person to another. The particular case we consider is surgical operations where nurses and surgeons routinely pass instruments to one another. Through fine-grained analysis of specific instances we address,- the preparatory work engaged in prior to passing, the ways in which the layout of artefacts is organised with respect to the temporal ordering of the activity, and how this arrangement can be reconfigured in the light of problems and circumstances that arise in an operation. We examine how passing an implement is finely shaped within the course of its articulation with regard to emerging actions of the participants. We suggest that an analysis of fine details of seemingly simple activities with objects may have implications for our understanding of collaborative work, and a one or two key concepts that have informed the design of advanced solutions.

Introduction

Despite the rich and varied ethnographic tradition within CSCW and the long-standing interest in the analysis of technologies in action, the ways in which physical objects and artefacts are arranged, grasped, manipulated, exchanged, and deployed remains surprisingly neglected. Many studies, including our own, have ascribed a certain analytic primacy to talk in collaboration and paid less attention to the ways in which seemingly simple objects and artefacts serve to underpin and enable the concerted accomplishment of complex activities. In this regard, the surgical operation is of particular interest, since despite its organisational complexity and the highly specialised knowledge and skills it demands, many of the tasks performed by surgeons rely upon relatively mundane objects and artefacts;

indeed artefacts that are not too dissimilar to tools that one might find in the kitchen or in a shed at bottom of the garden – scissors, knives, saws, pliers, tweezers and the like. The skilled and timely use of these tools, their availability, exchange and manipulation, is an integral feature of the accomplishment of this highly complex collaborative activity.

In this paper, we consider how personnel within the operating theatre, in particular the surgeon and the scrub nurse, systematically, yet unobtrusively, accomplish the timely exchange of implements; an exchange that preserves the smooth and largely unproblematic production of highly complex tasks and activities. In particular, we address the ways in which instruments are configured, displayed, held, handed and received, to enable the practical accomplishment of particular actions in specific, situatedly relevant ways. In surgery, the very passing of an instrument to another, rests upon a sensitivity to, an awareness, an understanding, and an anticipation of how and when the implement will be used at this moment on this occasion. The analysis of this subtle yet systematic and robust form of collaborative activity is used to reflect upon three areas of longstanding interest to research in CSCW – awareness, affordance and ubiquitous computing.

Despite the long-standing tradition of research on work and interaction in the delivery of health care, both in CSCW and more generally the social sciences, the operating theatre and surgery remains relatively neglected. This may come as some surprise when one considers the complex organisational structure of surgery, the array of tools and artefacts that are brought to bear in its accomplishment, and the various initiatives designed to enhance, even transform, current practice though the introduction of new technologies and digital resources. There are a number of important exceptions, carefully crafted studies that have begun to chart the complex interactional and communicative organisation that underpins practical accomplishment of the surgical operation including for example Nardi et al (1993), Mondada (2001), Moreira (2004), Goodwin et al (2005) and Koschman et al (2006). A number of these researchers have considered operations that use video-mediated ('key hole') techniques either to support the work of co-present colleagues (Nardi et al 1993 and Koschman et al 2006) or to also support distributed collaboration (Mondada, 2001). For example, in detailed studies Mondada and Koschman et al show how the surgeons coordinate their talk and delicate gestures with their hands and instruments when operating on a patient to create and configure a shared workplace and establish references to particular locations and features of the surgical field. Moreover, Hindmarsh and Pilnick (in press, 2007) describe how the passing of instruments by the nurses in the anaesthetic room is timed and designed to anticipate how and when an instrument will be used. These studies point to the distinctiveness of surgical operations and the ways in which their organisation differs from the sites that have more predominantly formed the focus of analytic interest in CSCW. Suchman (1993) has aptly characterised these other work sites as 'centres of coordination', and shown the ways in which they encompass such seemingly diverse domains as air traffic control, station operation rooms, emergency dispatch, and airport operation centres. It is worth noting that such domains not infrequently involve a range of personnel with overlapping skills and knowledge that are primarily concerned with coordinating the activities of a range of physically dispersed individuals. In this regard surgical operations are rather different. They involve a complex division of labour that involves personnel from various occupations, with very different skills to collaboratively accomplish a single, principal activity that is performed by a particular individual namely the surgeon. The principal activity accomplished (and accountable) with respect to a prescribed set of specialised conventions and procedures relies upon the timely and organised contributions of others including the anaesthetist(s), registrar and nurses. The seemingly simple arrangement and exchange of instruments that enable the surgeon to undertake the various aspects of the procedure(s) provides the foundation to the collaborative accomplishment of the operation and in some cases the very survival of the patient.

Aside from providing an interesting and distinctive ethnographic opportunity, the analysis of the collaborative accomplishment of the surgical operation raises a number of interrelated issues that have been of some interest within CSCW. Firstly, as Schmidt (2002) points out the concept of 'awareness' has not only provided a vehicle to address the complex processes of organisational interaction that enable personnel subtly and unobtrusively to coordinate their actions and activities with each other, but also informed the design and development of a number of technical environments designed to support and enable, in many cases distributed, collaboration. Surgical operations and their reliance on instruments and implements, raise some interesting issues with regard to awareness, and point to the ways for example in which contingent assemblies and configurations of tools are designed, and can serve, to enable a number of participants to see and envisage, the structure of the procedure and 'where we are now and about to be'. In our analysis we suggest that awareness does not simply rely on participants possessing the same information or knowledge about a particular activity but more on how they are able to contribute actively to the contingent organisation of awareness and interaction – in this case, the ways in which the participants in and through the grasping, handling, organisation and use of instruments can orientate prospectively to the upcoming actions and concerns of others.

Secondly, over the past decade or so we have witnessed a burgeoning interest in tangibility and the ways in which the physical manipulation of objects and artefacts can enable computational resources and capabilities. The contributions of Weiser (1991), Fitzmaurice et al. (1995), Ishii and Ulmer (1997) amongst others are critical in this regard, in particular for how they reveal the significance and enormous potential of creating interdependencies between the physical, the tangible and the digital. However, as Hornecker (2005) recently suggested, notwithstanding the growing commitment to tangibility and tangible user interfaces, developments have primarily focused on individual or single-user interfaces rather than collaborative aspects of tangible interaction and interactivity.

Thirdly, CSCW has understandably treated the concept of 'affordances' with some reservation and care and yet it is widely recognised that it does provide a rich resource with which to reflect upon the qualities and design of artefacts and technologies (e.g. Gaver, 1991; Norman, 1988). As we have suggested, many of the implements used during the surgical operation, are not unlike familiar tools and artefacts that one can purchase from a kitchen shop or home care store. There are, of course, subtle differences between many of the implements used in surgery and their more common counterparts. More importantly however, in the surgical operation we can see how the qualities of implements, their 'affordances', are oriented to, and constituted, collaboratively to enable the smooth and unproblematic exchange and deployment of particular tools and artefacts. It is also interesting to note, that not withstanding the principal qualities and design for particular users, implements enable a broad variety of applications and uses not conventionally associated with the activities in question.

An ecology of instruments

In the daily work of undertaking surgical operations surgeons are dependent on the availability of many specially designed surgical instruments – the tools of the trade. Every surgical case has its own requirements and demands a variety of different instruments for the performance of particular procedures involved. Instrument modification varies from the strength needed for bone work, to length required to reach depth, and to delicacy required to approach microscopic structures. The design of these surgical instruments has evolved over many years and has provided the surgeon with an array of different instruments suited to the specifics of particular interventions and procedures (Figure 1).

Given the range of different instruments used and the intricate demands of the actual surgical procedures, including the complex and frequent interaction and communication with other members of the surgical team, the surgeon is supported by one or several scrub nurses. The role of the scrub nurse, among other duties, is to provide assistance by passing the correct tools to the surgeon during the course of procedure. The key to the successful accomplishment of a surgical intervention is the timely availability and efficiency of tools. Surgical instruments not working properly or not immediately available may delay procedures, interrupt other activities or sometimes even jeopardise the safety of the patient.

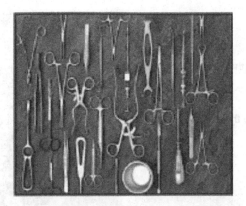

Figure 1. A great variety of surgical instruments

Let us join the action in the course of a surgical procedure when a surgeon gives a simple request for an instrument to a scrub nurse and the scrub nurse passes that instrument to the surgeon (fragment 1). At this moment the surgeon (S) is using a drill and a suction tool to gain access to an osteoma, or tumour, in the area above the patient's eyebrow. Two surgical trainees (T1 and T2) have joined the operation to function as skilled assistants to the surgeon and also to learn about this procedure. To the far left (in the images) is the scrub nurse (N), looking down on the instrument table. When we enter the scene, the surgeon is engaged in an elaborate discussion with the trainees about the case and procedures (image 1a). Within the discussion the surgeon intersperses a request for an instrument – "the (1.0) freer please". Shortly following the instruction the scrub nurse fetches the instrument (an elevator tool) from the instrument table and passes the instrument to the surgeon (1b). The surgeon takes the instrument and continues to address her trainees by redirecting their attention to the surgical phenomenon by saying "you can just see there" and using the instrument just received to expose the osteoma for the trainees (1c).

Fragment 1

S: (…) septation becomes part of
     the intersinus septum which is in-
     tegrated into the osteoma (0.1)
     that's the problem and that's what
     we are on here what I am doing is
     drilling around it (0.3) and you
     can just see::   →

     (1.0)

S: the::
     (1.0)

Nurse (N)   (T1)   (T2) Surgeon (S)

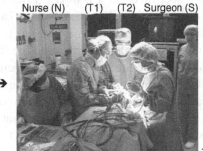

1a

S: freer please

(Scrub nurse passes the instrument)   →

    (0.2)

S: you can just see there:::

    (1.0)

S: the::

    (1.5)

S: juncture (1.0) (just there) [(0.5)   →
    between the osteoma

T1:   [mmm

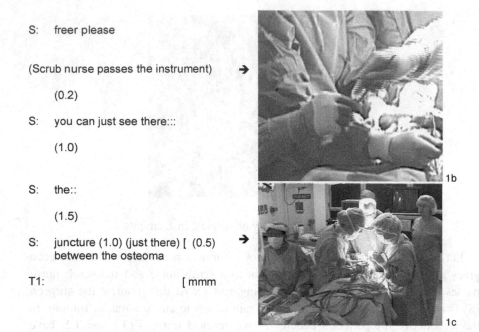

1b

1c

   In this fragment we witness the smooth and seemingly unproblematic handling
and passing of instruments. It involves the surgeon giving an instruction to which
the scrub nurse immediately responds by fetching a tool and placing it in her
hands. One of the challenging aspects of passing the correct tools to the surgeon
is for the scrub nurse to know the names of all the range of different instruments.
Learning the names can be difficult as there is no standardised nomenclature for
the instruments. Sometimes the brand of the instrument is used and sometimes the
inventor has given the instrument a name. Moreover, the same surgical instruments may have different names at different hospitals. Surgeons themselves do
not always use the correct name and sometimes they use blanket terms or make
up their own. However, the scrub nurse does not just respond to a request by
quickly recognising its name and passing the correct instrument; the act of passing an object involves a complex series of actions and activities drawing on a
range of important skills and resources. Even in this simple fragment we can see
how the use and handling of instruments is embedded in a complex weave of multiple interrelated activities and responsibilities. For example, the passing is done
in relation to other distinct and parallel activities. It is done in relation to the conduct of a delicate procedure involving the demands and use of a range of different
surgical tools. It is also done in relation to other competing activities of the surgeon, in this case whilst she give elaborate characterisations and descriptions of
the disease and to the trainees, or within the developing course of the surgery, the
surgeon now and then may also have to direct particular attention towards the
work of the anaesthesiologist and their joint concerns with the management of the

patient's condition. In this way it can be recognised how the passing of instruments are often secondary to other activities such as teaching and medical work. Given such circumstances, there may not be the opportunity to make an explicit request or instruction about what might be required at a particular moment. This will then place demands on others to prepare and communicate the timely availability and smooth transfer of instruments during the course of the operation. In such circumstances we find the smooth accomplishment of the use and handling of instruments relies upon a tacit body of skills, competencies and practice.

Before the operation begins the scrub nurse prepares the supplies and equipment needed for this particular surgical case. Different types of operations require specific tools and accessories. One of the most important aspects of selecting the instruments for the operation is to be familiar with the surgical approach and the anatomy involved - the instruments selected and prepared have to support the specific case and the ways in which the function of particular instruments can do the work. During the course of the operation, the surgeon uses a variety of tools that can be classified by their function: for cutting and dissecting, grasping and holding, clamping and occluding, exposing and retracting, and so on. Many of these categories include different types of instruments. For example, instruments for cutting and dissecting include a variety of scalpels, knives and scissors of different sizes and configurations.

The principal way of preparing for surgery is to assemble sets of instruments. Every set may include all the appropriate instruments needed for the case or a particular part of the procedure. There are standardised sets that may include all the instruments needed to open and close the incision, along with the ones needed to complete the surgical procedure. Commonly, the nurse also includes additional instruments based on information about the physiological status of the patient, proposed incision site, the character and conduct of a single procedure, and the surgeon's personal preferences. By obtaining information during the preoperative assessment and consulting particular preference cards, nurses know how to complement the selection. The instruments in these sets are carefully selected with regard to the procedure and the particular manoeuvres expected to be performed by the surgeon. For example, the type and the location of the tissues to be cut determines which scissor or knife the surgeon will use; the length may provide the means through which the surgeon can reach depths of body cavities; and the size and depth of incisions may determine the width and length for appropriate exposure of the surgical site. Also, as all surgeons have different ways of using their hands and fingers, the surgeon may want instruments that fit particularly well with their own way of grasping and manipulating instruments during particular manoeuvres.

Based on this competence and knowledge about the organisation and procedures of the particular case, the scrub nurse makes available the sets of instruments on tables next to the operating bed. For most cases, the nurses prepare two tables: the instrument (back) table and the Mayo stand. The instrument table provides an area for all the instruments and the sterile supplies to be used during the procedure. The Mayo stand is used to hold instruments that will be used more frequently during the current stage of the surgical operation (see figure 2).

The preparation of sets of instruments laid out on the instrument table is one fundamental way of contributing to the smooth passing of instruments. So, for example, in our first fragment the scrub nurse responded quickly to the request for the "Freer" instrument simply because it was anticipated. The instrument was already made available on the instrument table in front of her, together with other currently relevant instruments, because the scrub nurse knew the case and the current stage of the procedure - a stage where particular instruments are needed to open and lift a flap of the scull in order to expose the tumour. Also, the scrub nurse knew about the particular instruments – in this case, the "Freer", which is an instrument frequently used for separating and lifting bone structures when exposing a tumour.

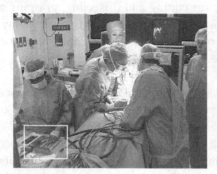

Figure 2 – Instruments selected for the particular case

Scrub nurses then do not merely need to learn the names of specific instruments, their shapes, qualities and physical attributes or to develop the ability to identify and pass instruments quickly. Assisting the surgeon requires them to organise and make assemblies of what potentially could be the relevant tools used in the operation. They configure the ecology in order for them to provide an efficient and timely response to a request.

Dynamic arrangements of instruments

It is not always possible to have all the instruments required for an operation laid out on one instrument table. We can see in previous examples how a Mayo stand is used to hold instruments that will be used more frequently. Even though each hospital normally has procedures for how tools should be laid out for particular operations, we frequently observe the scrub nurse are re-configuring and altering the organisation of instruments laid out on the Mayo stand. Consider an example (Fragment 2).

The surgeon is currently at a stage of a surgical intervention where she has exposed the area of the bone structure on the forehead (surgeon right; surgical assistant left). She is currently using a drill and other supplementary tools for exposing the cavity area (the frontal sinus) under the bone structure. On the instrument table (image 2a) the scrub nurse has placed the drill holder in the middle of the table next to the patient's bed (right); far to the left is a tray of additional instruments and behind the drill holder (for the nurse) is a pile of swabs. These are currently used by the surgical assistant (standing opposite the surgeon) holding the scalp and exposing the surgical area. The most relevant instruments are laid out in front of the drill holder.

When we enter the action the scrub nurse removes an instrument from the collection and then lays out the remaining ones on the table. The scrub nurse moves one instrument - (the "Freer") – to the first position in a collection of four instruments on the table (2b). A moment later, the surgeon asks for the "Freer". The scrub nurse looks down on the table and immediately finds it, first in the row of instruments next to the surgeon. She picks up the tool (2c) and hands it over.

Fragment 2

Nurse   Surgeon

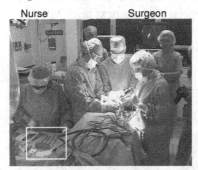

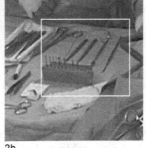

2a   2b   2c

In this fragment the scrub nurse orients to the relevance of a dynamic arrangement of instruments – that is, she organises the available instruments in a particular order with regard to the contingencies of the surgical activity. The scrub nurse has laid out those instruments and accessories that are going to be used during this procedure – for example the drills, the elevator instruments, the swabs (other instrument are kept on the instrument table behind her back). However, on this table the scrub nurse has also created a small area dedicated for the 4-5 most frequently and currently used tools (see frame in image 2b). These instruments are placed in a particular order. In this example the scrub nurse places the instrument anticipated to be used next, nearest to the surgeon. She creates an assembly of instruments where their spatial arrangement is related to their temporal relevance – the current assembly mirrors the temporal organisation of the activity it supports.

This dynamic arrangement of instruments may not only designed to support the nurse's own contribution so that she can pass the next instrument in a timely manner. There are many occasions – say when the surgeon is engaging in a procedure which only uses one or two instruments and is located a position next to the instrument table - when surgeons take instruments from the table directly. One way for the scrub nurse to support the surgeon to do this is to expose single instruments or organise the instruments into distinct groups. In the next fragment (3) the surgeon has just started to take and return a number of instruments laid out on the table. As a result of this, the layout of instruments has become disorganised making it increasingly difficult for the surgeon to find the next relevant tool. The scrub nurse notices the problem and helps the surgeon find the next one (3a). She removes the unused instruments (3b) and places another one further away from the rest (3c) – one of the two instruments the surgeon is currently using at this particular point.

Fragment 3

nurse   surgeon

3a   3b   3c

By noticing the difficulties the surgeon is facing in finding the next instrument, the scrub nurse clears the area on the table and places a relevant one next to the surgeon. The scrub nurse knows that it is the knife that the surgeon needs after using the elevator instrument – because she has been able to observe that those two instruments are working as a pair at the moment. By doing this she reconfigures the assembly of tools on the table so that the surgeon can freely return and find the two instruments currently being used. The dynamic arrangement of instruments on the table supports the ways in which the scrub nurse and the surgeon can coordinate how instruments are made available, here and now. A working division of labour emerges that is made possible by the nurse not only remaining sensitive to the moment-to-moment demands of the activity, but anticipating what will be required next. The dynamic arrangement of surgical instruments is a spatial and material interface – an ecology – that makes possible very fine moments of co-ordination.

A practical orientation to the passing and handling of instruments

In the examples provided so far, we have shown how the assembly and organisation of the instruments provides ways for the scrub nurse to make available a relevant set of instruments for the current surgical procedure. However, handling instruments can also be seen to be coordinated in other ways.

Consider the previous fragment once more (Fragment 4). We noticed that the scrub nurse creates gaps between the tools (4a). These not only support the visibility of the individual instrument for the surgeon but also support the practical task of grasping and taking the instrument from the table (4a-4b). Moreover, the orientation and direction of the instruments placed on the table also can facilitate how the scrub nurse transfers an object from the table directly into the hand of the surgeon (4c).

Fragment 4

 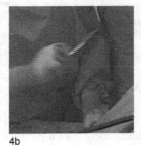 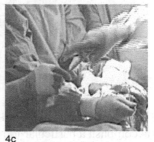

4a   4b   4c

In this fragment the scrub nurse takes the first instrument in a sequence of four (4a), where the spaces between the instruments allow her to easily grasp each individual instrument. The tools are positioned and orientated on the table, with the sharp end facing away from the scrub nurse. This facilitates how each is passed on to the surgeon (4b-4c), so knives and scissors can be passed without the risk of cutting herself or the surgeon. In this arrangement the instruments can also be safely taken directly from the table by the surgeon. The instrument has been positioned and orientated for the purpose of being grasped or handed safely and appropriately to someone else. It is important to note that whilst performing procedures and collaborating with others on a complex procedure surgeons may have limited opportunities to look at the instrument made available to them or have little possibility to re-position the instrument in their hands before use. For the one passing the instrument then, they need to take, present and transfer the instrument in ways that are congruent with how the instrument is going to be used and handled by another participant in a particular activity. Let us consider another example.

We will consider a procedure in which the surgeon uses an instrument called a clip applier (Figure 3). Many operations involve skin incisions and one of difficulties when making an incision is that the skin can easily start to bleed. Sometimes when it is not possible to stop bleeding by conventional measures the surgeon uses small clips to prevent the loss of blood. When the surgeon has made the primary incision in the head scalp, the surgeon controls the bleeding from the wound by applying clips around the scalp edge. This procedure requires the clip applier. The clips are placed on the tip of this applier. Preparation of the clip applier involves the scrub nurse opening the applier, placing the clip on the point and closing the applier to make the clip open. Between the shanks of clip applier is a locking mechanism that keeps the instrument locked with the clip opened and ready for applying (as in Figure 3). When the surgeon wants to apply the clip he or she pushes the open clip against the scalp edge and attaches the clip by releasing the mechanism (by separating the shanks).

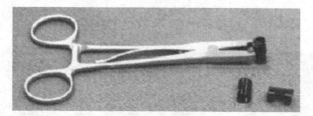

Figure 3. Clips and the Clip Applier

Clearly, the clip applier, like most instruments, has its own design and is made to accomplish a particular job and function in a particular fashion. When using the clip applier, for example, surgeons inserts their fingers through the finger rings and orient the tip of the applier and the actual clip towards the scalp edge. They then separate the finger rings and the shanks to release and close the clip around the scalp edge. These practical actions are what the scrub nurse orientates to in the passing of the instrument.

As we enter fragment 5 the surgeon is asking for the next clip and returns the empty clip applier to the scrub nurse (5a). The surgeon keeps her hand in the air waiting for the next instrument; whilst waiting, the surgeon looks at the surgical field and uses a towel with her other hand to stop the bleeding. The scrub nurse fetches another clip and makes the instrument available for the surgeon (5b). The scrub nurse displays the instrument for the surgeon by placing it in her field of view. The scrub nurse presents the clip applier in a position with the ring handles facing up and the clip facing down (see frame in 5b). The surgeon starts to move her hand towards the instrument and adjusts her hand so that her finger and thumb fit the position and orientation of the ring handles. Her gaze shifts briefly towards the instrument as she inserts her finger and thumb through the rings. The surgeon moves the instrument away from the scrub nurse and moves it directly into position at the edge of the scalp and releases the clip (5c). Already at this point, the scrub nurse has prepared and made available the next instrument (see 5c).

Fragment 5

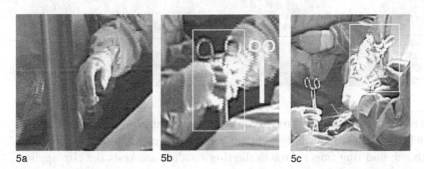

5a   5b   5c

This brief fragment points to the ways in which participants accomplish a smooth passing of the instrument. First, the scrub nurse displays the instrument and its availability (5b). Despite focusing on other matters, the surgeon can still notice that the next instrument is available. Second, the scrub nurse holds and configures the instrument in the air so that the surgeon can easily grasp and take it (5b). Third, the scrub nurse presents the instrument in a way (5b) that enables the surgeon to take the instrument, so it can be used directly (5c). Thus, the instrument is not only presented for easy grasping, but also passed on for immediate use so that this does not demand any reconfiguration of the instrument by the surgeon afterwards – enabling the surgeon to focus on the procedure and other necessary activities such as teaching work and communicating with the anaesthetic team.

One might expect that given the design of any particular instrument there would be little variation in the ways an instrument can be passed. However, if we consider a series of passings of similar instruments it becomes apparent that the ways in which it can be presented and transferred can be transformed within a given procedure. For example, in the two subsequent passings of clip appliers we see subtle differences in the ways the implements are positioned and orientated.

Fragment 6

6a

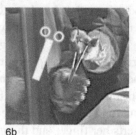

6b

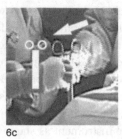

6c

Fragment 7

7a

7b

7c

In the next passing (fragment 6) we can see how the surgeon is holding the clip applier in her hand when attaching a clip on the skin edge (6a), as in (5c). She has put her thumb and ring finger through the ring handles and rests the clip applier against the palm of her hand with her elbows pointing downwards (see image 6a). The surgeon returns the empty clip applier in the same way as she positioned the instrument when releasing the clip (6b). We can then see how the scrub nurse in the next passing presents a clip applier using the same orientation of the instrument just employed by the surgeon (6c). In this example (fragment 7), we see how the configuration of the passing is informed by the previous use and handled in a similar manner. The surgeon puts her thumb and long finger through the ring handles but now rather than resting it against the palm of the hand (as in 6a) she directs the shanks away from her hand with her elbows pointing upwards (7a). This is also how the instrument is handed back to the scrub nurse (7b) who then presents the next clip applier in a way that allows the surgeon to grasp it that way again (7c).

What we can see in these two instances is that the instrument is being passed rather differently: in the first instance it is held in a "up-position" with the ring handles facing upwards (6c); and in the second instance it is held in a "side-position" with the ring handles directed horizontally towards the surgeon, in line with the hand (7c). These different instrument configurations seem to be informed by the scrub nurse's observation of how the surgeon is progressively holding and applying the clips.

In these fragments the scrub nurse seems to orientating to the changing practi-calities of accomplishing this particular procedure at this particular moment. For example in this case the way the instrument is applied depends on the position of the surgeon relative to the patient or the area of the surgical site, or the instrument may be held in a slightly different way depending on the distance or orientation to the area on the scalp edge where the next clip is going to be attached. Again, we see how the passing and handling of an instrument is intimately connected with the character and progression of the surgical operation and the material and func-tional features of instruments being used. Indeed, both participants may be sensi-tive to quite fine details of the other's conduct when passing and grasping an in-strument. Consider the following example where the scrub nurse has just prepared the next clip and the surgeon is about to hand back the instrument currently being used. The surgeon is now applying clips further around the scalp.

Fragment 8

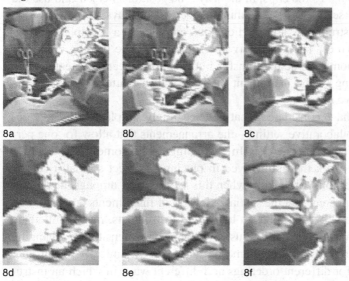

The scrub nurse observing the surgical procedure begins to move the new clip applier that is in her right hand slowly towards the surgeon. She holds the instru-ment in the field of view of the surgeon, keeping it still and waiting to be grasped (8a). A moment later, the surgeon releases the clip and removes the instrument from the surgical field. The scrub nurse opens her left hand displaying readiness to receive the used instrument (8b). As the surgeon places the used clip applier in the nurse's left hand, the scrub nurse continues to move the new instrument with her right hand towards the surgeon's right hand (8c). The surgeon briefly turns her attention to the instrument now being passed on to her and moves her hand towards it (8d). As the surgeon is about to put her thumb and index finger through the ring handles, she makes a delicate adjustment of her hands and fingers: seemingly rotating her hand to the right, bending and straightening her index and long fingers. The scrub nurse, who is looking at these reconfigurations, accordingly makes a slight shift of the instrument to the right whilst continuing to direct the ring handles in a motion towards the surgeon's pointing fingers (8e). The surgeon then thrusts her thumb and long finger through the ring handles and then upwards bringing the instrument towards her. The scrub nurse follows through the movement upwards for a brief moment before releasing it into the sole grasp of the surgeon (8f).

This fragment reveals a complex configuration and reconfiguration of hands and instruments by both participants as an implement is transferred from one hand to another. It is not simply that one person holds an instrument still for another then to grab, but, in passing the instruments is sensitive to how another is going to grasp, hold, orient and manipulate an instrument for a particular purpose in given circumstances. In this case as the surgeon moves around the scalp she has to change the way she applies the clips, in the ways she positions herself and use the clip applier. The nurse is sensitive to this change and displays this in how she passes the next instrument. The participants engage in a complex micro-coordination of activities. The progressive performance of the passing embodies not only an orientation to an actual transfer but also a prospective orientation to an upcoming handling of the instrument in the practical matters of putting the instrument to effective use.

In this paper we have considered what is a seemingly simple activity that occurs in a complex collaborative setting – the arrangements that allow for one person to pass an object to someone else. In examining this in some detail we have seen the preparatory work that is involved in placing an object so that it can be passed in a timely fashion, particularly when this is one object amongst an assembly of objects. It is apparent that the spatial assembly of instruments is sensitive to their potential temporal organisation. In laying out instruments, nurses anticipate the order in which implements will be used. They also are sensitive to changing circumstances and problems that may emerge. They can dynamically reconfigure the scene, allowing for different orderings and different ways in which an instrument can be passed or not passed at all but picked up by another. We can also see how even the ways in which objects are passed can be transformed, either in the light of current circumstances, the activities of the recipient or prior actions, like in the way another person passes back an object or whether they needed to shift it in their own hand before use. A simple passing of an instrument is accomplished by a fine micro-coordination of activities involving activities by both the passer and the recipient.

Discussion

For a number of years researchers in CSCW and cognate disciplines have suggested we look beyond conventional technologies and studies for ways to develop innovative systems to support everyday activities. Particular attention has focused on the possibilities of augmenting artefacts with digital capabilities so that individual appliances can provide novel kinds of information and computational support; support that can be embedded in, and resonate with, the local environment (Weiser, 1991). In order to develop ubiquitous technologies, it has been argued that we need to have a wide-ranging understanding of the ways in which ordinary artefacts are used within the accomplishment of everyday practical activities and in particular to explicate the characteristics and competences that enable such tools and appliances to be deployed to serve a range of practical purposes. The handling and exchange of instruments during the surgical operation raises issues that may bear upon the development of ubiquitous technologies; issues that resonate with long-standing concerns within CSCW.

Awareness remains a pervasive resource in reflecting upon the design and deployment of ubiquitous technologies to support collaboration and yet, as Schmidt (2002) notes, further analytic attention is required to unpack its organisational characteristics and significance. In this regard, there are a number of aspects of the instrument handling in the operating theatre that raise some interesting and perhaps relevant issues with respect to our understanding of awareness. In the first place, we can see, for example, how the arrangement, or configuration of an assembly of instruments, objects and artefacts, provide resources to enable the structure or trajectory of action to be seen, anticipated and accomplished. The arrangement is organisationally, interactionally and contingently implicative: its reconfiguration transforms the field of expected possibilities. Secondly, awareness, is not an abstract, nor simply a general competence, but rather depends upon, and is inseparable from, highly specialised skills and competencies that are part and parcel of the accountable accomplishment of the tasks at hand. In others words it is by virtue of practiced familiarity with, and engagement in, the activities at hand, that participants can be 'sensibly' aware of each others conduct, its implications and the matters at hand. Thirdly, the simple passing of an instrument in a timely and appropriate manner, directs attention to the ways in which 'awareness' relies upon the participants' abilities to prospectively anticipate particular actions and to recognise, and orient to the emerging and contingent, trajectories of action. In turn, particular events, activities, happenings and like, inevitably require that participants retrospectively reshape and reconfigure a sense of what's next, and what's after that. To treat 'awareness' as a 'state' or a general competence, or render it a 'fat moment', to corrupt Garfinkel's (1967) expression, rather than as ongoingly accomplished within the specialised demands and arrangements of particular environments might prove a misnomer when reflecting upon the design and development of ubiquitous and collaborative systems.

Our observations of the arrangement, handling and use of instruments during the surgical operation might also have some bearing on the concept of 'affordance'; a concept that has been roughly treated within CSCW and HCI. Despite the important debates concerning the criteria and characteristics of affordance (e.g. Gaver, 1991; Norman, 1988), we can begin to see how particular properties of an artefact are situationally and contingently constituted by participants themselves, in and through interaction and collaboration. Notwithstanding the characteristics of implements and the 'constraints' that they may place on, or engender from, action, we can see the very different ways in which the same instrument is handled and used by different participants within the same setting. These ways of approaching and handing instruments are of course inextricably embedded within the practicalities and practices that inform an activity's accomplishment. They may also be sensitive, as we have seen, to a co-participant's anticipated use, here and now, of the implement. In other words, we might need to readdress the analytic horizon of affordances and begin to take seriously the highly variable and contingent ways in which the 'same' object might inform and be informed by action and interaction.

These observations also bear upon the growing interest in CSCW and cognate fields of enquiry on, 'tangibility' (e.g. Ishii and Ullmer 1997) and allowing people to communicate through 'touch and feel' (e.g. Strong and Gaver, 1996). It has been suggested that the design of systems to support collaboration might fruitfully benefit from novel developments in haptic technologies (e.g. Adcock et al 2004). These recommendations have largely focussed on providing individuals with haptic feedback including a sense of the object's size, position or movement. Moreover, research into tangible and haptic interaction has not focused much attention on the relationship between form (appearance), function and action, and its relevance to interaction and collaboration, as pointed out by Sitorus et al (2007). With requirements for training surgeons so they can learn the 'feel of an operation' and the introduction of robotic and other sophisticated technologies to support medical interventions, it is not surprising that there has been considerable interest in haptic technologies in the surgical setting (e.g. Gerovich et al 2004). The simple of exchange of implements during a surgical operation raises, we believe, some interesting issues concerning tangibility. The smooth exchange of instruments, for example, relies upon the participant's ability to sense the shifting weight and balance of particular implement, to enable the passing hand to withdraw and the recipient to grasp and remove the object (in the situationally appropriate manner). The shifting tactile qualities of the implements, and the activities of exchange, are critical to collaboration and the performance of accomplishing the highly complex task of surgery. In this, and one suspects many other circumstances, we need to begin to consider how tactile properties of 'objects' can be reproduced to support distinctive, collaborative, in some cases simultaneous use of the same artefact. In other words, in rendering the digital, tangible, to support for example the performance of remote tasks, we may well need to prioritise the differential, yet collaborative aspects of an instrument's practical application or deployment. In turn, we suspect this will demand more detailed empirical studies that begin to delineate the ways in which touch and feel inform the concerted accomplishment of many workplace activities.

We believe that one of the most important contributions of CSCW since its inception has been the emergence of a burgeoning body of naturalistic research concerned with the social organisation of everyday activities and in particular cooperation and collaboration in the workplace. For many of these studies, it has proved a challenge to draw out their specific implications for the design and development of advanced technologies, and some cynicism, perhaps rightly, has accompanied these attempts. It may however be inappropriate to assess the contribution of such studies with regard to their short term implications for the design of particular technologies; indeed as we are all aware, given the institutional constraints that frequently bear upon system development, it is unlikely that ethnography will meet with much more success than other methods used within the field of CSCW and, more generally, in HCI. As others have suggested, it might be more worthwhile to begin to delineate more systematically the ways in which our findings concerning collaboration, communication and the situated use of tools and technologies, ranging from the banal to the highly complex, may provide resources for developing a re-specification, a more profound realignment of the ways in which we conceptualise technology and action and the ideas and theories that currently pervade both academic and applied research. In the longer term, one suspects that the judgement of CSCW will not lie its small scale contributions to particular systems, but in the ways in which it encourages designers, developers, managers and the like, to take the mundane seriously, as inspiration, and to prioritise technology in ordinary action.

Acknowledgements

We would like thank everyone in the Royal National Throat, Nose and Ear Hospital in London for granting us access to their workplace and for their willingness to talk about their work. We are particularly grateful to Dr. David Enderby and Dr. Maxim Nicholls. We would like to thank those people, including members of the WIT Group, Charles and Marjorie Goodwin, Jack and Marilyn Whalen, Lorenza Mondada and others who have informed our analysis through insightful discussions of the data presented here. This study was supported through funding by the EU IST Palcom and PaperWorks projects.

References

Adcock, M., Hutchins, M. and Gunn, C. (2004): 'Haptic collaboration with augmented reality'. *Proceedings of the* 2004 *International conference on computer graphics and interactive techniques*, p. 41, Los Angeles, USA.

Fitmaurice, G., Ishii, H. and Buxton, W. (1995): 'Bricks: Laying the foundation for graspable user interfaces'. *ACM Conference on Human Factors in Computing Systems (CHI'95)*, pp. 432-449, Denver, Colorado, USA.

Garfinkel, H. (1967): *Studies in Ethnomethodology*. Englewood Cliffs, N.J.: Prentice-Hall.

Gaver, W.W. (1991): 'Technology affordances'. *ACM Conference on Human Factors in Computing systems (CHI'91)*, pp. 79-84, New Orleans, Louisiana, USA.

Gerovich, O, Marayong, P. and Okamura, A. M. (2004): 'The Effect of Visual and Haptic Feedback on Computer-Assisted Needle Insertion', *Computer-Aided Surgery*, Vol. 9, No. 3, pp. 243-249.

Goodwin, D., Pope, C., Mort, M. and Smith, A. (2005): 'Access, boundaries and their effects: Legitimate participation in anesthesia'. *Sociology of health and illness, vol 27, no. 6, pp. 855-871.*

Hindmarsh, J. and Pilnick, A. (in press, 2007): 'Knowing bodies at work: embodiment and ephemeral teamwork in anaesthesia'. *Organization studies*, vol. 28, no. 9, September.

Hornecker, E. (2005): 'A design theme for tangible interaction: Embodied facilitation'. *Proceedings of the 2005 Ninth European Conference on Computer-Supported Cooperative Work*, pp. 23-43, September, Paris, France.

Ishii, H. and Ullmer, B. (1997): 'Tangible bits: towards seamless interfaces between people, bits and atoms'. *ACM Conference on Human Factors in Computing Systems (CHI97)*, pp. 234-241, Atlanta, Georgia, United States.

Koschmann, T., LeBaron, C., Goodwin, C., and Feltovich, P. (2006): 'The mystery of the missing referent: objects, procedures, and the problem of the instruction follower'. *Proceedings of the 2006 Conference on Computer-Supported Cooperative Work (CSCW2006)*, pp. 373-382, Banff, Alberta, Canada.

Mondada, L. (2001): 'Operating together through videoconferencing'. *Conference on Orders of Ordinary Action*, July 9-11, Manchester, UK.

Moreira, T. (2004): 'Coordination and embodiment in the operating room'. *Body & Society*, vol.10, no.1, pp. 109-129. Sage Publications.

Nardi, B. A., Schwartz, H., Kuchinsky, A., Leichner, R., Whitakker, S. and Sclabassi, R. (1993): 'Turning Away from Talking Heads: The Use of Video-as-Data in Neurosurgery'. *Proceedings of INTERCHI'93*, pp. 327-334, 24th-29th April, Amsterdam, The Netherlands.

Norman, D. A. (1988): *The Psychology of Everyday Things*. New York: Basic Books.

Schmidt, K. (2002): 'The Problem with 'Awareness': Introductory Remarks on 'Awareness in CSCW''. *Journal of Collaborative Computing*. 11, 3-4, pp. 285-298, Springer Netherlands.

Sitorus, L., Cao, S.S., and J. Buur (2007): 'Tangible interaction for configuration practices'. In *Proceedings of TEI '07*, February 15-17, 2007, USA.

Strong, R., and Gaver, W. (1996): 'Feather, scent, and shaker: Supporting simple intimacy'. *Proceedings of CSCW'96*, November 16 - 20, Boston. New York. ACM Press.

Suchman, L. (1993): 'Technologies of Accountability: On Lizards and Aeroplanes'. In G. Button (ed.): *Technology in Working Order*, pp. 113-126. London: Routledge.

Weiser, M. (1991): 'The Computer for the 21st Century', *Scientific American*, vol. 265, no. 3, September, pp. 94-104.

L. Bannon, I. Wagner, C. Gutwin, R. Harper, and K. Schmidt (eds.).
ECSCW'07: Proceedings of the Tenth European Conference on Computer Supported Cooperative Work, 24-28 September 2007, Limerick, Ireland

Prior-to-request and request behaviors within elderly day care: Implications for developing service robots for use in multiparty settings

Keiichi Yamazaki, Michie Kawashima
Department of Liberal Arts, Saitama University, Japan
BYI06561@nifty.com, kawashima411@nifty.com

Yoshinori Kuno, Naonori Akiya, Matthew Burdelski
Graduate School of Science and Engineering, Saitama University, Japan
kuno@cv.ics.saitama-u.ac.jp, akiya0427@hotmail.com, mburdie@yahoo.co.jp

Akiko Yamazaki
Department of Media Architecture, Future University-Hakodate, Japan
akikoy@fun.ac.jp

Hideaki Kuzuoka
Institute of Engineering Mechanics and Systems, University of Tsukuba, Japan
kuzuoka@iit.tsukuba.ac.jp

Abstract. The rapidly expanding elderly population in Japan and other industrialized countries has posed an enormous challenge to the systems of healthcare that serve elderly citizens. This study examines naturally occurring interaction within elderly day care in Japan, and discusses the implications for developing robotic systems that can provide service in elderly care contexts. The interaction analysis focuses on prior-to-request and request behaviors involving elderly visitors and caregivers in multiparty settings. In particular, it delineates the ways caregivers' displays of availability affects elderly visitors' behavior prior to initiating a request, revealing that visitors observe caregivers prior to initiating a request, and initiation is contingent upon caregivers' displayed availability. The findings are discussed in relation to our work in designing an autonomous and remote-controlled robotic system that can be employed in elderly day care centers and other service contexts.

Introduction

The rapidly expanding elderly population in Japan and other industrialized countries has posed an enormous challenge to the systems of health care that serve aging citizens. The field of robotics, in particular the development of service robots that can provide various forms of care, poses promises and challenges. Recent advances in robotics have led to the development of robots that can interact with people in public settings. For example, researchers have developed both autonomous (e.g. Imai et al. 2000) and remotely controlled robots that support human-to-human communication (Paulos et al. 1998; Jouppi et al. 2002; Kuzuoka et al. 2004). Such trends have led to an exploration of Human-Robot Interaction (HRI) and Robot-Supported Cooperative Work (RSCW) (Machino et al. 2006).

Several of the present authors have also been developing human-assisting robots through collaboration between robotics engineers and human interaction sociologists. We have discovered that seemingly mundane actions that occur between humans are not easily implemented in robots for human-robot interaction. One category of such actions is request-grant pairs. In order to provide service in contexts such as elderly care, robots need to be able to recognize human behaviors that require assistance, and then carry out assistance either autonomously or with the help of a human caregiver. While several of the authors have recently collaborated in the development of a robot that can approach a person who makes a summons by waving a hand (Miyauchi et al. 2004), we have not yet designed a robot that can respond to a person's request through hand waving or other semiotic means within natural settings.

In order to begin to address this issue, we have been examining human-human interaction within elderly day care facilities in Japan with a focus on verbal and non-verbal behaviors surrounding requests. This paper focuses on pre-request and request behaviors in order to show how visitors select a particular caregiver, and how caregivers acknowledge and grant a request. These findings are then discussed in relation to our work in developing an autonomous and remote-controlled robotic system that can be employed in elderly day care and other service contexts.

Background

Through the collaborative efforts of robotics engineers and human interaction sociologists, we have been working towards developing a robotic system that can provide 'service' within elderly day care facilities. Due to a rapidly expanding elderly population in Japan and other industrialized countries, elderly care has become a critical social issue, and robots are considered a means of providing a partial solution. In order to undercover the potentialities of robots for use in elderly day care, as a first step we video-taped interaction in three elderly day care centers in Japan. In Japan, people who provide elderly day care service include nurses, assistants, and part-time volunteers, all of whom will be referred to here as 'caregiver'. Japanese day care facilities typically support elderly persons in routine, everyday activities such as bathing, eating, and playing games. In the centers we observed caregivers often circulate around the room in order to monitor visitors who might need assistance (e.g. getting a drink, going to the bathroom). That is, multiple caregivers and multiple visitors are co-present in the same room, and any caregiver may provide assistance to any visitor.

In analyzing interaction, we focused on behaviors surrounding requests, including the initiation of requests by visitors and the granting of requests by caregivers. Our initial observations can be characterized as follows:

(1)   Among multiple caregivers and visitors, requests occur within a context in which multiple tasks are managed simultaneously.

(2)   When a visitor requires assistance, the visitor makes verbal and non-verbal actions before initiating a request.

(3)   Since multiple parties are engaged in different kinds of tasks, a visitor may seek out an available caregiver, establish a channel to communicate, and then initiate a request.

These initial observations raise several questions. How do visitors search for a caregiver among several caregivers in the room, choose a specific one, and then create a one-to-one connection with a particular caregiver?

Interaction analysis

Interaction analysis by C. Goodwin, C. Heath, G. Lerner, and others has revealed the importance of gaze and bodily posture at the initiating stage of a request or other social action. For example, Goodwin (1981) and Heath (1984) have shown that hearer gaze and bodily orientation relate to a speaker starting or re-starting talk. Lerner (2003) has observed that a present speaker's selection of a next speaker is highly related to the present speaker's gaze direction. For example, when a present speaker begins making a request towards a potential recipient the speaker gazes towards that recipient.

In this paper, we focus on prior-to-request and request behaviors among elderly visitors and caregivers. In relation to this, Heath (1984) makes a distinction between 'display of availability' and 'display of recipiency': '...whereas a *display of availability* serves as a pre-initiating activity providing an environment for the occurrence of a range of actions, a *display of recipiency* specifically initiates a sequence' (p. 250). In our data, caregivers typically displayed availability to multiple recipients (visitors) and then displayed recipiency to a particular recipient (visitor) before the visitor made the request as will be explicated below.

Lerner (2003) has pointed out that gaze has limitations as a tool for selecting next speaker. That is, the speaker's gaze is effective only when the recipient can see the speaker's gaze. In our data, visitors who displayed that they wanted to make a request to a caregiver typically first observed whether or not the caregiver was displaying availability or recipiency by gazing towards the caregiver before making the request. These initial observations led to the formulation of five central questions.

Q1   How do caregivers display availability to visitors?

Q2   How do caregivers display recipiency to a visitor?

Q3   How do visitors behave prior to making a request to a caregiver?

Q4   How do visitors behave when a caregiver is not displaying availability and/or recipiency?

Q5   How do visitors and caregivers display acknowledgment that establishes a connection for initiating requests?

Setting and methods

Ethnographic observations and videotaped recordings were made at three elderly day care centers in Japan. Day care center 1 is a mid-size facility located in a rural area of Western Japan. At this center we videotaped approximately fifteen hours over three days with two fixed cameras and two handy cameras. Day care facility 2 is a mid-size facility located in a suburb of Tokyo. At this center we videotaped approximately five hours with two fixed video cameras and three handy cameras. Day care facility 3 is a small facility in a suburb of Tokyo. At this center we videotaped approximately five hours with three fixed cameras. At each of these centers we set the fixed cameras on an overview of the main room, which allowed us to film from various angles. We videotaped using multiple cameras in order to capture gaze, bodily actions, and the use of objects. We had several caregivers wear a wireless microphone, and we used both remote microphones and directional microphones in order to record clear sound.

Behavior of caregivers

Caregivers display availability to visitors in various ways. Figures 1 and 2 show a lunch scene at facility 1. Caregiver F is circulating among the tables while looking around at the participants who are eating lunch (Fig. 1). The caregiver displays availability towards multiple visitors through bodily posture, head turning, and gaze. When F momentarily faces towards visitor G, visitor G lifts up a packet of medicine (a pre-request for the caregiver to open the packet for him) (Fig. 2), to which caregiver F responds by saying 'Yes' (*hai*) while approaching G.

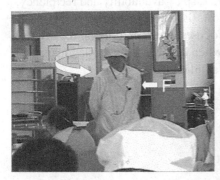

Figure 1. F displays availability to visitors.   Figure 2. F displays recipiency to G.

As indicated in these figures the caregiver distributes her gaze and bodily posture in such a way so as to display availability to multiple visitors. When the caregiver momentarily faces a specific visitor, the visitor ceases the split second to hold up the medicine, which results in his gaining the caregiver's recipiency.

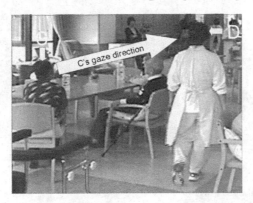

Figure 3. D not displaying availability towards C.

In the previous example, display of availability was done through bodily posture and gaze direction. In displaying availability it seems crucial that the caregiver is (at least partially) facing towards the visitor. A visitor may delay initiating a summons or other pre-request actions until a caregiver is facing him or her. For instance, in the next example (also from facility 1), visitor C has just finished taking a bath and is sitting down at a large table with several other visitors. When visitor C gazes towards caregiver D, caregiver D is facing the opposite direction, with her back turned walking away from C (Fig. 3). Although caregiver D is currently circulating around the room monitoring what visitors are doing (and consequently displaying availability to them), at this moment she is facing in the opposite direction of visitor C. Visitor C then begins looking around the room for another caregiver.

This section has shown ways that caregivers display availability and recipiency, and suggests that visitors' initiation of requests is contingent upon displays of availability and recipiency. The next section focuses more centrally on the behavior of visitors, in particular comparing cases when a caregiver is displaying availability and when a caregiver is not displaying availability.

Behavior of visitors

When caregiver is displaying availability

This section focuses on what visitors do prior to issuing a request when a caregiver is displaying availability. In such a situation, we find two crucial behaviors. First, visitors often monitor through gaze what a caregiver is doing. Such gaze allows the visitor to seize a moment that a caregiver is displaying availability towards a visitor who has a request. Second, visitors initiate requests after gaining recipiency, waiting until a caregiver faces towards him or her before initiating a request.

Figure 4. A begins to lift teapot while gazing towards B who then lifts up his teacup.

```
[Data1] Facility 3   07/22/05   [10:09am]
01A[gaze]   :   ,,,,,,----------,,,,,,---------,,,,,,,
                     □(Cups on the table)
   A[action]  :   (Walks to teapot at back counter)
   B[gaze]    :   A----------------------------,,,,,
02A          :                                                    (nod and lifts arm)
   A[gaze]   :   ,,,,,,,,,,,,,,,,,,,,,,,,,,,,,,,,,,,,,,,,,,,,,,,,,,,,,,,,,,,,,,,,,,,,,,Bxxxxx,,,,,,,,,,,,
   A[action]  :   Walks to A's seat ,,,, Puts A's cup,,,,,Walks towards teapot_____,,,,,,,
```

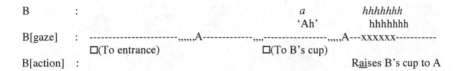

```
B        :                                                a          hhhhhhh
                                                        'Ah'        hhhhhhh
B[gaze]  : ----------------------,,,,,A-------------,,,,-----------------,,,,A---xxxxxx----------
            □(To entrance)                    □(To B's cup)
B[action] :                                                          Raises B's cup to A
```

Transcription conventions:
,,,, (movement of gaze, not fixed towards anything specific), A---(gaze fixed towards A; □ below indicates gaze is fixed on an object), underline (contextual explanation), italics (Japanese), h (laughter tokens).

The above points are illustrated in Data 1. This example comes from a scene in which visitors and caregivers are seated around tables having tea. The transcript begins at the point when caregiver A stands up and goes towards the teapot at the back counter (Fig. 4).

In line 1, visitor B is looking towards caregiver A, who is looking at the cups on the table while walking towards the teapot at the back counter. After caregiver A reaches for the teapot and pours her own tea, visitor B stops looking towards caregiver A. In line 2, visitor B again looks towards caregiver A just as A walks towards her own seat and puts down her cup on the table. When caregiver A starts lifting up the teapot and gazes towards visitor B, visitor B lifts up his cup towards caregiver A, and A responds by nodding and lifting her arm slightly, and then bringing the teapot to B to pour him more tea.

In this example, visitor B first gazes towards caregiver A as A looks at others' cups on the table, displaying an intention to serve more tea. Visitor B's continuous gaze towards caregiver A allows him to seize a brief moment him to lift up his teacup when the caregiver gazes towards him. In this way a visitor can initiate a non-verbal action, which in this case is interpreted as a request, at a brief moment when the caregiver displays recipiency towards the visitor.

The next excerpt illustrates how visitors behave when a caregiver displays availability but does not display recipiency. In Data 2, visitor H is seated around a table with other visitors engaged in coloring pictures. Visitor H observes caregiver K passing by while lifting her picture slightly, which displays some trouble with coloring the picture. Through caregiver K walks towards visitor H, he does not direct his gaze towards H (Fig. 5). In other words, at this moment K displays availability (visitor H is nearby and likely within K's peripheral vision) but does not display recipiency towards H. K then stops at the desk of another caregiver (J) and begins to address this caregiver (Fig. 6).

Figure 5. Caregiver K walks towards visitor H.   Figure 6. K addresses caregiver H.

```
[Data2] Facility 2    06/12/27    [10:07am]
  K           :                              suimasen cho[tto              hai
                                             'Excuse me a bit'             'Yes'
  K[gaze]   : ,,,J----------------------------------------------------------,,,,,,,,,,H----------------
  K[action] : ,,,Stops walking, walks to J                                  Turns to H
  H           :                                             [sensei kore dooyotte
                                                            'Sir, what do you think about this?'
  H[gaze]   : ,,,K------------------------------------------------------------------------------------------
  H[action] :                                             Prepares to show her picture to K
```

As K begins to address caregiver J, visitor H immediately interrupts K's talk using the addressee term, 'Sir' (*sensei*). Following this term of address, caregiver K turns his head towards visitor H and H then initiates a request, 'What do you think about this?'

As we can see in this data, a visitor may attempt to gain a nearby caregiver's recipiency to initiate a request when the caregiver is engaged in concurrent talk with another. The visitor then initiates her request upon gaining the caregiver's recipiency.

This section has examined the behavior of visitors when a caregiver is displaying availability, and either is or is not displaying recipiency. The next section will examine visitor behavior when a caregiver is not displaying availability.

When caregiver is not displaying availability

This section considers cases in which a caregiver is not displaying availability. In such a situation, a visitor who has a request does extra work in order to gain the caregiver's availability. We will show two points here. First, a visitor often displays a need for assistance by looking around to determine which caregiver is available. Second, a visitor may gain other visitors' help in achieving a caregiver's availability.

Let us examine the first point. By continuously looking around and searching for a person, visitors may attempt to locate an available caregiver who is relatively far away. This is illustrated in Data 3. Prior to this interaction (as discussed earlier in relation to Figure 3), visitor C had just finished taking a bath and is sitting down at a table. Visitor C continuously looks around but fails to locate a caregiver displaying availability towards her. After some time she locates caregiver E who is a bit far from her. Visitor C then waves her hand, as a non-verbal summons, towards caregiver E who then approaches her (Fig. 7). When caregiver E arrives at visitor C's table, C makes a request.

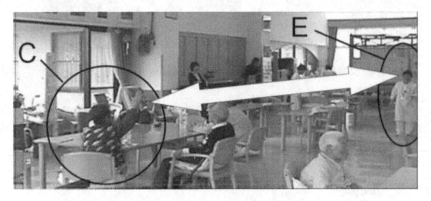

Figure 7. Elderly visitor raises her hand towards caregiver who is far away.

```
[Data 3] Facility 1    07/02/15    [11:12am]
C            :                      furo kara agatta kara karupisu cho::dai
                                    'I've gotten out of the bath, so get me a Calpis drink.'
C[gaze]      :  E--xxxxxxxxxxxxxxxxxxxxxxxxxxxxxxxxxxxxxxxxxxxxxxxxxxxxxxxxxxxxxxxxxxx
C[action]    :      Waving her hand towards E.
E            :                      doshita                    yossha wakatta
                                    'What happened?'           'Okay'
E[gaze]      :  ,,,Cxxxxxxxxxxxxxxxxxxxxxxxxxxxxxxxxxxxxxxxxxxxxxxxxxxxxxxxxxxxxxxxxxxxx
E[action]    :      Runs towards C
```

As can be seen in this data when there is no caregiver displaying availability a visitor may search for a caregiver until locating a caregiver who is displaying availability. When an available caregiver is far away, a visitor may summons a caregiver using non-verbal means.

We now examine the second point. In some cases, visitors engage in pre-sequences with other visitors to establish the legitimacy of a request when they do not identify a caregiver displaying availability. In the following example, visitor A notices that there is no footrest while sitting down at a table with other visitors (line 1). While this trouble report receives other visitor's agreement (line 4), it is not noticed by caregiver E who is currently talking to other visitors at the adjacent table. After other visitors agree with the trouble (lines 7 and 8), visitor A initiates a request towards the caregiver who is next to their table (line 12) (Fig. 9).

Figure 8. Talking about a missing footrest.   Figure 9. Initiating a request.

[Data4] Facility 2   06/12/27   [11:13am]
01A   :   *Ara mo::o okashi:to omottara, kyoo <u>ashi</u> ga nainda ne?*
                  'Oh I was thinking something is wrong today, there aren't any feet, right?'
02B   :   e?
                  'What?'
03A   :   *ashi* ↑ =
                  'Feet?'
04C   :   *aa::: a[shi.*
                  'Oh , the feet (=footrest).'
05D   :   *aa:::*
                  'Ah:::'
06A   :   *Are na::nka ashi ga darui to omotta[ra.*
                            'I was thinking my legs feel a bit tired.'
07B   :   [*un.*]
                                                            'Yeah.'
08C   :   *Dokonimo nai desu[ne:::::*
                  'I don't see it (=the footrest) anywhere, right:::::.'
09A   :   [*Nee   (itsumo atta-)*
                                     'Yeah.   (They [=the footrests] are always there-)'
     A[gaze] :   C--,,,,,E--------------------
10C   :   *Wasurechyatta[nokana*
                  'Maybe they (=the caregivers) forgot it?'
11A   :   [*Dasete moraoka.*
                                 'Should we have them bring it?'
     A[gaze] :   E------,,,,,C and B---------------------
12 (0.3)
13A   :   *Ne::* ↑ *:::* ↓   *chotto   nee   suima[sen   kashite kuremasu ka*
                  'Hey,   a bit   hey   excuse me   Can we borrow?'
     A[gaze] :   ,,,,,E--------------------,,,,,,,EXXXXXXXXXXXXXXXXXXXXX
     A[action] :   <u>(turning her body toward left, facing toward E)</u>
14D[gaze]   :   ,,,,,,,,,,,,,,,A-----,,,,,E-------,,,,,A-------
     D[action] :   (touching E's arm   Pointing at A)
15E   :   [*Hai?*
                                                            ['Yes?'
     E[gaze] :   ,,,D---,,,A--------,,,,,, ,
     E[action] :   <u>(coming close toward A) (putting</u>
                                                              <u>her face toward A's ear)</u>

In this example, visitor A does two crucial things prior to making her verbal request. First, she establishes the legitimacy of the request by talking to other visitors. In line 1, she notices that there is no footrest. After other visitors also recognize the problem (line 4 and 5), she gives an account for why she noticed the problem by mentioning her tired legs (line 6). Visitor C agrees with the problem (line 8) and provides an account saying, 'Maybe they (=the caregivers) forgot it?' (line 10). By engaging in this talk, visitor A is able to confirm the legitimacy of the problem and gain other visitors' support for initiating the request.

Second, prior to making the verbal request, visitor A achieves the caregiver's recipiency with the assistance of visitor D. In particular, as visitor A utters a summons towards caregiver E (line 13) (Fig. 9), visitor D starts looking towards caregiver E. When caregiver E does not respond to visitor A's verbal summons, visitor D touches caregiver E's arm and points at visitor A. This directly assists visitor A's initiation of the request. In line 13, visitor A makes a request to the caregiver.

In summary, this section has shown what visitors might do when they need a nearby caregiver's assistance but the caregiver is not displaying availability. The final section of the interactional analysis reviews the above analysis in relation to displays of acknowledgment.

Displays of acknowledgment

This section describes displays of acknowledgment in relation to establishing a connection for initiating a request. It specifically focuses on what caregivers do in response to a visitor after a visitor indicates a need for assistance. We found the following four patterns in caregivers' behavior in relation to visitors who had requests, and explicate these by reiterating data previously discussed.

(1)   When a caregiver displays both availability and recipiency towards a visitor, the caregiver responds to the visitor with a minimal utterance and/or non-verbal action, and then approaches the visitor. In Figure 2, when the visitor catches the caregiver's gaze, the caregiver responds by saying 'Yes' and then quickly approaches the visitor. In Data 1, when the caregiver caught the visitor's gaze, the caregiver responded by nodding towards the visitor and then brought the teapot to the visitor to pour the visitor more tea.

(2)   When a caregiver displays availability but does not display recipiency (as he or she is engaged in a concurrent activity), the visitor may interrupt the caregiver's activity; the caregiver may then respond by directing his or her attention towards the visitor and then verbally responding. In Data 2, following the visitor's summons, the caregiver turned his head towards the visitor and then responded by saying 'Yes'.

(3)   When a visitor does not locate any caregiver displaying availability, the
       visitor may search for a caregiver until locating one, and then wave his
       or her hand to call for the caregiver; the caregiver may then move
       quickly towards the visitor and verbally respond. In Data 3, upon locat-
       ing an available caregiver, the visitor waved her hand, and then the care-
       giver hurried to the visitor and initiated the question, 'What happened?'
(4)   When a visitor requires another visitor's support in accomplishing a re-
       quest (such as when a caregiver is nearby but not displaying availability
       towards a visitor who needs assistance), the caregiver attempts to re-
       spond to the visitor who gave help first and then displays recipiency to-
       wards the visitor who then grants the request. In Data 4, when the visitor
       attempted but failed to summons the caregiver, another visitor sum-
       moned the caregiver by touching the caregiver's arm on behalf of the
       visitor who initially needed assistance. The caregiver stopped her imme-
       diate engagement with other visitors, and then brought her body posture
       and face towards the visitor who touched her arm, saying 'Yes'.
   This section has discussed caregiver acknowledgment of visitors' prior-to-
request and request behaviors, which are done through verbal and/or non-verbal
means (e.g. rushing to the visitor, nodding, saying 'Yes').
   The preceding analysis suggests that visitors' and caregivers' behaviors prior
to requests play a crucial role in carrying out requests within elderly day care centers in which multiple parties are co-present. The next section applies this analysis
to a discussion of our work in developing robotic systems that have the potential
to be employed in the service of elderly care.

Towards development of a service robot

Three-step approach

In relating the above findings to developing service robots for use in elderly care,
it will be helpful to review our overall approach, one that we have taken in developing robots for use in other multiparty settings (Kuno et al. 2007). The first step,
as indicated in the previous section, is to analyze human-human interaction
through interaction analysis, in particular the non-verbal and verbal resources that
participants use in carrying out action. The second step is to consider the findings
in relation to developing a robotic system that can provide particular types of
service (e.g. responding to visitors' requests). The third step is to examine how
humans and the robot interact, and then evaluate the effectiveness of the robot in
order to refine it. This approach helps clarify in what ways human-like interaction
may be accepted and preferred, and in what ways it may be possible to employ
robot caregivers alongside human caregivers. It should be noted that our research

is not aimed at developing robots that can replicate human-human interaction, but rather is aimed at developing robots that can be 'user friendly.' Towards this end, we consider both cognition and action in design, including what types of verbal and non-verbal actions that we need to have robots do, and what types of verbal and non-verbal actions we need to have robots recognize in humans.

This section discusses our developments in relation to the second step: considering the findings from the interactional analysis in relation to the design of a robotic system that can be employed in multiparty elderly day care settings. The analysis of human-human interaction suggests that we should consider the following four issues. The related questions that these address were presented earlier and are shown here in parentheses.

(1) Display of availability: A service robot should be able to circulate among visitors engaged in activities and effectively display availability to them. (Q1, Q3)

(2) Display of recipiency: Following a visitor's verbal and/or non-verbal actions indicating that assistance is required, the robot should be able to display recipiency through gaze, and head and body orientation. (Q2, Q3)

(3) While (1) and (2) apply to typical situations, as suggested in Data 2 and 4 the robot should be able to deal with alternative situations such as when a visitor is in need of assistance when the robot is not displaying availability (e.g. engaged in another task). In such cases, the robot should be able to determine the priority between its current task and the new task. The robot should then be able to either signal a delay or immediately attend to the new task. (Q4)

(4) Acknowledgment: The robot should be able to recognize the reaction of the visitor against the robot's display of recipiency, and judge if the visitor is calling for the robot's help. The robot should then display acknowledgment, such as saying 'Yes' or raising its hand (Q5)

In order to address these issues, we have been developing two robotic systems. One is an autonomous robot and the other is a remote-controlled robot. The autonomous robot does not currently have high capabilities for responding to many of the problems and needs that arise within elderly day care centers. In such cases, it is imperative for the robot to be able to change to remote-control mode and let a remote caregiver respond to the problem. Since a remote caregiver only has to deal in person with the robot that cannot respond to a problem on its own, the remote caregiver can oversee several robots simultaneously. We are working towards this and expect the implementation to be cost efficient. As our study is still in the early stages, however, we first want to assess to what extent the autonomous robot and the remote-control robot can provide support to caregivers and visitors in elderly daycare centers. We will then be able to determine in what situations the robot could change from autonomous to remote control modes. We are currently developing an autonomous robot and a remote control robot independently and planning to conduct experiments with these robots.

Design implications for autonomous robot

As we have discussed above, the robot should be able to display availability to multiple visitors simultaneously and display recipiency to individual visitors in establishing a connection for service. The robot can display availability in part by rotating its head. A simple mechanical turn of the head, however, may not be sufficient. We believe that the robot should move its gaze from one person to another similar to the way human caregivers did in our observation. We have developed a robot that can make eye contact with humans (Kuno et al. 2005; Miyauchi et al. 2004, 2005), and while we can basically use this eye contact method, the observations indicate that humans use a range of verbal and non-verbal means to display recipiency such as nodding, approaching the visitor, and/or saying 'What happened?'

Figure 10. Service robot.

We are developing a robot that has the capabilities mentioned above (Fig. 10), using ROBOVIE-R ver.2 (ATR) as a system platform. Although the human vision system works fast enough to detect a person looking towards us, and the human field of view is wide and can often notice a person looking at us even though he/she is far away, computer vision does not work as fast and efficiently. Even if the robot uses an ultra wide lens with the same field of view as a human, it is difficult to obtain enough resolution to detect people in images. To help alleviate this, we attach three cameras on the robot's chest. Regardless of the head direction, the robot continues observing the scene with these three cameras. Although several faces can be detected at the same time, the robot moves its head from one detected face to another to display availability. If the robot detects a face that is looking at it, the robot turns its body in the direction of the face, then examines if the face is still looking at it with the camera (eye) on its head. The robot then makes eye contact, approaches the person, and says, 'What happened?' In the above process, if the face direction is not apart from the robot's front and the robot does not need to turn its body, the robot proceeds to the eye contact process without saying anything.

Design implications for a remote control robot

An important result of employing robots in elderly care is that robots enable a remote human caregiver to display availability to multiple visitors simultaneously. This display of availability can be done crucially through a robot's movements (e.g. circulating around the room while turning its head). Several of the current authors have presented the results elsewhere (Kuzuoka et al. 2004). This robot has three camera units on its body so that its horizontal field of view is about 180 degrees in total. On the remote control caregiver's side, the image of the camera unit is displayed on three horizontal screens (Fig. 11). Since the robot's head motion and a remote controller's head motion are synchronized, the remote controller's natural head motion when he or she scans the three-display units is reflected in the robot's head motion. Recently, we have added a display on the robot's chest to display a remote controller's face and named it GESTUREMAN-3.5 (Fig. 12). When this robot is used for elderly day care, we expect that visitors will be able to recognize a remote caregiver's availability both through the robot's head movement and the remote caregiver's face displayed on the robot's chest.

Figure 11. Remote operator's environment   Figure 12. Robot with chest display

As was shown in Data 4, a visitor may reach out and touch a caregiver's body to attract his or her attention. A robot thus should be able to sense such physical contact so that the remote caregiver can orient his or her head and make eye contact with the visitor.

We are aware of some existing remote control robots that have displays that show a remote participant's face (for example, Jouppi 2002). We have to clarify, however, how a Mona Lisa effect caused by 2D face images on a display affects eye contact between a remote caregiver and a visitor. Although we need further studies to clarify this, we expect that the combination of a display and a robot's head orientation can alleviate this problem.

Combination of autonomous and remote control modes

Recently we have started a project to combine the autonomous mode and the remote-control mode. The prototype robotic system is being developed for a museum (Fig. 13). The robot makes eye contact with a visitor, and approaches him or her. Then it faces the visitor and starts explaining the exhibit. If the robot finds that the visitor keeps looking at the robot during the explanation, the robot turns its head towards the visitor and asks, 'Do you have any questions?' The autonomous mode then changes to the remote-control mode. A human operator watches the three displays. The head direction of the visitor is sent to the robot to move its head. The robot shows which direction the visitor is paying attention to through its head motion. Such head motion, which is similar to the autonomous mode, facilitates smooth communication between the visitor and the robot. We are aware that needs and behaviors of visitors are very different between the museum and the elderly day care centers. Based on ethnographic studies, we need to modify the robot so that it works effectively in the elderly daycare center.

Figure 13. Guide robot and remote site.

Conclusion

In this paper, we have analyzed naturally occurring interaction in elderly day care centers in Japan with a focus on prior-to-request and request behaviors, and related the findings to implications for developing robots for use in elderly day care centers. Though we did not fully cover issues such as the details of request behavior (Zaliyana et al. 2004), we have attempted to understand what is going on in those centers, and use those understandings to develop robotic systems by focusing on 1) how prior-to-request and request behaviors are initiated between visitors and caregivers, and 2) how prior-to-request and request behaviors are coordinated between them.

In situations in which multiple parties are co-present while engaging in multiple tasks, a caregiver has to deal with a range of issues. How is it that a caregiver establishes a connection with other visitors who need assistance and then provides service? Such issues cannot be fully examined under experimental situations in which it has already been established that individuals perform requests to a specific other person. In order to design a robotic system that can function in naturally occurring, multiparty contexts, we have proposed a three-step approach that begins with an examination of human-human interaction. We believe that any attempts to design and implement robots in service care settings should take into account the socio-culturally organized interaction that goes on in those settings. The use of ethnographic approaches is crucial to uncovering the lived details of socio-cultural practices prior to, and alongside, the design phase. Our results are applicable for developing robots that can work collaboratively not only with humans but also with other CSCW systems. That is, as our study deals with problems related to request behaviors among multiple parties, our findings are applicable to system development for other service related areas. Along these lines, we hope that such a robot will be developed not only for elderly care centers but also within a range of other service contexts.

Acknowledgments

This research was supported by a Strategic Information and Communications R&D Promotion Program (SCOPE) from the Ministry of Internal Affairs and Communications, Grants-in-Aid for Scientific Research 16330095, Grants-in-Aid for Scientific Research 19203025, Grants-in-Aid for Scientific Research 17530373, Grants-in-Aid for Scientific Research 19024013, Grants-in-Aid for Scientific Research 18049010, the International Communications Foundation (ICF), and Oki Electric Industry Co. Ltd.

References

ATR. http://www.irc.atr.jp/productRobovie/robovie-r2-e.html.

Goodwin, C. (1981): *'Conversational Organization: Interaction between Speakers and Hearers'*, Academic Press, New York.

Heath, C. (1984): 'Talk and recipiency: sequential organization in speech and body movement' in J. M. Atkinson and J. Heritage (eds.): *Structures of Social Action: Studies in Conversation Analysis*, Cambridge University Press, Cambridge, pp. 247-65.

Imai, M., Ono, T., and Ishiguro, H. (2002): 'Physical relation and expression: joint attention for human-robot interaction', *IEEE Transactions on Industrial Electronics*, vol. 50, no. 4, pp. 636-643.

Jouppi, N. (2002): 'First steps towards mutually immersive mobile telepresence', *CSCW 2002 Conference Proceedings*, pp. 354-363.

Kuno, K., Nakamura, A., and Miyauchi, D. (2005): 'Beckoning robots with the eyes', *Proceedings of the International Workshop on Intelligent Environments*, pp. 260-266.

Kuno, Y., Sadazuka, K., Kawashima, M., Yamazaki, K., Yamazaki, A., and Kuzuoka H. (2007): 'Museum guide robot based on sociological interaction analysis', *CHI2007 Conference Proceedings*, pp. 1191-1194.

Kuzuoka, H., Kosaka, J., Yamazaki, K., Yamazaki, A., and Suga, Y. (2004): 'Dual ecologies of robot as communication media: thoughts on coordinating orientations and projectability', *CHI2004 Conference Proceedings*, pp.183-190.

Lerner, G. H. (2003): 'Selecting next speaker: the context-sensitive operation of a context-free organization', *Language in Society*, vol. 32, pp. 177-201.

Machino, T., Nanjo, Y., Yanagihara, Y., Kawata, H., Iwaki, S., and Shimokura, K. (2006): 'Proposal of robot-supported cooperative work −remote-collaboration system based on a shared field of view', *Journal of Robotics Society of Japan*, vol. 24, no. 7, October 2006, pp. 830-837.

Miyauchi, D., Sakurai, A., Nakamura, A., and Kuno, Y. (2004): 'Active eye Ccontact for human-robot communication', *CHI 2004 Extended Abstracts*, pp. 1099-1102.

Miyauchi, D., Sakurai, A., Nakamura, A., and Kuno, Y. (2005): 'Bidirectional eye contact for human-robot communication', *IEICE Transactions on Information and Systems*, vol. E88-D, No.11, pp. 2509-2516.

Paulos, E. and Canny, J. (1998): 'ProP: personal roving presence', *CHI' 98 Conference Proceedings*, pp. 296-303.

Zaliyana M., Yamazaki, C., Nakamura, A., and Kuno Y. (2004): 'Human-robot speech interface understanding inexplicit utterances using vision', *CHI2004 Extended Abstracts*, pp.1321-1324.

L. Bannon, I. Wagner, C. Gutwin, R. Harper, and K. Schmidt (eds.).
ECSCW'07: Proceedings of the Tenth European Conference on Computer Supported Cooperative Work, 24-28 September 2007, Limerick, Ireland
© Springer 2007

Designing Family Photo Displays

Alex S. Taylor
Microsoft Research, Cambridge, UK
ast@microsoft.com

Laurel Swan
School of IS, Computing and Mathematics, Brunel University, UK.
laurel.swan@brunel.ac.uk

Abigail Durrant
Digital World Research Centre, University of Surrey, UK
A.Durrant@surrey.ac.uk

Abstract. We present efforts to explore the relatively underdeveloped area of digital photo display. Using examples from two empirical studies with family homes, we develop our results around three broad themes related to the display of photos and their arrangement. The first theme highlights the collaborative as well as individual work that goes into preparing photos for display. The second attends to the obligations families have to put particular photos on display. The third introduces the notion of curatorial control and the tensions that arise from one person controlling a home's photo displays. Drawing on these themes, we go on to describe how we have used a critical design approach to open up the possibilities for future display innovations. Three critical design proposals are presented as sketches to illustrate the development of our ideas to date.

Introduction

This paper presents some of our ongoing efforts to think innovatively about digital photographic displays. We present materials based on two empirical studies of photographic displays in family homes. We then go on to describe our use of critical design practice for developing these materials in an exploration of new design possibilities.

In both our empirical studies, our intention was to investigate how families display photographs in their homes and to use the gathered findings as a means of informing the design of situated digital displays. Taking an exploratory stance, we wanted to avoid making any definitive statements about the display of photos in family homes. The purpose of the research was rather to open up new possibilities for display design in an area that appears to have received little attention in CSCW (as well as HCI). Positioned as an early foray, our aim has thus been to draw on a small set of our empirical materials in order to provide an interesting perspective from which to consider the collaborative aspects to family portrayal.

In the following, we give specific attention to three themes associated with photo displays that emerged during our investigations. The first considers the work involved in the co-construction of family photo displays. In particular, we discuss the coordination of activities that can occur in the preparation of photos for display, describing how different family members as well as distant relatives can contribute to a display's content. The second and third themes relate to this collaborative workflow, so to speak. The second attends to the sense of *social obligation* family members can feel in displaying photos of particular people (usually family members), and how this sense of obligation is played out within different families. The third gives heed to the observation that although, as noted above, the processes associated with photo displays can be collaborative, there appears to be a centralized control over a home's displays, or at least some of them. We came to think of this as a form of *curatorial control* whereby one person fashions the final appearance of their home's various displays.

Critical design and qualitative methods of inquiry

Introduced to HCI in the last decade, largely through research undertaken at the Royal College of Art in the UK, critical design has built a niche following, one for the most part involved in proposing *provocative* concepts in order to critically examine technology and people's everyday interactions with it (see, for example, Dunne (1999) and Martin and Gaver (2000)). Broadly speaking, this form of critical design (drawing from *critical* approaches in the arts and humanities) serves an *inquiring* function. Unlike product-oriented design that is directed towards producing complete and ideally marketable results, critical design is aimed at provoking questions, reflecting on design and thus shaping future possible directions. The result is not merely a physical product, but also a way of thinking about and articulating a conceptual space for design.

In the latter sections of this paper, we present three proposals—taken from several ideas inspired by our fieldwork—that draw on this notion of critical design. What we wish to demonstrate is how the concepts, in sketched form, have enabled us to further our thinking on the subject of domestic display and to think innovatively about display design.

By presenting three critical design proposals in conjunction with materials from our empirical studies, this paper also incorporates a secondary, methodological component. Several notable publications in both the CSCW and HCI literature have highlighted a disparity between design and qualitative and specifically ethnographic methods of inquiry (e.g. Button and Dourish, 1996; Plowman, Rogers and Ramage, 1995). Put simply, the general consensus is that the descriptive character of qualitative investigations presents something of a mismatch *vis-à-vis* design; design, largely aiming to be prescriptive, is seen to run counter to the product of qualitative methods of inquiry, namely, description. In light of this apparent problem, proposals for re-casting ethnography's contribution to design have been written by such notables as Anderson (1994) and Dourish (2006). Presenting similar arguments, but drawing on different subject matter, these two authors suggest that ethnography has its place in *opening up the play of possibilities* for design (to borrow on Anderson's oft-used phrase). That is, some forms of qualitative inquiry in systems design are considered not to be in the business of eliciting design requirements or even the vaguely termed 'implications for design', but rather provide opportunities for re-thinking ordinary, everyday practices that might be the subject of design.

It is this position that our use of critical design aims to build on. Attempting to take the contribution of empirical inquiries a step further, we investigate the use of critical design to refine the play of possibilities. Our hope is that this will enable us to attend not only to the observable features in everyday practice, but also provide scope for innovation. We consider this last point key, as it is aimed at over-coming a common criticism of qualitative methods, one suggesting that methods like ethnography give extraordinary privilege to people's existing methods, without sufficient thought to what might be. As Dourish writes (citing the anthropologist Geertz), there is "a certain ethnographic tendency to operate as 'merchants of astonishment'" (2006, pp. 3-4). In using critical design, our aim has been to further explore the conjoining of qualitative methods of inquiry and design, and specifically how the innovation of photo display design might result from such a combination. The turn to design practice, more broadly, is seen as a means to engage with the creative ways photo displays are made in homes and the very tangible ways they are interacted with. By combining empirical and critical design approaches, our hope is thus to explore research methodologies for better understanding home life and specifically CSCW in the home.

On a related point, we also believe such an investigation to be particularly relevant in designing for the home. The home presents a difficult set of challenges for innovative design, challenges that contrast with many of the problems faced in designing for the work place. The home incorporates many different motivations and practices that cannot be simply optimized through technological support. Actions are not always purposeful, sometimes fleeting and regularly bound up with the unremarkable aspects of home making. Indeed, in setting an agenda for systems design in the home, O'Brien and Rodden (1997) give early emphasis to this:

> The home is at different times a place of escape, a place of work, a place of privacy and a place of public exhibition of the tastes and values of the householders living there. (p. 257)

The coordination of activities in the home are not merely, then, about getting somewhere, finishing this, or sharing that; they are also about making a house feel like home. As we hope our materials will demonstrate, even the seemingly banal reasons for organizing, displaying and viewing photos are tightly interwoven with a family's sense of itself and its ongoing social organization.

Related Literature

A significant motivation for this research emerges from an apparent disparity. Currently, we are witnessing an unparalleled proliferation of capture devices capable of producing still-picture and video content. With digital cameras now outselling their analogue counterparts (Chute, 2003), and the increased incorporation of cameras in devices such as personal computers, PDAs, music players and, of course, mobile phones, it seems reasonable to assume that the quantity of digital photographs will only increase—and considerably so. Moreover, various research projects including work from Martin and Gaver (2000) have speculated on proposals relating to emerging practices of digital photography, with emphasis on capture.

What is somewhat surprising is that this growth in both products and research has not been matched with a parallel output in novel photo display technologies. If anything, the options for photo display have remained fairly limited (see Kim and Zimmerman 2006b for similar discussion). This is particularly true in homes, where we largely remain tied to our tried and tested paper-based displays. There are, not surprisingly, good reasons why paper-printed photos remain prolific; as more general research into work-practice reminds us, paper has affordances that are often hard to beat in the digital realm (Sellen and Harper, 2002). What's more, the distinctive qualities of a paper-printed photo appear to exhibit certain 'instructions' that shape how we think about and recall the photographed moment (Chalfen, 1998). Indeed, the conventional framing practices associated with paper photos appear so well established that it seems difficult to imagine how they might be minimally adjusted, never mind supplemented with innovative alternatives. Drazin and Frohlich (2007), for example, write of the deeply expressive qualities associated with conventional framed photos in family homes and detail how established 'framing activities' serve to materialize memories and intentions (foreshadowing a number of points we have discovered in our empirical studies).

Given families' well-established practices with framing, it is perhaps not surprising that research in CSCW and CHI concerned with photo displays has tended to focus on the distribution of media between and within households rather than the redesign of the displays themselves. Kim and Zimmerman's (2006a/b) work on smart digital photo frames uses interviews with families to map out the different locations of photos displayed in homes and broadly characterises different spaces for photos as formal or informal. Their findings also explain how households display photos to share narratives and prompt social interactions. They purposefully avoid, however, altering the interactional properties of the frame or how we relate to its displayed content, focusing instead on novel methods for managing and distributing photos to electronic frames.

Work from Mynatt et al. (2001) is perhaps the most comprehensive and complete in terms of display design. They implement a picture frame designed to support remote presence with an eye to enhancing the links between families and their distant, aging relations. Their work though is understandably more concerned with the issues of awareness rather than the arrangement or inherent properties of the frame itself. The CareNet display is of a similar nature, using a technologically augmented display that looks similar to a photo frame to support the relations between an elderly person and the network of people involved in their care (Consolvo, Roessler and Shelton 2004).

Beyond physical photo displays, there are several examples of what could be seen as research into the practices of looking at photos. A number of studies, for example, have focused on the sharing of photos; i.e. looking at them together, between people who are physically collocated (Balabanovic, Chu and Wolff, 2000; Frohlich et al.; 2002; Crabtree, Rodden and Mariani, 2004), as well as distributed (Counts and Fellheimer, 2004; Kindberg et al., 2005; Van House et al., 2005; Voida and Mynatt, 2005). Looking at photos, in this sense, has been seen to be something that mediates social relations, whether between family and friends perusing a paper-based photo album or online communities navigating large electronic collections (Kapoor, Konstan and Terveen, 2005). Frohlich et al. (2002), for example, have given close attention to the ways in which people talk about photos when looking at them, both remotely and when co-located, and in doing so describe different forms of what they refer to as *photo-talk*. Relevant to the materials in this paper, they demonstrate how memories are jointly produced in the sharing of photos, and how our ways of looking and understanding are shaped by some of the common social and material practices involving photos.

Research focused on *photowork* (Kirk et al., 2006) is less immediately relevant to photo displays, but has strong implications for the ideas we will present. Kirk et al. set out the common practices associated with digital and paper-based photos and reveal that although people manage their photos in idiosyncratic ways, the workflow, or what they call photowork, broadly follows a number of possible trajectories. They describe the activities performed to get photos from the device of capture to prepare them to be archived, shared, put on display, and so on. Kirk and his colleagues do not address collaboration around photowork directly, but do lay the groundwork for what we will go onto describe as the coordinated efforts of getting photos to a place of display and the subsequent tensions that can arise.

Fieldwork findings

In the following empirical section of this paper, we present a number of examples drawn from interviews and observations conducted with fifteen households in London and Hertfordshire, U.K. Two qualitative studies have contributed to this corpus. One, an ongoing field study of home life, has been running for nearly three years, involving extended engagements with eight family households and several one-off visits to homes that have been introduced along the way. A range of topics and practices has been addressed in this study, identified and guided in large part by issues raised by the participants and their observable routines. The attention given to photos in this paper, for example, came from recurring discussions in several of the participating homes around family photos and their display.

Of the households visited in this first study, seven were two-parent families with children, ranging in age from less than a year to twelve years old. One household was composed of an elderly widow living with two grandchildren. As well as the observations and interviews, three of the participants also videotaped themselves for extended periods. Due to the nature of what we were looking at, i.e. photo displays, all the households also ended up giving us tours of their homes in one fashion or another.

The second empirical study also involved visits to eight family households, but was structured differently with one teenager and one parent participating from each household. Participants were invited to identify photo displays in their home in response to tasks set by the researcher. Responses were subsequently discussed, first with participants, individually, and then between the two family members. Discussion took the form of semi-structured interviews and home tours.

The points raised in the empirical sections came about through informal discussions between the paper's authors and more structured workshops with members of the research group the authors participate in. Both discussions and workshops focused on the transcripts, video and photographs gathered during the home visits and involved working up this data into broad thematic groupings. Particular focus in the presented research was given to the material features of photo displays and how they interleave with the ways families are collectively organised.

The three design proposals we will present—part of a significantly larger collection—were generated with involvement from numerous researchers with different backgrounds, e.g., computer science, hardware engineering, sociology, psychology and interaction design. Two design workshops were held with these researchers, the first brainstorming design ideas related to the empirical materials and the second discussing and critiquing a number of design proposals outlined by two of the papers authors. Between the first and second workshop, the proposals and reasonings for them were added to an online blog, allowing the workshop participants to gain an early sense of the designs and the thought processes behind them, and to add preliminary comments. As we shall elaborate on later, only three proposals from this process are presented here in order to pay closer attention to the issues raised in the empirical sections and highlight their critical contribution.

Collaborative photowork

In the first example from our fieldwork, we want to draw attention to the collaborative efforts involved in *photowork*. Before presenting this material, worth noting is our broad definition of photo displays, including those photos arranged to be seen in albums, frames and wall-mounted assemblages, and even casually distributed around a home, on pin-boards, fridge doors, etc.

Jim and Karin are an American couple living in London with their three small children. Both parents have digital cameras and regularly take photos. Karin describes their photo displays as a 'joint effort' but adds that Jim "takes the lead on digital photo management". As Karin explains, Jim spends more time on the computer with the photos, taking it upon himself to sort through photos on a monthly basis, deleting certain pictures, editing others, removing red-eye or altering the brightness, etc., and then choosing which photos to print. Karin, on the other hand, is mostly in charge of how photos are displayed and has constructed various photo arrangements or displays throughout the house. As she describes it, she is more involved with displaying and archiving paper photos.

On further inspection, we found this division between paper and digital not to be hard and fast. Observing video they recorded of themselves, we found Karin spending considerable time on the computer looking through digital photos, while Jim can be seen combing through storage boxes of printed photos to find one for a particular frame. Of interest to us in this apparent contradiction is not whether Karin and Jim do what they say, but rather that the joint work around the photos, whether in paper or digital form, is performed more or less unproblematically. For the most part, the coordination work appears to go unnoticed, accomplished as a matter of course in getting photos from digital cameras, onto computers, to print and ready for display. The coordinated efforts are often asynchronous and usually not co-located but there are, it seems, systems in place for the work to be successfully accomplished. The dedicated place for photowork (their home's attic), the single PC, its systematic arrangement of folders and files, the storage boxes of paper-photos, and the photo albums on shelves all have their part in making the workflow visible and enabling the photowork to be performed collaboratively.

Turning our attention to a particular display in Jim and Karin's house we see the result of an ongoing collaborative activity. In the hallway leading to Jim and Karin's sitting room, there is an impressive collection of black and white photos of past and present family members. Pictures are added once or twice a year, and rarely, if ever, removed. All the pictures are either black and white or sepia-tone, and they are all framed in black, white or gold frames (Fig. 1). This assembly has come about through the combined efforts of Karin and Jim, and also includes contributions from friends and extended family. For the most part, Karin arranges the pictures, although both she and Jim choose which pictures to use and a friend, Lawrence, takes family photos once a year that have been framed and added to the wall. Extended family participate remotely. During one of our interviews, Karin explains how some of the pictures have been sent by family members in the post or sometimes brought from the US in person. Lately, distant family members have also started to create digital copies and send them by email. Karin recounts how her mother contributes: "And my mom is always sending photos and saying 'oh I thought this might be good for the wall'". She also draws attention to a long picture with white crease marks, placed prominently in the bottom row of the framed photos. The picture is of a family reunion held by Jim's family in the early 1900's, sent by his mother. The picture, it emerges, has been copied and sent via email (with creases and all).

Figure 1. Family wall.

The transition from paper to digital and back to paper again, and the re-rendering of the picture's physical features (i.e., its creases), raises questions concerning the preservation of age and authenticity, and of the methods for invoking history. Relevant to our argument here, however, is how the movement of media from person to person and transitions between digital and paper formats seem completely unremarkable to Karin and Jim, and no doubt to their extended family as well. That Karin and Jim, and their families and friends might participate in assembling the pictures for the family wall and using a variety of means to do so is, if anything, an assumed feature of family relations.

Obligations

In the following, we consider another simple but interesting feature of collaboration around family photo displays: the idea of obligation. In our studies, we found photographs of certain people were placed on display because they were needed to be seen to be on display. We found this intriguing on two fronts. The first was the tacit understanding that pictures of certain family members must be displayed, unquestioningly. The second was the ingenuity in reconciling the sometimes opposing claims of needing to display family members but not necessarily wanting to. Two examples, one relating again to the family wall and a second to to. Two examples, one relating again to the family wall and a second to family wedding photos illustrate this role of obligation.

When Karin is asked if all the photos sent by the collective grandmothers as "good for the wall" end up on the wall, she says no, that she effectively finesses anything she doesn't want up there. However, certain situations override this; she gives an example, explaining how a photo of her sister has ended up where it is.

> Well, I did get a little bit of grief from my sister. The reason we did this photo shoot with my sister before she left London was because she was like "There aren't any photos of me on your wall!", you know, and so I was like [*sotto voce*] 'oh you know, that's true' so I scrambled, we had this present for her done, and we had those photos done and I put the one of her and me as kids up on the wall. I definitely made sure that was up before her last visit.

Karin's explanation reveals how her family is accountable for her sister's absence on the wall. Completely unnecessary, however, is any explanation of why this should be the case. It is taken for granted that *all* family members should be on display and any exclusion is a form of disloyalty.

Turning to two wedding photos on display in another household, we see that this obligation to family can be achieved in ways that are less elaborate, but nonetheless inventive and that still reflect the tensions of displaying particular family members. In a household of three (mother: Trish, father: Des, and daughter: Tina), we find something as simple as a frame placed in light and another in shadow can cast emphasis on one photo over another. The two frames in question both contain posed photos from different family weddings and both are of Trish, Des and Tina. They are placed near to one another, one on the living room sideboard and the other on top of a shelving unit holding CDs (Fig. 2).

Figure 2. Wedding portraits on CD rack in shadows (far left) and on sideboard (left of centre).

Explaining why the frames have been arranged as they are, Trish, Des and Tina produce an elaborate story behind the two pictures. Talking, first, about posing for the framed photo placed in the shadows and then about the photo placed in the light, Trish recalls the circumstances under which they were taken:

> Yeah this one [picks up frame from shadows], which is really quite funny, because it shows you the difference in the weddings... My second youngest brother, it was his wedding in April

and everybody was kinda of like: 'hmmm, let's make an effort' you know, 'it's a wedding.' Whereas this one [points to photo on sideboard in light] you can see people were actually happy and they enjoyed it more. You know it's not being nasty but [looks back to frame she's holding]… but nobody kinda liked his partner and it was all like, 'oh, let's make an effort'. You know it's his choice of who he marries and we just have to kinda lump it. So everybody's like, 'hmm, yeah smile' [said with sarcasm]. Whereas that one [points to frame on sideboard again], because it was a really nice day and people enjoyed the wedding, it kind of comes across more in the photo.

To the undiscerning eye, there is little difference between the two framed pictures and certainly no visible difference in how happy (or unhappy) the family are on each occasion. Salient though is the display of both pictures so that one is given visual prominence over the other. We are cautious about making any strong claim about the intended meanings of photo display arrangements and, in this example, the relative positioning of the framed photos. Trish and her family are clearly involved in producing an account for us as part of our fieldwork exercise; in fact, when returning the frame she has removed from the shelving unit, Trish swiftly retracts the lengthy explanation given for the photo arrangement. Jokingly, she retorts "… but that's mainly cause there's no backing" to offer an alternative explanation for the frame's placement in the shadows, against the back wall.

Whatever the reasoning, plainly visible is that both photos are on show despite the family's ambivalent feelings towards one of the weddings. This suggests that like the addition of Karin's sister to the family wall, this inclusion comes down (at least to an extent) to obligation. One can easily imagine the offence caused if Trish and Des chose to display one wedding picture but not the other. No doubt most of us, upon reflection, have photos or other objects in our homes not because we want them there, but because we feel obliged to. What seems crucial to this is that the photos are seen to be on display, day in day out. It wouldn't do for Karin to have an obviously temporary photo of her sister amongst the framed photos on the wall or if, somehow, Trish's brother was able to detect his wedding photo being placed on display only for his visits. There appears then, to be a sensitivity to the ways in which photo arrangements are viewed jointly in households and that this sensitivity has, as it were, a demonstrable quality—that households have to be seen to be putting certain sorts of photos on display of and for others. In some sense, the idea, or even the fiction, of family needs to be maintained, and displaying photos of particular people is one way of doing this.

Curatorial Control

In this last section of empirical materials, we address what we saw as a tension that can arise in the movement of photos through the processes of photowork to their eventual display. We've suggested that both aspects of photo display—that is, the processes of getting photos to a display on the one hand, and the viewing of the display on the other—involve forms of collaboration or at least shared involvement. A recurring theme we found in our fieldwork, however, was that often one particular family member took overall control of a household's display of photos. Having what we've come to call *curatorial control*, this family member would make decisions around how the processes of photowork fed into the display of photos and how the obligations of display were met (for further evidence of this see Drazin and Frohlich, 2007). Even where we saw effort put into distributing this decision making, the curatorial control often ended up in one person's hands. Tension arose over shifting from, one, the collaborative elements of photowork to photo display and, two, the display to the shared viewing of the photos. To elaborate on the first of these issues we present an example from another household and the negotiations played out through digital and conventional, paper-based photowork. To address the second, we consider the tensions that arise between a mother and daughter over a photograph displayed in their bathroom.

The first example centres around a household made up of Charlotte, Hamish and their three children. During one of our visits, Charlotte and Hamish discuss what each of them does with photographs. Charlotte explains how she organizes her family photo albums, describing the activity as "making decisions about what you keep as a kind of 'family thing'". Characterizing the selection process, she explains how she sorts through various types of family memorabilia to determine what should be put away in a box in the attic and what can be thrown out, taking into account factors such as whether elderly grandparents are involved, whether the occasion was particularly memorable, etc. As with the family wall and wedding photos above, a strong sense of obligation motivates this selection procedure. Charlotte goes on to describe how she physically divides the photos that go into albums: the albums are kept in a cupboard in the sitting room, with the day-to-day albums on the top shelf and the 'special' albums on the bottom shelf. She is fairly assiduous about keeping up with putting photos in her albums, not liking to have photos piled up. Charlotte reveals how she approaches this preparation of photos with zeal:

Charlotte: So I'll wait till there's a quiet evening, and my, my big investment is my guillo-tine, because I used to spend hours drawing straight lines on them and then cutting them with scissors...

Interviewer: To get them to fit into certain...?

Charlotte: Well, so that if it's a nice photograph but there's somebody's thumb, or there's somebody, you know,..., somebody in the background...

Hamish: It's Stalinism! It beats airbrushing them out.

Charlotte: ... (laughing) a bit of, a bit of a doorframe, you know, or someone's nose, you know, ...you just *chop it off!!* (makes slicing sound with paper-cutter)

With Charlotte's photo albums, we see how family histories can be filtered and fashioned. Although this particular excerpt runs the risk of sounding vaguely Machiavellian (thanks to Hamish's comment about Stalinism), it does capture how an influence over the processes that make up photowork can produce a certain rendering of family, one 'designed', intentionally or not, by the family member with curatorial control.

A revealing point to examine further relates to Charlotte's choice of the guillotine, enabling her to act out her curatorial control rather viscerally. On investigation, we find a seeming division in Charlotte and Hamish's family between digital versus conventional paper-based photowork. Charlotte operates in the paper-based realm, continuing to use a conventional film camera, to have her pictures printed and to give the prints a definitive chop when necessary. Hamish, meanwhile, uses a digital camera; he views, manages and edits many of his photos on his personal laptop and the household computer, as well as having some of them printed to paper. Interesting for this study is how this division in practice relates to photo display; to illustrate this point, we consider some photos Hamish has taken with his digital camera during a family trip to Canada that have since been printed onto paper. When asked about what happens with digital photos, they answer the following:

Charlotte: I don't have anything to do with those. There's a whole bag of digital photographs from Canada sitting in the bedroom that we've done nothing with, which we keep saying, oh we must do something. But we're never going to get down to doing anything with them.

Hamish: The only time we look at them is because they're on the screen saver.

Interviewer: Yes, I saw them on the screensaver and I was curious...

Hamish: They've never made it to an album... You see, it's funny, because Charlotte, you take pictures yourself, and they're the ones that go in the album. I take the digital ones and they never go in the album.

As Hamish points out, it is Charlotte's photos that end up in albums. Even though Hamish's digital photographs have now assumed physical form, they remain excluded, nominally due to the fact that they began life digitally. When Charlotte says "We're never going to get down to doing anything with them" we get the sense that this isn't so much about *how*, technologically, the photowork is performed but arguably more about *who* takes and processes the pictures. In short, the tension arises around the control of photos to the possible sites of display. In this case, the digital divide has come to be the resource for determining control; although the material differences between digital and paper photographs can certainly affect how they are used, in some instances the use of the distinction can mask something altogether different, e.g., how it is one delimits control.

In our final example, we consider how representations of individual family members can be 'curated' by one member, and how photographs can privilege certain portrayals of family, whilst excluding others. Yvonne has created a permanent home display in her family bathroom by printing photographic images on bathroom tiles, making a conscious effort to include representations of each member of her immediate family. Here, we focus on one photo in particular, that of her daughter, Cat (Fig. 3). Yvonne describes what the photo means for her:

I got Cat to pose. I never force stuff because- I mean it works two ways- they [the household members] also know I remove photos that are bad: I don't see why anyone should have a photo on display that they hate; and that's partly because he [her husband], also a photographer, keeps every photo, every bad one, and I just think life's too short! I believe in editing. So, I just look at that and I think of Liv Tyler: there's a neat film called Stealing Beauty, which I love, I really love; I play it when I need to get energy when I'm cooking. But I think it's provocative. Fathers don't like that film if they have daughters, because they think of their daughter losing her virginity. But I just think she looks – not even Rock Star, but just stunning there. It surprises me how beautiful and grown up she is. Surprises me and makes me proud! And she's not embarrassed by it, fortunately.

In fact, Cat is embarrassed by the photograph: "everyone puts too much importance on it". Cat's mother has emphasised a certain representation of her daughter, creating a tension that is captured in Cat's description of the T-shirt she is wearing in the photo:

Yeah, I suppose it surprises me, how they got me to do that. What you can't see is that the t-shirt is actually, erm, splattered with fake blood saying: 'no one's perfect', [laughs] which I, which always amuses me as well cause I don't think Maman remembers that: it was a T-shirt that she absolutely loathed. But, yeah, I can't remember how she persuaded me to stand in lavender field like that.

But Cat is resigned to its display, saying: "I've got no choice". Paradoxically, further discussion reveals that she finds a certain comfort in knowing that she is displayed alongside the rest of her family. Despite the photo's content and its location, she says that being included makes her feel 'like one of the family'.

Figure 3. (a) Tiled bathroom and (b) tile with picture of Cat.

Yvonne's bathroom photo arrangement and Cat's ambiguous feelings towards it illustrate the tensions that can arise with one person as family curator. It appears that Yvonne is asserting a certain idea of her family, despite the fact that her idea is not one held in common by all her family members. The fact that Cat is actually embarrassed by the photo, and that Yvonne's husband might be uncomfortable with the photo, suggests that Yvonne is representing the 'family' as interpreted by Yvonne, rather than as a collaborative endeavour.

Overall, both examples above demonstrate not just that one person has curatorial control in the display of family photos, but that tensions over displays get played out in an ongoing fashion. Interestingly, these tensions are not solely between household members, but can also be within an individual. Despite her discomfort with the photo, the fact that being excluded from the bathroom shower grouping would be worse for Cat than her present embarrassment illustrates tension, this time from an individual perspective.

Designing domestic photo displays

The materials above hopefully foreground a number of issues we found to be of particular interest in studying photo displays in family homes. Of course, the materials do not address the entire range of practices families engage in when preparing and displaying their photos, nor do they cover the entire set of results from our larger corpus of data. Rather than aim to address breadth of coverage, we've attempted to work through specific points raised in our empirical studies in order to consider spaces for novel digital display design. To recap, the three themes we've focused on are (i) how family's collaborate around the practices associated with getting photos to a point of display; (ii) how social obligation influences the kinds of photos placed on display and the material arrangement of displays; and (iii) the how one person's curatorial control in a household raises tensions around the organization and presentation of family. We've also sought to reveal that a collaborative process can be seen to underlie most of these practices, yet not always in obvious ways. Though the task of placing a photo on display is often performed by just one person, the journey of the photo into that person's hands might have involved the joint intent of others and certainly involves viewings from household members as well outsiders. As we've implied earlier, these less visible forms of collaboration around photo displays have been seemingly overlooked in CSCW and HCI. Indeed, we would take this a step further and suggest the very idea of such collaboration may well be constrained by the lack of existing technologies to support it: 'framing' activities are generally designed for individual use and, to date, collaborative display technologies are rare (if they exist at all).

We've seen this seemingly under-explored design space to present interesting methodological and analytic challenges for CSCW and HCI. Clearly, it is hard to design for practices that do not yet exist. Insights from empirical studies can sensitize the researcher to a new design space, but engagement with a 'fictional' set of new experiences on the basis of studies like ours pose an on-going challenge for inter-disciplinary fields (hence the long-standing discussions about empirical studies and their relationship to design, as reviewed in the introduction).

In this section, we present a strategy that we have been investigating for opening up the possibilities for display design, aiming, in particular, to build upon the themes discussed above. To illustrate our use of this strategy, we present three design sketches positioned not as design *solutions* to issues surrounding the themes, but as concepts enabling further, empirically grounded investigations. The strategy we have adopted, incorporating a critical perspective, is thus aimed at promoting grounded exploration, offering a point of departure from the *problem-solving* or stylistic concerns that can preoccupy design (Dunne, 1999).

We specifically aim for the sketches to give a degree of form to our thematic tensions so that they provide a tangible basis for inquiry. Also to facilitate the probing of the issues, the design concepts have been purposefully left simple in terms of functionality and technical detail. Broadly, for the purposes of our inquiry, sketching was chosen because it was seen to have a particular strength in facilitating the generation of ideas and the exploration of design spaces whilst avoiding the need for commitment to detailed specifications that could be distracting or convey resolution. To use Tabor's terms (2002), sketching offers "a space for half-formed thoughts".

Photo Mesh

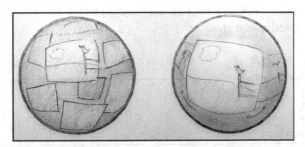

Figure 4. Photo Mesh.

The first of our concepts, *Photo Mesh* (Fig. 4), plays with the possibility of making a digital media archive visible in a shared domestic space. It is envisaged that the family's archival content would be open to contributions from an entire family. Here, Photo Mesh takes the form of a circular, wall-mounted screen for displaying many photographs simultaneously. In its default state, it behaves as an ambient or peripheral surface, with its displayed content (randomly) cycling through the associated archive. However, it also allows a 'walk-up' set of interactions: a user or group of users can make intuitive gestures to navigate through the archive in a temporal fashion. A specific photo can also be selected from the collage to fill the entire surface. As such, Photo Mesh experiments with how displays may support a shift in engagement, from periphery to foreground, and from a multiple to single image-viewing platform. In this way, it offers a novel kind of flexibility in a shared domestic space. Importantly, through the collaborative interactions afforded, this simple system also probes the notion of a 'shared display' and the possible tensions that this creates between family members.

Let us briefly expand upon the inquiring function of this sketch. Although the technology that Photo Mesh comprises is not in itself innovative, we believe its *configuration* to be. The display enables an exploration of the themes above—particularly collaborative workflow and curatorial control—by enabling the serendipitous discovery of photographs and the immediate selection of a given photo to display in a shared space. Photo Mesh condenses some of the aspects of workflow with the actual display of a photo, allowing both to be achieved with a simple and easily performed set of interactions. Of interest in the context of the presented work, Photo Mesh sets up hypothetical conditions for a dynamic family display which is openly accessible and jointly editable. Because the preparation and physical display of a photo is achieved with ease and potentially in collaboration, the display offers no inherent hierarchy of control to any member. In practice, we'd expect rules to be imposed on its use within a household, perhaps around the inclusion of content in the archive or what is displayed when, and by whom. It is this, in part, that we see contributing to the critical character of the design. The concept encourages us as designers (and potentially as users) to attend to the activities associated with workflow collaboration and control and, through *provocation*, draws attention to the ways in which the features of the digital artefact can interleave with these.

Photo Switch

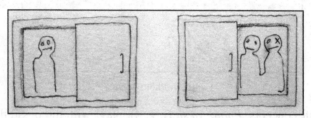

Figure 5. Photo Switch.

A second concept, entitled *Photo Switch*, again proposes the installation of a situated display in a family household (Fig. 5). This second design has, in contrast to Photo Mesh, significantly reduced functionality. Photo Switch comprises a wall-mounted casement for two display surfaces and a sliding door that constrains viewing to no more than one photograph at a time. In its most basic form, Photo Switch does not need to incorporate digital technology; other iterations of the design, however, are connected to a digital archive.

As an interventional artefact, Photo Switch provokes questions around the curatorial control (or distribution of control) of family representations. This is because, as with Photo Mesh, household members would have to make choices and engage in negotiations around what to display and when. By forcing a choice to be made over the photo displayed, Photo Switch immediately demands one to question how particular representations are obscured whereas others are privileged. Perhaps unexpectedly, the design reveals the relationship between choice over physical form, on the one hand, and social judgment on the other; shown is that choice in display arrangement and social obligation can rub up against each other, sometimes in uncomfortable ways. This in turn raises questions concerning the family curator and the ways in which one person comes to physically fashion family photo displays to meet the obligations of their idea of family. The immediate, visible tensions that can arise with Photo Switch offer the opportunity for such curatorial authority to be openly contested.

Photo Illume

Figure 6. Photo Illume.

The final design idea to be presented here is *Photo Illume*, which differs from the other two proposals because it takes the form of a portable display frame for single image-viewing (Fig. 6). This display comprises an LCD screen that fades to black if the displayed photo doesn't receive sunlight; it behaves as if solar-powered. Photo Illume artefacts are networked to a digital archive, and, once faded to black, another image from the archive automatically replaces the current one. It is envisioned that Photo Illumes could be moved around for certain effects, literally 'illuminating' the handling of content.

There are obvious parallels between Photo Illume and the arrangement of the wedding photos in Trish and Des's home. Photo Illume offers a provocative position, however, as it associates the 'handling' of the display with a photo's form (i.e., its brightness) and the duration of the photo's display. In effect, a responsibility of sorts is bound up with the sense of obligation because one must actively attend to Photo Illume to ensure it shows what it should. At the same time, the need for particular placement of the display in light and the need to repeatedly interact with it makes one accountable for the control they have. Yvonne's choice of photo in the bathroom would no longer be quite so set in stone, so to speak, but instead demand an active accountability for its location and persistent display.

This need for active engagement with the display also raises issues around photowork. Photo Illume can distribute photowork to the system in that the photos change as a result of the system's own measurement of time. This confounds the purposeful 'framing' of photos that we have seen families engage in, but rather than reducing responsibility, it reconfigures the 'framing' work to be more tightly interwoven with the physical act of display. The action, as it were, shifts from the preparatory shared workflows to some negotiated activity around 'display-making' itself.

Conclusions

Above, we've illustrated how we've used critical design practice to think innovatively about photo displays and their shared use in family households. We've made a particular effort to show how empirical studies can serve to ground critical design, and how critical design proposals can, in turn, build on descriptive empirical accounts by providing direction and form to the play of possibilities.

Three broad themes drawn from our empirical studies have been the main impetus for this design work. In short, we've highlighted the collaborative as well as individual practices associated with photowork. We've described how there are obligatory social pressures that influence what families put on display and how they compose their photo arrangements. Lastly, we've suggested it is one person in a household that often takes control of many of the home's photo displays. This curatorial control can, we've shown, raise tensions in households, tensions associated with the social organization and presentation of family. The three concepts above, Photo Mesh, Photo Switch and Photo Illume, have been presented to show how each of these themes can be developed while sensitizing them towards design concerns. In our concluding remarks, we want to briefly detail several possibilities for further design exploration that we've found useful from this use of critical design. For purposes of clarity, we list these:

• Photo Mesh opens up questions around photo displays designed to merge the collaborative aspects of photowork and the act of display. It opens up possibilities for where the collaboration might lie and how it can be reconfigured by a set of design interactions.
• Photo Switch raises the association between choice and obligation. A choice in the photo displayed binds one to a single representation at the cost of another. This opens up design possibilities around making visible or hidden the choices made in arranging photos. Importantly, it does not dictate whether a display should promote one or the other. Rather, it suggests that thought should go into how a display might be designed to suggest either.
• Photo Switch also draws attention to how choices in photo display are likely to demand negotiation between family members around where and when to display photos. It thus provokes inquiry into design's role in engaging family members in active and sometimes playful participation around photo display.
• Photo Illume draws attention to the 'display-making' activity itself because one is repeatedly made accountable for the choice of photo displayed. Possibilities exist here for photo displays that make visible the ongoing engagement with display-making, revealing not only the process of getting a photo to a display but also the act of keeping it there.
• All the designs highlight the dynamic qualities afforded by digital displays, either in the changing photos or in the physical arrangement of the display itself. Possibilities here are vast, but hopefully one value of the three proposals is in how they exemplify particular directions to explore in this respect.

In sum, at this exploratory stage of design, the sketches and the possibilities they've provoked hopefully draw attention to several simple but what we see to be important areas in designing photo displays for the home. Broadly, we've raised questions around collaboration both in the processes of preparing photos for display and with the displays themselves. Through our sketches, we've highlighted how collaboration can be afforded in different ways and at different stages of preparation and display. By foregrounding some of the collaborative features involved in photo display, we've also aimed to encourage a sensitivity in display design towards the negotiations, obligations and accountabilities that families play out in displaying their photos. We've chosen not to prescribe the ways in which these issues should be addressed. Instead, we've aimed to show how they can be further examined, sometimes provocatively, through specific designs.

To further the work presented, we are currently building working artefacts based on the proposals above (as well as others) with the intention of situating the, in family households. This notion of locating artefacts 'in the wild' draws from Hutchinson et al.'s (2003) use of Technology Probes. However, unlike Technology Probes, our designs do not explicitly pursue the goal of assessing a technology in use. In keeping with our particular design sensibility, the designs are framed as critical interventions into family homes. Their presence attempts to catalyze some of the tensions we have highlighted with the aim of provoking idiosyncratic reflection on our themes *by* family members themselves and in the context of their everyday lives. In this respect, we draw on Gaver et al.'s (2006) contribution to the Equator project. Essentially, our ambition is to use these designs to encourage households to think about their photo displays in new ways.

We imagine that output from such interventions would form qualitative accounts of people's encounters with the designs. These accounts may offer us design inspiration. In parallel, they may enrich our understanding of how members of a family household collectively use displays to create, constrain and control their shared representations, and the challenges presented by digital technology for doing so.

Acknowledgments

We are indebted to the families who participated in this study for their time and thoughts. Special thanks must also go to David Frohlich, David Kirk, Evanthia Lyons and Abigail Sellen for their contributions throughout the research. Part of the presented research is supported by the Microsoft European PhD Scholarship Programme.

References

Anderson, B. Work, ethnography and system design. In *The Encyclopaedia of Microcomputers* (eds Kent, A. & Williams, J. G.). Marcel Dekker, New York, 1997, 159-183.

Balabanovic, M., Chu, L. L. & Wolff, G. J. Storytelling with digital photographs. *Proc. CHI '00.* ACM Press, 2000, 564-571.

Button, G. & Dourish, P. (1996) Technomethodology: Paradoxes and possibilities. *Proc. CHI '96,* ACM Press, 19-26.

Chalfen, R. Family photograph appreciation: dynamics of medium, interpretation, and memory. *Communication and Cognition*, 31 (1998), 161-178.

Chute, C. *Worldwide still camera forecast, 2003-2007: the emerging digital solution*. Report #29662, IDC, 2003.

Consolvo, S., Roessler, P. & Shelton, B. E. The CareNet Display: Lessons Learned from an In Home Evaluation of an Ambient Display. *UbiComp '04*. Springer, Nottingham, 2004, 1-17.

Counts, S. & Fellheimer, E. Supporting social presence through lightweight photo sharing on and off the desktop. *Proc. CHI '04*. ACM Press, 2004, 599-606.

Crabtree, A. & Rodden, T. Domestic routines and design for the home. *JCSCW*, 13 (2004), 191-220.

Crabtree, A., Rodden, T. & Mariani, J. Collaborating around collections: informing the continued development of photoware. *Proc. CSCW '04*. ACM Press, 2004, 396-405.

Dourish, P. (2006) Design implications. *Proc. CHI '06*, ACM Press, 541-550.

Dunne, A. *Hertzian tales: Electronic products, aesthetic experience and critical design*. RCACRD Publications, London, 1999.

Drazin, A. & Frohlich, D. (2007) Good Intentions: Remembering through Framing Photographs in English Homes. *Ethnos*, 72, 1, 51–76.

Frohlich, D., Kuchinsky, A., Pering, C., Don, A. & Ariss, S. Requirements for photoware. *Proc. CSCW '02*. ACM Press, 2002, 166-175.

Gaver, B., Dunne, T. & Pacenti, E. (1999) Design: Cultural probes. *Interactions*, 6, 1, 21-29.

Gaver, W. Bowers, J. Boucher, A. Law, A. Pennington, S. Villar, N. The History Tablecloth: Illuminating Domestic Activity. *Proc. DIS'06*, ACM Press, 199 – 208.

Hutchinson, H. et al. (2003) Technology probes: inspiring design for and with families. *Proc. CHI '03*, ACM Press, New York, NY, 17-24.

Kapoor, N., Konstan, J. A. & Terveen, L. G. How peer photos influence member participation in online communities. *Ext. abs. CHI '05*. ACM Press, New York, NY, 2005, 1525-1528.

Kim, J. & Zimmerman, J. Cherish: smart digital photo frames for sharing social narratives at home. *Ext. abs. CHI '06*. ACM Press, 2006, 953-958.

Kim, J. & Zimmerman, J. (2006b). Cherish: smart digital photo frames. *Proc. Design & Emotion*.

Kindberg, T., Spasojevic, M., Fleck, R. & Sellen, A. The ubiquitous camera: an in-depth study of camera phone use. *Pervasive Computing*, 4, 2 (2005), 42-50.

Martin, H. & Gaver, W. Beyond the Snapshot: From Speculation to Prototypes in Audiophotography. *Proc. DIS '00*, ACM Press, 2000, 55-65.

Mynatt, E. D., Rowan, J., Jacobs, A. & Craighill, S. Digital Family Portraits: Supporting Peace of Mind for Extended Family Members. *Proc. CHI '01*. ACM, 2001, 333-340.

O'Brien, J. & Rodden, T. (1997). Interactive systems in domestic environments. *Proc. DIS '97*, ACM, New York, NY, 247-259.

Plowman, L., Rogers, Y. & Ramage, M. (1995) What are workplace studies for? *Proc. ECSCW '95*, 309-324.

Sellen, A. J. & Harper, R. The Myth of the Paperless Office. MIT Press, Cambridge, Mass, 2002.

Tabor, P. A space for half-formed thoughts. In *Doors of Perception 7: Flow*. 14-16 Nov, 2002. http://flow.doorsofperception.com/content/tabor_trans.html.

Van House, N., Davis, M., Ames, M., Finn, M. & Viswanathan, V. The uses of personal networked digital imaging: an empirical study of cameraphone photos and sharing. *Ext. abs. CHI '05*. ACM Press, 2005, 1853-1856.

Voida, A. & Mynatt, E. D. Six themes of the communicative appropriation of photographic images. *Proc. CHI '05*. ACM Press, 2005, 171-180.

L. Bannon, I. Wagner, C. Gutwin, R. Harper, and K. Schmidt (eds.).
ECSCW'07: Proceedings of the Tenth European Conference on Computer Supported Cooperative Work, 24-28 September 2007, Limerick, Ireland
© Springer 2007

The Awareness Network: *To Whom* Should I Display My Actions? And, *Whose* Actions Should I Monitor?

Cleidson R. B. de Souza
Faculdade de Computação, Universidade Federal do Pará,
Belém, PA, Brasil
cdesouza@ufpa.br

David Redmiles
Department of Informatics, University of California, Irvine
Irvine, CA, USA
redmiles@ics.uci.edu

Abstract. The concept of awareness has come to play a central role in CSCW research. The coordinative practices of displaying and monitoring have received attention and have led to different venues of research, from computational tool support, such as media spaces and event propagation mechanisms, to ethnographic studies of work. However, these studies have overlooked a different aspect of awareness practices: the identification of the *social actors who should be monitored and the actors to whom their actions should be displayed*. The focus of this paper is on how social actors answer the following questions: *to whom* should I display my actions? And, *whose* actions should I monitor? Ethnographic data from two software development teams are used to answer these questions. In addition, we illustrate how software developers' work practices are influenced by three different factors: the organizational setting, the age of the project, and the software architecture.

Introduction

Schmidt (2002) discusses some important findings about the concept of awareness recognized by the CSCW community. These findings are based on seminal studies of work practice (Harper, Hughes et al. 1989; Heath and Luff 1992; Heath, Jirotka et al. 1993), and they conceptualize awareness as a range of coordinative practices performed by competent actors to accomplish their work (Heath, Svensson et al. 2002). The nature of these coordinative practices is dual: it involves (i) displaying one's actions, and (ii) monitoring others' actions. That is to say, social actors *monitor* their colleagues' actions to understand how these actions impact their own work and, while doing their work, social actors *display* their actions in such a way that others can easily monitor them[1]. The displaying and the monitoring of activities are thus complementary aspects: the displaying of one's actions is facilitated by the monitoring of the others and vice versa.

The practices by which social actors became aware of their colleagues' work usually have been associated with actors' achievements—"hidden" results of work arrangements—and not viewed as the result of deliberate, explicit actions (Schmidt 2002). However, this is not the case. In fact, according to Schmidt, social actors deftly choose the degree of obtrusiveness of their actions:

> "no clear distinction exists between, on the one hand, the coordinative practices of monitoring and displaying, normally referred to under the labels 'mutual awareness' or 'peripheral awareness', and, on the other hand, the practices of directing attention or interfering for other purposes. In fact, by somehow displaying his or her actions, the actor is always, in some way and to some degree, intending some effect on the activities of colleagues. The distinction is not categorical but merely one of degrees and modes of obtrusiveness."

Despite the undeniable importance of these findings, one aspect has not received enough analytical attention by the CSCW community: the identification of social actors involved in the coordinative practices of awareness, that is, *how social actors identify the colleagues who should be monitored and those colleagues to whom their actions should be displayed*. We argue that a change of focus is required: instead of focusing on the coordinative practices, one should focus on how social actors answer the following questions: *to whom* should I display my actions? And, *whose* actions should I monitor? It is also necessary to understand how the organizational setting facilitates the identification of these two sets of actors.

These questions have been looked at from a technological point of view in event notification servers (Lövstrand 1991; Fitzpatrick, Kaplan et al. 2002), usually through subscriptions that allow one to define the notifications to receive. Empirical studies, however, have not focused on these aspects, partly because the studies of work practice that helped to establish the concept of awareness used the perspectives of ethnomethodology and conversation analysis (Garfinkel 1967). Studies using these perspectives focused on the organization of the work in "small time frames"; consequently, social actors did not change. The settings studied (control rooms, newsrooms, trading rooms, etc.) required individuals to monitor their colleagues' immediate actions at the same time they were engaged in other activities (Heath, Svensson et al. 2002). Note that this is not a criticism of these sociological perspectives; rather, it is an observation that this focus has led CSCW

---

[1]   Implicit in this discussion is the notion of interdependent activities, i.e., displaying and monitoring are especially relevant because the outcome of one's action can affect others' actions (Malone and Crowston 1994; Schmidt 2000).

researchers to overlook other aspects of awareness, as discussed further in this paper.

We can thus describe the focus of this paper as the identification of the "awareness network"—the network of actors whose actions need to be monitored and those to whom one needs to make one's own actions visible. Through the presentation of ethnographic data from two software development teams, we illustrate how software developers identify their awareness networks, the size and fluidity of these networks, and how these aspects influence the practices by which they become aware of the actions of their colleagues. We also discuss how organizational settings facilitate or hinder the identification and maintenance of awareness networks. In this regard, this paper briefly illustrates how software developers' knowledge about the software architecture is used to guarantee a smooth flow of work.

The remainder of this paper is organized as follows. The next section describes the two research sites studied, Alpha and Beta, as well as the methods used to collect and analyze data from these sites. Next, the ethnographic data of the Beta and Alpha teams is presented, and a discussion follows in the subsequent sections. Finally, the last section presents the final comments and future work.

Research Site and Methods

We conducted two qualitative studies at different large software development organizations. The first field study was conducted during summer 2002, and the second one was performed during summer 2003. We adopted observation (Jorgensen 1989) and semi-structured interviews (McCracken 1988) for data collection. The role of the software architecture in the work practices was evident during the data collection; therefore, we explicitly tried to collect information about this aspect. Data analysis was conducted by using grounded theory techniques (Strauss and Corbin 1998). Details about each team as well as the methods used are described next.

Alpha

In this study, the first team has developed a software application called Alpha (not the real name), a software composed of ten different tools in approximately one million lines of C and C++ code. Each one of these tools uses a specific set of "processes." A process for the Alpha team is a program that runs with the appropriate run-time options and it is not formally related to the concept of processes in operating systems and/or distributed systems. Running a tool means running the processes required by this tool with their appropriate run-time options. Processes are used to divide the work: Process leaders and process developers, usually work with only one process. Each developer is assigned to one or more processes and tends to specialize in each of these. This is an important aspect because it allows developers to deeply understand a process's behavior and structure, allowing them to deal with the complexity of the code. Process leaders are responsible for reviewing each change made to their process.

The software development team is divided into two groups: the developers and the verification and validation (V&V) staff. The developers are responsible for writing new code, fixing bugs, and adding new features to the software. This group comprises twenty-five members, three of whom are also researchers who write their own code to explore new ideas. V&V members are responsible for testing and reporting bugs identified in the Alpha software, keeping a running version of the software for demonstration purposes, and maintaining the documentation (mainly user manuals) of the software. This group comprises six members. Developers and V & V team members are located in several offices across two floors in the same building.

The Alpha group adopts a formal software development process (Fuggetta 2000) that prescribes the steps to be performed by the developers. For example, all developers, after finishing the implementation of a change, are supposed to integrate their code with the main baseline. In addition, each developer is responsible for testing his or her code to guarantee that when the changes are integrated, bugs will not occur in the software. Another part of the process prescribes that, after checking-in files in the repository, a developer must send an email to the software development mailing list describing the problem report (PR) associated with the changes, the files that were changed, and the branch where the check-in will be performed, among other pieces of information.

The first author spent eight weeks as a member of the Alpha team. He made observations and collected information about several aspects of the team, talking with colleagues to learn more about their work. Additional material was collected by reading manuals of the Alpha tools, manuals of the software development tools, formal documents (such as the description of the software development process and the ISO 9001 procedures), training documentation for new developers, PRs, and so on. All Alpha team members agreed to the data collection. Furthermore, some of the team members agreed to be shadowed for a few days. These team members belonged to different groups and played diverse roles in the Alpha team. They worked with different Alpha processes and tools and had varied experience in software development, which allowed a broad overview of the work being performed at the site. Eight Alpha team members were interviewed during 45- to 120-minute sessions, according to their availability. To summarize, the data collected consist of a set of notes that resulted from conversations and documents as well as observations based on shadowing developers.

Beta

The second field study was conducted in a software development company named BSC. The project studied, called Beta, is responsible for developing a client-server application. The project staff includes 57 software engineers, user-interface designers, software architects, and managers, divided into five different teams, each one developing a different part of the application. The teams are designated as follows: lead, client, server, infrastructure, and test. The lead team comprises the project lead, development manager, user interface designers, and so on. The client team is developing the client side of the application, whereas the server team is developing the server aspects of the application. The infrastructure team is working in the shared components to be used by both the client and server teams. Finally, the test team is responsible for the quality assurance of the product, testing the software produced by the other teams. In the remainder of this paper, members of the client (server) team will be called Beta client (server) developers.

The Beta project is part of a larger company strategy focusing on software reuse. This strategy aims to create software components (each one developed by a different project/team) that can be used by other projects (teams) in the organization. Indeed, the Beta project uses several components provided by other projects, which means that members of the Beta teams need to interact with other software developers in other parts of the organization.

To facilitate the reuse program, BSC enforces the usage of a *reference architecture* during the development of software applications. The BSC reference architecture prescribes the adoption of some particular design patterns (Gamma, Helm et al. 1995), but at the same time gives software architects across the organization flexibility in their designs. This architecture is based on tiers (or layers) so that components in one tier can request services only to the components in the tier immediately below them (Buschmann, Meunier et al. 1996). Data exchange between tiers is possible through well-defined objects called "value objects." Meanwhile, service requests between tiers are possible through Application Programming Interfaces (APIs) that hide the details of how those services are performed (e.g., either remotely or locally, with cached data or not, etc.). In this organization, APIs are designed by software architects in a technical process that involves the definition of classes, method signatures, and other programming language concepts, and the associated documentation. APIs are both a technical construct and an organizational mechanism that allows teams to work independently (de Souza, Redmiles et al. 2004).

Regarding data collection in this field study, we also adopted non-participant observation (Jorgensen 1989) and semi-structured interviews (McCracken 1988), which involved the first author spending 11 weeks at the field site. Among other documents, meeting invitations, product requests for software changes, emails, and instant messages exchanged among the software engineers were collected. All this information was used in addition to field notes generated by the observations and interviews. We conducted a total of 15 semi-structured interviews with members of all five sub-teams. Interviews lasted between 35 and 90 minutes. To some extent, an interview guide was reused from the Alpha field study to guarantee that similar issues were addressed. These data were analyzed using grounded theory (Strauss and Corbin 1998) to understand the role of APIs in the coordination of Beta developers, as reported elsewhere (de Souza, Redmiles et al. 2004).

Data Analysis

After the second data collection, datasets from the two different organizations and projects were integrated into a software tool for qualitative data analysis, Max-QDA2. After that, the data collected was analyzed by using grounded theory (Strauss and Corbin 1998) with the purpose of identifying a framework to explain the results observed in both field studies. Interviews and field notes were coded to identify categories that were later interconnected with other categories.

The following sections describe the work practices of the Alpha and Beta teams, how their developers identify their awareness networks, and the organizational factors that influence the identification practices. More details can be found in the dissertation of the first author (de Souza 2005).

The Awareness Network in the Alpha Team

The Task Assignment

For accountability purposes, all changes in the Alpha software need to be associated with a problem report. A PR describes the changes in the code, the reason for the changes (bug fixing, enhancement, etc.), and who made the changes, among other pieces of information. An Alpha developer is usually delegated new tasks by being assigned to work with one or more PRs. These PRs are reported by other team members, who are responsible for filling in the field "how to repeat," which describes the circumstances (data, tools, and their parameters) under which the problem appeared. When software developers report a PR, they also might divide a it into multiple PRs that achieve the same goal. This division aims to facilitate the organization of the changes in the source code, separating PRs that affect the released Alpha tools from those PRs that affect tools or processes not yet released.

As mentioned in the previous section, each developer is assigned to one or more processes and tends to specialize in that process. A manager will follow this practice and allocate developers to work on PRs that affect "their" respective processes. However, it is not unusual to find developers working in different processes[2]. In this case, Alpha developers need to identify and contact the process owner to find out whether there is a problem in the process[3]. If there is a problem, developers will start working to find a solution to this problem. Even if the problem is straightforward, before committing their code, Alpha developers need to contact process owners to verify, through a code review (a prescription of the software development process), whether their changes in the process are going to impact the work of these process owners.

Finding Out Who to Contact

The need to contact process owners means that the developer working with the PR needs to identify the owner of the process being affected. This is not a problem for most developers, who have been working in the project for a couple of years and already know which developers work on which parts of the source code. In contrast, developers who recently joined the project face a different situation because they lack this knowledge. To handle this situation, newcomers use information available in the team's mailing list. The software development process prescribes that software developers should send email to this list before integrating their changes in the shared repository. Developers thus associate the author of the emails describing the changes with the "process" where the changes were occurring: Alpha team members assume that if one developer repeatedly performed check-ins in a specific process, it was very likely that he or she was an expert on that process. Therefore, a developer needing help with that process would know who to contact for help. According to Alpha-Developer-04:

> "If you are used to looking at the headlines and know that [tool1] stuff seems to always have [Alpha developer1]'s name on it and all of a sudden you get a bug, for us with the GUI because you can get it from any point, I could end up with a GUI bug that ends up being [tool1]-ish in the PGUI and what do I do? I don't understand why this thing behaves the way it does but most of those PRs seem to have [Alpha developer1]'s name on them. So you go down and see [Alpha developer1] so by just reading the headline and who does what, you kind of get a feeling of who does what, which isn't always bad. (...) [Alpha developers2] does [tools2] sort of stuff and although I have never had to talk to him about it, but if I run into a problem, by reading the email or seeing them, he tends to deal with that kind of stuff so they [the broadcast email messages] tend to be helpful in that aspect as well. If you have been around 10 years, you don't

---

2   This might happen due to various circumstances. For example, before launching a new release, the entire workforce is needed to fix bugs in the code; therefore, developers might be assigned to fix these bugs no matter where they are located. Or, a developer who already started working on a bug, because it seemed to be located in his or her process, might later find out that the bug is located in a different process. In this case, it is easier to let that developer continue to fix the bug due to the time already spent understanding it, than to assign it to a different developer at that point.

3   Sometimes bugs are reported because of an abnormal behavior that *might* be considered a problem; the role of the developers in this case is precisely to find out whether there is a problem. This happens due to the complexity of the Alpha code and the lack of domain knowledge of Alpha software developers (Curtis, Krasner et al. 1988). In this case, developers discuss the issue face-to-face and/or by email, and a PR is not inserted in the bug-tracking tool until the existence of a bug is confirmed.

care, you already know this. I have only been here two years and that stuff can make a difference– who you ask the question to when you get in trouble."

The quote above illustrates how new members have difficulty in identifying
who to contact for help, that is, their awareness network is unknown. This also
illustrates how software developers use an organizational guideline (broadcast
cmails for each check-in) to handle this problem.

The Code Reviews

The Alpha software development process also prescribes the usage of code reviews to be performed by process leaders whose processes are affected by the
changes in the code. This means that after a developer is done with changes in the
Alpha software, he or she needs to request a code review in that code. If the
changes involve more than one process, a request for a code review has to be
made to the owner of each process affected by those changes. Furthermore, developers' changes can be reviewed as many times as required until they are allowed to be checked-in. More specifically, according to the Alpha development
process:

"If the appropriate CSCI Lead(s) decide that the Developer's code changes are not sufficient
for the task, then the Lead(s) communicate with the Developer, then steps 6.1.13 through
6.1.16 are repeated until the CSCI Lead(s) decide that no further changes are required to accomplish the task." *[Alpha Software Development Process Description]*

As discussed in the previous section, developers need to identify process leaders in order to request code reviews; they therefore need to identify their awareness networks. Again, this is not a problem for most developers, but newcomers
use emails to obtain that the information.

The PR Work

After having his or her changes approved by the process owner(s), a developer
fills in the other fields of the PR, describing not only the changes made in the
code (through the designNar field, for example), but also the impact these changes
are going to have on the V&V staff[4]. The information about the impact on the
V&V staff is recorded in two PR fields: (i) the "how-to-test-it" field is used by the
test manager, who creates test matrices that will later be used by the testers during
the regression testing; and (ii) another field that describes whether the Alpha
manuals need updating. The documentation expert uses this information to find
out whether the manuals need to be updated, based on the changes introduced by
the PR. In some cases, developers are even more specific:

"Developers will be very helpful and they will say 'Figure 7-23 in the [tool] manual needs to
be changed.' If they do that, it makes my job easier and I appreciate it, but I don't expect it."

---

4   Process leads also use information about changes in the code to perform code reviews.

In short, problem reports facilitate the coordination of the work among Alpha team members. They provide information that helps team members to understand how their work is going to be impacted, which is useful for different members of the team according to the roles they are playing.

Sending Email

To conclude the work required to make changes in the Alpha software, developers need to inform their colleagues that they are about to commit their changes to the shared repository. This is done by sending an email to the rest of the team. These emails are necessary due to the lack of modularity of the Alpha software: a change in one particular "process" could impact all other "processes." According to a senior Alpha developer:

> "There are a lot of unstated design rules about what goes where and how you implement a new functionality, and whether it should be in the adaptation data or in the software, or should it be in [process1] or should it be in [process2]. Sometimes you can almost put functions anywhere. *Every process knows about everything*, so just by makefiles and stuff you can start to move files where they shouldn't be, and over time it would just become completely unmaintainable. ... *yeah, every process talks to every other one.*..." [emphasis added]

We discuss later how the structure of the Alpha software, in particular its non-modular software architecture, influences the strategies used by software developers to identify their awareness networks.

Using Email

Emails exchanged among team members are also used by software developers to find out whether they have been engaged in parallel development. Parallel development happens when several developers have the same file checked-out and are simultaneously making changes in this file in their respective workspaces. Note that if a developer, John, is engaged in parallel development with another developer, Mary, and Mary already checked-in her changes in the main branch before John did, John will necessarily have received an email from Mary about her check-in's. By reading these emails, John will be aware that he is engaged in parallel development with Mary because her email describes, among other things, the files that have been checked-in. In this case, John is required to perform an operation known in the Alpha team as a "back merge." This operation is supported by the configuration management (CM) tool adopted by the team and is required before a developer can merge his or her code into the main branch.

Parallel development happens because the Alpha software is organized in such a way that parts of it contain important definitions that are used throughout the rest of the software. This means that several developers constantly change these parts in parallel; back merges thus are performed fairly often:

"It depends on ... there are certain files, like if I am in [process1] and just in the [process2] that [back merges] is probably not going to happen, if I am in the [process3] there is like ... there is socket related files and stuff like that. I think [filename] and things of that sort. There's a lot of people in there. The probability of doing back merging there is a lot higher. What I will probably try to do is discard my modifications and/or I'll save my modifications and then, right now I'll see if I can put myself on top of it because at that point there's stuff supposedly already committed so there's nothing I can do except build on top of them."

To avoid back merges without avoiding parallel development, Alpha developers perform "partial check-in's." In a partial check-in, a developer checks-in some of the files back to the main repository, even when he or she has not yet finished all the changes required for the PR. The checked-in files are usually those that are changed in parallel by several developers. This strategy reduces the number of back merges needed and minimizes the likelihood of conflicting changes during parallel development. In other words, Alpha developers employ partial check-in's to avoid being affected by other developer's changes in the same files because these changes can generate additional work for the developers.

The Awareness Network in the Beta Team

The Organizational Context

As mentioned previously, applications developed in the BSC organization should be designed according to a *reference architecture* based on layers and APIs, so that components in one layer could request services only to components in the layers immediately below them through the services specified in the APIs. By using this approach, changes in one component could be performed more easily because the impact of these changes is restricted to a predefined set of software components. In addition, changes in the internal details of the component can be performed without affecting this component's clients. As a consequence of this approach, it is not necessary to broadcast changes to several different software developers, but instead just to a small set of them. That is, by decoupling software components, it is possible to facilitate the coordination of the developers working with these components (Conway 1968; Parnas 1972).

Unfortunately, organizational factors decrease the effectiveness of this approach. For example, the large-scale reuse program adopted by BSC leads Beta developers to interact with developers in different teams who can be located anywhere: in the same building, in different cities, or even in different countries. This is necessary to allow software components to be reused within the organization and to reduce software development costs. However, due to the size and geographical distribution of the organization, this was problematic. During our interviews, we found out that Beta server developers do not know who is consuming the services provided by their components, and Beta client developers do not know who is implementing the component on which they depend. Because of that, developers do not receive important information that affects their work (e.g., important meetings they need to attend).

This problem is aggravated by the young age of the project, according to Beta Developer-15:

"When you sit on a team for two years, you know who everybody is. Even peripherally you know who people are. So if we had to get answers about [another BSC product in the market for years], we have so many people on the team who were on the team for so long [a] period of time they can get the answer immediately. They know who the person is even if they have never met them. We don't have that in this group because it takes time for those relationships to develop ... like I talked to so and so and talked to so and so and so on. You only have to go through that once or twice because once you have gone through that you know the person. I think part of that frustration is how you spin up those relationships more quickly. I don't know if you realize this but this team has only been in existence since last year. So it is a ten-month-old team."

In short, Beta developers have difficulty identifying who they need to contact to get their work done, and they acknowledge that this is problematic. A developer, for instance, reported talking to up to 15 people before finding the right person:

Interviewer: "So have you experienced this problem?"

Beta Developer-15: "Totally. That is what I have said. I am kind of merciless in trying to find the right person. I have shotgunned up to four or five people at once to say 'do you know who is responsible for this?' and then gotten some leads and followed up on those leads and talked to as many as 10 to 15 different people."

Another developer complained about the need to simplify the "communication channels" in the organization to avoid having to interact with different managers to find out who was the person responsible for implementing a particular software component. This same developer reported that one of the teams providing a component to his team is not even aware of his team's need. On another occasion, a developer tried to find out whether she could use a particular user-interface (UI) component. The UI designer working with her indicated a developer in Japan who was using this same component. It was this Japanese developer who recommended to her another software developer, back in the U.S., who was implementing the UI component she wanted! Finally, a developer suggested that a database containing information about who was doing what in the organization was necessary: "sometimes you wanna talk to a developer ... the developer in the team who is working in this feature [that you need]."

Architects and managers also recognized this situation as problematic:

"The problem with that [not knowing who to contact] too is that there is another case where people are thinking that there is someone else doing something [but] when push comes to shove and it gets pushed on to you; it is an empty void because they don't stand up and say that they have tried to identify their server counterpart and my client counterpart and there is not one. We have a problem here."

Finding Out Who to Contact

In order to identify who they need to contact, developers adopt different approaches. First, they rely on their personal social networks. Managers also play an important role in this process due to their larger social networks. Beta developers contact them so that these managers can identify the person they want to find.

In one occasion, a client developer "followed" his technical dependency in order to switch teams: his software component had a dependency on a component provided by the server team, who actually had a dependency in a component from the infra-structure team, who depended on an external team's component. To simplify the communication channels and make sure that the client team would have the component, the manager of the client team decided to "lend" this developer to the external team[5]. By doing this, the manager, to some extent, could guarantee that the services he needed would be implemented. This approach provides another advantage: managers would guarantee the stability of part of their awareness network.

Identifying who to contact is a problem in the entire BSC organization. Indeed, BSC managers create a discussion database that developers can use to identify the people necessary to answer their questions. However, due to the large number of databases already in use, managers have to slowly convince BSC developers of the importance of this particular database:

> "The management team is really trying to socialize the idea that that [the discussion database] is the place to go when you have a question and you don't know who can answer it. They are really trying to socialize that people should give a scan to it every once in a while to see if they can help and answer a question. The amount of traffic there has picked up quite a bit in the last couple of months, especially in the past couple of weeks. My team has not gotten that message a hundred percent yet. There is a tool for it and a place to go that I have had a lot of success with when I use it; it is just that the message has not gotten out yet that that is the place to go. One of the things that happens when you have so many databases [is] it takes a while for one to emerge as the place to be. This is turning out to be the place to be."

Not everything is hectic in the BSC organization, though. An organizational aspect facilitates the identification of the awareness network: the API review meetings. Within the Beta team, these meetings are scheduled to discuss the APIs being developed by the server team. The following people are invited: API consumers, API producers, and the test team that eventually will test the software component's functionality through this API. In addition to guaranteeing that the API meets the requirements of the client team and that this team understands how to use it, this meeting also allows software developers to meet. After that, the server team provides APIs to the client team with "dummy implementations" to temporarily reduce communication needs between them, thus allowing independ-

---

5   In software engineering, artifact dependencies (such as the ones that exist among the components of a software system), often imply dependencies among software developers (Grinter 2003; de Souza, Froehlich et al. 2005).

ent work. This approach is useful only in some cases, due to the time that passes between API meetings and the actual implementation of the API. In the meantime, changes in developers' assignments may cause communication problems because developers do not know about each other anymore. In short, changes in assignments change the awareness network, thereby making the work of software developers more difficult to coordinate.

On the Effectiveness of Notifications

Beta developers have an expectation that major changes in the software are preceded by notifications, so that everyone is informed about changes that could affect their work. In fact, developers reported warning their colleagues of major changes in the code and their associated implications. This is done in group meetings, which provide an opportunity to developers to inform their teammates. Developers also inform their colleagues on other teams. For instance, server developers inform the installation team of new files being added or removed so that installation procedures can be updated with this information. In other cases, Beta server developers may negotiate with client developers changes in APIs that existed between the teams before actually performing the changes.

However, the usefulness of these notifications is contingent upon knowing who to contact. As discussed in the previous section, not all Beta developers know their awareness networks and therefore, are not able to provide and receive important notifications. For instance, according to Beta-Developer-15:

> "Let me give you an example. Our database developer [name] had certain files that were used to create databases. He changed the names of the files at one point so we lost some time while people were trying to deploy because they went to follow the instructions that I had written and they could not find the files that I was telling them to run. ... But that is the flavor of the type of thing I am talking about."

Because developers can miss important information, a strategy adopted by this same developer is to read everything to find out what could impact him:

> Interviewer: "In your particular case, have you not received an email that you should have received? And because you did not receive it, have you wasted one day of work, for instance?"
>
> Beta Developer-15: "Partly that. *I sort of make up for that by reading everything.* Obviously, it is not a generically good solution because it means that you waste a lot of time. I basically stay in a hyper alert state constantly looking for things that impact me. The problem is that you read through a lot of things that you are not really interested in. I have reviewed a lot of these design documents [that I mentioned earlier] and I probably don't ever have to necessarily read but I did not know if there was anything in there that was relevant to installation. ... Part of it is attention, being able to remind somebody that you are interested in what it is that they are doing." [emphasis added]

Other developers are similarly concerned about receiving too many notifications about things that are not relevant to them, especially when dealing with discussion databases. That is, they are concerned about not being in one's awareness network and still receiving notifications of changes. According to Beta Developer-13:

> "I think that in the beginning when it [the discussion database] was small, we used to go in everyday, at least I did, and look for new documents and keep updating. Now it is like, if someone has sent me an email that said that they have related a document and here is a link that is when I go to it. Because otherwise it is massive amounts of things and I cannot even make sense of it and how it is relevant to me." [6]

Even if the notifications are delivered to the right personnel, notifications are useful only to some extent: once an API is made public, control of who is using it is lost, and therefore notifications are no longer necessary because these APIs cannot change. As described by a server developer (Beta Developer-10):

> "We have latitude to change it [the API] as long as we are talking about an unpublished or semi-private API. If it is a contract between us and the client people, we probably have more latitude to change it and therefore they can trust it a little less than if it was a published API. At that point it would be very difficult to change it because people would be relying on ... right now we control everything that has a dependency, we control all the dependencies because the only people who are using the API are our own client teams and test teams and we can negotiate changes much easier than if they were external customers that were unknown to us or people in the outside world who we don't control and who also could not readily change their code to accommodate our API changes. We would have to go about carefully deprecating, evolving ... some features."

Discussion

Before proceeding with the analysis of the data, it is important to clearly establish the differences and similarities between the Alpha and Beta teams, as presented in Table 1.

Table 1 - Alpha and Beta Teams

	Alpha	**Beta**
Project duration	9 years	9 months
Team size	34	57
Sub teams	2	5
Formal software development process?	Yes	Partially. Only regarding the APIs
Software architecture	Non-modular and not-documented	Modular, defined through a reference architecture
Division of labor	Based on PR	Based on APIs
Interaction with other teams?	Not necessary	Often, due to the reuse program

---

[6]   This problem occurred because the BSC was already using several different databases, which were not organized nor updated often. This is a common problem reported by Beta developers.

The Identification of the Awareness Network

The empirical data presented in the previous section stresses the importance of the proper identification of a software developer's awareness network. Observations from the Beta team suggest that when the awareness network is misidentified, the collaborative endeavor is severely damaged; most of the problems faced by Beta developers (delays in their work, uninteresting notifications, notifications overflow, missing notifications, and so on) are due to difficulty in identifying their awareness network. To deal with this problem, these developers need to adjust their work practices accordingly. They have to use several approaches ranging from activations of their personal networks to discussion databases. The situation is better in the Alpha team: due to the duration of the project, most developers already know their colleagues' expertise. The only exception is newcomers, who do not know this information and use email to identify the process leaders.

The identification of the awareness network is difficult because awareness networks are fluid. That is, they easily change components (the software developers) and size. For instance, once an Alpha developer starts working in a PR, his or her awareness network is limited to the owners of the processes that the PR involves. This is necessary because these owners can provide information about the potential problem investigated in the PR (they are the ones who can answer the question: "is it really a problem?"). Note that developers do not know beforehand all the processes involved in the change—a common situation in software systems (Sommerville 2000). Therefore, this network might change as a software developer explores the problem described in the PR. When developers need to fill in the PR fields to complete their work, their awareness network becomes the V&V team members who will be affected by their changes. In this case, the identification of the awareness network is facilitated by the PRs because these artifacts already provide useful information about the impact of changes. Finally, before checking-in their changes, software developers' awareness networks become the entire software development team and they need to broadcast their changes to their colleagues. This is necessary because Alpha's software architecture is nonmodular, and a change in a process can impact all other processes. During this whole process, if developers are engaged in parallel development, their awareness network includes the other developers who are changing the same files. To deal with this situation, developers perform partial check-in's of files that are more likely to lead to parallel development. In this case, software developers use their knowledge about the software architecture to reduce the size of the awareness network and, by doing so, reduce their coordination efforts.

The same fluidity can be observed in the Beta team: changes in developers' assignments lead to changes in their awareness networks. In addition, when new developers start to reuse a software component through its API, this means that the awareness network of both the component's provider and consumer increases. To be more specific, APIs go through a publication process: they are initially private (without clients), then they are made semi-public (they have internal clients), and finally they are publicized (external clients can use it). Private APIs can be changed without a problem because no one is affected. Semi-public APIs require changes to be negotiated to minimize their impact on their clients. Finally, public APIs cannot be easily changed; they have to go through a slow process of change in which services are marked to indicate that API consumers should stop using them. As an API goes through this publication process, the awareness networks of the developers implementing the API expand: initially the awareness network is small because almost no one is affected, but in the end it becomes so large that it is unknown. As the awareness network expands, software developers' work practices need to change as well to accommodate this situation.

Note, however, that the fluidity of the awareness networks in the Alpha and Beta teams is different: whereas it changes somewhat rapidly during the course of work on a PR for Alpha developers, it changes slowly in the Beta team. Furthermore, changes in the Alpha developers' network are temporary (they last only while the PR work lasts), whereas in the Beta teams they are permanent, at least until the next change in assignments.

At this point, it is important to compare the concept of awareness network with the one of intensional networks (Nardi, Whittaker et al. 2002). The former concept calls attention to the set of social actors that one needs (i) to be aware of, and (ii) to be made aware of, as well as the work required to identify those actors. Intensional networks focus on the work necessary to create, maintain, and activate personal social networks. To simplify, one could argue that the latter is a prerequisite for the former.

Factors Influencing the Awareness Network

The data clearly present how three different factors influence the awareness network: the organization-wide reuse program, the young age of the project, and, finally, the software architecture.

The organizational reuse program in the BSC corporation influences the size of the awareness network: a Beta developer can need information from any other software developer in the organization, if the first developer's code depends on the second's. The result of this approach is that a software developer's awareness network could potentially be any software developer in the organization. API team meetings alleviate this situation because they allow component providers and consumers to meet; however, changes in team membership make the situation vulnerable again. To deal with this problem, Beta developers adopt approaches to identify their networks (social networks, databases, etc.) and broadcast messages, but this causes complaints about information overflow that isn't related to one's work. In other words, Beta developers may receive notifications from developers who do not belong to their awareness network. This situation is identified throughout the entire organization.

The second aspect that influences the identification of the awareness network is the software developers' experience in the project. Whereas the Alpha project had been going on for more than nine years at the time of the study, the Beta project and the BSC organizational reuse program existed for little more than nine months! As one developer pointed out, this was *not* enough time to allow software developers to establish the social connections among themselves required for the accomplishment of their work. Similarly, novice Alpha developers mentioned the importance of knowing who to contact in the project in order to finish their work without impacting their colleagues.

Finally, software architecture is the third factor that influences the awareness network. Alpha software developers recognize that the Alpha software architecture is not modular, and as a result, a change in one software process can affect several other processes (and their developers). In contrast, Beta software has an architecture defined according to best practices in software engineering with controlled dependencies through layers, APIs, and so on. This architecture, called modular, implies a small number of developers being impacted by changes. On the one hand, a non-modular architecture leads to larger awareness networks, and as a result, specific coordinative practices: the displaying of actions is done by email broadcasts and PR fields, whereas the monitoring is performed by reading emails. Alpha software developers also use their knowledge about the software architecture (some processes are often changed in parallel) to avoid needing to monitor other software developers. On the other hand, modular architectures lead to more manageable awareness networks, which could not be fulfilled in the Beta team due to organizational factors. In this case, developers also display their knowledge about the software architecture when they "follow the dependency" to find out to which team they should switch in order to provide the necessary services. Note that the influence of the software architecture result is not surprising because this influence has long been recognized to affect the coordination of the work (Conway 1968; Parnas 1972; Grinter 2003; de Souza, Redmiles et al. 2004; de Souza 2005). What is important here is finding out *how* software developers make use of that information to facilitate their work.

Concluding Remarks

The term "awareness" is used to describe a range of practices by which social actors coordinate their work through the display of their actions to their colleagues and the monitoring of actions from their colleagues. Most empirical studies focus on the identification of these coordinative practices and assume settings in which the social actors who display and monitor actions do not change often. This happens because the seminal studies of awareness practices usually adopted perspectives (ethnomethodology or conversation analyss) that focused on actions in a small time frame. Furthermore, these studies focused on settings such as control rooms, newsrooms, and trading rooms, which have characteristics that make necessary for individuals to monitor each other's conduct on an ongoing basis while engaged in distinct but related activities (Heath, Svensson et al. 2002).

This paper departs from this view and takes a different approach. It focuses on the software developers' work practices necessary to accomplish their work over a somewhat extended period of time. By doing that, it is possible to observe how these practices are influenced by the organizational setting, and, more important, how developers' coordinative practices require proper identification and maintenance of the list of actors whose actions should be monitored and to whom actions should be displayed. We call this list the "awareness network." The practices of displaying and monitoring are useful only to the extent that social actors do know who they should monitor and to whom they should display their actions. Previous studies had largely overlooked this aspect.

We have drawn our results from empirical data from two software development teams that were observed and interviewed. Their data were analyzed by using grounded theory techniques (Strauss and Corbin 1998). Our results suggest that the awareness network of a software developer is fluid (it changes during the course of work) and is influenced by three main factors: the organizational setting (the reuse program in the BSC corporation), the software architecture, and, finally, the recency of the project. In addition, software developers even try to manage their awareness networks to be able to handle the impact of interdependent actions.

Acknowledgments

This research was supported by the Brazilian Government under grants CAPES BEX 1312/99-5 and CNPq 479206/2006-6, by the U.S. National Science Foundation under grants 0534775 and 0205724, and by an IBM Eclipse Technology Exchange grant.

References

Buschmann, F., R. Meunier, et al. (1996). *Pattern-Oriented Software Architecture: A System of Patterns*. Wiley, Chichester, West Sussex, UK.

Conway, M. E. (1968). 'How Do Committees Invent?' *Datamation*, vol. 14, no. 4, pp. 28-31.

Curtis, B., H. Krasner, et al. (1988). 'A Field Study of the Software Design Process for Large Systems.' *Communications of the ACM*, vol. 31, no. 11, pp. 1268-1287.

de Souza, C. R. B. (2005). On the Relationship between Software Dependencies and Coordination: Field Studies and Tool Support. Department of Informatics, Donald Bren School of Information and Computer Sciences. University of California, Irvine. Ph.D. dissertation, p. 186.

de Souza, C. R. B., J. Froehlich, et al. (2005). Seeking the Source: Software Source Code as a Social and Technical Artifact. *ACM Conference on Supporting Group Work, Sanibel Island, FL, November 06-09, 2005*, pp. 197-206.

de Souza, C. R. B., D. Redmiles, et al. (2004). Sometimes You Need to See Through Walls—A Field Study of Application Programming Interfaces. Conference on Computer-Supported Cooperative Work, Chicago, IL, November 6-10, 2004, pp. 63-71.

Fitzpatrick, G., S. Kaplan, et al. (2002). 'Supporting Public Availability and Accessibility with Elvin: Experiences and Reflections.' *Journal of Computer Supported Cooperative Work*, vol. 11, no. 3-4, September, 2002, pp. 299-316.

Fuggetta, A. (2000). Software Processes: A Roadmap. Future of Software Engineering, Limerick, Ireland.

Gamma, E., R. Helm, et al. (1995). *Design Patterns: Elements of Reusable Object-Oriented Software*. Addison-Wesley, Reading, MA.

Garfinkel, H. (1967). *Studies in Ethnomethodology*. Prentice-Hall, Englewood Cliffs, NJ.

Grinter, R. E. (2003). 'Recomposition: Coordinating a Web of Software Dependencies.' *Journal of Computer Supported Cooperative Work*, vol. 12, no. 3, 2003, pp. 297-327.

Harper, R., J. Hughes, et al. (1989). Working in Harmony: An Examination of Computer Technology in Air Traffic Control. *European Conference on Computer Supported Coooperative Work. Gatwick, London.*

Heath, C., M. Jirotka, et al. (1993). Unpacking Collaboration: The Interactional Organisation of Trading in a City Dealing Room. *European Conference on Computer-Supported Cooperative Work, Milan, Italy, September 13-17*, pp. 155-170.

Heath, C. and P. Luff (1992). 'Collaboration and Control: Crisis Management and Multimedia Technology in London Underground Control Rooms.' *Journal of Computer Supported Cooperative Work*, vol. 1, no. 1-2, 1992, pp. 69-94.

Heath, C., M. S. Svensson, et al. (2002). 'Configuring Awareness.' *Journal of Computer Supported Cooperative Work*, vol. 11, no. 3-4, September 2002, pp. 317-347.

Jorgensen, D. L. (1989). *Participant Observation: A Methodology for Human Studies*. SAGE Publications, Thousand Oaks, CA.

Lövstrand, L. (1991). Being Selectively Aware with the Khronika System. *European Conference on Computer Supported Cooperative Work, Amsterdam, The Netherlands, September 24-27, 1991*, pp. 265-279.

Malone, T. W. and K. Crowston (1994). 'The Interdisciplinary Study of Coordination.' *ACM Computing Surveys*, vol. 26, no. 1, 1994, pp. 87-119.

McCracken, G. (1988). *The Long Interview*. SAGE Publications, Thousand Oaks, CA.

Nardi, B., S. Whittaker, et al. (2002). 'NetWORKers and their Activity in Intensional Networks.' *Journal of Computer Supported Cooperative Work*, vol. 11, no. 1-2, 2002, pp. 205-242.

Parnas, D. L. (1972). 'On the Criteria to be Used in Decomposing Systems into Modules.' *Communications of the ACM*, vol. 15, no. 12, 1972, pp. 1053-1058.

Schmidt, K. (2000). The Critical Role of Workplace Studies in CSCW. In *Workplace Studies: Recovering Work Practice and Informing System Design*, P. Luff, J. Hindmarsh and C. Heath, Cambridge University Press, Cambridge, UK, pp. 141-149.

Schmidt, K. (2002). 'The Problem with 'Awareness'—Introductory Remarks on 'Awareness in CSCW'.' *Journal of Computer Supported Cooperative Work*, vol. 11, no. 3-4, September 2002, pp. 285-298.

Sommerville, I. (2000). *Software Engineering*. Addison-Wesley Publishing Co., Boston, MA.

Strauss, A. and J. Corbin (1998). *Basics of Qualitative Research: Techniques and Procedures for Developing Grounded Theory*. SAGE Publications, Thousand Oaks, CA.

L. Bannon, I. Wagner, C. Gutwin, R. Harper, and K. Schmidt (eds.).
ECSCW'07: Proceedings of the Tenth European Conference on Computer Supported Cooperative Work, 24-28 September 2007, Limerick, Ireland
© Springer 2007

"...and do it the usual way": fostering awareness of work conventions in document-mediated collaboration

Federico Cabitza and Carla Simone
Università degli Studi di Milano-Bicocca
cabitza,simone@disco.unimib.it

Abstract. In this paper, we concentrate on how conventions among practitioners are put at work for the sake of cooperation in those work settings where coordination is mediated at a large extent by complex webs of documental artifacts. Our case study focuses on *coordinative conventions* exhibited in the hospital domain and mediated by compound patient records. We conceive of the provision of *document-mediated awareness information* as a "learning device" by which these conventions can be made explicit in all those situations where practitioners need support in coping with and solving cooperative problems in the articulation of their activities. To enable such a context-dependent and user-centered provision of awareness, we also present and outline the WOAD framework that provides users and designers with a conceptual model and language aimed at facilitating the construction of a convention- and collaboration-aware layer on top of traditional architectures of electronic documental systems. To this aim, we take the case of the Electronic Patient Record (EPR) as paradigmatic.

Awareness as a "device" for local conventions

The idea of considering the provision of suitable awareness information as a way to support cooperative work by facilitating the learning of work-related conventions and their inclusion into practice was first seminally introduced by Mark (Mark, 2002). We share Mark's suggestion to address the requirement of establishing and maintaining appropriate conventions within a distributed group of co-operating actors in terms of *collaboration awareness* as "an active learning device", i.e. as a means that takes the innovative function of helping cooperating partners to learn about each others' conventional ways to coordinate; and even of *shaping* these normative conventional behaviors. Moreover, we share the idea of providing actors with *awareness on conventions* in order to reinforce (or better yet, *promote*) desirable behaviors and to encourage the "correction" of undesirable behaviors in the group. Our common assumption here is that making conventional behaviors explicit and, above all, making actors aware of them *only* whenever these behaviors are suitable for the current context might support actors in making apt and timely decisions on how to proceed with their work, on the basis of well-founded expectations of others' behaviors. Instead of focusing on distributed groups, as Mark did, we rather focus on groups where communication and coordination are mediated by a web of cross-referenced documental artifacts, i.e., on *coordinative conventions regarding the use of complex document systems*. Instead of providing users with *further* information besides what documents show, we propose to change the *way* the same documental content is provided. In doing so, we aim to make actors more aware of the work conventions which are based on documental content; and also reduce the risk of information overflow that Mark said occurs once users have fully internalized cooperative models of usage. In synthesis, we propose considering awareness information as a *"reactive presentation device"*, by which conventions are made present-at-hand when needed. Awareness provision is aimed to (a) foster fruitful and on-the-point-of-work discussions about the conventions put at work in the given cooperative setting (i.e., on what is usually "taken for granted" and can hence lead to unexpected breakdowns if not actually conformed by all the stakeholders involved); (b) to mildly and unobtrusively remind actors of how-and-when their colleagues rely on actions made upon the documental content, and (c) to facilitate working habits on proper documentation settle into place seamlessly, especially in the case of apprenticeship and frequent collaborator turnover.

In the next sections, we give the reasons for our focus on *document systems* – either paper-based or digitized– and their coordinative role in cooperative work settings. Giving some examples from our field studies in the hospital domain, we propose the concept of *coordinative convention* as a general umbrella that encompasses conventional practices –e.g. of using documents, of naming and classifying things– by which actors articulate their activities seamlessly. During our study and empirical observations, we identified several coordinative convention regarding document use for both information production and retrieval and gave this kind of convention the name of *document-mediated coordinative convention*s (DMCCs); accordingly, we also use the notion of *document-mediated awareness* (DMA) to answer the question of "what can actors be made aware of, when reading or writing official documents?". Lastly, we illustrate an example of computational mechanism that correlates contextual conditions to occasions for providing DMA for the sake of CC promotion and support; and we outline the functionalities of DMA provision that we agreed upon with practitioners in order to augment documental systems with a CC-oriented support*.

The silent work of documents

Documents are used extensively by practitioners in the execution of their own work and as a means for sharing information with others (Hertzum, 1999) and they manage the flow of information throughout the enterprise. For this reason, researchers from different disciplines have been studying the ways and extent documents are used and managed within professional practices for a long time. As a result, evidence has been collected from very different settings of how documents (far from being mere subsidiary tools where bits of information are passively stored) are woven into work activities and part and parcel of those activities that characterize work in its purpose and sense (e.g., Malone, 1983). On the other hand, the transition from paper-based traditional documents —and the correlated habitual practices— to their fully digital counterparts and to practices intended to exploit these new functionalities, has proven to be highly problematic (e.g., Braa et al., 1998, Sellen et al., 2003). Consequently, the role of documents in work practices has become a central point of interest in several and complementary research fields, and its analysis from observational and ethnomethodological approach has become a way to inform a proper design of computer-based documental systems. Recent studies have considered that documents are not to be regarded as isolated artifacts, but rather as intertwined in a heterogeneous network of people, places and other artifacts used to support communication and the articulation of work activities (Braa et al., 1998, Bardram et al. 2005). In the observational studies we undertook, we found confirmation of other contributions from the specialist literature (e.g. Luff et al., 1992, Berg, 1999) reporting how documents, as versatile and flexible coordinative artifacts (Schmidt et al., 2002), play an essential role in coordinating work and enabling synchronous as well as asynchronous collaboration.

In this paper, we concentrate on document systems that are compounded by a network of mutually cross-referenced documents that mainly play the role of *records*, i.e., official, inscribed artifacts that are written to preserve memory or knowledge of facts or events which have occurred in a cooperative arrangement (cf. the *accumulative* function Berg refers to in (Berg, 1999)) and to support the articulation and coordination of work activities that are tightly coupled with data production and consumption (cf. their *coordinative* function). Such systems are collections of *templates* in-use that we call *webs of documental artifacts* after the suggestive account of a *web of coordinative artifacts* described in (Bardram et al., 2005). More specifically, we focus on the role that these webs play in mediating

*   This work has been made possible by the F.A.R. grant of the Italian Research Ministry.

and supporting cooperative work, especially in those arrangements that are not necessarily highly physically distributed, but in which practitioners need to heavily rely on asynchronous communication to articulate their decisions and interventions on multiple and complex trajectories of work. After having surveyed works on the use of documents for information sharing (e.g., Bannon et al., 1997, Harper et al., 1995), we conducted a field study to uncover how physicians and nurses coordinate with each other in two wards of the same regional teaching hospital by means of their official documentation, the patient-centered *clinical record* [1]. In order to envisage supportive functionalities, we observed situated practices of making sense of records that characterize how hospital practitioners articulate their actions across wards and shifts and along different clinical cases while relying on local conventions and ad-hoc agreements. From the method point of view, we followed a "quick and dirty" approach (Hughes et al., 1995): we undertook observations in the wards in as much an unintrusive way as possible and intertwined them with informal and semi-structured interviews with key practitioners to discuss the results of our observations and to collaboratively identify problematic situations and technological means that could play a role in alleviating the uncovered problems. In the last part of the study, we mocked-up these supportive means using the WOAD computational framework (read more below), and we used the mock-ups as a basis for further discussions about the optimal functionalities by which to promote document mediated awareness.

The nature of conventions in cooperative work

In our research, we used the term *convention* with the common-sense meaning of 'shared agreement and related practice that is either established or consolidated by usage'. In what follows, we denote as *coordinative conventions*, those conventions that regard *modalities* by which practitioners *articulate their activities* in any mutual cooperative effort. Among the myriads of coordinative conventions that can be detected in any cooperative arrangement, we will focus on *Document-Mediated* Coordinative Conventions (in the following, DMCCs or just CCs), i.e. conventions that regard how and when documents are used to either articulate or document work activities. Coordinative conventions are usually formed in an *ad-hoc* manner with respect to the domain and work arrangement at hand and can be considered as fairly flexible agreements that actors share on 'what should be done if a certain condition occurs' (i.e., actions), or about 'what a certain condition means from the coordination point of view' (i.e., interpretations). Following Lewis (Lewis, 1960), we also consider CCs as "regularities in the behavior", which actors of a cooperative arrangement *prefer to* conform to, relying on the

---

[1]   Other authors prefer speaking of patient records and call electronic patient records (EPR) its digitized counterpart. We will use the EPR acronym for its widespread use in the specialist literature.

fact that also others do, so that mutual coordination and comprehension is facilitated. The expression "prefer to" hints two important aspects of CCs: on the one hand, conformance to CCs is a voluntary act, that is not imposed by an organizational entity (either role or unit) acting as a superior authority. Even when conventions are established *intentionally* and do not simply emerge from habitual practice, actors follow them since they want or need to, not because some organizational entity has forced them to. On the other hand, conventions are conformed to since they are *worth* complying with, even irrespective of the number of actors that have agreed upon them. In fact, differently from Lewis, we prefer to relax the requirement that "everyone or almost everyone" has to conform to a behavior to make it a convention: we rather conceive of conventional use of documents as any *meaningful habit* that has been established between actors, even between two single ones. *Reciprocity* is hence the condition 'sine qua non' by which conventions can be applied, since they are built upon and are part and parcel of the common ground that is essential for any ensemble of actors to cooperate and even communicate with (Mark 2002, Schutz, 1970). This common ground is by nature cumulative and is developed as actors share experiences and solve coordination problems while on the job. Consequently, conventions are also temporary agreements, i.e., they slowly change according to what actors agree upon by managing in conventional ways. This aspect of CCs calls for the intertwined requirement that conventions must be *flexibly* defined (and possibly redefined) and applied. Since our main concern is the design of computer-based technologies that are supportive to cooperative work, we make an important point about the difference between conventions and what are usually called *business rules*, especially in regards to policies and organizational requirements on document use and work reporting (Cabitza and Simone, 2006). From the information systems point of view, business rules are commonly conceived as the definitions, operations, and constraints that pertain to *which data* can be processed and *how* these data can change in the ordinary achievement of business goals. Business rules, different from conventions, are intrinsically normative and are set "from above", i.e., by the management of an organization, in order to "mold" document-based business practice, rather than to be influenced by it. Consequently, the corresponding *business logic* that is to enact these rules into an electronic document application is usually hardwired in the data schema and manipulation methods that the users of a organizational information system are usually provided with. In an organizational domain, the functionalities of institutional document systems tend then to mirror the constraints and needs of business rules, and the rigidity due to their hard-wiring into even complex work-flows is deemed by management more as an opportunity for compliance and efficiency, than as a hindrance to smooth "practice flowing", as often reported in the CSCW literature (e.g., Florijn, 1994). Conversely, CCs are the expression of the users' needs and spring out from practice, which not necessarily is a "best practice" (besides for those who prefer to conform to the convention) nor an *institutional* praxis. Conventions on document use thrive for their local and possibly temporary ability to solve and even prevent coordination problems on an ad-hoc basis. For this intrinsic difference, for the temporary, voluntary and local nature of conventions, our point is that DMCCs should be treated differently from business rules and be addressed by a *logically different* layer "on top of" the hard-wired application logic of electronic document systems as EPRs are (see Fig. 1). Historically, EPRs are among the "most closed" organizational applications and hence are a paradigmatic case of applications whose logic can hardly be augmented "from within" with coordinative and user-centered functionalities. Some EPRs give access to their data just after business rules and corresponding constraints have been applied and there is no way to either change or make those rules more convention-oriented. Even if these rules were at some time convention-based, their change would require a massive intervention on the corresponding business logic, rather than a simple rewriting of a specific statement, as in our proposal. This is the most critical case in which the two-tier approach can yield its fruits: irrespective of the way organizational rules mold information, a system endowed with computable expressions of coordinative conventions can provide actors with meta-information in order to make them aware of which conventions on data use are the most appropriate to the intended purpose or current occasion. For this reason, in what follows we concentrate on the medical domain and we take the EPR as paradigmatic case for our reflections.

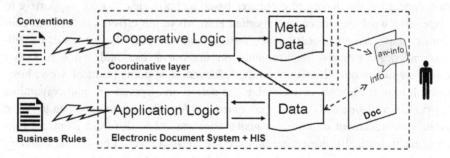

Fig. 1 The two-tier architecture to enhance closed electronic document system with collaboration awareness. Aw-info in the balloon stands for awareness information.

Coordinative documental conventions in hospital work

The clinical record is the main documental artifact used in hospital care as the composite repository for the information concerning a single patient stay. The clinical record can be further decomposed in two partly disjointed sets of documents: the medical record and the care (nursing) record, where doctors and nurses are supposed to document their interventions and activities, respectively. Indeed, the dyad medical- and nursing- record constitutes a clear and impressive example of *web of documental artifacts* since they are not intended as watertight compartments and each of them is consulted as a unique multi-page artifact only at patient's discharge from the hospital: during the patient's stay, the whole clinical record is split up into several sheets and documents scattered throughout the ward, each being very specific for a certain aspect of care and hence possibly used by different actors at the same time. In order to circumscribe the object of observation, in both an Internal Medicine ward and in a Neonatal Intensive Care Unit (NICU) we have focused on a family of artifacts that within the clinical record are called *single sheets*. They are denoted as "single" since they are sheets conceived to integrate in one single sheet sections which for their function should be parts of either the doctors' or nurses' record. Single sheets are used by physicians to order drugs, prescribe treatments or referrals and establish particular therapies: in short, they are supportive tools and "mediators" of the so called Physician Order Entry (POE). The POE is one of the most crucial document-mediated coordinative moments in hospital work. In the POE doctors give nurses orders about either diagnostic or therapeutic interventions, and nurses give doctors clinical accounts upon which doctors can take appropriate clinical decisions, though with a rigidly differentiated assignment of concerns and responsibilities. The artifacts used in the POE then mediate two kinds of coordinative behaviors: a more *prescriptive* one, in which doctors commit and delegate nurses to accomplish an intervention on the patient and nurses make themselves accountable for that intervention to be executed as doctors expect; and a more *descriptive* one, where nurses give doctors feedback on the completion of the related task and corresponding clinical data, thus enabling further activities that were waiting for the order execution. In both cases, conventionality plays a fundamental role as we are going to illustrate in the following sketchy vignettes.

Conventions on proper timing – Documental artifacts can be used to convey meaning besides what practitioners annotate on them, i.e., by means of their boilerplate contents and structure. For instance, in the case of the prescription of laboratory tests, the doctor requiring a test is supposed to indicate whether the examination is urgent or the blood sample can be taken and sent to the laboratory with all the other routine examinations. Since the indication 'routine' conventionally refers to the next day early in the morning, for routine examinations the physician is usually exempted from recording the precise time and even the date of the request. Conversely, for requests marked as 'urgent' this indication is necessary because only in this way nurses can correctly prioritize due tasks and realize whether they must hurry up and take the blood sample. The conventional nature of urgency was made clear during our observational studies in both the observed Internal Medicine ward and NICU: at the former ward, whenever the doctor checked the 'urgent' box on the single sheet for a request, she meant "please, send me back the lab results in half an hour", while at the NICU, "urgent" meant "right now" with no exception, due to the typical critical conditions of the admitted premature newborns. Right timing on order completion is therefore a clear example in which unwritten CCs are at work, specifically on the notion of urgency that is taken for granted in a given setting with all the coordinative consequences of deeming something urgent: for instance, consider the CC by which nurses make sense of the time elapsed from a request, in order to understand whether they are late or not about an order. Or the CC by which nurses are supposed to explicitly notify doctors that lab reports have just been sent back from the lab and are ready to be reviewed (as in the case when they are urgent) instead of letting doctors look the reports up in the clinical record on their own. This and the following considerations must be seen in the light of technological support to work: therefore the point on proper timing CC is not whether ward practitioners need to be supported in realizing what an urgent order means every time, but rather it is how a digital documental system could remind them of urgent orders *at an appropriate time*.

Conventions on proper redundancy – In a previous analysis of cooperative work in the Internal Medicine ward (Cabitza et al., 2005), we pointed out the manifold ways the phenomenon of data redundancy occurs in the daily documental work of nurses and doctors, and we denoted with the expressions *redundancy by duplicated* and *replicated data* those cases in which the *same* data are reported either in two or more documents of the clinical record or in different points of the same artifact, respectively. Also at NICU, redundancy can play an important role in supporting both coordination among practitioners and their decision making. For instance, it is only on a conventional basis that members of a specific NICU team want to have data on the weight, age and height of newborns reported in every single sheet of drug prescription only when a newborn is in life-threatening conditions. Conversely, the fixed and good-for-the-whole hospital business rule on data replication that is irrespective of patients' condition would neglect this local and team-based conventional requirement, and expose practitioners to the risk of both being provided with irrelevant and overloading information and losing the unobtrusive reminder on critical conditions that the presence or absence of this data could play at the very point of order entering.

Conventions on proper compilation – A similar case regards the infusional therapy sheet and the conventions we observed pertaining to whether a compiled sheet is considered complete/accurate or not within some practitioners' community. At the NICU, nurses are conventionally used to not reporting liquid intake values –or to reporting them only by a rough estimate– whenever these values are within normal range for two main reasons. On the one hand for the sake of conciseness; on the other hand, to convey an implicit reminder that "all is well" to the colleagues of the next workshifts. We then observed how traditional dimensions of data quality like accuracy and completeness, which are usually taken as intrinsic to a document or data set, assume a more conventional and context-dependent nature in a highly dynamic and frantic domain which clinical work is. We also observed that actors perceive how well work is documented depending on local conventions, which determine what fields are really mandatory or what could be the most convenient order of their compilation on the basis of the current workload and kind of work (e.g., whether critical or stable patients). This is also a case in which CCs and the business logic of a Hospital Information System (HIS) could be discordant with each other in that administrative managers and biostatistical researchers could have their quality requirements (e.g., for accurate and complete clinical data) embedded into the EPR forms and workflow in terms of corresponding constraints that straightjacket the coordinative and informational needs of clinicians at the point of care (Cabitza and Simone, 2006).

Conventions on documental content – The variable content of a document, i.e., what is jotted down in the clinical record by practitioners in the act of documenting and making their daily work accountable, can be produced and consumed in the light of conventions that affect the very meaning it conveys. For instance, as a result of a long and continuous frequenting of its members, in almost any ward a pretty complex but still yet unofficial jargon can end up by developing and thriving, a jargon by which medical terms and habitual examinations and treatments are abbreviated in shorthand. As the novices and frequent job-hoppers that we interviewed confirmed to us, besides pretty ordinary ways to shorten medical expressions that are common to a certain discipline or scientific community, also other much less common naming conventions are employed, especially in spoken language. For example, in the very same hospital, practitioners referred to their ward as either 'reparto' or 'divisione', or with abbreviations such as U.O. (for Unità Operativa) or S.C. (for Struttura Complessa) according to their length of service: corresponding "ward-wide" conventions became then consolidated according to the average age of ward staffs. These and similar conventions, once introduced even by chance within a certain group of practitioners, then become more and more consolidated over time, either by sheer habit or even for the often implicit intention of fencing off outsiders or ward patrons that are better not to catch every thing said in the ward (e.g., patients or their relatives). While cascading and drop-down menus employed in EPR pages and forms usually disregard these local abbreviating conventions or, even worse, tend to impose their own "standard" acronyms, doctors usually fill free-text fields with these ward-wide abbreviations. Forgetting these conventions in design undermines the effectiveness of any computer-based support for the mutual articulation of ward activities.

Conventions on document-based practices – Other times, naming conventions come from the clash between precise marketing strategies of pharmaceutical companies and regional-wide or hospital-specific drug supplying policies: practitioners make sense of what is written on clinical records from these conventions. It is on the basis of these conventions that some doctors prescribe name-brand drugs while, in so doing, they mean any drug with the same active principle; or that, viceversa, nurses administer specific branded drugs instead of others once that doctors have prescribed a generic drug. The point here is that doctors and nurses cooperate about pharmaceutical treatment more on the basis of ward- or even doctor-specific conventions, rather than on what it is actually written on the single sheets. Again, forgetting these ordering conventions undermines the effectiveness of automatic drug dispensers (Balka et al., 2007) and can hinder their actual inclusion in clinical practice.

We also observed a set of even more articulated conventions that – consolidating *across*, rather than *within* single wards– "regulate" how nurses should prepare patients for certain treatments or tests, especially when the latter are accomplished in an external facility or another ward. EPRs and request forms are usually intended to mediate the booking of a time slot at the external facility and they limit themselves to supporting just the "scheduling" dimension of articulation work between multiple wards: instead, the *pragmatic* dimension of articulation, i.e., handing over patients so that their care trajectories result in no seams or discomforts, is left to the ad-hoc externalization and combination of CCs across different communities of practice. The fact that a patient must fast a predefined number of hours before undertaking a test, or that she must be provided with either a local or systemic sedative and even how and to which extent she should be informed about the very sequence of treatments she will undergo, is a matter of more or less externalized conventions between nurses of the referring and of the accepting wards. We have seen as frustrating and unrealistic how it can be to try to embed these conventions into any business logic that is irrespective of doctors' idiosyncrasies, particular testing modalities and other contingencies.

What actors need to be aware of

Within the CSCW community, recent surveys have ended up by listing and describing up to nineteen different types of *awareness information* (e.g., Jang et al., 2000). In these and similar listings, researchers have tried to shed light on the manifold and often very situated use that actors can make of some specific (usually visual) information to become aware of aspects related to the current work, like "what others are doing" and "where they are" (Gutwin et al., 1997, Bång and Timpka, 2003) in order to fulfill either tacit or explicit informational needs. Generalizing the situated phenomenon of awareness can be useful to detect common features and recurrent patterns of provision of this kind of information and hence to extract similar requirements for a supportive technology. Nevertheless, one should never overlook the domain *specificity* of awareness information: much of what an actor needs to know about others heavily depends on the application domain. Moreover, the very nature of the awareness information provided depends on the very means actors use to get this information. For this reason, in our study we have concentrated on *document-mediated awareness* (DMA), i.e., awareness that can be conveyed through documents. DMA concerns either document content or the work practices that closely relate to the basic ones of reading and writing. We collected requirements about DMA provision mainly by (a) interpreting what the users of the reference document system -i.e., the clinical record- did and said in light of some awareness aspects selected for their relevance on specialist literature; and (b) by explicitly challenging these interpretations during scheduled interviews by means of some "key questions" that were inspired from those proposed in (Schmidt 2002) and (Gutwin et al. 1997). The questions and answers we collected led to drawing up a list of "kinds of awareness" that, far from being comprehensive of all the possible nuances, is oriented towards what interviewed practitioners have claimed are their awareness needs and desirable support about "conventional" articulation work. The main reasons why actors felt they needed to be reminded of conventions lay on the wide range of different needs that novices and experts perceive as the most urging. The former ones advocated awareness provision as a support for their 'practice learning' and inclusion in the ward habits. The latter ones appreciated the possibility of being reminded of conventions when hectic action and frequent interruptions could hamper their full and seamless compliance to them. The list of awareness kinds detected by explicit interviewing encompasses:

Browsing awareness - This kind of awareness can be provided when a certain textual item (e.g., a content entry, a whole passage) is recognized as correlated (e.g., hyperlinked) to some other ones, possibly in different documents (what has been called *redundancy by supplementary data* (Cabitza et al., 2005). The provision of this kind of awareness concerns the aim of supporting data interpretation and mutual consistency of correlated data.

Alerting awareness - This kind of awareness can be provided to make actors aware that there is something (that can be purposely left underspecified) that must be checked about what they are reading or writing since things are not going as expected (obviously with respect to some convention). The intentional underspecification of this kind of alert is conceived to find application in domains characterized by openness, ambiguity and unpredictability. Let us consider the case in which the convention of a hospital ward states that, whenever the temperature of a patient is higher than forty degrees, an alert should be raised to the accountable nurse: this case is about alerting awareness for "absolute conditions". Conversely, let us consider a "subtler" convention about "relative conditions". The doctors we interviewed during our field studies gave us the significant example of operated inpatients, whose low blood pressure is normal *unless and until* signs of an anaemia also show up, when that could be an indication of internal hemorrhage. Similar conventions can be applied to all those cases in which data become significant only after insertion. In those cases, an alert should be raised as soon as a vital sign becomes serious under some other condition, although when it was reported into the documental system it did not raise a particular warning since under the contextual conditions it was negligible.

Provisionality awareness - This kind of awareness can be provided according to conventions by which, in a given cooperative arrangement, either data are consolidated or committed to some official repository. Or alternatively, according to conventions by which data are purposely conveyed as still provisional and pertaining to an unfinished job. For instance, in the paper-based practices we observed, actors often relied on the convention that if notes were (still) written in pencil, then practitioners *did* have to consider those notes but were to take them as not yet definitive, or even as an invitation for further checking. The need for actors to be aware of what is still provisional with respect to what conversely constitutes an unmodifiable and legal account of accomplished clinical deeds is essential to cooperatively structure the formation of decisions and judgments. This holds even when the peculiar affordances of paper-based artifacts are not replicated in their digitized counterparts and their business logic does not specifically address this requirement (Hardstone et al., 2004). In fact, we observed the case of an electronic parenteral nutrition calculator used at the NICU, where actors relied on the convention that values inserted long before the scheduled feeding time were not to be considered definitive, but just as prospective formula so as to prevent unnecessary preparations.

Inconsistency awareness - This kind of awareness can be provided according to either the semantics of the data or more local conventions by which data are considered lacking in consistency with respect to their type or with respect to other data previously recorded in the documental system, respectively. In the former case, inconsistency awareness can regard, e.g., body temperature data that are higher than fifty degrees (i.e., an impossible physical condition), or dates for prospective examinations being scheduled in the past, and similar cases that concern the definition of a data type in a given application domain. In the latter case, inconsistency can regard more abstract aspects of the medical application domain, like that between some drug administration with some particular disease or allergy, or between patient-centered and work-related conditions (e.g., a pregnant woman scheduled for a C.A.T. examination, or a meat-based meal ordered for a vegetarian inpatient). Inconsistency awareness does not necessarily require an amendment, since actors can find a reason to cope with a partial inconsistent state of the world anyway, or even to supersede the business rules by which a sound situation is fallaciously considered inconsistent.

Amending awareness - This kind of awareness can be provided according to either some formal data model or more local conventions by which data are considered mistakes with respect to their type or data representation. This case is slightly different from the former, in that it regards data resulting in syntactic mistakes, like a date where a name is supposed to be filled in, an e-mail address that is filled in without the at sign ('@'), or even a tax number field that is empty (where a predefined 'not available' value is expected for those cases in which such number cannot be timely filled in). This DMA derives from the fact that doctors and nurses deemed any automatic correction in their records as unsuitable and even potentially harmful: they preferred speaking of proper warnings that are raised according to flexible data constraints that have to be taken as maps rather than as scripts (Schmidt, 1997).

Accounting awareness - This awareness information concerns either who did something (or was responsible for, in the case of work activities) or when she did it. According to the degree of granularity of the work context representation, such awareness information can be characterized also in terms of other contextual information besides merely accountability and time: e.g., which was the activity that enabled or triggered the record; where it has been accomplished; whether it is traceable back to some routine task or to a handling of an exception, etc. For instance, a convention holding at the observed hospital wards states that if a certain item has been recorded by a nurse long after the scheduled end of her work-shift, this could mean that it refers to a serious emergency handling and also that recorded items should be taken with some caution. The provision of such DMA is particularly desirable when an actor consults the documentation to interpret the history or log of updates for a certain data field.

Reminding awareness - This kind of awareness information can be provided to point out that some task *should* be executed. It can be used to remind some specific actor or role that it is due time for the execution (or completion) of a previously scheduled task as in the case of urgently due lab examinations reported in the single sheets.

Coordination awareness - This awareness information can be provided to make actors aware of some activity interdependency and hence to prompt them to actively manage it. The provision of such DMA could be sensitive to conditions related to either activities that must wait until some other activity has been accomplished, thus keeping resources underutilized and having other practitioners waste their precious time. For instance, this was often observed when patients had to be brought to external facilities for examinations on a roughly staggered schedule. Coordination awareness could then be conveyed in order to make the actors involved in the blocking activities feel committed and determined in supporting the dependent colleagues.

Enabling/Inhibition awareness - These two DMAs were recognized as very desirable and very difficult to achieve at the same time. In fact, the former was seen as capable of improving uniformity and effectiveness in routine interventions by reminding which alternatives are to be evaluated according to some conventional and referential "best practice", like in the case of a growing suspicion of GBS infection (Beta hemolytic streptococcus group B). In this case, doctors can be presented with the opportunity to either undertake an antibiotic therapy or just keep observing for a couple of days (the so called 'wait-and-see' prescription). Even more significantly, the *inhibition awareness* was seen useful at preventing unconventional or erroneous behaviors in that it can be provided whenever at least one of the preconditions of an activity are not met by the current context, i.e., whenever some convention or business rule makes actors deem an activity as "inhibited". This can happen for a number of reason, e.g., whenever a "conflicting" activity is in execution, either in regards to its logical precondition (e.g., a drug prescription can not come after the corresponding drug administration) or the use of common but not shareable resources. These resources can be even patients that have to undertake two diagnostic examinations at the same time. Since these DMAs can be provided only when the preconditions of an activity are recognized as either true or false by the current context, only activities that are very specific to a given situation or are critical should be suggested as either *enabled* or *inhibited*. In the former case, actors are suggested to begin the activity, while in the latter case the activity is indicated as leading to unconventional or undesirable situations. In doing so, a potential problem of information overload can be prevented. Moreover, these activities should be clearly identifiable by contextual conditions or by a direct action of the involved actors in order to avoid nagging warnings about what the actor can/cannot do at a given time.

A framework to express conventions and provide awareness about them

As a result of our interaction with the hospital practitioners, we conceived of the above mentioned typologies of awareness as kinds of *suggestions* that the augmented document system could convey to actors in promoting awareness on CCs, irrespectively of the way these types of awareness are represented through proper changes in affordance or formatting of the interface of a specific document system. The identification of proper suggestions requires the cooperative effort of actors and designers to make the relationship explicit and symbolic, which occurs between *recurrent patterns of context* and *conventional, reactive ways* to cope with this context. To this aim, it was natural to express these relationships in terms of conditional statements, i.e. *if-then* statements: context patterns are represented in the antecedent (the if-side), while the corresponding reactive behaviors in the consequent part (the then-side), respectively. Consequently, as designers, we adopted a *declarative and reactive (production-based)* approach in defining the computational framework (called WOAD – see below). The idea behind this choice is twofold: on one hand, to keep the same linguistic paradigm; on the other hand, to simplify the translation from an informal expression of habitual behaviors and domain knowledge into a computational formalization; this is accomplished by leveraging on the well known advantages of declarative and production-based approaches in terms of flexibility (Lloyd, 1994) and modularity. Our point is that expressing the conditions by which the main DMCCs must be applied to the current content of documents in terms of simple bunches of reactive code (i.e., in terms of the if-side of a production) could respond, at least partially, to the urging requirement of frequent tuning, production or dismissal of conventions that regard the electronic document system. In other words, we propose WOAD as a *programming interface* with which to "program" (i.e., make computable) mechanisms of awareness provision about conventions on data use and consumption, at a problem oriented level. In fact, WOAD users can concentrate on the specification of the functionalities supporting the coordination needs of the target setting and avoid considering the technical details of the underlying operational infrastructure. Since our goal is *not* to develop a full-fledged electronic document system but to endow these systems with cooperation-oriented functionalities, we conceive an upper layer of convention-aware application logic that would be conceptually "on top of" them and support awareness provision in a computable but yet platform-independent way.

The WOAD framework

The WOAD framework (an acronym for 'Web of Documental Artifacts') encompasses a conceptual model and a reference software architecture to make symbolic and declarative expressions of coordinative conventions computable by a rule-based interpreter[2]. The WOAD model encompasses a set of high-level concepts – like those of *actor, documental artifact, fact space*, and *facts interpreter* – that could guide the design of a context-aware and coordination-oriented level on top of electronic document systems. WOAD also provides designers with a set of language constructs – the L*WOAD language – that are made executable by a full-fledged interpreter that enables the distributed and context-aware execution of rules. L*WOAD encompasses a set of both static and dynamic constructs – namely *facts* and *mechanisms*, respectively – by which the designer can express both contextual, organizational and procedural knowledge about a work arrangement in a declarative manner.

Specifically, conventions and awareness provision mechanisms are expressed by two specific constructs: *convention-facts* and the related *mechanisms*, respectively. In L*WOAD, the suffix *-fact* is associated with static *key-value data structures*, by which the programmer can characterize the relevant entities of a documental domain by simply assigning a value to specific attributes. A *convention-fact*, for instance, is characterized by four attributes: a *name*, a *description* and two further attributes, *condition* and *action*. *Condition* slots contain the symbolic expression of conditional statements regarding either the existence of some facts within the *fact space* (i.e., the memory of the computational system) or, more specifically, some condition over the values of these facts. The *action* slot contains a declarative description of the convention in terms of either conventional behaviors or interpretations (proper sequences of WOAD assertions are usually used to ex-

---

2   For more details, please refer to http:// http://www.mac.disco.unimib.it/docs/Cabitza-PhD-thesis.pdf

press this information). It is important to notice that in this notation, CCs are sort of "knowledge" represented as static data structures: they are not intended to generate an automatic or computationally supported flow of work. Instead, they serve as sources of information to conceive mechanisms to provide awareness *regarding conventions*, as depicted in Fig.2.

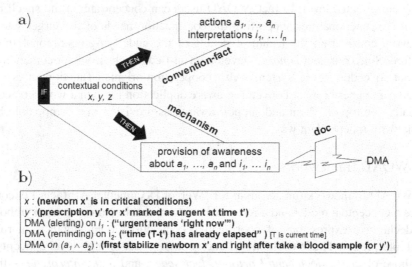

a)

actions $a_1, ..., a_n$
interpretations $i_1, ... i_n$

THEN
convention-fact

IF contextual conditions
    x, y, z

THEN
mechanism

provision of awareness
about $a_1, ..., a_n$ and $i_1, ... i_n$

doc

DMA

b)

> x : **(newborn x' is in critical conditions)**
> y : **(prescription y' for x' marked as urgent at time t')**
> DMA (alerting) on i_1 : **("urgent means 'right now'")**
> DMA (reminding) on i_2: **("time (T-t') has already elapsed")** [T is current time]
> DMA *on* $(a_1 \wedge a_2)$: **(first stabilize newborn x' and right after take a blood sample for y')**

Figure 2.a The relationship between the L*WOAD constructs of convention-fact and mechanism. Figure 2.b An example of instanced mechanism on a NICU convention.

The main rationale behind the design of proper WOAD mechanisms is to support convention adherence by suggesting to actors either which behaviors could be compliant to the anticipations and presuppositions of co-workers in a given situation (i.e., suggestions on what-to-do) or which conventional interpretations co-workers would rely on to seamlessly coordinate with them (i.e., suggestions on what-is-conventionally-meant under specific and well defined work conditions). L*WOAD mechanisms can then be seen as *conditional statements*, like *if-then* rules made of an antecedent and a consequent: the clear similarity between conventions' condition-action pair and mechanisms' antecedent-consequent one is not fortuitous. In fact, there is a tight coupling between *convention-facts* and corresponding *mechanisms*, since they both make explicit the relationship between the *same* contextual conditions and some conventional way to cope with or be aware of them, respectively (see Fig.2.a). The only output of L*WOAD mechanisms is to make explicit what kind of *DMA type* should be provided to users of a document system so that they can recognize the conventional nature of the situation at hand (the shared antecedent), and make sense of it according to locally agreed interpretation and conventions (the consequent instantiated on the actions contained in the pertinent conventions).

From the notational point of view, the consequent part of a mechanism concerning a convention CC_i would contain WOAD primitives that assert (make true) into the *fact space* a corresponding *awareness-fact* representing an awareness message that is provided for actors' consumption at artifact level. Each *awareness-fact* refers to a given class (or type) of awareness information, whose description has been outlined in a previous section. From the template point of view, an *awareness-fact* is a fact with three attributes: (1) as just said, a *type*, which at instance level can be taken from the DMA list or any other taxonomy; (2) a *content* attribute that, at instance level, refers to the piece of information actors should be aware-of. This information can be conveniently rendered as a message –be it either an alert or reminder or whatever according to the awareness type– conveyed to actors in some way through the interface (see next section); and (3) a *source* attribute that, at instance level, encompasses all those facts that constitute the source of the awareness information, i.e., the "reason" for actors' attention, in terms of actual aspects of the current context calling for a conventional action or interpretation (see x and y in Fig.2.b).

Conveying awareness through documents

The next step was to put WOAD at work in order to construct the mechanisms supporting the identified kinds of awareness within a coherent technological framework. For our "experimental" sessions with some key actors of the ward personnel, the NICU management put a web-based Electronic Patient Record at our disposal that the head physician had commissioned approximately one year earlier from a small local IT firm that had been providing the ward with a number of lean and task-specific applications over the last ten years. By leveraging on the long-time acquaintance and acquired familiarity between the designers of the small firm and some of the physicians working at the ward, a full-fledged prototype of electronic clinical record was built to allow for incremental improvements and further validation by the hospital management. Due to interoperability issues and other red-tape hindrances at the whole hospital level, this prototype was never amended and failed to be fully deployed at the ward, but nevertheless it constituted an ideal platform on top of which we could conceive and illustrate the awareness-providing mechanisms to their intended beneficiaries in terms of "mocking up" sessions, in which the graphical interface was just instrumental and not a primary concern. The goal was to evaluate how properly the uncovered conventions were rendered into WOAD mechanisms calibrated on the prototype's structured pages according to the model of ward conventions expressed in terms of L*WOAD constructs. These "mocking up" sessions led us to collect a number of interactional requirements, that the full-fledged electronic documental platform should satisfy for tow main reasons: to make secretarial work by clinicians smoother; but also, and above all along the WOAD perspective, to make the cooperative effort between practitioners and designers toward the construction of computational mechanisms supporting DMA easier and more effective. These requirements are not to be intended as valid just for the clinical application at hand or for the clinical ward we studied, but they can also be made more general by correlating them to the main functionalities exerted by documents and to the taxonomy of awareness we propose. Such functionalities can be summarized in the following enumeration: 1) *Function of alerting actors* about data previously inserted by other actors, regarding either inconsistencies/errors or suggestions for their correction. This functionality can be harked back to the requirements pertaining to the archival dimension of the record at hand and to the provision of either *alerting, inconsistency* or *amending* awareness. 2) *Function of highlighting data values* that could be useful for actors to consider, so as to provide them with awareness information about linkages with other data and well characterized relationships between what they write (or are about to write) and other data written in the past or by colleagues. This functionality pertains to the articulation dimension of the record at hand. In fact, it aims to support the task of making sense of what is recorded and is correlated with the provision of *browsing, inconsistency, accounting* and *coordination* awareness. 3) *Function of highlighting data fields* that users must fill in during a given documental activity (e.g. error-free form compilation); and the correlated function of providing users with information about the *reason and way the form completion must be done*. This functionality pertains both to the archival and articulation dimension of the record (Cabitza and Simone, 2006): the former benefits from a higher data quality (i.e., more complete records, more accurate data), while the latter benefits from a support to documental activities that have some priority over others. This functionality regards the provision of *browsing, inconsistency/amending* and *coordination* awareness information. 4) *Function of highlighting data fields* so that the activities associated with those fields are suggested *as possible choices*; in addition, in the case none of the suggested activities is selected by actors, then *occasion for justification* would prompt them. This functionality clearly regards articulation of tasks: in fact, by the proper highlighting of fields, a corresponding flow of work is suggested to actors along a descriptive rather than prescriptive perspective. Moreover, even when the suggestion is disregarded by actors, a justification space is proposed in order both to increase the accountability of the accomplished deeds and to provide colleagues with the rationale of the deviation from conventional or purely routine work trajectories. This functionality regards the *coordination, enabling* and *inhibition* awareness.

Conclusions

The paper presented a research path that combines the study of the literature about the role of documents in cooperative work, with a field observation in two hospital wards of the practices of coordination and usage of documents from the related clinical record. Our point is that a supportive technology could help actors by providing them with awareness information about in-use conventions. In turn, the interaction with doctors and nurses allowed us to participatively identify different kinds of that specific document-mediated awareness (DMA) information as well as different ways in which these actors would like to be supported to strengthen the mutual adoption of conventions. Since both conventions and awareness provisions are triggered by context conditions, we adopted a declarative and production–based approach to make DMA provision computational and decoupled from any specific implementation platform. To this goal, we developed the WOAD framework, whose main component is the L*WOAD language. By using the L*WOAD constructs, designers can express the relationship between conventions and pertinent awareness information through specific interface functionalities. The approach has been informally tested through mock-up sessions with satisfactory outcomes in terms of clear requirement identification and fruitful discussions about useful interface functionalities. The research path will continue with the full implementation of the WOAD framework, to both consolidate its interoperability with existing document systems (via XML-based API) and improve the interaction between various stakeholders in their joint effort of designing awareness mechanisms and their representation.

References

Balka, E., Kahnamou, N. and Nutland, K. (2007). Who's in Charge of Patient Safety? Work Practice, Work Processes and Utopian Views of Automatic Drug Dispensing Systems. *International Journal of Medical Informatics*.

Bannon, L. and Bødker, S. (1997). Constructing Common Information Space. In Proceedings of the ECSCW'97, p. 81–96, Lancaster (UK). Kluwer Academic Publishers.

Bardram, J. E. and Bossen, C. (2005). A web of coordinative artifacts: collaborative work at a hospital ward. In Proceedings of GROUP '05, p. 168–176, New York, USA. ACM Press.

Bang, M. and Timpka, T. (2003). Cognitive tools in medical teamwork: The spatial arrangement of patient records. *Methods of Information in Medicine*, 42:331–336.

Berg, M. (1999). Accumulating and Coordinating: Occasions for Information Technologies in Medical Work. *Comput. Supported Coop. Work* 8(4): 373–401.

Braa, K. and Sandahl, T. I. (1998). Approaches to Standardization of Documents in Information and Process Integration in Enterprises. *Rethinking Documents*. Kluwer.

Cabitza, F. Sarini, M. Simone, C. and Telaro M. (2005) ``When Once Is Not Enough": The role of redundancy in a hospital ward setting. In GROUP'05: Proceedings of the 2005 International ACM SIGGROUP Conference on Supporting Group Work, 158-167, Sanibel Island, Florida, U.S.A. ACM Press.

Cabitza, F. and Simone, C. (2006) ``You Taste Its Quality": Making sense of quality standards on situated artifacts. In MCIS'06: Proceedings of the First Mediterranean Conference on Information Systems, Venice, Italy, October 2006

Florijn, G. (1994) Workflow Management - A Limited View on Office Processes. Position paper for the CSCW'94 Workshop on Workflow Systems and Office Information Systems.

Gutwin, C. and Greenberg, S. (1997). Workspace awarness. Position paper for the ACM CHI'97 Workshop on Awareness in Collaborative Systems, organized by Susan E. McDaniel and Tom Brinck, Atlanta, USA.

Hardstone, G., Hartswood, M., Procter, R., Slack, R., Voss, A., and Rees, G. 2004. Supporting informality: team working and integrated care records. In Proceedings of CSCW '04. p. 142-151 Chicago, USA, ACM Press.

Harper, R. and Sellen, A. (1995). Collaborative tools and the practicalities of professional work at the international monetary fund. In Proceedings of CHI '95, p. 122–129, New York, NY

Hertzum, M. (1999). Six roles of documents in professionals' work. In Proceedings of ECSCW'99, p. 41–60, Norwell, USA. Kluwer Academic Publishers.

Hughes, J., King, V., Rodden, T., and Andersen, H. (1995). The role of ethnography in interactive systems design. *Interactions*, 2(2):56–65.

Jang, C. Y., Steinfield, C., and Pfaff, B. (2000). Supporting awareness among virtual teams in a web-based collaborative system SIGGROUP Bulletin, 21(3):28–34.

Lewis, D. K. (1969). *Convention: A Philosophical Study*. Cambridge, Harvard University Press.

Lloyd, J. W. (1994). Practical Advantages of Declarative Programming. Proceedings of 1994 Joint Conference on Declarative Programming, GULP-PRODE, Peñiscola, Spain, EU.

Luff, P., Heath, C., and Greatbatch, D. (1992). Tasks-ininteraction: paper and screen based documentation in collaborative activity. In Proceedings of CSCW '92, p. 163–170, New York, USA. ACM Press.

Malone, T. W. (1983). How do people organize their desks?: Implications for the design of office information systems. *ACM Transactions on Information Systems*, (1):99–112.

Mark, G. (2002): 'Conventions and Commitments in Distributed CSCW Groups'. *Comput. Supported Coop. Work*, 11(3-4), 2002, 349-387

Schmidt, K. (1997). Of maps and scripts: the status of formal constructs in cooperative work. In Proceedings of GROUP'97, p. 138–147, Phoenix Arizona USA. ACM Press.

Schmidt, K. 2002. The Problem with 'Awareness': Introductory Remarks on 'Awareness in CSCW'. *Comput. Supported Coop. Work*, 11, 3 (Nov. 2002), 285-298.

Schmidt, Kjeld and Ina Wagner (2002): Coordinative Artifacts in Architectural Practice. In Proceedings of COOP 2002. p. 257-274. Saint Raphaël, France, Amsterdam IOS Press,.

Schutz, A. (1970). *On Phenomenology and Social Relations*. The University of Chicago Press.

Sellen, A. J. and Harper, R. H. R. (2003). *The Myth of the Paperless Office*. MIT Press, Cambridge MA.

L. Bannon, I. Wagner, C. Gutwin, R. Harper, and K. Schmidt (eds.).
ECSCW'07: Proceedings of the Tenth European Conference on Computer Supported Cooperative Work, 24-28 September 2007, Limerick, Ireland
© Springer 2007

A safe space to vent: Conciliation and conflict in distributed teams

Matt Billings & Leon A. Watts
University of Bath, UK
[m.j.billings : l.watts] @bath.ac.uk

Abstract: This paper considers the nature of conflict in relation to the environments within which distributed teams cooperate. Effective conflict management can bring great benefits to distributed teams, while inadequate conflict resolution strategies can incur significant personal and resource costs. The increased geographical, cognitive and emotional distances between members can stimulate and amplify conflict. Parties may display disinhibited behaviour (flaming) or may be reluctant to accept reconciliatory overtures (low trust). These factors can be attributed to the impact of communication technology on social structures that underlie interaction. Shifting to face-to-face meetings can be impractical or involve prohibitive cost, so it is important to establish how best to deal with conflict in technologically-mediated settings. Dispute resolution practitioners (conciliators) have evolved strategies and techniques to construct and regulate "safe-spaces"; settings that are conducive to finding creative solutions to entrenched conflicts. Building on interviews with expert conciliators, we discuss the potential for learning from the structure and constraints of conciliation environments in order to improve conflict management through technologies.

Introduction

Many interpersonal concerns affect people whose collective activities are supported by technologies. From time to time, conflict naturally arises in our dealings with others - it is a familiar part of the team experience. Friends and colleagues can boil over with frustration or anger, becoming prone to extreme outbursts of emotion. This 'venting' behaviour can have disastrous consequences for cooperative work, alienating colleagues and causing potentially terminal breakdowns in communication.

If managed effectively, conflict can be productive: team-members will improve their understanding of each other, plans may become more robust as problems are mitigated, and the team may develop strategies for dealing with future conflict. However, ineffective conflict management can compromise the team's activities: resources will be expended on servicing the conflict rather than constructively, on matters of value to the individuals and to the group as a whole.

Consideration of the setting and conditions of work, in terms of conflict management practice, can enhance co-operation. When people work together through technologies, such as email or videoconferencing systems, the factors introduced to conflict by mediating technologies must be accounted for. In this way, workable strategies can be formulated to maximize the potential benefits to teams and minimize the risks of negative outcomes. In this paper, we consider the connection between the environment created for people to cooperate and strategies that can help them to manage conflict.

We begin by describing conflict as an interpersonal process: how disputes arise and are perpetuated, along with strategies for their resolution. We then outline existing research that investigates characteristics of conflict through mediating technologies, to discover what strategies these theories propose for dealing with conflict in distributed teams. The paper goes on to consider the practice of 'conciliation', a rarified form of conflict management. This is used to outline strategies that practitioners use for resolving entrenched conflict. We then consider the question, 'how might conflict be managed in distributed teams?' Our investigation reports conciliators' experiences and concerns about their ability to deploy conflict-resolution strategies in a distributed environment. It also examines the way that conciliators' practice is affected by mediating technology. The findings of this investigation are used to provide guidelines for managing conflict in distributed teams.

Conflict and communication through technologies

Conflict is a natural periodic state of affairs to exist between people. The causes of conflict are complex and have been widely interpreted as: competition for resources, whether as remuneration or status (Deutsch, 1987); manifestations of power imbalances (Bush & Folger, 2005); or incompatible explanations of the other's behaviour (Winslade & Monk, 2000). However, it may be helpful to conceive of conflict as a process (Laue, 1987): conflict involves movement from the situational variables that create it, through behaviours that perpetuate it, to strategies for bringing it to an end.

Research in CSCW has shown that teams using computer-mediated communication systems face difficulties in managing interpersonal conflict. There is clear value in understanding how technologies might be used "to reach a solution that preserves and builds relationships among group members" (Poole, Homes, & Desanctis, 1988, p. 228).

Early attempts to resolve differences of opinion using CMC focused on mechanisms for achieving consensus, and on excluding emotional issues. They relied upon the definition and imposition of schemes for structuring exchanges among parties (Flores, Graves, Hartfield, & Winograd, 1988; Poole, Homes, & Desanctis, 1988). Later work showed the difficulties in practice of formalizing collaborator states and actions. Attention has moved towards finding "malleable coordination mechanisms" (Schmidt, 1997, p. 142) that might serve as resources for situated action. Still more recently, the focus has shifted to defining constraints on the appropriation of collections of technologies as flexible support for collaborative work (Balka & Wagner, 2006; Dourish, 2003). It is necessary to create sociotechnical conditions within which teams can define their own norms for engagement through technologies. In terms of communication, technologies have been found to exacerbate interpersonal conflict and hinder conflict management practices (Hinds & Bailey, 2003). These findings demonstrate a need to move toward designing systems to support existing conflict management processes.

Conflict Management in Computer-Mediated Communication

Conflict encourages those involved to invest heavily in strategies that are designed to achieve their desired outcome and to mitigate the significance of their potential loss. This investment might be in terms of resources or of personal emotion. Once participants are heavily invested in a conflict, each tends to become committed to a particular defined outcome rather than exploring alternatives. Conflict is perpetuated by perceived power differences, necessitating an investment of resources in the outcome of the conflict.

To manage conflict effectively, these power and resource differentials need to be addressed (Coleman, 2000). Participants can then reach some lasting agreement as to the outcome of the dispute. This agreement, in broad terms, will be: recognition of dominance, avoidance, or resolution. In the dominance case, one party will accept that the other has been victorious, thus forfeiting their own invested resources, simply "cutting their losses". This outcome may result in resentment and hostility, potentially reducing the team's immediate operational effectiveness, undermining morale and sowing the seeds for future conflict.

Avoidance requires parties to the conflict to agree to disagree, or sidestep the conflict. These parties may still forfeit the resources they have so far invested and may have to work to avoid issues that trigger conflict. They will remain prepared to re-open hostilities should a similar situation occur. In a team setting, the potential for the problem to begin again depends on the centrality of the trigger issues to collective objectives and also on the likelihood of parties encountering them in the lifetime of their collective activities.

Resolution is the third general form of agreement. Participants adopt a 'win-win' attitude to address their conflict. They identify shared goals and look at ways of pooling their resources to achieve this. To achieve a lasting resolution, parties will be willing to sacrifice some of the resources they have invested (Folger & Baruch-Bush, 1994).

The idea of a lasting resolution to conflict is the most appealing for the day-to-day running of teams, especially where there is a longer horizon for their collective activities. Resolution can be of positive benefit to the team, as hitherto unconsidered alternative plans and outcomes must be generated to move from the conflict stalemate. Jarvenpaa & Leidner (1999) found that one of the predictors of successful distributed collaboration was a "phlegmatic attitude to crisis" (p. 809). Teams that are able to manage crises such as interpersonal conflict are more likely to be successful. However, research into conflict in CSCW indicates that there are additional hurdles for distributed teams who wish to resolve conflict effectively.

Flaming

In a conflict situation, for one party to achieve their goal, others will be unsuccessful, thus forfeiting the resources they have invested. Awareness of this potential loss of resources further encourages parties to commit to a particular outcome. Behaviour may become more extreme as individuals seek to dominate or intimidate the other parties into capitulation.

Computer-mediated communication (CMC) has a propensity to escalate conflict, with less regulated emotional expression, or 'flaming', and greater polarization of opinion (Mabry, 1997). In this way, interpersonal communication can quickly become hostile and aggressive. Parties are likely to become entrenched in their position and a cycle of hostility will further escalate the conflict (Thomson & Nadler, 2002). If flaming has occurred, either on- or off-line, those involved in the conflict will have a negative view of the other, and will be disinclined to trust their intentions. This reduction in trust is further exacerbated when parties are interacting in a mediated environment.

Trust

Trust is constructed and experienced differently in distributed teams (Bos, Olson, Gergle, Olson, & Wright, 2002; Olson & Olson, 2000). Research shows that trust in others is reduced when parties do not perceive themselves to be co-located. This can result from a lack of personal information about the other party, or from the perception of a large social and geographical distance between parties.

The general reduction of mutual trust presents another problem for managing conflict in distributed teams. Their investment in a specific outcome at the expense of the other (and their perception that the other is committed to an outcome that will disadvantage them) will reduce their willingness to risk forfeiting these resources by trusting the other party. So, in situations of conflict, trust is already at risk. If the communication medium serves to further reduce trust, it will be difficult to encourage parties to engage in strategies designed to reduce conflict

To understand how these properties of technological environments can impact upon conflict and conflict management processes, it is necessary to consider more carefully those theoretical accounts that attempt to explain the roots of CMC effects.

Theoretical accounts of CMC effects

Researchers have examined the effects of CMC on relationships in both organizational and informal settings. Accounts of these effects focus on what the salient and significant aspects of communication might be, and how the presence of mediating-artifacts might impact upon them. All argue that the most compelling differences are to do with social information, not with objective matters (Spears, Lea, & Postmes, 2000).

Social Cues and Social Information

Early explanations of CMC effects, often referred to as 'cues-filtered-out' models (Culnan & Markus, 1987), focused on differences in the capacity of mediating technologies to carry social cues. The notion that CMC restricts the transfer of cues is associated with reduced social sensitivity. Specifically, this includes a reduction in interpersonal warmth, an increase in uninhibited behaviour, and more extreme attributions (Hancock & Dunham, 2001).

Studies also report a reduction in the ability of CMC systems to deal with uncertainty and ambiguity, and proportionally more task-focused talk. The reduced opportunity for leveraging social cues makes it hard to handle contentious communication. Conflict may be exacerbated by undetected misunderstandings, fewer opportunities to repair misunderstanding, and less effective attempts at repair, all feeding a spiral of increasing mistrust. They are also likely to encourage misunderstanding by reducing contextual information that parties may use to build common ground, enhance feelings of anonymity and reduce a sense of accountability.

However, these 'cues-filtered-out' models fail to adequately explain how social information might be leveraged to manage something as emotionally intensive as conflict.

Relational CMC

More recently, the emphasis has shifted from cue-transference, to the relational impact of CMC systems (Walther & Parks, 2002). Findings show mediated relationships to be: less socio-emotionally oriented; less inhibited (Joinson, 2001), and more prone to conflict escalation and risky behaviour (Thomson & Nadler, 2002). Conversely, CMC can encourage self-disclosure (Joinson, 2001); allow greater control over self-presentation (Walther, Loh, & Granka, 2005); and can helpfully reduce uncertainty (McKenna, Green, & Gleason, 2002).

CMC effects are likely to be moderated by: familiarity between the participants (Holton & Kenworthy-U'ren, 2006); user experience of various combinations of communication channels (Burgoon et al., 2002); and duration of joint activity and anticipation of future interaction (Walther, 1994).

Thus the specific impact of CMC on particular disputes may be highly variable. Where parties are heavily invested in a particular outcome, the situation cannot be characterized just in terms of technology effects and hence the success of conflict management is hard to predict without controlling relational factors.

Strategies for Managing Computer-Mediated Conflict

All accounts of the effects of CMC point towards conflict management problems for distributed groups. They attribute difficulties to: a) reduced social information; or b) an unpredictable interaction between the presence of the medium and a host of other variables. Therefore, existing models of CMC suggest that, for effective conflict management, it is necessary to move communication to: a) a richer communication environment; or b) a more predictable interaction of variables. Both of these recommendations would point toward face-to-face (FtF) communication being the most appropriate environment for conflict management.

However, given the nature of distributed teams, the costs and disruption associated with shifting conflict to a FtF setting may be difficult or impossible to bear. Team members may have little option but to attempt to deal with conflict through available technologies, such as in large and voluntary collective enterprises like Wikipedia (Kittur, Suh, Chi, & Pendleton, 2007). It would be of benefit to those who operate in CSCW teams to build a deeper understanding of the way in which communication can be managed under duress. In our attempt to understand how conflict management processes operate in a technological environment, we need first consider how conflicts can be managed effectively. To this end we examine the work of conciliation professionals.

The setting of conciliation

Conciliation is concerned with the resolution of entrenched conflict and revolves around the use of strategies for managing conflict. It introduces an impartial, and non-judgmental, third-party into a conflict situation (Wall & Lynn, 1993). All manner of circumstances will lead people to seek this kind of intervention, from employment disputes and community grievances, to marital breakdown. In each case, they are acting in response to conditions which have made "unmediated" communication extremely difficult. The conciliator represents a medium for communication between parties, the intervention of which is intended to help them find a mutually acceptable resolution to their conflict.

Conciliation usually takes place with all parties co-present and in a carefully arranged setting. Conciliators have no vested interest in outcomes, nor do they have enforcing powers on any agreed outcome. They may not pass judgment on the behaviour of the parties in dispute. Their intervention is limited to influencing the progression of the dispute through their expert use of language and deep understanding of conflict processes (Kressel, 2000). Their reputation for impartiality and behaviour within the conciliation process provides the conciliator with their mandate for controlling the exchange: it is not a mandate for setting the agenda of the dispute itself. This mandate enables the conciliators to take the initiative in response to the situation. Their use of techniques and strategies is specifically designed to position themselves so that they may most effectively help parties resolve their conflict.

Reflection and positioning within a conflict

Conciliation is a practice-based discipline. Initial training may involve lectures and discussion, but the main focus is on the development of skills through practice. This has led to a tradition of role-play in conciliator training and development. Role-play and rehearsal are central to the practice both for ethical reasons and to promote reflective self-awareness. Throughout their career, conciliators are expected to continue training to improve their practice. This often takes the form of role-play or observations. The focus on practice and continual development encourages conciliators to think reflexively about the way that they deploy their skills and the impact that they have in a conflict. The techniques deployed by the conciliators are themselves designed to create an environment in which parties are encouraged to reflect upon and reposition their actions and attitudes. The aim of this reflection is to allow the conciliator to exercise reframing strategies that encourage parties to think about the conflict and the other party in new ways. They re-present information at intervals, serving as an active record of the key steps in transforming the conflict. The distance between the two parties is progressively reduced, encouraging a willingness to share or relinquish some of the resources invested in a particular outcome.

Conciliation settings, strategies and techniques

Conciliators begin by structuring the physical environment and preparing parties for the conditions they must observe whilst engaging in this special form of communication. These strategic preparations are used to create a safe space in which parties feel free to express themselves without fear of committing to an outcome. Secondly, they work to improve communication, by encouraging parties to listen to what the other is saying and address their own behaviour. Thirdly, they encourage parties to recognize the other's interests. The techniques used by conciliators to pursue these ends include: 1) reframing - subtle changes in the language used invite parties to view situations and behaviours from a different position, thus encouraging parties to move from their heavily-invested positions; 2) control over the floor or the topic - this ensures that irrelevant power differences between the parties can be mitigated to ensure that any agreement reached is fair; and 3) demonstrating listening behaviour - this encourages parties to be open and honest about their interests, desires and resources. It also encourages them to 'vent', which in turn helps them to feel as though their concerns have been heard. Before deploying these techniques, conciliators reflect on the situation, drawing on their experience of conciliation practice to decide when it is necessary to shift from one to another.

In this section, we have argued that conciliation involves the creation of a setting in which communication may be structured in particular ways. We consider that conciliation functions as a kind of mediation environment or setting. Parties for whom trust has been seriously undermined are given mechanisms for coping with lack of trust. These include the opportunity for emotional venting, by altering the nature of communication exchanges in a way that is distinct from their communication in the 'real-world'.

Studying conciliation in CMC conflicts

It is apparent from CMC research that, in situations such as conflict, the effects of the medium are likely to be profound. The changes in interactivity, the paucity of social cues or information, the increased physical and cognitive distance, are all likely to exacerbate conflict. For a conciliator, the impact of these properties of the communication medium is likely to be a reduction in the efficacy of their practice - their ability to reflexively assess the appropriateness and impact of techniques and strategies may well be distorted by the medium.

Conciliation has a successful track-record in transforming entrenched conflict into a manageable form of dispute. We wanted to assess the potential of mapping the structures of conciliation settings into technological mediation settings. This would help to uncover ways in which properties inherent in a technological environment can be leveraged to aid conflict management processes. To this end, we report an investigation of the potential for adapting conflict management techniques and strategies to distributed environments. First, we discuss professional conciliators' experiences and concerns about the use of CMC in their practice. We then describe how a highly experienced conciliation professional followed up their interview by conciliating two conflicts using a video-mediated communication system.

Conciliator experiences and attitudes

Twelve expert conciliators practicing in the UK were interviewed as part of a study to develop a Grounded Theory of conciliation (not reported here). Grounded Theory (Glaser, 1978; Glaser and Strauss, 1967) is a qualitative method which does not presuppose any theoretical assumptions. We adopted this approach because it is suited to the development of formative accounts of phenomena of investigative interest. Analytic categories are developed with direct reference to the data gathered by the analyst, guided by the principle of parsimony. Relationships between these categories are used to develop a theory about the phenomenon under investigation.

All subjects are active professional conciliators, together representing more than 90 years' experience in conflict resolution practice. Between them their experience covered the majority of domains of conciliation (family, community, neighborhood, business, domestic violence, victim-offender, employment, divorce). In the UK, videoconferencing is not currently used by professional conciliators. However, telephone and email communications are used extensively to manage cases and are incorporated into dealings with clients at each conciliator's discretion, and with the express agreement of the clients concerned.

Method

Interviews were semi-structured with open-ended questions. These aimed to elicit their concerns and goals with regard to the process of shifting conflicting parties out of entrenched positions. Questions also prompted interviewees to provide grounded (case-based) accounts of the various techniques they apply in their conciliation practice. We asked them about their motivations in deploying the techniques they described, and their reflections on the impact of the technique in question. They were specifically asked for their views on the way that mediating technology might affect their conciliation practices.

Analysis

The interviews ranged from 30 minutes to 90 minutes in length and were conducted over the telephone or in person at the participant's place of work, depending on geographical and time constraints. Each interview was transcribed and the transcripts subjected to an analysis in accordance with a Grounded Theory method. Our intention was to construct an account of conciliator concerns about the use of mediating technologies, based on the identification of common concerns. In this way, conciliators' comments about the use of technologies were grouped into three separate categories: 1) use of cues; 2) moderation of presence; 3) experience differentials.

1) Use of cues for inferring underlying concerns

All conciliators raised the issue of non-verbal cues for conflict management. The ability to detect and to draw out the implied meaning and inter-party significance of literal statements is a central element of the conciliator's work. Conciliators must have confidence in their ability to properly reflect these underlying meanings in their own use of language, to acknowledge and "surface" the concerns of each party. Conciliators are adept at deciphering the relationship between what is said, how it is said and what is left unsaid. This assessment then influences the strategies and techniques that the conciliator chooses to deploy.

Conciliators rely on various cues and gestures to infer understanding and to communicate information. In conciliation, this is a reflexive activity: the conciliator must monitor what one party does, what the other does in response, and how the first party consequently moderates their behaviour, all in relation to their own conciliation activities. Responses from the conciliators indicated that this was dependant upon having all of the behavioural information present in the interaction. CMC was perceived to reduce the transmission of significant social cues, and would therefore have an impact upon their practice, as the following quotations demonstrate:

> The lack of gestures and body-language make it difficult to understand their true meanings . . . you have to keep checking that they understand. (Conciliator 10: 13 years' experience)

> There may be a loss of body-language . . . It may also be hard for one party to see the effect that their words have on the other party. (Conciliator 9: 4 years' experience)

Conciliators discussed the way that CMC distorts or retards the transfer of cues. The specific worry for conciliators was that this potentially restricts their ability to demonstrate listening behaviour, encouraging parties to reflect upon their own behaviour. Without this reflection, parties will fail to recognize how they are presenting themselves and are understood by the other side. Self-recognition and rebuilding a viewpoint on the conflict are critical for moving towards a productive outcome. Any threat to reflection is potentially serious as it is the basis for parties to move from their heavily-invested positions.

However, by the same token, retardation of the process can be viewed as having some potential for positive effects. The asynchronicity of text-based conciliation can positively encourage reflection before parties communicate.

> The time lapse may mean that clients will reflect on their response, or provide a considered response. (Conciliator 7: 13 years' experience)

A more considered response may prevent parties from reacting destructively in the heat of the moment. If the medium encourages reflection, and the conciliator is able to instigate reframing strategies, the conflict may be progressed.

This observation contrasts with the 'flaming' literature, and may be explained by the lack of anonymity that exists in established distributed teams and the kind of conflict that would arise in such situations. This paper is concerned with conflicts amongst people who know or have some established and demonstrable relationship with one another. The dynamics of accountability are very different in these situations than for those who only know one another as a collection of nick-names in cyberspace and without consequence beyond it.

However, it is interesting to note that there is a relationship between qualitative experience of social cues and the degree to which the conciliator is able to encourage reflection. In a face-to-face setting the conciliator is able to encourage direct and explicit reflection, alongside 'venting' behaviour. In a cues-filtered-out environment, such as text-based communication, reflection may also occur, but the conciliator is less in control of its duration and focus. This raises concerns for conciliators about the appropriateness of the use of CMC in certain disputes. To successfully leverage the reduction of cues afforded by technology, it will be necessary to consider the stage in the conflict management process at which CMC technologies might be deployed.

2) Moderation of presence

The second concern reported by conciliators is a reduction in presence or a sense of being there. One of the aims of conciliation is to develop a working relationship between parties. When people are in conflict, they will tend to have a very polarized view of the other. The conciliator will seek to alter this by encouraging parties to view each other in fuller, more social terms. This requires a sense of presence. The conciliators interviewed for this study believe that there is something inherent in CMC that reduces this sense of presence and thus impacts on their role.

> When parties are together in a room . . . responsibility is on people in the room, you are saying 'these are your problems' . . . they need to take the decisions away and make them work . . . [in the real world] they must learn to deal with each other. (Conciliator 5: 20 years' experience)

The conciliator must encourage parties to view each other as social individuals. This then encourages them to listen to the other parties' concerns and consider the impact of their own actions upon them. Without the ability to engender presence, the parties may remain distant, and not be encouraged to work toward a shared resolution. Conciliators felt that there was something significant in the parties committing to meet together in the same room that enabled them to practice conflict resolution. The lack of presence engendered by CMC could inhibit parties from developing the level of commitment necessary to engage in the difficult, but necessary activities of reflection. This is echoed by:

> "It's a little bit safer on video – you haven't got so much to lose." (Conciliator 1: 9 years' experience).

However, conciliators also indicated that, in some instances, a reduction of physical presence is beneficial or even necessary. In situations of high-conflict or extreme power differentials, such as domestic violence, "shuttle mediation" is used by conciliators for precisely this reason. The sense of distance engendered by CMC may create a useful environment for encouraging parties to communicate.

> It might be a useful tool for kick-starting the process . . . if there is something getting in the way of parties coming together [for example] threats of violence. (Conciliator 6: 13 years' experience)

So, level of presence may be something that conciliators are able to deploy to alter power differences in useful ways. The relationship between power and presence is something which is not prominent in the CMC literature but which conciliators have indicated is highly salient for conflict management strategies.

3) Experience and power differentials

Conciliators discussed the effect of differences in level of experience and familiarity with conflict environments. The effective use of CMC systems requires a skill set that may not necessarily be assumed as equal for all parties. Conciliators must address any power differences that are hindering parties from reaching resolution. They felt that experience differentials of CMC have a significant potential to skew these power differences in unpredictable ways. Those more familiar with the medium might be more comfortable with the changed body language, or other differences to FtF communication.

> People can hide behind technology . . . they are adept at presenting themselves through technology. (Conciliator 3: 6 years' experience)

Similarly, the environment in which they are situated for the interaction also may distort the conciliator's practice. Conciliators try to bring the disputants together in neutral territory, and exercise control over who is able to attend. This ensures that the conciliator is highly aware of all of the stakeholders and determinants of conciliation with which they must contend. Differences in the communication environment bring with them the risk of divorcing the conciliator from this degree of control. They do not know who might be 'off-screen', or on which resources the parties might be drawing in their local environment.

> The presence of others also changes behaviour . . . [the conciliator] does not know who's off-camera. (Conciliator 4: 3 years' experience)

From this, it is evident that the use of CMC results in a change in the information that the conciliator is able to use. This increases their uncertainty about the reasons behind parties' behaviours, making it difficult for them to accurately predict or ascertain the motivations behind an individual's observed behaviour.

Here we can see that the introduction of uncertainty can exacerbate concerns about power and experience differentials. For effective conflict management, conciliators require an awareness of the salient power differences in the interaction. They then attempt to address these in a way that encourages parties to use them cooperatively rather than competitively. If the conciliator is uncertain about those resources the parties possess and have invested in a particular outcome, they will be unable to confidently address these differences. This uncertainty may erode parties' trust in the conciliator to effectively manage the conflict.

Implications

CMC is likely to have a very real impact on the identification and resolution of conflict in distributed teams. The above examples demonstrate that conciliators are reluctant to use CMC for their practice because of its unpredictable effect on communication. Conciliators need to be sure that they are able to deploy their strategies and techniques in an effective manner. The issues they raised echo findings in the CMC literature, but with an important difference that connects propensity to flame with accountability that extends beyond the mediation environment. CMC can be instrumental in altering power differentials. It can also affect the availability and interpretation of social cues, inhibit parties from fostering a sense of presence, and exacerbate communication problems such as misunderstanding or misattribution. In normal circumstances, these may have an impact on the way that participants co-operate. In groups where there is a high potential for conflict, these traits of the medium are likely to have a significant affect on the ability of the group to manage their co-operation effectively.

Perhaps one of the more interesting findings about the conciliators' perceptions of CMC is that it could foster both positive and negative behaviours in conflict. They suggest that properties of CMC that may cause difficulties in one situation may be constructive and beneficial in others. The primary factor, moderation of presence, can have positive or negative consequences for the both the conciliator and for conflict management. This is congruent with relational accounts of CMC, but with a twist: too much presence can be destructive.

However, it appears that the impact of CMC technologies is more complicated than simply exacerbating existing tensions. These findings of the interview-study go beyond some of the existing CMC theories. They offer novel insights into relationships on three levels: social information and reflection; presence and power displays; and uncertainty and power differentials. Control over the availability of social information is instrumental in promoting effective reflection. Control over presence makes it possible to moderate displays of power such as physical intimidation and dominance behaviour. Uncertainty must be responded to so that parties do not retrench into their initial power-differentiated positions.

Follow-on study: Adaptive video-mediated conciliation

The findings from the above interviews suggest that a number of factors combine to shape the way parties in conflict respond to one another, notably the ability to moderate presence, to resolve uncertainties, and the opportunity to reflect on the ongoing conversation. The operation of each of these factors is linked to a recognized element of conflict management processes: interpretation of social information, display of power and moderation of power differentials. All three must influence the way that the conciliator deploys, and parties react to, conflict management techniques and strategies. Our interview data was limited in terms of the insight it could offer on how these factors dynamically interact. We wished to gain insights into how an experienced conciliator might dynamically adapt her practice to deepen our understanding of the expressiveness, presence and control categories of action. To this end, we augmented our interview data by setting up two special video-mediated role-play sessions with one of the conciliation professionals who had participated in our interview study.

Setting and method

We installed a small multi-party video-mediated communication (VMC) system between three separate and sound-isolated rooms. The system used a dedicated LAN bridge to connect three personal computers running Apple 'iChatAV' fullscreen on 17" monitors. Sessions were recorded directly from iChatAV via a third-party application.

Two role-play conciliations were performed. As discussed earlier, it is important to note for the validity of this investigation that role-play is a familiar and established element of conciliator practice and continuing professional development. Professional actors were employed to play the conflicting parties in order to mitigate the possible effects of using the role-play method. The role-plays differed in terms of the content and intensity of conflict (low and high conflict). The actors prepared for their roles with character descriptions and a story briefing. The conciliator had over 12 years' experience in a variety of conciliation domains and is considered expert within her community of practice. She trains new conciliators and runs professional development courses, as well as serving as a conciliator in a variety of domains. She is used to operating in unfamiliar environments and to reflecting on the effects these have on her practice.

Each role-play was run by the conciliator as they would a 'normal' conciliation within a 40-minute meeting slot, but an interview followed each session.

Analysis and findings

The conciliator's post-session remarks were cross-compared with statements under the analytic categories derived from our interview study. Audio transcriptions were prepared from the iChatAV recordings and used to contextualize these remarks. A report was prepared to summarize them and then sent to the conciliator for validation. The report identified differences between conciliator perceptions of the medium and their experiences. We noted those changes that conciliators could not overcome, alongside those which added advantages to the conciliation process. The conciliator felt she was able to take steps to adapt to the limitations of the medium, and even to use its properties to her advantage. Quotations are taken from the post-session interviews.

She found it difficult to understand parties' intentions due to the reduction or distortion of social cues. The conciliator drew attention to the way that the medium hindered her ability to identify and create a shared understanding between parties. She "didn't trust parties' understanding so much". This statement reinforces our earlier observation that parties must be able to agree that they have understood something and that additional conversationally relevant actions serve to compliment and confirm this understanding. The conciliator was concerned that there was "nothing else to convey understanding", again reflecting the importance of cue usage to ensure that parties are developing an appropriate understanding of the conflict and of each other.

This finding is important because it opens up the nature of uncertainty as a multi-faceted problem in conflict. Uncertainty applies to the immediate understanding of the specific points each party is making. It also applies to the uncertainty with which they make their points, i.e. the degree to which they might be prepared to shift their positions. Furthermore, it applies to the global understanding of the degree to which trust among parties has been re-established. From the conciliator's viewpoint, it is necessary to be clear about degrees of uncertainty because they are material to progressing the conflict.

Similarly, the conciliator felt that it was: "not as easy to make things visible". In this instance, 'visible' is not to do with video but about raising the salience of issues in the discussion. The conciliator had difficulty in drawing parties' attention to various aspects of the interaction or process that would help to move parties through the conflict. A technique she used was to suggest that certain issues be temporarily sidelined, allowing the focus of the dispute to move in a more productive direction. She felt that parties did not trust that the issues they had raised would be dealt with later, inhibiting her use of this technique. In the video transcript, a participant continually raised an issue despite advice to move on. In an FtF setting, the participants may have seen the conciliator make a note of the points as they were raised. Without this information being conveyed, parties may feel that they are becoming lost in the issues, and be unable to know when an understanding has been reached. This offers one way that the limitations of the medium can be overcome – through explicitly verbalizing her actions.

For the conciliator, this affects their practice. They can no longer be sure that a participant is reverting to an issue because it has suddenly become salient, or if they feel that it has been forgotten and they wish it to remain on the list. In this way, CMC can distort trust in the understanding that parties feel that they share. This combination of effects forced the conciliator to: "have to spell out what was understood." In situations of conflict, parties may be reluctant to expend the effort to do this, stalling the dispute. However, by the same token, an impetus to make certain points in the process explicit could be helpful. Rephrasing to promote reflection on the framing of the conflict is absolutely central to the business of discovering creative resolution perspectives.

The conciliator also discussed the presence theme. The medium's ability to engender an appropriate level of presence has a direct impact on their role, in terms of the control strategies they deploy and the emotion experienced by the other parties. In this study, the conciliator felt that the presence of the medium reduced the propensity for parties to start 'venting', i.e. uncontrolled emotional outbursts. Venting is considered to be an integral part of conflict resolution, provided that it occurs in a controlled environment. If parties do not feel that the medium engenders a suitable degree of presence, they will not feel engaged with the other and therefore be disinclined to start 'venting'. The conciliator adapted to this in terms of the control strategies she used to engage the parties and to draw out their concerns. She reported that her interventions were perceived to have a greater effect. When parties did begin to vent, "the level of conflict ramped up quickly". However, once the conciliator deployed conflict management techniques, the conflict "settled down much quicker than expected". This demonstrates that the conciliator's techniques may have more of an impact in a technologically mediated environment.

A conflict management technique for situations of high-conflict, is to "get them [the parties] to talk directly to you [the conciliator]", including establishing mutual gaze. In doing this, the other party gets to hear how their actions have affected someone else, without it being viewed as a direct threat. It is a presence moderation technique for use within an FtF setting. In VMC, if someone talks directly to the camera, both parties will have a sense that they are being directly addressed, since they both 'share the same eye' in the form of a single camera. This makes it difficult for one individual to directly address another individual in this way. Therefore, it is likely that the social cues appropriate for interaction with the conciliator, rather than the other party, will be more salient. Parties are unlikely to vent *directly at* the conciliator, so will be less likely to vent overall.

Despite the difficulties reported above, and given the adaptive responses to manage the interaction between parties, the conciliator's overall view of the process was that it was: "not as hard or as different as I thought it might be. It wasn't wildly different." This does not invalidate the concerns raised in the interview study but suggests that managing conflicts through technologies is a matter of refinement rather than an entirely alien process. The changes we observed demonstrate that the conciliator was able to alter her practice to moderate the impact of the medium. In other words, the strategies and techniques deployed by the conciliator can translate to a CMC environment.

The hyperpersonal model of CMC (Walther, 1996) argues that a reduction of social information attunes parties to the cues that they do receive, and consequently makes them 'work harder'. The conciliator's interventions are intended to reinforce parties' perceptions of one another as legitimate social agents. According to the hyperpersonal model, the individuating strategies employed by the conciliator should have a greater impact, because of the lack of contradictory information. However, it may be that parties to a distributed conflict will have 'further to go'. If the conflict has arisen or been conducted on-line, then instead of a hyperpersonal relationship, the parties may have developed a 'hypercritical' relationship: the reduced social information that they have received during the conflict has led to parties developing and reinforcing a negative picture of the other. This increases the importance of effective conflict management at an early stage.

Extrapolating from our investigation, we can say that the use of conflict management techniques could be more effective in environments where social information is sparse. However, this suggestion must be tempered by the conciliator's concerns about the degree to which any settlement would be lasting. The conciliator was concerned that their control techniques led to a general 'lack of venting'. If indeed they were unable to vent effectively, feelings of frustration would follow that they hadn't been able "to have their say". Venting certainly seemed to work differently compared to the conciliator's experience of other role-plays and in other settings.

Our investigation indicates that there is potential for elements of strategies and techniques employed by a conciliator to be utilized in distributed team settings. However, the concerns raised by conciliators about the impact of CMC on their practice are significant. The evidence suggests that attempting to translate these practices to the new setting requires a combination of the unique properties of CMC and special organizational facilitation in terms of the status and progression of conflicting talk. We now turn our attention to the implications of our investigation for helping to manage conflict in distributed teams.

Discussion

Technological mediation can exert a powerful influence on conflict processes. Distributed collective activity can be conducted in formally constituted teams or informal groups of people with common interests. In either case, members must work to create sociotechnical settings for their communications. These settings must be conducive to establishing outcomes that are consistent with their concerns. In this paper, we have addressed the particular challenges that people face as they attempt to manage conflict in such settings. Our discussion has framed conflict management as a part of the additional effort to be expected when working in collaborating groups. As such, we have focused on the process side of conflict; namely, the necessary conditions and strategies for moving from states of outright hostility through to some form of agreement.

Accounts of media effects broadly suggest that an appropriate response to conflict is to shift to 'richer' media, or to abandon mediation altogether in favor of familiar FtF confrontations. However, distributed individuals who are engaged in collective activity are often obliged to cooperate within the constraints of the media at their disposal. We have argued that much can be learnt from conciliation professionals about managing conflict. Conciliators focus on the conditions that come together to create an effective setting for contentious communication to take place. The limits of "more bandwidth" as a solution are all too apparent when even the gold standard of co-present communication is insufficient in itself to resolve conflict. We have shown how conciliators work to create a setting for finding resolutions. For conciliators, a setting is at once a safe, neutral space and also a platform to exert control and direct attention towards new accounts of antecedent behaviour and so to new possible outcomes.

For distributed teams, the main challenge is to create a setting that properly fosters attention on what and how things are said, even when they are said harshly. The setting must support the tentative process, exposing values and finding mutually satisfactory new perspectives on the power and resources at stake. Accountability must be preserved so that confidence is built in proposed actions. However, the way in which accountability is preserved must be selective: judgment must be reserved and delayed sufficiently to disambiguate emotional and objective statements. Individuals need to communicate their concerns and depth of feeling to others, to feel that these concerns have been properly acknowledged. They can get more frustrated and entrenched in their positions when they can't actually let their anger out. "Venting" is necessary but comes with the attendant risk that it will amplify the antagonism of other parties unless the setting is designed to cope with the legitimacy of emotional outbursts.

Being on- or off-record is an organizational decision, not a product of technological design. Mediating technologies can always be used to create a record of communication, whether the value of communication history has been a central design concern (as with email) or is more of an afterthought (as with instant messaging). This suggests a tension in technology choice: in high conflict, conciliators say that venting is most productive when it is off-record, but conciliators also say that parties have an equal need to take time to reflect on mutual positions and values. We are confident that in extreme cases, it would be beneficial to make use of an access-controlled and separate communication environment to that used for other team communication. The very fact of its separateness could underline the special status of things that are said within, i.e., in an invite-only chatroom. We are less confident about the politics of migrating a dispute, where the dispute has emerged in a 'normal' channel but must be moved across to a nominated 'safe space'. Migration would at least require the explicit agreement of the conflicting parties. There are significant challenges still to be met in understanding how relational communication can cope with the generation and usage of technological expressions of dissent and confrontation. More research is needed to see how to preserve relevant emotional and accountable context whilst maintaining the safety of the safe space, in order that productive reflection on statements and records of talk may take place.

ACKNOWLEDGMENTS

We thank the professional conciliators for the generosity with which they gave us their time and for sharing their experiences so openly, those actors who took part in our 'emotionally charged' role-plays, and ACAS and the UK EPSRC scheme for supporting our work.

References

Balka, E., & Wagner, I. (2006). Making Things Work: Dimensions of Configurability as Appropriation Work In Proceedings of ACM CSCW'06 (pp. 229-238). New York: ACM Press.

Bos, N., Olson, J. S., Gergle, D., Olson, G. M., & Wright, Z. (2002). Effects of four computer-mediated communications channels on trust development. Paper presented at the Proc. CHI 2002, Minneapolis, Minnesota, USA.

Burgoon, J. K., Bonito, J. A., Ramirez Jr, A., Dunbar, N. E., Kam, K., & Fischer, J. (2002). Testing the Interactivity Principle: Effects of Mediation, Propinquity and Verbal and Nonverbal Modalities in Interpersonal Interaction. Journal of Communication, 52(3), 657-677.

Bush, R. A. B., & Folger, J. P. (2005). The Promise of Mediation. San Francisco: Jossey-Bass.

Coleman, P. T. (2000). Power and Conflict. In M. Deutsch & P. T. Coleman (Eds.), Handbook of Conflict Resolution: Theory and Practice: Jossey-Bass.

Culnan, M. J., & Markus, M. L. (1987). Information Technologies. In F. M. Jablin, L. L. Putnam, K. H. Roberts, & L. W. Porter (Eds.), Handbook of organizational communication: An interdisciplinary perspective, (pp. 420-443). Newbury Park, CA: Sage

Daft, R. L., & Lengel, R. H. (1986). Organisational Information Requirements, Media Richness and Structural Design. Management Science, 32(5), 554 - 571.

Deutsch, M. (1987). A Theoretical Perspective on Conflict and Conflict Resolution. In D. J. D. Sandole & I. Sandole-Staroste (Eds.), Conflict Management and Problem Solving: interpersonal to international applications. (pp. 38 - 44). London: Pinter.

Dourish, P. (2003). The Appropriation of Interactive Technologies: Some Lessons from Placeless Documents. Computer Supported Cooperative Work, 12(4), 465-490.

Flores, F., Graves, M., Hartfield, B., & Winograd, T. (1988). Computer Systems and the Design of Organisational Interaction. ACM Trans. Office Information Systems, 6(2), 153-172.

Folger, J. P., & Baruch-Bush, R. A. (1994). Ideology, Orientations to Conflict and Mediation Discourse. In J. P. Folger & T. S. Jones (Eds.), New Directions in Mediation: Communication and Research Perspectives. Thousand Oaks: Sage.

Glaser, G. B. (1978). Theoretical Sensitivity, The Sociology Press, California.

Glaser, G. B. & Strauss, A. L. (1967). The Discovery of Grounded Theory: Strategies for Qualitative Research, Aldino Publishing Company, New York

Hancock, J. T., & Dunham, P. J. (2001). Impression Formation in Computer-Mediated Communication Revisited. Communication Research, 28(3), 325-347.

Hinds, P. J., & Bailey, D. E. (2003). Out of Sight, Out of Sync: Understanding Conflict in Distributed Teams. Organisation Science, 14(6), 615 - 632.

Holton, B. C., & Kenworthy-U'ren, A. L. (2006). Electronic Negotiation: A Teaching Tool for Encouraging Student Self-Reflection. Negotiation Journal, 22(3).

Jarvenpaa, S. L., & Leidner, D. E. (1999). Communication and Trust in Global Virtual Teams. Organisation Science, 6(10), 791 - 815.

Joinson, A. N. (2001). Self-disclosure in computer-mediated communication: The role of self-awareness and visual anonymity. European Journal of Social Psychology, 31, 177-192.

Keisler, Siegel, & McGuire. (1984). Social Psychological Aspects of Computer-Mediated Communication. American Psychologist, 39, 1123 - 1134.

Kittur, A., Suh, B., Chi, E., & Pendleton, B. (2007, April 28 - May 03 2007). He Says, She Says: Conflict and Coordination in Wikipedia. Paper presented at the CHI 2007, San Jose.

Kressel, K. (2000). Mediation. In M. Deutsch & P. T. Coleman (Eds.), Handbook of Conflict Resolution: Theory and Practice: Jossey-Bass.

Laue, J. (1987). The Emergence of Institutionalisation of Third-Party Roles in Conflict. In D. J. D. Sandole & I. Sandole-Staroste (Eds.), Conflict Management and Problem Solving: interpersonal to international applications. (pp. 17 - 29). London: Pinter.

Mabry, E. (1997). Framing flames: The structure of argumentative messages on the net. Journal of Computer-Mediated Communication, 2(4).

McKenna, K. Y. A., Green, A. S., & Gleason, M. E. J. (2002). Relationship Formation on the Internet: What's the big attraction? Journal of Social Issues, 58(1), 9-32.

Olson, G. M., & Olson, J. S. (2000). Distance Matters. Human-Computer Interaction,15, 139-178.

Poole, M. S., Homes, M., & Desanctis, G. (1988). Conflict management and group decision support systems. In Proceedings of ACM Conference on Computer Supported Cooperative Work (pp. 227-243). Oregon: ACM Press.

Schmidt, K. (1997). Of maps and scripts: The status of formal constructs in cooperative work In Proceedings of ACM GROUP97 (pp. 138-147). New York: ACM Press.

Short, J. A., Williams, E., & Christie, B. (1976). The Social-Psychology of Telecommunications. New York: Wiley.

Spears, R., Lea, M., & Postmes, T. (2000). Social Psychological Theories of Computer-Mediated Communication: Social Pain or Social Gain? In W. P. Robinson & H. Giles (Eds.), The Handbook of Language and Social Psychology (2nd ed.). Chichester: Wiley.

Thomson, L., & Nadler, J. (2002). Negotiating via Information Technology: Theory and Application. Journal of Social Issues, 58(1), 109-124.

Wall, J. A., & Lynn, A. (1993). Mediation: a current review. Conflict Resolution, 37(1),160 - 194.

Walther, J. B. (1994). Anticipated Ongoing Interaction Versus Channel Effects on Relational Communication in Computer-Mediated Interaction. Human Communication Research, 20(4), 479-501.

Walther, J. B. (1996). Computer-Mediated Communication: Impersonal, Interpersonal, and Hyperpersonal. Communication Research, 23(1), 3-43.

Walther, J. B., Loh, T., & Granka, L. (2005). Let Me Count the Ways: The Interchange of Verbal and Non-Verbal Cues in Computer-Mediated and Face-to-Face Affinity. Journal of Language and Social Psychology, 24(1), 31-65.

Walther, J. B., & Parks, M. R. (2002). Cues Filtered-Out, Cues Filtered-In: Computer-Mediated Communication and Relationships. In M. L. Knapp & J. A. Daly (Eds.), Handbook of Interpersonal Communication (Vol. 3rd Edition): Sage.

Winslade, J., & Monk, G. (2000). Narrative Mediation: A New Approach to Conflict Resolution. San Francisco: Jossey-Bass.

L. Bannon, I. Wagner, C. Gutwin, R. Harper, and K. Schmidt (eds.).
ECSCW'07: Proceedings of the Tenth European Conference on Computer Supported Cooperative Work, 24-28 September 2007, Limerick, Ireland

Semi-Synchronous Conflict Detection and Resolution in Asynchronous Software Development

Prasun Dewan

University of North Carolina

dewan@unc.edu

Rajesh Hegde

Microsoft Research

Rajesh.Hegde@microsoft.com

Abstract. Previous work has found that (a) when software is developed collaboratively, concurrent accesses to related pieces of code are made, and (b) when these accesses are coordinated asynchronously through a version control system, they result in increased defects because of conflicting concurrent changes. Previous findings also show that distance collaboration aggravates software-development problems and radical co-location reduces them. These results motivate a semi-synchronous distributed computer-supported model that allows programmers creating code asynchronously to synchronously collaborate with each other to detect and resolve potentially conflicting tasks before they have completed the tasks. We describe, illustrate, and evaluate a new model designed to meet these requirements. Our results show that the model can catch conflicts at editing time that would be expensive to manage at later times.

Introduction

Complex software must be developed collaboratively. While recently there has been some interest in synchronous pair programming, traditionally the collaboration is asynchronous, with programmers working independently on the same or different parts of the software. Even in pair programming, different pairs work asynchronously on the same project. In asynchronous software development, there is a need for coordination mechanisms to manage conflicts. Traditionally, such mechanisms are provided by version control systems, which require programmers to individually address the conflicts at check-in time. Inspired by the findings that distance collaboration aggravates software-development problems (Herbsleb et al. 2000) and radical co-location reduces them (Teasley et al. 2000), we identify a new distributed computer-supported model of software development that provides semi-synchronous conflict-management in asynchronous software development. By conflict management we mean determining if there is a conflict, identifying how to resolve it, and performing the fix. By semi-synchronous collaboration we mean a mix of synchronous and asynchronous collaboration.

The general concept of breaking collaboration into diverging asynchronous and converging synchronous phases has been presented in previous work (Munson et al. 1994). Here we consider a concrete realization of this concept in which the synchronous phases are used only for conflict management. Lightweight system-provided mechanisms are used to make transitions between the two phases.

To investigate this and other ideas, we have extended the user interface of the Visual Studio software development environment – we call the extended user-interface CollabVS. The design, implementation, novelty, and all possible uses of the extensions are not a focus of this paper. In fact, some of the extensions are also provided by recent programming environments and can be easily improved. Here we focus on the narrower issue of the application of these mechanisms in developing a new conflict-management model.

The rest of the paper is organized as follows. We first derive the collaboration model based on the results of previous research. Next we present a simple but realistic joint programming example to illustrate the model. We then identify a joint software development task also designed to exercise the model that is more elaborate than the example but small enough to be carried out in a lab study. Next we present the actual study performed using the task, and end with conclusions and future work.

Deriving the Model

In this paper, we will talk about both previous work and our own contribution at the model level. A model abstracts out details of the user activities supported by a single tool or a set of integrated tools. As these activities are supported directly by the tool (set), we assume there are lightweight mechanisms to transition among them that do not require the use of the OS to explicitly start applications. By abstracting out tool details, it is easier to reason about them and improve their shortcomings. In fact, in this section, we will derive our conflict management model by identifying and refining the models supported by previous work on collaborative software engineering tools. Before we do so, let us first identify the problems these models address.

Brooks (1974) found that adding more people to a software team does not necessarily increase the productivity of the team because of coordination costs. This observation seems unintuitive for two reasons. First, documentation should reduce the need for direct communication. Second, modular decomposition of software products should isolate software developers. However, studies have found that documentation and partitioning approaches do not work in practice. Curtis et al. (1988) found documentation is a not a practical alternative because requirements, designs and other collaborative information keep changing, making it hard to keep their documentation consistent. After finishing an activity, software developers often choose to proceed to the next task rather than document the results of what they have done. Perry et al. (2001) studied Lucent's 5ESS system and found a high level of concurrency in the project - for example, they found hundreds of files that were manipulated concurrently by more than twenty programmers in a single day. Often the programmers edited adjacent or same lines in a file.

Version control systems, when used in conjunction with programming environments, address the problem of concurrent accesses. After programmers have completed an editing task to their satisfaction, they switch to the version control system (window/perspective/tab), check in their changes for all programmers working on the project, and use the diff tools of the system to identify conflicts. If no conflicts are found, they can end the task. Otherwise, after viewing/processing one or more potential conflicts reported by the version control system, they can check-out the code, switch to the editing system (window/perspective/tab), and fix the real conflicts to carry out another iteration of this process. As mentioned above, this process involves editing and conflict detection phases, all of which are carried out asynchronously by the programmers, though they may use check-in notifications (Fitzpatrick et al. 2006), email, IM, virtual "ticker tapes" (Fitzpatrick et al. 2006) and other communication mechanisms to trigger synchronous collaboration supported by some external tool that is not integrated with the version control system.

Even though this model provides conflict management, (Perry et al. 2001) have found it does not work well. They found a positive correlation between the amount of concurrent activity and defects in a file, despite the use of state-of-the-art version control mechanisms to find and merge conflicting changes. Based on other studies, it is possible to derive some of the reasons for this situation. Programmers do not accurately document their planned and finished tasks and do not look at such documentation. As one programmer put it, "I will just blast ahead and cross my fingers and hope I have not screwed up" (Grinter 1998). Thus, programmers are not able to prevent conflicts themselves during the editing phase (as opposed to check-in time) of their activity because of *insufficient information about the activities of others*.

Another reason for the current problems is that conflicts are detected by a *file-based* diffing tool. Such a tool can only detect direct conflicts, that is, conflicting changes to the same file. Even then, it can give many false positives and negatives because it does not know the structure of the file. It cannot detect indirect conflicts involving different files. Moreover, few people have a sense of the overall picture or the broad architecture (Curtis et al. 1988; Grinter 1998), which is required to prevent conflicts. One way to reduce indirect conflicts is to have well-defined APIs between the various components of the system. However, API's may change (Grinter 1998). In fact, new people may be hired simply for the task of adapting to concurrent changes to a new API (de Souza et al. 2004).

Yet another issue with the traditional model is that the conflicts are detected at *check-in* time after a user has performed the task, rather than earlier, when the task is being performed. Because programmers do not have the benefit of a "stitch in time," the repair is costly, leading to the productivity problems reported by Brooks.

Finally, when two programmers make conflicting changes, the person who checks-in or saves later is responsible for detecting and repairing the conflict *individually*, though, as mentioned above, he/she can use informal channels to involve others in synchronous or asynchronous conflict management. In fact, programmers concurrently working on different private spaces (created from the same base) often race to finish first to avoid having to deal with merging problems (Grinter 1995) and/or re-run test suites on the merges (de Souza et al. 2004). The fact that distance collaboration aggravates software-development problems (Herbsleb et al. 2000) and radical co-location reduces them (Teasley et al. 2000) implies the need for lightweight channels for allowing programmers to collaborate with each other more closely to prevent and resolve conflicts.

Thus, the studies above motivate a new collaboration model that meets the following requirements:

Early conflict detection: Conflicts should be caught while programmers are implementing their tasks rather than at check-in time after they have finished their tasks.

Dependency-based conflict notification: The system should use information about the dependency among program elements in checked-out versions to notify programmers about both direct and indirect conflicts.

Collaborative conflict detection and recovery: Ideally, the system should automatically find all conflicts, but this is impossible, in general, because of the halting problem in computer science, though heuristics could be used to do semantic merging in special cases. Therefore, it should provide mechanisms for programmers to collaboratively detect and fix conflicts.

Usability: A model supporting the above features is bound to be more complex than the existing model. Therefore it is important to additionally require the model to be usable. This implies that the model should be easy to learn and provide few false positives about potential conflicts, and the programmers should find each of the activities of the model useful and should not feel that the synchronous phases of the model violates their privacy.

Based on the previous works cited above, we take these requirements as axioms, though (Gutwin et al. 2004) present a study of three open-source software projects that seems to contradict these other works. Based on interviews with fourteen people working on these projects, they found that the developers were hard pressed to recall examples of duplicated or conflicting work. One can argue that that this study does not necessarily contradict the other findings above as open source projects are different from other projects in that they are more loosely coupled, do not have as firm deadlines, and make all information public. Thus people are more in control and aware of the software development process, and hence can better prevent conflicts. Our work and that of several other projects described below is based on the assumption that conflicts do occur, as reported by other papers addressing this issue.

To the best of our knowledge, ours is the first work to explicitly state and derive the set of above requirements, though some subsets of it have been the implicit design goals of many projects. One approach to support early conflict detection is to synchronously show the activities of co-developers. This can be done by showing the exact concurrent edits of collaborators interacting with a synchronous non-WYSIWIS editor (Dewan and Riedl, 1993; Cook et al 2005), or by continuously displaying diffs between different versions of a file (Minor et al. 1993). A user study found that concurrent synchronous editing done by pairs of programmers can, in fact, reduce conflicts and task completion times (Cook et al 2005). (This productivity gain is consistent with the studies of pair programming using a WYSIWIS editor.) However, the also study found that users wished to have the option of disconnected workspaces to work privately. The results of the study imply that it would be useful if changes made to private workspaces could also get the benefit of early conflict detection. Therefore, other systems such as (Hupfer et al. 2004; Josephine Micallef 1991; Cook et al. 2005; Molli et al. 2001; Schummer et al. 2001) show more abstract information about remote activities such as editing of the same checked-out file or method. However, they do not provide enough code contexts to find faults. Moreover, none of the previous semi-synchronous systems provide special code merging mechanisms to fix the conflict before check-in time. In fact, when a potential conflict was identified, users of Tukan (Schummer et al. 2001) resorted to pair programming – in other words, moved to a completely synchronous collaboration model.

Based on the previous findings and system designs, we have developed and evaluated a new semi-synchronous model, in which the editing phases are always asynchronous and the conflict detection and recovery phases may be synchronous or asynchronous. Of course, as mentioned earlier, an asynchronous phase may be executed synchronously by a team of programmers working independently from other programmers. This model is shown graphically in Figure 1. Not all transitions are shown to reduce clutter. Though not shown in the figure explicitly, as in the traditional model, after finishing their tasks, programmers can transition to the

version control system to check-in their changes and detect and fix additional
conflicts.

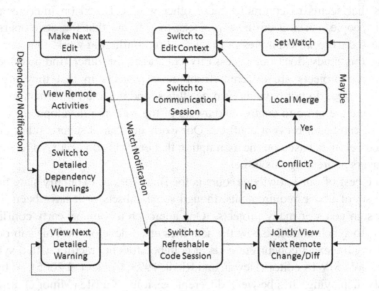

Figure1: Semi-Synchronous Conflict Resolution Model

In our model, as in Jazz, JSE and SubEthaEdit, programmers (a) can be constantly made aware of the program elements accessed by others, which include
not only files, as in the previous systems, but also methods and classes, and (b)
can easily switch to communication sessions involving team members, which can
include not only an IM session, as in the previous systems, but also an
audio/video session. Also, as in Mercury (Josephine Micallef 1991) and Tukan
(Schummer et al. 2001), they get warning about potential conflicts based on dependency checking among different checked-out versions. The remaining parts of
the model described below are entirely new.

Programmers can control the level of synchrony in the conflict detection phase
by requesting that dependency checking be delayed by a specified number of edits. They can also choose the granularity of program elements for which dependency checking is done (e.g. method, class, file). Based on the coupling among
their tasks, different granularities would be appropriate. It is important to not
choose a higher-granularity than appropriate as programmers would then get unnecessary false positives. Moreover, our model requires that the same warning not
be displayed twice. Our expectation is that on the first conflict between two program elements, programmers would communicate the work they plan to do on
these elements in their checked-out versions, and thus would not need to resolve
conflicts between the methods multiple times. Based on the monitoring and warnings, programmers can switch to a conflict inbox, so called, because it can be

considered a persistent collection of detailed conflict messages regarding the current project. As with a regular inbox, the user can iteratively look at each of the items.

After viewing one or more warnings, they can either go back to the edit context, perhaps adapting their work to reduce conflicts, or switch to a code session that can be shared with other programmers. In this session, they can browse the checked-out versions of a remote programmer to identify potential conflicts. Because these versions have not been checked-in, the code in it may not be complete enough to determine if it indeed conflicts with the code of the local user. In this case, the local programmer may set a watch asking the programming environment to inform him/her when the remote user finishes editing a program element, assuming the remote programmer agrees to such monitoring of his/her activities. The local programmer may then switch to editing tasks that are less likely to conflict with the remote developer's current activity. When a watch notification arrives, the programmer can revisit the code session, and continue with the process of identifying conflicts.

Once a real dependency between a local and remote version has been identified, remote changes can be incorporated in the local code to prevent future conflicts. This merge is different from the kind of merge in version control systems in that it affects the local editing buffer rather than a global checked-in version. As these changes are made to the editing buffer by the system to resolve an identified conflict, in our model, they do not trigger conflict warnings.

At any stage in this process, programmers can switch to any of the boxes shown in Figure 1 that are labeled with a title that begins with "switch to". In particular, at any point they can switch to a communication session to identify and resolve conflicts. These boxes represent areas of the screen (such as windows/tabs/panels) that can be displayed/viewed at any time using lightweight commands such as change tab. We have not shown arrows from all tasks to these boxes to reduce clutter.

By simply looking at the model design, it trivial to see that the model meets the requirements of early conflict resolution, dependency-based conflict notification, and collaborative conflict detection and recovery. To determine if it meets the usability requirement requires a programmer study described later.

The model ignores the exact approach for session-creation, notification, dependency checking, diffing, merging, determining when programmers have finished editing a program element, and refreshing code sessions in response to remote changes, which are implementation-dependent. To evaluate and illustrate the model, we have had to resolve these aspects. However, as they don't belong to the model, their nature is not a contribution of this paper.

Illustration and Motivation

To motivate and illustrate the various aspects of the model, we present a realistic two- developer programming exercise that is small enough to be described completely and yet rich enough to benefit from all the of activities of the model.

Consider a drawing tool under development. Assume that the current version of the project contains an abstract class, AShapeWithBounds, that represents a geometric shape with rectangular dimensions. It declares four variables, x, y, width and height, which define the location and size of the shape. It also has the following constructor to initialize the variables:

```
public AShapeWithBounds (int initX, int initY, int initHeight, int initWidth) {
   x = initX; y = initY; height = initHeight; width = initWidth;          }
```

Alice is the one who created and checked-in this class. A while after doing so, she realizes that the positions of the height and width parameters should be reversed. She had sorted these two parameters alphabetically – however, the convention is to put the dimension along the X axis before the dimension along the Y axis.[1] Therefore she has checked out the class and is about to correct the ordering. In the meantime, Bob is adding a new subclass of AShapeWithBounds, ARectangle in a separate file. The constructor of the new subclass will call the constructor of the above class to initialize the coordinates and size of the bounding box of the rectangle. As a result the two activities conflict with each other.

We will assume that the developers are unaware of each other's tasks and thus do not know they conflict. This is realistic. Bob may be using the API developed by Alice, and developers and users of the API may not communicate with each other (de Souza et al. 2004). Thus, this is an example of an indirect conflict involving different files rather than a direct conflict involving the same file. As Bob is unaware of Alice's change of mind, his constructor follows the parameter order of the base class constructor in the original version of AShapeWithBounds.

```
public ARectangle(int initX, int initY, int initHeight, int initWidth):base (initX, initY,
   initHeight, initWeight){ }
```

This code will not work correctly with Alice's new version of the base class constructor. When the collaborators rely only on the version control system, even one that is fine-grained, to coordinate their changes, the earliest point at which they can detect the conflict is when the later user commits. As the changes occur in two different files, the version control system, in fact, cannot detect the conflict. As the original and changed constructors have the same signature, ARectan-

---

[1]   This is a mistake the first author actually made, and like many errors, seems uncharacteristic of a proficient programmer only in retrospect.

gle, will compile correctly with the new version of AShapeWithBounds, and thus a build will also not catch the conflict. If appropriate testing or code reviews is not done, then the conflict would be caught at usage time.

We show below how our collaboration model supported by CollabVS can help prevent this conflict or catch it earlier without relying on expensive testing or code reviews.

Let us assume that Alice has started changing the constructor parameters of AShapeWithBounds() when Bob starts editing the constructor ARectangle(). CollabVS displays to Bob a user-panel for Alice showing the log-in name of the remote user, whether the user is online, the file, class and method on which the user is focusing (currently has cursor in), and status of the current activity – editing, viewing or debugging (Figure 2). This information is synchronously updated. Bob could look at Alice's user panel to realize she is editing a method he intends to call.

As Bob is not expecting a conflict, it is likely that he does not actually look at the user tile. As soon as he starts editing the constructor, however, CollabVS automatically detects a potential conflict. In general, it detects a potential conflict when a user starts editing a program element that has a dependency on another program element that has been edited but not checked-in by another developer. It looks for dependencies among three kinds of program elements: file, type (class or interface), and method. Each of these program elements depends on itself. In addition, a type depends on a subtype and supertype, and a method depends on a method it calls or is called by. Such dependencies extend recursively beyond one level. For example, a subtype may have another subtype of its own, and CollabVS works at any depth of such dependencies.

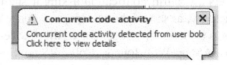

Figure 2: Coding Awareness.   Figure 3: Notification Balloon (Alice's View).

On detecting a conflict, CollabVS displays a notification balloon that gradually fades away (Figure 3) so that, in case of a false positive, programmers can ignore it much in the way they ignore junk-mail notifications today. (In fact setting the dependency-checking parameters can be expected to be similar to the process of defining junk mail filters.) Clicking on the notification balloon automatically takes the user to the conflict inbox (Figure 4) displaying a persistent collection of detailed conflict messages regarding the current project. In general, the person whose edit created the conflict is responsible for initiating the (possibly collaborative) resolution of the conflict. This means that Bob must decide on the next step.

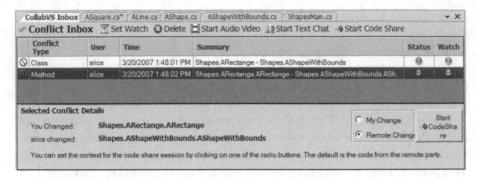

Figure 4: Conflict Inbox

Bob realizes from the notification and inbox that Alice is in the middle of changing the called method. He has other changes to make, and therefore, decides he should delay editing the constructor until Alice has decided what she wants to do with the called method. Therefore, he sets a watch on the conflict by selecting the conflict (Figure 4) and pressing the *set watch* command. Based on the selected conflict, CollabVS knows the dependent program element edited by the collaborator. It gives the active user the option of waiting until the collaborator moves away from editing the current program element and starts editing a different one. As a user may make a temporary movement from a method, it also gives the option of waiting for a certain time period (Figure 5). In this example, Bob knows that the constructor on which Alice is working is simple, and infers that any movement from it will probably be permanent. Therefore, he chooses the first, *by code context*, option (Figure 5), filling in some text explaining to Alice why her actions must be tracked by him. When he commits the dialog box, Alice gets a confirm-notification asking if she is OK with Bob setting a watch on her activity, as she might have privacy concerns. When Alice accepts the watch, Bob gets a success message. Once Alice moves the insertion point out of the constructor AShapeWithBounds, CollabVS notifies Bob.

As mentioned before, ColabVS only knows that a potential conflict exists between the two methods – to determine if it is an actual conflict, Bob must actually see what Alice has done. To do so, he selects the conflict and invokes the *start code session* command in the conflict inbox. This command automatically defines a potentially collaborative session for viewing the contents of Alice's conflicting remote program element – Alice's constructor. A code session (Figure 8) shows the local and remote version of the (manually or automatically selected) program element side by side. If Bob had selected the *my change* option in the conflict inbox, then the code session would have shown his conflicting program element in comparison with Alice's version of it. The code session would also be created in Alice's programming environment if the *collaborative code session* setting was chosen. To locate the exact change, he goes to the code-session panel and exe-

cutes the *show diff* command to show the difference (Figure 6) between two program elements (method, in this case). Bob is now easily able to find the change
and adjusts the parameters of his own constructor when he codes it. As mentioned in the model description, when he re-edits the constructor he does not get a
new conflict notification.

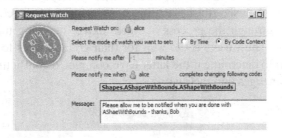

Figure 5: Request for completion Notification

```
public AShapeWithBounds(int initX, int initY, int initHeight, int initWidth   )
public AShapeWithBounds(int initX, int initY, int initWidth, int initHeight)
        : base(initX, initY)
    {
        width = initWidth;
        height = initHeight;
    }
```

Figure 6 Diff-ing in the Code Session

Once Bob finishes his constructor, he needs to test it. However, the code he
has written assumes Alice's version of the AShapeWithBounds() constructor,
while his workspace has the old version. Thus, he uses the local merge facility
provided by the model to merge his version of the constructor with Alice's version of it to test his code. Currently, CollabVS provides a very simple implementation of this facility that simply replaces the local program element with the remote version of it. Since the code displayed in a code session is a snapshot at the
time of starting the session, users can execute the *refresh* command on the code
session to get the latest remote version of the program element. Typically such a
command would be executed in response to a watch event indicating that the remote user has finished editing the program element that must be imported.

Communication Sessions

We assumed above that Bob had other activities to do when the conflict was detected, and thus could postpone editing of the ARectangle() constructor until Alice had finished editing the AShapeWithBounds() constructor. If this is not the
case, he cannot use the code sharing session as Alice has not yet completed her

changes. Therefore, he can use a chat, audio, or video session to communicate with her to determine her intentions. A communication session is shown in-place within the programming environment (Figure 7), so that switching to it is light-weight, as required by the model As Bob does not expect a complicated conversation, he simply opens a text channel. Alice quickly tells him what she intends to do, and Bob adapts his code. When she finishes her edits, he would like to test his code with her version. Therefore, he selects the conflict from the conflict box and sets a watch for when she finishes editing it. When he gets the completion notification, he goes through the process outlined above involving the use of a code sharing session. Thus, users could wait for their collaborators to finish editing a method both (a) to determine if the latter have completed conflicting code, and (b) import remote changes into their workspace.

Figure 7: In-Place Communication Sessions

As we see above, the implementation of the model in CollabVS is able to give early and more sophisticated notification about possible conflicts in comparison to a file or version-control system. In a file or version-control system, however, the interleaving of the actions of the two programmers and their tasks does not matter. In our collaboration model, as we see above, it matters, because of the support for early conflict management. When Bob had other activities to perform, he did not need to start a communication session with Alice to determine her intent – he could simply look at her finished method before writing his dependent method. Our model is able to accommodate both schedules.

There are other variations to the scenarios above that are also supported by the model: Bob might edit the ARectangle() constructor before Alice edits the AShapeWithBounds() constructor. In this case, the conflict would be detected when Alice starts her edits, and she would be responsible for managing it. She can start a communication session with Bob and tell him how to adapt his code. Again, he can set a watch on her activity, incorporate her code into his version, and use it to test his code. In all of the cases above, Alice may also incorporate

Bob's changes into her version, or let the version control system correctly merge the two versions.

When a conflict is detected with uncommitted code of another user, the latter may not have an open CollabVS session. In this case, traditional communication channels must be used to contact the other user, which are external to the model. These channels can also be used to completely resolve the conflict – however, for complicated cases, a CollabVS session can be opened by the second user, and then conflict resolution can occur as explained above.

Finally, when a user creates a potential conflict, the other user may have already checked in the code involved in the conflict and exited CollabVS. In this case also the model and its implementation in CollabVS will report the conflict. For each user, the model tracks all concurrent edits since that user checked out a project, including both checked-in and uncommitted edits. These edits persist until the user commits the project to the version control system.

Evaluation

As mentioned above, the assumption behind our work is that the requirements described earlier are axioms as are the findings that motivate them. In particular, we assume that many conflicts occur that cannot be automatically merged in traditional version-control systems. We do not try to provide new research to motivate these requirements, relying entirely on previous work. What we wished to determine is that when conflicts do occur, how usable is our model to detect and resolve them at edit time. This, in turn, requires us to determine if users can easily transition among the various activities of the model, whether these transitions help users identify and resolve conflicts, whether users feel the model violates their privacy, whether the model creates an unacceptable level of false positives, and whether it is easy to learn. To provide preliminary answers to these questions, we decided to conduct a lab study. This task was particularly challenging because it involved multiple distributed programmers working together and we had to assign problems that were "realistic," led to conflicts, and consumed about an hour of work.

We looked hard for examples and/or characterization of such conflicts in the published literature, but were unsuccessful in our search. About this time, the first author was building a whiteboard application in incremental steps. These steps were taken alone and serially by the author, but we tried to determine if the above kind of conflicts would occur if pairs of these steps were taken in parallel by different programmers. We found several pairs of tasks that would cause such conflicts including the motivating example given in the previous session, and chose one of these pairs for our study. One of the tasks in the pair was to add a new feature while the second one involved refactoring existing code for extensibility. The first task is consistent with the practice of continuously adding features (Perry et al. 2001) while the second is consistent with modern programming philosophies (such as extreme programming) espousing constant refactoring, which is used, for instance, in the development of Mozilla (Reis et al. 2002). We invited pairs of programmers for a lab session and assigned each person one of the tasks in this pair.

Both participants in a pair were given a whiteboard implementation that displayed circles, points and squares. When this program was written, it was assumed that a shape should be oblivious to the display task, which is carried out by a special view class. Unfortunately, this approach has its own disadvantages – the view class used the C# *is* operator to check the class of a shape to determine how to display it. This makes the task of adding new shapes error prone – it is easy to forget to check for the new kind of shape. Therefore, one of the participants ("B") was asked to re-factor the code so that the display operation is implemented by each shape. The other participant ("A") was asked to add a new kind of shape, a line, to the whiteboard. A was responsible for processing input commands to create a line, storing its coordinates, and displaying it. The code session of Figure 8 shows the original code and actual changes made to it by one of the pairs of users. As we see in this picture, a version control system, even a fine-grained one, cannot correctly merge the two sets of changes, which requires that the displaying of a line be done in the model class that stores the line coordinates, and not the view class. Both direct conflicts involving the view class, and indirect conflicts involving the view and model class, occur in this exercise. The goal of our study was to determine if the users were able to easily use our mechanisms to detect and fix the conflict at editing time. We could not evaluate aspects of the model that interface it with traditional conflict management such as email and version control systems as the level of asynchrony in such conflict-management cannot be realistically simulated in a lab study. As mentioned earlier, the model allows programmers to choose the granularity of dependency checking. In the evaluation, we turned on the finest-granularity checking. We did not evaluate the usage of dependency-checking parameters in this study as they depend on the task and programmers' previous experience with the tool, and the participants used out tool for the first time to perform a single task.

We recruited 16 participants from a pool of developers from Microsoft. The pool of participants was gender balanced and included a mix of people with intermediate, advanced, and expert software development skills. Participants were randomly grouped into pairs, assigned to separate rooms, and told that they would be co-workers for the duration of the study. The study involved training participants to ramp them up to speed in getting familiar with the system for about 20 minutes. Then they were given about 60 minutes to complete as much of the assigned tasks as possible. In the end, 10-15 minutes were used to fill in a survey and for debriefing. We recorded participants' actions using LiveMeeting.

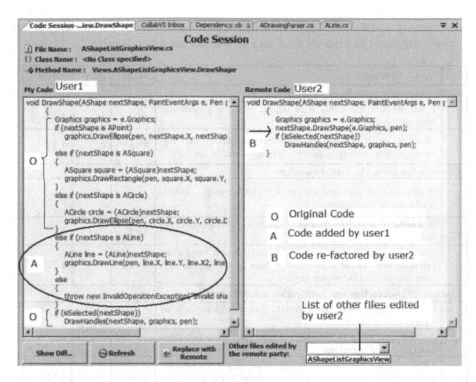

Figure 8: Example of Actual Code Session in Lab Study

Table 1 shows the result of survey questions we asked the participants at the end of their tasks. All survey questions were answered using a 7-point scale where 1 = "strongly disagree" and 7 = "strongly agree". We interleaved positive and negative questions in the survey so the participants did not follow a specific pattern in answering. As mentioned earlier, several programming environments such as Jazz support monitoring of the focus of a collaborator. Telling others the exact method a person is working on goes beyond existing awareness systems. The responses to the first question show that users were not bothered by this invasion of their privacy because, as indicated by responses to the second question, users felt they were able to better plan their work. Not surprisingly, users found it easy to start a communication session with collaborators as lightweight commands were available from the programming environment to transition to them. More interestingly, they found synchronous communication sessions useful to resolve conflicts. They agreed that the collaboration model found conflicts that would have been hard to find otherwise, and interestingly, were mostly not distracted by false positives. In fact, it was possible to do better with false positives. The model allows users to set conflict detection be delayed by a specified number of edits (we had set this to zero for the study). Moreover, the implementation of the model in CollabVS does not currently use program slices to detect conflicts

(Gallagher et al. 1991) as such a capability was not available to us. Finally, Table 1 shows that users found code sessions and watches useful and usable.

	Survey Question	Mean	Med	SDEV
Code-awareness related questions				
1	I was **NOT** comfortable with others seeing my presence information.	2.00	1	1.55
2	Knowing what method or type(class/interface) my co-developer was editing helped me plan my work better	5.50	6	1.51
Communication-tools related questions				
3	It was easy to start and end a conversation(audio, video, text) with my co-worker	6.63	7	0.72
4	It was NOT useful to start an audio, text, video conversation.	1.75	1	1.18
5	I liked having the audio/video/text conversation tools integrated within Visual Studio rather than as a separate tool such as a general IM application.	6.19	7	1.22
Code-conflict-detection and notification related questions				
6	ColabVS helped me find conflicts that would have been hard to find otherwise.	4.84	5	1.69
7	Automatic conflict detection gave too many false positives and thus was **distracting**.	2.31	2	1.08
8	The fact that I was able to see my co-developer's code (using the code share session) was very useful to me to resolve conflicts.	6.16	6.5	1.12
9	It was easy to use code share session	5.97	6	1.16
10	It was **difficult** to understand the conflict notifications that the system provided.	3.13	2.5	1.54
11	It was easy to set a watch on my co-worker's activity	5.69	6.5	1.48
12	It was useful to set watch on my co-worker's activity	5.31	5.5	1.57
13	Setting a watch helped me concentrate more on my work than polling for information through CollabVS awareness information.	5.38	5.5	1.53
General questions				
14	Overall, it was easy for me to use CollabVS to collaborate with my co-worker	5.66	6	1.35
15	Overall, the CollabVS tool window was **distracting**	2.63	2	1.82
16	Overall, I liked working with CollabVS ON in my Visual studio (than working without it)	6.00	6	1.03

Table 1: Survey Questions and results (1: Strongly Disagree, 7: Strongly Agree)

Some participants did not answer questions about the *watch* feature because they did not use it (9 out of a total of 288). We ignored their answers in the calculations. Based on the LiveMeeting video recordings, we were able to determine that text chat, audio conversation, watch, asynchronous code session, and synchronous code session were used by 4, 6, 4, 5, and 6 teams, respectively. This implies that these aspects can be learnt in about twenty minutes of training time – as we see each feature was used by at least half of the participants. Thus, we believe the results show that these features of the model are easy to learn, easy to use, and useful. This data also shows that synchronous code sessions were used by all participants and some also used asynchronous code sessions. The former were used in deciding how to fix the conflict and the latter to merge changes. We must rely only on the subjective answers of Table 1 to determine the usefulness of monitoring others' activities, which cannot be determined by examining the videos.

Overall, users said they were happy with the features of our model and were not distracted by the CollabVS window. This is not only reflected in the answer to questions 14-16, but also the free-form comments they filled at the end of the survey and remarks during debriefing, some of which are reproduced below: "Watch is extremely useful when people have different working hours." "This is really cool system for a small team." "Very useful not just for code, but also for SQL queries, documents etc if supported." "It's really nice to know when someone is about to add some constructor, about to make a method virtual, about to add new class etc" "Would love to have it now." "This tool has the ability to spark discussion rapidly and get to a decision really quickly. This has got to be great money and time saver. It not only keeps the project cost down but also leads to higher quality software." "I first thought it would be annoying to have all these awareness. But as I used them, I loved them." Some participants had a few suggestions as well. "While the tool is definitely useful, it has the potential to "bug" others. A do not disturb mode will help reduce this." "I would have liked to see the popups not steal my focus." "I do not like popups, it's very easy to just dismiss it without seeing. Some integration with messenger may help, or some notification in the sidebar would be great." Popups are provided for accepting watch and audio/video session requests. "Conflict detection inbox takes away space from the code editor. Maybe this should be a window at the bottom." "I would have loved to see what code share my co-worker is watching right now." "Good to know which ones (files) I already copied from a remote version and which ones I didn't". Some of these negative comments can perhaps be overcome in a better implementation of our model.

Thus, this initial user study shows that our model is promising and worth more investigation. It is possible that the participants were primed by the tutorial to think about conflicts. However, this does not detract from the results as our goal was to determine how easy it is to catch conflicts with our model at editing time that cannot be caught by the traditional model, and not to determine if conflicts actually occur. The programmers were not told in advance what the conflicts were.

All of the pairs did indeed detect and completely fix the conflicts in the time period. The tasks would have taken less time had the programmers not had to detect and fix the conflicts while programming, but the checked-in code would have had faults. Even if all of the 60 minutes were used for conflict management, our results are encouraging because this time period is about an order of magnitude less than the average time required to fix a bug - the literature reports it to be between 5 and 15 hrs (Humphrey 1997). We did not directly compare how well the given problem-pair would be solved with and without our tools because (a) The bug detection and fixing time of 5-15 hrs given above is much more than the time available for a lab study, and (b) all participants had used Visual Studio without our tools and thus could give informed comments about the benefits and drawbacks of the tools. Thus, we assumed the earlier findings about the cost of late conflict management, and in our study were interested only in determining if our tools were effective in enabling conflict management at edit time. In general, our model can catch conflicts that are also caught by code reviews and other systems (possibly using semantic information) at file-save, check-in or later times. Even in the case of these conflicts, it can prevent programmers from taking actions that depend on the conflict. Moreover, as mentioned in the introduction, our approach could also allow different pairs of programmers to manage conflicts.

Conclusions and Future Work

This paper makes several contributions. It distills earlier work into a set of requirements that have not been explicitly identified before, and presents a new model that meets these requirements and subsumes and extends previous models. Another important contribution of the work are two concrete realistic examples of conflicting coding, a small one used to illustrate the model and a longer one used in the study, that are small enough to be presented in a paper and rich enough to bring out the limitations of the traditional conflict management model.

These examples could be the bases for concrete illustration of future models/tools and motivate other detailed conflicting tasks that serve as benchmarks for conflict-management tools. Perhaps the most important contribution of the paper is an experiment that allowed the use of several conflict-management features, both existing and new, that have never been evaluated before by a programmer study.

Conflicting code is an old and complex problem that will not be solved by any one result. It requires advances in many areas such as visualization and project management not addressed here. The contributions of this paper take us closer to finding the ideal collaboration model to address this problem. They also suggest several future steps towards this goal. It would be useful to perform a lab study involving teams that are larger than two members. Many aspects of our model assume a small team-size – in particular the approach of showing and logging the conflicts with each team member, which scales better than synchronous (WYSIWIS and non-WYSIWIS) programming but worse than traditional asynchronous development. This does not make such aspects impractical because a team typically has less than eight members (Booch et al. 2002), though it may occasionally have hundreds of members. It would be useful to create scaleable version of our model that accommodates larger teams. Programmers may have been more concerned about privacy if they were doing real work rather than a lab exercise. To answer these and other questions with the evaluation, the most important next step for us is to make the system more robust and perform a field study with it. We can imagine this happening in two stages. In the first one, we would simply detect conflicts without reporting them, thereby obtaining a set of real-life conflicts. These could form useful benchmarks for research in this area. More important, based on these conflicts, we could refine, configure, and turn on our dependency reporting; and determine qualitative data regarding how well the users found the system usable and useful, and quantitative data regarding changes to defect rate. It would be useful to explore the use of some of these features for purposes other than conflict management in software development. For example, a user seeing a collaborator working on a method may ask him a question about the method. Moreover, we have seen here examples of awareness and notification mechanisms tied to the context of software development. It would be useful to explore analogous mechanisms in other contexts such as paper writing. For example, it may be useful to determine the exact section on which a user is working and to get a notification when a collaborator finishes working on a section of a paper. These results can be then used to improve and refine the collaboration model and resolve issues that have been left as implementation-defined in this paper.

Acknowledgments

This research was funded in part by *Microsoft* and NSF grants ANI 0229998, EIA 03-03590, and IIS 0312328.

References

Booch, G. and A. W. Brown (2002). 'Collaborative Development Environments', www.jorvik.com/alanbrown/files/cde-v4.1.pdf.

Brooks, F. (1974). "*The Mythical Man-Month.*" Datamation 20(12): 44-52.

Cook, C., W. Irwin, et al. (2005). A User Evaluation of Synchronous Collaborative Software Engineering Tools Proceedings of the 12th Asia-Pacific Software Engineering Conference (APSEC'05) - Volume 00 IEEE Computer Society: 705-710

Curtis, B., H. Krasner, et al. (1988). "*A field study of the software design process for large systems.*" Commun. ACM 31(11): 1268-1287.

de Souza, C. R. B., D. Redmilles, et al. (2004). 'Sometimes You Need to See Through Walls - A Field Study of Application Programming Interfaces'. *Proc. Computer Supported Cooperative Work* pp. 63-92.

Dewan, P. and J. Riedl (1993). 'Towards Computer-Supported Concurrent Software Engineering '. IEEE Computer 26(1) pp. 17-27.

Fitzpatrick, G., P. Marshall, et al. (2006). "CVS integration with notification and chat: lightweight software team collaboration" Proc. Computer Supported Cooperative Work pp. 49-58.

Gallagher, K. B. and J. R. Lyle (1991). "Using Program Slicing in Software Maintenance." IEEE Transactions on Software Engineering 17(8): 751-761.

Grinter, R. E. (1995). 'Using a Configuration Management Tool to Coordinate Software Development'. Proc. Organizational Computing Systems pp. 168-177.

Grinter, R. E. (1998). 'Recomposition: Putting it All Back Together Again'. Proc. Computer Supported Cooperative Work pp. 393-402.

Gutwin, A. C., R. Penner, et al. (2004). 'Group awareness in distributed software development'. Proc. Computer supported cooperative work pp. 72-81.

Herbsleb, J. D., A. Mockus, et al. (2000). 'Distance, dependencies, and delay in a global collaboration'. Proc. Computer Supported Cooperative Work pp. 319-328.

Humphrey, W. (1997). A Discipline for Software Engineering.Addison Wesley

Hupfer, S., L.-T. Cheng, S. Reiss, J. Patterson (2004). 'Introducing collaboration into an application development environment'. Proc. Computer Supported Cooperative Work pp. 21-24.

Josephine Micallef, G. E. K. (1991). "Extending the Mercury System to Support Teams of Ada Programmers." 1st International Symposium on Environments and Tools for Ada pp. 49-60.

Minor, S. and B. Magnusson (1993). 'A Model for Semi-(A)Synchronous Collaborative Editing'. Proceedings of European Conference on Computer Supported Coopearative Work. 219-231

Molli, P., H. Skaf-Molli, et al. (2001). 'State Treemap: An Awareness Widget for Multi-Synchronous Groupware'. Proc. International Workshop on Groupware.

Munson, J. and P. Dewan (1994). 'A Flexible Object Merging Framework'. Proc. Computer Supported Cooperative Work. 231-242

Perry, D. E., H. P. Siy, L. G. Votta (2001). "Parallel Changes in Large-Scale Software Development: An Observational Case Study." ACM TOSEM 10(3): 308-337.

Reis, C. R. and R. P. d. M. Fortes (2002). 'An Overview of the Software Engineering Process and Tools in the Mozilla Project'. Proc. Open Source Software Development Workshop.

Schummer, T. and J. M. Haake (2001). 'Supporting distributed software development by modes of collaboration'. Proc. European Computer Supported Cooperative Work pp. 79-98.

Teasley, S., L. Covi, M. S. Krishnan, J. S. Olson. (2000). 'How does radical collocation help a team succeed?'. Proc. Computer Supported Cooperative Work pp. 339-346.

L. Bannon, I. Wagner, C. Gutwin, R. Harper, and K. Schmidt (eds.).
ECSCW'07: Proceedings of the Tenth European Conference on Computer Supported Cooperative Work, 24-28 September 2007, Limerick, Ireland
© Springer 2007   179

Tag-Based Metonymic Search in an Activity-Centric Aggregation Service

Michael J. Muller, Werner Geyer, Beth Brownholtz, Casey Dugan, David R. Millen, and Eric Wilcox
IBM Research
{*michael_muller, werner.geyer, beth_brownholtz, cadugan, david_r_millen, eric_wilcox*}*@us.ibm.com*

Abstract. Knowledge workers often need to find, organize, and work with heterogeneous resources from diverse services, information stores, and repositories. This paper analyzes two problems that knowledge workers frequently encounter: difficulty in finding all relevant resources across diverse services, and difficulty in formulating and executing searches for resources related to their current activity-of-interest. The Malibu project explores solutions to these problems through a dynamic peripheral display that aggregates knowledge resources from multiple services to support activity-centric work. Of particular interest is the ability to select a knowledge resource and use it as a metonym (a proxy) for its social-tagging metadata in a tag-based search for related resources among heterogeneous services. We evaluated our solutions to these two problems through convergent analyses of quantitative (data log) and qualitative (interview and discussion data) data. Our partial successes show the strength of these new ideas, and indicate areas for future research.

Introduction

While working on a single, integrated activity or concept, knowledge workers often need to find, organize, and save heterogeneous resources. Using the concepts of activity theory, Bardram and colleagues have studied the assembly of diverse resources in medicine (Bardram, 200f5). Others have noted the heterogeneous resources needed for knowledge work in activity management in offices (Bellotti et al., 2003; Ducheneaut and Bellotti, 2001; Halverson et al., 2004; Kaptelinin, 2003; Moran et al., 2005; Muller et al., 2004; Whittaker, 2005). A number of projects have explored systems for supporting knowledge workers in assembling and using such heterogeneous resources (Bardram, 2005; Bellotti et al., 2003; Geyer et al., 2006; Muller et al., 2004).

During the same period, researchers have described knowledge workers' issues with interruptions and interruption management. Knowledge workers frequently change tasks, either by choice or through interruptions (González and Mark, 2005; Iqbal and Horvitz, 2007; McFarlane and Latorella, 2002). Interruptions are commonly blamed for impairments in attention, task completion, and quality of work (Cutrell et al., 2001; Hudson et al., 2002; Monk et al., 2004). Several systems have intended to support knowledge workers by managing interruptions and/or by preserving or restoring context (e.g., Sen et al., 2006; Sullivan, 2006; Whittaker, 2005).

Organizing and Using Activity Resources

Several research programs have explored support for context switching and resource rediscovery by organizing and integrating resources, tools, and people around the computational concept of a work activity (e.g. Bardram, 2005; Bellotti et al., 2003; Geyer et al., 2006; Gwidzka, 2002; Kaptelinin, 2003; Muller et al., 2004). Many of these approaches have in common that they provide some structure within which all records of an activity may be collectively located and (re)discovered.

In our research, an "activity" is a structured set of diverse objects that are shared among specified collaborators to accomplish a shared task (Geyer et al., 2006; Moran et al., 2005; Muller et al., 2004). An activity can begin with something as simple as a chat or an email, shared between two people, and can grow into structured collections of over a hundred files, messages, chats, links, etc., that are shared among dozens of users, and that have lasting corporate value long beyond the time of the last update to any of the objects in the activity (Muller et al., 2004). Alternatively, an activity can be instantiated from a stored customizable template (Moran et al., 2005).

Representation Gap

Activity-centric computing provides powerful tools to support collaborative work. However, one problem with activity support systems is that the user is burdened with manually managing the resources and the structure of many activities simultaneously. Worse, despite the fact that the various activity-based approaches allow the collection of heterogeneous resources inside a single structure, users often must continue to store some information in multiple services – e.g., documents and tasks in an activity-centric store *plus* feeds in a feedreader *plus* bookmarks in a social-bookmarking system *plus* communications events or logs in email or instant messaging clients. As a consequence, much information that is part of the cognitive model or otherwise related to the activity might not get captured or displayed in the formal representation (e.g., Bardram, 2005; Moran et al., 2005; Muller et al., 2004). We call this problem the **representation gap**.

Currently, as noted above, users have to manage multiple information stores. Many of these stores do not even have the ability to link to relevant resources in other information stores. This problem is further complicated by the fact that, in complex activity environments, new resources are always being added to the community's or enterprise's various storage services by colleagues. Users need to be able to find these newly added resources whose relationship with their current activity structures has not yet been determined. With today's tools, users must monitor multiple stores and services, including feeds from individual sources of information, and then must take manual actions to aggregate these diverse resources into their activities.

A few corporate services have experimented with socially-informed feeds, such as the ability to subscribe to individual users' bookmarks in Dogear (Millen et al., 2006) and the ability to receive alerts as colleagues added new information to team-based activities (Geyer et al., 2006; Muller et al., 2004; Sen et al., 2006). However, some of these experiments have led to a deluge of alerts with limited relevance to the user's actual needs (e.g., Muller et al., 2004), and this problem has led to additional research into ways of limiting those information feeds and subscriptions according to individual actions or social recommendations (Sen et al., 2006). The research in this paper intends to aggregate many of these sources of new information, and to use a single, user-tunable method to control and limit the information from these sources.

Metonymic Search

In order to satisfy their information needs beyond what's represented in an activity, knowledge workers typically use standard web or desktop search tools. However, this requires the user to interrupt their work and actively seek out information. Since today's search technologies do not take into account the user's current activity, users need to manually encode their information needs through appropriate search terms. Users typically try to identify key phrases that can be used in a search engine to find related resources. This strategy is labor-intensive, error-prone, and fails to take advantage of available metadata about the user's current activity or any object in general. Users would have an easier time searching if they could base their search on automatically derived attributes of the item of interest. In rhetorical terms, this could be called **metonymic search** – i.e., the use of the item itself as a metonym (a referent) for its attributes, and the execution of the search by specifying the item as a placeholder for its attributes.

Several schemes have been developed that follow the Superbook model (Egan et al., 1989) of (a) selecting an item of interest and then (b) invoking an operation that is typically called "more like this." However, these approaches generally work only within their own domain (e.g., documents for Superbook, or webpages for Internet search engines), and are often procedurally opaque to end-users (e.g., the concept of vector-space cosine similarity in latent semantic indexing is difficult for most users to grasp). There appears to be no solution for our problem domain, namely helping users to cope with the representation gap by easily invoking a metonymic search for related items across multiple stores of heterogeneous resources. The "Malibu System" Section (below) provides examples of tag-based inter-service search, and the scenario of use (below) provides examples of how tag-based searches can help to resolve the representation gap, and how a metonymic approach to those searches can make them easy to initiate and manage. We used a stack architecture for all of our tag-based searches, which manifested in the user interface as the ability to return to previous states of our client. We believe that this design not only addresses the representation gap but also provides better support for recovering from interruptions since each stack represents a search context that can easily be restored. In order to support interruption management We we provided Malibu as a peripheral display that could be invoked and dismissed with a single gesture, leaving the user's display with preceding, underlying work intact.

Summary and a Look Forward

We developed the experimental Malibu system to assist knowledge workers in their activity-centric work, with the goal of improving or overcoming the limitations of the current activity management approaches. Malibu aggregates and provides fast access to information from different data sources; it finds relevant information across data sources using social tags and person information; it allows the user to rapidly switch and restore contexts; and it helps users manage discovered resources by flagging them as tasks.

The organization of this paper is as follows. We describe the Malibu system, and we describe three issues that our design addresses to deliver value to our end-users. We describe a field trial, in which we provided Malibu for download by employees in IBM. We then present usage data (logs and interviews); these data allow us to test our hypotheses of Malibu's value. Finally, we close with a self-critique and questions to be addressed in future work.

Malibu System

Malibu runs as a desktop side bar ("Malibu Board") that slides out when users hover with their mouse at the left or right side of the screen.[1] Malibu provides peripheral access to and awareness of multiple data sources contained in a series of

---

1   Malibu is a research prototype. A full version of the system would include appropriate accessibility
     features.

configurable views, each one displaying multiple instances of a single type of data, such as tasks, bookmarks, and activities (see Figure 1). We envisioned that the user would invoke Malibu with a mouse gesture, would be able to work with old or new objects there, and would be able to dismiss Malibu with a second gesture, returning to the pre-Malibu context of her or his work. As we will describe, some users preferred to work in this way, while others maintained a Malibu window open all the time (often on a secondary display), and yet other users complained that the gestural-display user interface was annoying.

Similar to the Google side bar (Google, n.d.), Malibu can be extended with new views and data sources. The system currently supports the following views and data sources: My Tasks (A), My Activities (B) from the Lotus Activities system (Geyer et al., 2006), Dogear Bookmarks (C) from the Dogear social bookmarking system (Millen et al., 2006), and My Feeds (D), a feed reader that supports RSS and ATOM.

We decided to implement Malibu as an extension to IBM's latest corporate instant messaging client Sametime 7.5 because the client gives us access to the people information for Malibu's search engine. All the aforementioned data sources (tasks, feeds, activities, bookmarks) have people information associated with them, i.e. an instant messaging client becomes an ideal launching pad for pivoting on people, e.g. search for all bookmarks of a certain user. There are also technical reasons why we used Sametime 7.5 as a platform. Sametime 7.5, based on Eclipse and Java, is designed to be an extensible framework. In particular, Sametime 7.5 includes an infrastructure for easy deployment of extensions (plug-ins). Since Sametime 7.5 has a large install base in IBM, it allowed us to easily target a large user group. People are usually more reluctant to install new applications rather than plug-ins to existing applications. The download web site of the Sametime 7.5 client also offered other plug-ins, so employees were accustomed to searching for new functionality there. Finally, the Sametime platform allowed us to leverage corporate directories and authentication resources.[2]

Malibu Views

Each view has a different set of features. Consider first the Activities view. As mentioned above, an activity is a shared structured collection of heterogeneous objects, assembled by members of a team, to accomplish a group objective; the objects in an activity may include documents, messages, files, and so on (Geyer et al., 2006; Muller et al., 2004).

---

[2]   We explored possibilities to develop a Malibu-based people view, with enhanced capabilities. However, we thought it might be confusing to offer a second, seemingly redundant view of people ("buddies"), even if our second view had greater functionality than the conventional buddylist.

Figure 1. Malibu Board

Users of an activity (also known as "members") often need to know the current status of the activity, or of one of the component objects within that activity. Malibu displays activities with updated information in bold, and sorts activities in terms of their relevance to the user. Malibu also supports user operations that are specific to activity management, such marking activities as important or unimportant. The Activities view also has filters to show only important and modified activities. This way, users can manually manage and prioritize their activities.

Similar filters are available in the Dogear view, which shows recent bookmarks from an enterprise social-bookmarking system (Millen et al., 2006).

In contrast to Activities and Dogear, the feeds view allows people to add or delete feeds, and to mark any feed as "read."

We also implemented a task view that provides the ability for other views to designate any item in Malibu as a task (including a user-controlled completion indicator) with a pointer to the original item. The main purpose was to provide some capability for the user to flag (or bookmark) resources discovered during the tag-based search as follow-up tasks for later review.

Malibu Navigator

At the top of the Malibu Board, is the "Navigator" (E) which can be used to bring any Malibu item, including people from the instant messaging client, into focus, i.e. items can be selected as pivot objects on which Malibu performs a tag-based or people-centric search ("Surf in Malibu").[3] When a user pivots ("surfs") on an item, views are reconfigured to display contextual information related to the current pivot object; which becomes the current focus of the board. For example, if the user pivots on a bookmark, the system uses the tags associated with that bookmark to execute tag-based searches for other Dogear bookmarks, activities, feeds, and tasks. If the user pivots on a person, the system uses that person's name to search for bookmarks created by that person, activities in which that person is a member, and feeds that mention that person. The search can be refined by selecting individual tags or manually adding key words to the query. The details box (F) shows information about the current focus item, including the social tags from that focus item (which were used to perform the tag-based search in all of the views). Similar to a browser, the navigation buttons and the history drop-down menu can be used to restore the search results of previous pivot objects. Details such as tags, description and author information can be also viewed in a slide-out window by clicking on items in any view.

Extensible Tag-Based Resource Aggregation

Malibu thus provides views of several different types of data, including activities, feeds, shared bookmarks, and tasks. In practical business settings, users are likely to have a large number of these resources. As we noted earlier, the sheer number and diversity of these resources is likely to present problems to users. We described the representation gap as the difficulty in discovering all of the resources relevant to a current activity or task. Malibu assists with that problem through the

---

[3] In our environment, tags are used to describe not only resources (Millen et al., 2006) but also activity records (Geyer et al., 2006), selected feeds, and people (Farrell and Lau, 2006).

use of automated tag-based search. Most of the resources in our environment have been tagged by users.[4]

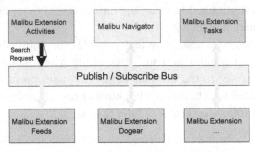

Figure 2. Malibu Publish / Subscribe infrastructure.

We designed Malibu to be extensible, i.e. developers can add new data sources and views to Malibu if the predefined set is not sufficient. Each Malibu extension implements the visual representation (view) and a search interface for tag-based retrieval that is registered with the Malibu Navigator component when the new Malibu extension is installed. In order to allow for a decoupling between the Malibu extensions (i.e. they do not need to know about one another), Malibu components communicate through an internal publish / subscribe system.

When a user executes a "Surf in Malibu" operation on an object in one of the Malibu views, the corresponding Malibu extension submits a search request to the publish / subscribe bus as illustrated in Figure 2 for the Activities Extension. The search request contains the metadata of the focus item: name, description, tags, and people information. Each Malibu extension can register with the Malibu Navigator to receive search requests from the internal publish / subscribe system. Malibu extensions receiving a search request, analyze the tags associated with the selected item, and conduct a tag-based search. Each Malibu extension can independently decide how to implement the search, e.g. whether or not to search the local cache versus issuing a request to a server, or both. Local search in our four out-of-the-box extensions is done through basic pattern matching of tags. The Dogear and the Activities plug-in also issue search requests directly to the servers of their data using REST APIs. Each Malibu extension updates its view with the search results ordered, for example, by recency of the item. The Malibu Navigator also receives the search request from the publish / subscribe bus and displays the search item as a focus item.

In the same way, Malibu is also aware of the identities of users (encoded in the search request), and extensions can conduct searches based on identity as well as on tags. For example, we added a buddy list context menu and a button into the

---

4   Tags are user-generated descriptive words or phrases that are, in general, visible to other users of a
     social bookmarking system such as del.icio.us (http://del.icio.us). For reviews, see Cameron et al.
     (2005); and Golder and Huberman (2006).

Sametime 7.5 chat window (see Figure 3) that allows users to trigger a "Surf in Malibu" action on their buddies. This also submits a search request to the publish / subscribe bus and Malibu extensions can perform a similar search on the buddy's identity, showing items related to the searched person. Future versions of Malibu may make use of tags that have been associated with users, e.g., through an enhanced directory service that allows one user to write tags to characterize another user (Farrell and Lau, 2006).

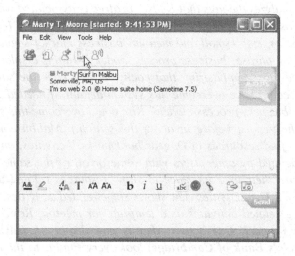

Figure 3. "Surf in Malibu" action integrated in the chat window.

The tag-based and people-centric search are designed to help address the representation gap by finding relevant resources across heterogeneous resource domains and by providing sufficient data to evaluate the relevance of each returned object through tag-comparisons with the "surfed" object.

Thus, in a simple sense, Malibu acts as a resource aggregator by collecting views of heterogeneous resources into a single user experience. In a more substantive sense, Malibu acts as a sophisticated resource aggregator by finding and displaying related and relevant resources through automated tag-based search leveraging common, social metadata of objects.

Scenario of Usage

The following usage scenario illustrates some core features and demonstrates how Malibu can be used to support activity-centric work.

Kim, the lead member of a customer care team, opens the Malibu *Board to start her day. The Activities view (B) shows her activities filtered by importance. Kim sees that there is a new collaborative activity named* **Roxy's Boxes of Roxbury**. *It is marked unread (bold) and shows up at the top of the activities list. Kim clicks on the activity and a details view slides out. Kim sees that the date of the* *activity was yesterday afternoon; and the creator was Kelly from sales. The description says "Roxy's Boxes of Roxbury needs a business process model". Kim knows that Kelly will expect to see Kim's responses and relevant resources added to that activity. Because Roxy's Boxes is an important customer, Kim knows that Kelly will be waiting anxiously for Kim's response.*

*Kim right-clicks on the **Roxy's Boxes** activity and chooses "Surf in Malibu" to find resources related to the **Roxy's Boxes of Roxbury** activity (i.e., an object pivot). Malibu analyzes the tags that Kelly has already associated with the **Roxy's Boxes** activity (as shown in Figure 1, these tags are "boston, bpm [business process model], custom, smb (small-and-medium business market segment], and the components of the phrase 'business process model'." In this display, Malibu has alphabetized the tags, emphasizing that each one will have the same weight in searches. Kelly could have overcome this system default, if needed, by hyphenating the phrase "business-process-model." Kim could overcome this system default by modifying the tag list before invoking the search.). Malibu conducts a tag-based search to find resources in Dogear bookmarks, Activities, and Feeds, that have been associated by other users with some or all of the same tags. Malibu views reconfigure their user interface to show resources related to the **Roxy's Boxes** activity (E). The Activities view shows some related activities. Kim hopes to use one of these related activities as a template for meeting Roxy's needs for a business process model. One activity that is now displayed, **Business Process Model for People's Bank of Cambridge,** looks very similar to the new Roxy assignment, and might contain useful modeling information. Kim right clicks on the **People's Bank of Cambridge** activity and selects "Create Task". A new task linked to that activity shows up in the task view and Kim renames it as **Evaluate usability of BPM for Roxy's**. Kim can use this task both as a memory aid and as a link to the resource that is the basis of the task.*

*An incoming chat from Mary interrupts Kim. Mary is asking for the planning documents for the "Pharma" project. Kim interrupts the current task, and the configuration of the Malibu board to support that task, confident that Malibu will be able to return to that configuration when the interruption is over. Kim right-clicks and surfs on Mary's name in the buddy list (i.e., a person pivot). Malibu views use information about Kim and Mary to reconfigure, now showing all activities that Kim shares with Mary. The activity **Pharma Customer Planning** appears in the list. Kim had previously finished the planning document that Mary was asking for, Kim drags the document from her desktop onto the **Pharma Customer Planning** activity. As a result of the drag operation, Malibu automatically uploads the document as a new object in the **Pharma Customer Planning** activity. Kim replies to Mary in the chat, informing her that the document is complete and now available in the activity.*

To recover from the interruption, Kim presses the back button. Malibu reconfigures into the pre-interruption state, showing Kim the context of her work before

Mary's interruption and the consequent reconfigurations that Kim had to make in order to work with Mary. Because Malibu preserves context, Kim can recover from Mary's interruption.

*Kim knows little about business process modeling in Roxy's business domain. She looks at the Dogear Bookmarks (C) and Feeds (D) views for related information. Kim notices a feed entry with a news article that could be interesting to all the members of her Roxy customer care team. She drags and drops the entry onto the **Roxy's Boxes of Roxbury** activity to share it with the team; Malibu creates a new object in that activity containing a link to the feed item. Kim also sees an interesting shared bookmark referring to a BPM tutorial she would like to look at later. She drags and drops the bookmark into the task view, creating a new task linked to bookmark. In this way, Kim prevents a self-interruption: She avoids having to read the BPM tutorial now, because she can create a link to it in a task that she can execute later. In the task view (A), Kim is reminded of the **Evaluate usability of BPM for Roxy's** task that she had created previously. She double-clicks on the task which opens up the activity the task is referring to.*

After reviewing the activity in the browser, she decides to take a new look at all her current activities. She presses the "home" button to restore overall work awareness again, clearing the previous focus on Roxy's. The Activities view shows all her activities newly filtered by importance, in keeping with updates and new resources that have been added since the last time Kim engaged in this overview.

Intended Benefits to End-Users

In summary we hoped that Malibu would improve knowledge workers' experiences in the following ways:

Issue 1. Representation Gap: Malibu should help users to view resources relevant to their current activity, even if those resources occur in diverse services or stores.

Issue 2. Metonymic Search: Malibu should support simple (one-click) operations to execute complex searches based on the attributes of an index item, across multiple services.

Issue 3. Recovery from Interruptions: Malibu should allow users to recover from interruptions by through a simple "back" operation to access previous searches and views. Also, Malibu's operation as a slide-out/slide-in sidebar should provide a useful peripheral display, providing and preserving work context when needed, but easily dismissed when not needed.

We explored these three issues in an eight-month field trial.

Malibu in Practice

We provided the Malibu client for download at an internal company website for early adopters of new technologies. Usage was entirely voluntary. As part of the installation procedure, we informed users that we would be collecting their data for study purposes. Users were at liberty to halt the installation if they did not want their data to be collected. The data reported in this paper come from a subset of the users who downloaded and installed the experimental Malibu client. The data were collected in three ways:

- Usage logs were automatically recorded from each user's client.
- Telephone interviews were conducted with thirteen users. A fourteenth interview was conducted via instant messaging, at the informant's request.
- A discussion database (internally called a "forum") was maintained for asynchronous dialogue among users and the members of the Malibu team. Ultimately, this database contained both informal comments, requests for assistance, and answers, and also a somewhat more organized survey process conducted by the company department that operates internal trials.

We will organize the presentation of results around themes, rather than around the sources of our data. We precede those results with a discussion of some of the issues in conducting this kind of large-scale, elective trial.

Description of the Sample

Offering Malibu for company-internal download by a diverse employee population was a good way to collect data and feedback, but it was also more difficult from a research perspective. Malibu was one of a large number of experimental plug-ins to the Sametime 7.5 instant messaging (IM) product, which was itself undergoing rapid beta-version development iterations during our trial. Company culture encouraged employees to download any and all of the plug-ins, whether or not the employee was using the services that were accessed through each plug-in. In order to filter out noise from users who had never used any of the services leveraged in Malibu, or one-time curious early adopters or beta testers, we focused our report of early experiences with Malibu on a subset of 57 users who participated in one or more of the services, and who made strong use of Malibu functionality.[5] We consider these 57 users to be representative of usage in the kind of "ideal case" that is often involved in the first usage of an experimental system – i.e., a small, carefully selected sample of users who have motivation to use the new system.

Our sample of log records from 57 employees included women and men from 16 countries. Most were not part of the research organization. Users' jobs and

---

5   We excluded logs from members of the Malibu team (authors of this paper plus two summer interns), because we didn't want to treat our testing protocols and/or demonstrations as if they were real usage.

roles ranged from sales and distribution, to service delivery, to operations management, to training, to market intelligence analysts, to a researcher, and a variety of information systems responsibilities (e.g., architect, developer, designer). Users' clients ranged from small and medium businesses up to US federal government contracts. Roughly 20% were in IBM's consulting organization Participants in the interviews were men and women from five countries, with a range of 0.5 to 20 years in the company, and a range of Malibu usage history of 1.5 to 8 months. Interviewees were chosen from the same pool as the employees whose logs we studied, so their backgrounds spanned a similar range. Comments in the forum were from a wide range of employees; the comments ranged in content from one-line "me too" messages to lengthy discussions of features and problems.

Issue 1: Addressing the Representation Gap

We designed Malibu to help users deal with resources scattered across multiple systems. One way to work on this issue was to examine how many times there was search content in more than one Malibu view for each of the 57 users. The lowest percentage of searches with content returned was 64.91 for the FeedsView. Thus, most of the views presented content most of the time. More than 70% of our sample received resources in at least two of the three views, and just over half of the sample received resources in all three views. On a statistical basis, there is evidence that Malibu was successful in reducing the representation gap for more than two thirds of our sample.

A second source of data about the representation gap came from interviews. While discussing "best" and "worst" features of Malibu, users spontaneously commented that

I use Malibu to level-set what I need to get done. I live and breathe in an interrupt-driven environment. I use Malibu to return me to sanity. About half the time I need to dive into the details of an activity or a task (business operations manager)

you could capture all the bits and pieces you are involved in… it's a good idea to have it captured somewhere, for future use or if an auditor walks in (procurement program manager)

Comparing Malibu with a similar web-based service, one user noted,

The level of integration among all the component [services], that plugged in this, is what gives it the edge. (communications manager)

Comments in the forum were convergent:

It is great because [of] the decision to integrate Malibu with [instant messaging] and Activities… (designer)

The concept "find everything related to the activity I'm working on ", is very powerful (business operations manager)

Users were also critical of aspects of these features. Several users argued that we had not completed the integration work: Malibu allows users to view and open *existing* activities, but

You can't actually create a new Activity from... Malibu... you have to create in the web inter-
face [to the Activities server], then refresh the Malibu UI to see it, and work with it. (business
operations manager)

We were particularly intrigued with the critique that

The collaboration capabilities of Activities are largely ignored in Malibu... Ideally, I'd like
to... PUSH those... results out to the members [of my team]... (business operations manager)

With regard to our first issue, Malibu has made some progress toward repairing
the representation gap. The statistical results from the log analysis demonstrated
that Malibu provides access to diverse resources from heterogeneous sources.
User remarks in interviews and in the online forum indicate that people found
those diverse resources useful. In some ways, the users understood our solution
better than we did, and recommended ways to extend our solution to the representation gap into new services and features.

Issue 2: Exploring Tag- Based Metonymic Search

Our second Issue was that it would be valuable for people to be able to select an
object and initiate a search across heterogeneous services for diverse objects similar to the selected object. We called this operation "metonymic search," because
the selected object was being used as a referent (a metonym) for its attributes.
Searching ("surfing") a unitary object (metonym) was equivalent to specifying all
the attributes of the object (tags), in searches in all of the available services. More
than 89% of the 57 users surfed on one or more persons, and over half of the sample surfed on Activities. About a quarter of the sample surfed on Dogear bookmarks, Feeds (some of which had tag or person metadata), or Tasks (which could
optionally have tag metadata). The number of objects returned from each service
was roughly proportional to the number of searches.

Crucially for part of our claim of metonymic search across diverse services,
surfing on each type of object produced results from at least two types of services.
Thus, the metadata from the surfed object was useful in finding resources not only
in the same type of service (e.g., surf an activity to find other activities), but also
in different types of services (e.g., surf an activity to find bookmarks and feeds).
In this way, metonymic search also helped to reduce the Representation gap (the
scatter of related resources across multiple services).

As in the previous section, the statistical results demonstrate that the data are
available to support tag-based metonymic search. The next question is whether
users experienced it that way.

Users' views on what was, to them, the "surf in Malibu" operation, were
mixed. Some users found the concept straightforward and obvious:

Once you get the hang of the 'surf in Malibu' concept, it begs to be used, and more impor-
tantly, applied to more and different data sources, such as emails, [IM] chat transcripts, Goo-
gle desktop, etc.etc.etc. (business operations manager)

Put an item in focus ["surf"], surfing [is] supposed to be able to provide things that are related, based on the thing you are pivoting on (developer)

Some users seemed less confident of the concept, or its utility;

Trying to figure out exactly how it was supposed to work was a problem. The desire to be able to have that right-click context-sensitivity was useful. (senior consultant)

And um the ability to see a filter – surfing in Malibu – that hasn't been – either I don't have enough in there... It doesn't seem to bring up anything of help yet.... I don't know where it's looking, maybe in the title... (sales executive)

About a quarter of the users were confident enough of their understanding of the tag-based search mechanism to critique it or their own practices:

Yeah that's the pivot thing. I think it works really well, but you need the tagging stuff to support it. (communications manager)

It only surfs by the tag associated with the activity. I'm trying to be more diligent about tagging things. (business operations manager)

Most disturbingly, some users considered surfing to return bad results:

I could IM [instant-message] somebody, and then I could open another window in which it would show me other activities or maybe something else associated with that person... [Surfing on objects] sometimes the relevance of what came back with – was questionable. (chief engineer, federal systems)

With regard to our second Issue, Malibu has made some progress toward a functional tag-based metonymic search, but there is clearly room for improvement. The statistical results from the log analysis demonstrated that Malibu is capable of retrieving resources via tag-based metonymic search. User remarks in interviews and in the online forum indicate that some people found the concept quite clear, and most users had at least an intuitive understanding that surfing would produce related resources. However, several users remain confused or "struggling" with the concept, and some users were not convinced that the resources returned by the search were relevant to the surfed object. Other research (Muller, 2007) has showed that there is relatively low overlap of vocabularies from one service to another, so we will be investigating multiple normalization strategies (e.g., lower-case normalization, stemming, prefix-removal, lexical lookups) with the hopes of increasing the number and relevance of returned objects. We also hope to add machine-learning methods to automate and improve the effectiveness of the search in the near future.

Issue 3: Recovering from Interruptions

Our third Issue was to support recovery from interruptions. We provided two features to address this problem, with two very different outcomes. First, we implemented the tag-based search feature as stack of searches. Users could navigate through previous states of the stack (and the contents of views that were produced by those states) with a simple "back" operation. In session logs, we coded this feature as a type of "focus" event – counted similarly to a focus (or pivot) on an object. The "back" operation was the most frequently observed focus event (768 events among 57 users, or 34%), with a focus on a person as the next most frequent focus event (654 events, or 29%). Users had few comments about this feature, other than to note that it worked, apparently as expected.

Our second feature for interruption recovery was to provide a peripheral display. We hoped that this feature would be allow users to preserving their work context *outside* of Malibu, as needed, because users could easily dismiss Malibu when it was not needed. We hoped that the gestural invocation (move the cursor to the edge of the screen) would help users differentiate between Malibu and conventional applications (typically invoked with a click or a command).

The log data show a very large number of event sequences in which the Malibu window slid out and then back in with no Malibu operations occurring between those two events. These data suggest that users may have invoked Malibu by accident, and then either dismissed it or waited for it to time-out and slide back into the screen border.

User comments confirmed that this was sometimes a problem:

The slide-out – at first I thought it was quite handy, but often out comes Malibu, and you start getting irritated... (procurement program manager)

You know the window, you can hide the window, but if you move your mouse cursor over a certain part of the screen, then the window appears ago [sic]. My intention was not to re-open the Malibu window, and so I stop now to use it. (information architect, whose first language was not English)

However, some users considered the slide-out/slide-in behavior to be an useful:

[it] runs in the background. I have it to be hiding, and then I bring up to kind of look at my bookmarks (business process developer, whose first language was not English).

It uses a bit of your brain that has peripheral vision, it's not the kind of thing that other [applications] on your desktop use very well. I can look at Malibu without having to open my feedreader. I need to stay aware of new things, because I'm in Communications... For me, picking up my feed when I'm popping into other stuff... When it broke, I was gutted.... I love the slideiness... (communications manager)

One user engaged in lengthy remote access to other machines. The "slide-in" feature of the client – a thin four-pixel bar at the side of the screen – persisted during the remote access, allowing the user to continue to use Malibu-accessed resources despite the fact that her/his current desktop view was of another machine. This user-based insight taught us that a peripheral display may provide two types of value: (a) allowing users to maintain/regain context in their own machines, and (b) allowing users to access their "home" (local) services while "remote desktopped into another machine," one informant added.

Earlier versions of Malibu included an option to run the client as a separate window. Some users remembered that feature, and asked us to restore it. Several of these users had dual monitors, and had developed practices that allowed them to treat one monitor as secondary, where they placed windows that functioned in a manner analogous to a peripheral display.

It appears that user reaction to our peripheral display feature was quite varied. For some users, it contributed to Malibu's success. For other users, it became a reason to stop using Malibu. We will probably return to providing options for operation as either a peripheral display or a stand-alone application.

Related Work

In addition to the large array of activity-related research we presented in the introduction of this paper, researchers have studied the usefulness of side bars for peripheral awareness in Side Show (Cadiz et al., 2002). Side Show evolved into a side bar for Microsoft Vista. Other similar products are DesktopSidebar (DesktopSidebar, n.d.), and Google Sidebar (Google, n.d.). These products focus on providing a side bar user interface framework for controlling and managing views. They do not provide tag-based or other forms of aggregated search across different data sources displayed.

Watson (Watson, n.d.) is a side-bar-like product that features automated search based on the active application on the desktop. Watson is an implicit query system that is similar to our notion of metonymic search in that it extracts key words from an object (e.g., a Word document) in focus. However, the keywords are neither social tags nor metadata, and the system sends queries via traditional search engines to find related information. Dashboard (Dashboard, n.d.) provides similar functionality. As the user reads email, browses the web, writes a document, or chats with friends, the system proactively finds objects that are relevant to the user's current desktop activity, and displays them in a separate window. Henzinger (Henzinger et al., 2005) tries to automatically find news articles on the web relevant to the ongoing stream of TV broadcast news. Their approach is to extract queries from the ongoing stream of closed captions, issue the queries in real time to a news search engine on the web, and present the top results to the user. All these implicit query systems do not leverage social tags to perform search, but rather automate the process of generating a query from content and submitting it to a search engine.

Social tags have become increasingly popular to organize and find information. Numerous systems on the Internet, -- e.g. Flickr (Cameron et al., 2006) or Delicious (Golder and Huberman, 2006), use tags as a way of managing information. However, tags are used only inside those repositories to manage a single content type. We leverage tags to search across repositories, and our search approach is metonymic, i.e. we implicitly use metadata of an object (tags) of interest to find related resources across data sources.

Conclusions and Next Steps

The Malibu Board was intended to help knowledge workers engaged in complex and intermixed collaborative activities. We outlined two particularly vexing problems: the scatter of relevant resources among multiple services, and the difficulty of searching for information relevant to the current item-of-interest.

We addressed the problem of scatter in our discussion of the representation gap. Malibu provides access to multiple stores of data and documents, and allows searching by using the attributes of other users, as well as of objects. Malibu thus provides a form of social navigation through complex information spaces, in the context of real-time social awareness via its IM environment. Statistical evidence from usage logs showed that Malibu often finds and displays resources from these multiple services, and users' comments showed that in general the combined information, in a social-awareness context, makes sense and is of value to users. The next steps are to explore the feasibility, utility, and desirability of the many extensions that users proposed to us. We will also enhance our use of person metadata from recent advances in person-tagging (Farrell & Lau, 2006).

We addressed the problem of search in complex, heterogeneous domains through a multi-service, tag-based re-implementation of the familiar "more like this" search user interface – we called this approach "metonymic search," because the item-of-interest (person or object) is used as a referent (metonym) for the attributes that are actually searched. This kind of pivoting from object to person and back again has become a strong feature in social software and social navigation: We hoped that our metonymic search could provide a more powerful basis for this emerging new socially-informed search paradigm. As we did with the representation gap analyses, we used two convergent types of evidence. We used statistical analysis of log data to show that our approach was technically feasible and functional, and we consulted with users to explore the utility and meaningfulness of our solution. User reaction ran from uncertainty to enthusiasm, with one user stating that "the 'surf in Malibu' concept... begs to be used, and more importantly, applied to more and different data sources"; this statement was repeated in the official internal evaluation of the experimental client.

Most of our users evidenced at least an intuitive understanding of the concept of tag-based search. In a subsequent experiment, we have exposed the tags associated with a surfed object for user inspection and manipulation. Early results show that users take the opportunity, when appropriate, to refine their search by selecting a subset of the tags of the surfed object. We have not been able to compare the quality of search that results from user-modification of the tag-list. At this stage, all we know is that the feature called "surf in Malibu" (tag-based metonymic search) does indeed make sense, and that users understand it well enough to want to adjust its parameters while using it.

Malibu also addressed the problem of preserving the context when users switch activities or during interruptions through a "back" operation to return to previous Malibu states, and through a peripheral sidebar user interface (the "Malibu board"). Users' reactions to this set of features were sharply divided. For the short-term, we are considering restoring the option to run Malibu as either a sidebar or a separate application. Over the longer term, we hope to conduct a more ethnographic study to understand how people use Malibu in situ, and to understand perhaps which settings or activities make sidebars more attractive to some users and stand-alone applications more attractive to others.

Acknowledgements

We thank all our anonymous users and the Lotus Activities product team for their support, and the ECSCW 2007 reviewers for their insightful recommendations.

References

Bardram, J.E. (2005): 'Activity-based computing — Lessons learned and open issues', Position paper at ECSCW 2005 workshop, *Activity — From a theoretical to a computational construct.* Paris, September, 2005.

Bellotti, V., Ducheneaut, N., Howard, M., and Smith, I. Taking email to task: The design and evaluation of a task management centered email tool. *Proc CHI 2003*, ACM, Ft Lauderdale, FL, USA, pp. 345-352.

Cadiz; J.J., Venolia, G.D., Jancke; G., Gupta, A. (2002): 'Designing and deploying an information awareness interface', *Proc. ACM CSCW 2002,* ACM, New Orleans, LA, USA, pp. 312-323.

Cameron, C., Naaman, M., boyd, d., & Davis, M. (2006): 'HT06, tagging paper, taxonomy, flickr, academic article, toread', *Proc. Hypertext 2006*, ACM, pp. 31-40.

Cutrell, E., Czerwinski, M., & Horvitz, E. (2001): 'Notification, disruption, and memory: Effects of messaging interruption on memory and performance', *Proc INTERACT 2001*, ICS press, Toyko, pp. 263-269.

Dashboard (n.d.): http://www.nat.org/dashboard/, retrieved 9/28/06.

DesktopSidebar (n.d.): http://www.desktopsidebar.com/index.html, retrieved: 9/28/06.

Ducheneaut, N., and Bellotti, V. (2001): 'E-mail as habitat: An exploration of embedded personal information management', *ACM interactions*, vol. 9, no. 5, 2001, pp. 30-38.

Egan, D.E., Remde,J.R., Gomez, L.M. Landauer, T.K., Eberhardt, J., and Lochbaum. C.C. (1989): 'Formative design evaluation of superbook', *ACM TOIS*, vol. 7 no. 1, January 1989, pp. 30-57.

Farrell, S., & Lau, T. (2006): 'Fringe contacts: People-tagging for the enterprise,' Workshop paper at WWW2006, Edinburgh, 2006.

Geyer, W., Muller, M.J., Moore, M., Wilcox, E., Cheng, L., Brownholtz, B., Hill, C.R., Millen, D.R. (2006): 'ActivityExplorer: Activity-Centric Collaboration from Research to Product', *IBM Systems Journal*, vol. 45 no. 4, 2006, pp. 713-738.

Geyer, W., Vogel, J., Cheng, L., Muller, M. (2003), 'Supporting Activity-Centric Collaboration through Peer-to-Peer Shared Objects,' *Proc. ACM Group 2003*, ACM, Sanibel Is., FL, USA, pp. 115-124.

Golder, S., & Huberman, B.A. (2006): 'Usage patterns of collaborative tagging systems', *J. Info Sci*, vol. 32, no. 2, pp. 198-208.

González, V., and Mark, G. Managing currents of work: Multi-tasking among multiple collaborations. Springer, Paris, *Proc ECSCW 2005*, Springer, Paris, pp. 143-162.

Google Desktop (n.d.): http://desktop.google.com/, retrieved 9/28/06.

Gwidzka, J. Reinventing the inbox — Supporting the management of pending tasks in email. *CHI 2002 Doctoral Consortium*, Minncapolis, 2002.

Halverson, C.A., Erickson, T., and Ackerman, M.S., (2004): 'Behind the help desk: Evolution of a knowledge management system in a large organization', *Proc CSCW 2004*, ACM, Chicago, pp. 304-313.

Henzinger, M., Chang, B. Milch, B., and Brin, S. (2005): 'Query-free news search', *World Wide Web*, 8(2):101–126, 2005.

Hudson, J.M., Christensen, J., Kellogg, W.A., & Erickson, T. (2002): '"I'd be overwhelmed, but it's just one more thing to do": Availability and interruption in research management', *Proc CHI 2002*, ACM, Minneapolis, pp. 97-104.

Iqbal, S.T., & Horvitz, E. (2007): 'Disruption and recovery of computing tasks: Field study, analysis, and directions, *Proc. CHI 2007*, San Jose, CA, USA, ACM, pp. 677-686.

Kaptelinin, V. (2003): 'UMEA: Translating interaction histories into project contexts', *Proc. ACM CHI 2003*, ACM, Ft Lauderdale, FL, USA, pp. 353-360.

McFarlane, D.C. (2002): 'The scope and importance of human interruption in human-computer interaction', *Human Computer Interaction*, vol. 17, no. 1, pp. 1-61.

Millen, D.R., Feinberg, J., Kerr, B. (2006): 'Dogear: Social bookmarking in the enterprise', *Proc CHI 2006*, Montreal, ACM, pp. 111-120.

Monk, C.A., Boehm-Davis, D.A., & Trafton, J.G. (2004): 'Very brief interruptions result in resumption cost', Poster at 26th Annual Cognitive Science Society meeting, Chicago, 2004.

Moran, T.P., Cozzi, A., and Farrell, S.P., 'Unified Activity Management: Supporting People in eBusiness,' *Communications of the ACM* **48**, No. 12, Special section on Semantic eBusiness Vision, 67–70 (December 2005).

Muller, M.J.: 'Patterns of tag usage across four diverse enterprise tagging services', paper at HCIC 2007, Winter Park, CO, USA, February 2007.

Muller, M.J., Geyer, W., Brownholtz, B., Wilcox, E., and Millen, D.R. (2004): 'One-hundred days in an activity-centric collaboration environment based on shared objects', *Proc. CHI 2004*, ACM, Vienna, pp. 375-382.

Sen, S., Geyer, W., Muller, M.J., Moore, M., Brownholtz, B., Wilcox, E., & Millen, D.R. (2006): 'FeedMe: A collaborative alert filtering system', *Proc. CSCW 2006*, ACM, Banff, Alberta, CA, pp. 89-98.

Sullivan, S. (2006): 'A generalized interruption manager', short paper submitted to CHI 2006, Montreal.

Watson (n.d.): http://www.intellext.com/, retrieved 09/28/06.

Whittaker, S. (2005): 'Supporting collaborative task management in email', *Human Computer Interaction 20*, 1&2, 49-88.

L. Bannon, I. Wagner, C. Gutwin, R. Harper, and K. Schmidt (eds.).
ECSCW'07: Proceedings of the Tenth European Conference on Computer Supported Cooperative Work, 24-28 September 2007, Limerick, Ireland
© Springer 2007$

The Distributed Work of Local Action: Interaction amongst virtually collocated research teams

Dylan Tutt[1], Jon Hindmarsh[1], Muneeb Shaukat[2] and Mike Fraser[2]

[1]Work, Interaction & Technology Research Centre, Dept. of Management, King's College London, London, SE1 9NH. U.K. *{dylan.tutt; jon.hindmarsh}@kcl.ac.uk*
[2]Department of Computer Science, University of Bristol, Merchant Venturers Building, Bristol, BS8 1UB. U.K. *{muneeb; fraser}@cs.bris.ac.uk*

Abstract. Existing research on synchronous remote working in CSCW has highlighted the troubles that can arise because actions at one site are (partially) unavailable to remote colleagues. Such 'local action' is routinely characterised as a nuisance, a distraction, subordinate and the like. This paper explores interconnections between 'local action' and 'distributed work' in the case of a research team virtually collocated through 'MiMeG'. MiMeG is an e-Social Science tool that facilitates 'distributed data sessions' in which social scientists are able to remotely collaborate on the real-time analysis of video data. The data are visible and controllable in a shared workspace and participants are additionally connected via audio conferencing. The findings reveal that whilst the (partial) unavailability of local action is at times problematic, it is also used as a resource for coordinating work. The paper considers how local action is interactionally managed in distributed data sessions and concludes by outlining implications of the analysis for the design and study of technologies to support group-to-group collaboration.

Introduction

Over recent years we have witnessed the emergence of what have been termed "collaboratories"; formal collaborations between distributed research laboratories or groups that are connected via communications technologies. There is significant encouragement (through funding and other means) for inter-institutional research teams to be distributed nationally and internationally. However, time, monetary and scheduling constraints restrict opportunities for research teams to congregate, to engage in research meetings and to collaborate on the analysis of data. Therefore there is a strong demand for systems and technologies to support virtually collocated research meetings. A particular challenge in the development of the collaboratory, then, centres on an obdurate problem in the development of CSCW systems – namely designing effective support for *synchronous* collaboration over and around common documents, objects and datasets.

Whilst "collaboratories" are primarily considered in relation to research in the natural sciences they are equally relevant to social scientific research. This paper explores one case concerning the use of new tools to support the real-time analysis of video data amongst distributed social scientific research teams. The tool they use, MiMeG, is designed to support a common practice for social science research communities engaged in video analysis - the 'data session'. In standard data sessions multiple individuals meet to view, comment on and collaboratively analyse video data. Thus, MiMeG is attempting to support 'distributed data sessions', where groups of geographically remote researchers can view video data simultaneously and conduct meaningful analytic work with those data.

The technical development of the MiMeG software has been introduced in an earlier paper (see Fraser et al., 2006) but here we discuss how it is used in practice to support the collaborative analysis of video data. In doing so, the paper highlights an issue rarely given serious consideration in the existing CSCW literatures on synchronous remote working – the organisation of 'local action'. Often studies report *that* action occurs at one site which is hidden from remote colleagues. However such action is generally treated as incidental, peripheral, disruptive, problematic or otherwise a distraction to the main business of a virtually collocated meeting. Few studies have focused on its interactional organisation in any detail. What is particularly interesting in this case is that, in contrast to other studies, it is not straightforwardly problematic and indeed at times is used as a resource by members of the research team to coordinate the business of the distributed group as a whole.

Remote Working & Virtually-Collocated Teams

There is a great deal of research in CSCW and cognate disciplines that highlights how remote working is a poor cousin to face-to-face meetings. Indeed physical collocation is usually considered "the gold standard of work environments" (Hinds & Kiesler, 2002: 56) and numerous studies powerfully reveal our "compulsion for proximity" (Boden & Molotch, 1994) and how "distance matters (Olson & Olson, 2000). However there is significant and increasing demand for various forms of virtual collocation and within CSCW there is a long-standing tradition of developing and evaluating systems to support synchronous remote working, from groupware through to various forms of media space and collaborative virtual environment. A common concern for many of these systems has been an attempt to support group meetings focused on and around documents, objects and other media.

Studies of these technologies in use often highlight the lack of interactional cues available to remote participants and the difficulties that arise as a result. In particular they note how the bodily and material contexts of actions are 'hidden' from remote participants leading to a range of troubles for participants to assess the sense and significance of those actions. Cursor movements, avatar actions or even displays of conduct on video are somehow, and in various ways, disembodied and disembedded. Thus action at one site ('local action') is unavailable to remote participants and is disconnected from the work of the group as a whole.

The focus for many of these studies has been on systems that support collaboration between two or more *individuals* distributed across workplaces (Mark et al., 2003). However there is a growing demand for groups to be virtually connected to other groups, especially (but by no means exclusively) within research communities.

Studies of group-to-group collaboration also discuss how the lack of access to local action at remote sites is problematic in various, although somewhat different, ways. For example Olson & Olson (2000: 147) suggest that in co-present team meetings "[p]articularly important is the spatiality of human interaction ... If a team member wants to observe his manager's reaction to a point someone made he can just glance quickly in her direction", whereas in virtual meetings this is not possible. In studies of virtually collocated, interdisciplinary teams at Boeing, Mark et al. (1999) found that participants had difficulty identifying who was talking over the audio conferencing link and that they were distracted by parallel activities that they undertook whilst attending the meeting. Ruhleder (2000) has also argued that the interactional demands in local sites can distract from the mediated communication. Aoki et al. (2003) dismissed 'casual conversation' in local sites as incidental to the business of the meeting. Sonnenwald et al. (2002: 125) also consider local action to be peripheral, as they report that it has become common practice in videoconferences for participants to "cover the microphone closest to them" to mute or muffle talk and action that may be heard at other locations "including whispers or side comments, munching on chips, sneezes and page turning".

Furthermore it is argued that asymmetries in access to local action can lead to the formation of 'sides' in distributed groups. Bos et al. (2004, 2006) pay careful attention to the dynamics of 'partially distributed groups' in which some participants are collocated while other individuals join in remotely. They show how participants "experienced 'collocation blindness' and failed to pay enough attention to collaborators outside of the room" (Bos et al., 2006: 1313) and have argued that distributed teams tend to form subgroup identities based on their shared physical location, where people typically enjoy more interaction and share more information with each other than they do with remote partners and even begin exhibiting in-group behaviours (Bos et al., 2004).

So, the widespread research on remote working and virtually collocated teams reveals how the unavailability or partial availability of 'local action' at remote sites is treated as incidental or straightforwardly problematic (a nuisance, a distraction, etc.) or leads to undesirable conduct (e.g. the development of in-group behaviours). However none of these studies takes the interactional organisation of local action as a topic of inquiry in its own right or explores the wider range of ways in which 'local action' bears upon 'distributed work'. Our studies of the use of MiMeG to support distributed research teams provides opportunities to begin to treat these issues seriously.

The System: MiMeG

Within the social sciences, many researchers working with video materials recognise the value of being able to share, show and discuss data with others. One dominant means for doing this is the 'data session', where colleagues and peers congregate to view and collaboratively analyse video data. This enables participants to explore tentative formulations and analyses and to receive immediate comment, contribution and feedback from colleagues in relation to their data. Participants can range in number from a minimum of two to a quite sizeable small group, of possibly up to twenty or so – although beyond that the dynamics transform significantly. The data session can be relatively formally structured with an introduction to the data, the viewing of the data, time for participants to make notes and subsequently opportunities for each participant to make comments. Alternatively someone can just start the video and anyone can ask questions or raise issues. Whilst data sessions may vary in form, they are common activities for many in the video analytic research communities of sociology, psychology, education, anthropology, linguistics, geography, CSCW, HCI and more.

As mentioned earlier, there is increasing support for inter-institutional national and international research projects, consortia and networks. As a result there is growing demand for technologies to support 'distributed data sessions', where remote participants can see, discuss and collaboratively analyse video data in real-time. MiMeG is a preliminary attempt to do this and it enables members of a research team located at two or more sites to simultaneously watch and discuss fragments of video data. Note that it is not intended to replace face-to-face meetings – indeed there is evidence to suggest that tools for remote collaboration tend to work better if participants do meet up regularly aside from their virtual meetings (Olson & Olson, 2000). However there is demand for such systems to *supplement* existing face-to-face meetings.

The design of the system (for more detail, see Fraser et al. 2006) was founded on an understanding that the visibility and control of video data is central to the data session. There are of course many systems designed to support distributed co-working on different media, however the support for work on video materials is rather primitive. Therefore the system ensures that high quality video is played simultaneously at all sites. There is no built-in video view of the other group(s) as we wanted to begin with a system that distributed the data coherently. Indeed recent studies have shown that, especially for visually complex tasks in which the focus of attention changes frequently (such as identifying and orientating to features in video data), a shared view of the 'task space' is essential, and can be more useful than a limited view of the 'person space' afforded by traditional videoconferences (see Kraut et al., 2002). The research team is however connected via Skype (free audio conferencing software) and whilst Skype can provide a basic video conferencing link, early trials indicated that it provides too basic an image of other sites for it to add value.

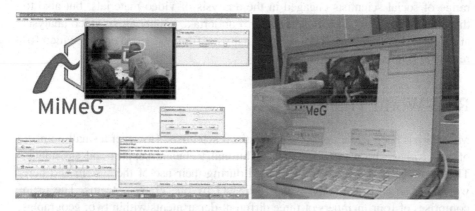

Figure 1: The Interface includes video windows, playback controls, annotation controls and windows for other media (transcripts, images, etc.). The system can be used with computer screen and mouse or projection screen and pen-based input.

The repeated playback of a video fragment is a routine practice in data sessions, whether to help participants become familiar with the sequence of actions in the data, or for more focused, finer grained video analysis. Therefore a range of controls for playback is available. Playback controls rest at a single site, although participants can choose to formally pass control to other sites.

Another key concern in design was to support participants in indicating features in the video. One of the major activities in data sessions generally is that participants encourage colleagues to notice phenomena on screen. This then forms the basis for analytic discussions regarding the significance of those phenomena. As video is not static (unless on freeze frame), the phenomena to be discussed are fleeting – they may only appear on screen for a second or less. A glance, a gesture, a nod, a movement of a pen, a stroke on a keyboard or whatever are difficult enough for an individual to *spot* on video, let alone to reveal to others. Thus there can be substantial coordination work involved in getting a group of others with different viewpoints in the room to see some action on screen. Therefore MiMeG enables all sites to *annotate* the video stream in real time by drawing on it using mouse or pen input – these annotations appear on all screens simultaneously. Annotations can be added whilst the video rests on a single frame or indeed during playback.

Data sessions also routinely involve additional media, such as transcripts of talk, images, photographs, etc. Transcripts in particular tend to form a fundamental resource for participants to locate interesting features in the data. As a result, MiMeG enables all sites to display common additional media. Furthermore it allows transcripts to be time-stamped so that participants can navigate the video clips using the transcript that they have produced.

The development of this system will potentially be of value not only to the range of social scientists engaged in the analysis of video materials, but also to the broader range of practitioners keen to undertake collaborative video analysis at distance – for example, performance analysts, film and video editors, video forensics specialists and the like.

Real-World Trials

MiMeG has been widely distributed to social scientists. However a small number of groups have been provided with additional technical support and assistance. These groups have agreed to be studied during their use of the system and here we report on early experiences with MiMeG by one of these teams. The team comprises of four members of three different departments within two, geographically remote UK universities. In the past, members of the team regularly met for informal data sessions. However in the present context they are collaborating on a funded research project concerned with car sharing. They have collected a large corpus of audio-visual recordings of action and interaction in cars and regularly hold data sessions in which they explore issues concerning way-finding, instruction-giving, domestic routines and the like. They are interested in using MiMeG for two key reasons: firstly it would enable them to continue to hold data sessions when one or more of the team is visiting a more remote third institution for a significant period (which is often the case); and secondly it would provide opportunities for more ad-hoc, unplanned, less time consuming data sessions to discuss specific issues that arise during data analysis by an individual team member.

We recorded two one-hour distributed data sessions. As the participants already know each other well they can be seen as a "gelled social group" (Aoki et al., 2003). This situation can be placed in contrast to experimental groups brought together for a trial, or established groups facing a work task in which the system might be viewed to be of dubious benefit to them. This case provided a highly relevant test of the technology. The research team was engaged in a meaningful data session, on real project issues, and where the team were keen to adopt the system more generally. For comparative purposes we recorded a regular, co-present data session involving this team as well as a number of co-present data sessions with other similar research groups.

We video-recorded the distributed data sessions by using two camcorders at either site – one to depict the participants clearly and the other to display a close-up image of the on-screen activity. We obtained written consent from all participants for the presentation of the data in this paper, although we decided to give them pseudonyms. In working with the data we adopted an analytic approach common to CSCW, namely video-based field studies informed by ethnomethodology and conversation analysis (e.g. Heath and Luff, 2000). In analysing the use of the technology the concern should not be seen as a traditional evaluation of the system properties or functionality. Rather we are attempting to explicate the interactional practices that emerge in managing the technology in use. Our understanding of these practices is intended to stimulate further issues for research and to inform the design of future technologies.

Local Action as 'Side Work'

Numerous studies of distributed collaborative work have described the nature of action at one site that is (at least partially) unavailable to remote colleagues. However such actions are usually dismissed as being off topic or incidental (Aoki et al., 2003) or a distraction from the core meeting activities (Ruhleder, 2000). Within the distributed data sessions under consideration, there were numerous instances of such 'local action', action that fell beneath the remote site's horizon of notice. However on close inspection such action can *at times* be seen to be a central resource for the coordination of the distributed team's work.

Consider the following example from a distributed data session involving the research team. Eddie and Ivor are based in one UK city (Site 1) and their colleagues Ben and Henry are in another UK city (Site 2). In **Fragment 1**, the two sites are tackling a common problem that emerged in our early trials with MiMeG – that is establishing whether or not the video playback is running in unison at each site. This is in order to ensure that they are discussing the same part of the scene. As the fragment begins Eddie asks about the positioning of the traffic in the paused video as a means of assessing video alignment (L.1-3).

After asking Ben about the relative positioning of the car and the van on their screen in Site 2, Eddie (to the right of Image 1.1, partly obscured) moves on to describe what can be seen at Site 1 (L. 9-13). As he does this, Ivor leans in towards the screen and alongside Eddie and slowly extends his right arm, holding his pen as a pointer (during the word "overlapping", L.12). The gesture arrives at the playback control window on the screen during Eddie's stretching of the word "by:::" (L.12), but does not intrude on Eddie's view of the video window. Eddie is therefore made aware of Ivor's upcoming contribution, but is able to describe the scene in the video window, without having his view obscured or his account otherwise disrupted by Ivor's gesture.

Fragment 1 (Bold in the transcript marks the line where the image occurs)

```
1  Eddie:  and in yours is- are the
2          van and the car right
3          beside each other?
4  Ben:    er (.) no:: the van's behind
5          the car
6  Eddie:  by a ↑lot?
7          (0.9)
8  Henry:  er- fifteen ↑feet
9  Eddie:  we've got them (.) pretty
10         much parallel (.) in
11         fact the van's (0.4)
12         overlapping by::: one or
13         two foot probably
14 Ivor:   °the code reads°
15 Eddie:  erm (.) our time code
16         ends 06↑4
```

Image 1.1 (L.14)

At the end of Eddie's utterance, Ivor moves his pen to the time code in the playback window and, as Eddie looks down, Ivor slides the pen across the scale and suggests that Eddie use the time code to specify the paused video frame. Spoken softly with his head tilted close to Eddie, Ivor's utterance "the time code reads" is designed to be heard locally and not remotely. Eddie subsequently reads out the code for their remote colleagues in order to assess the extent of the video misalignment by comparing frame numbers.

There are three points to raise here. Firstly, Ivor's actions are designed explicitly for his local colleague – the gesture is invisible remotely and his talk is very softly spoken so that he cannot be heard by the others. Secondly, his action is delicately coordinated such that it does not disrupt Eddie's talk to the remote site. Thirdly, it is designed to *contribute*, to support and not to distract from the general activities of the data session. It is not peripheral to the business at hand, but rather very much on topic. Ivor not only encourages Eddie to notice the time code, but to elaborate on his description and announce the accompanying time code to the remote site.

This sort of 'side work' at local sites is a fairly common feature in our data. Consider **Fragment 2,** which is a further example of how side work contributes to the meeting as a whole. Here, with the same arrangements of participants, Henry faces the problem of getting others (at both the local and remote sites) to see something that he has noticed in the video data – in particular evidence of 'no entry' to a particular side street. The research team is studying a car journey through a city and at this time they are interested in the organisation of directions given by one passenger. Eddie (at Site 1) questions how Henry (at Site 2) knows that there is 'no entry' to a road in the route under examination. Henry and Ben (both at Site 2) look for evidence in the video.

Fragment 2

```
1  → Henry:   that was it there I think
2    Ben:     °oh was it
3    Henry:   yep
4             (3.1)
5    Henry:   we're just going back a bit
6             (3.8)
7    Henry:   °mark it on the screen°
8             (0.8)
9    Ben:     where ↑is it?
10   Eddie:   yeah so there's right hand turn markings on the
11            road there
12            (0.4)
13 → Henry:   °back a bit°
14   Ben:     Henry thinks he can see it °but I'm no(t)°
15   Eddie:   yeah there's a (.) you- there's markings ↑on the
16            road (1.9) so you can do a right turn
17            (1.1)
18   Henry:   there
19   Ben:     have we ↑missed it have we h[ere?
20   Henry:                              [no no:: (.) that's
21            just coming up
```

In data sessions, participants are routinely called upon to ground their analytic claims in observable evidence in the video data. Therefore much of the work of data sessions involves getting others to see such evidence. This often involves the rewinding, pausing and playing of the fragment at moments relevant to the observation being made. This is complicated considerably when the phenomena being pointed out are in the moving video rather than a paused image and thus may only be on screen for a moment or two.

In this case, the matter is further complicated as the data are from a moving vehicle and they are trying to spot something at the side of the road – thus it is at a distance from the camcorder (therefore small) and only visible momentarily (as the car passes by). When Ben plays the clip, Henry leans in to the screen to prepare to spot and point out evidence of 'no entry'. Moments later he reaches out and points to the laptop screen – an action only available to Ben in the local site. As he points, Henry leans towards Ben and quietly says to him: "that was it there I think" (L.1). This is only available locally and the participants at the other site display no orientation to the utterance to indicate that it was audible to them. However at the local site Ben's hand immediately moves to the playback controls to rewind the fragment, thereby displaying his understanding that the relevant moment in the video has passed.

Once that section of the clip begins to play again (L.6), Henry promptly points towards the screen (Image 2.1) and softly suggests that Ben "mark it on the screen". However this time Ben keeps the video playing. Indeed he asks quietly "where ↑is it?". At this moment, having drawn back his pointing gesture a little (Image 2.2), Henry transforms the poised finger into a more substantial and cruder backwards-thumbing gesture to request rewinding (Image 2.3). This 'hitch-hiking' hand gesture suggests a sizeable rewinding required from Ben, and that the phenomenon is well past. Ben immediately pauses the clip before rewinding it. Much of this co-occurs with Eddie's comments in lines 10-11. Thus they are able to re-position the video without interrupting him.

Image 2.1 (L.7)   Image 2.2 (L.8)   Image 2.3 (L.11)

When the clip begins to play for a third time, Henry again points firmly towards the screen. Of particular note here is that as Ben continues to let the clip play, Henry's pointing finger starts to slide to the right of the screen as if to mark how the feature (the 'no entry' sign) is passing off screen. So, Henry transforms his referential practice into a representational gesture that 'marks up' a virtual route extending out of the screen. His finger indicates where the feature is going if the route could be seen trailing off screen. Indeed Ben treats it as if the phenomenon has gone off screen – he stops the video immediately and says "have we ↑missed it have we here?", but he is assured that it is still on screen.

This fragment reveals how side work rests upon the rich interactional resources available to co-present colleagues. The visibility of subtle and delicate gestures and movements facilitate the close coordination of conduct. These are of course unavailable to remote sites. However, crucially the side work is organised in parallel and in between contributions to the group as a whole. In Aoki et al's (2006: 398) discussion of 'aside' turn types, local talk in remote sessions is described as the production of a "turn in a soft voice (especially when produced in overlap) [which] targets the action towards people who are not attending to the main conversation as primary participants". However these fragments show that side work is not an "aside" to the meeting but rather conduct that contributes to the very core of the business at hand. Thus local action and distributed work in these distributed data sessions are deeply co-implicated.

Revealing Local Action

Often within these distributed data sessions, aspects of local action are explicitly announced or revealed to the remote site. That is to say, participants somehow describe or narrate what is unavailable remotely. The following fragments allow us to explore when and how these announcements are produced and how they are orientated to by participants at remote sites. Consider, for example, the previous fragment, **Fragment 2.** Both Henry and Ben produce accounts of their side work at certain moments. Their local action is only partially available to Eddie and Ivor. It is partially available as they are able to see that the video is jumping around and at times playing, but they cannot see the delicate embodied work of Henry's instructions and Ben's control of the playback.

At two moments Henry and then Ben reveal the nature of their side work. The first (L.5) follows a 3.1 second pause in talk, during which the video is stopped and jerks through a couple of still frames as Ben rewinds it. Henry accounts for the movements of the video when he explains that "we're just going back a bit". As with most turns in these data sessions the recipients are clear (indeed few problems regarding the intended recipient for a turn emerge in our data). The turn is designed for the remote audience. Henry leans towards the microphone and employs the pronoun "we" to mark out his local 'side', thereby further identifying the remote site as addressees. Its production at this moment accounts for the ongoing pause in the discussion and the movements of the video playback.

The second instance (L.14) comes moments after a comment from Eddie. Neither Henry nor Ben attend to Eddie's turn immediately. However after a pause, and quiet local instruction from Henry, Ben starts to rewind the clip again. He says "Henry thinks he can see it °but I'm no(t) °", again revealing that they are engaged in ongoing side work to position the video clip. It accounts both for the visible rewinding of the clip and for the lack of response to Eddie's turn. However, in contrast to the previous instance, the design of the turn seems to mark this as Henry's perspective.

The next fragment shows how the activity of revealing local action may not necessarily take the form of a clear announcement in talk. Rather this one takes the form of a 'response cry' (Goffman, 1981). In **Fragment 3**, Ben and Henry are based at one site, while Eddie is the sole 'full' participant at his respective site. However, also in Eddie's room is Muneeb who is providing technical support on the use of MiMeG. He joins the action because Eddie experiences problems manipulating the video. The fragment begins with Ben introducing a new line of inquiry, which focuses on one particular utterance ("now we've got a problem") spoken by one of the people in their data. In response to this new topic (L.1-4), Eddie, who has the playback controls, starts to try to find that point in the video.

Fragment 3

```
1    Ben:    so erm (.) I >don't know if I've said this before<
2            but one thing I've been thinking about was the
3            (0.2) we've got a ↑problem >now we've got a
4            problem< line
5            (1.2)
6    Eddie:  yea↑h
7    Ben:    do you know where that ↑is?
8            (1.1)
9    Eddie:  yep hold on
10           (4.2)
11   Henry:  °you mean in the sense of [how does it become a=
12   Muneeb:                           [drag it
13   Henry:  =a problem?°
14   Eddie:  do I have to drag it
15   Ben:    no [I was thinking of just [what was the guy
16   Muneeb:    [ye↓ah
17→  Eddie:                             [↑tsh hhh
18   Ben:    doing (.) wi[th hh.
19→  Eddie:              [URGH↑hhh::
20   Ben:    wi[th ha::
21   Henry:    [ha hhh
22           (1.9)
23   Ben:    with that line and her reaction to it
24   Eddie:  er:: I think it's ↑here
```

| Image 3.1 (L.3) | Image 3.2 (L.5) | Image 3.3 (L.19) |

In data sessions, someone quoting a line in a transcript often initiates new topics. They may raise an analytic puzzle for others to explore or simply express interest in the utterance design. However it will routinely lead to that part of the video being played (and replayed) for analysis. In this case, after Ben quotes one line from their transcript, Eddie starts to search for the relevant part of the video. He first turns away from the screen to the paper transcript on the desk to his left in order to find the relevant line of transcribed talk (Images 3.1-3.2). This will be used to help locate the right position in the video fragment. This takes place during the 1.2 second pause (L.5) in which Eddie's activity is unavailable or observable to Ben and Henry. When Eddie says "yea↑h", the higher intonation at the end of the utterance works to request more from Ben, who then asks explicitly "do you know where that ↑is?" (L.7). As Ben cannot see that Eddie is looking for it, this maybe raises uncertainty about how he is participating during these moments.

Eddie's next utterance ("yep hold on", L.9) reveals to the remote site that he is engaged in the task and 'buys' him some time to find the relevant part of the video. Whilst Eddie tries to work the system, the video remains static at the remote site. However Muneeb, in the room with Eddie, notices his difficulties with the controls and advises him to "drag it" (L.13).

As Eddie repeatedly fails to 'drag' the bar on the playback controls, he produces two "response cries" (Goffman, 1981) which interrupt a comment by Ben (L.17: "↑tsh hhh"; L.19: "URGH↑hhh::"). Goffman defined response cries as "exclamatory interjections which are not fully-fledged words. *Oops!* is an example", which display "evidence of the alignment we take to events" (Goffman, 1981: 99-100). In this case, considering that the task involves the movement of a finger across a laptop touchpad, rather than one demanding physical exertion, the second cry (Image 3.3) is somewhat overstated. However this 'strain grunt' demonstrates his difficulty in operationalising Muneeb's prior suggestion to "drag it" and more generally reveals problems in working the system to the remote site. Thus it reveals problems to both the local audience (Muneeb) and the remote audience (Ben and Henry).

Ben and Henry's laughter acknowledges the trouble (L. 20-21) and Ben pauses for a while before completing his turn (L. 23) – indeed Goffman argues that these cries serve as "a warning that at the moment nothing else can claim our concern" (Goffman, 1981:105). Thus Eddie's 'strain grunt' both interrupts Ben's turn and simultaneously accounts for the interruption, by alerting the remote site to the extent of, and his preoccupation with, local problems.

Revealing local action to the remote site at opportune moments is significant to the success of the distributed data session. In particular, these moments when participants announce, describe or otherwise reveal key aspects of their local action often follow, or are produced, during pauses in conduct. Revealing the character of local action often indicates that a moment or two is needed before they can resume with the distributed work of the research team (cf. Hindmarsh et al., 2000). They are timed and designed to do this work. Another example we have is when a participant leaves the room. This is not announced immediately but rather timed and designed with regard to practical issues at hand. It only comes to light after the end of an ongoing turn and a pause where the absence of the other may be accountable. As much of the local action in these clips is partially available to remote colleagues through the video playback, participants render visible the hidden work that makes sense of the movement of video on display. However it is of course not only about revealing what can be seen at this moment, but informing remote colleagues of what can be expected in the moments to come. Thus local action is revealed to support the smooth coordination of the distributed work.

Tag Work: Re-working local action

In these distributed data sessions, there are a number of examples in which local actions are *re-worked* to be made available to the distributed team as a whole. There is not an explicit description or announcement of local action, as with the activities of revealing local action, but rather the utterances are built upon and re-designed in subsequent contributions to the data session. We term this 'tag work' as it usually takes the form of one person taking on or building up the local action of a co-present colleague.

As an illustration, consider **Fragment 4**, from a data session involving Ben and Henry at one site, with Eddie at the other. We join the action after a long 10.4 second pause. The team has been discussing the 'duties' of the driver to the passenger during a journey. Following the pause, Ben quietly quotes an utterance spoken in their video data – "I just need to get to the bottom of this" (L.1) – which is only hearable at the local site.

Fragment 4

```
1    Ben:    °I just need to get to the bottom of this:°
2            (3.0)
3→   Henry:  I suppose there in that statement too about I just
4            need to get the- to the bottom of this there's
5            also a sense in which (.) it will be her: that
6            takes over the task once again once they've- when
7            they've arr↑ived (.) you know that (.) th[at
8    Eddie:                                            [that's
9            nice
```

Towards the end of the long pause Ben sits back, strokes his forehead and raises his eyebrows (Image 4.1). This embodied display of 'thinking' or 'pondering' is accompanied by the quote from the data, which is only clearly audible to Henry. Eddie, at the remote site, cannot be seen to acknowledge or in any way display having heard this utterance, and from our recordings it seems that it only comes across faintly as muffled talk. It is clear that the turn is not designed to *demand* response from any party, but it does offer opportunities to take it up, especially to Henry.

Of particular interest here is the way in which Henry *re-works* the turn moments later ("I suppose there in that statement too", L.3). Essentially Ben's quote encourages Henry to pursue this line of analytic inquiry. As such Ben's local talk is 'picked up' and transformed by Henry. He uses the fact that the talk was clearly hearable to him to proffer an analysis of the utterance to which Ben is referring. However his comments are not just designed for Ben (in the form of side work), but are rather re-directed to the whole research team.

He does not look at Ben, but rather turns towards the screen and microphone, and makes his talk clearly audible remotely by raising his voice (Image 4.2). In doing so he orients to the team as a whole, rather than simply the colleague alongside him. Talking more loudly and leaning towards the microphone ensures that the remote site can hear. This is a common trend in our data and interestingly 'general' talk seems to have the flavour of addressing the remote site as opposed to the local site. So, in this case, Henry transforms the audience for, and potential participants to, the comments.

Image 4.1 (L.1)   **Image 4.2** (L.7)   **Image 4.3** (Beyond transcript)

His vocal stress on the words "there" and "too" acts as key building blocks in the transformative activity. They position Henry's talk as not designed to display a *new* point, but rather to display that it is built on, and is adding to, a prior. Furthermore, by repeating Ben's quote "I just need to get to the bottom of this" Henry reveals uncertainty as to whether Eddie will have heard Ben's talk. By integrating the quote into his new contribution, it ensures that whether or not Eddie has heard Ben's turn, he will still understand his comments. So the turn *does not require* that the prior has been heard to be made sense of, and yet it very much builds on and attends to that prior.

After he receives positive alignment from Eddie ("that's nice", L.8-9), Henry turns to face Ben (Image 4.3) while continuing with his tentative analysis of the utterance originally quoted by Ben. In doing this Henry then draws a series of nods from Ben. This local action, which is unavailable to the remote site, provides visible alignment to (parts of) Henry's analysis and encourages him to continue.

Local action can also be re-worked for the remote site through the shared MiMeG workspace. Consider how **Fragment 2** continues beyond the point that we previously discussed. Once Ben and Henry reach a frame of the video that features the relevant side road, Ben's draws on the frame, using the annotation tool, to ask Henry whether the sign on-screen is the no entry sign that he is looking for. Prior to this point, Henry had been gesturing over the screen – gestures that were not available to Eddie and Ivor. However Ben's annotation crucially transforms the audience by making it available to the remote site through the shared workspace (Image 2.4).

Fragment 2 con't

```
19   Ben:    have we ↑missed it have we h[ere?
20   Henry:                              [No no:: (.) that's
21           just coming up
22→ Ben:    about there?
```

```
23          (2.2)
24  Henry:  think [so
25  Eddie:        [erm (.) you've got the guy on our monitor
```

Image 2.4   **Image 2.5**

During "No no:: (.) that's just coming" (L.20-21), Henry holds a pointing gesture still while Ben scrolls the cursor arrow up to an on-screen location. He starts
to draw a red circle at the no-entry road and Henry pulls back his pointing finger.
Once the annotation is complete, Ben asks Henry "about there?". While the annotation tool features in the discussion between Ben and Henry to clarify a feature
locally, it renders previously unavailable features of that discussion available to
the remote site for their scrutiny. Thus Ben 'builds on' Henry's pointing gestures
and adds to them by specifying them on screen.

Interestingly it is only when the annotation is committed to the video stream
that a problem with video alignment between the two sites is revealed. Ben's data
mark-up appears a sizeable distance from the relevant feature on the remote
screen ("erm (.) you've got the guy on our monitor"). Unbeknown to the other,
each site had set their video window to a different size during the course of the
data session, which caused the annotation to mark up different parts of the scene
across the sites (Image 2.5). The extent of the misalignment is revealed across
sites as the teams set about circling the heads of the subjects in the video stream.

So 'tag work' involves the transformation of locally available conduct,
whether purely vocal or additionally non-vocal, to make it available to the distributed team as a whole. As we have seen, this transformation can be undertaken
purely through talk or through the additional affordances of the shared digital
workspace. This sort of transformation marks something as relevant or significant
enough to be shared more generally rather than remain as side work. Also the
new comment or contribution builds on the prior local action. It is designed in
such a way that it indicates that local action is being referenced, but it also captures and re-iterates that local action; the prior action is integrated into the new
contribution. Thus the new turn ensures that it can be understood even if the prior
has not been heard or seen by remote colleagues. This also reveals that participants can be uncertain whether local action has been heard remotely.

Discussion

This paper has begun to unpack the nature and organisation of local action within data sessions held by virtually collocated teams. In CSCW, often such local action has been treated as straightforwardly problematic, peripheral, irrelevant, a nuisance, or a distraction to distributed group work. However the data presented here reveals a more complex picture of local action. It should be noted that we did not search out 'constructive' local action. Rather we were interested in the interactional practices that underpinned the work of the distributed data sessions and in taking such an interest we found local action to be critical to that work. Let us also be clear that we are not suggesting that the unavailability of local action is *always* beneficial. Indeed we have a number of instances in the data that demonstrate troubles that arise due to the lack of information of activities at the other site (e.g. the start of Fragment 3). However we are keen to emphasise that local action should not be straightforwardly glossed as peripheral or problematic, so we have attempted to redress the balance by focusing on examples that do not routinely appear in the literature.

A key message here is that local action should not be disregarded in analysis, evaluation or design. The examples of local action in our data cannot be disconnected from the work of the distributed group, but rather feed into the central organisation of the group's work. Taking it seriously in the study of emerging group-to-group conferencing systems may involve challenges in terms of capturing such action, but it may also reveal critical practices. In terms of design, if anything the implications are really rather positive. The fragments certainly do not focus on a problem to be solved. Rather they show how participants exploit the technological asymmetries to coordinate work. So while there are good reasons for designers to consider technically complex solutions that reveal local action to overcome well-known problems (indeed we are pursuing such a line in parallel work), designers should not be put off more lightweight solutions that may be more immediately deployable (at least for the group sizes that we have discussed here). In doing so they might do well to consider the best configurations of technology to embrace local action.

There are two further implications that we would like to raise, which concern our understanding of 'schisms' in virtually-collocated meetings and our understanding of how 'sides' form in distributed work.

The phenomenon of 'side work' that we discuss relates to the concept of 'schisms' familiar to studies of co-present interaction. In studies of co-present meetings multiple parallel conversations, or 'schisms', often break out. The examples in the section on 'side work' could be seen as schisms. However unlike the literature on schisms, side work represents local action that is very much *in-topic* rather than off-topic in that it contributes to the immediate work of the distributed group as a whole. 'Side work' is also similar to the 'side sequences' discussed by Jefferson (1972). Again however there are notable differences. Side sequences refer to breaks in activity that clarify problems or issues before that activity resumes. While side sequences are inserted within the flow of conversation, due to the configuration of MiMeG, side work occurs *in parallel* to ongoing talk. Furthermore, the environment makes the side work potentially *invisible* to some participants. In a co-present meeting one can see someone whispering to or gesturing at another. Here such conduct is invisible. As we have seen, this provides opportunities for participants to do local work to make the distributed data session work. This makes it possible for Ivor to design his contribution in Fragment 1 so that it is not seen or heard remotely. It is positioned *alongside* the ongoing talk but such that it then re-shapes the work of the group as a whole. Thus standard concepts in the analysis of co-present interaction take on a new form, organisation and significance in these mediated encounters.

A number of studies have noted *that* co-present colleagues in distributed groups tend to develop 'sides' (e.g. Bos et al. 2004) and the reason for this is often linked to the additional social cues available to co-participants in local sites. The findings presented here contribute to this work by revealing some of the interactional practices that underpin *how* sides emerge. Take for example the case of 'tag work' presented in Fragment 4. In a co-present data session with four participants, all parties would be able to hear what Ben said. Thus all parties would be able to build on his comment to progress the analysis. However due to MiMeG, Henry is given *unique access* to the comment of his co-present colleague and is the only party able to build on from it. Sacks (1992) writes of the ways in which finishing another's sentence can give an impression of a team. Here we can extend that to suggest that building on the contribution of another also does so. Furthermore in revealing local action, participants routinely announce what 'we' are doing, again giving the flavour of a co-operative. Moreover as talk to the team as a whole seems to be directed to the remote site, it possibly gives the remote site primacy in claiming next turn, giving rise to a site-to-site (side-to-side) turn-taking system. Each of these practices fosters some sense of 'local team' and provides the turn-by-turn basis in and through which sides emerge.

These observations may be of interest to those studying or developing large group conferencing systems. Sometimes people at the same site do not represent the same interests and maybe more importantly people that represent the same interests are not necessarily at the same site. Therefore they are denied opportunities for side work; to coordinate contributions, check facts, help out, etc. Our study here helps us to encourage work that is exploring mechanisms that could facilitate *cross-location* side work. To this end, Access Grid and other conferencing systems might consider text chat (Mark et al. 1999) or 'space like systems' which can support sub-conferences or allow directed comments through "whispering" (Berc et al., 1995; Yankelovich et al., 2005). Whichever tools are selected it is critical to ensure that they do not distract from the meeting but provide resources for side work to be intertwined with ongoing team activities or even to facilitate opportunities for tag work.

That said, clearly this paper is presenting early findings from our programme of studies. In our concern to provide support for 'real-world' teams, we are directed in part by their group composition and the technologies that they use. This particular team had four members and ran data sessions using standard computers or laptops. In future work we are keen to explore larger group sizes and the use of different display technologies to see how practices translate or 'scale'. For example we are interested to see if the relationships between local action and distributed work become more complex when there are opportunities for parallel instances of side work in local sites. How then does *simultaneous* side work get drawn into the meeting as a whole? We are also eager to consider the impact of different technological ecologies, ranging from multiple screens, to tabletop displays, to wall projections and the like on the organisation of action at local sites. It is likely that these different ecologies impact on how local participants can manage relationships between local action and distributed work.

In conclusion, the data in this paper reveal practices that are quite distinct from co-present data sessions. Whilst the tasks are the same – finding and showing phenomena, making analytic claims, supporting claims with video evidence, etc. – the interactional asymmetries imposed by MiMeG lead to new forms of coordination. With the development of "collaboratories" there will inevitably be further study of group-to-group(s) systems and, as we have started to see here, the focus on groups interacting at distance and over and around data may well reveal intriguing practices; practices that allow us to refine our understanding of concepts such as 'awareness', 'involvement' and even 'activity'. Indeed these systems give rise to novel and complex participation frameworks that may contribute as much to our understating of the dynamics of social interaction as to the design of new technical solutions.

Acknowledgments

We are extremely grateful to the research team featured in this paper for allowing us to study their use of MiMeG. We would also like to thank Paul Luff, Christian Heath, Dirk vom Lehn and the anonymous reviewers for their comments on earlier versions of this paper. This work was funded through the MiMeG ESRC e-Social Science Research Node (Award No. RES-149-25-0033).

References

Aoki, P., Romaine, M., Szymanski, M., Thornton, J., Wilson, D. & Woodruff, A. (2003): 'The Mad Hatter's Cocktail Party: A social mobile audio space supporting multiple simultaneous conversations', *Proc. CHI 2003*, ACM Press, New York, pp. 425-432.

Aoki, P., Szymanski, M., Plurkowski, L., Thornton, J., Woodruff, A. & Weilie, Y. (2006): 'Where's the "party" in "multi-party"?: Analyzing the structure of small-group sociable talk', *Proc. CSCW 2006*, ACM Press, New York, pp. 393-402.

Berc, L., Gajewska, H. & Manasse, M. (1995): 'Pssst: Side Conversations in the Argo Telecollaboration System', *Proc. UIST '95*, ACM Press, New York, pp. 155-156.

Boden, D. & Molotch, H. (1994): 'The Compulsion of Proximity', in R. Friedland & D. Boden (Eds.) *NowHere: Space, Time and Modernity*, University of California, London. pp. 257-286.

Bos, N., Olson, J., Nan, N., Shami, N., Hoch, S. & Johnston, E. (2006): 'Collocation blindness in partially distributed groups: is there a downside to being collocated?', *Proc. CHI 2006*, ACM Press, New York, pp. 1313-1321.

Bos, N., Shami, N., Olson, J., Cheshin, A. & Nan, N. (2004): 'In-group/out-group effects in distributed teams', *Proc. CSCW 2004*, ACM Press, New York, pp. 429-436.

Fraser, M., Hindmarsh, J., Best, K., Heath, C., Biegel, G., Greenhalgh, C. & Reeves, S. (2006): 'Remote Collaboration over Video Data: Towards real-time e-Social Science', *Computer Supported Cooperative Work*, 15, 4, pp. 257-279.

Goffman, E. (1981): *Forms of Talk*, University of Pennsylvania, Philadelphia.

Heath, C. & Luff, P. (2000): *Technology in Action*, Cambridge University Press, Cambridge.

Hindmarsh, J., Fraser, M., Heath, C., Benford, S. & Greenhalgh, C. (2000): 'Object-Focused Interaction in Collaborative Virtual Environments', *ACM ToCHI*, 7, 4, pp. 477-509.

Hinds, P. & Kiesler, S. (Eds.) (2002): *Distributed Work*, MIT Press, Cambridge, MA.

Jefferson, G. (1972): 'Side sequences', in D. Sudnow (Ed.) *Studies in Social Interaction*, Free Press, New York, pp. 294-338.

Kraut, R., Gergle, D. & Fussel, S. (2002): 'The Use of Visual Information in Shared Visual Spaces', *Proc. CSCW 2002*, ACM Press, New York, pp. 31–40.

Mark, G., Abrams, S. & Nassif, N. (2003): 'Group-to-Group Distance Collaboration: Examining the "Space Between"', *Proc. ECSCW'03*, Kluwer, Dordrecht, pp. 99-118.

Mark, G., Grudin, J. & Poltrock, S. (1999): 'Meeting at the Desktop: An empirical study of virtually collocated teams', *Proc. ECSCW'99*, Kluwer, Dordrecht, pp. 159-178.

Olson, G. & Olson, J. (2000): 'Distance Matters', *Human Computer Interaction*, 15, 2/3, 139-178.

Ruhleder, K. (2000): 'The Virtual Ethnographer: Fieldwork in distributed electronic environments', *Field Methods*, 12, 1, pp. 3-17.

Sacks, H. (1992): *Lectures on Conversation. Vols. 1 & 2.* (Ed. G. Jefferson), Blackwell, Oxford.

Sonnenwald, D., Solomon, P., Hara, N., Bolliger, R. & Cox, T. (2002): 'Collaboration in the Large: Using video conferencing to facilitate large group interaction', in A. Gunasekaran, O. Khalil, & M. Syed (Eds.) *Knowledge and Information Technology Management in 21st Century Organizations*, Idea Group Publishing, Hershey, PA, pp. 115-136.

Yankelovich, N., McGinn, J., Wessler, M., Kaplan, J., Provino, J., & Fox, H. (2005): 'Private communications in public meetings', *Proc. CHI 2005*, ACM Press, New York, pp. 1873-1876.

L. Bannon, I. Wagner, C. Gutwin, R. Harper, and K. Schmidt (eds.).
ECSCW'07: Proceedings of the Tenth European Conference on Computer Supported Cooperative Work, 24-28 September 2007, Limerick, Ireland
© Springer 2007   219

Bringing Round-Robin Signature to Computer-Mediated Communication

Takeshi Nishida   Takeo Igarashi
The University of Tokyo   The University of Tokyo / JST PRESTO
tnishida@ui.is.s.u-tokyo.ac.jp   *takeo@acm.org*

Abstract. In computer-mediated group communication, anonymity enables participants to post controversial comments without risking accusations of improper behavior. While this may encourage more open and frank discussion, it diminishes accountability. In addition, anonymous comments are perceived as weaker than non-anonymous comments. We propose a communication protocol that allows a user to send a strong message to the group without having to assume sole individual responsibility. The system posts an anonymous comment, and then calls for supporters. When sufficient numbers of supporters have been gathered, the system reveals the names of all supporters as a round-robin signature. This prevents the originator from being identified. We describe the implementation of this protocol in a text-based chat system, and report our experience operating it at two technical conferences.

Introduction

Group communication plays a major role in group decision-making, information exchange, and other social processes. However, it can be difficult to express honest thoughts to a group. For example, a new group member may feel uneasy about submitting a controversial comment that might irritate established members. This kind of difficulty is more profound in Asian cultures, where modesty is valued and improper comments by junior members are strongly punished by senior members.

Anonymity lowers this entry barrier by allowing such participants to submit a comment without the risk of being accused of impropriety. Anonymity is common in Web-based communications. For example, the news and commentary

Web site Slashdot posts both anonymous and non-anonymous comments. On the Japanese BBS site 2channel, nearly all of the posts are anonymous. Anonymity also appears in closed-group communications, such as group decision-making systems, and its effectiveness is a hot topic in psychological research (Jessup and George, 1997; Nunamaker et al., 1997; Joinson, 1999, 2001; Postems and Lea, 2000).

However, anonymous comments are often valued less than comments with signatures, and it can be difficult to send a strong message to the community through anonymous comments. On Slashdot, for example, anonymous posts are given lower default scores by the moderation system. Anonymous users are called "anonymous cowards," and their posts are likely to be skipped or filtered out (Lampe and Resnick, 2004). In other situations, such as in educational communications in schools or at academic conferences, anonymity is discouraged.

We propose a communication protocol that overcomes the inherent weakness of anonymous comments. Users can send a strong message to the community while avoiding the risk of assuming a large individual responsibility. The original comment is submitted anonymously and displayed to the group, along with a request for supporters. When the number of supporters reaches a certain number, the system reveals the names of all supporters as a round-robin signature, which conceals the identity of the first person to submit the comment. In this way, the protocol combines the advantages of anonymous and non-anonymous communication. It is most useful when provided as an extension to normal anonymous or non-anonymous communication.

We implemented the protocol on a non-anonymous text-chat system. The system was used during two technical conferences as a communication backchannel during presentation sessions. We analyzed the chat log and found that our system encouraged non-anonymous postings of sensitive comments.

Round-Robin Communication Protocol Design

We combined the round-robin signature method, which is traditionally used in petitions, with modern computer-mediated communication (CMC).

Round-Robin Signature

Round-robin is a group signature method in which the names of the signatories are arranged in a circle to represent equality (Figure 1). This form of signature list has been used in petitions throughout history when a risk of severe punishment was imposed to help groups conceal their leaders and prevent them from assuming all of the responsibility for the petition.

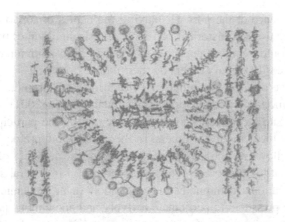

Figure 1. Example of a round-robin sigunature (from the work of Yamamoto, 1994).

This method has been practiced in many countries. For example, it was adopted by sailors petitioning officers in the British Royal Navy (Rediker, 1987), and Japanese farmers and peasants of the Edo period used this signature style when they presented a petition against misrule (Hosaka, 2002). We believe that this practice is universal, and can be effective in modern CMC.

Communication Flow

The protocol begins with an anonymous post by a user. Other users see the post and can choose to support the comment. These responses are hidden by the system until the post gathers a sufficient number of supporters. When this is achieved, the names of the originator and the supporters are revealed as a round-robin signature. At this point, everyone in the group knows who supports the original post, but no one knows its originator—except for that person. If the post fails to gain enough supporters, it remains anonymous. The number of supporters required to show the round-robin signature can be customized by the originator.

This communication protocol is designed to be an extension to anonymous or non-anonymous communication. When the protocol is combined with anonymous communication, users can enhance their influence with minimum risk. When the protocol is combined with non-anonymous communication, users can contribute to a discussion without the risk of being accused of making improper comments.

Benefits and Promising Situations

The protocol combines the best properties of anonymous and non-anonymous communications. Like anonymous communication, it lowers the barriers to entering a discussion, and yet, as in non-anonymous communication, gives weight to the comment. Furthermore, like moderating systems, it appropriately enhances or weakens the influence of the post. Displaying the names of supporters in round-robin reminds the users of historical petitions, and strongly unites the signatories. These effects would be more apparent in closed-group communications, when users are able to easily identify others by their name.

In addition, the protocol is similar to a ritual in that it promotes coordination by forming common knowledge among participants (Chwe, 2001). With CMC, it is difficult to create a common knowledge base among the participants because they cannot view the activities of others. In the round-robin protocol, anonymous communication allows participants to safely examine the activities of their peers.

We believe that the proposed protocol can be useful in several situations. For example, in educational communication in schools or at academic conferences, when people are pressured to participate actively and anonymous participation is discouraged, the proposed protocol serves as an intermediate stage between anonymous and active non-anonymous participation. It can be provided as a backchannel for face-to-face communication in the classroom, as in Rekimoto et al. (1998) and Barkhuus (2005). This is particularly helpful in Asian cultures, in which people are generally too reserved to actively participate in a discussion.

In situations with asynchronous decision making by teams or groups, which typically occur on mailing lists or online discussion boards, silent members prefer to be seen as passive supporters. As a result, the responsibility for decisions is usually concentrated within a small group of active supporters. The proposed protocol can encourage active support by silent members and the sharing of responsibility.

User Interface Design

We implemented a chat system with the proposed protocol, Lock-on-Chat IKKI. It is based on Lock-on-Chat (Nishida and Igarashi, 2005), a text-chat system in which the users can share images and chat about the images in anchored windows. It has been used by audiences to exchange comments on slides during live presentations. 'Ikki' is a Japanese word meaning "riot" or "petitions."

Figure 2(a–d) shows a screenshot of the Lock-on-Chat IKKI client. It consists of four components: thumbnails for managing received images (a), a main image window for viewing and chatting about images (b), an icon palette for initiating the round-robin communication protocol (c), and a log that displays all of the messages in chronological order (d).

The user can upload images to the server by drag-and-drop to the client window and the uploaded images will be instantly shared by all clients. One of the images is shown in the main image window, and the user can switch to different images by clicking the corresponding thumbnails.

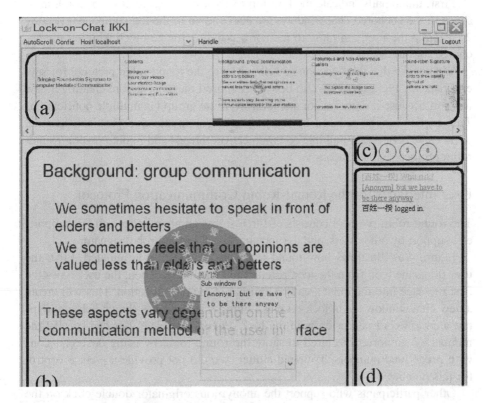

Figure 2. Screenshot of the Lock-on-Chat IKKI client.

Lock-on Message Posting

The user creates a new chat window anchored to an image (lock-on) by clicking on the image and typing in the first message (Figure 3). Other members are notified about the lock-on through multiple components.

Figure 3. Creating a new chat window (lock-on).

First, thumbnails indicate the location of lock-ons (Figure 2(a)). Second, messages in the anchored chat windows are also shown in the log component (Figure 2 (d)), and the user can jump to the corresponding image by clicking on the anchored messages.

We believe that this function is well suited to the round-robin protocol for several reasons. First, users have to be well prepared mentally before creating a new lock-on because it draws major attention from the group via multiple notifications. This barrier can be reduced by the proposed communication protocol. Second, users can easily create multiple communication threads and initiate several round-robin protocols simultaneously.

User Interfaces for the Round-Robin Communication Protocol

The round-robin protocol consists of three steps: an anonymous call for supporters, support by other users, and the appearance of a round-robin signature.

Figure 4(a) illustrates how round-robin communication is initiated. First, the user drags the icon from the icon palette onto the image. Then, the user types the first message into the input area that appears at the drop location. This will create a new chat window, as in lock-on messaging. A reminder is shown below the input area to avoid confusion with the lock-on function. The user can specify the number of supporters required to show the round-robin by using different icons with predefined numbers. To avoid clutter, we did not provide a precise control for this number.

Other participants who support the anonymous originator double-click on the anchor or select 'Support this topic' from the context menu (Figure 4(b)). All users will be notified immediately when the number of supporters has increased.

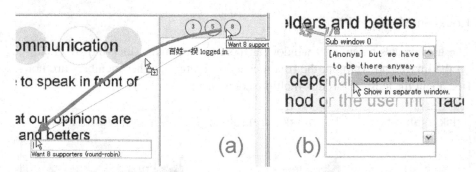

Figure 4. User interfaces for round-robin communication in Lock-on-Chat IKKI: (a) initiation and (b) response as a supporter.

The names of the originator and the supporters are revealed as a round-robin signature when the number of supporters reaches the threshold specified by the originator. The round-robin appears with an animation effect (Figure 5).

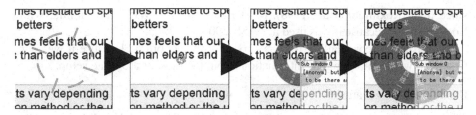

Figure 5. Animation effect when the round-robin appears.

Experience as a Backchannel at Conferences

We operated Lock-on-Chat IKKI at two technical conferences as a communication backchannel during the presentation sessions. During the presentations, most attendances were in the main conference room, equipped with their own laptop computer (Figure 6). The contents of the main screen were captured manually and uploaded to the server by an operator.

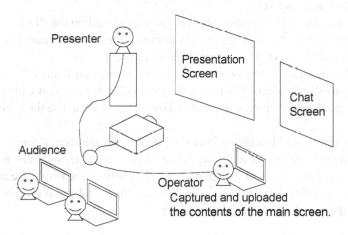

Figure 6. Operational setup.

First Trial Experience

The first operation took place at the Workshop on Interactive System and Software (WISS) 2006. WISS is an annual workshop in Japan focusing on user-interface technologies. It is a single-track conference and approximately 150 participants attend the workshop each year. Presentation sessions have been augmented by chat systems since WISS'97 and various chat systems have been tested since then (Rekimoto et al., 1998). Most participants at WISS are familiar with Lock-on-Chat because it was used at WISS 2004 and 2005.

We provided icons calling for 4, 8, 16, and 32 supporters. Because it was our first trial, we had no previous information about the most appropriate setup.

Results and Observations

The system was used by 108 users. However, in the first day, they did not use the round-robin protocol except in some test trials. The users had to play with the user interface a few times to see what happened when they used it. Interestingly, most users agreed to use their real names or easily identifiable nicknames (91 users), although it was generally common for participants to use an unidentifiable nickname (59 out of 95 users at WISS2004). The round-robin protocol encouraged the use of real names.

Practical uses of the round-robin protocol were seen after the second day. It was mostly used to express critical opinions that were constructive but difficult to express. Examples were 'I'm suspicious of the scalability of this user interface,' 'I think this one (a related work) is more interesting,' and 'Is this an appropriate target with which to compare?'

More casual uses of the round-robin protocol increased on the third day. Some of them were just for fun and games. Examples were 'Crash, crash! (during the live demo)' and 'Anybody like the night session better?'

Just before the end of the conference, an anonymous call stated 'I will definitely come to WISS again.' While this kind of post is not risky, it can be a little embarrassing, and might represent another kind of situation to use the round-robin protocol.

The first operation highlighted issues related to the number of supporters required to reveal the round-robin signature. Many anonymous calls remained anonymous because they had gathered only about half of the original call. Some users commented that they felt disappointed when the round-robin was shown and the system did not allow them to join afterward.

Log Analysis

Figure 7 shows the number of calls and the number of revealed round-robins (the calls that gathered sufficient supporters). In total, about one-third of the calls gathered a sufficient number of supporters. Originators tended to require a larger number of supporters than actually joined. This low rate does not necessary indicate the failure of our approach, as it is preferable for only important posts that attract sufficient support to be revealed.

Most of the calls were for 4 or 8 supporters, but some users tried larger calls of 16 or 32. Larger calls were obviously more difficult to accomplish. The only exception involved a call for 32 supporters for the message previously mentioned: 'I will definitely come to WISS again.'

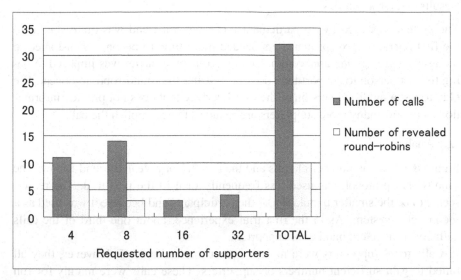

Figure 7. The number of calls for supporters and the number of revealed round-robins during the first trial experience.

Second Trial Experience

The second operation took place at the 48th Programming Symposium. The Programming Symposium is an annual meeting in Japan, focusing on programming and software technologies. It is a single-track conference with approximately 100 participants each year. Presentation sessions have been augmented by a normal text-chat, so very few participants had experience with Lock-on-Chat. We were not allowed to operate our system exclusively and it was run as a second chat system in parallel with a normal text-chat.

We modified the round-robin protocol so that it can welcome new users after the message is revealed. Such new members are not immediately added to the round-robin, but are included when certain numbers of additional supporters are obtained. A new goal was set higher than the original, in the manner of a Fibonacci sequence, such as 3, 5, 8, 13.... We chose this design to preserve the sense of accomplishment achieved when the post first gathered a large number of supporters.

Based on the first trial experience, icons for 3, 5, and 8 supporters were available. We also anticipated lower numbers of users because the symposium had fewer participants. We removed the icons for large numbers because of the protocol modification described above.

Results and Observations

The system was used by 30 participants. The general trend was quite similar to the first operation, except that users needed more time to become accustomed to the user interface. One user commented that a mental barrier was imposed to being the last person to support the post, and causing the round-robin to appear. We plan to test a modified version of the user interface that does not provide information as to how many more supporters are required to accomplish the call.

Log Analysis

Figure 8 shows the number of calls and the number of revealed round-robins. The round-robin protocol was used less frequently than in the first trial. The reason seems to be the smaller population of the participants and because it was used as a second chat system. As in the first trial experience, about one-third of the calls gathered a sufficient number of supporters.

Calls for 8 supporters were more frequent than calls for 5; however, they all failed to gain sufficient numbers of supporters. These calls were mainly for fun and games, with the protocol serving in a similar manner to normal anonymous communication. We could not completely remove these behavioral problems, but adding some penalties for unaccomplished calls might improve the method.

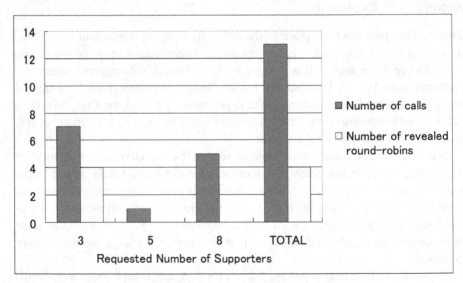

Figure 8. The number of calls for supporters and the number of revealed round-robins during the second trial experience.

Related Work

Anonymity is a hot topic in psychological research. Joinson (1999) studied the effect of anonymity on the results of Internet-based questionnaires and also examined the relationship between self-disclosure and visual anonymity (Joinson, 2001). Anonymity was considered the key to improving performance in group decision support systems (Jessup and George, 1997; Nunamaker et al. 1997), but these works were questioned by Postems and Lea(2000).

The effect of providing communication backchannels to face-to-face communication was reported by Rekimoto et al. (1998) and Barkhuus (2005). One of the most important characteristics of these backchannels is that they can add anonymity to the communication space. Here, we report the effect of adding another protocol, round-robin, as a backchannel to reality.

Conclusion and Future Work

This paper addresses anonymous and non-anonymous dualism in communication. We explored the design space between them by incorporating round-robin signature, a sophisticated method used historically in human society. We believe that the exploration of this space can enrich CMC.

We built a working system and operated it at two technical conferences. We observed both expected and unexpected uses of the round-robin protocol during the operation; the system gathered a great deal of controversial comments in addition to playful comments. Users also had difficulty in assigning an appropriate number of supporters.

Several areas require further revision. First, we plan to explore variations of the protocol. For example, imposing penalties to anonymous calls that cannot gather any supporters might improve the behavioral problems often observed in anonymous communication. We will also examine the effect of displaying or concealing the number of additional supporters required to achieve the round-robin signature.

Next, we plan to apply the protocol to other situations. For example, decision making in a smaller group would allow us to observe the effect of the protocol in detail. We will observe longer terms of use because the effects may change over time. It would also be interesting to apply it to anonymous communication, especially in open Web communication.

Acknowledgments

We thank Prof. Ikuo Takeuchi for his comments and advice. We also thank the programming committees of WISS and the Programming Symposium for giving us the opportunity to operate our system. Finally, we thank all of the participants in the operation for their active discussion and helpful comments. This work was funded in part by grants from the Japanese Information Technology Promotion Agency (IPA).

References

Barkhuus, L. (2005): "'Bring your laptop unless you want to follow the lecture': alternative communication in the classroom," In the *Proceedings of GROUP'05*, 2005, pp. 140–143.

Chwe, M. S.-Y. (2001): *Rational Ritual: Culture, Coordination, and Common Knowledge*, Princeton University Press, Princeton, NJ, USA.

Hosaka, S. (2002): "Hyakusyo ikki to sono saho," Yoshikawa Kobunkan, Tokyo, Japan. (in Japanese)

Jessup, L. M., and George, J. F. (1997): "Theoretical and methodological issues in group support systems research: Learning from groups gone away", *Small Group Research*, Vol. 28, No. 3, 1997, pp. 394–413.

Joinson, A. N. (1999): "Social desirability, anonymity, and Internet-based questionnaires," *Behavior Research Methods, Instruments, & Computers*, Vol. 31, No. 3, 1999, pp. 433–438.

Joinson, A. N. (2001): "Self-disclosure in computer-mediated communication: the role of self-awareness and visual anonymity," *European Journal of Social Psychology*, Vol. 31, No. 2, 2001, pp. 177–192.

Lampe, C., and Resnick, P. (2004): "Slash(dot) and burn: distributed moderation in a large online conversation space," In the *Proceedings of CHI 2004*, 2004, pp. 543–550.

Nishida, T., and Igarashi, T. (2005): "Lock-on-Chat: boosting anchored conversation and its operation at a technical conference," In the *Proceedings of INTERACT 2005*, 2005, pp. 970–973.

Nunamaker, J.F. Jr., Briggs, R. O., Mittleman, D. D., Vogel, D. R. and Balthazard, P. A. (1997): "Lessons from a dozen years of group support systems research: a discussion of lab and field findings", *Journal of Management Information Systems*, Vol. 13, No. 3, 1997, pp. 163-207.

Postems, T., and Lea, M. (2000): "Social processes and group decision making: anonymity in group decision support systems," *Ergonomics*, Vol. 43, No. 8, August 2000, pp. 1252–1274.

Rediker, M. (1987): *Between the Devil and the Deep Blue Sea: Merchant Seaman, Pirates, and the Anglo–American Maritime World*, 1700–1750, Cambridge University Press, Cambridge, UK.

Rekimoto, J., Ayatsuka, Y., Uoi, H., and Arai, T. (1998), "Adding another communication channel to reality: an experience with a chat-augmented conference," In the *Conference Summary of CHI'98*, 1998, pp. 271–272.

Yamamoto, T. (1994): *The History of Fukui*, Modern History 1, chapter 3, section 3, Fukui Prefecture, Japan. (in Japanese)

L. Bannon, I. Wagner, C. Gutwin, R. Harper, and K. Schmidt (eds.).
ECSCW'07: Proceedings of the Tenth European Conference on Computer Supported Cooperative Work, 24-28 September 2007, Limerick, Ireland
© Springer 2007

Asymmetrical collaboration in print shop-customer relationships

Jacki O'Neill[1], David Martin[1], Tommaso Colombino[1], Jennifer Watts-Perotti[2], Mary Ann Sprague[2], Geoffrey Woolfe[2]
Xerox Research Centre Europe, Grenoble, France[1]
Xerox Research Centre Webster, Rochester, USA[2]
{firstname.lastname@xerox.com}

Abstract. The service provider-customer relationship, although not perhaps considered a typical collaborative relationship, is clearly collaborative work. However, such work is constrained by the very (service) nature of the relationship. Customer-service provider interaction can be characterised as interaction at the boundaries of organisations, each of which is likely to have their own workflows and orientations. Many service organisations attempt to facilitate this interaction by configuring their customers, using standardised forms or applications. In this way they bring the customers workflow into line with their own. In this paper we describe field work examining one particular service relationship; that between print shops and their customers. A notable feature of print shop-customer relationships is that customers prepare the material that the print shop then prints. This makes the standardization of workflows difficult, particularly within the service relationship. Technologies exist which aim to automate and standardize the workflow from customers to print shops. However, they have, up to now, largely failed to live up to their promise, leaving print shops to adopt ad hoc solutions. This paper describes the hidden work that the print shops do to make the service relationship work.

Introduction

The service relationship, between service provider and customer, is an important one for CSCW. Although it may not typically represent what we think about when we talk about collaboration, examining the customer-service provider interaction demonstrates that it is clearly collaborative work (cf. Hughes, Randall & Shapiro, 1991). Such collaboration may be necessary for that service relationship to work, but at the same time it is constrained by the very (service) nature of the relationship. It is not one of straightforward cooperation with both parties on an equal footing, and the relative responsibilities for ensuring a satisfactory service provision for both sides may be unequal. This is especially true in the print industry where, as we shall see, the service relationship is maintained through collaborative work to make the artefacts from the customers workflow fit into the print shops workflow. The asymmetry in the collaboration comes from the print shop taking on the bulk of the work to make the service relationship work. In this paper, we explore this asymmetrical collaboration between print shops and their customers.

In business there is an increasing move to remote channels for service provision, with organisations interacting with their customers using information and communication technologies (ICTs), the Internet and so on. In addition many service organisations have technologically managed workflows and thus make use of on-line forms, standardised files and applications – web interfaces and such like – in an attempt to create a smooth process across organisational boundaries, minimising the need for face-to-face and even telephone contact. In this Internet age large portions of the service sector now do business online from government services to on line banking and insurance. A recurring theme with industries that have made this change is that moving customers to remote channels may be highly profitable but that doing so requires some re-configuration of the relationship with the customer and carefully thought through technology design (Bowers and Martin 2000; Rouncefield, Harper & Randall, 1999). Focusing on printing we see that it is a service industry that is moving in this direction. Technologically managed workflows are being widely adopted. Job submission is often remote, with files frequently being sent by email. In addition many print shops are seeking to conduct more business online, whereby customers submit jobs using standardised templates. In some areas, attempts have been made to fully automate aspects of the workflow so that collaboration between print shops and their customers is minimised. Many jobs are submitted as 'ready to print', that is, jobs which can be printed out and dispatched to the customer with, in theory, no extra work required to prepare the document for printing on a digital production press.

Digital print shops cater for a wide range of customers with diverse requirements and this is part of their selling point. However, that very diversity of customers, as well as the service provider role, presents problems in process standardization and movement to remote channels for customer-organisation interaction. Their customer diversity means that it is difficult to employ standard workflows across various customers and consequently learning and re-use from customer to customer is not optimised. Moreover, the service banner means that they are often involved in doing extra (often not 'costed') work in order to produce a printed product that is good enough in terms of content and aesthetics.

In this paper we report on a series of ethnographic studies of digital print shops which examine the print shop-customer relationships from the side of the print shop. For CSCW, the paper provides some interesting new material on problems and concepts that have drawn interest for a number of years:

1. How do we understand the nature of cooperative work in customer-organisation interaction, and what does this mean for process and technology integration?
2. What is the work involved in supporting cooperative (service) work across organisational boundaries? What is the work involved for service organisations (and customers) when their workflows do not match?
3. To what extent can print shops configure their customers (cf. Woolgar 1991; Bowers and Martin, 2000), in the sense of both better understanding the customers they work for and in getting their customers to interact with them (preferably through technology) in standard, tractable, predictable ways?

In the print shops we noticed a large amount of extra 'collaborative' work was involved in the print shop-customer relationship. The print shops in particular undertook much work to make the service relationship work. As we shall see this collaborative work goes on despite attempts at automation. Much of this work comes about because the customer, or some agency working for the customer, prepares the files which the print shop must turn into a finished product. The customer creates the file within their own workflows and according to their concerns and then passes the file to the print shop. The file then enters the print shop's technologically supported workflow through which it passes to become a finished product. As we will explore in this paper, the two workflows often do not converge well, despite there being, in some cases, tools designed to support (or partly automate) the workflow from customer to print shop. This non-alignment of workflows creates additional work for both print shops and customers, although the bulk of this work is handled by the print shop. In this paper we will explore the solutions implemented by the print shops in an attempt to address the problems caused by the disparate workflows and their contingencies, within the constraints of a service, rather than a straightforward collaborative, relationship.

Related work

Studies of the workflow and workflow technologies in print shops are not new to CSCW. Papers by Bowers, Button and Sharrock (1995) and Button and Sharrock (1997) examined workflow and communications technology in large print shops. This work examined offset printing which poses different challenges to digital printing. Even so we can see that the use workflow technology, has long been a facet of print shop work. These papers clearly reveal the problems that such systems can introduce *within* the print shop organisation. In this paper, however, we focus on the customer-print shop interaction *across the organisational boundary*.

Although over the years technological innovation in both workflow and communication systems has moved on, we will see in this paper that technology has by no means solved all the challenges.

There has been some research in CSCW that has addressed the customer-service provider relationship, most notably in the banking sector (see, for example, Hughes et al (1999)). One notable feature of many of these papers is their consideration of how the technology is used by the bank to configure the customer (see also Bowers and Martin, 2000). Some research has considered the customer-service provider relation in the printing sector, but has focused on the interaction with the customer around technical support (Whalen & Vinkhuyzen, 2001; O'Neill et al, 2005) or around sales and support (Whalen, Whalen & Henderson, 2002).

There is one essential difference, however, between these service relationships and those discussed in this paper; that is, here the print shop customer often prepares the file or the components of the file that the print shop is to print. In the technical support and banking situations any shared artefact that is created can be strictly controlled by the service organisation. For example, banks have standardised forms or internet banking applications which the customer must complete or use to access the banks services. These forms and applications are the external face of the service provider's organisation, they are designed to be a bridge between the customer and the service provider and specifically to fit with the workflows of the service organisation. They could be considered to be what have been referred to elsewhere as boundary objects (Star, 1989; Star & Greisemer, 1989).

The print shop situation is different because, in most cases, such a standardised object does not exist, rather the client prepares the file in their workflow and the print shop prints it in theirs. Various attempts at standardisation have been and continue to be made and these will be examined in this paper along with other methods for dealing with the issues that arise. One major attempt at standardisation is 'colour management' (discussed below). However, as is often the case when two (or more) diverse organizations attempt to integrate and standardise the process between them through the implementation of technologies, difficulties often arise (Martin et al. 2007; Lee, 2005). More often than not this is due to not fully considering the *social* – the work practices of those on both sides and in particular those at the organisational boundaries – in the design of the *technical* (see Woolgar, 1991). Resolution of these difficulties tends to (re)involve the social, that is the various parties work together to come to some solution. This suggests perhaps that rather than attempting to automate processes which are currently collaborative, tools which facilitate the collaboration may be more appropriate. At the very least, we emphasise once again that a careful consideration of the social nature of the processes to be automated is essential for success.

The print shop studies

During 2006 a multi-sited ethnography of digital colour production print shops was carried out in the US and Europe. Observation was carried out in six sites: four commercial print shops and two printer testing sites. The print shops varied in size, customers, core business and workflow organisation. The ethnography consisted primarily of observations, with total time on site around three months. The observations were supplemented by some in-situ interviewing and data was collected through field notes, digital photographs and video and audio recordings.

During these studies we noticed that a large part of the work of the print shops was managing the files that they received from the customer - be they assorted pictures and text for creating a document, data files for variable data printing, or 'ready to print' files. This in itself is not strange, however what struck us was the amount of routine work that went into fixing problems with the files which originated upstream at the customer site. This work turned what might at first glance be seen as a simple service relationship into a relationship requiring collaboration, moreover this collaboration was asymmetrical, with the print shop doing much of the work to rectify problems caused upstream, with much of this work, and even at times the existence problems, being hidden from the customer.

Digital production printing offers the promise of high quality prints in short runs, on demand, often from files submitted by customers. However, for such printing to be cost effective and timely, the submitted files need to adhere to certain characteristics, for example, to have international colour consortium (ICC)[1] colour management profiles attached, which our studies and others (Riordan, 2005) show rarely occurs. Where the customers do not submit files suitably adjusted to fit the digital production printing workflow, the print shops must engage in considerable work to make the workflow work. They are in addition constrained by the service relationship, limiting to some extent their ability to 'configure' the customer or certainly all customers, such that they receive 'suitable' input into their processes. In the following sections we will examine the work the print shops do currently to address the everyday troubles of making the files ready to print.

Exploring print shop-customer relationships

Digital production printing has advantages over traditional offset printing for both black and white and colour prints in two main areas 1) short runs (approx. <2500 prints) and on-demand printing, where the cost and set up time of offset printing can be prohibitive, and 2) variable data printing, where the printed output

---

[1]   The ICC - http://www.colour.org/ - is a body set up by several large players in printing and associated industries which has set up standards for colour management

changes, often for each item e.g. promotional material individually tailored to each recipient or bills and statements.

A variety of workflows and divisions of labour can be found in digital print shops. Such print shops typically consist of sections covering *sales*; *pre-press* - where work is carried out on the files to be printed, their components or the data prior to being sent to the printer; *production* – where the printing itself is carried out; *finishing* – turning the printed pages into the end product (booklet, letter, etc.); *dispatch* and *billing/accounts*. Print shops may also include graphic design sections. The division of labour and workflow varies across print shops, with roles being combined or separated out. For example, pre-press in some print shops is separated from production both physically and in the division of labour, whereas in others there may be different areas for pre-press and production but the same people working both. Our study covered print shops with both separate and combined pre-press sections. Most print shops have implemented some sort of workflow tool(s) to manage the flow of work from the customer, through the sections described above and back to the customer. Digital printing is a highly competitive environment and digital print shops are constantly looking at ways to improve their processes and offer new services, with technology at the heart of this process.

In this paper, we will be examining workflows within each of two areas:

1. *Workflows for high-quality colour digital printing.* Such printing typically consists of short runs and may or may not be subject to a short turn around time. An additional feature of some of the jobs we examine is that they are submitted as 'ready to print', that is, as files that can in theory be printed straight off without requiring any additional work and are costed as such.
2. *Workflows for variable data printing.* Such printing ranges from large black and white jobs such as bills to simple colour jobs such as place cards and complex colour jobs such as promotional mail outs, pension statements, etc.

In examining these workflows we will describe the everyday troubles (the "normal, natural troubles," if you like (Garfinkel, 1967)) that the print shops encounter in dealing with the content submitted by the customer.

Workflows for high quality colour printing

The colour managed workflow

The aim of digital colour printing is to produce high quality, consistent colour prints which the customer is happy with. In principle, ICC colour management is meant to assist greatly in achieving this. Reproducing colour across devices (monitors, printers) and on different media (LCD, paper, etc.) is a complicated business and colour management is a technology designed to enable translation between different colour spaces[2] and colour devices (monitors, printers, etc.). This is necessary to ensure that a colour shown on one monitor or printed on one device (e.g. the customer's office printer) will appear the same when printed on another device (e.g. the print shops production printer). 'ICC profiles' should be attached to the file at creation and then can be interpreted by any other device to accurately represent the colours in the file.

The aim of the colour management system is that the communication of 'perceptual intent' between customer and print shop is automated. The print shop should be able to receive the files from the customer and print them out to achieve colour that the customer is satisfied with, without having to engage in lengthy colour adjustment work. Unfortunately, colour management is a complex technology that many people find difficult to understand and use. Furthermore, successful colour management requires both the document designer and the print shop to rigorously follow all ICC colour management procedures and use fully colour calibrated and characterized displays and printers. Colour management tools are rarely used as intended (Riordan, 2005) In our studies none of the files received were treated as part of a colour managed workflow. Some of the reasons why it is not used are: (1) it is a fragile (non-robust) system requiring strict adherence to procedure throughout the entire colour document lifecycle, from conception to consumption; (2) it requires that the customers' monitors are calibrated and that the customers attach the appropriate colour management tags to the files; (3) this fragility is exacerbated by the technical complexity of the current system, its tools and their user interfaces, all of which can easily overwhelm users without considerable training in colour science; and (4) colour management requires that the customers do work at their end to make their files fit into the workflow of the print shop, when they may not even be aware of this workflow and its requirements. For the print shops, because the files they receive lack usable colour management tags, the system cannot be used as intended.

Ad hoc solutions to non colour managed workflows

The print operators nevertheless have to try and get good quality colour prints. In some cases they might have a hard copy proof which they are trying to match. In other cases, where no hard copy is provided, they do not know just what colours the customer wants (their 'perceptual intent'). This is because the customer's screen or printer may be calibrated differently, which will affect the appearance of colours. The print shops we observed had put in place different ad hoc solutions to get around the problems caused by a non-colour managed workflow, we will examine two of these solutions here; manually adjusting the colour and customising

---

[2]   Colour data is represented using numerical colour spaces, each space being a language to describe colour. The same numbers can be used in different colour spaces to represent different colours, thus the same set of colour values will look different in two different colour spaces.

the libraries of specifically defined 'spot' colours. These are two distinctly different approaches taken by different print shops which fitted in with the make-up of their customers and contracts. Elements of each of these approaches were seen at the other sites that we studied.

The manually adjusted workflow

One ad hoc solution to achieving desired colour despite the lack of colour management information was a manually adjusted workflow, in which operators manually adjust colours in the file, and then print it out to see the effects of their adjustments. This is an iterative process that can result in significant time spent before an acceptable print is achieved. This manually adjusted workflow can be performed in prepress or at the Digital Front End (DFE), which is the computer that drives the print engine. When done at the DFE, operators must perform manual aesthetic adjustments using tools that were designed to perform automated mathematical transformations using colour management tags. When done at the DFE, tools such as *tonal reproduction curves* (TRCs) which make adjustments to concentrations of individual colours and *emulations*, designed for the colour managed workflow, which make changes to the whole file, are used. To illustrate the difficulties of the manually adjusted workflow we will describe the use of emulations.

Choices for alternative colour spaces are called emulations in the DFE interface. A change from one emulation to another effects all of the colours in a file, often in unpredictable ways. In our studies emulations were frequently used by the print operators for aesthetic control, even though they are not designed for that purpose. The problem with this is that the effect is difficult to predict and categorical rather than directional. Hence the outcome of one test emulation, if not fully satisfactory, will not necessarily inform the user on which steps should be taken next.

Different print shops used emulations to different extents, however all the shops observed used them for aesthetic control rather than as part of the colour managed workflow they were designed for. The internal testing site tried each job with a number of different emulation settings to get the best colours possible. This shop was a special case since their aim was to show the colours that could be achieved by the printer to the best effect. Whereas in this internal site we observed up to seven emulations being tried on a single job, in the commercial print world we did not see more than three emulations being tried on one job, with the ultimate choice often being a compromise between some aspect of colour or image quality. This is because the commercial shops do not have unlimited time and manpower to spend on each job and proofing is a costly process. Of the commercial shops, two use emulations extensively whereas two shops used them more rarely, having developed other systems for colour control.

In the next section we will describe the the the printing of an interior design catalogue at Europe1 to illustrate the work that the print operators must do to achieve good quality colour.

Interior design catalogue

In this job, the interior design catalogue came as a ready-to-print file i.e. one not requiring work by the print shop, with a hard copy proof. In theory the print shop could have just printed out the entire run, however they on looking at the file they predicted some potential problems and carried out some proofing. As predicted there were problems with the colour between the customers proof and the print shops proof. The print operator then had to undertake extra work to produce a good quality output, this work is hindered by the tools available and is hidden from the customer.

In this example we can see some of the difficulties of using emulations for aesthetic adjustment, in particular trying to find a good balance between the different parts of the document whilst using a transform that applies to the whole document. In this case the print operators had a hard copy proof submitted by the customer to match. A first print was printed using Direct (which takes the settings straight from the file). However, the colours of the catalogue did not match the hard copy closely enough, for example, a pink background was considerably lighter than the hardcopy proof. The print operators then produced a subsequent proof using an emulation called Euroscale. This produced a closer match to the colours in the catalogue but a considerably less deep and rich black on the front and back covers of the catalogue. The print operators attempted to get around the problem with the black by making some adjustments to the way in which the emulation was applied. The parameter pane for the selection of emulations at the DFE, allows for some selections that modify how the transform is applied to the document, so the print operator, using Euroscale (which provided the best colour match) selected the options to "Preserve pure colours" and "100% Black TextGraphics". The rationale of the selection was to bypass the transform the Euroscale emulation was applying to the 100% black process colour background on the front and back covers, thus changing the way it was being printed. This in fact worked, with the exception that the parameter selection did not affect a small tiff logo with a black background present on the front cover, producing a clearly visible gradient between the black cover and the black in the tiff logo. This contrast between the two blacks was seen as an unacceptable outcome. However, to get a rich black the print shop would need to use Direct, which gave poorer coloured images. In this case the print shop decided to prioritize the quality of the images in the catalogue over the richness of the black of the covers, having been forced to choose one over the other.

We saw many other examples of compromises being made between one part of the document and another. For example, in another print shop, US1, an operator was tasked with printing an advertisement containing people holding a tray of biscuits. Given the current tools, adjustments to optimize the look of the biscuits made the people's faces look very pink. However, when the faces were brought back to a more normal hue, the biscuits began to look too yellow. This occurred because the biscuits and faces had the same percentage of yellow in the colour mix and the tools only operated on the entire page, hence if you changed one it affected the other. The operator eventually compromised by creating a print in which neither the biscuits nor the faces were optimal. A frequently used heuristic by the print operators is to prioritise flesh tones, however, because the aim here was to sell the biscuits, the colour of the biscuits somewhat overrode this. It may seem that compromise such as these may be easily pre-specified by the customer, however, as we will see customers 'perceptual intent' is often only worked-up as the contingencies and compromises of any job become apparent.

Better tools could be designed to support the actual workflow between customer and print shop, rather than leaving the print shops to develop ad hoc ways to get around the problem of producing high quality colour prints from customer's files. However, better tools would be unlikely to eliminate the extra, hidden work that the print shop must carry out, although reducing it would be advantageous.

Customised spot library

Another print shop, Europe2, attempted to get colour consistency and quality by customising the spot colour library on their printer for some of their customers. The spot colour library allows operators to define specific cyan, magenta, yellow and black (CMYK) values for specific named colours within a file[3]. Many of their customers were long-term customers whose prints used standardised colours which remained consistent across jobs. For example, a major customer, who we will call 'Home Seller Collective' (HSC) represented a large group of solicitors who printed out window cards, leaflets and so on, illustrating houses for sale. Each of the solicitors had their own template, with their own colours, e.g. logo, border colours and so on, into which the pictures and text about the property were inserted. This was done by HSC who then transferred the resulting PDF files directly to a shared folder on the print server. The files were submitted as ready-to-print and, in theory at least, all the print operators had to do was to print them out and pass them onto finishing and dispatch. These jobs came in daily, throughout the day, and tended to be short runs (between 1 and 50 copies), however a large number of jobs could come in on any one day. These jobs had a very short turn around time (a few hours at most), being submitted to one of a number of deadlines throughout the day. HSC jobs are run under tight deadlines and there is no time for customer and print shop to engage in a proofing cycle, however the cus-

---

[3]   Printing involves creating colours from the basic four colour palette (CMYK) on the basis of combining toners or inks.

tomer demands high quality consistent colour and keeping the contract relies to a large extent on Europe2's guarantees that they can provide this to tight deadlines.

When the current printer was purchased, Europe2 engaged in a collaborative process with the customer to try to introduce some predictability into the colour workflow. The customers sent a sample file to the print shop, with the background colours specified as spot colours. The print shop then printed a proof and sent this back to the customer. The customer returned the proof with comments on the colour such as 'Different colour of red needed'; 'Green should be darker', etc. The print operators made adjustments to the spot colour library according to these comments, re-proofed and returned to the customer. This went on for a number of cycles and took an extended period of time to complete for all the solicitors (a couple of months). The finally approved hard copy versions of the files were kept in a 'bible' next to the printer to be used for colour matching, although the print operators rarely used it having become familiar with the colours for each solicitor. The customers then used the templates with the specified spot colours to submit their jobs. This process did provide a level of consistency, however problems with colours did still arise – often with the photographs and such like which were not covered by this process - which then had to be addressed with the same manual adjustments described above.

Here the print shop engaged in a long-term collaborative process with their customer to ensure good quality prints through the setting up of a spot colour library. In doing so they emphasised the benefits to the customer of working to produce an aligned workflow – consistent colour on a short turn around time without proofing. So here the solution was a moving of the two workflows, print shops and customers, together through a process of (partial) standardisation. Taking, for example, the concept of configuring the customer, the print shop could be said to have configured the customer *and* themselves such that they could achieve a smoother, more consistent workflow. As a solution it is only suitable for long term contracts with clients who are willing to work with the print shop to achieve a fit between workflows. In addition, there is a trade-off between the predictability introduced by customising the spot colour library and being able to use the printer flexibly for whatever colours a particular job might have. In effect Europe2 were doing their proofing in advance.

Proofing as collaborative work

In the case of the interior design catalogue discussed above, the print shop had a hard copy proof they were trying to match and so they carried out all the proofing cycles internally. They did not engage in a proofing process with the customer. Even so this process is costly. All the sites used the production printer for proofing. Thus, not only is there the cost of the materials and the direct time of producing the proof to be taken into account but this also takes the printer out of production runs. Proofing, along with all the other work of the print shop, needs to be considered in the constraints of the print shop as service provider. The print shop must of course attempt to do the best possible for each customer, but just what that 'best' consists in is not a matter of quality alone, rather it is quality in the context of time, money, customer relationships, expected ongoing business, urgency, etc. hence the compromises described above.

In many other instances, both where hard copy proofs are provided by the customer and when they are not, the proofing cycle involves the customer. In these cases the print shop may do one or more internal proofs until they have what they think is a good quality print, this is then sent to the customer for approval. The customer may approve this or suggest changes, which then involves a subsequent proofing cycle.

Through the proofing cycle the print shop and the customer collaboratively work up an understanding of what will be good enough for this job, given the various constraints and compromises. The priorities of the print job may emerge as the potential compromises become evident. In these cases (and perhaps more widely) the 'perceptual intent' of the customer is worked up collaboratively in the process of communication with print shop (rather than being pre-specified). Thus in many cases some proofing appears necessary, however a reduction in the number of proofing cycles, both internally and externally would be financially and temporally beneficial.

'Ready to print' jobs

As we have mentioned, there is a large category of jobs known as 'ready to print' which are submitted to the print shop in a state that theoretically means the print shop can just go ahead and print them. The estimate for these jobs is given without including any fee for work beyond production and finishing. In practice, many of these jobs actually do require some work and although the print shop would be within its rights to either give the customer whatever output came from the file or to charge the customer extra, there is often a reluctance to do this. This is because the print shops are operating under the constraints of the service provider-customer relationship in a competitive market, with its orientation to producing good quality work and building customer relationships.

Jobs that are provided to a print shop as "ready to print" can present obvious defects which are self-evident as such to the operator. Fig. 1 shows the output of a print-ready file where the page layout and creep settings[4] have produced an image at the bottom of the page where the edge is printed across the spine of the booklet.

---

[4]   These ensure that images on book pages are positioned correctly in relation to the spine when it is assembled out of separate sheets

Figure 1: Creep and bleed   Figure 2: Unacceptable cast on paper rolls

The print operator can, and often does, make a judgment as to how serious a defect is and whether to proceed with a production run, given that such jobs do not foresee an exchange of proofs between the print shop and the client and/or extensive corrective work on the part of the print shop. It is reasonable after all to expect more tolerance on the part of the client given that they are not paying for the print shop's professional expertise in preparing the job. It is still possible, however, that the client will be disappointed with the results and, regardless of who is responsible for the defects in the final printed product, this can reflect badly on the print shop. This puts pressure on the print shop to do as much as is practicable to correct defective ready-to-print files. What that amounts to will depend on the relationship with and perceived importance of the client, whether further business depends on the client being satisfied with that particular job, etc.

There are also situations where the issue with a job is not self-evident to the print operator, often because it is a question of aesthetic requirements which have not been clearly communicated, and are therefore not visible as matters of perceptual judgment, to the print operator. For example, a company selling paper-making machinery submitted a job as ready-to-print and it was printed without any obvious quality problems, and consequently delivered to the client. Fig. 2 shows a page from this job. The client returned the job claiming the image quality was unacceptable, due to a yellow cast on the photographs which had a negative impact on the reproduction of 'white' paper rolls. This is a problem that the client clearly did not anticipate, so consequently did not give specific warning to the print shop. The print operator's own judgment can only go so far in trying to anticipate the client's preferences, and in this instance the cast, which is not unusual in pictures taken indoor with artificial lighting, was unwittingly aggravated by the client who encoded the file with an inappropriate colour space when creating the PDF file. Had the client expressed this priority from the outset, the print operator might have been in a position to instruct the client on how to better prepare the file for production, or negotiated to do it themselves. Ultimately the print shop agreed to reprint this job because this was a first-time client which they were keen to do more business with, but the job itself was run at a loss.

Of course by rights when the files do not print out as expected the print shops could charge the customer for them anyway, as the contractual agreement is for printing with no work. However, most print shops rely on repeat business and therefore work hard to maintain both a good relationship with the client and a good reputation. In addition, who may be held accountable is a somewhat fuzzy business – the print shop might say the fault lies with the clients files but if the client can see one thing on screen or on their own local printer this might be a difficult case to make. Problems with ready-to-print files are often additionally costly as not only is the cost of work on the print not included in the pricing, but the print shops might print the whole run before any problems are noticed.

Summary of colour workflow

Many troubles for the print shops originated upstream at the customer site; the customers were preparing files without usable colour management tags attached, leaving the print operators to try to get a good quality print using the resources available to them. This often required a compromise on some part of the document. The customers' and the print shops' workflows are poorly aligned and this causes problems for the print shops in terms of efficiently producing documents for the customer. The two ad hoc solutions that we have examined approach the problem from different angles. In the first, the print shops try to deal with the customers files as best they can as they receive them (or on an ad hoc basis), this gives them flexibility but requires extra work at the point of printing. In the second, the workflows of the customer were brought into line with those of the print shops, which produces greater predictability (for at least some parts of the job!) but reduced flexibility and required extra work in advance to standardise the two workflows. In both cases the bulk of the extra work was taken on by the print shops in the name of maintaining good customer relationships. Ideally a colour managed workflow would have avoided many of these problems, but *ideally* seems to be the operative word, since colour management is a system that print shops and customers seem unwilling and unable to implement.

In this paper we are examining the issues of printing, including colour, from the perspective of the print shop. Thus far our only access to the customers perception of colour comes through the proofing process, e.g. which files are accepted or returned. We would contend that what is important here is the print shops professional understanding of the customers' colour requirements which has developed over their years in service to and collaboration with their customers. However, in our ongoing work we are investigating document creation and in particular colour from the perspective of the document creators, that is the print shop customers. To this end we are investigating colour (colour preferences, perceptual intent, aesthetics etc.) as a situated activity, taking into account the different ways in which it is construed, measured, articulated and so on at different points in the document production process. We have reason to believe, drawing on the work of Armour (1996) and Goodwin (1997) that the model on which colour management is based, that of communication of 'perceptual intent' and colour consistency across devices, may be based on a misconstrual of the way colour and aesthetic preference manifest themselves in practice. We hope to explore these issues further in future work.

The next section will examine how the files created at the customer site cause problems for the print shops in variable data printing.

Workflows for variable data printing

Similar to the problems in colour printing, we observed problems in variable data printing caused by the different, non-converging, workflows of the print shop and customer. Variable data printing refers to the printing of a unique printout for every member of a potentially large group of recipients. Text, images, and graphics can change for each printout. For example, an advertisement postcard may include text personalised for a specific recipient, pictures of products that the recipient might be interested in (based on past buying behaviour), and unique graphics which vary based on recipient and/or product characteristics. At the other extreme, only the recipients name and address may vary with all other text and graphics remaining the same.

We observed several kinds of problems with variable jobs at print shops originating at the customer site. One problem was the significant challenge of maintaining 'data integrity' (i.e. the right data in the right place) within variable print jobs. In jobs where images, text, and graphics can all vary at once, print shops and their clients must make sure the correct data lines up for each recipient (i.e. each recipient receives a postcard with the correct name, as well as the intended messages etc.). Data integrity is especially important in jobs where personal information like financial data is included. Sending personal information to the wrong recipient can lead to severe consequences, such as governmental fines in some countries or unintentional disclosure of personal information that could have legal repercussions.

Data integrity problems can originate at the print shop or in the customer files that are sent to the shop. The customer can send incomplete or inaccurate data and/or the print shop can make mistakes in their processing and assembly of the data into a printed piece. It is important to note that the data is not actually merged into the printed piece until after it reaches the print shop. Ultimately, print shops serve as the final checkpoint in ensuring data integrity, even though they have less background understanding to help them recognise problems. One way print shops attempt to address this issue is by sending a proof sample to customers for their approval. Print shops often collaborate with customers to determine what this sample should include. However, the sample may not capture all of the mistakes that may exist and time pressures can mean that proofing is not always feasible.

In addition to sending samples back to customers, print shops often conduct their own internal checks of data integrity, e.g. checking customer's data for missing data fields and problems with images. When information was missing from the data stream, print shops went back to customers to request the missing information. The process of preparing the files for variable data printing is a collaborative one, although perhaps one that might be considered as implicit collaboration, since the customers and the print shops do not explicitly set out on joint file preparation, rather it emerges in the course of the workflow. To illustrate, in Europe2 a routine part of the work of client services, who received the file from the customer, was to check the data files, for missing fields, duplications (e.g. same name at same address) and so on. They would notify the customer of problems with the file, which the customer could then clean up and return, perhaps over a number of iterations.

Checking did not stop at this stage, however, pre-press would also check the file while working on it. In one example, client services had already received new 'cleaner' files from the customer for a letter inviting retail businesses to a conference and passed the files onto pre-press. The pre-press operator in looking at the data files, noticed that in one entry the same name 'Mr Tunnels' was in both the name field and the organisation field. The operator at first considered this was a mistake and went to remove the duplicated entry in the organisation field. However, he then reasoned that 'Mr Tunnels' might in fact be the name of a shop and left the entry in. This example illustrates the judgements that print shop workers must make; the data is somewhat ambiguous to them, being that of the client, yet they routinely carry out such checks and make such judgements.

We can see then that, as with the colour workflows, the print shop carries out work on the customers files to make them printable. Whereas some of this work is in collaboration with the customer, other work is hidden from them, with time constraints and so on meaning it is not feasible to take every 'little' thing back to the customer. There are a number of reasons why this work may take place: (1) the customer does not necessarily know exactly what the print shop requires to produce a good print job, not being party to their workflows; (2) because the merging of the data takes place at the print shop this may be an ideal time to check for problems; (3) since the print shop carries out this work, the client may take it to be part of the service. As with the colour printing described above, who is accountable for what is not always clear cut; for example, sending a letter out twice or with the wrong information may reflect badly on the customer, but also on the print shop. This type of integrity checking was not formally billed to the customer, but was instead another example of extra work performed by print shops in an effort to provide quality products for their customers. To several sites this additional quality checking was considered a value-added service and was considered necessary for customer satisfaction.

Co-creation and co-design

Another problem encountered by print shops is that customer data files did not always include all of the information and/or formatting that the shops needed to do their job. For example, one shop modified customers' files by adding the date that data was received and renaming customer fields to create consistency across jobs. They were adjusting the files to make them fit with their own workflows and in this way the files that were ultimately printed were often co-created by print shops and their customers.

One solution to the difficulties which caused by disparities between customers and print shops workflows is to take on responsibility for creation and design of files earlier in the process, typically at stages previously done by the customers. So for example, in US1 the print shop was printing a job which included variable images pulled from a master asset database. This job was a daily job in which new data streams arrived at the print shop every day. When a new data stream arrived, the print shop broke the data stream into smaller print jobs based on recipient information (and other parameters), and then integrated those jobs with the relevant subset of images from the master asset database. The print shop approached this process by creating image bundles for each subset of the data stream that was printed as a separate job. Originally, the print shop requested that the client provide the image bundles. The client owned the master asset database, updated it when necessary, and created and supplied the image bundles to the print shop along with the data streams. However, there were problems with producing accurate, timely bundles and to address these the print shop took over the master assets database, relocating it to the print shop site and enabling the customer to push files to the database via ftp whenever updates were necessary. The print shop then created scripts which examined the daily data streams and automatically created the image bundles necessary for each daily job. This new process worked better because the print shop had more detailed information about how the data stream needed to be subdivided, based on mailing regulations and other parameters that affected the creation of individual jobs from the daily data streams.

Discussion

The fieldwork described in this paper reveals the extra collaborative work that is needed to make the artefacts - print-ready files, data files, pictures and other content - from one workflow, the customer's, fit with a second workflow, the print shop's. Previous work has described how workflows of different organisations need to converge where the artefacts and processes of one have an impact on the other. When these processes are not smoothly aligned, extra 'management' work is required at and across the organisational boundary (cf. Bowers and Martin 2000; Lee, 2005; Martin et al, 2007). Our studies reveal that although this extra work in printing can be described as collaborative in a broad sense (cf. Hughes, Randall & Shaprio, 1991), it is asymmetric in that the print shops take on more of the ameliorative work (on behalf of the customers) to ensure data, images and files print out well. Reasons for this include the competitive market place, the location of skills (print shops may be best placed to prepare files for their own workflow requirements) and, particularly in colour printing, the haziness that surrounds problem location and 'blame' assignment. Cases where customer and print shop form a more equal collaborative partnership to align their workflows are less usual. Taking the print shop's perspective, the question then arises as to how they might manage this asymmetry, and crucially, how might they reduce the amount of 'boundary management' work they take on, or charge for more for this?

Print shops in general deal with a wide variety of customers, with widely ranging requirements. From one-off jobs to long term repeated business, from basic to high quality, from simple to complex data, from 'concept-to-design-to-print' to 'ready-to-print'. There is just not the place for print shops to work with all their customers to standardise their practices and create 'boundary objects' to smoothly manage the business of printing – too much business is one-off or short term and is based on a model of minimal communication.

The route through which the manufacturers of printing technology (print devices, workflow systems etc.) have sought to assist in dealing with the great variety of customers has been to develop technologies that are meant to ensure an integration and standardisation of format and process across customers and print shops. For example, the technology of 'ICC colour management' is meant to facilitate this, as are workflow systems that are meant to reach out into customer operations or 'configure the customer' (guide and constrain them) through for example, a web portal. Thus far, as we have seen, these systems have not delivered on their promise. Among their problems being the fact that if technologies are going to be adopted and fully utilised, in a way that allows for smooth workflow from customer to print-shop, they need to be straightforward and painless (and cheap!) to deploy and operate, or to yield some other obvious benefits. For example, 'colour management' is complicated to deploy and operate and requires strict adherence from start to finish. Our evidence would suggest that there is not the will or the capability to properly deploy it within customers and print shops, save perhaps for a specialised few. In general, it must be noted that for many customers the 'extra' work that the print shop does on their files may be largely invisible, or only partially visible, and therefore be all part of the service. It is only in particular cases that the print shop will send files back. This makes the situation more complicated for the print shops to enforce process alignment, or start charging for the work.

When we look at the situations where workflows between customers and print shops have been aligned we can see that there are a number of shared features about these situations. Firstly, and maybe obviously, these involve long-term, repeat business customers, for example for the 'HSC' property job in Europe2, or the variable data job in US1, where the print shop took on the database management, scripting and so forth. In these cases the benefits are clearer to the customers (and to the print shops). In the HSC job, the work to set up the spot colour libraries benefits both – it makes the job easier for the print shop and ensures certain quality standards can be met within time constraints. In the US1 job the customer hands over the database management to the print shop which again helps ensure quality, and the print shop can charge extra for this enhanced service. Both situations have the benefit to the print shop of tying the customer in. And they hint at a potential tension in the situation for print shops – the current complexity of aligning workflows and reaching an agreed upon product is inefficient and sometimes costly when dealing with one-off or short term customers or ready-to-print files. However, it may be capitalised upon to charge a little extra to long-term customers or to at least 'gear them in' to a bespoke workflow and a contract – one they view as having been difficult to set up.

In fact, in many ways we now reach the heart of situation for print shops (and common in many service relationships). Long term, high value relationships pay better and are worth extra effort in setting up. However, these customers only make up some of the customer base in this industry – the question then becomes how to deal with the 'long tail' (Anderson, 2006), of many customers who sign up for one-off printing jobs, or cheaper 'ready-to-print' options, given that quality will remain crucially important. Technology seems like the obvious route to achieve quality control through standardisation, however, it has largely failed so far. Although we should note here that more complex online ordering systems are being put into place by some print shops, we have yet to see the impact of them. Although, in for example, Europe1, they were predicting troubles as the customer took on some of the work that had previously been done by the print shop. If, in the future, they needed the print shop to carry out that work, they would have to pay extra for it.

Thus far technologies like 'colour management' have been predicated on the idea that what customers want (their 'perceptual intent') for a printed product is necessarily or can be fully encapsulated in the file they send. Our research has shown that what a customer wants is often the product of a process of 'rework' and relative prioritisation given circumstances and contingencies undertaken collaboratively with the print shop. Given the difficulty of achieving the ideal of colour management it seems like it might be a more fruitful route to consider how to develop tools to accelerate the collaborative process of working towards an acceptable solution for both parties.

References

Anderson, C. (2006) *The Long Tail*. Hyperion, New York.

Armour, L. (1996) *A Study of Colour: Wittgensteinian and Ethnomethodological Investigations*. PhD thesis, Department of Sociology, Lancaster University

Bowers, J., Button, G., & Sharrock, W. (1995) Workflow from Within and Without: Technology and Cooperative Work on the Print Industry Shopfloor. *Proc. ECSCW'95*. 51-66

Bowers, J., & Martin, D. (2000). Machinery In The New Factories: Talk and Technology in a Bank's Call Centre. *Proc. CSCW 2000*. 49-58

Button G & Sharrock W. (1997) The production of order and the order of production. *Proc. ECSCW'97*. 1-16

Garfinkel, H. (1967) *Studies in ethnomethodology*. Englewood Cliffs, N.J.: Prentice-Hall

Goodwin, C. (1997) The Blackness of Black: Color Categories as Situated Practice. In Resnick, L., Säljö, R., Pontecorvo, C. & Burge, B. (Eds.) *Discourse, Tools and Reasoning: Essays on Situated Cognition*. 111-140. Springer

Hughes, J., Randall, D. & Shapiro, D. (1991). CSCW: Discipline or Paradigm? *Proc. ECSCW 91*. 325-336

Hughes, J. O'Brien, J., Randall, D., Rodden, T., Rouncefield, M. & Tolmie, P. (1999) Getting to know the 'customer in the machine' *Group'99*. 30-39

Lee, C. (2005). Between Chaos and Routine: Boundary Negotiating Artifacts in Collaboration. *Proc. ECSCW 2005*. Paris, France, Kluwer. 387-406

Martin, D., Hartswood, M., Slack, R. & Voss, A. (2007). Achieving Dependability in the Configuration, Integration and Testing of Healthcare Technologies. To appear in *JCSCW SI: CSCW and Dependable Healthcare Systems*. Springer, Dordrecht, NL.

O'Neill, J. Castellani, S., Grasso, A., Roulland, F. & Tolmie, P. (2005). Representations can be good enough. *ECSCW'05*. 267-286

Riordan, M (2005) *Variation in premedia colour and the potential automation of imaging tasks*. PICRM-2005-05 Printing Industry Research Center at RIT

Rouncefield, M., Harper, R., & Randall, D., (2000), *Organizational Change in Retail Finance: An Ethnographic Perspective* Routledge Studies in Money and Banking, ISBN: 0415202647

Star, S. L. (1989). The Structure of Ill-Structured Solutions: Boundary Objects and Heterogeneous Distributed Problem Solving. In M. Huhns & L. Gasser (Eds.), *Readings in Distributed Artificial Intelligence*. Menlo Park, CA: Morgen Kaufman

Star, S. L. & Greisemer, R. L. (1989). Institutional Ecology, 'Translations and Boundary Objects: Amateurs and Professionals in Berkeley's Museum of Vertebrate Zoology, 1907-1939. *Social Studies of Science* 19: 387-420.

Whalen, J. & Vinkhuyzen, E. (2001) Expert systems in (inter)action: diagnosing document machine problems over the telephone. In Luff, P., Hindmarsh, J., & Heath, C., (eds) *Workplace studies: recovering work practice and information system design*. CUP. 92-140.

Whalen, J.; Whalen, M. & Henderson, K. (2002) Improvisational choreography in teleservice work. *British Journal of Sociology*. 53 (2). 239-258.

Woolgar, S., (1991). Configuring the user: the case of usability trials. In J. Law (Ed.), *A Sociology of Monsters: Essays on Power, Technology and Domination*. London: Routledge.

L. Bannon, I. Wagner, C. Gutwin, R. Harper, and K. Schmidt (eds.).
ECSCW'07: Proceedings of the Tenth European Conference on Computer Supported Cooperative Work, 24-28 September 2007, Limerick, Ireland
© Springer 2007

Dressing up for School Work: Supporting a Collaborative Environment with Heterogeneous Technologies

Christina Brodersen[1] and Ole Sejer Iversen[2]
[1]Department of Computer Science, University of Aarhus, Denmark
[2]Department of Information & Media Studies, University of Aarhus, Denmark
sorsha@daimi.au.dk, imvoi@hum.au.dk

Abstract. This paper approaches heterogeneity and heterogeneous technology as assets, rather than limitations, in the development of computer supported cooperative work. We demonstrate how heterogeneous technologies sustain teachers' and students' school work by presenting four different prototypes (the HyConExplorer, the eCell, the iGame-Floor and the eBag) that complement one another because they offer different functionalities and are, at the same time, designed with the wholeness of school activities, particularly group-based ones, in mind. Thus, they provide teachers and students with a broad range of IT support to aid them in and outside of the classroom. We take the school domain as our point of departure, but argue that the focus on heterogeneous technologies is applicable for the general area of CSCW.

Introduction

The scope of heterogeneity and heterogeneous technologies is vast within the field of CSCW. Many research contributions focus on heterogeneity as it is present between the different groups of actors in an organisation, for example within healthcare (see Bossen, 2002, Færgemann et al., 2005, Reddy et al., 2001), and describe possible solutions for the design of technology that may accommodate the disparate groups. Other studies of cooperative work within organisations have focused on the organisational aspects and work-arounds found when people are forced to juggle a number of heterogeneous applications and systems to get their work done; for example Bødker et al. (2003) describe work to which heterogeneity is a hindrance, because the technology in use is very poorly integrated, and thus 'heterogeneous technologies' becomes synonymous with 'devices and applications that do not work well together, if at all'.

With this paper, we approach heterogeneity and heterogeneous technology as assets rather than limitations. A common problem encountered when dealing with heterogeneity in technology design is the challenge of combining technology designed with different purposes and disparate design strategies, and this is what the term heterogeneity most often conveys. However, with this paper we want to present a new view on heterogeneity that lets us design with the disparate hardware and software capabilities in mind. In this sense we align our work with that of Fraser et al. (2003), who aim to "provide assemblies of artefacts to support a coherent experience.." (p. 181) when designing technology for museum visitors.

Our point of departure is collaborative activities, primarily project work, in Danish elementary schools, but even though the examples we present originate in a school context, the ramifications of designing *for* heterogeneity are applicable to CSCW in general.

We align ourselves with the work of Rist (1999) and Correa & Marsic (2005), among others, who are concerned with providing access to shared resources through a variety of heterogeneous devices in a way that takes advantage of the individual device and its capabilities (and recognises its limitations). However, the scope of group work in elementary schools, as described below, transcends the needs for accessing a collection of materials, and focuses on providing means for gathering, producing, assessing and presenting material in the course of a group project. We see a strong resemblance between our approach to heterogeneous technology, and the work by Anderson et al. (2000), who present the Chimera hypermedia system. This system allows programmers to use the tools to which they are most accustomed, and provides a variety of views of the same material to support the heterogeneity inherent in software development environments, thus allowing the programmers to choose the tool they find best suited to the task at hand or their particular style of programming.

In this paper we present four prototypes based on heterogeneous technologies that meet current educational challenges and provide teachers and students with new, flexible tools for engaging in the variety of different activities they encounter at school, and particularly in group-based project work: the HyConExplorer, the eCell, the iGameFloor and the eBag. The prototypes presented here are effective *because* they are heterogeneous rather than *despite* their heterogeneity; they complement one another because they offer different functionalities, and because they are, at the same time, integratable and designed with the wholeness of school activities, particularly group-based ones, in mind. These prototypes are but a few of the possible examples of novel IT concepts that can be introduced, and coexist with the 'common' types of technology we find in schools, for example PC's,

SMARTboards™ and laptops, and should be seen as an enhancement rather than a replacement of the already existing technologies. Together, they present a *medium* for collaboration rather than a *mechanism* (Bentley & Dourish, 1995); a flexible framework within which teachers and students can work and add content in accordance with the current topic, learning style and curriculum, and thus choose the right tool to 'dress up' for school work.

School work

The Danish elementary school system is changing, as new educational visions are gaining ground and shaping pedagogical strategies and practice, and technological advances introduce new tools for learning. The Danish Ministry of Education set out, in their vision for learning in elementary schools in the year 2010, a number of skills they consider important for the students to acquire, for example, learning to navigate increasingly heterogeneous sources of information, collaboration and fellowship, participation and responsibility, and problem solving and knowledge sharing (Undervisningsministeriet, 2000); the overall aim being to give students the right tools for entering a work force where *innovation* is becoming an important quality sought by employers. In this context, teachers' and students' roles are changing: Teachers are no longer lecturers but coaches; students are no longer passive recipients of information from a single source, but active, knowledge-producing actors who need to juggle and assess many disparate sources of information in and outside of the school. Thus, the teachers are faced with the challenge of creating an educational environment that nourishes innovation and constructivism, and treats children in a more individualised way, for example through differentiated teaching. To support these issues, we see a general movement within the educational practice of the elementary schools towards interdisciplinary project work where the students collaborate in semi-autonomous groups, not unlike the structure of *loosely coupled workgroups*, as described in Pinelle & Gutwin (2005). The project work aims at creating involvement and relevance in relation to the surrounding environment, drawing on resources from society as well as school facilities. Moreover, the project work form is characterised by reaching beyond the traditional boundaries of the classroom, calling for a more flexible use of the school's physical space and resources. The students move between different locations, for example the classroom, library, hallway etc., utilising available resources and transporting materials across locations, as well as moving beyond the school borders to get hands-on experience with the topics in question. An added educational as well as technical challenge thus lies in enabling teachers and students to carry their information with them in a way that allows easy access to whatever technology they have available during the project work, that is, supporting collaboration in mixed environments. Our locus of design in this context in many senses resembles the discussion dealing with the support of mobile work presented by Bellotti & Bly (1996), and Luff & Heath (1998), in that, rather than focusing on providing increasingly complex PC-based support for distributed activities, we should consider it in terms of mobility, and the understanding that support for mobile work must be realised through a combination of different technologies that supports "...an individual's ability to reconfigure him or herself with regard to ongoing demands of the activity in which he or she is engaged." (Luff & Heath, 1998, p. 306)

Looking specifically at project work, we move beyond the work of the individual, and look at how collaboration may be supported as the students move between different locations and assignments during the group work sessions, and which challenges this poses to the design of new technology for this field. Project work in elementary schools carries aspects of both local and remote mobility (Bellotti & Bly, 1996, Luff & Heath, 1998), in that the work requires them to move around locations outside of the school area to find project information in the 'real world', while maintaining contact with teachers and other students, or being able to save and access information gathered in and outside of the physical school environment. The importance of mobility for children's group work is well documented by, for example, Cole and Stanton (2003), Danesh et al. (2001) and Inkpen (1999), and we take these aspects of mobility seriously when designing IT support for group work in elementary schools.

With this paper we present four prototypes based on heterogeneous technology that, in combination with one another and the already available technology in the schools, meet the educational challenges and provide teachers and students with a very strong technological toolbox that lets them experiment, learn and explore to achieve their educational goals: the HyConExplorer, the eBag, the iGameFloor and the eCell. However, before presenting the prototypes in detail, we will present the setting and our research method.

The iSchool project

The iSchool project was a 5-year research project with the vision of creating learning spaces wherein everyday cultural competences, the curiosity, and the narrative skills and desires of children and adolescents meet the outside world that surrounds them, the teacher and the school. The project aimed to develop an open and 'fluid' information technology with sufficient accessibility and robustness to support learning in and outside the physical limits of the school, based on the development of software infrastructure, GUI's and spatial concepts for new interactive school environments. Teachers and students were provided with the means of experiencing coherence between the use of digital and physical materials across school libraries, classrooms and on fieldtrips.

We believe that good design cannot be achieved without the committed involvement of the teachers and students, who are the usage experts when we deal with teaching and learning in the schools. In the following, we briefly present the schools with which we have worked and the research methods we have applied in this setting.

Research method

We belong to the action-oriented research tradition that has grown out of the Scandinavian cooperative design tradition (e.g. Bødker, 1991, Bødker et al., 2000, Greenbaum & Kyng, 1991 and Schuler & Namioka, 1993) and consequently, we understand design as a cooperative, iterative process which crosses boundaries between work practices, and which must involve active participation from a wide range of contributors. Consequently, the techniques for supporting design in inter-disciplinary groups must support this 'multi-voicedness' (Engeström, 1987) by creating an open and dynamic design space for all stake holders. This is reflected in the methods we have employed to both attain a fundamental understanding of the challenges present in the school environment, and to elicit design requirements for our prototypes. Thus, we have relied on more traditional ways of getting in-sight into a use practice (e.g. field studies and open-ended interviews) as well as devised new methods to understand the impact of the introduction of new tech-nology, and to access areas of the children's lives to which we had poor or no di-rect access (i.e. after-school and family activities) (e.g. see Dindler et al., 2005, Iversen & Nielsen, 2003, Nørregaard et al., 2003).

During the iSchool project we collaborated with four different elementary schools situated in and around Århus. In the process of designing the four proto-types, we hosted more than 30 design workshops and prototype evaluations with the active participation of teachers, students, school administrators, designers, ar-chitects, engineers, programmers and HCI researchers. Each prototype has been evaluated several times in context for periods ranging from 2 weeks to one year. In our collaborative design process with teachers and students, heterogeneity emerged as a shared objective in the design of technology for school work; the teachers, in particular, searched for tools that would allow them to cover a wider range of teaching styles. Rather than expressing a need for more complex, PC-based solutions, the teachers and students requested a more diverse palette of sup-port for their everyday work. In the following, we present the four prototypes we designed with this request in mind: the HyConExplorer, the eCell, the eBag and the iGameFloor. For each prototype, we present a scenario that demonstrates the prototype in educational use, emphasising the relationship between the diverse prototypes. The scenarios are synthesised from our empirical material to show key aspects of the prototype and are thus all based on authentic observations but do not necessarily originate from one episode.

Dressing up for school work with heterogeneous technologies

To meet the educational challenges described above, and address the needs for more diverse tools for school work, we experimented with many different types of technologies to test their strengths and weaknesses within the school context. While the PC offers adequate support for many individual tasks, the teachers put particular focus on acquiring tools for collaboration that also supported:
- Learning by doing and constructing new content and meaning
- Nomadic aspects of school work to support learning in context
- Differentiated education that allows each student to progress according to his or her current level and potential
- Collaboration in adhocracies
- A variety of learning types, for example, kinaesthetic learning

Each of the resulting prototypes provides strong support for one or more of these issues, but none of them cover all; their diversity encourages teachers and students to select or reject any given tool in the toolbox, depending on the task at hand.

The HyConExplorer – supporting nomadic learning in context

As described above, it is becoming didactically desirable as well as technically possible to move school work outside of the classroom, and take advantage of the rich sources of information available beyond books and computer screens. It is, for example, possible to read a book about construction work and gain basic knowledge of what constitutes working at a construction site, but the book has no way of conveying how work is coordinated, how noisy the environment is, how safety is ensured through the action of the workers, etc. Taking a field trip to a construction site is a much richer source of information if we wish to properly grasp the working conditions (Figure 1).

Figure 1 - school work in the field

We have been inspired by a number of projects that aim to move education out of the classroom. Gay et al. (2002) present some interesting pedagogically founded perspectives on how mobile technology may support the natural science subjects in the field, e.g., data gathering and cooperative learning. However, they do not consider how context specific information and services can support field-work. Ambient Wood (Rogers, et al. 2005) is another fine example of how we may move education out of the classroom. Their goal was to provide pupils with: *"contextually relevant digital information during their explorations of the wood-land at pertinent times that would provoke them to reflect and discuss among themselves and the facilitators its significance and implications for what else was around them."* (Want, et al., 1995 p. 45) We agree with the importance of sup-porting reflected learning but we also see a great need and great possibilities in supporting constructive contextual feedback from the pupils, allowing them to produce material tied to the current activity and location. Providing teachers and pupils with tools of contextualization is thus essential to support the learning process in the field and project based education in general.

Figure 2 - The HyConExplorer prototype pack and the HyConExplorer in the field

The HyConExplorer is a geo-spatial hypermedia system that supports project based education and learning outside of the classroom through contextualisation of information, and is in itself an example of an integrated collection of heteroge-neous technologies (see Figure 2). The basic concept of the HyConExplorer is to augment physical space with digital information structures. The HyConExplorer *tablet* edition is designed to run on tablet PC's equipped with a mounted camera for capturing low resolution images, video, and audio, and a Bluetooth enabled GPS unit for recording the user's physical location. HyConExplorer/J2ME is the second generation of mobile hypermedia systems developed on the HyCon framework. The system is designed to run on a much simpler hardware setup than the tablet PC version, namely directly on *Java enabled SmartPhones* with built-in cameras and microphones, which communicate with sensor equipment using Blu-etooth. For more information about the technical aspects and the use of the Hy-ConExplorer, see Bouvin et al. (2005), Bouvin et al. (2003) and Hansen et al. (2004).

An example of usage: part of the curriculum for 8th graders is the study of consumerism, particularly how products are marketed towards teens and tweens. In addition to traditional textbook material about the subject, a group of 8th graders were equipped with the HyConExplorer prototype during a one-day workshop session. To bring the classroom closer to the real world, the session was conducted in the shopping district of central Aarhus where teachers presented the purpose of the day after which the students were split up in smaller groups and went to explore retail consumerism at first hand (Figure 2). They visited different shops in the vicinity where they interviewed shop keepers and customers, took pictures of store fronts and merchandise to identify and discuss the different strategies used for marketing products for teenagers. The HyConExplorer kept track of where and when the different types of material had been collected, and gave the students an overview of the entire set of collected material with geographical markers on a map. After returning to base, the students could look through, discuss and rearrange the collected material into a presentation for the rest of the class, and for publication on a project website[1].

Thus, the HyConExplorer supports both access to existing digital information, and the production and collection of information in context. Furthermore, as the students leave traces of their project activities behind, by tying picture, text or video annotations to a physical location, it becomes possible for them to revisit the information in context, or let other students with a similar project 'bump into' this, and use it to enhance their own work. In this way, the layers of annotations will eventually form a rich, constantly expanding tapestry of information, in situ.

The use of a mobile phone, particularly in combination with the HyConExplorer software, is an example of a dedicated technology directed towards school work beyond school premises. The HyConExplorer provides support for nomadic learning, learning by doing and the construction of new content and meaning.

The eCell – supporting collaborative work in adhocracies

Remote learning has been the focus of many research efforts within the CSCL research community as networked computers provided learners with the possibility to contribute to a common learning environment without being physically present together. E.g. web support for learning has been on the agenda in the computer supported learning communities for many years, introducing a number of primarily administrative systems for sharing documents and awareness about classes and group work (Clulow & Brace-Govan, (2003), Hampel & Keil-Slawik (2001), Heo (2003) and Neville et al. (2003)) and examples of how collaborative technologies can create virtual classrooms (Neal, 1997) or 'Resource Rooms' (Lau et al., 2003). Other systems for remote collaborative learning environments use a strong didactic focus as the point of departure. Abowd (1999) focus on promoting social

---

1　　See http://www.daimi.au.dk/~fah/hycon/konsumus/konsumus-avis.html

awareness in learning communities like the Viras system (Prasolova-Førland & Divitini, 2003). eLearning has thus been primarily concerned with developing advanced technology for supporting distributed, remote learning because the gain and flexibility of this area is so obvious.

However, more efforts are being put into investigating how in-formation technology may also improve collocated, collaborative learning because there is equally much to be gained from enhancing the current learning practices through mindful development of technology to support collaboration in the primary schools. Ulicsak et al. (2001) propose tools for supporting young children (9 – 10 years old) in cooperating with each other as well as reflecting on what they're doing. Scott et al. (2003) provides an excellent study of how technologies such as large screen displays and handheld devices impact children's face-to-face collaboration and stress the importance of designing flexible hardware and software.

The eCell is a temporary collaborative niche for group/project activities in school environments, consisting of a private, inner display and a public, outer display (Figure 3). The eCell was envisioned as a flexible IT-supported installation to be placed in the unused public spaces of the school. Our intention was to include the entire school premises in the learning environment, including the corridors. The intention was to create a dynamic school environment in which the students' could claim unused space as the need occurred, and thereby work with their private materials *in* the public space. In return, the group of students would be able to give something back to the public school environment by sharing parts of their current work with people passing by the eCell.

The inner display of the eCell consisted of a 42"plasma screen with a SMARTboard™ overlay. This setup was powered by a Dell Dimension XPS PC, and provided access to the students' digital portfolios through a BlipNet access point network and a BlueTooth dongle. Peripheral devices included a LogiTech wireless keyboard and mouse. The outer display consisted of 60" diffusion screen for back projection, combined with a 1700 lumen InFocus™ projector. The outer display was powered by another Dell Dimension XPS PC. For more information about the eCell, see Brodersen & Iversen (2005).

An example of usage: a group of students have just attended a briefing session with their teacher to start on their new, interdisciplinary project about moving away from home. The group has to investigate the numerous practicalities related to getting a place of one's own for the very first time, including making a budget, looking at insurance options, and opening a new bank account. Trying to determine how to approach the task, they go to the nearest eCell and access their project folder on the inner display. They brainstorm about all the things they need to cover, and take turns using the SMARTboard™ pens to write down their agreed-upon plan for proceeding with the project over the next few days (Figure 3). The teacher drops in to hear how the group is doing, and suggests that they plan a meeting with a financial advisor at the local bank to help them get an overview of the many expenses connected to moving away from home. They save the plan and the brainstorming notes in their project folder, and the group leaves the eCell. During their work with the project, the group use the eCell on several occasions, and they start posting some of their project material on the outer screen to inform the rest of the school of what they have been up to. The publication of the project material provides the group with new input about the project theme from other students and teachers who have been watching their progress on the public screen of the eCell.

Figure 3 – the eCell from without and within

Whereas the HyConExplorer technology provided IT support for project work in the field, the eCell provides a flexible space for ad-hoc collaboration 'at home', where small groups can work in private on the inner screen, while engaging the rest of the school through what is made public on the outer screen.

The iGameFloor

IT support for public schools has primarily been designed to support traditional class-room teaching placing the students in front of a PC monitor using mouse and keyboard as input technologies. However, current literature (e.g. Carbo et al., 1991) points to the fact that children have different learning styles (kinesthetic, visual, and auditory) and thus technologies for educational purposes must reflect the same range of learning styles. IT support for kinesthetic learning has, so far, not been fully covered in CSCW literature. In the iSchool project, we wanted to experiment with the use of an IT supported kinesthetic learning environment that used an interactive floor technology.

Interactive floors have emerged in recent years, and can be divided into two main categories: sensor-based and vision based interactive floors. Sensor-based interactive floors are typically utilized in dance and performance set-ups e.g. the prototype Magic Carpet (Paradiso et al., 1997) and Litefoot (Fernström et al 1998). The prototypes are sensor intensive environments for tracking the move-ment of feet and in the case of the Magic Carpet the sensor floor has been sup-plemented with sensor technologies for tracking the movements of the upper body and arms. The Z-tiles concept (Leikas et al. 2001, Richardson et al., 2004), and the LightSpace™ technology are existing interactive floors based on tiles and sensors to provide entertainment environments. In contrast to the sensor-based floors, the vision based floors support a more fluid and natural interaction on a floor surface. iFloor (Krogh et al 2004) introduces an interactive floor facilitating debate based on SMS and email contributions. A projector mounted on the ceiling is connected to a local computer to provide a display on the floor. The floor interaction works on the basis of a vision-based tracking package (Nielsen & Grønbæk, 2006) analyzing the rim of the interface based on a video feed from a web-cam also mounted on the ceiling. We wanted to combine the best features from existing sensor based and vision-based interactive floors in a novel interactive floor setup with vision tracking limb contact points from below the floor surface.

Figure 4 - the iGameFloor in use and the game construction interface on PC

The iGameFloor is built into the physical floor of the assembly hall (Figure 4). The iGameFloor is a 3 m deep well, covered with a projection surface. The projection surface is a 3x4 m glass sheet, approximately 9 cm thick, divided into four tiles. The glass surface consists of 8 cm of load-bearing glass, a 3 mm Fresnell diffusion layer, and a 6 mm thickness of hard protective surface glass. The four tiles are supported at the outer edges, and have an internal conical frame resting on a central supporting pillar. The four Web cams associated with the projectors are managed by a tracking client running on a Dell 9150 that runs the vision software, supporting fine-grained tracking of limb positions. The limb positions are communicated to the application machine feeding the four projectors. The tracking client can be switched to a mode in which it uses a ceiling mounted wide-angle Creative™ webcam for coarse-grained tracking of body contours from above. For more information on the iGameFloor, see Grønbæk et al. (2007) and Iversen et al. (2007).

An example of usage: A group of hearing impaired students, aged 9-12, is studying the relationships of individual words to broader language concepts as part of a school project. The teacher and a group of older students have formulated a learning target aimed at understanding how words are related according to their kinship within broader concepts (e.g. banana, apple and orange belong to the broader concept fruit). Initially, they talk about different broader concepts (furniture, cutlery, flowers etc) and find examples in books and on the internet.

Using the iGameFloor game construction interface, they formulate different exercises for the interactive Floor. To the question: "Which animals belong to the category of rodents?" the students choose a number of correct answers (mice, rats, etc.) and a number of incorrect answers (dogs, cows, frogs, etc.). A total of 10 questions constitute a learning game, which can be played by the students individually or with others at the interactive floor (The iGameFloor) in the assembly hall. They submit the game that they have made to a group of younger students, and they play it as a collaborative game with 4 participants (Figure 4). The questions are spoken aloud, and the participants then choose correct and incorrect answers from the visual areas. The collaborative game environment makes them negotiate the correct answers through oral communication. As the hearing impaired students use their hands and feet as cursors, they have limited access to their use of sign language. Thus, they practice their speech and hearing skills in a motivating and collaborative learning environment.

The iGameFloor concept is inspired by Gardner's (1993) work on multiple intelligences which is based on the hypothesis that there is a connection between body movement and language development. By stimulating bodily skills (movement), as a supplement to traditional speech and listening instruction, we could enhance the linguistic capabilities of hearing impaired students in particular. Thus, the iGameFloor supports kinaesthetic interaction and collaboration.

The eBag

Looking at how mobile technology has been introduced in education, we discover that many systems focus on introducing mobile technology to support a traditional classroom type teaching in (Abowd, 1999, Scheele et al., 2003) and outside (Chang & Sheu, 2002) the classroom. A possible explanation for this is that a considerable number of the projects are dealing with higher education (Haderrouit, 2003, Schneider & Synteta, 2002) and consequently the lecture format which is still predominant for teaching at universities. However, the introduction of the concepts of mobile learning (m-learning) (Georgiev et al, 2004) and particularly ubiquitous learning (u-learning) (Jones & Jo, 2004, Ogata & Yano, 2004, Verdejo et al., 2006) emphasises the development on technology and general learning environments to support learning through different mediums and in different places. Verdejo et al. (2006) and Weal et al. (2003) present two fine examples of how we may move education out of the classroom. Verdejo et al. (2006) describes technology for learning activities involving tasks of preparation, data gathering, data analyzing, visualization and modelling aimed at 12-year old students. The Ambient Wood project (Weal et al., 2003) presents an example of how we may provide students with contextually-relevant digital information that would support them in discussing and reflecting on what they were doing and learning. However, the use of mobile technology is, naturally, not limited to use outside. Ogata & Yano (2004) presents JAPELAS (Japanese polite expressions learning assisting system), a context-aware system to help learners choose the correct form for addressing other people in-situ based on information about the social hierarchy. Common to these examples and a parallel to our work is the understanding that ubiquitous learning requires the seamless support of learning activities across technologies, social settings and physical locations.

Figure 5 - an open eBag

The eBag is a digital counterpart to each student's physical school bag (Figure 5). It is a web based portfolio system with seamless proximity-based login from all interactive surfaces in the physical school environment, for example in the eCell or on a traditional PC. Consequently, it serves as a link between different types of displays, through which its contents can be accessed, and it allows the students to collect, carry, access and share digital information very easily. Thus, the eBag is the student's personal, digital repository in which they can place pictures, video, music, text documents and other digital material for use in and outside of school. With the eBag, focus is on the ubiquitous aspects of web support in learning environments that allows the digital information to travel seamlessly across technological platforms. Taking advantage of the current context when placing and retrieving information provides the teachers and students with a sense of seamless interaction with the digital material.

The eBag infrastructure is written on top of the context-aware HyCon framework and collaborative web services based on Web-DAV. The proximity-based login is based on a Bluetooth sensor network and the eBag itself is 'tied' to a mobile phone with Bluetooth capabilities or a BlueTag which the students carry with them. Thus, whenever the students are within reach of a sensor, their eBags will appear on the display connected to that sensor. For more information about the eBag system, see Bouvin et al. (2003) and Brodersen et al. (2005).

An example of usage: An 8th grade class is working with Ohm's Law, and the physics teacher presents the project to the class (Figure). She divides the class into groups by dragging selected eBag icons into close proximity. She distributes a new project folder about Ohm's Law to the different groups by dragging the project folder onto the group icon; for some of the weaker students, the teacher has prepared additional material, and the stronger students receive more challenging assignments, thus supporting a differentiated teaching strategy. Now, the students can access the new group folder on any PC, SMARTboard™ mobile phone, eCell, iGameFloor, etc, on which the eBag application and a Bluetooth sensor is installed. One of the groups chooses to work on laptops, and as they open the computers, their eBags immediately become available on the screen (Figure 6).

The eBag provides a flexible infrastructure for students and their teachers across different technologies, including all the other prototypes. It supports differentiated education because it is personalised, and serves as a digital portfolio as well as a communication tool between the teacher and the students.

Figure 6 - eBags in use across technologies

Heterogeneous technology in and beyond school work

The four prototypes we have presented provide teachers and students with a rich collection of resources to equip themselves for doing school work, that is, we deal with a palette of technologies that have been designed with the same conceptual line of direction, but are based on, and take advantage of different technological platforms. Thus, the prototypes create a structure that allows, but which does not prescribe, differentiated teaching, which offers support for teachers and students when they work in adhocracies, lets the students seek out different places of learning in and outside of the school, and allows, for example, the use of the body in interaction with the technology. The prototypes provide a very flexible framework within which teachers and students can define the contents to suit their curriculum and style of teaching, and as such should be seen as enabling rather than dictating learning. This is not unlike the approach presented in Bentley & Dourish (1995) which calls for a new orientation in supporting flexibly organised work by providing "... a framework within which activity can take place, rather than structuring activities themselves.", that is, providing a *medium* for cooperation rather than a *mechanism*. (p. 135). Our vision for educational technology has never been to banish stationary and laptop PC's from the school setting, but to demonstrate that they can be complimented by different types of heterogeneous technologies that represent different opportunities (and limitations) in an educational setting, and which transcend the practice of sitting students in front of a traditional PC. The four prototypes presented here are our first examples of how this may be achieved, and we hope to see many more tools to enhance the educational toolbox, and that make it easier for teachers and students to 'dress up' for school work.

However, the message of this paper is not limited to academic settings, but has applicability for CSCW in general: for example, the dynamics of school work, that is the flexibility and ad-hoc nature of project work, as well as the constant focus shift as students and teachers go from one class and topic to another, is comparable to the multi-tasking within multiple collaborations observed, for example, by Gonzalez & Mark (2005), where people continually switch between different collaborative contexts throughout their day. Thus, we firmly believe that we could benefit by mindfully seeking heterogeneity, in accordance with the purposes for its implementation within any area of application. The vision of ubiquitous computing is the fluid transfer of data and services across different environments via various available resources, and the design of technology to support this, particularly with respect to supporting collaborative work in the ubiquitous computing environments, which should exploit the advantages (and keep in mind the limitations) of the many different types of heterogeneous technologies available today. Like Bellotti & Bly (1996), we are 'moving away from the desktop computer', but we have not abandoned it altogether; it may be likened to a Swiss-army knife, with an application area unparalleled in the area of information technology, if we design for its strengths rather than its weaknesses. The key in CSCW, as in the support of mobile work, is to think in terms of creating flexible toolboxes of technologies that let users select from a variety of tools, and thus embrace heterogeneity as a core constituent in the design of CSCW systems.

Conclusion

In this paper we propose a view of heterogeneity as an asset to design, and have demonstrated how designing for heterogeneity in a school environment resulted in four very different prototypes. Each of these has its strengths and limitations, but together they represent a wide selection of diverse but interconnected tools which allow teachers and students to 'dress up' for work, depending on the task at hand. This approach has the power to inform the design of CSCW systems in general, by focusing on the advantages of the various available technologies, without sacrificing the wholeness of the context of their implementation, and thus creating a wider selection of tools, systems and applications for collaboration.

Acknowledgements

The work reported comprises that which was conducted for the iSchool project at the Center for Interactive Spaces, at the University of Aarhus. We would like to thank all project participants and our colleagues for their invaluable contributions. We would also like to give special thanks to the teachers and students at 'Møllevangskolen', 'Skovvangskolen', 'Katrinebjergskolen' for participating in the workshops and collaborative design sessions.

References

Abowd, G. D (1999). Classroom 2000: An experiment with the instrumentation of a living educational environment. In IBM Systems Journal, vol 38, no. 4, 1999, p. 508 – 530.

Anderson, K. & Taylor, R.N. and Whitehead, E.J. (2000). Chimera: Hypermedia for Heterogeneous Software Development Environments. In *ACM Transactions on Information Systems, 18*(3), pp. 211-245.

Bellotti, V. & Bly, S. (1996). Walking away from the desktop computer: Distributed collaboration and mobility in a product design team. In Ehrlich, K. & Schmandt, C. (Eds.), *Proceedings of ACM 1996 Conference on Computer Supported Cooperative Work*. New York: ACM Press, pp. 209-218.

Bentley, R. & Dourish, P. (1995). Medium versus Mechanism: Supporting Collaboration through Customisation. *Proceedings of the Fourth European Conference on Computer-Supported Cooperative Work ECSCW'95*. Dordrecht: Kluwer, pp. 131-146

Bossen, C. (2002). The parameters of common information spaces:: the heterogeneity of cooperative work at a hospital ward. In *Proceedings of the 2002 ACM Conference on Computer Supported Cooperative Work*. New York: ACM Press, pp. 176-185.

Bouvin, N.O., Brodersen, C., Hansen, F.A., Iversen, O.S. & Nørregaard, P. (2005). Tools of Contextualization: Extending the Class Room to the Field. In *Proceedings of the 2005 Interaction Design and Children Conference*. New York: ACM Press, pp. 24-31.

Bouvin, N.O., Christensen, B.G., Grønbæk, K. and Hansen, F.A. (2003). HyCon: A framework for context aware mobile hypermedia. In *The New Review of Hypermedia and Multimedia, 9(1):59-88, January 2003*.

Brodersen, C., Christensen, B.G., Grønbæk, K. and Dindler, C. (2005). eBag - a Ubiquitous Web Infrastructure for Nomadic Learning. In *Proceedings of the Fourteenth International Conference on World Wide Web*. New York: ACM Press, pp. 298 - 306.

Brodersen, C. & Iversen, O.S. (2005). eCell - Spatial IT Design for Group Collaboration and Learning in School Environments. In Schmidt, Pendergast, Ackermann & Mark (Eds.) *Proceedings of the International ACM SIGGROUP Conference on Supporting Group Work*. New York: ACM Press, pp. 277-235.

Bødker, S. (1991). *Through the Interface: a Human Activity Approach to User Interface Design*. Lawrence Erlbaum Associates, Inc.

Bødker, S., Ehn, P., Sjögren, D. & Sundblad, Y. (2000). Co-operative Design—perspectives on 20 Years with 'the Scandinavian IT Design Model'. Keynote presentation in J. Gulliksen, A. Lantz, L. Oestericher, K. Severinson-Eklundh (Eds.), *Proceedings of NordiCHI 2000*, STIMDI, pp. 1-10.

Bødker, S., Kristensen, J.F., Nielsen, C. & Sperschneider, W. (2003). Technology for Boundaries. In *Proceedings of the 2003 International Conference on Supporting Group Work (GROUP'03)*. New York: ACM Press, pp. 311 - 320.

Carbo, M., Dunn, R. & Dunn, K. (1991). *Teaching Students to Read Through Their Individual Learning Styles*. Prentice Hall.

Chang. C. & Sheu, J. (2002). Design and implementation of ad hoc classroom and e-schoolbag systems for ubiquitous learning. In *Proceedings of IEEE International Workshop on Wireless and Mobile Technologies in Education*, pp. 8–14.

Clulow, V. & Brace-Govan, J. (2003). Web-based learning: experience-based research. In *Web-based education: learning from experience*. Idea Group Publishing, pp. 49–70.

Cole, H. & Stanton, D. (2003). Designing mobile technologies to support co-present collaboration. In *Personal Ubiquitous Computing*. 7(6), Dec. 2003, pp. 365-371.

Correa, C.D. & Marsic, I. (2005). An optimization approach to group coupling in heterogeneous collaborative systems. In *Proceedings of the 2005 international ACM SIGGROUP conference on Supporting group work*. New York: ACM Press, pp. 274-283.

Danesh, A., Inkpen, K., Lau, F., Shu, K., & Booth, K. (2001). GeneyTM: designing a collaborative activity for the palmTM handheld computer. In *Proceedings of the SIGCHI Conference on Human Factors in Computing Systems*, CHI '01. New York: ACM Press, pp. 388-395.

Dindler, C., Eriksson, E., Iversen, O.S., Ludvigsel, M. & Lykke-Olesen, A. (2005). Mission from Mars - A Method for Exploring User Requirements for Children in a Narrative Space. In *Proceeding of the 2005 Conference on interaction Design and Children* (IDC '05). New York: ACM Press, pp. 40-47.

Ellis, J.B. & Bruckman, A.S. (2001). Designing palaver tree online: supporting social roles in a community of oral history. In *Proceedings of the SIGCHI conference on Human factors in computing systems*. New York: ACM Press, pp. 474-481.

Engeström, Y. (1987). *Learning by expanding*. Helsinki: Orienta-Konsultit.

Fernström, M. & Griffith, N. (1998). Litefoot – Auditory Display of Footwork. In *Proceeding of ICAD'98*, Glasgow, Scotland.

Fraser, M., Stanton, D., Ng, K. H., Benford, S., O'Malley, C., Bowers, J., Taxén, G., Ferris, K., & Hindmarsh, J. (2003). Assembling history: achieving coherent experiences with diverse technologies. In K. Kuutti, E. H. Karsten, G. Fitzpatrick, P. Dourish, and K. Schmidt, (Eds.) *Proceedings of the Eighth Conference on European Conference on Computer Supported Cooperative Work* (ECSCW'03). Norwell, MA: Kluwer Academic Publishers, pp. 179-198.

Færgemann, L., Schilder-Knudsen, T. & Carstensen, P.H. (2005). The dualistic nature of articulation work in large heterogeneous settings – a study in health care. In H. Gellersen et al. (Eds.): *Proceedings of the 9th European Conference on Computer Supported Cooperative Work*. Dordrecht: Springer, pp. 163-184.

Gardner, H. (1993). *Frames of Mind: The Theory of Multiple Intelligences*, 2nd ed. New York: Basic Books.

Gay, G., Reiger, R. & Bennington, T. (2001). Using mobile computing to enhance field study. In Miyake, N., Hall R, & Koschmann, T. (Eds.), *Carrying the conversation forward*. Mahwah, NJ, Erlbaum, pp. 507-528.

Georgiev, T., Georgieva, E., and Smrikarov, A. (2004). m-learning: a new stage of e-learning. In *Proceedings of the 5th international Conference on Computer Systems and Technologies* (CompSysTech '04). New York: ACM Press, pp. 1-5.

Gonzalez, V. & Mark, G. (2005). Managing currents of work: Multi-tasking among multiple collaborations. In K. Kuutti, E. H. Karsten, G. Fitzpatrick, P. Dourish, & K. Schmidt (Eds.) *Proceedings of the 8th European Conference of Computer-supported Cooperative Work (ECSCW'03)*. Paris:Springer, pp. 143-162.

Greenbaum, J. & Kyng, M. (Eds.). (1991). *Design at Work - Cooperative Design of Computer Systems*. Hillsdale, NJ: Lawrence Erlbaum Associates Publishers.

Grønbæk, K., Iversen, O.S., Kortbek, K.J, Nielsen, K.R., & Aagaard, L. (2007). Interactive Floor support for Kinaesthetic Interaction in Children Learning Environments. To appear in the *Proceedings of the International Conference on Advances in Computer Entertainment Technology* (ACE 2007), Salzburg, Austria.

Haderrouit, S. (2003). Implementing web-based learning in higher education: An evolutionary software engineering approach. In Lassner and McNaught (Eds.) *Proceedings of ED-MEDIA 2003*, pp. 483–490.

Hampel, T. & Keil-Slawik, R. (2001) Steam - designing an integrative infrastructure for web-based computer-supported cooperative learning. In *Proceedings of the 10th International World Wide Web Conference*, pp. 76–85,

Hansen, F.A., Bouvin, N.O., Christensen, B.G., Grønbæk, K., Pedersen, T.B. & Gagach, J. (2004). Integrating the Web and the World: Contextual trails on the move. In *Proceedings of the 15th ACM Hypertext Conference*. New York: ACM Press, pp. 98–107.

Heo, M. (2003). A learning and assessment tool for web-based distributed education. In *Proceeding of the 4th Conference on Information Technology Curriculum*. ACM Press, pp. 151–154.

Inkpen, K.M. (1999). Designing handheld technologies for kids. In *Personal Technologies*. 3(1&2), pp. 81-89.

Iversen, O.S. & Brodersen, C. (2007). Building a BRIDGE between children and users: a sociocultural approach to child–computer interaction. To appear in P. Markopoulos, J. Höysniemi, J. Read & S. MacFarlane (Eds.) *Cognition, Technology and Work for the special issue on Child-Computer Interaction: Methodological Research*.

Iversen, O.S. & Nielsen, C. (2003). Using Digital Cultural Probes in Design with Children. In *Proceedings of the 2003 Conference on Interaction Design and Children (IDC'03)*. New York: ACM Press, p. 154.

Iversen, O.S., Kortbek, K.J., Nielsen, K.R. & Aagaard, L. (2007). Stepstone - An Interactive Floor Application for Hearing Impaired Children with a Cochlear Implant. To appear in the *Proceedings of the 6th Interaction Design and Children Conference,* June 6-8, 2007, Aalborg, Denmark

Jones, V. & Jo, J.H. (2004). Ubiquitous learning environment: An adaptive teaching system using ubiquitous technology. In R. Atkinson, C. McBeath, D. Jonas-Dwyer and R. Phillips (Eds.), *Beyond the comfort zone: Proceedings of the 21st ASCILITE Conference*. Australiasian Society for Computers in Learning in Tertiary Education, pp. 468- 474.

Jordan, B. & Henderson, A. (1994). Interaction Analysis: Foundations and Practice. In *Journal of the Learning Sciences, 4*(1). Lawrence Erlbaum Associates, Inc., pp. 39 - 103.

Krogh, P.G., Ludvigsen, M., Lykke-Olesen, A. (2004): "Help me pull that cursor" - A Collaborative Interactive Floor Enhancing Community Interaction. In special issue of *Australasian Journal of Information Systems, 11*(2), pp. 75-87

Lau, L. M. S., Curson, J. Drew, R., Dew, P. M and Leigh, C. (1999). Use of Virtual Science Park resource rooms to support group work in a learning environment. In *Proceedings of the international ACM SIGGROUP conference on supporting group work*. New York: ACM Press, pp. 209-218.

Leikas, J., Väätänen, A. & Räty, V. (2001): Virtual space computer games with a floor sensor control: human centred approach in the design process. In Brewster, S., & Murray-Smith, R. (Eds.) *Proceedings of the First international Workshop on Haptic Human-Computer Interaction, Lecture Notes In Computer Science, vol. 2058*. London: Springer-Verlag, pp. 199-204.

Luff, P. & Heath, C. (1998). Mobility in collaboration. In S. Poltrock, & J. Grudin (Eds.) *Proceedings of ACM 1998 Conference on Computer Supported Cooperative Work*. New York: ACM Press, pp. 305-314.

Neal, L. (1997). Virtual Classrooms and Communities. In Payne, Stephen C., Prinz, Wolfgang (ed.): Proceedings of the International ACM SIGGROUP Conference on Supporting Group Work 1997. New York: ACM Press, pp.81-90

Neville, K., Adam, F., and McCormack, C. 2003. A web-based platform to mentor distance learners. In A. K. Aggarwal, (Ed.) *Web-Based Education: Learning From Experience*. Hershey, PA: IGI Publishing, pp. 189-202.

Nielsen, J. & Grønbæk, K. (2006): MultiLightTracker: Vision based simultaneous multi object tracking on semi-transparent surfaces. In proceedings of the International Conference on Computer Vision Theory and Applications (VISAPP 2006), 25 - 28 February, 2006 Sctúbal, Portugal.

Nørregaard, P., Andersen, J., Dindler, C., Frich, J., Iversen, O.S. & Nielsen, C. (2003). Networking News—a method for engaging children actively in design. In *Proceedings of the 26th Information Systems Research Seminar in Scandinavia* (IRIS'26).

Ogata, H. & Yano, Y. (2004). Context-Aware Support for Computer-Supported Ubiquitous Learning. In *Proceedings of the 2nd IEEE international Workshop on Wireless and Mobile Technologies in Education (Wmte'04)* Washington, DC: IEEE Computer Society, pp. 27-35.

Paradiso, J., Abler, C., Hsiao, K., and Reynolds, M. (1997). The magic carpet: physical sensing for immersive environments. In *CHI '97 Extended Abstracts on Human Factors in Computing Systems: Looking To the Future* (CHI '97). New York: ACM Press, pp. 277-278.

Pinelle, D. & Gutwin, C. (2005). A Groupware Design Framework for Loosely Coupled Workgroups. In K. Kuutti, E. H. Karsten, G. Fitzpatrick, P. Dourish, & K. Schmidt (Eds.) *Proceedings of European Conference on Computer-Supported Cooperative Work (ECSCW'05)*. Paris: Springer, pp. 65-82.

Prasolova-Førland, E. and Divitini, M. (2003). Collaborative virtual environments for supporting learning communities: an experience of use. In *Proceedings of the 2003 ACM SIGGROUP International Conference on Supporting Group Work*, ACM Press, pp. 58 – 67.

Reddy, M. C., Dourish, P. & Pratt, W. (2001). Coordinating Heterogeneous Work: Information and Representation in Medical Care. In W. Prinz, M. Jarke, Y. Rogers, K. Schmidt & V. Wulf (Eds.) *Proceedings of the Seventh European Conference on Computer-Supported Cooperative Work. (ECSCW'01)*. Dordrecht:Kluwer Academic Publishers, pp. 239-258.

Richardson, B., Leydon, K., Fernstrom, M., and Paradiso, J. A. (2004). Z-Tiles: building blocks for modular, pressure-sensing floorspaces. In *CHI '04 Extended Abstracts on Human Factors in Computing Systems* (CHI '04). New York: ACM Press, pp. 1529-1532.

Rist, T. (1999). Using Mobile Communication Devices to Access Virtual Meeting Spaces. In *Personal and Ubiquitous Computing, 4*(2). London:Springer, pp. 182-190.

Rogers, Y., Price, S., Randell, C., Fraser, D. S., Weal, M. and Fitzpatrick, G. (2005) Ubi learning integrates indoor and outdoor experiences. Communications of the ACM, 48(1):55–59, 2005.

Scheele, N., Seitz, ., Effelsberg, W. & Wessels, A. (2003). Mobile devices in interactive lectures. In Lassner and McNaught (Eds.) *Proceedings of ED-MEDIA 2003*. AACE, pp. 154–161.

Schneider, D. & Synteta, P. (2002). Eva pm: Towards project-based e-learning. In *World Conference on E-Learning in Corporate, Government, Healthcare, and Higher Education*, volume 1. AACE, pp 2755–2756.

Schuler, D. & Namioka, A. (Eds.). (1993). *Participatory Design, Principles and Practices*. Hillsdale, NJ: Lawrence Erlbaum Associates.

Scott, S.D., Mandryk, R.L. & Inkpen, K.M. (2003). Understanding children's collaborative interactions in shared environments. In *Journal of Computer Assisted Learning* 19(2), pp. 220-228.

Thomas, A.N., Pellegrino, J., Rowley, P., Scardamalia, M., Soloway, E. & Webb, J. (1992). Designing collaborative, knowledge-building environments for tomorrow's schools. In *Proceedings of the SIGCHI conference on Human factors in computing systems*. New York: ACM Press, pp. 427 – 430.

Ulicsak, M., Daniels, H. & Sharples, M. (2001). CSCL in the classroom: The promotion of self-reflection in group work for 9-10 year olds. In *Proceedings of the European Conference of Computer Supported Collaborative Learning*, pp. 617-624.

Undervisningsministeriet (The Danish Ministry of Education). (2000). *Vision 2010 - en udviklingssamtale med skolen*. Undervisningsministeriets forlag. ISBN 87-603-1708-6.

Verdejo, M. F., Celorrio, C., Lorenzo, E., and Sastre, T. (2006). An Educational Networking Infrastructure Supporting Ubiquitous Learning for School Students. In *Proceedings of the Sixth IEEE international Conference on Advanced Learning Technologies* (ICALT). Washington, DC: IEEE Computer Society, pp. 174-178.

Want, R., Schilit, B., Norman, D.A., Gold, R., Goldberg, R., Petersen, K., Ellis, J., & Weiser, M. (1995). An overview of the PARCTab ubiquitous computing experiment. In *IEEE Personal Communications*, 2(6), pp. 28–43.

Weal, M. J., Michaelides, D. T., Thompson, M. K. & DeRoure, D. C. (2003). The ambient wood journals: replaying the experience. In L. Carr and L. Hardman (Eds.) *Proceedings of the 14th ACM Hypertext Conference*. ACM Press, pp. 20–27.

L. Bannon, I. Wagner, C. Gutwin, R. Harper, and K. Schmidt (eds.).
ECSCW'07: Proceedings of the Tenth European Conference on Computer Supported Cooperative Work, 24-28 September 2007, Limerick, Ireland
© Springer 2007

Exploring cooperation through a binder: A context for IT tools in elderly care at home

Alexandra Petrakou

School of Communication and Design, University of Kalmar, Sweden.
School of Engineering, Blekinge Institute of Technology, Ronneby, Sweden.
Alexandra.petrakou@hik.se

Abstract. This paper examines the empirical findings of a study of the work and cooperation taking place within and between the home help service and home health care in a Swedish county. The aim is to explore the current context for the design and development of IT tools that may facilitate cooperation and coordination in elderly care at home. The focus of the study is the use of a tool, a binder, which collects material considered as important to sustain cooperation between and within the two services. The paper illustrates concrete aspects of how different types of material is utilised and how the actual use of the binder reveals both advantages and disadvantages. Through focusing on the binder, aspects that are crucial to consider also when designing IT tools are made visible. These aspects include the need to support the integration of home care information and the importance of assisting asynchronous communication through the facilitation of informal information. It is also necessary to consider the mobile nature of the home care work, and the importance of a patient-centric view that promotes information sharing between the heterogeneous network of actors involved in the home care process, including the care receiver and relatives.

Introduction

The challenges that face the developed countries in respect of elderly care urge health and social care systems to change their current work practices and to increase their collaborative activities. The growing number of elderly people, in combination with a decreasing number of young people, requires not only new approaches to the organisation of elderly care but also new ways of working (Gröne and Garcia-Barbero, 2001; Leichsenring, 2004). In addition, there is an endeavour to make it possible for the elderly to live at home for as long as possible instead of moving them to an institution (Anderson and Hussey, 2000; SALAR, 2006). This challenge is complex and demands different kinds of solutions. One approach that is considered crucial when providing care of good quality to the elderly in the home is improving the cooperation between health care and social care providers (Bricon-Souf et al., 2005; Reed et al., 2005; SALAR, 2006). Furthermore, technology, and information technology (IT) in particular, is often proposed as a means to facilitate aspects of the work practice and to support cooperation between different care providers (Bricon-Souf et al., 2005; Koch, 2006; Koch et al., 2004; Vimarlund and Olve, 2005).

Research regarding IT tools for elderly care at home has been conducted by different research fields and various IT solutions have been discussed. Koch (2006) presents an overview of the research on IT in the home care setting. The overview shows that the majority of the papers concerns the measurement of vital signs and audio-video teleconsultation, while a minority of the research papers is focused on IT tools that improve information access and communication in order to facilitate cooperation. Furthermore, research conducted within the field of Computer Supported Cooperative Work (CSCW) has shown that cooperation is a complex issue that requires more than the improvement of information access and communication (Bannon and Schmidt, 1989; Heath and Luff, 1991; Schmidt, 1994).

Care settings are often collaborative in nature and studies conducted from a CSCW perspective have explored these settings. These studies focus on the use of medical records – paper-based as well as computerised (Heath and Luff, 1996; Luff and Heath, 1998) – transformations in the collaborative work caused by the introduction of new technology (Bardram et al., 2005), the use of a shared information system to coordinate work (Reddy et al., 2001), temporality in collaborative work (Reddy et al., 2006), the formal and informal character of information sharing (Hardstone et al., 2004) and the use of different non-digital artifacts (Bardram and Bossen, 2005) etc. CSCW studies relevant to this paper are focused on the work and cooperation carried out in different care settings with co-located personnel, in contrast to elderly care at home. In fact, in-home elderly care has not been extensively studied from a CSCW perspective. Only a few studies have explored the implications for design of IT tools intended to support the cooperation between health care and social care providers conducting elderly care at home (e.g. Bricon-Souf et al., 2005; Koch et al., 2004; Pinelle, 2004; Pinelle and Gutwin, 2003a; 2005). Most importantly, there is a lack of research on how the workers providing care for the elderly in their homes actually manage to work and cooperate at the present time, and how the workers use the tools currently available to support cooperation and coordination.

The aim of this paper is to explore the current context for the design and development of IT tools that may facilitate cooperation in elderly care at home. The paper analyses the empirical findings of a study of the work and cooperation taking place within and between home help services and home health care in a county in Sweden. The focus of the study is the actual use of a tool that supports cooperation and coordination. This tool is a binder that contains a collection of material considered as important for supporting cooperation between and within the two services. With the binder in focus, issues crucial to consider also when developing an IT tool are made visible. In contrast with the loosely coupled home care cooperation studied by Pinelle (2004) and Pinelle and Gutwin (2003a; 2005), the setting examined in this paper depends to a much greater extent on cooperation and coordination between workers. Furthermore, compared to hospital wards and medical units, in-home elderly care is clearly more complex. To begin with, the work is carried out in the care receivers'[1] homes, environments that cannot easily be changed. Secondly, the work activities need to be coordinated between different actors not only within but also across organisational boundaries. Thirdly, work activities need to be coordinated across time.

The paper is structured as follows; first I describe the research setting and method. Then, I give a general description of the binder and outline the material collected in the binder in detail. I also illustrate some concrete aspects of how the material in the binder is used to support cooperation and coordination. This is followed by an analysis and discussion of crucial aspects that must be considered also when developing IT tools related to elderly care at home. Finally, I conclude by summarising the findings from the analysis of the binder.

Research setting and method

The findings examined in this paper are the result of empirical material collected from a study of the work and cooperation conducted in elderly care at home in a county in Sweden during 2002-2004 (Broberg and Petrakou, 2003). In the county where the study took place, as in more than half of the counties in Sweden, two parties provide the elderly with care at home: social care at home is provided by the municipalities through the organisation of home help service groups (in Swedish: hemtjänst), while health care at home (in Swedish: hemsjukvård) is supplied by the county council. Therefore, care of an elderly person at home may well involve both organisations and engage different providers in the task. Several reports have shown that this cooperation does not always function properly and it is often suggested that the use of information technology may improve the situation

---

[1]   A person in need of home help service is called a care receiver, while a person in need of home health care is called a patient. However, later on in the paper we will use the word 'care receiver' to indicate a person in need of both home help service and home health care.

(SALAR, 2006; SOU, 2004). The problems with cooperation between home help service and home health care were also observed by health and social care managers in the studied county and a project was therefore initiated with the purpose of improving the problematic situation. One part of the project consisted in a study of the work and cooperation taking place in and between home help service and home health care in order to define the problems that occurred in the daily work. In this paper, I examine some of the empirical material collected by that study.

The empirical material was collected through observational studies, interviews and group discussions. During the observational studies, a number of selected workers were observed during their work shift. A total of 30 work shifts taking place during the day, the evening and the night were observed. During these studies, field notes were taken and transcribed the day after the observations were conducted. To continue, some 15 interviews were conducted with managers in both organisations while district nurses, assistant nurses and home help service workers participated in the group discussions. The aim with the interviews was to enable a holistic understanding of the work and the cooperation between and within the two organisations. Questions were therefore asked concerning the rules and obligations for home help service and home health care. The group discussions focused on four themes: problematic issues concerning the inter-organisational cooperation between home help service and home health care, problematic issues concerning work activities, problematic issues concerning co-operative activities and finally general issues concerning information needs and tools.

Home help service

The home help service units (10 units) in the studied municipality belong to the Administration of Health and Social Care and are headed by a unit manager who is responsible for the staff, the budget and the administration. A home help service unit consists of two or more home help service groups. Every group has a meeting point, which is often situated in an apartment. The home help service units consist of 22 day shift groups that are reorganized in the evenings to form approximately 10 evening shift groups which cover different geographical areas. In addition, a unit also consists of 4 night groups that handle the entire municipality. The number of workers in each group varies between 10 to 15, depending on the number of care receivers in the area.

The home help service provides help with food, getting dressed, cleaning, care assistance, practical services and social care and they also respond to alarms. To apply for home help service, the care receiver or his/her relatives sends an application to a care administrator who is located in a special department within the care administration of the municipality. When an application is granted, a notification is sent to the home help service group and to the unit manager. The group includes the new care receiver in their planning and a contact person is chosen from the staff. The contact person is ultimately responsible for the care receiver and for his/her living accommodation and care. For example, it is the contact person who should contact other care providers such as primary care if needed.

In order to obtain information about a new care receiver or to acquire updated information about a care receiver's needs, all meeting points have a fax machine. Fax messages with information regarding new care receivers and the care interventions they should receive are sent from the care administrator. In addition, the care workers send information through the fax machine to the care administrator if they observe a need to change the interventions.

The studied day shift group shared two mobile phones that were provided by the municipality. These mobile phones are used mainly for receiving alarms. Naturally, the mobile phones are also used if the care workers need to communicate. If they need information which is stored at the meeting point, they can call the fixed telephone which is located there. However, they cannot be certain that someone will answer since no one is assigned to monitor that phone. During the evening, all personnel have mobile phones, since only two people from each day shift group work during the evening. In addition, all night personnel have mobile phones.

Home health care

Health care in Sweden is provided by the county councils which are responsible for organising hospitals and primary care. Primary care is administered by primary care centres situated in every municipality. Every municipality is geographically divided into districts and a primary care centre is responsible for one or more districts depending on the number of inhabitants. The primary care centres are staffed by physicians, district nurses, nurses and assistant nurses. At the studied county council, home health care is a task performed by district nurses supported by assistant nurses in primary care. Home health care is provided during the day and in the evening. During the day, home health care is provided by every primary care centre. In the evening, an evening group handles all patients in the municipality.

The district nurses have a greater responsibility and conduct more advanced interventions than the assistant nurses. A district nurse may give a care diagnosis. This means that when a district nurse examines a patient, she judges if the patient should be treated through interventions provided by her (care interventions) or if the patient needs to consult a doctor to receive a medical diagnosis. Furthermore, the district nurses have a reception where the people of the district can make an appointment. The care interventions provided by district nurses both at the reception as well as in the patients' home include checking the blood pressure, binding up wounds, giving insulin, taking samples for testing, insert pharmaceuticals into medical dispenser units, dispensing medicine and eye drops, helping with surgical stockings and also giving advice and support to their patient. Assistant nurses assist the district nurses with minor treatments such as helping with surgical stockings, binding up wounds, treating wounds with cream, administering eye drops and insulin. Some of the interventions conducted by assistant nurses in home health care could be delegated to the home help service workers.

The home health care personnel use a computerised patient record system which can only be accessed through computers located at the reception. This system is used within all primary care and contains functionalities other than the record system such as booking appointments at the reception and sending messages to personnel within primary care. Of the items included in the patient record, the nursing care plan (in Swedish: omvårdnadsplan) is the most important document for a district nurse. This plan is created at the beginning of a patient's care process. In addition to this, the district nurse needs to document every contact that she has had with the patient throughout the care process. She must thus specify what has been done during a visit, in what condition the patient was in when she arrived, and also which people have been contacted. While working in the patients' homes it is impossible to access the patient record system. If the nurse wants to bring information from the patient record to a home care visit, she has to print information from the system or enter the information into her calendar before she leaves her office. Otherwise she has to phone someone who is at the reception or go back to the reception herself to get the information needed. In contrast to home help service workers, all district nurses and assistant nurses have mobile phones.

Since the evening group also belongs to primary care, each person must document his or her interventions using the same computerised patient record system as the dayshift personnel use. However, workers in the evening group also send faxes to all the day shift districts to report items of special interest. Similarly, the dayshift personnel send faxes to the evening group if there is a new patient that is in need of home health care during the evening, and they also phone the evening group if there is something this group should pay special attention to.

Elderly care at home

Elderly care at home involves not only home health care and home help service but also, for instance, hospital visits, physiotherapy at the hospital, physiotherapy at the primary care unit as well as family and relatives. It is of utmost importance that the care process is discussed with the care receiver. Furthermore, during the late 1990s the National Board of Health and Welfare (SOSFS1996:32) issued new requirement regarding information sharing and cooperative care planning to the municipalities and county councils. Therefore, when an individual is scheduled to receive care at home for more than two weeks, a care plan meeting (in Swedish:

vårdplanering) with all parties involved is mandatory. Usually, this happens after an elderly person has been treated at the hospital. During this meeting, the care providers and the care receiver with relatives discuss the care interventions that need to be conducted in order for the care receiver to be able to live in his/her own home. Approximately 4-7 people attend these meetings; the nurse at the hospital who initiates the meeting, the care receiver and his/hers relatives, personnel from the home help service and home health care and finally the physiotherapists from both the hospital and from primary care if needed. Home health care is represented by a district nurse or in some cases an assistant nurse. The home help service is represented by the care administrator, who writes the application for home help service. If possible, the presumptive contact person is also at the meeting.

The SVOP binder: A tool for cooperation and coordination

In order for the home help service and the home health care workers to be able to cooperate and coordinate their efforts during the care process, there is a great need of information and communication. Since the new guidelines were issued in the late 1990s this is even more so the case. Therefore, in 2001-2002 a project called Rehab 300 was conducted. As a part of this project, workers and managers at the studied municipality and county council constructed an information and communication tool, the SVOP binder, that may provide sufficient material for cooperation. SVOP stands for "coordinated health care and care planning" (in Swedish: Samordnad Vård- och OmsorgsPlanering). The binder has been modified a couple of times over the years and is here described in its most recent form.

The SVOP binder, Figure 1, is considered the care receivers' property and is used for storing, documenting and communicating information about the care receiver and his/her care process. Essentially, when an elderly person is in need of both home health care and home help service, as detailed by the care plan meeting, the district nurse compiles the SVOP binder. The binder is placed in the care receiver's home (often in the kitchen) and consists of different types of material. The binder collects two types of material: material that used to be kept separately by the two organisations and material needed to support cooperation. What the latter type of material should consist of was initially discussed during the Rehab 300 project. Furthermore, the inside of the binder provides space for inserting cards such as the patient's identification card, needed when visiting primary care or the hospital. There is also space for inserting medical prescriptions and a pharmacy card shown when purchasing pharmaceutics from a pharmacy. See Table I for a complete description of the documents in the binder. If needed, addi-

tional material is included in the binder such as a wound status, catheter reports
and fluid charts.

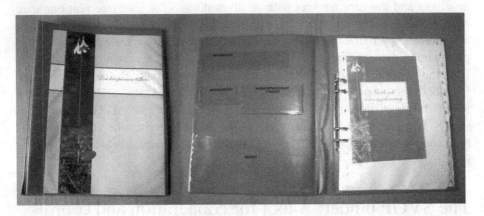

Figure 1. Left – The front of the SVOP binder. Right – A view of the inside of the binder.

In Table I, the documents collected in the binder are divided according to their
function. "Read-only" refers to documents that are only updated when the complete document is replaced. "Writeable" refers to documents that may be annotated. "Other" is material that is not always required to coordinate the home care
process but is needed in other situations. The table also describes the proposed
use of each document, the worker/s responsible for updating each document and
from where the document is collected. Along with the material in the binder, observation of the actual use of the binder showed that material was also attached *to*
the binder such as post-it notes and/or a note pad. This is not included in the table
but described later.

As shown in Table I, the binder consists of several documents which provide
the workers with information for administering home care interventions and for
supporting cooperation and coordination between the workers involved. During
the observations, it was found that the actual use of the binder has both advantages and drawbacks. More importantly, the binder and its use highlight many
important issues essential to cooperation. In what follows, I illustrate some concrete aspects of how some of the material collected in the binder is used.

Table I. The material in the SVOP binder

Read-only	Use	Responsible	Collected from
Work plan	Description of home help service interventions during morning, afternoon, evening and night.	Contact person	Home help service
Contact information	Information about all involved in the care process and their contact information.	District nurse and contact person	Only in the binder, facts collected from patient records and home help service
Summary of care interventions	Overview of the care receiver's social situation and health condition.	District nurse, contact person, care receiver and relatives.	Only in the binder
Prescribed pharmaceuticals	Information about medicines and prescriptions.	District nurse	Patient records from hospital and primary care.
Discharge information	Information from the hospital after discharge or from a physician in primary care after a visit.	Hospital personnel or physician in primary care	Hospital or physician in primary care
Physiotherapy interventions	Documented if needed by describing the problem, the procedure and the follow up.	Contact person	Only in the binder
Current health condition	Description of the care receiver's current health condition, which is needed during a hospital admission.	District nurse and contact person	Only in the binder
ADL status (Activities of Daily Living)	Description of the daily activities that the care receiver is able to handle personally and those which he/she needs help with.	Contact person	Home help service, Hospital
Writeable	**Use**	**Responsible**	**Collected from**
Current events document	Irregular events during the care process are documented but also messages between the care providers.	All personnel	Only in the binder
Signature list for pharmaceuticals	Confirms which medicine is given and by whom.	All personnel	Patient records
Signature list for physiotherapy interventions	Documents each visit by describing the problem, the procedure and the follow up.	All personnel	Only in the binder
Appointments	Appointments to the hospital, the primary care unit and other relevant places are documented.	All personnel, relatives and the care receiver	Only in the binder
Note pad	Care receiver and relatives write messages to the home care personnel.	Care receiver and relatives	Only in the binder
Other	**Use**	**Responsible**	**Collected from**
Signature clarification	Clarifies to whom the signature belongs.	All personnel	Only in the binder
Care receiver's approval	Care receiver signs this document to approve information sharing between the organisations.	District nurse and unit manager in home help service	Only in the binder

Read-only: Contact information

A SVOP binder is used mainly for elderly people who need multiple care interventions from both the home help service and home health care. These people are often in need of other types of care interventions such as physiotherapy treatment or they require continuous contact with the physicians at the primary care unit. In order to provide an overview of all the people involved in the care receiver's care process, the SVOP binder contains these people's contact information, including name, title and telephone number. Furthermore, the relatives' contact information is also included. If there is a need to contact some of these people during a home visit, this makes it easier to reach the right person at the right time. One such example was observed during a home help service visit:

> During a home visit the home help service worker asks an elderly care receiver how she slept the night. She describes a pain she felt all night. When the care worker helps the care receiver to get out of bed she complains about a pain in her arm. The care worker gets worried and tells the care receiver that if it hurts so much, they need to contact the district nurse. The care receiver agrees and the care worker looks in the SVOP binder for the telephone number to the district nurse. She phones the district nurse and informs her about the situation. The district nurse says that the care receiver must come to the emergency ward immediately. However, the care receiver does not want to go and the care worker tries to calm her. Since the care receiver is very anxious someone must be with her in the ambulance and at the emergency ward. The care worker consults the SVOP binder in search of a telephone number to a relative to discuss if he/she is able to meet the care receiver at the hospital.....

Having instant access to the contact information was essential in the above situation. With this, the care worker could contact both the district nurse and the relative so quickly. During the observation, the care worker declared that anxiety may have a detrimental effect on the health condition and that it was therefore necessary to contact the relative so he or she could be with the care receiver at the emergency ward and calm her down. Being able to contact the right person at the right time is often crucial in elderly care at home, not only in these situations, but also if the needed information is not available in the SVOP binder, as will be discussed later in the paper.

Writeable: Signature list for pharmaceuticals

One of the intentions with introducing the SVOP binder is to support the shared care interventions, that is, interventions that could be conducted by both the home help service and home health care workers. These interventions consist mainly of minor tasks such as administering insulin or prescribed pharmaceuticals, or treating minor wounds. When administering medicine, the workers must sign their names and write the time on a signature list. Therefore, the SVOP binder contains material for these interventions such as a document called prescribed pharmaceuticals and a signature list for pharmaceuticals. The general planning of who should do what and when is often done during the care plan meeting. However, this plan can be changed during the care process if the health status of the care receiver alters. For example, if a care receiver has been prescribed pain killers that are supposed to be administered during night time, the medicine could instead be given during the evening if the care receiver is in a lot of pain. Thus, the signature list for pharmaceuticals also provides important information for the night personnel as illustrated by the following observed situation:

> The night group is visiting a care receiver who is in a lot of pain. There should be a pharmaceutical for this among the prescribed medicines that the night group is allowed to administer if necessary. However, they notice that there is no medicine to administer on this particular night. They start wondering why and look at the signature list for pharmaceuticals to see if anyone else administered the medicine. On the signing list they see that a care worker gave the medicine to the care receiver during the evening shift.

In this particular situation the signature list gave essential information to the night personnel; without it they could not have known why there was no medicine available. If the SVOP binder did not exist, the workers would have had to sign one document within each organisation since it is obligatory to document all such shared care interventions. It should also be noted that the signature list for pharmaceuticals not only provides information to the involved parties, it is also important when a care receiver's health status is followed up on.

Writeable: Current events document

One of the most important parts of the binder is considered to be the document called current events. In this document the workers involved write notes to inform each other and to report current and irregular events that occurred when they treated the care receiver. In this document, the workers can also find out if there is anything that the other care providers should pay special attention to. In addition, this document makes it possible to see patterns in the care receiver's physical condition during the home care process. For example, if it turns out that a care receiver often falls, this indicates that something is needed to prevent the person from falling and injuring him/herself, such as special shoes or an adjustment of the care interventions.

Although the current events document could in theory be a very important co-operation tool, it was found during the observations that it is used rarely. Since the binder, and thus the current events document, is located in the care receiver's home, the workers can only access this information when visiting the care receiver. This is unfortunate, since some of the information is needed before they visit the care receiver (this is so they can coordinate visits or prepare relevant material before the visit). Therefore, when the workers add to the current events document, they also try to reach the person who needs the information by phone, by leaving messages with other persons or, if possible, by using voice mail. Unfortunately, sometimes the messages do not reach the right person. The following observed situation describes the actual consequences of a message not reaching the right person:

> The district nurse is visiting a care receiver that previously had a wound that was treated with cream. During this visit the district nurse observes that the wound has gotten worse again. Therefore, she writes in the current events document to the home help service workers that they should resume the treatment of the wound with cream. Since the binder is seldom used, it took a couple of days before the home help service worker saw this message.

Reaching personnel in home care by phone is not an unproblematic task. While all district nurses and assistant nurses have mobile phones, the home help service workers during dayshifts share only two mobile phones, and these are used primarily for receiving alarms. Therefore, district nurses often have trouble contacting a specific home help service worker. Instead of talking directly to the person that needs the information, district nurses often leave a message with another person who answers either one of the mobile phones or the fixed phone at the home help service meeting point. Sometimes, the day shift personnel do not even bother to make notes in the binder, especially when the information is intended for other day shift personnel. Instead, they prefer phoning each other to ensure that the right information will reach the right person at the right time, even though reaching people by phone may be difficult. Unfortunately, if the day shift personnel phone each other instead of making notes in the current events document, this can lead to difficulties for the night shift personnel, since there is no other way to keep informed during night visits. The following observed situation describes one such occurrence:

> When the nightshift personnel visit a care receiver, they notice that the care receiver has trouble breathing. The care workers discuss the possible reasons for this and study the SVOP binder to see if the other care providers have made notes about this. The information in the binder is not up-to-date and the care workers do not know what they should do. They know that the care receiver recently went to the hospital, but they do not know why. They decide to visit the care receiver several times during the night and talk to the dayshift group about the care receiver's condition. When the care workers report to the dayshift it is revealed that the day shift care workers already knew about this problem and discussed it with the district nurse. Finally, the day shift tells the night shift that the care receiver's condition will not improve and that there is nothing they can do.

The lack of adequate information not only complicated the work of the night shift personnel, it also made it more difficult to see patterns in the care receivers' physical condition during the home care process. In addition to this, since information is not always available in the SVOP binder, personnel must sometimes spend a great deal of time phoning the people that may have the required information.

Material attached to the binder

Another important aspect concerning the binder is the use of post-it notes and a note pad. Post-it notes and/or a note pad are often placed on the front of the binder to highlight that information has been added to the binder, or to inform the other personnel of something that falls outside the scope of the current events document or of other document sections in the binder. For example, home help service workers may inform of interventions that have been postponed or left for other workers to do. Relatives also attach notes to the binder with messages to the home help service or home health care personnel such as shopping list. It is interesting to observe that there actually is a document called "note pad" included in the binder for the relatives to use, see Table I.

A context for IT tools in elderly care at home

The studied setting of elderly care at home is clearly complex. The care workers need to cooperate within their own group, within their own organisation between work shifts and also across organisations. In other words, the workers are required to cooperate and coordinate their efforts across both their disciplines and their organisational boundaries while being distributed across time and/or space. Furthermore, the work is conducted in the care receivers' homes, and these are environments that are difficult to change. Compared to the loosely coupled home care setting studied by Pinelle (2004) and Pinelle and Gutwin (2003a; 2005), the setting examined in this paper is much more dependent on cooperation and coordination between workers. In addition, there is a development towards even more extensive and tighter cooperation since health care and social care systems are required to increase their collaborative efforts in order to provide in-home elderly care of good quality. To meet these demands, the involved personnel have constructed a tool, the so called SVOP binder. This binder contains collected material that the care providers consider important for supporting cooperation between and within the two services.

In the previous section I illustrated some concrete aspects of how different types of material in the SVOP binder are used to facilitate this cooperation. The actual use of the binder reveals both advantages and drawbacks with its construction, and it highlights issues critical for cooperation in elderly care. In this section I analyse the findings from the binder case and discuss aspects that are crucial to consider when developing IT tools in the context of elderly care at home.

Coordinating by integrating home care information

One aspect that needs to be considered from the perspective of elderly care at home is the importance of coordinating the activities conducted across groups and organisations. The SVOP binder is intended to help gather and disseminate relevant information that may make cooperation and coordination easier for all involved care providers. By integrating information as shown in Table I, the SVOP binder aids care personnel awareness of the other care providers; it describes the

activities that have been conducted, and it outlines the events that have occurred
during the home care process. Without the binder some of this information would
not be known to co-workers from other groups, both within and across the organisations.

The integration of health care information has been the focus of studies regarding the development of electronic patient records, also called integrated care records (Fitzpatrick, 2004; Hardstone et al., 2004). An electronic patient re-
cord/integrated care record could certainly support some aspects of the cooperation in elderly care at home, but it is important to emphasize that the documents
compiled in the SVOP binder cannot simply be replaced by an electronic patient
record. Although some parts in the binder are gathered from the patient record, as
illustrated in Table I, the SVOP binder is not a copy of the patient record. All the
medical information of the patient record is not relevant for those involved in elderly care at home. Similarly, the binder does not provide all the home help information that is kept by the home help service. Furthermore, it should also be noted
that while the electronic patient records contains information on a person's life-
long health record, the SVOP binder is focused on supporting information sharing
and communication in the daily work. Fitzpatrick (2004) highlights a similar observation in a study of a medical unit at a hospital. In this study, the health care
staff conducted their work by using what Fitzpatrick calls the working record.
The working record is defined as a diverse collection of documents and forms
used by the health care staff to help them plan and manage their work. This is
similar to the intention with the SVOP binder, with the difference that all material
is gathered in one specific place, namely in the binder.

Various degrees of informal information

Another important element of working with elderly care at home that the SVOP
binder highlights is the need to communicate both asynchronously and informally. Since the home help service group of the case study only has two mobile
phones to share, it is often problematic for the district nurses to reach the right
person by phone. Providing all home help service workers with mobile phones
might improve the situation to some extent, but phones will not eliminate the need
for asynchronous communication. When administering care in the home the attention must be on the care receiver, and the care worker's main responsibility is not
to be accessible by phone to everyone. As for the night shift personnel, they
communicate primarily asynchronously. Therefore, asynchronous communication
is essential for supporting the cooperation within and between home help service
and home health care. Bricon-Souf et al. (2005) also highlight this issue by stating
that a major feature of home care is its asynchronous character and that "team
members cannot directly communicate during task realization or in an informal
way during a meeting or a coffee break" (p. 811). Furthermore, the kind of asyn-

chronous communication that is needed is not only an exchange of formal information regarding the care receiver's health status, but also an informal discussion during the care process. The importance of supporting informal discussion has been emphasized by several researches. Hardstone et al. (2004) state that work gets done through the sharing of informal information within organisations. They also emphasize the importance of informal discussion and provisional judgement for effective cooperation within a multidisciplinary team. Furthermore, Westerberg (1999) shows how decisions are often reached in an informal way, through negotiations and discussions with others.

In this study, the current events document in the SVOP binder and the post-it notes attached to the SVOP binder allow asynchronous communication. The use of these two materials has not been legislated. Rather, they spring from a need to cooperate and to provide the best home care possible. Therefore, they also support different levels of informality, in contrast to the information gathering that characterises the construction of the patient record. Fitzpatrick (2004) makes a similar observation in her analysis of the working record where she finds various degrees of formality to coexist.

The current events document is much more formal than the post-it notes. In the current events document the personnel write notes to inform each other of irregular events that have occurred in relation to the care receiver, or if there is anything that the other care providers should pay special attention to. It is also possible to identify patterns by examining the irregular events that take place over time in a care process. The use of the current events document thus offers an overview which allows for easy monitoring of a care receiver's health progress. The notes in the current events document also make it possible to formally store the information. In contrast to the current events document, the post-it notes are not formally stored since the message is usually disposed of after it has been received. The post-it notes that are attached to the binder also have another type of function: they can be considered as asynchronous pointers. Even though the post-it notes might be viewed as containing redundant information, they are sometimes used to indicate that new information has been added, to remind care workers to search for information in the binder.

Patient-centric view

The third important aspect that needs to be considered in the context of elderly care at home is how the SVOP binder supports a patient-centric view. As a complement to the "clinician-centric view of work" described by Fitzpatrick (2004), the patient-centric view is essential to the context of elderly care at home. From the perspective of this context, the main intentions with the binder are to share information, to enable care providers to communicate with each other about the care receiver and also to include the care receiver and the relatives in the care process.

The working record studied by Fitzpatrick (2004) provides a clinician-centric view of work. In that study, each member of the care team contributed to the official patient chart through progress notes, examination notes etc. They also worked with various forms and documents where they could reflect on "their own view of the patient and their role in the care of that patient" (Fitzpatrick, 2004, p. 294). These clinician-centric documents were always carried around by the health-care workers of the clinic, thus helping them plan and manage their work. In home care, the care providers also work with their own "clinician-centric" documents while conducting their individual work tasks and while coordinating work within their own group. As a complement to this, the SVOP binder as such is focused on the care receiver since it assembles the information and communication necessary for the heterogeneous network of actors surrounding the care receiver to cooperate. What is more, the SVOP binder makes it possible for relatives and the care receiver himself/herself to actively participate in the care process. Therefore, the binder can reflect the views of both formal and informal care providers as well as the views of the care receiver. It is also important to note that the binder is always with the care receiver as it is placed at home and follows the care receiver to hospital and to visits to primary care.

By providing a patient-centric view of care, the SVOP binder may be considered as a boundary object (Star and Griesemer, 1989) for the heterogeneous network of actors involved in the home care process.

> Boundary objects are objects which are both plastic enough to adapt to local needs and the constraints of the several parties employing them, yet robust enough to maintain a common identity across sites ... they have different meanings in different social worlds but their structure is common enough to more than one world to make them recognizable, a means of translation. The creation and management of boundary objects is a key process in developing and maintaining coherence across intersecting social worlds (Star and Griesemer, 1989, p. 393).

The SVOP binder serves as a boundary object in the sense that it provides all the involved actors with a common ground through supplying joint information material and enabling communication between different groups and individuals. In addition, the material and documents in the binder are not only used to coordinate the care process, but are also used to support involved individuals in daily work situations. For example, the current events document brings together current information regarding the care receiver's general health status, information that may indicate to individual care givers that they must make a particular contribution to the care process.

The management of tools that provide a patient-centric view differs slightly from the management of clinician-centric tools. The main difference is that care providers who work with patient-centric tools need to consider that the patient and his or her relatives should be able to access the documentation that the tool provides. Therefore, the care providers should not write messages to each other that they do not want the relatives or the care receiver to read. Examples of such messages are informal medical remarks that might upset the care receiver. This constraint may be one of the reasons why the current events document is seldom used. In addition to this, privacy issues need also be considered since visitors are able to access the information in the SVOP binder.

The patient-centric view is valuable in the home care process as it facilitates the active participation of relatives and care receivers. However, the SVOP binder should not be regarded as a replacement of clinician-centric tools. Both views are required in order to provide in-home elderly care of good quality.

Accessibility and mobile work

In order to make proper use of the information and communication possibilities that the binder provides, it has been placed in the care receivers' homes and it is also considered the care receivers' property. The advantage of this is that the binder is easily accessible not only for the home help service and home health care, but also for all other care providers. For example, if a care receiver must go to the hospital, the SVOP binder is sent with the care receiver so that the personnel at the hospital can make notes in the binder or get a quick overview of what has happened during the home care process. Most importantly, the binder is accessible to the care receiver himself/herself and to relatives.

The placement of the binder in the care receivers' homes and the fact that it is considered as the care receiver's property certainly contribute to the patient-centric view described previously. However, it was observed that this placement also hampered accessibility and that it therefore failed to fully support the way the workers in home help service and home health care conduct their care. Since the binder is placed at the care receivers' home, the material in the binder is only accessible during the actual visit. This may be unfortunate since some of the information contained by the binder needs to be reviewed before the visit, for example the messages written in the current events document. Furthermore, the information on current events is evidently of such importance that the care workers try to reach each other by phone instead of making notes in the current events document. This has resulted in important information being left out of the binder, which in turn forces the care workers to phone each other in order to become updated by the people who presumably have the information. Synchronous communication may work during the day shift, but without proper information in the binder, the night shift personnel cannot know what has happened to the care receiver or comprehend the discussions that have been conducted between the care workers during the day. Due to the restricted accessibility of the binder, the potential for asynchronous communication provided by the SVOP binder is not fully realized.

Several researchers propose mobile technology such as PDAs and laptops to support home care since their work is mobile to a great extent (e.g. Bricon-Souf et al., 2005; Koch, et al., 2004; Pinelle and Gutwin, 2003b; Scandurra et al., 2004). Such technology may be applicable also in this case to support the mobile nature of this type of care work and to make it possible for workers in home help service and home health care to receive and disseminate information wherever they are. However, to substitute the SVOP binder with mobile technology intended to support home help service and home health care is not a straightforward task. It is of utmost importance to consider the advantages in cooperation currently provided by the SVOP binder. These advantages include the integration of home care information, the varying degrees of informal information and the participation of care receivers, relatives and other care providers.

Conclusions

In this paper I have examined empirical findings from a study of the work and cooperation taking place in the home help service and home health care. The focus of this study has been how a so called SVOP binder is used to support cooperation and coordination. With the binder in focus, issues crucial to consider also when developing an IT tool were made visible.

The binder was designed to meet the demands of the complexity of elderly care at home. Furthermore, the material collected in the binder has been carefully considered by workers and managers in the home help service and home health care. The care workers' holistic understanding of the elderly care process is one of the cornerstones of the SVOP binder. The binder integrates home care information with the relevant information needed for coordinating the home care process. However, the SVOP binder is not only a collection of information; it also helps support the degrees of informal information needed in the daily work characterising care service. Furthermore, the SVOP binder promotes a patient-centric view since the aim with the binder also is to inform and communicate with other care providers and to include the care receiver and relatives in the care process. In order to make this information accessible, and to facilitate communication between these parties, the binder has been placed in care receiver's home and is considered the care receiver's property. Clearly, the binder provides all involved in the elderly care context with useful material for cooperation and coordination. At the same time, the SVOP binder suffers from some problems. In particular, the placement of the binder in the care receiver's home means that the material is not accessible to the mobile care givers at all times. In addition to this, privacy issues must also be considered since everyone who visits the care receiver is able to access the information provided by the SVOP binder.

Mobile Technology such as PDAs may be used to make it possible for workers in the home help service and home health care to receive and disseminate information wherever they are. However, to merely replace the information in the SVOP binder with a mobile tool for the home help service and the home health care workers may not be the ultimate solution. It is necessary to consider the advantage of various degrees of informal information that is supported by the post-it notes, the note pad and the current events document. There is also a need to consider how the information currently compiled in the SVOP binder can be made to accompany the care receiver in the care chain so that all care providers can access the information and communicate with each other. Finally, it is important to consider the inclusion of the care receiver and relatives in the care process when developing IT tools in the context of elderly care at home.

Acknowledgements

The study was sponsored by the eHealth Institute at the University of Kalmar. I want to thank the district nurses, assistant nurses, home help service workers and managers who participated in this study. I also wish to extent my warmest gratitude to Bo Helgeson and Päivi Jokela for reading, discussing and giving invaluable comments on the different versions of this paper.

References

Anderson, G. F. and Hussey, P. S. (2000): 'Population aging: A comparison among industrialized countries', *Health Affairs*, vol. 19, no. 3, pp. 191-203.

Bannon, L. and Schmidt, K. (1989): 'CSCW: Four characters in search of a context', *Proceedings of ECSCW 1989*, pp. 358-372.

Bardram, J. E and Bossen, C. (2005): 'A web of coordinative artifacts: Collaborative work at a hospital ward', *Proceedings of GROUP 2005*, pp. 168-176.

Bardram, J. E, Bossen, C. and Thomsen, A. (2005): 'Designing for transformation in collaboration: A study of the deployment of homecare technology', *Proceedings of GROUP 2005*, pp. 294-303.

Bricon-Souf, N., Anceaux, F., Bennani, N., Dufresne, E. and Watbled, L. (2005): 'A distributed coordination platform for home care: analysis, framework and prototype', *International Journal of Medical Informatics*, vol. 74, no. 10, pp. 809-825.

Broberg, H. and Petrakou, A. (2003): *Verksamhetsanalys av Hemsjukvård och Hemtjänst i Kalmar län*, Research Report (2003:2), University of Kalmar.

Fitzpatrick, G. (2004): 'Integrated care and the working record', *Health Informatics Journal*, vol. 10, no. 4, pp. 291-302.

Gröne, O. and Garcia-Barbero, M. (2001): 'Integrated care – A position paper of the WHO European office for integrated health care services', *International Journal of Integrated Care*, vol. 1, June 2001, www.ijic.org.

Hardstone, G., Hartswood, M., Procter, R., Rees, G., Slack, R. and Voss, A. (2004): 'Supporting informality: Team Working and Integrated Care Record', *Proceedings of the CSCW 2004*, pp. 142-151.

Heath, C. and Luff, P. (1991): 'Collaborative activity and technological design: Task coordination in London underground control rooms', *Proceedings of ECSCW 1991*, pp. 65-79.

Heath, C. and Luff, P. (1996): 'Documents and professional practice: 'bad' organisational reasons for 'good' clinical records', *Proceedings of CSCW 1996*, ACM Press pp. 354-363.

Koch, S. (2006): 'Home telehealth – Current state and future trends', *International Journal of Medical Informatics*, vol. 75, no. 8, pp. 565-576.

Koch, S., Hägglund, M., Scandurra, I. and Moström, D. (2004): 'Towards a virtual health record for mobile home care of elderly citizens', In M. Fieschi, E. Coiera and J. Li (Eds.): *Proceedings of MEDINFO 2004*, IOS Press, Amsterdam, pp. 960-963.

Leichsenring, K. (2004): 'Developing integrated health and social care services for older persons in Europe', *International Journal of Integrated Care*, vol. 4, September 2004, www.ijic.org.

Luff, P. and Heath, C. (1998): 'Mobility in collaboration', *Proceedings of CSCW 1998*, pp. 305-314.

Pinelle, D. (2004): *Improving Groupware Design for Loosely Coupled Groups*, Ph.D. Dissertation, Department of Computer Science, University of Saskatchewan.

Pinelle, D. and Gutwin, C., (2003a): 'Designing for Loose Coupling in Mobile Groups', *Proceedings of GROUP 2003*, pp. 75-84.

Pinelle, D. and Gutwin, C. (2003b): 'Awareness-Based Scheduling in a home care clinical information system', *Proceedings of American Medical Informatics Association* (AMIA) Annual Symposium 2003, pp. 519-523.

Pinelle, D. and Gutwin, C., (2005): 'A groupware design framework for loosely coupled workgroups', *Proceedings of ECSCW 2005*, pp. 65-82.

Reddy, M. C., Dourish, P. and Pratt, W. (2001): 'Coordinating heterogeneous work: Information and representation in medical care', *Proceedings of ECSCW 2001*, pp.239-258.

Reddy, M. C., Dourish, P. and Pratt, W. (2006): 'Temporality in medical work: Time also matters', *Computer Supported Cooperative Work*, vol. 15. pp. 29-53.

Reed, J., Cook, G., Childs, S. and McCormack, B. (2005): 'A literature review to explore integrated care for older people', *International Journal of Integrated Care*, vol. 5. January 2005, www.ijic.org.

SALAR - The Swedish Association of Local Authorities and Regions (2006): *Care of the Elderly in Sweden Today*.

Scandurra, I., Hägglund, M. and Koch, S. (2004): 'Integrated care plan and documentation on handheld devices in mobile home care', In S. Brewster and M. Dunlop (Eds.): *Proceedings of Mobile Human-Computer Interaction – Mobile HCI 2004*, LNCS 3160, Springer-Verlag, pp. 496-500.

Schmidt, K. (1994): 'Cooperative work and its articulation', *Le Travail Collectif (Travail Humain)*, vol. 54, no. 4, pp. 345-366.

SOSFS (1996:32): *Socialstyrelsens Föreskrifter och Allmänna Råd om Informationsöverföring och Samordnad Vårdplanering*.

SOU (2004:68): *Sammanhållen Hemvård*, Betänkande av äldrevårdsutredningen.

Star, S. L. and Griesemer, J. R. (1989): 'Institutional ecology, 'Translations' and Boundary Objects: Amateurs and professionals in Berkeley's Museum of Vertebrate Zoology, 1907-39', *Social Studies of Science*, vol. 19, pp. 387-420.

Vimarlund, V. and Olve, N-G. (2005): 'Economic analyses for ICT in elderly healthcare: questions and challenges', *Health Informatics Journal*, vol. 11, no. 4, pp. 309-321.

Westerberg, K. (1999): 'Collaborative networks among female middle managers in a hierarchical organization', *Computer Supported Cooperative Work*, vol. 8, no. 1-2, pp. 95-114.

L. Bannon, I. Wagner, C. Gutwin, R. Harper, and K. Schmidt (eds.).
ECSCW'07: Proceedings of the Tenth European Conference on Computer Supported Cooperative Work, 24-28 September 2007, Limerick, Ireland
© Springer 2007

Common Information Spaces along the illness trajectories of chronic patients

Glenn Munkvold[1] and Gunnar Ellingsen[2]

[1] Nord-Trøndelag University College, Department of Information Technology, Norway; [2] Dept. of Telemedicine, University of Tromsø, Norway.
glenn.munkvold@idi.ntnu.no; gunnar.ellingsen@unn.no

Abstract The notion of Common Information Spaces (CIS) is extensively used as a framework to analyse cooperative work. Drawing on recent contributions to the discourse on CIS, this paper develops a perspective on how information is shared in heterogeneous contexts. We study the introduction of an electronic nursing plan in the psychogeriatric ward at the University Hospital of North Norway. The plan was expected to improve information sharing among the healthcare practitioners and in that sense contribute to their CIS. However, although the nursing plan was regularly updated, it was less used *in practice* than initially expected. We suggest that this can be ascribed to the temporal and evolving character of both medical information and work. Drawing on the notion of trajectories, we elaborate on these findings and develop a perspective on CIS, emphasising its situated, temporal and negotiated character.

Introduction

The notion of Common Information Spaces (CIS) is extensively used within the CSCW field as a framework for analysing cooperative work. A CIS denotes the context in which information is shared between actors whose work practices interleave. With a particular focus on the interrelationship between actors, artefacts, information and the situations in which these meet, it aims at refining our understanding of how artefacts support coordination and articulation work in cooperative settings (Schmidt and Bannon, 1992; Bannon and Bødker, 1997; Randall, 2000; Bossen, 2002).

CIS comes in many forms and is used in various contexts (for example, see Bannon and Bødker, 1997). As illustrated by Bossen (2002), it is of particular interest as a framework to analyse problem-solving activities in heterogeneous work settings. These typically involve places and situations with a high degree of inter-communication and "where the meanings of the shared objects are debated and resolved" (Schmidt and Bannon, 1992, p.27).

In this paper, we explore the notion of CIS by drawing on empirical data from the healthcare context. Healthcare services today typically are profoundly frag-mented across technical, organisational and professional boundaries, thus resem-bling the heterogeneity described above. Knowledge about treatment and care is increasingly dispersed among many people and many technologies, and single doctor-patient relationships are gradually being replaced by a shared-care ap-proach in which the individual patient's healthcare is handled by a team of pro-fessionals, each specialising in one particular aspect of care (Grimson et al., 2000). Throughout the illness trajectory, patients today face individual healthcare practitioners and/or organisations whose knowledge of each other's activities is limited. Accordingly, expressions such as shared care, integrated care and conti-nuity of care are commonly used to denote more general ambitions of creating coherent and effective health care services for patients across disciplinary and in-stitutional boundaries (Winthereik and Vikkelsø, 2005).

Fundamental to the ongoing efforts of overcoming institutional and interdisci-plinary boundaries are infrastructural arrangements such as electronic patient re-cords (EPRs), standards, procedures, classification schemes and the like (Grimson et al., 2000). These form the link that is assumed to enhance information sharing and coordination of work so that patients are given a coherent service where every professional perspective is accounted for. The assembly of infrastructural arrangements and the various work practices they entrench delineate what is de-noted as CIS in the CSCW literature.

Empirically, we have studied the implementation of the nursing care plan at the psychogeriatric ward in the University Hospital of North Norway (UNN). The ward serves elderly patients who suffer from a combination of chronic and psy-chiatric conditions. Work at the ward thus entails extensive cooperation across professional boundaries. Aligned with contemporary efforts to promote the nurs-ing profession in the health sector, the nursing plan was expected to improve in-formation sharing among the healthcare practitioners. This included an improved documentation practice together with enhanced predictability and a clearer over-view. However, although the nursing plan was regularly updated and contained current status information about all patients, we observed that it was less used in practice than its primary users, the nurses, wanted. For example, the plan was used to a lesser degree in close cooperative settings such as during admission of patients, in nursing handover conferences and in interdisciplinary meetings.

We suggest that this can be ascribed to the temporal and evolving character of both medical information and work. Drawing on the notion of trajectories, we elaborate on these findings. In particular, we pay attention to how the nursing plans were integrated into the work practice. Our main objective is to contribute to a conceptualisation of CIS (see Reddy et al., 2001; Bossen, 2002; Rolland et al., 2006) by providing a temporal dimension to *how* information is made common in heterogeneous work practices. Analytically, we draw on the notion of trajectories (Strauss et al., 1985; Timmermans and Berg, 1997) in which we explore how work is accomplished along the trajectories of chronic patients. In this sense, trajectories "refer not only to the physiological unfolding of a patient's disease but the total *organization of work* done over that course, plus the *impact* on those involved with that work and its organization" (Strauss et al., 1985, p.8). We proceed along the following dimensions:

Firstly, we explore what kind of information sources and artefacts are in use in cooperative settings that cut across professional boundaries. We elaborate on the nature of CIS (manifested by the points at which the work trajectories of physicians and nurses intersect) as situated, temporal, regularly (re)negotiated and achieved in practice. The nursing plan, we argue, is only one entity in a larger information infrastructure. Its particular value is in constituting the nursing perspective on the care process, as the medical cardex does for the physicians' perspective.

Secondly, we discuss how medical data is not fixed and self-contained, but evolves over time during the patient's illness trajectory. To portray this evolving trajectory, the plan had to be linked with a variety of information entities and practices. We develop our argument by providing an example from the nursing handover conference, which is a setting where it is crucial to know how a patient is progressing.

Thirdly, we illustrate the unpredictable nature of the plan. We analyse the trajectory of the nursing plan and stress its uncertain and contingent character and how it eventually became an infrastructural entity that appealed to a new reality. In our case, it increasingly became entangled with managerial concerns for resource management and control.

The remainder of this paper is organised as follows. First we elaborate on the theoretical foundation for the paper. We then describe the setting for our empirical investigation and describe the method used, followed by a description of the case. Subsequently the case is analysed. In the conclusion, we consider some implications contributing to the conceptualisation of CIS.

Theory

Related work on Common Information Spaces

The notion of CIS was originally proposed by Schmidt and Bannon (1992) as a response to the, at that time, somewhat objectified perceptions of how information is shared among actors whose work activities interleave:

> "Cooperative work is not facilitated simply by the provisioning of a shared database, but rather requires the active construction by the participants of a common information space where the meanings of the shared objects are debated and resolved, at least locally and temporarily" (Schmidt and Bannon 1992, p.27).

Human interaction is always mediated by representations of information. Hence our experiences and the way we perceive the world can never be replicated perfectly. Schmidt and Bannon (1992) in particular point out that information entities always have to be interpreted by human actors. By doing so, a clear distinction is made between the carrier of information and its meaning. The common information space then is said to encompass "the artifacts that are accessible to a cooperative ensemble as well as the meaning attributed to these artifacts by the actors" (Schmidt and Bannon, 1992, p.28). At the core of their argument is how information is continuously decontextualised to make it commonly available, and how it is subsequently recontextualised within the framework of its new work context (Schmidt and Bannon, 1992). In this process, the notion of articulation work is crucial as a mechanism to handle the contingent nature of cooperation and preserve the flow of work (for example, see Strauss et al. 1985; Gerson and Star 1986). A main objective in CIS, then, is to reduce the complexity in articulation work.

Bannon and Bødker (1997) refine the notion of CIS by providing an account of how information is made common. They argue that a CIS is dialectical in nature - both open and closed at the same time. "Openness" refers to the way information is always malleable and interpretatively flexible in local communities of practice. 'Closed' refers to the way information goes through a process of closure and becomes boundary objects (Star and Griesemer, 1989) - immutable and portable across different communities of practice. A further refinement of the CIS, they argue, needs to address the interplay between these two perspectives (Bannon and Bødker, 1997, p.87). In their refinement of the concept, they identify five domains in which the degree of closure is increasingly visible. At the one end they identify coordination centres, such as control rooms, in which the participating actors are co-present and where it is crucial that the CIS remains open and malleable. At the other end they place the web, in which information is packaged and made available to a larger, distributed audience.

The assumed idea of commonality is however problematised by Randall (2000). In demonstrating how classification scheme maintenance increasingly becomes difficult as the number and range of users increases, Randall argues that:

"... the very notion of CIS is radically underspecified. It is not possible to distinguish its puta-
tive features by reference to technology, to information or to organizational structure. At very
least we might begin to recognise that the problems of classification use in CIS are likely to
range along a continuum which stretches from shared, small group, work tasks to complex in-
ter-organizational chains." (Randall, 2000, p.17)

A more recent contribution in this respect is proposed by Bossen (2002). Based
on ethnographic fieldwork within a hospital ward, Bossen delineates seven parameters that can be used to position a CIS. The parameters include the degree of
distribution of work, the multiplicity of webs of significance, the level of required
articulation work, the multiplicity and intensity of means of communication, the
web of artefacts, the immaterial mechanisms of interaction, and the need for pre-
cision and promptness of interpretation (Bossen, 2002, p.176). Erickson and Kellogg (2003) add to this picture by describing how artefacts are socially translucent
and thus make visible the various professional activities in cooperative settings.

In studying how information is incorporated into the diverse work practices of
an intensive care unit, Reddy et al. (2001) contribute to our understanding of the
dialectical nature of CIS. In studying how a group of healthcare practitioners
made use of a shared information system, they found that the particular strength
of a computer-based system was its ability to decouple information from its representation. Although the healthcare practitioners had a common focus on patient
care, decoupling enabled the production of more specialised representation of information, which subsequently allowed the various professionals to work more
effectively together.

Rolland et al. (2006) provide another relevant contribution. Based on a study
of different CIS in a major international oil and gas company, they argue that
some CIS appear as much more situated, momentary and malleable when embedded within extremely heterogeneous contexts. They claim that infrastructural arrangements for a CIS that attempts to cut across various communities of practice
and heterogeneous collections of information inevitably will produce new instances of fragmentation (Rolland et al. 2006, p.499).

Nursing Care Plans as infrastructural arrangements in CIS

Nurses are commonly referred to as the ones "who weave together the many facets of the [health care] service and create order in a fast flowing and turbulent
work environment" (Allen, 2004, p.279). Therefore, their associated tool, the
nursing plan, is an infrastructural arrangement that will inevitably play a key role
in producing CIS. Located at the very core of patient care delivery, nursing care
plans are assumed to contribute to higher quality of care and better cost contain-
ment (Reed and Stanley 2003; Sexton et. al 2004). In addition, it is assumed that a
nursing plan provides for appropriate treatment and continuity of care for the patient within and across institutional boundaries (Reed and Stanley 2003). As argued by Voutilainen et al (2004, p. p72):

" (…) its [the nursing plan's] primary purpose is to ensure the individuality and continuity of care (…) When documentation is accurate, individual, pertinent and up-to-date, it promotes consistency and effective communication between nurses and the other team members involved in care."

Similar arguments are also echoed in Norwegian policy documents (KiTH 2003, p. 18)

"(…) documentation of this work process [nursing process] is also called the care plan, it is interdisciplinary and can be used by all professions."

Basically, a nursing plan is an overview of nurse-related diagnoses (problems) combined with relevant interventions for a patient with a chronic disorder. At the core of the nursing plan is its shared terminology. The nurses apply this terminology to describe the patients' problem (i.e. nursing diagnoses) and link this to one or several interventions, detailing what to do in certain situations and several outcomes to enable an evaluation of what nursing care can affect. Some of the most well-known systems are that of the North American Nursing Diagnosis Association (NANDA), the Nursing Intervention Classification (NIC) and the Nursing Outcome Classification (NOC) (for example, see Gordon, 1998).

Another 'promise' associated with the electronic nursing plan, and a more structured documentation process, is that it is expected to replace a variety of existing dispersed information sources in the hospital. In terms of sharing information, this is considered to be a major problem, for example during handover conferences:

[The nursing handovers] however often lack formal structure and this is compounded by a lack of guidelines for the nurse giving the report. Consequently, the information presented may be irrelevant, repetitive, speculative or contained in other information sources" (Sexton, 2004, pp.37-38).

Integrating the information in the plan is implicitly assumed to enhance information sharing among the nursing practitioners. However, the literature reveals a nursing community whose actual compliance with a structured documentation process is rather low (Björvell et al., 2002; Sexton et. al 2004). Studies have indicated that "nurses have problems integrating the nursing process and care planning into their daily record-keeping" (Björvell et al., 2002, p.35). In a survey cited by Sexton et al. (2004, p.38) "nursing care plans were referred to in handover only 1% of the time and this was probably because care plans were not being updated".

Trajectories

In hospitals, there have been many efforts in integrating heterogeneous information sources (Ellingsen and Monteiro, 2003), thus contributing to a CIS. However, work in hospitals is clearly depending on the patient case and how the patient's illness develops. This draws attention to a temporal and evolving character of both medical information and work. Thus, adding a temporal dimension to CIS is necessary. Therefore, we draw on the notion of trajectories (Strauss 1993; Strauss et al. 1985). Strauss describes it as follows:

> "(1) the course of any experienced phenomenon as it evolves over time (an engineering project, a chronic illness, dying, a social revolution, or national problems attending mass or "uncontrollable" immigration) and (2) the actions and interactions contributing to this evolution" (Strauss 1993, pp53-54)

The lens provided by such an approach is particularly useful for explicating (i) the multiple perspectives and meanings surrounding new medical technologies and (ii) how these evolve over time. In this regard, Orlikowski and Yates (2002, p. 687) emphasis that there is "ongoing constitution of multiple temporal structures in people's everyday practices".

Healthcare work is shaped by the patient's illness and how this illness is expected to develop. The term "trajectory" has been suggested to conceptualise the chain of tasks associated with the course of the illness of a patient. This concept emphasises that patients follow a trajectory that refers to a past, a present, and a possible future. As indicated above, this refers not only to the physiological unfolding of a patient's disease but to the total organisation of work done over that course, plus the impact on those involved with that work and its organisation (Strauss et al. 1985, p.8). Reddy et al. (2006, p. 37) emphasises the temporal logic with illness trajectories by underscoring that:

> A patient's particular illness trajectory also creates a structured "timeline" of activities, events, and occurrences – a temporal trajectory.

This is illustrated by the way nurses (from a care perspective) continuously construct "histories" and "futures" when writing reports between nursing shifts (for example, see Munkvold et al. 2006).

However, the resulting patient trajectory will never be the result of consciously developed plans or a particular sequence of decisions. Rather, it is the emergent effect of the interlocking of entities doing subtasks. This, (Berg, 1997, p.138) explains, gives rise to an understanding of plans as a kind of trajectory which "is continually reset on the spot, as the outcome of the continual articulation work". The nursing plan, for example, conceptualised as a process, is a trajectory that is constantly changed, altered, negotiated in response to changes in the surrounding nodes that constitute the heterogeneous network of planning.

Method

Research setting

The research was conducted at the University Hospital of North Norway (UNN), which has some 5000 employees, including 450 physicians and 1000 nurses. The hospital has 600 beds, of which 150 are psychiatric. The actual study took place in the psychogeriatric ward, which is one of four wards in the Department of Special Psychiatry

The psychogeriatric ward is a closed unit. Nobody can enter or leave it without explicit permission (such as a key). The ward has 15 rooms, and treats 95 patients a year with an average length of stay of 6-8 weeks. There are 45 people working permanently here, including nurses, unskilled workers and substitutes, social workers, occupational therapists and physiotherapists. In addition, three physicians and one psychologist pay regular visits. The turnover at the ward is high, with up to 5 new unskilled workers starting each month.

Patients here are 65 or older and have usually been diagnosed with a psychiatric disorder such as dementia or anxiety. Many of them have been transferred here from high-security closed units, where they have come close to breaking doors and walls. They might thus constitute a danger both to themselves, to other patients as well as staff. The first room you come into is the day room. Typically the patients sit in this room, often with a nurse nearby. The room is usually strikingly silent. Occasionally, low whispering can be heard when nurses talk with the patients. As some patients may have severe psychoses with serious mental and behavioural disorders, the situation might change abruptly and dramatically. A patient might start to yell and upset other patients. In such situations, resources are mobilised quickly. The activities in which the staff were involved (writing, feeding, discussion, meetings, etc) are suspended and attention is focused on the agitated patient.

A set of formal regulations is important in shaping the resources needed to treat individual patients. Broadly, these differentiate between patients who have been admitted voluntarily and those who have been committed to the ward involuntarily. For example, a patient who has been committed must be treated and followed up one-to-one and is not allowed to leave the ward without being accompanied by a member of the staff.

The diagnoses mentioned above and the fact that medical treatment may have little or no effect on these disorders result in a work environment whose activities are directed towards a interdisciplinary approach to care and treatment. In this ward, environmental therapy and individual attention are considered crucial in creating a safe and stable situation for patients. Observations made by the staff are considered particularly important for the treatment that is given, for instance, in feeding situations, self-care, etc.

Research method

This study adheres to an interpretive research tradition (Walsham 1993; Klein and Myers 1999) in which reality is assumed to be socially constructed. The interpretative approach assumes no predetermined relationship between information technologies and social contexts. As researchers we thus "[seek] an understanding of the context of the information system, and the process whereby the information system influences and is influenced by the context" (Walsham, 1993, page 4-5).

The methodological strategy of this study is based on the qualitative research paradigm. We are inspired by ethnography in particular, and rely to a large extent on participant observations as a primary method.

The empirical material was collected from May to December 2005. In addition to observing work, we conducted semi-structured interviews, engaged in informal discussions, analysed various documents and participated in internal project meetings.

In total we conducted 80 hours of observation, including nursing handovers, interdisciplinary meetings (e.g. cardex and treatment meetings), and the process of updating the nursing plan and writing reports. Handwritten field notes were transcribed shortly after each observation session. While observing, we made an effort to cover different types of actors and interactions in order to highlight potentially different interpretations of what was going on.

Fifteen interviews were conducted. The interviews lasted an average of 1 to 1.5 hours. In addition, we spent some time in project meetings as well as studying various documents, such as project specifications, newsletters and training material. The overall process of collecting the data was open-ended and iterative, with the earlier stages being more explorative than the later ones.

The analysis of the data is based on a hermeneutic approach, where a complex whole is understood "from preconceptions about the meanings of its parts and their interrelationships" (Klein and Myers, 1999). This implies that the different sources of field data are all taken into consideration in the interpretation process.

Case

Implementing the nursing module

The introduction of the electronic nursing module took place in the context of a larger, hospital-level implementation of a new EPR infrastructure, also containing a nursing module. A decision to replace the existing EPR, in 2003, marked the start of a prolonged undertaking to create an all-encompassing information infrastructure cutting across departmental and professional boundaries.

The Department of Special Psychiatry was highly motivated to implement the nursing module in its four wards. Expectations related to improved efficiency and a better overview of the planning process were also important. Not only should it improve the care provided by nurses; another important aspect was the way it could facilitate coordination of work across disciplinary boundaries.

"I believe that this system [care plans] might help us better articulate what we do. I believe this is a huge challenge within the psychiatric sector: that we are able to explain to others what we do and how we think" (Nurse).

The implementation process was carried out over a half-year period. Three persons (two nurses and one secretary) were recruited internally to run the project. For two days a week, they were able to pay full attention to the implementation of the nursing module in the department's four wards. After some months of in-house training, the system was introduced in February 2005, both in the psychogeriatric ward and in the three other wards in the department. By May 2005, all wards had started to use the new nursing module.

The nursing module included functionality for writing daily reports and for creating nursing care plans - one plan per patient. The first part was the report section, where users wrote reports on a patient several (usually three) times a day. In this section, the users could write free text (that is, construct a narrative of the patients' problems). The second part was the nursing care plan. Unlike the report, it was highly structured and contained international codes for identifying diagnosis and related interventions for a patient.

The nursing plan was based on the NANDA and NIC classification systems. A NANDA diagnosis might spawn one or more NIC interventions. Also, for each NIC intervention there might be several ordinances or instructions (direct actions). The ordinances are written as plain-text extensions in the plan (see figure 1).

Treatment elements	FA	Frequency/situation	Start	End	Status
Nursing diagnoses					
Anxiety -- rt confusion	2		09.08.05		Active
Impaired mucous membrane	4		30.08.05		Active
Insufficient sleep	8		10.08.05		Active
Nursing interventions / Ordinances					
Reducing anxiety -- Objective: security, patient trust	2		09.08.05		Active
Wake up before breakfast		Always	30.08.05		Active
Encourage sleep	8		09.08.05		
Make sure the patient get enough sleep			09.08.05		Active
Consider medication		Together with physician	09.08.05		Active
Record sleeping pattern		Make list, record in report	09.08.05		Active
Help patient maintain diurnal rythm			09.08.05		Active
Sense of reality	2		09.08.05		
Clear messages about what to be done during the day		Written, Oral	09.08.05		Active
Improve feeling of security -- introduce yourself, tell when you are about to finish your watch, offer contact	2		23.08.05		
Heal wound -- No denture lower jaw; objective: prevent wound in the gums	6		30.08.05		
Activity-therapy -- follow week-schedule	7		23.08.05		
Independent nursing ordinances					

Fig. 1: The nursing plan with diagnosis, interventions and ordinances

The user writing the report was expected to use the plan with its diagnosis, interventions and instructions as a basis for the reports. Whenever deviation from the plan occurred, it was supposed to be documented in the report. As a result, the content of the report was kept to a minimum:

"The goal is to write as little as possible in the report, and to write in relation to what is in the nursing plan and describe any deviation from it" (Project group nurse)

In other words, the written report and the nursing plan were mutually dependent. For a complete understanding of the case, the users thus had to read them both. The plan provided the current status of the patient's nursing diagnosis (problems) and interventions, while to understand how it had evolved the nurses had to read the written reports. Deviations from the plan, what had happened over time, and how the nursing plan had changed were only documented in the reports.

In use, the nursing module was considered to be successful, especially by the nurses. It was also argued that the plan facilitated communication and had potential:

"People attending the meetings have already read the reports and the nursing plans. So now we focus on the core of the case (...) and we don't have to read everything aloud in the meetings" (Nurse).

"After having used the system for a while, I think we will improve and become more precise in what we write in the reports" (Nurse).

Two important arenas for information sharing

As indicated by the quotations above, nursing plans were assumed to enhance information sharing within and across disciplinary boundaries. In this ward, it is in particular at regular meetings that the various professionals meet and try to make sense of patient cases. One obvious reason for this is that the physicians have responsibility for patients in several wards, and thus are not always available outside the regular cardex meetings. Likewise, for the nursing practitioners, the meetings between working shifts are crucially important in ensuring coherence and continuity over the patient trajectory.

The interdisciplinary *cardex meeting* is held twice a week. Its main purpose is to clarify and exchange patient information and discuss further treatment. The name, cardex, denotes the presence of the various documents holding information about patients, and in particular the medication charts. The meeting is held in the conference room, which is the only room suitably configured for such occasions. The room contains a very large conference table with a dozen chairs around it. In one corner is a computer, the only one in the room. Its screen is positioned away from the centre of the room, so that it is visible only to the person using it. A projector is safely fastened to the ceiling above the conference table, and on the wall behind the door is a large whiteboard. The whiteboard is extensively used. It holds an overview of all the patients, indicating their names, the main therapist and care provider, their follow-up status and going-out status, and in some cases general information such as the date and place planned for the patient's discharge from the ward. Finally, next to the whiteboard is a small table holding various magazines, registration forms and documents.

The cardex meeting is well organized. It has a prearranged division of labour and a given sequence of action. Managing the process is the coordinator, usually a nurse. He or she is the only person with direct access to the EPR during the meeting. The coordinator thus initiates the individual reports by browsing through the various documents and forms found in the EPR. During this process, an oral account is produced on the spot. Another nurse has been assigned the role of taking the minutes. She makes sure that vital questions and decisions are recorded in the minutes of the meeting. Also present are the physicians. They have been delegated the responsibility of handling medical concerns. Hence on the table in front of them are the medication charts, filed in one large binder. The remaining participants (nurses, physiologists, physiotherapists, etc) listen and, whenever appropriate, fill in with comments and questions. Typically, everybody brings a personal notebook. From time to time during the meeting, they make their own personal notes in their notebooks.

The *handover conference,* on the other hand, is vital in ensuring continuity between shifts. Only nurses are present during these meetings, which are essential as they provide the nurses with an arena to informally debrief, clarify and discuss patient information. In this ward there are four handovers a day, of which two are considered to be main handovers. The main handovers take place between the work shifts in the morning and in the afternoon. Like the cardex meetings, the main handover conferences take place in the large conference room. Two key tasks are carried out during these meeting. First, an oral briefing is given for each patient, primarily based on the written reports from the last 24 hours. Second, day plans are set up for the individual patients. In this respect the handover conference typically drifts from collective discussion to individualised preparation (planning).

Typically, an experienced nurse is delegated the task of coordinating the meeting. His or her description of the state of affairs is put across as a story. Various artefacts are used during the process, such as the written report, the ward list, and the whiteboard. In fact, as the coordinator does not have a complete overview of all patients, this presentation is highly reliant on the availability of a mixture of patient representations.

Analysis

The analysis is structured as follows: Firstly, we present the nature of CIS as where the work trajectories of physicians and nurses intersect (manifested by the intersection points of physicians' and nurses' work trajectories) as situated, temporal, regularly (re)negotiated and achieved in practice. Secondly, we discuss how medical data is not fixed and self-contained, but evolves over time during the patient's illness trajectory. Thirdly, we analyse the trajectory of the nursing plan and highlight its uncertain and contingent character.

CIS: temporal, contingent and achieved in practice

Instead of perceiving CIS as a common resource or shared space fixed in time and space, we argue that CIS is a short-lived arrangement, achieved in practice, and that constantly needs to be renegotiated. We develop our argument by focussing on the negotiations between physicians and nurses in interdisciplinary meetings in the course of the patients' illness trajectory. In their research on oncology protocols, Timmermans and Berg (1997, p. 276) argue along similar lines:

"[E]ach actor follows a <u>trajectory</u> which refers to a past, a present, and a possible future' (...) The doctor who orders the protocol, while, for example, following a research trajectory, sees the patient as one case in a project. The trajectory of the nurse who administers the protocol might be characterized by the tasks of her shift"

Following a similar line of argument, we argue that the CIS around a patient can be conceptualised as multiple disciplinary trajectories with only brief intersection points where the different professionals coordinate their activities. Below, this is spelled out more specifically by illustrating two of the most common trajectories, the care trajectory associated with nurses and the medical trajectory associated with physicians. Consider the first treatment meeting where the professional team of care providers tries to make sense of the case, including collecting information from very different sources. Notice in particular how professional boundaries delimiting the work of physicians and of nurses are being maintained and 'reinforced':

"Typically the nurses would be delegated the task of collecting information from home care, nursing homes and the like. The physician [responsible therapist] would be responsible for talking to the primary [referring] physician and ensuring that appropriate testing and examinations are carried out. For instance, Madres, MMS, Obsdement (...) and filling out the proper forms, etc. The psychologists carry out neuropsychological testing (...), we have a social worker who takes care of the individual plan, the physiotherapist has to do his thing, and so on" (Physician)

A similar situation occurs when the patients are discharged from the ward, only now in the opposite direction. The nurses prepare their own summaries for the nursing home, while the physician produces a formal discharge letter for the general practitioner. Accordingly, different artefacts and information sources (discharge letters, nursing summaries, etc.) enforce different professional perspectives.

However, if we look more closely at the heart of the interdisciplinary work in the ward, namely the interdisciplinary meetings, we can sense how the intersection points between physicians and nurses are really of a *momentary and contingent* character. The following field-note extract from a cardex meeting illustrates this:

The coordinator (Lisa) is managing the process. Positioned behind the computer, she is going through the information for all the patients in the ward based on the patient ward list in the EPR. Also seated at the table are the three physicians. On the table in front of them is a large binder holding the medical cardexes as well as the Physician's Desk Reference book. The rest of the staff is spread around the room. Based on the nursing reports in the EPR, the coordinator has started to elaborate on recent changes and the current status of a patient with anxiety and extreme hypomania:

Coordinator: *"The patient claims that she has benefited from earlier stays"*

Psychologist: *"Her son says that she has been taking better care of herself since the transfer to the nursing home?"*

Having remained in the background, silently listening to the discussion, the head physician interrupts the psychologist:

Head physician: *"Only standard specimens have been ordered for this patient...?"*

The head physician's head is bowed as he carefully reads the laboratory requisition lying on the table in front of him. He has the full attention of the other two physicians in the room. With the physicians' attention on the laboratory requisition, one of the nurses has started talking to the rest of the staff:

Nurse A: *"The patient had a tendency to complain about her own disorder. We have however made it clear to her that there should be no talking about her own disorder in the day room"*

With this comment, nurse A is in fact not responding to the comment made by the head physician, but rather adding details to the account put forward by the coordinator. The staff's attention is directed towards the coordinator. Meanwhile, the three physicians have quietly started an internal discussion about the specimens ordered. They are still occupied in this discussion as the coordinator ends the overall brief (signalling that the nurses are done) by asking if anyone has any further questions. There is no response and they move on to the next patient.

For the next patient, a similar situation emerges. In this case, however, one of the physicians replies to what the coordinating nurse says:

Coordinator: *"The patient's mood is unstable. He starts sweating rather quickly. Participated on a trip to Prestevannet earlier today and was very satisfied with that"*...

Physician A, whose attention suddenly seems to have been attracted, interrupts the coordinator:

Physician A: *"Sweating???"*

Coordinator: *"Well... like he was tense ..."*

Another physician, Physician B, writes something into the medical cardex, while at the same time looking in the Physician's Desk Reference (a book describing medication).

Physician B: *"Maybe we should reduce this specific medication"*

Physician B points at the patient chart, whereupon a discussion about medication starts between the three physicians. Physician B grabs the Physician's Desk Reference book and opens it again. The rest of the staff is silently listening; some are occupied with writing information into their own personal notebooks. For instance, a nurse makes a note in her notebook to remember to call the homecare service, and the psychologist writes something in her personal calendar to remind her that a specific test needs to taken. The professionals collectively agree on booking a treatment meeting for this patient.

Having completed the meeting, the various professionals (the nurses, physician, psychologist, etc.) would often write separate reports on what has been said and decided in the meeting.

Although both nurses and physicians want the best for the patient, they have different goals, practices and perspectives, making complete information sharing illusive. Work around a patient should rather be seen as taking place in parallel paths. At certain (intersection) points in the meetings, the various professionals poll the others, checking for potential changes to their own work.

In this light, the nursing plan is merely one element in a larger infrastructural arrangement, reflecting the nursing perspective on the care process as the cardex does for the physicians.

The evolution of medical data over time in the course of the patient's illness trajectory

Medical data is often considered to be fixed, self-contained and independent. In this sense, these data are considered to be pure facts, and all that is necessary to see. However, regarding medical data as "isolated givens, overlooks how medical data mutually elaborate each other" (Berg and Goorman, 1999, p. 54-55). One such mutual elaboration is how medical data evolves over time: "[i]n the course of a patient's illness trajectory, data items are constantly reinterpreted and recon-structed" (Berg and Goorman, 1999, p. 55). This underscores the temporal dimen-sion with illness trajectories and accordingly how "[t]emporality (...) lead[s] to expectations about the future based on past events" (Reddy et al. 2006, p. 48).

To illustrate this, Berg and Goorman (1999) showed how the sequence of blood pressure measurements of a post-operative patient in an Intensive Care Unit (ICU) was tightly interconnected:

> "Consider the following sequence of blood pressure measurements in the post-operative pa-tient mentioned above: at 6 am, 120:70; at 9 am, 125:75; at 11 am, 115:65. If all other clinical signs would remain unchanged, then this series of readings would be most likely read as a 'stable blood pressure'. But if the 1 p.m. reading were to be 100:50, then the 11 am reading would be reinterpreted as the beginning of the decline" (Berg and Goorman, 1999, p. 54-55).

A key problem for the nursing plan was exactly that it was not able to support an "evolvement" view on medical data on the patient's illness trajectory. It could only show the current status (diagnosis and interventions). As these data were de-pendent on each other, the nursing plan was used less than expected. Below, we elaborate on this problem by focusing on an extract from the field notes made during a handover conference. Among the four handover conferences during a day, this one is taken from the one carried out in the afternoon:

> With only nurses present, main handover conferences are normally carried out in the confer-ence room. Typically, an experienced nurse is delegated the task of coordinating the meeting, and today Anne has been assigned this role. Her description of the state of affairs is put across as a story. During the process various artefacts, like the written report, the ward-list, and the whiteboard, are used. In fact, not having the complete overview of all patients, her presentation is highly reliant on the availability of a mixture of patient-representations.

> Anne has positioned herself behind the only computer in the room. On the screen in front of her is the ward list. It holds an overview of all admitted patients and provides access to the in-dividual records during the brief. The ward list is visible only to Anne, so during the discus-sion reference is frequently made to the comparable overview found on the whiteboard. The

whiteboard is the only visible description of patients which is observable for all nurses during the handover. Anne starts off with the first patient:

Coordinator (Anne): *"The patient has been isolated this weekend due to aggressive behaviour. As you can see on the whiteboard, he has one-to-one follow-up."*

Handling the patient requires a considerable effort from the nurses. Behind the patients' name on the whiteboard, a column called 'going-out status' says *"No going out"*, while another one called 'follow up' says *"one to one"*. The oncoming nurses' attention is now directed towards the whiteboard.

Anne continues: *"The nursing care plan has been changed. Suicide is no longer a risk, so it has been removed from the care plan."*

Anne's remark about changes in the care plan is not deduced from the care plan module in the EPR, but from the last written report. In fact recent changes in the care plan are only to be found in the written reports. The care plan module only holds an up-to-date overview of nursing diagnosis and interventions. Hence identifying changes in the care plan entails having to browse through separate written reports:

Nurse: *"The electronic nursing care plans provide only the status, and not how things change over time"*

Anne has opened the nursing care plan to refresh her memory on the patients' current status. It does not seem necessary to add anything more, so she closes the window on the screen and looks at the rest of the group.

Anne: *"The patient is isolated in his room, but with the door open. One nurse is always nearby to keep him safe"*

She is interrupted by one of the incoming nurses: *"But the patient loves to go for a walk…"*

A discussion arises among the nurses regarding the patient's 'going-out status'. On the one hand the aggressive behaviour of the patient makes him difficult to handle; on the other hand outside access is an important part of the therapy.

Anne follows up on the patient: *"Today, when [nurse] Lise had her lunch, I sat in isolation for about an hour with the patient. He really seems nervous. Besides, he also had an [ECT] today."*

Electroconvulsive therapy (ECT), a rather controversial treatment method, is normally used when other forms of therapy, such as medications or psychotherapy, have not been effective. Usually ECT treatment is given three times a week for a month or less. Anne is trying to search backwards in the written reports to find out when the series of ECT treatment actually started, but is unable to find it. The remainder of the handover is accomplished in a similar way. An account is given for all patients. Typically all written reports from the last 24 hours are used. Occasionally older reports are studied, as when Anne was trying to find out when the ECT series had started.

This field extract underscores the importance of an historical overview of how medical data changed and how the patient developed. The nursing plan was therefore only used to a minor degree in handover conferences. Instead, the users still focussed on the reports. One of the nurses explained:

"We have some really unstable patients and this means that the plan changes all the time (…). We need to trace the changes that are made for the different entries and themes in the nursing plan (…) look at this! This is hopeless [she is pointing at the nursing plan]. Here are some important data from 08.02, but it is not possible to see how they have changed. The patient has had a lot of different wound treatments, but I don't even know when the first one was done"

This sequence illustrates how the patient developed (improved) along his illness trajectory. Perceiving this directly in the nursing plan alone is impossible. Also, this situation provides an overview of how long an intervention has been active. In contrast, the nursing plan did not provide information about when a diagnosis was initiated and the measures were taken out of the reports and put in the nursing plan; it only gives an overview of the current situation.

As elaborated in the field note extract above, suicidal patients can never go out alone, but must always be accompanied by one of the health personnel. Therefore, the two related parameters: 'going-out status' [whether a health worker needs to accompany the patient] and 'follow-up' are extremely important for the resource management in the ward; not least how these parameters develop:

"We are very interested to see how the patient develops. For me as a night watch nurse, covering several wards, it is particularly important (…) For instance, at one stage, you could see that the patient was not allowed to go out on a given date. Some time later, he could go out accompanied by two staff members, and at the moment, he must be accompanied by one staff member, etc."

The uncertain and contingent character of the nursing plan trajectory

It is often "thought that the trajectories of technological projects are contingent and iterative" (Law and Callon, 1992, p.49). From this perspective, implementing a large information system (cf. the nursing plan) into an organisation is seen as a rational process where goals, a clear overview and good planning lead the way to a given outcome. Sometimes, to be sure, this will be the case. However, "[there is] no necessity about such a progress. If all is smooth, this is because contingency has operated in that way" (Law and Callon, 1992, p.50).

For instance, an information system may appeal to a new reality, and become something completely different. In this case, the nursing plan turned into a resource management tool. Resource management in the psychogeriatric ward was a complex issue, depending on the current condition of the patient, the legal clauses in effect, the going-out status and follow-up. 'Going-out status' indicates whether a health worker needs to accompany the patient outside the ward or not. 'Follow-up' indicates what kind of attention a patient might need, and how often. Having a good overview of such issues was extremely important as "suicidal patients can never go out alone, but must always be accompanied by one of the health personnel" (Nurse). The rhetoric around the plan was modified to include resource management as well:

"The ideal situation would be to document going-out status and follow-up in the nursing plan; then we could have an overview of the resources needed and how they developed" (Project group nurse)

The users themselves had a key role in the transformation process of the plan. Even if the important factors, going-out status and follow-up, were not explicitly part of the plan, the staff used them implicitly to obtain an overview of the resources needed:

"By reading this plan, I can see that this patient will require a lot of time and resources" (Nurse)

Also in the maintenance of the nursing plan, it became increasingly important to include the resources needed. For instance, when a nurse was updating the nursing plan, one of the project leaders passed by and reminded her to include the staff resources needed:

"You must include that this patient needs one-to-one follow-up (...) we have to be precise about which resources are needed in order to succeed with the nursing plan" (project group nurse)

Although it had been intended primarily as a vehicle for tracking the ongoing delivery of nursing care, the nursing plan implementation process became increasingly entangled with managerial concerns for resource management and control. The use of clinical information was thus lifted out of its primary context in order to be used for completely different purposes.

Conclusion and implications for CIS

This paper develops a perspective on how to conceptualise CIS in which various perspectives are accounted for. We explore how CIS are *achieved in practice* by drawing on the notion of trajectories. A perspective on CIS is developed that emphasises its situated, temporal and negotiated nature. We demonstrate how it encompasses several disconnected trajectories (professional, medical and technological) and how each follows its own logic only with brief intersecting points. Also we stress the *temporal* dimension of the multiple trajectories - and how they evolve over time in the course of the patient's illness trajectory. Based on this, we call for a furthering of the discourse on trajectories and temporality within CSCW. From a practice perspective this implies adhering both to objective and subjective perspectives of time (Orlikowski and Yates, 2002) and how work unfolds along different temporal dimensions.

Ambitions, aims and goals related to medical technologies change and expand over time and in relation to multiple stakeholders. For example in our case, the nursing plan started out as tool for nurses, yet gradually turned into a resource management tool. Whether this is a trend that ultimately will turn the nursing plan into a major tool for management is of course too early to judge. Nevertheless, such transformations of ambitions are typical of information system projects and should not come as a big surprise. Primary work transforms into something different, and where technologies find new areas of application.

Implementing the nursing plans with the aim of improving information sharing is extremely difficult. In order to succeed, the first and indeed most important thing to do is to move beyond simplistic strategies of replacing the existing information sources. The strategy to pursue is rather to find mechanisms that strengthen the relations between the different nodes. Implicitly this also involves paying closer attention to the non-common – that is, the information that remains local to the various professionals. In this respect, we call for the need to rethink 'implication or design' by focussing more on process rather than the product.

References

Allen, D. (2004): 'Re-reading nursing and re-writing practice: towards an empirically-based reformulation of the nursing mandate', *Nursing Inquiry, Special Centenary Issue*, vol. 11, no. 4, 2004, pp. 271-83.

Bannon, L. and Bødker, S. (1997): 'Constructing Common Information Spaces', *Proceedings of the European Conference on Computer Supported Cooperative Work*, ECSCW'97., Kluwer, 1997, pp.81-96.

Berg, M. (1997): *Rationalizing medical work: decision-support techniques and medical practices*, Cambridge, Mass: MIT Press.

Berg, M. and Goorman, E. (1999): 'The contextual nature of medical information', *International Journal of Medical Informatics*, vol. 56, no. 1, pp. 51 - 60.

Björvell, C., Wredling, R. and Thorell-Ekstrand, I., (2002): 'Long-term increase in quality of nursing documentation: effects of a comprehensive intervention'. *Scand J Caring Sci.*, no. 16, pp. 34–42.

Bossen, C. (2002): 'The Parameters of Common Information Spaces: The Heterogeneity of Cooperative Work at a Hospital Ward', *Proceedings of Computer Supported Cooperative Work*, CSCW'02, ACM Press, 2002, pp.176-185.

Ellingsen, G. and Monteiro, E. (2003): 'A Patchwork Planet: Integration and Cooperation in Hospitals', *Computer Supported Cooperative Work*, vol 12, no.1, pp. 71-95.

Erickson, T. and Kellog W.A. (2003): 'Social Translucence: Using Minimalist Visualisations of Social Activity to Support Collective Interaction', In K. Höök, D. Benyon and A.J. Munro eds. *Designing Information Spaces: The Social Navigation Approach*, Springer, 2003, pp. 17-42.

Gerson, E. M. and Star, S. L. (1986): 'Analyzing due process in the workplace', *ACM Transactions on Office Information Systems*, vol. 4, no. 3, July 1986, pp. 257-270.

Gordon, M. (1998):' Nursing Nomenclature and Classification System Development', *Online Journal of Issues in Nursing*, Available from: http://www.nursingworld.org/ojin/tpc7/tpc7_1.htm (accessed March 22. 2007).

Grimson J., Grimson W. and Hasselbring W. (2000): 'The SI Challenge in Health Care', *Communications of the ACM.*, vol.43, no.6, June 2000, pp.48-55.

KITH (2003): *Requirements specification for electronic documentation of nursing. National standard 2003*, Available from: http://www.kith.no/upload/1101/R12-03DokumentasjonSykepleie-rev1_1-NasjonalStandard.pdf. (accessed March 22. 2007)

Klein, H.K. and Myers, M. D. (1999): 'A set of principles for conducting and evaluating interpretive field studies in information systems', *MIS Quarterly*, vol. 23, no. 1, pp. 67-94.

Law, J. and Callon, M. (1992): 'The life and death of an aircraft: A network analysis of technical change', in W.E. Bijker and J. Law (eds), *Shaping Technology/Building Society: Studies in Sociotechnical Change*, Cambridge, MA, MIT Press, 1992, pp. 21-52.

Munkvold, G., Ellingsen, G. and Koksvik, H. (2006): 'Formalising work – reallocating redundancy', *Proceedings of the Conference on Computer-Supported Cooperative Work 2006*, ACM, pp. 59 – 68.

Orlikowski, W. and Yates, J. (2002): It's About Time: Temporal Structuring in Organizations, *Organization Science*, Vol. 13, No. 6, pp. 684-700

Randall, S. (2000): 'What's Common about Common Information Spaces?', Paper presented at the Workshop on Cooperative Organisation of Common Information Spaces, Technical University of Denmark, 2000, Available at http://www.itu.dk/people/schmidt/ciscph2000/Randall.pdf (accessed March 22. 2007).

Reddy, M. C. Dourish, P. and Pratt, W. (2001): 'Coordinating Heterogeneous Work: Information and Representation in Medical Care', *Proceedings of the Seventh European Conference on Computer Supported Cooperative Work*, ECSCW'01, Kluwer, 2001, pp.139-158.

Reddy, M.C., Dourish, P, and Pratt, W. (2006): Temporality in Medical Work: Time also Matters. *Computer Supported Cooperative Work* vol.15, pp.29-53

Reed, J. and Stanley, D. (2003): 'Improving communication between hospitals and care homes: the development of a daily living plan for older people', *Health and Social Care in the Community*, vol. 11, no.4, 2003, pp. 356–363.

Rolland, K H, Hepsø, V and Monteiro E. (2006): 'Conceptualizing Common Information Spaces Across Heterogeneous Contexts: Mutable Mobiles and Side-effects of Integration', *Proceedings of the 2006 20th anniversary conference on Computer supported cooperative work*, ACM, 2006. pp. 493-500.

Schmidt, K. and Bannon, L. (1992): 'Taking CSCW seriously: Supporting Articulation Work', *Computer Supported Cooperative Work*, vol.1, no.1, 1992, pp.7-40.

Sexton, A., Chan, C., Elliot, M., Stuart, J., Jayasuriya, R, and Crookes P. (2004): 'Nursing handovers: do we really need them?', *Journal of Nursing Management*, no 12, 2004, pp.37–42.

Star, S. L. and Griesemer J. R. (1989): 'Institutional ecology, 'translations' and boundary objects: Amateurs and professionals in Berkeley's Museum of Vertebrate Zoology, 1907-39'. *Social Studies of Science*, vol. 19, no. 3, pp. 387-420.

Strauss A., Fagerhaugh S., Suczek B. and Wiener C. (1985): *Social Organization of Medical Work*, Chicago, The University of Chicago Press.

Strauss, A. (1993): *Continual Permutations of Action*, Thousand Oaks, CA: Sage.

Timmermans, S. and M. Berg. (1997): 'Standardization in action: Achieving universalism and localisation through medical protocols', *Social Studies of Science*, vol. 27, pp. 273-305.

Voutilainen, P., Isola, A., amd Muurinen. S. (2004): 'Nursing documentation in nursing homes – state-of-the-art and implications for quality improvement', *Scandinavian Journal of Caring Sciences*, vol.18, no. 1, 2004, pp. 72–81.

Walsham, G. (1993): *Interpreting Information Systems in Organizations*, Wiley, Chichester.

Winthereik B.R. and Vikkelsø S. (2005): 'ICT and Integrated Care: Some Dilemmas of Standardising Inter-Organisational Communication', *Computer Supported Cooperative Work*, vol.14, no.1, 2005, pp.43-67.

L. Bannon, I. Wagner, C. Gutwin, R. Harper, and K. Schmidt (eds.).
ECSCW'07: Proceedings of the Tenth European Conference on Computer Supported Cooperative Work, 24-28 September 2007, Limerick, Ireland
© Springer 2007

Gifts from friends and strangers:
A study of mobile music sharing

Maria Håkansson[1], Mattias Rost[1] and Lars Erik Holmquist[1, 2]

[1]Future Applications Lab, Viktoria Institute, Göteborg, Sweden
[2]Swedish Institute of Computer Science (SICS), Stockholm, Sweden
{mariah, rost}@viktoria.se, leh@sics.se

Abstract. Mobile technology has turned the traditionally *collective* activity of enjoying music into an often *private* one. New technologies such as wireless ad hoc networks have the potential to re-connect listeners who are now separated by headphones. We report on a field study of *Push!Music,* a novel mobile music sharing system. Push!Music allows both manual and automatic sharing of music between users through ad hoc wireless networking, and also provides a social awareness of other users nearby. The system was used by 13 subjects for three weeks. In post-study interviews, we identified four categories of results: *social awareness, sharing music with friends, sharing music with strangers,* and *sharing automatically.* Based on this, we present implications for design that can be applied not only to mobile music sharing systems, but to mobile media sharing in general: *Allow division into active and passive use; enhance the awareness of who, where and when; support reciprocity;* and finally, *support identity and impression management.*

Introduction

Enjoying and creating music is often a *collective* activity – people play in bands and orchestras, visit concerts, and dance together to music at clubs. Music fills a number of social functions, and plays an important part in how we identify and express ourselves (DeNora, 2000; O'Hara and Brown, 2006). Sharing music with others is an essential way to expand the listener's horizon and often also fills a social function, whether it is done through physical mix-tapes (D'Arcangelo, 2005) or using computer software such as iTunes (Voida *et al.*, 2005).

Thanks to portable radios, Walkmans and iPods, music has become a constant companion that gives us a personal soundtrack to our everyday life (Bull, 2000; Bull, 2006). At the same time, this mobile technology has turned music listening into a *private* activity – we listen in isolation while in our car, in public transport and at work. It might be that this private music sphere breeds a disconnectedness, even isolation, from others even when sharing the same physical space.

Emerging wireless technology such as WiFi and Bluetooth could create new possibilities of sharing music in the mobile setting – essentially turning a private activity back into a social one. We argue that mobile music sharing, and more generally mobile *media* sharing, still has a lot of untapped potential. The telecom industry wants to find new ways for people to share personal media such as photos, songs, and video; thus driving revenue in networks and terminals. For computer-supported collaborative activities, easier sharing of multimedia files in the mobile setting could heighten social awareness, facilitate communication, and support community discourse. However, services such as MMS (Multimedia Message Service) have so far not met any great success (Jaques, 2006). To construct successful systems there is a need to explore the emerging practices around mobile media sharing.

In this paper, we report from a 3-week field study of a novel mobile music sharing system, *Push!Music* (Håkansson *et al.*, 2007; Jacobsson *et al.*, 2005). Push!Music is implemented on handheld computers which connect wirelessly through ad-hoc networks. The system allows two ways of sharing music. Firstly, users can *manually* send songs as personal recommendations to other users in the vicinity. Secondly, songs can *automatically* copy and recommend themselves to other nearby users based on a similar music history. The system also provides users with a minimal social awareness resource by displaying the nicknames of other users in the vicinity. In the study we found a number of design implications for how to design not only mobile music sharing systems, but also mobile media sharing systems in general.

The Push!Music system

Push!Music is a mobile music player with ad hoc wireless sharing capabilities that allows music to be shared between users who are in the vicinity of each other (Håkansson *et al.*, 2007; Jacobsson *et al.*, 2005). It has been implemented on handheld computers with wireless networking (WiFi). In its basic function, the software provides a straightforward music-playing interface with standard controls.

To facilitate music sharing, as soon as another user is anywhere within the WiFi range of a Push!Music device, s/he is shown in the interface as a connected

Figure 1. The Push!Music interface.

user, identified by a personally selected nickname. In the main window (Figure 1) users can see at a glance if other users are nearby by checking the colour of a small icon. By switching views to a user list in the interface, users can see all currently connected persons listed by nicknames.

Music can be shared in two ways; both as a form of *recommendation* and as the copying of a specific song (i.e. MP3 file) from one device to another. The first way of sharing music is to manually send or *push* a song. Users can push songs to any nearby user who appears connected in the interface. Whenever a new song is transferred to another device, it is placed in a temporary pool of incoming music. After the current song has finished playing, the songs from the pool are automatically played one after the other in the playlist. While a song is playing, a history list of the most recent 'owners' of this song is displayed in the interface.

The second way of sharing is that songs *automatically* copy themselves to nearby players, based on collected information about a user's listening history. Each song is a so-called *media agent* that records and saves what happens to it and in what listening context it appears (for details see Håkansson *et al.*, 2005; Jacobsson *et al.*, 2006). For instance, a song will know if it has been pushed and to whom, if it is being listened to frequently, if it has been explicitly rated by the user (who can click 'good' or 'bad' in the interface), etc. Each song then uses this information to compare itself with songs on other devices. If the conditions on another device are satisfactory, the song automatically starts copying itself to the new device. This happens primarily with other nearby players that have a similar listening history, but not already a copy of this particular song.

Peer-to-peer file sharing inevitably brings up the question of legal rights. As a research prototype, Push!Music currently has no digital rights management (DRM) and no payment facilities integrated into the system. However, there are several DRM systems that are designed to facilitate legal peer-to-peer sharing, for instance the Potato system (www.potatosystem.com), Weedshare (www.weedshare.com) and Snocap (www.snocap.com).

Related work

While *awareness* was not initially a major function of the Push!Music system, its importance was accented in our study. Dourish and Bellotti (1992) defined awareness as "an understanding of the activities of others, which provides a context for your own activity". Awareness technologies have typically been designed to support users of distributed collaborative work systems (e.g. in the form of *Mediaspaces*; Bly *et al.*, 1993). In addition to sharing work data, such systems improve the awareness of users engaged in informal or non-work activities, with the argument that socialising, coordination, etc. are also important for the success of collaborative work systems. Peripheral awareness has also been used in other domains than work, exploring more ambiguous ways of conveying a sense of presence, for instance between remote lovers (Gaver, 2002). Presence awareness has further been an essential part in instant messaging (IM) systems where the status bar is often used to convey activity information (e.g. Grinter and Palen, 2002). A recent commercial system, *Twitter,* takes this to the logical extreme by in essence being an IM statusbar without any IM functionality (www.twitter.com).

Mobile awareness systems make it possible to provide awareness to users in the mobile setting. The Active Badge (Want et al. 1992) was an infrared device worn as a badge and detected by beacons in the ceiling, which made it possible to accurately detect a person's position in an office and communicate this information to other workers. The Hummingbird (Holmquist *et al.*, 1999) required no infrastructure, and instead used mobile devices with radio transceivers to alert users when others were nearby, thus supporting social awareness. The Hummingbird was tested in a group of ski instructors during a one-week ski trip, which showed that when a system provides for such open-ended use, it becomes important for users to collectively negotiate when and in which situations to use it (Weilenmann, 2001).

A number of other mobile systems have been designed to increase the awareness of and trigger interaction with other users with similar profiles, for instance the *Meme Tag* (Borovoy et al. 1998), *Social Serendipity* (Eagle and Pentland, 2005) and *Scent* (Jung *et al.*, 2006). In Scent, users can also exchange information about one's shared acquaintances. These systems have primarily been tested in conference settings or other events with a limited time-span. Paulos and Goodman (2004) took a different approach in Jabberwocky, an experimental system that detects and records over time the presence of so-called *familiar strangers* in our everyday life and then present it in an abstract way.

In the fields of CSCW and HCI, the research on *music sharing* and related practices has so far investigated primarily *stationary or online sharing.* This includes how people use online peer-to-peer file-sharing software (Brown *et al.*, 2001), how an interactive music system could allow people to collaboratively choose music for a public place such as a café bar (O'Hara *et al.*, 2004) or a gym (McCarthy and Anagnost 1998), and the social practices around iTunes music sharing (Voida *et al.*, 2005).

Several systems have also been designed to facilitate *mobile music sharing* in order to turn the usually private listening on mobile music devices into a more social experience. In *tunA* (Bassoli *et al.*, 2006), music was streamed between devices over a wireless ad hoc network, allowing nearby users to actively "tune in" and eavesdrop on nearby users' playlists. In *SoundPryer* (Östergren *et al.*, 2006), music was automatically streamed between encountering cars to create a shared music experience in traffic. Both these systems were only tested in short field trials, and unlike Push!Music did not allow for neither active nor autonomous recommendations or the copying of files between devices.

A recent *commercial mobile music sharing system* is Microsoft's *Zune* (www.zune.net), which allows users to wirelessly send songs to people in the vicinity, much like Push!Music, but without support for automatic sharing. A digital rights management (DRM) system allows the recipient to listen to the shared songs three times within three days for free. Songs can later be bought from an online music store. Users manage privacy by turning the wireless on and off, changing the privacy settings to control if other users should be able to see them online, or simply block other Zune devices from sending songs.

The study reported in this paper is the second of two consecutive user studies of Push!Music. A preliminary study was conducted in 2005 and involved a group of five male friends who used the system daily for two weeks, mostly on a local university campus (Håkansson *et al.*, 2007). In this group, the sharing of music was playful and triggered discussions about music. Friends pushed songs as recommendations or to disseminate particular songs they liked. They highly appreciated the automatically received songs, which they considered to be unexpected and spontaneous. Finally, we found that received songs could be viewed as 'gifts', much like SMS messages sent between teenagers on mobile phones (Taylor and Harper, 2002).

Method

We conducted a *three-week field study* of Push!Music, where the participants used the system in their everyday life. Below we present the set-up of the study.

Participants

The study involved 13 participants: 4 women and 9 men, all students in their early- to mid-twenties recruited from a local university campus. We knew that there is limited interaction between the classes at this particular campus, and therefore deliberately recruited people from several different classes and grades. This meant that all participants knew someone or a couple of people from his/her class but not the participants from the other classes/grades (see Table I). The participants *A1-A4* knew each other from class and socialised on campus; *B5* and

B6 went to the same large class and knew each other by face, but did not know of each others' participation in the study; *C7* and *C8* formed a very tight pair that met every day on campus and occasionally elsewhere; and *D9-D13* were a close group of friends from class who also occasionally socialised off campus. During the study we did not to reveal who the other participants were.

Group 1	Group 2	Group 3
A1 (M)	B5 (M)	D9 (M)
A2 (M)	B6 (M)	D10 (M)
A3 (F)	C7 (F)	D11 (M)
A4 (F)	C8 (F)	D12 (M)
		D13 (M)

Table I. Overview of users. The participants belonged to four university classes, A-D, and were divided into three group interviews 1-3. M = male, F = female.

Setting

The campus is a four-storey building with classrooms and various open areas for group work and socialising. Many students use the open areas to meet for group projects. The campus is small enough for the participants to encounter each other by coincidence on a more or less daily basis, yet large enough to prevent students from knowing everyone beforehand. Most of the students use the same local transport line to get to and from school, which meant that it would also be possible to encounter other Push!Music users outside the main building.

Procedure

Before the study, each participant was introduced to the overall concept and functionality of Push!Music in individual pre-study meetings. Everyone was equipped with a mobile device with Push!Music installed and a set of earphones. Each participant had selected roughly 100 songs as an initial music collection to be loaded onto the personal mobile device. They were thus not explicitly familiar with each other's music before the study. The participants were told to use Push!Music as they pleased, but were encouraged to use it as their main mobile music listening device during the study. They agreed to not change the music library on their device by adding or removing songs.

During the study we regularly met up with the participants in brief feedback and support sessions to check if any technical problems had occurred. At the same time we documented spontaneous comments and questions as well as our own observations by taking notes. For example, we realised that the instability of the ad hoc network sometimes limited the music sharing. As the participants moved around or sat in different places, the indoor architecture of floors and thick walls became obstacles that made the ad hoc network rather unstable. B6, for instance, who was the only one on the fourth floor using the system, occasionally saw other participants and also successfully pushed a couple of songs, but did not receive any songs during the study. Quantitative data such as the amount of time using Push!Music, the number of pushed and automatically sent songs, etc., was gathered during the study by logging events in each mobile device. The media agents' individually saved information also provided us with logged data.

After the study, we performed group interviews where the participants openly discussed their experiences of using Push!Music. Before each interview, we briefly analysed relevant log data to get an initial understanding of their use of the system. All in all we ran three group interviews with 4-5 participants in each that lasted between 50 and 80 minutes. The participants took part in an interview according to university class, so that they would know someone there (see Table I). We occasionally used open-ended questions as prompts to trigger their discussions or to follow up on things they were talking about, but most of the time the authors remained in the background. The open-ended questions were for example related to what they did in general with Push!Music, if they shared any music and if yes, why, and if they had seen other users and how this had affected their usage. The participants themselves brought up several topics, such as identity, impression management and privacy.

The group interviews were recorded for transcription and analysis. The analysis consisted of categorising the raw data, and finding repeated themes, issues and also conflicting ones. In parallel, we examined the quantitative data as well as the informal notes taken during the study. All user quotes in this paper have been translated from the native language.

Results

We will first give an overview of some factors that affected the overall use of Push!Music during the study. Thereafter, we will present four themes of qualitative findings: *social awareness, sharing music with friends, sharing music with strangers,* and *sharing automatically*.

The participants used Push!Music to and from campus (by bus, ferry and bike) and on campus when their class activities allowed them to do so. Some participants temporarily replaced their personal MP3-player with the Push!Music player during the three weeks, while others used both. Several users brought up the poor battery lifetime (due to the drain of WiFi and MP3 playback) and described how they tried to remember and plan for re-charging. This implied that they used it less often *on the move* than they had wished for, and more often in a 'semi-stationary' way on campus where they were close to power outlets.

Since the participants had different daily schedules, the use of the system naturally became spread out over time and place. Some users encountered each other daily, while others never met during the study. For instance, C7 and C8 used Push!Music together in the same location on campus almost every day but not on the local transport, whereas B5 only used it to and from campus because it was his opportunity to listen to music during the day. In this way, C7 and C8 encountered more participants and shared more music than B5 who only briefly encountered another participant as he was walking to the bus stop.

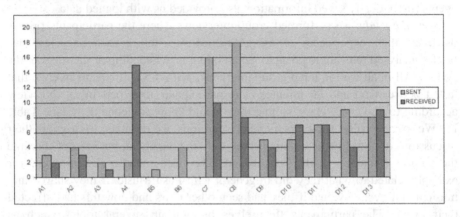

Table II. The amount of sent and received songs for each participant.

After talking to the participants and analysing the logfiles, we discovered that the system had not identified enough similar music on the different players to trigger any *automatic* sharing. For this to happen, it is not enough to just have Push!Music on; users need to listen to a lot of music on their players, in particular songs that others have pushed to them, so that songs get a similar listening history. A combination of circumstances – the number and kind of songs pushed between groups, not always listening to music (because of other activities) and each user only encountering a sub-set of participants – had a stronger than expected impact on the automatic sharing. Despite this, the participants had very valuable opinions about the concept of automatic sharing.

The number of *manually* sent (pushed) and received songs for each participant is presented in Table II. During the 3-week period, users sent 84 songs and received 70 (the difference can be explained by lost transfers due to bad network connections, e.g. if a user moved out of range while a song was being transferred). The table shows some clear differences between the groups. A1-A4 socialised on campus and primarily explored the system together. A4, however, spent more time on campus working alone with Push!Music on, and thus received more songs. She explained that she did not send many songs, but preferred to see "what happened" in the system. B5 and B6 used the system the least and did not know any other participants in the study. B5 only used it to and from campus and encountered one other user, while B6 mostly used his player alone on the fourth floor, where he was isolated from the others.

The ones who pushed most songs were C7 and C8 who always worked together. They pushed to each other, and "as soon as someone [of the others] appeared" in the vicinity. Together with A4, C7 and C8 spent most time on campus of the participants. Finally, the friends D9-D13 mostly used the system together and had a similar amount of shared songs. It was higher than A1-A4 who also knew each other from before, and one reason for this is that D9-D13 developed playful activities such as pushing songs as pranks.

Social awareness

Social awareness turned out to play a larger than expected role in the study. Many participants had the system on passively in the background even when they were not engaged in sharing or listening. One reason for this was to increase the probability of getting music, as B6 explains:

"... as you sit in school, you don't have to listen to it but you can... I had mine on anyway just in case anyone would pass by... by coincidence... so that you have a large probability of a [music] transfer to happen. I've had mine on every day, lying there, even if I didn't listen to it"

But another reason for keeping it on was simply curiosity and wanting to see if and when someone got connected. Every now and then the participants scanned the interface for people and new songs. For some, obtaining awareness of other users became an *ordinary part of playing music*, integrated with the usual activities of managing the music player and as unremarkable as glancing through a physical window to see what is outside. As D10 describes below, he would check the player when entering a new area, when turning it on or when taking the player out of the pocket/bag to change songs. His friend D9 follows up by suggesting that Push!Music could also be used simply as an awareness tool to see if friends are around in a crowded place:

D10: "But I think I checked a couple of times too when I got on the bus, you turn it on or you change songs, then you see if the lamp [indicating WiFi] of if the man [the icon indicating users nearby] were lit up, if there was anyone else on the bus..."

D9: "It would have been great if you know... like we go with bus 16 almost all of us and then you can see as you, there are so many people, as you enter the bus you could have the device to tell 'ah he's on the bus too'"

What D9 suggests is that the system also introduces enhanced *digital awareness* of people around you; like the Hummingbird (Holmquist et al. 1999) it makes one aware of users not directly visible. D10 experienced this when he thought he was alone on campus and suddenly discovered another user nearby:

"I have found people who you wouldn't have seen if... who you hadn't even seen nearby... you've been in school alone and then suddenly you see there is this Mats or what it was... someone who was called... And it was completely dead in school, I had no idea where he was at all, there was only this person there somewhere..."

It clearly added to the excitement of using Push!Music that there were other *unknown* users nearby. Some participants saw the same unknown users several times or even daily, which gave them more time to make guesses or theories about who these users could be and where they were located on campus:

C8: "… I used some process of elimination when not many were there and some poor guy was out in the kitchen [there is one on each floor for students to use] or maybe it was a few people… I tried to look for PDAs but it didn't go so well…"

Interviewer: "So you wanted to know who the others were?"

C8: "Yes, at least I did… I'm a very curious person."

These theories became a popular topic of discussion among the participants, similar to what happened in the study of the Jukola system (O'Hara *et al.*, 2004). This primarily concerned C7 and C8 (the tight pair) and A1-A4 (the group of class friends) who did not know each other but happen to be located on the same floor on campus. In the conversation below, A1, A2 and A4 are discussing C7 (Hans/Hansel) and her friend C8 (Greta/Gretchen) who they first believed were faked and not real users; partly because they always appeared visible and partly because of the intriguing and suspicious choice of nicknames:

A2: "… we thought Hans [Hansel] and Greta [Gretchen] were bots or something like that… they… they were two PDAs that were put in your office because of the name[s]…"

A1: "Plus, they were always visible too."

A2: "Yeah, those were the ones you saw, it was Hans and Greta, and Hans was kind of blinking…"

A1: "Is it them who sit in that room close to the coffee machine on the third floor? Those [two] who always sit there? That room that is kind of long, if you go from the coffee machine it is… Is it them?"

Interviewer: "Mm, yes."

A1: "I *knew* it!" [laugh]

A4: "Exactly."

A2: "Then we were right!"

C7 and C8 had made similar theories and assumptions about the group A1-A4. However, C7 and C8 clearly believed they gave enough cues to other users by frequently and visibly using their mobile devices. Below, C7 is also starting to wonder what the 'rules' of this technology are: if A1-A4 had figured out who she was, how come they did not push her any songs:

C8: "But I thought it was obvious because we always had the PDAs… how could they not see that?"

C7: "Yeah, exactly."

Interviewer: "I don't think they noticed."

C8: "I sat there and clicked hysterically [on the PDA] for some time… so it was MDI-people [from class A]? That's what I assumed… they do hang out there…"

C7: "Hm… how strange they didn't send me songs in that case…"

Despite the general curiosity about others, no actual *face-to-face interaction* took place between users who did not know each other before the study. They did push songs to strangers but there were no attempts made during the study to ask anyone or let someone know that you were a fellow participant.

The majority of the participants argued that a personally selected nickname is enough when sharing user information, as long as it could be used to simply recognise users you have met before. Having more information would imply that others as well as oneself could be looked up, and this was something they did not want everyone to be able to do. Some further argued that another possible implication of having more information, e.g. a picture, could be that it evokes prejudices that, in turn, affect the sharing of music negatively. This reveals a *tension about identity* in Push!Music, as music is usually much about expressing one's identity (see e.g. Brown *et al.*, 2001):

> B6: "I wouldn't want a picture... or to see any picture at all because [I] think it takes away some of the... you can still in some way make some judgement [about the received music] without "crap, he looks like a hard rock fan, I have to run away now to avoid getting music" or similar... it's not as spontaneous. You don't need to know who it is that you have shared music with, then you might get a more... then it is more fun to get music actually, when it is a totally anonymous... transfer [of music]"

> C7: "I wouldn't probably push my music to a hard rock fan for example... if I see, oh, he looks like a hard rock fan, I would think that he wouldn't like... "

Sharing music with friends

The participants had different motivations for pushing songs to friends. The majority thought pushing was an exciting feature, and therefore pushed songs *because they enjoyed it* and did so as soon as someone they knew (or did not) was nearby. Two other motivations (also present in an earlier study, c.f. Håkansson *et al.* 2007) were to *recommend* a song because you thought the receiver would like it, or to *disseminate* a song because you liked it yourself and wanted others to hear. The latter demonstrates some impression management (Goffman, 1959), as the sender might pick a song to tell something about him/herself: "... I wanted to spread 'Hello Saferide' to as many [people] as possible because I like that artist... I think people should listen to this if they haven't discovered it before..." (A2). D10 imagines how he could use Push!Music to push songs and maintain his identity and role as someone who knows about new music before everyone else does:

> "I look at different web sites, top-ten lists of the most popular downloads and those kind of things... everything that's new... and then you check almost every day to see what's popular today and if you see something you recognise then you get it... I know that I often see it before other people and then I could send it [using Push!Music] to other people earlier too... spread the word faster."

Another motivation was to push a song to *get something to talk about* as an important "side-effect". The sharing of music became a prompt for social interaction, but this happened only between users who already knew each other and were socialising face-to-face. In these cases, using Push!Music created a sense of togetherness:

A2: "... me and A3 talked a bit... we talked generally about music and so, because we both had Push!Music, and about me hearing the new [song] by Chemical Romance and then [she said] 'ah, but I've got that'..."

A3: "I was at their concert, it's my favourite band, I've got lots [of music] by them..."

A2: "'Ah, I've got that' she said and then maybe we pushed it to someone else..."

Yet another motivation was to push a "tasting sample" or a 'memory aid' that would then *help the receiver to remember* getting more of that artist, for instance at an online shop. A number of participants talked about how difficult it is to remember recommendations you get from friends, as D10 gives an example of: "we face that problem almost every day, we talk about applications or anything on the web really, and then when you come home and you have time to check these [things] up, you have no idea what they were called."

A final and noticeable motivation was to push songs to friends as *pranks*. This was something that mainly happened in the group of five friends (D9-D13) who knew each other well. We did not see any 'mischievous' use of Push!Music aimed towards strangers. The friends easily knew the difference between serious recommendations and pranks, and sometimes they would not waste time listening to the latter – as D13 says: "Blixten [D10] sent me all the music he knew I wouldn't like. [laugh] So I deleted it as soon as it appeared..." Pranks were also *in-jokes*, which helped creating a social cohesion. An example of this was one song in particular that was mischievously disseminated to everyone in the group (D9-D13). No one appreciated it as a 'good' song, but everyone enjoyed the prank in itself.

D9: "I think it didn't take long before everyone had 'Boten Anna' [a song]..."

Interviewer: "Who had it from the beginning?"

D9: "Yeah, who had it? No, it was D11 who had it from the beginning..."

Interviewer: "Why did you send it?"

D11: "I knew D9 would think it was fun! [everyone laughs] When I put together the list [of song for the study] I thought, well, I think I'll add this one..." [laugh]

Despite the 'non-serious' music as a result of pranks, D9-D13 believed that one has a greater tolerance towards music received from friends compared to strangers, and that this should be addressed in the system.

Sharing music with strangers

Some motivations were the same as when pushing songs to friends, such as disseminating particular songs. However, we also found motivations that were different, and some reasons *not* to push to strangers at all.

Participants pushed songs as 'Hello, I'm here'-messages to strangers to *let them know that they were around*, as C7 explains: "... if I don't push him [a song], how will he know that I'm there?" They pushed songs to *trigger some kind of contact*, often as *implicit requests for music* to be pushed back. These actions could be combined with disseminating a particular song, but several users just picked a random song when pushing to a stranger, as C7 explains: "Well, I just picked a song. I don't know that person so I don't know what taste in music he has... if he likes my song then he'll save it and if not, he can remove it, it doesn't matter."

Another reason to push was to *reciprocate* to a song one had received earlier. By considering songs as *gifts*, we here became aware of the "obligation to reciprocate" that comes with received gifts (Taylor and Harper, 2002). In Push!Music reciprocity was sometimes problematic. For instance, a number of users told us that they wanted to reciprocate, only to realise that it was no longer possible because the sender had moved out of the WiFi range.

They also expressed reasons *not* to push songs to strangers. One reason not to push (pranks as well as 'serious' recommendations) was simply because *one did not know the person*. Another reason was that some believed it could be *experienced as too intrusive*. The participants in the conversation below compare pushing songs to strangers with spamming and looking for random contacts on ICQ:

D13: "It really depends [if I would push songs to strangers]... if you have some music that maybe you have made yourself or something... sending [it] to all kinds [of users] just to disseminate... but I don't think, "I like this band", I wouldn't spread to all sorts [only] to the ones you know..."

D9: "Exactly, I wouldn't sit on the bus and spread music, that feels like..."

D13: "...like spam"

D9: "I don't look for random contacts on ICQ either"

Yet another important reason why some did not want to push songs to strangers was that as a sender, you could *not easily get any feedback* on what the receiver thought about the music. Currently the only way would be to ask the recipient face-to-face, and as mentioned before no face-to-face interaction was initiated between users who did not know each other. A related and equally important concern was that you could *not get credit* for pushing great songs (without face-to-face interaction). Neither could you build up a *reputation* for possessing great music, or maintain your *identity* as a person with great taste. A1, who gave the impression of being a true music aficionado (and a keen user of online file sharing systems), was the one who strongest expressed this concern:

A1: "It feels like the concept of pushing only works if you know who you send to, so you can follow up on it later. Because, if the system grows and there are 5000 users, I don't see any motivation in using [the] push [function] at all, to push music to someone specific..."

Interviewer: "How do you mean?"

A1: "I don't get credit for sending that song! Nobody will care..."

Interviewer: "You want credit?"

A1: "I want credit, yes, you want something. If it grows and gets really big I think you... the motivation to push music to people you don't know [...] then it is only interesting if you could perhaps build up some kind of reputation for pushing a lot of files or something..."

Participants acknowledged that pushing music to strangers could potentially be used as a trigger to get in touch with other people; however, they also brought up some concerns. In the discussion below, A2 claims that since the music is the most important part, he does not want any social consequences or obligations as a result of sharing music. Furthermore, he points out that *if* Push!Music were to be used as a means to get in touch with people, it would require everyone to have the same approach to avoid intrusiveness, similar to what Goffman (1963) calls *mutual openness*. That is, there has to be some (unspoken) mutual agreement that it is approved to engage in face-to-face encounters with unacquainted users:

A2: "It depends on how you use it [Push!Music], if you use it to meet... well, *the music* is the most interesting. I don't want to meet that person... maybe it's not that interesting to meet him, but maybe someone uses it as some social [device], "I want to meet people, I have no friends, but I listen to this music.""

A3: "Maybe you want to meet people who have the same taste in music and discuss music?"

A2: "Then you have to be more... then you need to have such an approach to it, *everyone* needs that approach if [s/he] uses the service. I wouldn't like someone to... sure, it [Push!Music] can push some of my music, but I don't want any person to look me up because of that."

The participants had different opinions about the fact that in Push!Music, songs can only be shared with people in the vicinity. A1 stood out from the others and did not see any added value in sharing only with nearby users – factors such as bandwidth, convenience and size of download were more important. However, the majority of the participants were positive to *ad hoc local sharing*. Despite their doubtfulness about direct interaction with unknown users, they still believed it was an *intriguing*, *fun* and *personal* way of getting new music compared to if the same songs had been analysed and sent out via computer. A2, who also claimed that the music itself was the most central part to him, brings up the importance of *context* when receiving a song from another person. A3 adds that moving in changing contexts could mean that one gets different music:

A2: "Let's say this other person has said this [song] is good, someone else should listen to this too, that means something right? Who that person is. I would never look that person up because I've received a song from him as I passed him in the city, but since this person listens to it in his player and maybe rated it and says it's good, then you should listen to it. Just because it's from a person in that context is very important, it is more personal in a way... compared to if a computer would have analysed it..."

A3: "Then maybe you can get different songs, different amount of songs, depending on where you are?..."

C8, who was very curious of the other users during the study, thought it was intriguing to know that users of Push!Music are *real* persons around you: "It was more fun, I think, to have them [other users] 'live', because knowing that someone is nearby but you don't know who it is, that's more exciting! Then it's a physical person, not just a name on a display..." As B5 expresses below, the nearby or local could also be seen as a sort of *security* or as a *filter*, implying that you cannot get music from anyone or any kind of music. The local aspect is also what he believes makes Push!Music different to online sharing systems:

"... this local part is some kind of security in itself and fun too. For example if you are on the bus and suddenly you receive music, that's fun, someone [else] is here [on the bus]... but if it would be over a larger distance, then... then you're basically back on the internet again, then I would have feared that suddenly there would be some song with five minutes of recorded screams"

Overall, receiving music from strangers often meant a welcome break from your own music. According to the participants, this music was more unexpected than something friends would have sent them. The majority of the participants were positive about the music they had received from strangers, although in general they wished they had received more during the study.

Sharing automatically

Because of technical reasons, the participants did not experience any automatic recommendations during the study. Despite this, they all talked enthusiastically about the concept of automatic sharing and referred to it as the most fun and "magical" part of Push!Music. They primarily seemed to think of the automatic sharing as something that would occur between strangers.

We recognised two possible reasons why the automatic sharing was so highly appreciated. The first reason is that the automatic sharing allows users to become introduced to new music *without being active*. The majority of the participants wanted new music, but said that they were "lazy" and wished they were more active looking for it. Push!Music could provide you with inspiration to listen to new music without forcing you to type in or actively search (which requires you to know roughly what you are looking for), as it is done in most online sharing systems. As A2 told us: "...you put it [the mobile device] there and thought it could share music and then when you checked it you would have received something... or sent something."

The second reason is that the automatic sharing could be looked upon as a *more balanced way of sharing* compared to directly pushing songs, which could be experienced as too intrusive. The automatic way would then allow the sharing of music among people in a non-intrusive but yet personal way. In the conversation below, A2 wants to specify which songs to share (as if he were to push them), but he wants the system to share them *automatically* and thereby *diminish* his role and responsibility in the act of sharing to strangers:

A1: "You trust it [the system] to get something automatically, because... I don't know, I don't get much out of pushing a song to someone I don't know, who I cannot ask afterward if he liked the song, it feels pointless [to push], it was fun at first to know now I've pushed a song,

I've spread 'Mäster spettaren' [a particular song] to five people [laugh], but that's about it what I can be satisfied with…"

A3: "But if you're with friends, ahh, have you heard that song, you can have it from me and you send it over and it's done really fast… that's when you're going to use [the] push [function]. But like he [A1] said, in the beginning it was fun to send stuff."

A2: "I would have liked a function: ok, I want to spread this song by Hello Saferide, so it's labelled "please push this when I meet someone" instead of… ok, I can see Hans but I don't know who it is, [so] I can't push to him, I don't know that person, but if I tell it [the system] to push this [song] if it meets people, then it will spread it [the song] to people…"

Interviewer: "… kind of automatically, but yet personal?"

A2: "Yeah, exactly, you decide what… then it can be random if it [the system] pushes or not […] instead of this active [the current push function] which you only use for… those who sit beside you or similar."

Implications for mobile media sharing systems

Push!Music was deliberately designed as an open system with few limitations. Users could push a song to *any* user in the vicinity, and there were no restrictions from who one could receive music – if someone pushes you a song, it will end up in your playlist. However, this openness was less than straightforward from a social perspective. Push!Music was quickly adopted by the participants to support *already existing* social networks and practices. For instance, users got a stronger social cohesion by using Push!Music to send songs as pranks or to prompt discussions about music and related things. Although the participants also pushed songs to strangers, this was something they did not feel equally comfortable with; for example, they argued that one "cannot" push to someone one does not know, and if one did, some worried that the recipient would think it was too intrusive.

We recognised a division in the use of Push!Music: users enjoyed being *active with friends* (sending songs as pranks, memory aids, recommendations, etc.) and felt most comfortable with the idea of being *passive with strangers* (sharing automatically). Perhaps this is not surprising, as we naturally do not have the same relationship with strangers as with friends. For instance, we do not greet or interact with strangers in public and densely populated areas because it would simply be too exhausting and overwhelming (Goffman, 1963). Nonetheless, we are still curious and intrigued about unknown people around us, and we can use this knowledge to build systems that enhance our sense of our surroundings (Paulos and Goodman, 2004). The fact that the participants talked enthusiastically about the idea of sharing automatically with people one encounters in everyday life is a demonstration of this.

The following design implications draw on the findings in the study. They are not only applicable to music sharing; we argue they have relevance for mobile media sharing in general, e.g. for digital photos.

Allow division into active and passive use

Most of the participants used Push!Music differently with friends vs. strangers. This suggests that media sharing activities could be divided into two separate parts: one *active* for friends, and one *passive* for strangers. This could ensure an *enjoyable* and *secure* experience of media sharing in the mobile realm. Similar to IM systems (see e.g. Grinter and Palen, 2002), the use of buddy lists could allow users to add people as friends or contacts to a particular list where pushing of songs and sharing of personal information is possible. Strangers encountered in everyday life would not be included in this list by default. It should still be possible to push songs to strangers, but it would require some sort of approval from the receiver before the song is actually sent. However, the system would still be open for sharing music *automatically* between strangers, which would provide users with new music in a non-intrusive and less socially demanding way. Moreover, we suggest that the active part could be extended to allow for sharing over larger distances, to support a more spontaneous sharing between friends who are not in the vicinity. After all, friends play a very important part in music sharing, implying that they should be possible to share with at anytime.

Enhance the awareness of who, where and when

Push!Music currently lets users know who has sent a particular song and if it was pushed or automatically shared. However, the system did not provide any notice when another user appeared in the vicinity or, importantly, when one received (or automatically sent) a song. We learned two things: firstly, as a result of this, users were sometimes unaware of the fact that they had received songs and did not notice them until later. Secondly, users talked about the importance of receiving music from "a person in that context", arguing that the setting or situation in which one gets a song is important and matters to the overall experience of sharing music. When evaluating a mobile social software system for motorcyclists, the researchers found that an exciting part of the experience was to hear a *notification sound* when one encountered another biker and some content was transferred (Esbjörnsson *et al.*, 2004). We therefore suggest enhancing the awareness of *who, where and when* with a vibration or sound (which should be possible to turn off). Such a notification would give the receiver a chance to know when others are around, to "be prepared" to listen to something new, and finally, a chance to reciprocate while the sender is still in the vicinity.

Support reciprocity

As Taylor and Harper (2002) report on gift-giving in their study of teenage mobile phone use, accepting a gift (for example a text message) means that the recipient is "obliged to reciprocate in kind". In our study of Push!Music, we also became aware of this obligation in the *sharing of music*, and how participants sometimes became frustrated when they could not reciprocate due to design and technical issues. This applied to the sharing with friends as well as with strangers. The ad hoc communication with users moving out of the WiFi range or one not noticing the received music until later made reciprocity difficult. As reciprocity has proved to be an essential part of the sharing of music using Push!Music, we suggest that there should be *support for reciprocity* to better support the practice of *sharing*. This could include improved methods for sharing media back, or simply sending a "thank you" to acknowledge a received song.

Support identity and impression management

We noticed a tension in Push!Music where the participants on one hand claimed that identity and impression management did not matter (it was the sharing of *music* that was important, not with whom) versus a strong wish for better support for it. For example, we learnt that for some users, getting *credit* was a very important motivation behind the sharing of music. Some users wanted to be able to build up a *reputation* for pushing good music or for being the first ones who disseminate new music. Although the majority of potential users might be 'average' consumers who just want to get to know new music, we recognise the need to better support music aficionados and their role in the system. We argue that they are important in sharing systems because it is through them that a lot of the sharing of music takes place. We therefore suggest a better support for maintaining one's identity and impression, and a better support to recognise other users. However, in a *mobile* sharing system, this puts other demands on privacy compared to online systems, which in turn limits how the impression management could be supported. We suggest that such information could be some sort of 'abstract accountability', similar to ambiguous awareness information that Gaver (2002) proposes or how the presence of familiar strangers is presented in (Paulos and Goodman, 2004).

Conclusions

In our study of the Push!Music system, we found that rather than triggering new face-to-face interactions with strangers, the system mainly supported existing social networks. At the same time, users did occasionally share songs with strangers – but would have preferred automatic sharing, as it implied less social intrusion. We believe that the findings could be valuable to the design of mobile *media* sharing systems in general, not just the ones related to music. For instance, people are happy to publish photos on on-line systems such as Flickr (wwwflickr.com), but are likely to use access management to exercise control over which photos are available to everyone in the world, and which are only available to close friends or family. Mobile sharing systems cannot simply allow sharing with everyone who happens to be in the same location, but at the same time, the presence of other users (or as one subject expressed it, "real people") was an exciting part of the experience of Push!Music and made the sharing feel more "live". Support for reciprocity in gift-giving, identity management, and credits for advanced users who contribute to the system are also important factors for the success of future mobile media sharing systems – perhaps even more so than for existing stationary applications.

Acknowledgments

We would like to thank our project colleague Mattias Jacobsson for help with practical issues and overall feedback. We would also like to thank Alex Taylor, Barry Brown and colleagues at the Viktoria Institute for very thoughtful and valuable comments on this paper and earlier work. Finally, thanks to the study participants for their time and enthusiasm. This work is supported by the ECAgents project (IST-2003-1940) funded by the European IST-FET programme.

References

Bassoli, A., Moore, J., and Agamanolis, S. (2006): 'tunA: Socialising Music Sharing on the Move', in K. O'Hara and B. Brown (eds.) *Consuming Music Together: Social and Collaborative Aspects of Music Consumption Technologies*, Springer, pp. 151-172.

Bly, S., Harrison, S., and Irwin, S. (1993): 'Media Spaces: Bringing People Together in a Video, Audio, and Computing Environment', in *Communications of the ACM*, January 1993, Vol. 36, No. 1, pp. 27-47.

Borovoy, R., Martin, F., Vemuri, S., Resnick, M., Silverman, B. and Hancock, C. (1998): Meme Tags and Community Mirrors: Moving from Conferences to Collaboration. Proceedings of CSCW'98, ACM Press, New York.

Brown, B., Sellen, A., and Geelhoed, E. (2001): 'Music sharing as a computer supported collaborative application', in *Proceedings of ECSCW 2001*. Kluwer Academic Publishers, pp.179-198.

Bull, M. (2000): *Sounding Out The City*, Berg, NY, USA.

Bull, M. (2006): 'Investigating the Culture of Mobile Listening: From Walkman to iPod' in K. O'Hara and B. Brown (eds.) *Consuming Music Together: Social and Collaborative Aspects of Music Consumption Technologies*, Springer, pp. 131-149.

D'Arcangelo, G. (2005): The New Cosmopolites: Activating the Role of Mobile Music Listeners. *Presented at the 2nd International Mobile Music Workshop,* at the 2005 "New Interfaces for Musical Expression" Conference, University of British Columbia, Vancouver, BC.

DeNora, T. (2000): *Music in Everyday Life*, Cambridge University Press, Cambridge, UK.

Dourish, P. and Bellotti, V. (1992): 'Awareness and Coordination in Shared Workspaces', in *Proceedings of CSCW'92*, Toronto, Ontario, pp 107-114. New York: ACM.

Eagle, N. and Pentland, A. (2005): 'Social Serendipity: Mobilizing Social Software', in *IEEE Pervasive Computing*, vol. 4, no. 2, 2005, pp. 28-34.

Esbjörnsson, M., Juhlin, O. and Östergren, M. (2004): 'Traffic Encounters and Hocman - Associating Motorcycle Ethnography with Design', in *Personal and Ubiquitous Computing*, Springer Verlag, vol. 8, no. 2, pp. 92-99.

Gaver, B. (2002): 'Provocative awareness', in *Computer Supported Cooperative Work*, Kluwer Academic Publishers, the Netherlands, Vol. 11, 2002, pp. 475-493.

Grinter, R.E. and Palen, L. (2002): 'Instant Messaging in Teen Life', in *Proceedings of CSCW 2002*, New Orleans, USA.

Goffman, E. (1959): *The Presentation of Self in Everyday Life*. Anchor Books, New York.

Goffman, E. (1963): *Behavior in Public Places. Notes on the Social Organization of Gatherings*, The Free Press, New York, USA.

Holmquist, L.E., Falk, J., and Wigström, J. (1999): 'Supporting Group Collaboration with Interpersonal Awareness Devices', in *Personal Technologies*, vol. 3, nos. 1-2, 1999, pp. 105-124.

Håkansson, M., Jacobsson, M., and Holmquist, L.E. (2005): 'Designing a Mobile Music Sharing System Based on Emergent Properties', in *Proceedings of AMT 2005*, Takamatsu, Japan.

Håkansson, M., Rost, M., Jacobsson, M. and Holmquist, L.E. (2007): 'Facilitating Mobile Music Sharing and Social Interaction with Push!Music', in *Proceedings of HICSS-40*, Hawaii, USA, 2007.

Jacobsson, M., Rost, M., and Holmquist, L.E. (2006): 'When Media Gets Wise: Collaborative Filtering with Mobile Media Agents', in *Proceedings of IUI 2006*. Sydney, Australia.

Jacobsson, M., Rost, M., Håkansson, M., Holmquist, L.E. (2005): 'Push!Music: Intelligent Music Sharing on Mobile Devices', in *Adjunct Proceedings of UbiComp 2005*, Tokyo, Japan.

Jaques, R. (2006): Cameraphone users fail to click with MMS. *Personal Computer World*, 08 Feb 2006.

Jung, Y., Blom, J., and Persson, P. (2006): 'Scent Field Trial – Understanding Emerging Social Interaction', in *Proceedings of MobileHCI 2006*, Helsinki, Finland.

McCarthy, J.F. and Anagnost, T.D. (1998): MusicFX: An Arbiter of Group Preferences for Computer Supported Collaborative Workouts. In Proceedings of CSCW '98, ACM Press, New York.

O'Hara, K. and Brown, B. (2006): Consuming Music Together: Introduction and Overview, in K. O'Hara and B. Brown (eds.) *Consuming Music Together: Social and Collaborative Aspects of Music Consumption Technologies*, Springer, pp. 3-17.

O'Hara, K., Lipson, M., Jansen, M., Unger, A., Jeffries, H., and Macer, P. (2004): 'Jukola: Democratic Music Choice in a Public Space', in *Proc of DIS2004*, Cambridge, MA, USA.

Paulos, E. and Goodman, E. (2004): 'The Familiar Stranger: Anxiety, Comfort, and Play in Public Places', in *Proceedings of CHI 2004*, Vienna, Austria.

Taylor, A.S., and Harper, R. (2002): 'Age-old Practices in the 'New World': A study of gift-giving between teenage mobile phone users', in *Proc of CHI 2002*, Minneapolis, USA.

Voida, A., Grinter, R.E., Ducheneaut, N., Edwards, W.K., and Newman, M.W. (2005): 'Listening in: Practices surrounding iTunes music sharing', in *Proc of CHI 2005*. Portland, USA.

Want, R., Hopper, A., Falcao, V., Gibbons, J. (1992): The Active Badge Location System. *ACM Trans. on Inf. Sys.*, Jan.1992.

Weilenmann, A. (2001): 'Negotiating Use: Making Sense of Mobile Technology', in *Personal and Ubiquitous Computing*, vol. 5: (2), 137-145 Springer-Verlag London Ltd.

Östergren, M., and Juhlin, O. (2006): 'Car Drivers using Sound Pryer – Field Trials on Shared Music Listening in Traffic Encounters', in *K. O'Hara and B. Brown (eds.), Consuming Music Together: Social and Collaborative Aspects of Music Consumption Technologies*. Springer, 2006, pp. 173-190.

L. Bannon, I. Wagner, C. Gutwin, R. Harper, and K. Schmidt (eds.).
ECSCW'07: Proceedings of the Tenth European Conference on Computer Supported Cooperative Work, 24-28 September 2007, Limerick, Ireland
© Springer 2007

Making the Home Network at Home: Digital Housekeeping

Peter Tolmie, Andy Crabtree, Tom Rodden, Chris Greenhalgh and Steve Benford

School of Computer Science & IT, University of Nottingham, Jubilee Campus, Wollaton Road, Nottingham NG8 1BB, UK.

{pdt, axc, tar, cmg, sdb}@cs.nott.ac.uk

Abstract. This paper exploits ethnographic findings to build on and elaborate Grinter et al's 2005 study of "the work to make the home network work". We focus particularly on the work involved in setting up and maintaining home networks, which we characterize as 'digital housekeeping'. Our studies reveal that it is through digital housekeeping that the home network is 'made at home' or made into an unremarkable and routine feature of domestic life. The orderly ways in which digital housekeeping 'gets done' elaborate a distinct 'social machinery' that highlights some important implications for the continued development of network technologies for the home. These include a requirement that designers take existing infrastructure into account and pay considerable attention to how future technologies may be incorporated into existing routines. The preoccupation of household members with making the home network transparent and accountable so that it is available to practical reasoning suggests designers should also consider the development of dedicated management interfaces to support digital housekeeping.

Introduction

Interest in the home as a site of technological research and development has burgeoned over recent years. Much of this is focused upon 'living laboratories' (Edwards & Grinter 2001). However, in a paper entitled *The Work to Make the Home Network Work*, Grinter et al. (2005) draw attention to the increasing presence of distributed computing in *ordinary* homes via the home network. This real world focus complements earlier efforts in CSCW to understand and inform the development of new agendas in distributed computing (e.g., Bowers 1994, Bowers et al. 1995, Button & Sharrock 1997). Similarly seeking to inform IT research as to the real world character of technology in homes, Grinter et al. present an ethnographic study that explores the work involved in making the home network work. The study reveals the complexity of the home network as it is manifest 'on the ground' and elaborates the work involved in incorporating the home network into the domestic routine; including practically managing network complexity, handling tensions that emerge between individual and communal needs, and meeting the demands of administration and troubleshooting.

Grinter et al's observations about network complexity complement concerns of other researchers in the field. Shehan and Edwards (2007) have sought to unpack the infrastructural origins of network complexity and associated problems. They explore different ways in which new approaches to infrastructure might help and note the current lack of tools supporting management of the home network. Others have also taken up the issue of complexity, focusing on mismatches between professional and ordinary user expectations (Bly et al. 2006), congruence and divergence between professionals and ordinary users (Brush 2006), and on improving understanding of how users ordinarily orient to complexity (Chetty and Grinter 2006). These investigations have been complemented by conceptual and technical work which is concerned to improve the coherence and visibility of the home network (Elmore et al. 2007, Lemhachheche 2006, Newman 2006, Shehan et al. 2006, Yang and Edwards 2006).

Whilst matters of complexity are not outside of our remit, we concentrate here upon elaborating the ways in which the management of the home network is becoming *an integral part of the larger management of the household*. Thus our focus is upon what is practically involved in leveraging the technology into everyday life such that it becomes an unremarkable feature of the household's domestic routines (Tolmie et al. 2002, Crabtree & Rodden 2004). This achievement relies on what might be described as 'digital housekeeping'. Here we seek to unpack some of the ways in which that achievement is organized across households so as to provide for 'making the technology at home' (Sacks 1992a) in the face of the endlessly variable social arrangements and activities that make up the 'routine' within any home. Domestic routines are not fixed but change from home to home and over time within any home. It is as if they were built on shifting sand and yet somehow household members can and do weave the home network into their daily lives. We want to understand something of what that 'somehow' consists as a socially organized accomplishment that extends beyond the particularities of the routines at work in any particular home.

We would start by drawing a contrast between digital housekeeping and traditional social science accounts of housekeeping, which emphasize the role of gender divisions to the accomplishment of housework in general (see Blythe and Monk 2002, Bell et al. 2005, Wyche et al. 2006). It is not that we dispute that gender can play an important role in the development of computing for the home.

Clearly it does (see, for example, Taylor and Swan 2005). Rather, and as our invocation of Sacks suggests, we prefer to suspend the broad concerns with gender that occupy mainstream social scientists, and instead seek to inspect the particular demands of digital housekeeping from the perspective *of household members* - particularly from the point of view of how members themselves see, understand and reason about the relationship between technology and the home in the course of situating it within their ongoing domestic affairs.

What we find when we do this is that members exhibit a number of preoccupations that revolve around setting the home network up and ongoing maintenance. These include locating the technology in the physical fabric of the home, maintaining the wider order of the home environment, and planning and preparing for change. They also include ongoing housekeeping, recurrent housekeeping, managing access and security, managing digital media, and restoring order when order breaks down. The concerns that members exhibit across different households in their practical efforts to make the home network at home draw attention to the importance of marrying technology development to existing infrastructure in the home (Rodden & Benford 2003) and put flesh on the bones of what Grinter et al. could be talking about when they say, "tools that provide views of the network oriented around the services the network provides - rather than the devices that comprise it - might greatly aid householders in working together on family solutions to not just media sharing problems, but also the set-up and administration of the devices and infrastructure itself."

Setting and Method

The findings on which this paper is based are drawn from 3 households in the UK. They are part of a longer term and ongoing course of research that seeks to explore the potential for, and inform the development of, new technologies in the home. The current studies focus on homes where the occupants have installed or are in the process of installing home networks. They involve:

- *House A*, which consists of two adults, 44 and 30 years old, both computing professionals, living in a large two-bedroom apartment.

- *House B*, a family consisting of 2 adults, 38 and 36 years old, and 3 children, 9, 7 and 15 months, living in a semi-detached house. One of the adults is a computing professional, all other members of the household have very limited technical experience.

- *House C*, a family consisting of 2 adults, both 43 years old, and 2 children, 12 and 9, also living in a semi-detached house. Once again one of the adults is a computing professional but all of the others in the household have no specialized experience of technology.

Whilst there is at least one member in each household involved in computing in some way, these homes cannot be said to constitute "advanced technology set ups" as in Grinter et al's study. In fact, all of the computing professionals involved expressed reluctance to get involved in computing activities at home as it already occupied their working days. Indeed, it quickly became apparent that having someone technical in the house does not make the home subject to rapid technology adoption. There are numerous other everyday household concerns that hold sway and any technical undertaking is *accountable to these*. Thus the building of home networks in these and other households seems indicative of an altogether different phenomenon. Broadband connections amount to over 70% of all Internet connections in the UK and this is accompanied by an increasingly widespread uptake of wireless technologies in the home. Home networks are no longer 'geek' experiments, they are an ordinary solution to burgeoning technological complexity. The participants in our study have, like others across the country and farther afield, installed home networks because it makes sense for them to do so in order to manage a host of technologies that are increasingly pervasive in character. Theirs are home networks *for* the home, not for professional curiosity.

The households were studied through direct ethnographic observation (Crabtree 2003). The study itself is ongoing but the reflections offered here are derived from monthly site visits and interviews conducted during the first 4 months of study. In keeping with the ethnomethodological approach that we adopt towards analyzing ethnographic fieldwork, we focus on what we can learn by inspecting particular 'instances' (Sacks 1984) in which members display the real world, real time competences and practices where they organize their interactions with computers (Button 1992). These 'embodied displays' (Dourish 2001) exhibit patterns of conduct that extend beyond the individuals involved (Garfinkel 2001). Think, for example, of the patterns of conduct made manifest by yourself as you walk down the road, buy goods in shop, and drive home, and how what you do is organized in very much the same ways as those around you who are engaged in the same activities. There is an 'incarnate' orderliness to human activity that we, as fellow members of the ordinary society, naturally observe and regulate (ibid.).

The fieldwork vignettes presented here should not, in that case, be read as being solely about the particulars of each observed instance. A whole range of *orderly concerns* that cut across households are manifest in the vignettes. They exhibit the kinds of reasoning that make 'homes' and 'households' recognizable for what they are. They are populated by such issues as where do you put the technology? Where do you plug things in? How do you organize your seating around it? What do you ask of your children with regards to its use? Working out answers to these and other routine problems of order in the home is of course subject to the local, the contingent, the endlessly variable and changeable. Thus, the particular physical characteristics of the home, the particular technological arrangements installed, the particular members that occupy the home, the particularities of the activities being undertaken, etc., all shape the ways in which household members actually come to make the technology at home in any particular setting. Nevertheless, the orderliness, or social organization, or 'machinery' as

Sacks called it, exhibited and displayed by members within particular instances is of much broader purchase and relevance. That purchase and relevance is located in the *broad recognizability of a set of mundane arrangements and activities* within which members find the resources to weave the home network into their everyday lives (Sacks 1992b).

The suggestion, then, is that despite local variation in their accomplishment, a particular assemblage or family of practices cuts across homes and that 'making the home network at home' relies on them. We treat this family of practices, or social machinery, in terms of 'digital housekeeping', a notion that is intended to denote that making the home network at home is not only about managing networks - it is also about managing the whole gamut of digital resources tied to it and rapidly populating the home environment. Furthermore, it is about *doing that* not as experts but as ordinary people who have to manage their digital resources as a part of their everyday lives. Most of what we speak of here does not trade on any profound computing expertise then. Rather it is a mixture of ordinary reasoning about what it takes to run a home and what it takes to use a computer, a digital camera, and a collection of other increasingly pervasive technologies within a local nexus of quotidian concerns. Our goal here is to begin to uncover the ordinary social machinery whereby household members make their digital resources available as resources within the broader organization of the home and accessible across a wide range of domestic activities. Key to this achievement is the ***setting up*** and configuring of digital resources so that they can be managed as part of the routine organization of the home, and the ***ongoing housekeeping*** of digital resources which provides for the maintenance and adaptation of the home network over time to meet the household's changing needs. Below we explicate important features of these primary constituents of the social machinery in turn.

Setting Up Digital Resources in the Home

When digital resources enter the home they cannot just be positioned in any way within the household and its routines. Their entry into the home is not only managed for the here-and-now by household members but for the *future* as well and this is an integral part of how people reason about them when setting them up. Furthermore, it is clear that there are features of the work of setting up that get oriented to as 'chores' to be done as part of the larger round of housekeeping in the home. Where technologies are placed, how this placement is achieved, how these fit with the everyday order of the household, and how this change is prepared for and planned play a key role in making the home network at home.

Locating Technology in the Home

One of the most important ways in which people provide for the future management of digital resources in the home relates to how they *physically position* technology. A number of constraints impact where we can place digital equipment in
our homes, of which power supply is the most evident. Additionally, certain
items of equipment may have to be placed within reach of where data/telecom
lines enter the home and, when wireless devices are being used, there may be
constraints upon where one can get a good signal.

However, there is much more to placement than just technological constraints.
For a start people routinely reason about the things or 'stuff' (Rodden and Benford 2003) in their homes in ecological or topological ways (Crabtree and Rodden
2004). They therefore position things in such a way that the connections between
things and the activities they engage in is transparent to household members.
Thus, the placement of digital stuff is framed by established routines in the home
and concerned with maintaining an appropriate relationship to those routines. For
example, places where people used to do written work (e.g., the kitchen table) become places where they also sit to do writing on their laptops. Even when technology opens up completely new possibilities, it continues to be located for its
availability to the routine. The positioning of things in the home, *including digital
resources*, is therefore intimately bound up with household routine and how it
may be reasoned about to support everyday household practice. In the following
vignette we can see how such consideration of other household concerns can
come to influence the positioning of technology.

House B
Ethnographer: Why did you put the hub on the windowsill? Was that necessary because of
lengths of wires?
Householder: I could have used an active extension cable, but I'd already anticipated that I might
have multiple USB things plugged in over there so I put the hub in straight off - and the windowsill
is sort of at least slightly out of the way and it's already got a pile of rubbish on it ...

Here, then, we can see how things may get positioned so that their 'untidy' aspect
will be hidden by the presence of existing physical disorder. Simultaneously, by
being 'out of the way' the routine concern with child safety in this home – they
have a young toddler – were solved. Thus we can see how the installation of digital resources can intersect with and become a part of other physical housekeeping
issues. Where this is the case the reasoning applied is always in terms of being
accountable to the broader issues in the household, not the other way round, and
the practices of installation *reflect* the logic of those concerns.

The following example reveals that the existence of even a wireless home network does not simply write anew the possibilities for how new technology gets
incorporated into practice:

House C
I have discovered that my favourite seat for viewing the television, which is on the other side of
the house from the PC, is just on the edge of network range, so I do tend to go through some

shenanigans of sitting in the right position in the seat to be able to put my laptop on the coffee table and trust the intermittent connection if I want to do something like read my mail while I'm
watching telly or whatever. You sometimes have to reorient yourself a bit to get back the signal.

In each of the households involved in our study, it can be seen how the set up of
home networks is shot through with a set of larger concerns regarding how best to
organize digital resources to facilitate not just personal use, but their routine use
within broader household activities. Matters such as 'tidiness', 'child safety',
'room usage', 'positioning of furniture', 'décor', 'where the power and phone
lines are', and so on, are critically implicated in the way the technology gets set
up and installed, and likewise, the positioning of technology becomes implicated
in how such things are reasoned about in the home.

Maintaining Order in the Home

The actual work of installing technology can be hugely disruptive to the household routine. It may involve the movement of furniture, the turning off of things
like televisions, the trailing of wires across floors so that whole rooms are out of
bounds, and, of course, one of the members of the household is physically unavailable for other activities at that time. Consequently one finds that the work of
installation gets organized around what else is happening in the household to try
and minimize the impact of these things.

House A
I'm going to be moving a new media PC in next. I'm going to do it next weekend when Rachel
isn't here because I know how disruptive it's going to be. I'm going to have to turn stuff on and off
- the TV for instance - and I know I'm going to have to move stuff around the living room and all
this has a knock on effect: I'm going to put the box in a targeted space – the TV has a cupboard
with a slot in it but there are DVDs in the slot at the moment - there's just not enough storage in
the house for all the DVDs -and then I'm also going to have to unplug lots of stuff.

Planning and Preparing for Change

The above comments about how the digital housekeepers we observed strive to
maintain order as they install technology are indicative of how important it becomes to undertake certain projects, especially larger-scale ones like installing or
extending home networks, in several stages. This involves knowing in advance
that the work can be accomplished within a certain amount of time and that, at the
end of it, everything can be restored to good order until the next time.

In view of the need to mesh installation with other household routines, those
who engage in setting up home networks can devote considerable attention to
thinking them through in advance. The critical problem here is figuring out how
to get a fit between a new technological arrangement and a well-established and
fine-tuned body of practice to which the household is already oriented. In this
situation inhabitants may overtly devote effort to making the technology at home.
Questions like where things are going to be stored, how people are going to get

access to them, where people are going to be able to access them from, what people will and won't need to be able to see, how they are going to be able to shift stuff around, how things are going to get linked up together and synchronized, and so on, all come to matter enormously, not as technical matters, but as matters of moment that can clearly impact upon any household member and their routine. Consequently, those setting up the network not only draw upon a range of online resources as Grinter et al. note, but also construct representations of their networks to address the issues that confront their efforts to make the home network at home. One householder's solution to being able to think these kinds of things through is shown below:

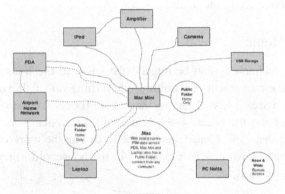

Figure 1. Making the home network transparent and reason-able.

Resources such as these make technological configuration of the home network visible and available to practical reasoning. As Grinter et al. note,

> "without the ability to understand the whole network, troubleshooting the network - let alone installing or modifying the network - becomes virtually impossible."

It would seem, then, that developing representations that enable household members to reason about the configuration of the home network at the level of device and service is an important feature of making the technology at home. A question that arises out of this, however, relates to how this might extend to service providers who are invited into the home to assemble and configure the home network (Verjee 2006). If the current work of configuration is oriented to a *local understanding* of how things are arranged and managed in any particular household, how will an external 'digital plumber' be able to anticipate or support this body of local reasoning? A part of the answer lies in developing representations that articulate the lines between digital plumbing and digital housekeeping. Either way, there is a serious need for the design community to make the home network much more transparent and available to practical reasoning by professional digital plumbers and DIY householders alike.

When the technology has been positioned, set up and installed, and everything is back in place, the orientation of household members shifts to living and engaging with the network as part of daily practice. Here the concern is not just with embedding particular devices in ongoing routines but about arriving at a point where managing the ensemble of devices can *become routine*. A major issue here is whether or not the technology is *stable* so that effort only needs to be devoted to keeping it that way rather than having to continually rebuild and reorganize. To that end those who set things up also seek to reassure themselves that such stability is present before adding any further layers of complexity.

House A
I've not got everything plugged in yet. Now one of the reasons for this - again a bit of natural caution - is, I want to see if the media PC collapses before adding more.

With the stability of the network established the practical concerns for digital housekeeping shift to maintaining the ensemble in the broader context of the household's everyday routines. We now turn our attention to that *ongoing* work.

The Ongoing Housekeeping of Digital Resources

As digital resources become more stable features of the home they require a different kind of housekeeping effort. Now it is a matter of keeping them in good order. From our studies it is clear that there are two principle ways in which household members reason about this ongoing housekeeping. Firstly there are predictable kinds of *necessary and recurrent housekeeping tasks* that are viewed as a part of having digital resources. Then there are *occasional housekeeping tasks* that arise as either a part of things breaking in some way or the kind of entropy that infects computational networks generally. The latter are 'one-offs' and it is hard to know when the need to undertake them might arise.

Recurrent Housekeeping as a Part of Domestic Routine

Some of the tasks that have to be undertaken as part of digital housekeeping in home environments are relatively invisible in work environments. Thus in most medium and large-scale enterprises the backing up of materials stored on the individual parts of the work network is the responsibility of dedicated support staff. The users of particular workstations or laptops connected to the network therefore have their materials backed up without any special effort on their part. The same is also likely to be the case for various upgrades and security patches. One can similarly schedule for automated back-ups and upgrades in home networks. However, we found that the work of setting that up and maintaining it was falling to *particular* members of the household who have to attend to the broader rhythms of the household when undertaking and scheduling such work.

The setting up of such systematic handling of routine digital housekeeping is either itself a job on an as-yet-to-be-realised 'to do' list, recalled as a requirement in the context of other household planning activities, or else wholly unreflected upon until things go wrong. Thus, backing up and upgrading are matters a) occasioned by other circumstances that arise, or b) are scheduled to be handled manually with some suitable periodicity. What does it take, then, for such tasks to be undertaken and what kinds of concerns are oriented to by the digital housekeeper? The following remarks reveal the extent to which, even for those members of the household who have considerable expertise with computers, and even where existing resources should make backing up relatively painless, it still turns upon the ways in which maintenance is *occasioned* within the household.

House C
I try not to leave anything I would cry about if it got trashed on the home machine. My partner's different, I think it's mostly her main machine. I, at various points, have shown her how to back stuff up onto various different media but I think it's always been enough of a pain that I'm damn sure she doesn't do it. I think she emails stuff to herself - she certainly does that - and occasionally I will say, "you need to back stuff up" when it occurs to me because I know she hasn't, and occasionally I do it for her but not regularly.

Occasionally upgrades are more to do with hardware, but once again these are an occasioned part of the wider concerns and routines of the household, rather than planned and structured as part of the ongoing business of 'keeping the system up to date' that one may encounter in larger enterprises. Upgrades could be prompted by any number of different household concerns such as someone who previously worked elsewhere beginning work at home; school work; more children reaching an age where they are playing games or going online; not to mention the increasing use of a growing number of linked leisure and entertainment resources (photos, music, films, chat, etc.). In the following case there are just too many people all trying to use the same desktop PC, with all of the attendant arguments about memory, applications, times of use, security, etc.

House C
At the moment, already under the pressure of our single PC ... I have retreated to working with my laptop, which means a wireless network. So... we've done the basics but now we're still under more pressure for that PC so now it looks like we'll introduce a second PC and that has to run right across the house and I'll connect that up. So the network's growing at the moment.

In the above excerpt we can see how it might be that more and more people are seeing the sense in setting up wireless facilities and constructing some kind of home network. Whatever the local reasons that occasion this, when it happens it involves a whole new set of housekeeping concerns that are of broader relevance.

Managing Access and Security

As computing facilities become more widespread throughout the home and are used in a wider variety of ways the range of routine concerns that manifest themselves can become quite daunting, involving things like password management, setting up and updating individual user accounts and profiles, and installing firewalls and virus checkers. One may also need to engage with more sophisticated interests such as the synchronization of resources such as file stores and calendars. However, all of this is as much an occasioned part of the evolution of the household as anything else, as is made clear by the following householder.

House C
The real maintenance is on the PC. That's because of ... different uses it's put to and the number of programs that are coming and going from it - particularly going. Initially it was worse because the previous PC - we didn't even bother with separate accounts because the kids were young ... and we didn't feel like we needed them and it just felt like more hassle for them to have to do that, but obviously, you know, as people have started to mess more and more with the configurations and do more different things, we did then introduce a system of accounts.

While many of these housekeeping issues prove to be one-off enterprises that only occasionally require further intervention, other features may require more regular consideration. In Household C the presence of children requires the management of NetNanny, for example, to ensure the children are not browsing anything unsavoury on the Internet. Yet here the actual management of it is not in any sense formulaic, but rather nuanced to each situation as it arises:

House C
As the kids got more into the Internet we kind of thought "yeah, we're not entirely sure what they're going to find, what they're going to browse" so we thought we'd install NetNanny. It's hard to be systematic about which sites you want to block and which ones you don't. It does take active control. So basically you've got a couple of options: you could go into the sites that NetNanny recommends by default, but it turns out that doesn't satisfy the kids. There are some things they want to look at that we are happy for them to look at that aren't on the list, so you can then either maintain the list of allowed and blocked sites yourself but you'd have to update that fairly regularly with a fair bit of discussion about each one or you end up saying "never mind all that, we'll log you in as 'grown up' mode". For us updating the list doesn't happen because it feels like just a bit too much hassle to do it. So when they log on, NetNanny will be set to kid mode and then if they want to look at something else they'll come to me and there'll be a bit of whingeing and they'll say "we hate Net Nanny, wurr-wurr-wurr" and then we'll decide whether to unblock it temporarily. The problem is we almost certainly won't remember to turn it back on for the remainder of that session and obviously we don't sit with them while they browse.

Managing Digital Media

A growing phenomena that runs to the heart of digital activity in domestic settings is the creation of blogs and community software such as Flickr. In many cases these may be personal resources with only limited interest in terms of how to maintain things for the rest of the household. However, the management of these things is indicative of an area of regular digital housekeeping that is rapidly becoming a chore. It is increasingly hard to find a home where there is not at least one digital camera and often there are several. Households are therefore increasingly confronted with multiple members of the household generating and then wanting to store, manipulate, and share digital photos. Downloading these photos, locating them in the right places, sorting them, sifting them, rotating some, deleting others, improving yet others, adjusting format, size and compression for different uses, often over and over across several directories, not to mention issues like naming and categorizing the photos so that they can be recovered easily from household repositories, can all add up to a significant amount of work. One of the households we have been looking at has adopted the practice of placing their photographs on a website for access by remote family members. This practice has evolved so that one of the household's members can make available to her mother, who lives in another country, photographs of the various places she has been recently. This practice is reciprocated by her mother. They are then able to phone one another and talk through the photographs. However, for the digital housekeeper in this situation the work involved is really quite substantial (Kirk et al. 2006), as the following account indicates.

House A
To start with I have to connect my camera with a USB to the laptop. The photos are then all collected into a single folder. However, whilst getting the images to the laptop is easy ... we can't then both look and discuss them because the laptop is too small for us to be able to view the photos together. The only screen we have that is big enough is on the PC in the office. But there's only space in the office for one chair. We have to review them because ... only about one in ten is interesting. I used to thin things on the camera but lately I've got into the habit of just dumping everything to the laptop. We can't display the raw material on the website so we have this painful thing to go through ... reviewing with only one chair in the office. We did the latest batch over two consecutive weekends. Once I know what we're keeping I have software that runs through the photos and creates a set of web pages including thumbnails and a navigation bar. So it's created in a folder as a website and this is then copied to our web-server. So, in order for it to happen at all I have to move files to a number of different locations which is tedious.

Restoring Order when Things Breakdown

In our study we found that many of the kinds of tasks that may get talked about as 'digital housekeeping' are the things that arise as a consequence of some kind of breakdown. Similarly, situations arise where the degree of disorder has become so great that it is harder to account for continuing to tolerate it than it is for getting on and fixing it. The latter kind of tasks can be motivated by things like problems with space, either in terms of machine memory or desktop 'real estate'. Ensuing work usually revolves around clearing out what one might call digital clutter. This can involve things like deleting shortcuts from desktops, getting rid of replicated or unwanted files including digital photos and music, moving larger files to other locations, or uninstalling software. Locating what can be deleted or moved in these circumstances can involve a great deal of work. Trawling through directories to compare them, sometimes even printing them, can be a significant part of the labour here, especially if there are multiple directories and multiple accounts on the same machine. Much of it is 'work of the eye', spotting things like the same size and date of creation, or the telltale tilde sign before the name of a temporary file. Furthermore, in the home situation resources open to disposal involve the application of local knowledge where reasoning is very much bound up with being a household member. The following is a case in point:

House C
Running out of disc space is a classic problem with games eating up huge amounts of memory. Particularly freebie games that are a nightmare that come with cereal packets, but the kids want to try them out. Eventually when everything's really falling over you have to go in and uninstall,

and you have to work out what to uninstall. I try and maintain a view as to what I think they are using at the moment. I think I have a sense of what are hot games right now. That may be wrong, but I think I have enough sense about their playing habits. So I know that right now we bought them Sims Two recently and everyone is playing Sims Two. So I know that uninstalling Sims Two would cause a riot. But I know that The Jolly Postman they probably haven't played for three or four years or mentioned. I imagine no one would notice if that slipped away.

The responsibility for the digital housekeeper in these circumstances can be onerous and installing and uninstalling resources can become a matter of identifying *accountably appropriate* courses of action. It is not just that one has not seen someone using something for a while. The apparent non-use provides for an account that is appropriate under the circumstances. When confronted with having to remove something an accountably appropriate course of reasoning is to remove what no one seems to use. Other criteria, such as 'this one is huge' and 'I don't think it's very good' might be applicable, may also be used. However, this would not provide an account that is attendant to the *communal* interests in the home. There is, of course, software available that can produce data regarding relative use of different applications. However, an application may be used only rarely but actually considered by some member of the household to be critical to what they do. Furthermore, if only one member of the household plays some particular game and others are played more often the preference of that person will become hidden in the statistics of use. Here such software is not enough. Arbitration falls instead to what is known of the habits of the household. Knowledge of this order is not often available to those outside of the local cohort.

An important thing to understand about things like running out of disc space, machines suddenly 'hanging', the appearance and settings being in need of reconfiguration, etc., is that the priority attached to restoring order, and the accountability of the digital housekeeper for dealing with it 'now', is completely different to those attached to more routine tasks. In this case, the problem has to be resolved here-and-now and may extend beyond the home itself:

House C
Games in particular mess with screen resolution so that's one of the most common and frustrating ones and no one else in the family really knows how to re-set those things. Quite often it happens in the middle of a game when the kids are really into it. They will complain - not really about the resolution, but about things hanging. I certainly find it a problem for myself if I sit down to use the computer and find it. So then I have to grumble a bit and re-set it.

My wife who uses it for her PhD work, she's definitely going to get on to me - "hey, the machine's broken, I don't know what's going on" - and then if I'm at work we have this whole protracted distant negotiation about stuff.

It might, of course, seem that handling of breakdowns is a relatively rare occurrence. However, as the range of digital resources in the home increases the likelihood of *something* causing trouble increases as well. In the case of one of the households we have studied the level of commitment here easily extends to several hours a week. As one household member put it to us,

House C

Of course you sit down with a problem that looks like it ought to be five minutes and it can take
you anywhere between five minutes and an hour depending on what it is.

Digital Housekeeping: The Social Machinery

If one concentrates on the particulars of the vignettes provided above, it may appear that the actual tasks involved in digital housekeeping are relatively trivial
and that the small number of households involved in the study tell us little about
the scope of the issue. Numbers, however, having nothing to do with the matter.
Nor are we suggesting that digital housekeeping is restricted to the particular
things we have presented and discussed here. Instead these particulars offer concrete occasions with which we might witness a much larger phenomenon at work:
a ubiquitous phenomenon that is invariably manifest *in the small details* of making the home network at home; in small details which vary from home to home
depending upon the technology installed; in small details that depend upon the
routines at work in any particular home; and in small details which testify to the
efficacy of members' methods for embedding the home network in their everyday
lives. It is very much the case that what is a big issue for household members in-
sofar as all must confront and address it, is nevertheless *reduced to an ongoing
series of small, routine tasks*. This is what makes it manageable. This is what the
incorporation of the home network into everyday life turns upon. Much like doing
the washing up, emptying the bins, washing clothes, etc., it may seem trivial yet
like such mundane activities it is critical to the domestic enterprise.

Digital housekeeping is done for the communal good of the household by certain individuals and is beginning to be recognized by household members as a
contribution to the overall management of the domestic environment.

House C
One of the things that has now happened is that maintaining the PC is seen as a household
chore rather than "messing about on the computer".

While one might be tempted to think of idealized versions of the organization of
the home that could support routine management of the home network through
things like task lists, alarms, stickies, etc., it is clear from our investigations that
occasioning is everything. Few people use generic resources to prompt this kind
of housekeeping activities. The use of such artefacts is itself occasioned - e.g.,
putting a post-it on the computer monitor saying 'back-up' after realising it hasn't
been done for a while. This is because shared computing resources in households
need to be *collaboratively negotiated* and reasoned about *in relation to ongoing
routines* in the home. By ongoing routines we speak of those activities undertaken
in the home without pause for special comment or account, recognizable by all in
the household as unremarkable because they are the things 'we usually do' being
done in the ways 'we usually do them' (Tolmie et al., 2002).

Many routine activities in the home are given priority: access to the bathroom before going to work, children's bedtime, and so on. However, housekeeping is notably oriented to as an activity of a *different order*. Forlizzi and DiSalvo (2006) found exactly this in their investigation of the use of domestic robots:

> "Most families engaged in primarily opportunistic cleaning, engaging in cleaning activities when time in their weekly schedule permitted. Many set a deadline of the weekend, noting that as long as cleaning tasks got done by Friday, it did not matter when they were done ... "

Indeed, to say something like "I need to get the kitchen cleaned before I get the kids to bed" could be unusual on many occasions. Digital housekeeping is the same in this respect. How could those responsible for it negotiate its priority above the other business of the home? Instead, it becomes something that will *fit in, around and with* other routines. The different routine activities visible in the homes we have been studying are too numerous to mention and their contingent and variable nature makes it pointless to do so. So it is not just that the home network is woven into a specific enumerable set of routines but that in the face of endless variety the home network is made at home by being made answerable to whatever passes as the routine in any particular home. The *accountability* of the technology to household routines simply cannot be underestimated.

The orientation to digital housekeeping as something that is *for* the household and something that needs to *fit with* the household is manifest in a number of ways that go beyond the small details of the particular instances we have considered here. There is a social machinery at work in making the home network at home – an orderliness to the enterprise that rises above the particularities of particular network configurations. Whatever the technology and whatever the activity involved in installing and maintaining it, it is always *somehow* accountable to 'just how we do things here'. Just what that 'somehow' might amount to is something we have opened up to examination above.

So, to sum up what we have uncovered so far about that machinery and its operation, we can see that household members order their relationship to the home network in the following ways:

- The components of the home network are placed both physically and socially in such ways as to *accommodate* existing infrastructure and established routines, such as the current placement of the television or the doing of work at the dining room table. The work of accommodation involves consideration of where things are done now and how things are done now such that the building of the network will not involve radically reinventing those placements and patterns of doing.

- The components of the home network are positioned so as to *reflect* abiding practical concerns in the home, such as keeping the technology out of view, attending to child safety, only making mess where mess already exists, etc. It is the placement of technology in such a way that, when inquired into, the accounts can pay testimony to these concerns that provides an exhibition of this kind of reflection in action.

• The work involved in setting up and adapting the home network is *accountable* to existing routines in the home, such that it will not unduly disrupt other courses of action central to domestic life. Thus we saw digital housekeepers actively accounting for how they ordered the work of installation around things like who would be in the household when and what other responsibilities they had to attend to.

Once introduced into the home, digital technologies are maintained in such ways that they resonate with existing routines in the home. Again, organizationally this means that household members order their relationship to the home network in the following ways:

• Ongoing digital housekeeping is characterized by recurrent and occasional housekeeping tasks that are *fitted in and around* other household routines as occasion permits or demands.

• All digital housekeeping tasks are conducted under the practical orientation of *appropriate priority*, which is to say that they 'get done' as and when time permits or demands and in such a way that their doing is manifestly accountable to other household routines. Thus, and for example, breaking off in the middle of washing up to sort out a machine that is hanging in the course of the kids doing their homework requires no special account. The account is manifest in the circumstance. Breaking off in the middle of doing the washing up to do a back-up or sort the digital photos is something different and others in the house may justifiably demand an explanation.

• Digital housekeeping tasks rely on *local understandings* of the configuration of the home network and what actions need to be carried out to maintain it. Thus deleting the Sims or only putting the family photos on your own desktop could be a source of future trouble. Yet, for an outsider, the currency of the Sims or just what might constitute a 'family' as opposed to a 'personal' photo cannot be guaranteed to be self-evident.

In these ways the home network becomes embedded in the social and physical fabric of the home. If some are dissatisfied with the unsystematic character of the social machinery at work, it needs to be remembered that the home is not the workplace. It is not subject to the order of action and control that inhabits paid labour. It exhibits a much looser organization that revolves around the daily articulation and coordination of domestic routines rather than procedures, processes, or workflows (Crabtree and Rodden 2004). Furthermore, the orderly ways in which the home network is made at home and embedded in domestic life raise serious challenges for the continued development of the home network.

Implications for Design

Making the home network at home is not simply a matter of installing and using the technology. It relies upon digital housekeeping. Through digital housekeeping household members weave digital resources into the larger constellation of routines that make up the social organization of the home, thereby keeping the home network in tune with the household's ongoing and evolving needs. The highly contingent, particular, and local character of digital housekeeping is underpinned by a social machinery that is of broader purchase to design. In outline, we think two main issues present themselves, issues that have been of longstanding concern within the design and CSCW communities:

• The need to develop the home network with *legacy* in mind.

• The need to provide for the *transparency* of the home network.

Legacy issues have been of concern in the design of workplace systems (e.g., Rouncefield et al. 2000). In the home they are less about developing technology with respect to previous computational systems and more about developing technology with existing infrastructure in mind. Looking back to how digital resources are set up in the home it can be seen that when introducing new technology household members exhibit an abiding preoccupation with legacy issues. These are couched in terms such as will the technology fit into the existing infrastructure? How will it fit? Where will it fit? These and more are key issues to the adoption and use of new technology in the home and are of some consequence to design. To be specific, it is not simply a case of providing for the 'piecemeal' entry of new technology into the home (Edwards and Grinter 2001), but also of ensuring that new technology is compatible with existing infrastructure such that household members might accommodate it within the physical and social fabric of the home.

While it will no doubt take a great deal of work to work out how legacy issues are to be addressed, the need to provide for the transparency of the home network is perhaps rather more tangible and available to design. Just as household members have an abiding interest in fitting technology into existing infrastructure and routines so too they have an abiding concern with the accountability of the home network. This is evident across set up, in planning and preparation for example, and ongoing housekeeping where household members draw on a host of resources to make network activity visible and available to practical reasoning. Indeed, it is by making the home network transparent and available to account that household members come to embed it in their domestic routines.

The design challenge here is not one that revolves around scheduling routine tasks but of making the home network *inspectable*. From the few particulars we have considered here it can already be seen that this will not only consist of representing the various devices constitutive of the home network, but also the services, user accounts, applications, and traffic that inhabit the home network in use. The challenge, then, is one of designing representations that make the day-to-day life of the home network *as articulated in user interactions with it* visible and available as a resource for supporting set up, maintenance, and change. Doing this will involve developing dedicated *management interfaces* that represent the network as a whole and in the details of its constituent parts, processes, and the transactions between its constitutive elements at a level that is intelligible to the ordinary household member. This intelligibility will turn upon being able to reason in the same way that one might reason about the interfaces one encounters on a daily basis if one is not a part of the computing profession. Clearly not all interfaces are of this order and we have already mentioned work that has begun to explore how to improve matters in this direction (e.g., Newman, 2006, Shehan et al. 2006, Yang and Edwards 2006). The efforts of household members to make the home network transparent and accountable, and the development of management interfaces that support this, articulates and elaborates what Grinter et al. allude to in talking about "developing tools" to support the work that makes the home network work. Indeed, the work of digital housekeeping that provides for transparency and accountability, and the development of systems support, are key ingredients in making the technology at home.

Conclusion

We have sought to build upon and extend the work of Grinter et al. (2005) on the work to make the home network work. We have focused particularly on the work involved in setting up and maintaining home networks, which we characterize as 'digital housekeeping'. Our ethnographic studies have revealed that it is through digital housekeeping that the home network is made into an unremarkable feature of the domestic routine. In examining digital housekeeping we have been concerned to move beyond the particulars of the work in participating households and identify a 'social machinery' that provides for the broad incorporation of the home network into domestic life. This machinery articulates the orderly ways in which household members set up, maintain and change the home network to meet their ongoing needs. This has some major implications for the continued development of network technologies for the home. It demands that serious attention be paid to legacy issues in terms of how technologies are designed to fit into the home environment. This requires that designers take existing infrastructure in the home into account and pay considerable attention to how future technologies may be incorporated into existing routines. Additionally, the concern household members exhibit with making the home network ordinarily available to practical reasoning suggests a need for resources such as dedicated management interfaces to support digital housekeeping.

Acknowledgment

The research on which this article is based was funded by the Equator Interdisciplinary Research Collaboration (EPSRC GR/N15986/01), www.equator.ac.uk

References

Bell, G., Blythe, M. & Sengers, P. (2005) "Making by making strange: Defamiliarization and the design of domestic technologies", in *ACM Transactions on Computer-Human Interaction (TOCHI)*, vol. 12 (2), pp. 149–173.

Brush, A.J. (2006) "IT@Home: Often Best Left to Professionals" *Position paper for the CHI 2006 Workshop on IT@Home*, April 23, 2006, Montreal, Canada

Bly, S., Rosario, B., Schilit, B., Saint-Hilaire, Y. & McDonald, D. (2006) 'Broken expectations in the digital home', in *Proceedings of the 2006 Conference on Human Factors in Computing Systems (CHI)*, Montreal, Canada, April 2006, pp. 568-573, Montreal: ACM

Blythe, M. & Monk, A. (2002) "Notes towards an ethnography of domestic technology", in *Proceedings of the ACM Conference on Designing Interactive Systems (DIS) 2002*, London, 2002, pp. 277-281, London: ACM.

Bowers, J. (1994) "The work to make a network work", in *Proceedings of the ACM Conference on Computer Supported Cooperative Work (CSCW) 1994*, pp. 287-298, Chapel Hill: ACM.

Bowers, J. Button, G., & Sharrock, W. (1995) "Workflow from within and without", in *Proceedings of the European Conference on Computer Supported Cooperative Work (ECSCW) 1995*, pp 309-324, Stockholm: Kluwer.

Button, G. (ed.) (1992) *Technology in Working Order*, London: Routledge

Button, G. & Sharrock, W. (1997) "The production of order and the order of production", *Proceedings of the European Conference on Computer Supported Cooperative Work (ECSCW) 1997*, pp. 1-16, Lancaster: Kluwer.

Chetty, M. & Grinter, R. (2006) "Making connections", *Position paper for the CHI 2006 Workshop on IT@Home*, April 23, 2006, Montreal, Canada

Crabtree, A. (2003) *Designing Collaborative Systems*, Springer.

Crabtree, A. & Rodden. T. (2004) "Domestic routines and design for the home", *The Journal of Computer Supported Cooperative Work (JCSCW)*, vol. 13, pp. 191-200.

Dourish, P. (2001) *Where the Action Is*, Cambridge, MA: MIT Press.

Edwards, K. & Grinter, R. (2001) "At home with ubiquitous computing" in *Proceedings of the International Conference on Ubiquitous Computing (UbiComp) 2001*, pp. 256-272, Atlanta: Springer.

Elmore, B., Subbarao, I. & Hamilton, S. (2007) "Designing software for consumers to easily set up a secure home network", in *Proceedings of the 2007 Conference on Human Factors in Computing Systems (CHI)*, San Jose, April 2007, pp. 1735-1740, San Jose: ACM

Forlizzi, J. & DiSalvo, C. (2006) "Service robots in the domestic environment", in *Proceedings of the 1st Annual Conference on Human-Robot Interaction (HRI)*, Utah, USA. 2-4 March 2006, pp. 258-265, Salt Lake City: ACM.

Garfinkel, H. (2001) *Ethnomethodology's Program* (ed. Rawls, A.), Lanham MD: Rowman and Littlefield.

Grinter, R. E., Edwards, W. K., Newman, M., and Ducheneaut, N. (2005) "The work to make the home network work", *Proceedings of the European Conference on Computer Supported Cooperative Work (ECSCW) 1995*, pp. 469-488, Paris: Springer.

Kirk, D., Sellen, A., Rother, C., & Wood, K. (2006) "Collecting and editing photos: Understanding photowork", in *Proceedings of the 2006 Conference on Human Factors in Computing Systems (CHI)*, Montreal, Canada, April 2006, pp. 761-770, Montreal: ACM.

Lemhachheche, R. (2006) "Inowiss", *Position paper for the CHI 2006 Workshop on IT@Home*, April 23, 2006, Montreal, Canada

Newman, M. (2006) "Now we're cooking", *Position paper for the CHI 2006 Workshop on IT@Home*, April 23, 2006, Montreal, Canada

Rodden, T. & Benford, S. (2003) "The evolution of buildings and implications for the design of ubiquitous domestic environments", in *Proceedings of the 2003 Conference on Human Factors in Computing Systems (CHI)*, Fort Lauderdale, April 2003, pp. 9-16, Ft. Lauderdale: ACM.

Rouncefield, M., Rodden, T., Sommerville, I. and Randall, D. (2000) "Remembrance of designs past", *Systems Engineering for Business Process Change* (ed. Henderson, P.), Springer.

Sacks, H. (1984) "Notes on methodology", *Structures of Social Action* (eds. Maxwell, J. and Heritage, J.), pp. 21-27, Cambridge: Cambridge University Press.

Sacks, H. (1992a) "A single instance of a phone-call opening", *Lectures on Conversation* (ed. Jefferson, G.), Lecture 3, Spring 1972, pp. 542-553, London: Blackwell.

Sacks, H. (1992b) "On sampling and subjectivity", *Lectures on Conversation* (ed. Jefferson, G.), Lecture 33, Spring 1966, pp. 483-488, London: Blackwell.

Shehan, E., & Edwards, K. (2006) "Pinning the tail on the networked donkey", *Position paper for the CHI 2006 Workshop on IT@Home*, April 23, 2006, Montreal, Canada

Shehan, E. & Edwards, K. (2007) "Home networking and HCI" *Proceedings of the 2007 Conference on Human Factors in Computing Systems (CHI)*, San Jose, April 2007, pp. 547-556, San Jose: ACM .

Taylor, A. & Swan, L. (2005) "Artful systems in the home", *Proceedings of the 2005 Conference on Human Factors in Computing Systems (CHI)*, Portland, April 2005, pp. 641-650, Portland: ACM.

Tolmie, P, Pycock, J, Diggins, T, MacLean A, and Karsenty, A (2002) 'Unremarkable Computing', in *Proceedings of the 2002 Conference on Human Factors in Computing Systems (CHI)*, Minneapolis, Minnesota, April 2002, pp. 399-406, Minneapolis: ACM

Verjee, N. (2006) "DSG shops to offer 'Tech Guys'", *The Times Online*, 5th September, 2006.

Wyche, S., Sengers, P. & Grinter, R.E. (2006) "Historical analysis", *Proceedings of the International Conference on Ubiquitous Computing (UbiComp) 2001*, pp 35-51, Newport Beach: Springer.

Yang, J. & Edwards, K., (2006) "ICEbox", *Position paper for the CHI 2006 Workshop on IT@Home*, April 23, 2006, Montreal, Canada

L. Bannon, I. Wagner, C. Gutwin, R. Harper, and K. Schmidt (eds.).
ECSCW'07: Proceedings of the Tenth European Conference on Computer Supported Cooperative Work, 24-28 September 2007, Limerick, Ireland
© Springer 2007

Behaviours and Preferences when Coordinating Mediated Interruptions: Social and System influence

Natalia Romero[1], Agnieszka Matysiak Szóstek[1], Maurits Kaptein[2] and Panos Markopoulos[1]

[1] Industrial Design, Eindhoven University of Technology, The Netherlands
[2] USI Programme, Eindhoven University of Technology, The Netherlands

{n.a.romero, a.matysiak, m.c.kaptein, p.markopoulos} tue.nl

Abstract. There is a growing interest in technologies for supporting individuals to manage their accessibility for interruptions. The applicability of these technologies is likely to be influenced by social relationships between people. This paper describes an experiment that examines interplay between a working relationship of an interruptor and an interruptee and two different system approaches to handle interruptions. We tested how system behaviour and the social relationship between the actors influence their interruption behaviours. Our results are consistent with prior research on the importance of relational benefit to understanding interruption. We found that interruptors were far more likely to be considerate of interruptees' activities, when they both shared a common goal. We have extended those findings by showing that interruptees display similar behaviours to those presented by interruptors. The results regarding the systems' influence show a clear trend towards the positive effect of the *Automatic* system on peoples' interruption behaviours which is based on: (i) visible interruption costs, (ii) social tension and (iii) system preference. We think that the results of this experiment translated into design implications can prove helpful in informing the design of computer–mediated solutions supporting interruption handling.

Introduction

Informal communication, both collocated and distributed, appears to be one of the most successful communication channels in nowadays offices (Kraut, Fish et al.

1990; Nardi, Whittaker et al. 2000; Nardi and Whittaker 2001). Such communication allows for rapid feedback, sharing local context, spontaneous conversations and referencing common depictions or values (Olson and Olson 2000). But there is a cost to it, interruptions. Nardi and Whittaker (2001), and Kakihara et al (2004) noted an asymmetry in control of interruptions between an interruptor and an interruptee that *'arises because while initiators benefit from rapid feedback, the recipients are forced to respond to the initiator agenda'*. To deal with this visible inequity in control over interactive attempts, awareness systems have been proposed as mechanisms to support interruption negotiation (Dourish and Bly 1992; Nichols, Wobbrock et al. 2002; Begole, Matsakis et al. 2004; Wiberg and Whittaker 2005). However, empirical evaluations of those systems have shown that, although they positively influence the behavioral patterns of interruptors, they do not prevent interruptions from occurring at wrong moments (Fogarty, Hudson et al. 2005). Such findings indicate that the relative behaviour of two interruption actors is not only determined by the existence of an awareness system but is likely to be influenced by other factors ranging from individual (McFarlane and Latorella 2002; González and Mark 2004; Bailey, Konstan et al. 2005) to social (Perlow and Weeks 2002; Jett and George 2003; Patil and Lai 2005) and to technical aspects (Cheverst, Dix et al. 2005; Wiberg and Whittaker 2005). A better understanding of the dependencies between social and technological influences on interruption behaviours for both interruption actors can prove helpful in informing the design of computer–mediated solutions supporting interruption handling.

This paper describes an experimental study evaluating the influence of two factors on the interruption behaviour of interruptors and interruptees; we wanted to test the impact upon the actors' behaviour caused by: (i) whether they share a common goal or not and (ii) whether the awareness system filters incoming interruptions or not. Finally, we wanted to assess how behavioural change enforced by automatic interruptions' filtering is perceived in terms of user preferences.

Related Work

A variety of behaviours in handling interruptions have been previously noted (Altman 1975; Sproull 1984; Jett and George 2003; González and Mark 2004; Minassian, Muller et al. 2004). In a face–to–face situation, when initiating an interruption the interruptor usually decides whether to interrupt or not by assessing the interruptee's availability status through verbal and non–verbal clues produced by the interruptee him/herself (e.g., does one appear stressed or relaxed) and through signals gathered from the environment (e.g., is one present or absent?) (Sproull 1984; Kendon 1990; Hudson, Christensen et al. 2002; McFarlane and Latorella 2002). The decision whether to continue or to withdraw from the interruption may be further based on the nature of its subject. The interruptor may decide to abandon a trivial question if the interruptee appears busy but may be less considerate about potential costs to the interruptee when dealing with an issue of greater importance or urgency.

Once the interruption has been initiated, the interruptee has a choice of how to deal with an incoming communicative attempt. (S)he can choose between immediately handling, postponing or rejecting an interruption and also between providing a comprehensive or a partial answer (Goffman 1967; Clark 1996). An adequate behaviour is often motivated by the social and professional relationship between the actors (Kendon 1990; Patil and Lai 2005). It is also contingent upon other aspects such as an interruptee's own time–pressure or the next activity planned (Hudson, Christensen et al. 2002; Adamczyk and Bailey 2004; Bailey, Konstan et al. 2005; Gonzales and Mark 2005).

In the case of mediated interruption handling, two approaches can be contrasted: an *automatic* and a *manual* approach. In the automatic approach, the system takes a role of an interruption mediator so that both actors fully rely on its performance. Begole and Tang (2003) explored the feasibility of automatic availability inference based on activity monitoring. Another example of automated availability management systems are Personal Reachability Management Systems (PRMS) (Reichenbach, Damker et al. 1997). The benefits of PRMS relate to minimizing interruptees' effort when dealing with undesired communicative attempts by shifting effort upon the interruptor. Processing an interruption request is automated and is based on what the interruptor has specified as the context of the communication attempt and what the interruptee has pre–defined as criteria for interaction agreement. Regarding the manual approach, a system such as Push–to–Talk (Nardi, Whittaker et al. 2000) implements a set of outeraction mechanisms that allow users to manually coordinate their availability without interfering with the lightweight of the communication protocol. With their system NEGOTIATOR, Whitaker and Wiberg (2005) have shown how manual availability management might create social tension for the interacting parties.

Apart from the benefits of each system there are also costs associated to ill-timed interruptions as well as effort to provide relevant context for reachability management. McFarlane (2002) experimentally compared different ways for coordinating interruptions in a computer–based multitasking context. Experiment subjects were asked to play a 'Jumpers Game' as their primary task, in which they had to save virtual game characters jumping from a building. While playing this game they were frequently interrupted by another task. McFarlane noted that participants' performance improved after they were allowed to control their interruptions by choosing the right moment for them to occur. The author concluded that in order to support mediated interruptions there is a need for tools that allow for assessing and announcing appropriate interruption moments.

Arguably, both automatic and manual approach can prove useful in different social relationships. Dabbish and Kraut (2004) extended McFarlane's experiment and investigated the use of awareness displays as instruments for supporting interruption coordination. They examined how awareness displays influence the choice of the interruption moment, how sharing a common goal increases their success ratio and, how the richness of presented information affects the interruption handling behaviour. They too used the 'Jumpers Game' as a primary task for the interruptee and introduced an 'Image Guessing' task for the interruptor. To complete their task successfully interruptors frequently needed help from their assigned interruptees. The results of this experiment showed that if the interacting parties share a common goal (Clark 1996), interruptors are more likely to display *altruistic behaviour* towards the interruptee: they will be more prone to assess interruptee's availability (Begole, Tang et al. 2003; Gonzalez and Mark 2004) and time–pressure (Adamczyk and Bailey 2004; Bailey, Konstan et al. 2005) before initiating the interruption.

The experiment by Dabbish and Kraut suggests that in a shared–goal situation an awareness display may, indeed, be an appropriate and sufficient stimulus for evoking *altruistic interruption behaviour* upon interruptors. However the experiment has also shown that in a non–shared–goal situation interruptors were likely to display somewhat *individualistic behaviour*: they were prone to interrupt whenever they were in need for help without paying attention to the interruptee's availability status. Considering that many interruptions in an actual working context arise not only from the team members sharing the same goal but also by other individuals, it seems reasonable to conjecture that a system assisting interruptions in a non–shared–goal situation cannot entirely rely on the awareness display and should be allowed to assess the interruption moment.

A number of interesting questions arise from the experiment of Dabbish and Kraut. Their study examined behaviours only for interruptors; it is also interesting to examine how the interruptees' behaviour is influenced by their relation with the interruptor. The authors contrasted two social relationships between the interruption actors: a *team* and an *independent* condition. The team condition was defined as: *"being in group with another person and having outcome interdependence"*; while the independent condition described a situation, in which: *"the interruptors were rewarded exclusively on their own performance"*. This distinction results in an effective experimental manipulation, but is arguably not representative of the interruptions concerning office workers. Clearly, while the *Team* (shared-goal) condition is very characteristic for the office environment, the *Independent* condition is fairly rare for workers who are not directly dealing with customers or the general public. A more common source of interruptions for them is from people working for the same organizational unit (department or sub-department) though not on the same project (so therefore not sharing goals) (Chrysanthis, Stemple et al. 1990; Patil and Lai 2005). In line with Chrysanthis et al. (1990) a *Group* is defined as: *"In the group, people can perform their tasks concurrently and independently, while interacting cooperatively to achieve own objectives"*. This social relationship is furthermore shaped by the existence of *social reciprocation* as defined by Perlow and Weeks (2002): "...*the likelihood of receiving an interruption from the interruptee in the near future*". Thus our experiment concerns a 'team condition' as defined by Dabbish and Kraut and a 'group condition' as defined by Chrysanthis et al. (1990) and Perlow (2002).

Finally, next to the social relationship between actors, our experiment also compares the manual and automatic approach to handle interruptions. The *automatic system* manages availability of the interruptee (Reichenbach, Damker et al. 1997) by filtering the flow of interruptions, while the *manual system* provides participants full control over their interruptions (Nardi, Whittaker et al. 2000). We examine the impact of these two system types on the behaviour of interruption actors in the two social conditions described above. We add to current literature with an experimental assessment of how differences between the two system types and the social relationship impact the behaviours of the interruption actors.

Experiment Description

Our experiment had a two–fold objective. Firstly, we aimed to assess if the presence of a shared goal equally motivates interruptors and interruptees to display *altruistic behaviours* when dealing with interruptions. Secondly, we wanted to test the effect of an *Automatic system* to motivate more *altruistic behaviours* in the case of an absence of a shared goal between the interruption actors.

For the purposes of this experiment we have implemented two systems for interruption management: a *Manual* and an *Automatic* system (which are described in more detail below). The common structure of the two systems was defined so that neither system intervenes with the interruptor's decision to initiate the interruption and so that both systems provide their users with an abstract awareness display representing the status of the interruptee (Dabbish and Kraut 2004). The difference between the systems rests in the way they deal with incoming interruptions. The *Automatic* system filters interruptions that are ill–timed according to the ratio between the number of tasks to be performed by the interruptee and the time left to do so; it also automatically notifies the interruptor that his/her interruption has been rejected. The *Manual* system allows all interruptions to get through to the interruptee, so that the interruptee has to decide whether to accept or reject each interruption request.

As in the experiments discussed above, our set–up aimed to create '*an abstract help–seeking situation, in which two parties are collaborating*' (Dabbish and Kraut 2004). In our experiment the two parties are: an *Asker* seeking help and a *Helper* who is engaged in an own task. We provided both actors with an abstract awareness display presenting them with the status of the Helper. Askers can choose the interruption moment and can also choose which out of a fixed set of questions to ask. Helpers can choose to answer immediately or reject the interruption, and they can also vary the quality of their responses.

Definitions and Hypotheses

We distinguish four interruption behaviours, two time–related behaviours and two content– related behaviours. Each behaviour pertains both to interruptions by Askers and to reactions by Helpers and has an altruistic or individualistic connotation (see: Table I).

ASKER	HELPER
Altruistic and individualistic behaviours that are time–related	
Timely interruption: Asker's altruistic behaviour to initiate an interruption when the awareness display shows Helper's low time–pressure.	***Timely reaction:*** Helper's altruistic behaviour to immediately accept an incoming interruption.
Untimely interruption: Asker's individualistic behaviour to initiate an interruption when the awareness display shows Helper's high time–pressure.	***Untimely reaction:*** Helper's individualistic behaviour to immediately reject an incoming interruption.
Altruistic and individualistic behaviours that are content–related	
High–value question: Asker's altruistic behaviour to initiate an interruption with a high score associated to its content.	***High–value response:*** Helper's altruistic behaviour to provide response with a high value associated to its content.
Low–value question: Asker's individualistic behaviour to initiate an interruption with a low score associated to its content.	***Low–value response:*** Helper's individualistic behaviour to provide response with a low value associated to its content.

Table I. Askers' and Helpers' time and content–related behaviours used as dependent variables in the experiment

We expect to find that interruptors and interruptees who share a common goal (*Team*) will display more *altruistic behaviours* when dealing with interruptions compared to those who do not share a common goal. For interruptors this means matching the interruption moment with the interruptee's availability status and interrupting with high–value questions. We also expect that interruptees in most cases will be willing to accept incoming interruptions and put effort in providing interruptors with a thorough, high–value response. Such behaviours will remain consistent disregarding the system the *Team* uses, so the *Team* members will show similar behaviour in both the *Manual* and the *Automatic* system. We assume that the *Manual* system will expose the *altruistic behaviours* of actors sharing a common goal and *individualistic behaviours* of those, who do not share a common goal. Interruptors who do not share a common goal will interrupt at all times without being concerned about the interruptee's availability status. Also interruptees will be willing to accept incoming interruptions only when they perform well and do not experience time–pressure imposed by their own task. Interruptees, in any case, will not be willing to put effort to sustain the quality of their answers.

Furthermore, we believe that the *Automatic* system will influence the behaviours of people who do not share a common goal, so they will change their behaviours comparing to those presented in the *Manual* system. As shown by related literature (McFarlane 2002; Bailey, Konstan et al. 2005) interruptions produce negative consequences if they occur at times when the interruptee might experience time–pressure, anxiety and annoyance related to his/her primary task. So, we introduce an *Automatic* system that monitors the interruptee's performance and automatically rejects interruptions occurring whenever the interruptee may experience time–pressure related to his/her primary task (so interruptions are allowed only when the interruptee performs well). We believe that such an additional filtering will encourage interruptors in the *Group* condition to pay attention to the interruptee's availability status and try to time their interruptions better. We also think that interruptees in the *Group* condition will be more willing to accept interruptions and more considerate about providing comprehensive response if interruptions appear at right moments. To test these expectations we have formulated three hypotheses, which are introduced below.

Hypothesis 1

Both Helpers and Askers show more altruistic interruption behaviours in the Team condition than in the Group condition. We expect H1 to hold for both time and content–related behaviours.

Hypothesis 2

Both Helpers and Askers show more altruistic interruption behaviours when using the Automatic system than when using the Manual system. We expect H2 to hold for both time and content–related behaviours.

Hypothesis 3

The positive effect of the system–type, thus using the Automatic system on interruption behaviour is the strongest in the Group condition. We expect H3 to hold for both Group–Helpers and Group–Askers, and to apply for time as well as content–related behaviours.

Participants

A number of 35 males and 25 females participated in the experiment (41 – 20 to 30, 17 – 30 to 40, 1 – 40 to 50 and 1 – 50 to 60 of age). 25 participants work in academia, 7 in industry, 26 were students and 2 were unemployed. They present different educational backgrounds: technical (18), design (18), psychology (3), economics (7) and others (8). Their educational level varies between: undergraduate (20), graduate (28) and PhD (12). Participants presented various nationalities and all were non–native English speakers. Most participants (42) reported having more than 2 years of experience using English on daily basis; the rest of the participants reported an experience between 1 and 2 years. All except one assigned pair were complete strangers to their partners in the game. In the familiar case the pair reported to be acquainted but had not worked together ever before or were they in any way professionally or socially linked.

Design

The experiment was a 2x2 mixed–subject design. The within subject factor was the *system condition*, which offered (i) a manual or (ii) an automatic approach to handling interruptions. This condition was randomized to avoid an order effect. The between subjects factor was the *social condition*, which identified two social relationships: the *Team* condition representing people sharing a common goal and the *Group* condition representing those who did not share a common goal but assumed social reciprocation.

Procedure

The experiment was conducted by the two first authors on the premises of the Eindhoven University of Technology and took form of a game, in which one Asker and one Helper won a prize of 25 euros each. Participants were divided in pairs and randomly assigned to their roles, and to the *Team* or *Group* condition. The players of each pair were placed in separate rooms so that they could not interact with each other in any way. Each pair played two rounds of the game: one using the *Automatic* and another using the *Manual* system (the order was randomised). The game began with an exploration phase, during which both players could become acquainted with the screens and controls. During the actual game, each round lasted 10 minutes. At the end of the second round a focus group was conducted.

In the *Team* condition, each Asker–Helper pair competed against other pairs; their scores were summed up and the best pair would win the prize. In the *Group* condition each Asker and each Helper competed individually with other Askers and Helpers; their individual scores were summed up, and the best Asker and the best Helper would win the prize. To create a feeling of a social reciprocation (Perlow and Weeks 2002) participants in both conditions were told that there would be a second phase of the game, in which they would swap their roles of Askers and Helpers.

Both *Automatic* and *Manual* system provided participants with an abstract awareness display (Dabbish and Kraut 2004) constructed out of two progress bars: the task bar that represents the progress of the Helper's task and the time bar that shows how much time was left for him/her to finish answering each question (see: Figure 1).

Figure 1. Left: the awareness display representing a timely interruption – the task bar is ahead of the time bar meaning that the Helper advances with the task and experiences low time–pressure; Right: the awareness display representing an untimely interruption – the time bar is ahead of the task bar meaning that the Helper stays behind the task and experiences high time–pressure.

Besides providing this information, neither system interfered with the Asker's decision to interrupt. The *Automatic* system filters the occurrence of an *untimely interruption* when Helper's task progress stayed behind his/her time progress at the moment the interruption was initiated. Any other interruption was interpreted as a *timely interruption*.

Asker's Game

The Asker receives an article divided in paragraphs, with 4 missing words per paragraph. (S)he has to fill in those missing words scoring points for each correct answer entered. The correct answer has to be chosen from a list of synonyms. Different words have different number of synonyms to choose from: some have one synonym and one correct word while others have four synonyms and one correct word to choose from. The word with one synonym and one correct word scores 2 points, while a word with four synonyms and one correct word scores 5 points. The Asker can confirm the chosen word with an assigned Helper who has access to the complete article, but who is busy playing another game. The Asker can check Helper's progress by recalling the awareness display.

Figure 2 shows the Asker's screen that is divided in two areas. The lower area contains the consecutive paragraphs of the article with missing words and a form to enter the chosen answers, with a 'Next' button to submit the words and move to the next paragraph. The upper area contains (from left to right) a form for sending questions, a timer and two buttons: the 'Progress Display' and the 'Option Display'. The 'Send Question' form is constructed out of a list with four numbers that represent the four lines containing missing words and a text field to enter the chosen word. The Asker sends a question by pressing the 'Ask Helper' button. The reaction of the Helper is shown at the same place on the screen and can be removed by using the 'Close' button. The timer counts down the time for each round in minutes except the last minute, which is counted in seconds. The 'Option

Display' button activates for 10 seconds the list with synonyms of all missing words. The 'Progress Display' activates for 10 seconds the awareness display of the Helper's task and time progress. The task bar represents the task progression with each block representing one of the 6 items to be filled in by the Helper and the time bar representing time progression with each block representing 10 elapsed seconds of each Helper's question (see: Figure 1). The awareness display is updated every 10 seconds and reset once the Helper receives a new question.

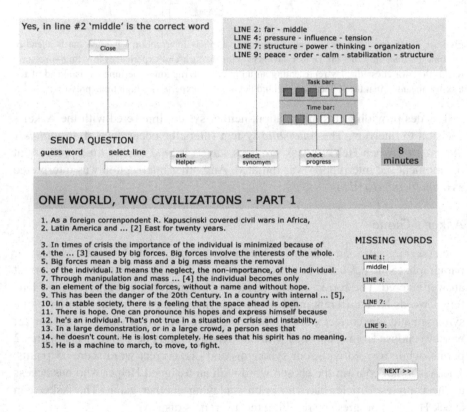

Figure 2. Asker's screen – the upper area contains of: (1a, 1b) the form to ask questions and receive answers from the Helper, (2) the timer, (3) the button activating the awareness display and (4a, 4b) the button with optional words to choose from; the lower area contains of: (5) the article and (6) the fields to enter missing words with a button to submit them.

Helper's Game

The Helper has to answer ten trivia questions by listing 6 related items (e.g., 'List six European capitals') and has 1 minute per question. Each consecutive answer scores more points (so the first answer scores 1 point and the sixth scores 6 points). After 1 minute a new question is displayed.

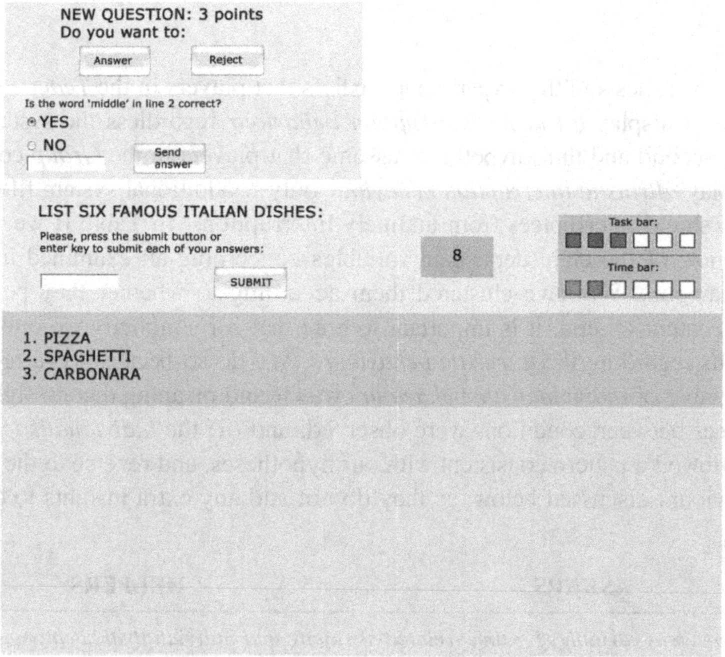

Figure 3. Helper's screen – the upper area contains of: (1) the question from the quiz, (2a) the notification of the new question from the Asker replacing the quiz question, (2b) the form to answer the Asker's question, (3) the timer and (4) the awareness display; the lower area contains (5) a list of answers submitted to the quiz question.

Figure 3 shows the Helper's screen that is also divided in two areas. The upper area displays the quiz questions and provides a text–field wherein the six answers should be entered, a timer and the awareness display representing Helper's own progress bar. In the lower area the list of submitted answers is displayed. When the Asker's question arrives, the upper area changes so that two buttons replace the quiz: '*Answer*' and '*Reject*'. If the Helper chooses to reject then the quiz is reactivated and the Asker receives an '*Ask later*' reaction.

If the Helper decides to answer, the lower area of the screen is replaced by the same paragraph that the Asker sees with lines numbered and missing words marked in brackets. The upper area is replaced by the Asker's question (e.g., Is 'earth' the correct word for line 2?). The Helper can either answer '*Yes*', if the selected word is correct or '*No*' is the word is incorrect. Optionally, (s)he can enter the correct word in the text field below, thus providing (with some extra effort) a high–value response.

Results

The first hypothesis in this experiment predicts that players in the *Team* condition will tend to display *altruistic interruption behaviour* regardless the system they use. The second and third hypotheses assume that players in the *Group* condition will display *altruistic interruption behaviour* only if additional system filtering is added to shield interruptees from untimely interruptions. In Table II we provide an overview of the eight dependent variables concerning all examined interruption behaviours. We have clustered them according to whether they pertain to time or content criteria. It is important to note that for simplicity we only report the results regarding the *altruistic behaviours*. We do so because (i) a relatively small number of *individualistic behaviours* was found meaning that no significant differences between conditions were observed, and (ii) the *individualistic behaviours* followed a pattern consistent with our hypotheses, and reverse to the altruistic behaviours discussed below, so they do not add any extra insights to our discussion.

ASKERS	HELPERS
Dependent variables for time–related altruistic and individualistic behaviours	
Timely interruption: interrupting when progress bars show task being equal or ahead of time.	**Timely reaction:** accepting of the incoming interruption.
Untimely interruption: interrupting when progress bars show time being ahead of task.	**Untimely reaction:** rejecting the incoming interruption.
Dependent variables for content–related altruistic and individualistic behaviours	
High–value question: asking about a word that scores 4 and 5 points.	**High–value response:** providing the 'No' answer and the correct word if the Asker's guess was incorrect.
Low–value question: asking about a word that scores 2 or 3 points.	**Low–value response:** providing 'No' answer only if the Asker's guess was incorrect.

Table II. Dependent variables for Askers' and Helpers' time and content–related behaviours used in the experiment

Testing the hypotheses

The three hypotheses as stated in section 3.1 were tested using two–way mixed subjects' ANOVA, with two independent variables (1 within and 1 between subjects). We tested each hypothesis separately for Helpers and Askers, both for time–related and for content–related dependent variables. Figure 4 shows the graphical representation of the obtained results with four graphs each showing the number of altruistic behaviours in each given case. For example, the graph in the upper right hand shows the number of timely interruptions initiated by Askers, thus those interruptions that were initiated when the progress bar showed the task progression was equal or ahead of time progress.

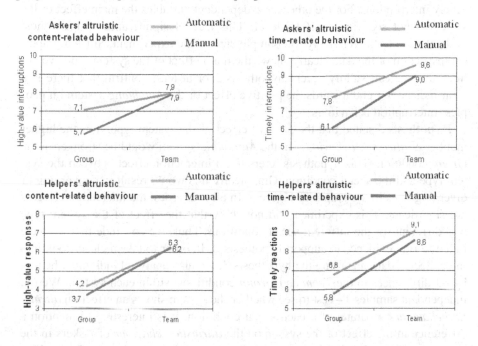

Figure 4. A graphical representation of the results of the quantitative analysis. Results are presented separately for Askers and Helpers, for both their time–related and their content–related behaviours.

Hypothesis 1 stated that in all cases, thus for all four dependent variables, players in the *Team* condition would show more *altruistic behaviours* than players in the *Group* condition. A graphical inspection of the data shows that for the altruistic measures presented in Figure 4 players in the *Team* condition indeed scored higher than players in the *Group* condition. This should result in a significant main effect of the social condition, which is not the case. However, the main effect of the social condition on Askers' timely behaviours is not significantly but indicative, $F(1, 28) = 3.228$, $p = 0.083$. This is also true for the effect on Helpers' content–related behaviour, $F(1, 28) = 3,571$, $p = 0.069$. Since the sample size of our experiment was relatively low to test this two–way model, we believe that a clearly visible overall trend in the graphical representation of the data confirm hypothesis 1.

Hypothesis 2 stated that players using the *Automatic* system would show more *altruistic behaviours* than players using the *Manual* system. From the graphs in Figure 4 it is visible that this is the case for all four of our dependent variables. For Askers' time–related behaviour the main effect of system is significant, $F(1, 28) = 4.388$, $p < 0.05$; Askers in the *Automatic* system initiated on average 8.7 timely interruptions, while Askers in the *Manual* system initiated on average 7.5 timely interruptions. For the other three dependent variables the main effect of the system is not significant at 0.05 level. This lack of significance is again most probably due to the relatively low sample size of the experiment. Since a graphical inspection of the data clearly shows the main effect of the system type, we believe that we can validly accept hypothesis 2 or at least confirm that there is a clear indicative trend towards the positive effect of the *Automatic* system on peoples' interruption behaviours.

Hypothesis 3 stated that the positive effect of the system type, thus the higher number of *altruistic behaviours* in the *Automatic* system would be stronger in the *Group* condition. This hypothesis refers to an interaction effect between the system type and the social condition. Graphically this would result in converging or diverging lines in the graphs in Figure 4. In all four cases, the interaction effect is not significant. This experiment did not show that the effect of the system type was different for the different social conditions. Thus, we conclude that we have failed to find evidence to support hypothesis 3. In order to take a closer look into the collected data regarding the hypothesis 3, we also analysed individual behavioural differences in the *Team* and *Group* conditions within each system. We ran independent samples T–Test to see whether the system shows an effect on *altruistic behaviours* separately for each social condition. It is interesting to mention a difference in the effect of the system on the *altruistic behaviour* of Askers in the *Group* condition that is not present in *Team* condition (*Automatic–Group M* = 7.8; *Manual–Group M* = 6.07; $t(14) = 2.284$, $p < 0.05$). However, the manipulations in our experiment were not strong enough to clearly show this interaction effect in the full two–way model. This result is by no means a sufficient evidence to support Hypothesis 3, however it opens a discussion about the potential influence of the system on behaviours in the group condition (see the discussion section).

Qualitative results

Statements (212) from six focus group sessions conducted with participants at the end of the experiment were audio recorded and transcribed with a notification whenever they were made by Askers or Helpers from either the *Team* or the *Group* condition. Next, passages describing participants' behaviours and motivations for each individual behaviour were extracted for further analysis (85 statements). These passages were coded by two independent coders according to whether they described participants' time or content–related behaviours and also according to comments about either the *Manual* or the *Automatic* system. Related statements within each group were clustered together, so that the differences between various motivations could be seen. The final step in the analysis was to reconnect the emerged clusters with data from the logs and examine how they relate to the quantitative results.

Askers' motivations for different interruption behaviours

Askers motivated initiating timely interruptions based on their individual and social concerns. The individual concern represented willingness to avoid rejection or to avoid waiting for Helper's answer. The social concern addressed willingness to avoid interrupting Helpers at wrong moments.

> **Team**: "With the first (*Automatic*) system, you check progress bars more often because you want to ask the question only when it is useful to avoid rejection."

> **Team**: "In this first (*Manual*) system I would check the progress bars and see if he had a lot of time left and then I would start asking."

> **Group**: "I looked at the progress bars all the time, it has helped me to develop my strategy when to ask and have high chances not to be rejected."

> **Group**: "… if the time bar were ahead of the task bar I would not ask any question. I was waiting a bit, checking again and if the situation didn't change, I would not bother him."

Interestingly, some Askers reported that the *Automatic* system relieved them of their social responsibility towards Helpers. They tended to check the progress bars less frequently and kept asking whenever necessary knowing that the system would notify them each time the interruption was untimely. In some cases, they checked the progress bars after interrupting to verify their chances for receiving a timely reaction. In the case of rejection, they would frequently perceive the '*Ask Later*' reaction to be provided by the system and not the Helper (even if sometimes it was not the case).

> **Team**: "But the second time (*Automatic*) I just asked whenever I felt like it because I knew that I would be rejected by the system if he was too busy. So, I let the system decide for me."

> **Group**: "In the other (*Automatic*) system I kept on sending questions because I knew that if timing was wrong, the system would deal with it. And I didn't mind the system refusing me."

Askers motivated initiating high–quality interruptions as a way to improve their score. They often decided to guess low–quality questions themselves since the eventual loss of points was limited and they did not want to waste time waiting. They also tended to ask high–quality questions when they perceived high–pressure in the Helper's game or if they wanted to avoid being too intrusive.

> **Team**: "I didn't want to wait for easy answers. So, I just started with the difficult ones, which gained more points and then put the rest in, while I was waiting for the answers."

> **Group**: "I got rejected on the third question and then I decided: I am not bothering him with any questions except from the most difficult ones".

Helpers' motivations for different interruption behaviours

Helpers perceived that their availability was not well assessed either by the system or the Askers. They noticed that whenever they had ample time they would not receive interruptions, while when they were rather busy with their own game, interruptions would feel to be more frequent. In the *Automatic* system, Helpers reported feeling unable to help Askers at times when they got blocked on their own quiz game. Some Helpers started deceiving the system by putting bogus answers to simulate progress in the quiz. Nevertheless, when Helpers were performing well, they appreciated the protection of the *Automatic* system allowing them to first complete their own task and attend Asker's requests later.

> *Team*: "At some point in the (*Automatic*) game I knew only three answers. So, I couldn't do anything anymore and I knew that the system wouldn't be sending any questions."

> *Team*: "With the second (*Automatic*) system I [...] felt I can at least finish my thoughts and as soon as I am done I can help."

> *Group*: "If I didn't know anything about the question, so I thought: 'I've already lost this one, I will at least help her'... So, I had more control over the game with the first (*Manual*) system than with the second (*Automatic*)."

> *Group*: "With the second (*Manual*) system I felt I was getting more questions. With the other one (*Automatic*) the questions came when I had ample time to answer them."

For some Helpers high–quality questions had higher priority than their own quiz game, while low–quality questions had not.

> *Team*: "With 5–point questions, I knew that no matter what I do, I could score only one extra point. So, it was definitely worth answering him."

> *Team*: "At some point I got a question, which had only few points and I thought: I am going to gain more points with my answers than this one, so I rejected."

For others providing high–quality answers was a way to optimise their performance (not giving the right answer would increase chances of receiving the same question again) or a method to show the pressure of their own game. Providing high–quality answers were for some Helpers a way to balance their inability to help at all times.

> *Team*: "I would check how many points the word was scoring. If it had more points than 2 then it was worthwhile for me to type in the whole thing, even if I missed my answer."

> *Team*: "I thought it's just a waste of time to say 'No' only. Then you get the same question again [...] It is just easier to give the answer."

> *Group*: "Then I answered the next questions putting the correct word but after that I felt more pressure and then I answered only 'No'."

Discussion

The quantitative results of our experiment provide a confirmation of *hypothesis 1* showing that players in the *Team* condition (shared goal) presented more *altruis-*

tic behaviours than players in the *Group* condition (non–shared goal). These results confirm findings of prior works and extend them by showing that interruptees display similar interruption behaviours to those presented by interruptors. Furthermore, our results suggest a positive effect of the *Automatic* system on peoples' interruption behaviour confirming *hypothesis 2*. Finally, we could not find evidence to either accept or reject *hypothesis 3* – there was no visible effect of the system type that over the two different social conditions.

Although we realize that the crudeness of the automation algorithm was a very simple scheme meant only to make sense in the experimental setup our results in fact represent a broader context, which we would like to elaborate further on. Specifically we would like to explain the outcome of *Hypothesis 2* based on our qualitative findings. Social interactions are dynamic and, even in our case where static team–group relationships was defined between the interruptor and the interruptee, the two actors did not always act in an equally straightforward way as a team or as a group. Looking closer into the effects of the *Automatic* system we consider it as a system protecting the interruptees and at the same time punishing the interruptors for improper timing of their interruptions. We use the notions of *protection* and *punishment* to translate our results into design implications. We argue that these effects put to an individual level the costs associated with different interruption behaviours. We cannot conclude that an *Automatic* system lead people to feel more considerate towards their partners. Nonetheless, we believe that participants behaved in a less individualistic manner mainly because they perceived the individual costs of their actions as more consequential comparing to their costs in the *Manual* system.

Askers associated costs with the way the *Automatic* system handled interruptions, namely that untimely interruptions were automatically rejected. As hypothesized, the *Automatic* system did not impact the behaviour of Team–Askers, who timed their interruptions well. On the other hand, it forced Group–Askers to be more conscious about timing their interruptions as a way to reduce the rejection ratio and to minimize time spent waiting for the Helper's response. At the same time the *Automatic* system made Askers feel relaxed to interrupt at any moment based on the knowledge that whenever they chose the interruption moment badly, the system would reject them automatically and the Helper would be in no way affected by their poor choice. Moreover, no costs were clearly associated with providing a wrong answer in the Askers' game, thus in both social conditions Askers showed to be little motivated to initiate interruptions that could bring low–value for either them individually or for the team and to be highly motivated to limit interruptions to only those with high score. A question, however, remains what would have happened if there was a cost associated with giving a wrong answer and how such a cost would have affected Askers' behaviours in both social conditions.

Similarly, Helpers saw the costs of providing low–value responses because of the high probability of being interrupted with the same question again. Once Helpers in both social conditions had decided to accept the interruption they tended to provide a comprehensive rather than a parsimonious response.

Interestingly, Helpers' preference between the two systems depended on their individual performance. They preferred the *Automatic* system whenever they performed their own task well; otherwise they preferred the *Manual* system allowing them to use time, which they would otherwise waste, for helping Askers.

These conclusions lead to design implications built on the notions of: interruption cost, social tension and system preference (see: Table III). Interruptees have demonstrated the need to modify the system behaviour in accordance to their performance and so it allows them to switch from synchronous to asynchronous communication whenever necessary. The chosen system behaviour should, however, be clearly indicated to both interacting parties, so interruptors would remain aware of the interruptees' choice and could adapt their expectations and behaviours accordingly. However, once the interruptee chooses for the automatic filtering, switching to the asynchronous communication, the system should provide interruptors with a buffer, in which they could store the content of their interruptions. Such a buffer would allow releasing the social tension guaranteeing to the interruptor that the interruption would reach the interruptee at an appropriate moment.

Interruption Costs	Social Tension	System Preference
Interruptees try to avoid being interrupted with the same content again. Interruptors try to avoid being idle waiting for an inconclusive response.	Interruptors shift the responsibility of assessing the appropriate interruption moment to the system.	Interruptees prefer additional system protection only when they perceive that their own task is worth to continue working on.
Design Implications		
Provide mechanisms to assign individual costs when one behaves socially inappropriate. Provide indicators to make these costs visible.	Provide a buffer to queue untimely interruptions. Allow interruptee to access interruptions in the buffer at any moment.	Design an availability communicator, where actors indicate whether they would like to coordinate interruptions manually or they prefer automatic interruption filtering.

Table III. Design implications built on the notion of interruption costs, social tension and system preference

Conclusions

We have presented an experimental study of interruption behaviours, in which we have compared an automatic versus a manual approach to handle interruptions. Our findings show that the automatic system encouraged *altruistic behaviours* more than the manual system. We have also compared the behaviour of interruption actors who share a common goal, versus those whom only dependency is potential reciprocation. Consistently with prior works our results indicate that altruistic behaviours are shown by interruptors who share a common goal with interruptees. We have also measured that interruptees presented similar behavioural patterns as interruptors. We did not find differences in the impact of the system type for the two social relationships.

Based on the qualitative analysis that tries to explain the results of this experiment, particularly of *Hypothesis 2*, we have deduced a number of design implications. Evidences show that the behaviour of the system depends on moment–to–moment activities of the two actors, suggesting the need for an adaptable interruption handling strategy. As an interruption brings individual costs to both actors a clear indication of these costs should be displayed to them. Consistent with the first conclusion the chosen strategy should be clearly observable by both actors to evaluate the potential costs of the interruption.

In the next steps of this research, we shall seek to verify the suggested design implications by applying them in the design of technologies to support interruption handling of collocated collaborators.

References

Adamczyk, P. D. and B. P. Bailey (2004). 'If not now, when?: the effects of interruption at different moments within task execution'. *CHI*, ACM Press.

Altman, I. (1975). *The Environment and Social Behaviour - Privacy, personal space, territory, crowding*. Monterey (Ca), Wadsworth

Bailey, B. P., J. A. Konstan, et al. (2005). 'On the Need for Attention-Aware Systems: Effects of Interruption on Task Performance, Error Rate, and Affective State.' *Journal of Computers in Human Behavior 1* (special issue on attention aware systems)

Begole, J. B., N. E. Matsakis, et al. (2004). 'Lilsys: Sensing Unavailability'. *CSCW*, ACM Press

Begole, J. B., J. C. Tang, et al. (2003). 'Rhythm modelling, visualizations and applications.' *UIST*, ACM Press

Cheverst, K., A. Dix, et al. (2005). 'Exploring bluetooth based mobile phone interaction with the hermes photo display.' *Mobile HCI*, ACM Press

Chrysanthis, P. K., D. Stemple, et al. (1990).' A logically distributed approach for structuring office systems.' *SIGGROUP*, ACM Press,

Clark, H. (1996). *Using language*. New York, Cambridge University Press

Dabbish, L. and R. Kraut (2004). 'Controlling Interruptions: Awareness Displays and Social Motivation for Coordination.' *CSCW*, ACM Press

Dourish, P. and S. Bly (1992). 'Portholes: supporting awareness in a distributed work group.' *CHI*, ACM Press

Fogarty, J., S. E. Hudson, et al. (2005). 'Predicting human interruptability with sensors.' *ACM Transactions on Computer-Human Interaction* vol. 12, no. 1, pp. 119-146

Goffman, E. (1967). *Interaction Ritual: Essays in Face-to-face Behavior*. Random House Inc.

Gonzales, V. M. and G. Mark (2005). 'Managing currents of work: Multi-tasking among multiple collaborations.' *CSCW*, Springer

González, V. M. and G. Mark (2004). 'Constant, constant, multi-tasking craziness.' *CHI*, ACM Press

Hudson, J. M., J. Christensen, et al. (2002). 'I'd be overwhelmed, but it's just one more thing to do.' *CHI*, ACM Press

Jett, Q. R. and J. M. George (2003). 'Work interrupted: A closer look at the role of interruptions in organizational life.' *Academy-of-Management-Review* vol. 28, no. 3, pp. 494-507

Kakihara M., Sorensen C. and Wiberg M. (2004). 'Fluid interaction in mobile work practices, The Interaction Society: Practice, Theories, and Supportive Technologies', *The Interaction Society: Practice, Theories and Supportive Technologies*, IDEA-group Inc.

Kendon, A. (1990). *Conducting interaction: patterns of behavior in focused encounters*, Cambridge University Press

Kraut, R. E., R. S. Fish, et al. (1990). 'Informal communication in organizations: Form, function, and technology.' *Human reactions to technology., Claremont symposium on applied social psychology*, Beverly Hills, CA, Sage Publications

McFarlane, D. C. (2002). 'Comparison of Four Primary Methods for Coordinating the Interruption of People in Human-Computer Interaction.' *HUMAN COMPUTER INTERACTION - HILLSDALE THEN MAHWAH* vol. 17, no. 1, pp. 63-139

McFarlane, D. C. and K. A. Latorella (2002). 'The Scope and Importance of Human Interruption in Human-Computer Interaction Design.' *Human-Computer Interaction* vol. 17, no. 1, pp. 1-61, 2002

Minassian, S. O., M. J. Muller, et al. (2004). *Diverse Strategies for Interruption Management in Complex Office Activities*.' IBM Watson Research Center

Nardi, B. and S. Whittaker (2001). 'The place of face-to-face communication in distributed work.' *Distributed Work*. P. Hinds and S. Kiesler, MIT Press

Nardi, B. A., S. Whittaker, et al. (2000). 'Interaction and outeraction: instant messaging in action.' *CSCW*, ACM Press

Nichols, J., J. O. Wobbrock, et al. (2002). 'Mediator and medium: doors as interruption gateways and aesthetic displays.' *DIS*, ACM Press

Olson, G. M. and J. S. Olson (2000). 'Distance Matters.' *Human Computer Interaction -Hillsdale Then Mahwah* vol. 15, no. 2/3, pp. 139-178

Patil, S. and J. Lai (2005). 'Who gets to know what when: configuring privacy permissions in an awareness application.' *CHI*, ACM Press

Perlow, L. and J. Weeks (2002). 'Who's Helping Whom? Layers of Culture and Workplace Behavior.' *Journal on Organizational Behaviour* vol. 23, pp. 345-362

Reichenbach, M., H. Damker, et al. (1997). 'Individual management of personal reachability in mobile communication.' *SEC*, IFIP TC

Sproull, L. S. (1984). 'The Nature of managerial Attention. Advances in Information Processing in Organizations.' *JAI Press*

Wiberg, M. and S. Whittaker (2005). 'Managing availability: supporting lightweight negotiations to handle interruptions.' *ACM Transactions on Computer Human Interaction* vol. 1, no. 12

L. Bannon, I. Wagner, C. Gutwin, R. Harper, and K. Schmidt (eds.).
ECSCW'07: Proceedings of the Tenth European Conference on Computer Supported Cooperative Work, 24-28 September 2007, Limerick, Ireland
© Springer 2007

Health Care Categories have Politics too: Unpacking the Managerial Agendas of Electronic Triage Systems

Pernille Bjørn and Ellen Balka
Simon Fraser University, Canada
pernille_bjorn@sfu.ca; ellenb@sfu.ca

Abstract. While investigating the resistance to the electronic triage system, ETRIAGE, at the emergency department of British Columbia Children's Hospital, we revisit the well-known CSCW-debate about THE COORDINATOR concerning the politics of standardized categories. Examining the history as well as the design of ETRIAGE, we reveal four basic assumptions about triage work in emergency departments, which are reflected in the design of the ETRIAGE application and related to the managerial agenda of controlling costs in hospitals. We find that ETRIAGE has an embedded surveillance-capability, which challenges the professional authority of nurses' work and removes discretion from the individual. We argue that the resistance towards ETRIAGE should be understood in terms of experienced nurses' disputing the assumptions about their professional practice that are embodied within such systems rather than general resistance to change or resistance to technology.

Introduction

Over two decades ago there was a huge debate within the computer supported cooperative work community about the role, use, and impact of standardized categories embedded in collaborative technologies. The discussion centred upon the collaborative communication technology THE COORDINATOR, designed by researchers Terry Winograd and Fernando Flores (Winograd and Flores, 1986). What was special about THE COORDINATOR was that the design was based on the ontology of speech acts proposed by Searle (Searle, 1979). THE COORDINATOR was developed by encoding and applying the standardized structures of speech act theory directly into the user interface.

"By teaching people an ontology of linguistic action, grounded in simple, universal distinctions such as those of requesting and promising, we find that they become more aware of these distinctions in their everyday work and life situations. They can simplify their dealings with others, reduce time and effort spent in conversations that do not result in action, and generally manage actions in a less panicked, confused atmosphere" (Flores et al., 1988, p. 158).

Suchman (1994) subsequently argued that applying standardized categories to collaborative technologies carried an agenda of discipline and control over members' action. Drawing on the work of Winner (1986), Suchman argued that THE COORDINATOR should not only be evaluated on its efficiency, productivity, and positive and negative side effects, but also in terms of how the application embodied specific forms of power and authority. It was argued that designers of technology not only design artefacts but also design organizations by embedding categories which constrain some work practices while enabling others, and that, by embedding speech act theory in its design, THE COORDINATOR became a device for social control. Suchman (1994) suggested that, in addition to investigating how artefacts support situated actions, we should also investigate how artefacts are themselves devices of social control that inscribe and encode organizational members' intentions by applying standardized categories for action.

We find the debate about THE COORDINATOR remains relevant today when investigating collaborative technologies in health care. Overcrowding in hospital emergency departments (EDs) is one of the major challenges facing health care in Canada (Ospina et al., 2006). With issues of long waiting times in EDs on the political agenda, it has been claimed that there is an urgent need to ensure consistent and comparable data collection between EDs (Rowe, Bond, Ospina, Blitz, Afilalo et al., 2006). To address this perceived need, a team of academic physicians in Canada has designed and implemented ETRIAGE: an electronic triage application designed to collect data during patients' triage examinations in emergency departments (Smith, 2005). The ETRIAGE application incorporates the national scale for triaging patients in Canada, the Canadian Triage Acuity Score (CTAS), in such a way that when nurses select a patient's chief complaint from a list, ETRIAGE requires the nurse to enter particular data in the exact manner established by the CTAS protocol. Other examples of standardized triage work also exist outside Canada, e.g., the Norwegian Index for Medical Emergency Assistance (Tjora, 2000).

ETRIAGE provides decision support for nurses triaging patients by using patients' chief complaints to generate a template of data fields and then using the data entered into these fields to generate acuity levels. By applying standardized categories for action (in this case the mapping of chief complaints both to field entries and to acuity scores), the designers have inscribed and encoded how nurses' intentions *should* be acted out according to rules and protocols that are built into the construction of the ETRIAGE application. Designs of IT-applications based upon idealized, rationalistic, and non-empirical views of healthcare work have been detected in previous studies as one of the key challenges of health care technologies (Goorman and Berg, 2000; Heath et al., 2000; Tjora, 2000).

In 2004, ETRIAGE was implemented in the emergency department at British Columbia Children's Hospital, Vancouver, Canada. After 18 months of use, the system was withdrawn. The reasons were that experienced triage nurses had found the inscribed categories embedded in the program problematic, that the use of the program had increased time required to triage, and that patients had been placed at risk during a busy flu season (Balka and Whitehouse, 2007).

In this paper we consider why the embedded categorization of ETRIAGE was perceived as obtrusive to nurses' triage practices. We investigate the characteristics and meanings of ETRIAGE by examining its history as well as the political relationships embedded in the software. Our study suggests that the design of ETRIAGE codified four assumptions about triage nurses' work, which demonstrate that the application is strongly compatible with the political agenda of standardizing triage work and less with an agenda of improving the conditions for triage nurses in emergency departments. Referring to the work of Dreyfus and Dreyfus (1986), we argue that the design of ETRIAGE decreases and limits the essential space for nurses' professional intuition and enactment of triage drift. By decreasing this space ETRIAGE becomes a device for social control forcing particular standardized procedures upon practice. Additionally, it removes the professional discretion of triage nurses by introducing impediments to the process of triaging patients. We argue this point through a discourse analysis of the journal articles published by the academic physicians who designed ETRIAGE combined with insights gained during observations of triage work and interviews with triage nurses about the introduction and withdrawal of ETRIAGE.

Standardization and Professional Intuition

The design of ETRIAGE is based upon a standardized classification scheme of triage work: CTAS. In 1995 the Canadian Association of Emergency Physicians recommended a five-level triage scale (CTAS) and a number of rules and protocols to be applied when assessing patients entering emergency departments (Murray, 2003). The CTAS guides triage nurses in assigning a triage score to patients and sets time thresholds for when patients should be seen by physicians. For example, a patient with a triage score of 1 (most urgent) should be seen immediately, whereas a patient with a triage score of 5 (least urgent) should be seen within 2 hours.

Applying CTAS involves a number of rules and protocols that dictate how triage nurses should evaluate the complaints of the patients based upon observations of, for example, the patient's respiration, eyes, ear/nose/throat, or skin.[1] The underlying rationale for CTAS was to distinguish between the emergencies of the patients in a more nuanced way and at the same time improve the possibilities for comparing performance across emergency departments. ETRIAGE incorporates the CTAS standard by stipulating a particular workflow for triage work and assigning acuity levels automatically. First, the triage nurse must choose a chief complaint from a nested, standardized list of chief complaints. The selected chief complaint then automatically generates a template with particular data fields related to the complaint. While examining the patient, the triage nurse enters information into the standardized template, which then calculates the acuity level.

The CSCW community has recognized for a long time that it is impossible to capture the richness of work by merely applying rational rules and protocols because work includes tacit and situated practices invisible to formal representations of work (e.g. Robinson, 1991; Schmidt and Bannon, 1992; Suchman, 1987). Designing computer supported systems requires us to pay equal attention to formal protocols as well as informal work practices. However, informal work practices have often been neglected when designing systems because they are invisible to rational models of work (Star and Strauss, 1999).

Dreyfus and Dreyfus' (1986; 1988)[2] five stages of human skill acquisition highlight the significance of professional intuition in experts' work, and can be used to explain the role and importance of the tacit, situated, and often invisible aspects of professional work. A *novice* bases actions on context-free elements, and rules, e.g., novice nurses can measure bodily outputs and decide whether they reach certain values. Through practical experience the *advanced beginner* starts to recognize situational elements, as opposed to context-free elements like distinguishing between breathing sounds indicating pneumonia from other breathing difficulties. For advanced beginners, rules for action might refer either to context-free (measures of numbers) or to situational elements (breathing sounds). *Competent* performers additionally adapt a hierarchical procedure for decision making. A competent nurse will not automatically address the patients in a prescribed order when entering a hospital ward, but will assess them based upon urgency of their needs. The *proficient* performer has highly developed perspectives on situations based upon recent events and experiences, which allows the proficient performer to recognize certain features and elements within situations as being more salient than others. The proficient performer relies upon a highly developed perspective, also referred to as "the intuitive ability to use patterns without decomposing them into component features" (Dreyfus and Dreyfus, 1986, p. 28). Professional intuition is "neither wild guessing nor supernatural inspiration, but the sort of ability we all use all the time as we go about our everyday tasks" (Ibid. p.

---

1   For an overview of CTAS and its application, see CTAS Implementation Guidelines (http://www.caep.ca/template.asp?id=B795164082374289BBD9C1C2BF4B8D32#guidelines).

2   This paragraph is based primarily upon Dreyfus and Dreyfus, 1986 pp. 19-36.

29). When the proficient performer intuitively organizes a task based upon salient features and elements, the performer at the same time thinks analytically about the task at hand. Already, when a patient enters into the emergency department a proficient triage nurse *notices* without conscious decision making if the new patient can or cannot wait in line. *Experts* generally know what to do based upon mature understandings. "When things are proceeding as normally, experts don't solve problems and don't make decisions; they do what normally works" (Dreyfus and Dreyfus, 1986, pp. 30-31). With expertise comes fluid performance: they know how to act without evaluating and comparing alternatives. Expert nurses "cannot always provide convincing, rational explanations of their intuition, but very frequently they turn out to be correct" (Dreyfus and Dreyfus, 1986, p. 34). Both the proficient performer and the expert make decisions and act without applying rules and protocols; instead they rely upon their professional intuition. Unlike a heuristically programmed computer, they do not solve problems, do not reason, or make inferences using strict rules. However, while the proficient performer sees the salient features and acts, experts just act.

This distinction between professional intuition used by highly experienced triage nurses and the rules and protocols which can be programmed within electronic systems raises questions about the whole foundation on which electronic triage is constructed. It raises the question of whether it is at all possible to construct decision support for triage work because the enforced categories represent only aspects of triage decisions-making that can be captured by rules and protocols. It also raises questions about whether decision support applications that embed rules and protocols will be useful in the professional work of experienced triage nurses when, in their work, they do not rely directly upon rules, but integrate rules into their actions constituted as professional intuition.[3] Unfortunately, this interplay between applying rules and using professional intuition is difficult even for experts to articulate.

Usually we do not consider whether a given technical application built upon a particular classification scheme has been designed in such a way that it produces a specific set of consequences for practice. However, technology is not a neutral tool; thus we must investigate and recognize the political dimensions of the devices (Winner, 1986). Standardization makes it theoretically possible to monitor deviations from anticipated workflows, but in a manner that fails to take the continuous exception-handling of work into account. Standardized categories do not have the power to capture the invisible, but often critically important, aspects of work. Standardization of nurses' work reflects a shift back to a narrow biomedical view of patients and neglects the holistic perspective of nursing, thereby reducing the professional discretion nurses have worked so hard to gain (Timmons, 2003). When constructing a classification of nurses' work, including the 'soft' tasks,

---

3   Rules can be used prescriptively or as guidelines. Prescriptive use of rules forces standardization. The use of rules as guidelines introduces a standard (rather than standardizing practice).

such as talking to patients and making them feel good, we run the risk of over-specifying what nurses *should* do, which can take discretion away from the individual (Bowker and Star, 2002). Thus, building categories to capture the richness of collaboration, including the informal aspects of work, brings a risk of control and surveillance (Suchman, 1994).

Recognizing the political dimensions of the design of technical applications does not necessarily reflect malicious intentions on the part of designers as much as it may reflect narrow conceptions of design work that do not pay attention to how system design changes may constrain work practices. However, although poorly designed systems may not flow from malicious intentions, it is important to reveal the political dimensions of technical applications because design choices tend to be fixed within the final artefact and therefore have huge implications for the practice in which a design is implemented. When developing new designs (e.g., electronic triage systems), it is important to recognize the flexibility within former designs (triage paper forms) in order to ensure that important aspects of flexibility of work are preserved when work is computerized. When investigating the basic assumptions behind particular electronic systems, we develop insights about whether these important aspects of flexibility are embedded or neglected within the design.

Unpacking Electronic Triage Work

Seventy-four-year-old Dorothy Madden died in a Winnipeg Emergency Department in 2003. After waiting six hours without seeing a physician and without being reassessed she went into cardiac arrest as a result of a heart attack she had suffered three days earlier (EmergencyCareTaskForce, 2004).

Triage is the process patients go through when they enter the emergency room and are assessed according to the urgency of their need for care. The word *triage* is a French verb meaning 'to sort.' In a medical care context, triage refers to "the process of sorting people based on their need for immediate medical treatment as compared to their chance of benefiting from such care. Triage is done in emergency rooms, disasters and wars when limited medical resources must be allocated to maximize the number of survivors."[4] Triage work requires complex knowledge about humans and symptoms. For this reason, triage is only conducted by highly experienced nurses who have been specially trained.

Media coverage of episodes such as Dorothy Madden's death (Eggertson, 2004; News, 2003) increased the public's interest in overcrowding within emergency departments in Canada and placed greater focus on the activity of triage. Following several negative media stories about long waits in emergency depart-

---

4   MedicineNet.com http://www.medterms.com/script/main/art.asp?articlekey=16736 retrieved on May 24, 2007.

ments, the Canadian Agency for Drugs and Technologies in Health (CADTH) published four reports in 2006 concerned with the issue of ED overcrowding (Bond et al., 2006; Ospina et al., 2006; Rowe, Bond, Ospina, Blitz, Afilalo et al., 2006; Rowe, Bond, Ospina, Blitz, Schull et al., 2006). The main conclusion of these reports is that "although there is a growing concern about ED overcrowding, there is currently no consistent standard for measuring this phenomenon" (Ospina et al., 2006, p. iii).

The series of reports commissioned by CADTH found that (1) there is a lack of standard methods for measuring overcrowding in EDs (Ospina et al., 2006); (2) the use of inconsistent methods of acquiring, collecting, and defining data in EDs creates a confusing picture of the problems of overcrowding (Rowe, Bond, Ospina, Blitz, Schull et al., 2006); (3) "overcrowding can be defined as a situation where the demand for emergency services exceeds the ability to provide care in a reasonable amount of time"; and (4) sixty-two percent of ED directors reported that overcrowding was a severe problem (Rowe, Bond, Ospina, Blitz, Afilalo et al., 2006, p. iii). Finally, (5) it was found that there exists a need for better reporting about the settings, characteristics, and outcome measures of treatments, in order "to improve the process of synthesizing evidence on interventions to reduce overcrowding" and support evaluation of the effect of various interventions (Bond et al., 2006, p. v).

It is widely claimed that improving health care in emergency departments is about reducing overcrowding, and determining the most effective strategies for reducing overcrowding requires the ability to compare initiatives and interventions at an institutional or national level. Meaningful comparisons across institutions, in turn, require collection and reporting of standardized data. Currently, many EDs do not acquire and collect standardized data, making it difficult to measure ED overcrowding. In this context, software that promises to deliver standardized data about ED waiting times appeals to management.

Having been endorsed as a national standard by the Canadian Association of Emergency Physicians (CAEP) and the National Emergency Nurses' Affiliation, CTAS plays an important role in the design, construction, and implementation of information systems used in EDs in Canada. The CAEP subsequently proposed a national standard data set for all emergency department information systems that included as one of the mandatory elements a CTAS score (Innes et al., 2001).

ETRIAGE at Children's Hospital

"People would walk in the door (...) we would just do an initial assessment, saying okay, they are safe to wait, and then over 90 minutes [would go by] before they got back to triage, which is totally unacceptable. And the nurses weren't feeling good about making people wait that long" (Interviewee from the ED at Children's hospital).

In 2002, a decision was made to acquire ETRIAGE in the ED of the Children's Hospital in British Columbia. It was implemented in 2004 and used by triage nurses for 18 months (Balka and Whitehouse, 2007). In 2006, amidst complaints from the staff that the system slowed down the process of triaging, a decision was made to discontinue the use of ETRIAGE. EDs are hectic and chaotic environments. Triage nurses are continually interrupted in their work. New patients arrive at the triage desk while the triage nurse is triaging other patients. Hence nurses must have mechanisms for interrupting triage interviews in order to assess whether or not the new patient requires more immediate care than the first one. In turn, the nurse may be required temporarily to set aside the first interview in order to attend to the more immediate needs of the second patient.

"So in high volume times, when you're continually stopping, using the pediatric assessment triangle, assessing whether they can wait, going back to your patient... it's so difficult to stay focused. You've got a sick person here, you've got four people waiting at the door" (Interviewee from Children's Hospital).

Since triaging requires the triage nurse to view the urgency of a patient in relation to the whole resource situation in the ED (e.g., how many patients of what level of urgency are waiting, how long the queue is in different parts of the ED), nurses conduct workarounds. For example, a patient whose clinical circumstances warrant assignment of a score of 4 might be assigned a 3 if the queue is particularly long in the non-urgent treatment area of the ED and the line is short in the urgent care area (where patients assigned a 1,2 or 3 are treated). There are also reported examples where the duty nurses assigned a score of 3 instead of 2 in situations where the CTAS protocol would recommend 2 (Dong et al., 2005).

"For example, an LOU 3 [CTAS 3] is your typical patient who comes in. Vital signs may be a little abnormal, gastro problems, a little dehydrated, and a mild fever. So it is a Level 3, and according to the CTAS they needed a reassessment every half an hour. However, after you've done a full assessment on the patient, he or she barely gets through registration before it's half an hour. You also have your other three patients to reassess and have interventions or whatever, so you're unlikely to get back to the LOU 3 patient for reassessment in 30 minutes, so it's really tough work to meet the guidelines" (interviewee from Children's Hospital).

The pre-ETRIAGE, paper-based system allowed nurses to assign a higher or lower score than might have been strictly warranted in order to manage the traffic flow between the two sides of the emergency department: the fast track (for CTAS score 4 and 5) and the acute area (for score of 1, 2 or 3). This process of 'under' or 'over' triaging is a well-know phenomenon, also referred to as "triage drift" (Dong et al., 2005). When ETRIAGE was introduced at Children's Hospital, the underlying classification system embedded in the software was a poor match for existing work practices, slowed work down, and constrained triage nurses from using their professional intuition and enacting triage drift. The computer-generated CTAS score also discouraged triage drift, making workarounds to smooth the flow of patients through the ED more difficult.

One of the main problems was the mismatch between the assumptions about workflow embedded within ETRIAGE and the logic of triage interviews at the Children's Hospital. Both the previous and current paper-based triage systems allow nurses to record information easily in check boxes in the order symptoms are presented to them. In contrast, the electronic triage system required the nurse to scroll down to the lower right-hand corner of the screen to a free text field connected to nested pull-down menus, and here the main examinations of the nurse are recorded. This process interrupted the patient's or parent's description of the patient's history by complicating the task of documenting examinations done at triage. Specifically, ETRIAGE required triage nurses to begin by selecting a chief complaint, which would then trigger a secondary template stipulating the kind of examinations the nurse should conduct related to the particular complaint specified. This differed from the paper-based system in which the nurses usually would listen to the patient before deciding what the chief complaint was. Some nurses felt that ETRIAGE also focused more on data input than assessment, whereas the paper-based system was more focused on the triage practice than on generating a complete data set in a prescribed order.

Applying the CTAS guidelines to triage practice by embedding them within ETRIAGE increased the amount of information documented on each patient, thereby adding time to the triage interviews. Some of these extra fields were perceived as improvements on triage practice by the nurses (e.g., the percentage of records that had complete vital signs recorded went up), whereas other fields were perceived as extraneous. For example, a SARS screen would pop up when typing anything connected to respiratory complaints, which is perhaps vital when in the midst of a known international outbreak, but frustrating the other 350 days of the year when no SARS outbreaks exist. Also, the electronic input forms included fields (such as a field indicating whether or not a patient had a tetanus shot) which may have been suitable for making comparisons between EDs at a national level, but were not appropriate in the local context because such records are not monitored by the emergency department, rather they are maintained in immunization records.

Other shortcomings of ETRIAGE included an inability to document and describe symptoms in the more nuanced manner appropriate for a pediatric population. For example, although parents of babies often come into the ED distraught because their child has been crying for a long time and triage nurses often wrote "crying baby" as a presenting symptom on paper forms, this common complaint was not embedded in the ETRIAGE classification system of presenting complaints. Consequently, triage nurses had to capture this complaint by selecting the category "altered level of consciousness", which is hardly the same as a crying baby. Moreover, the CTAS classification scheme did not reflect local terminology or practices and in some cases reflected medical diagnoses (such as asthma) rather than presenting complaint or symptom (such as wheeze). Other problems associated with the entry fields included difficulty in knowing which fields were mandatory and which fields were optional and could be bypassed.

Perhaps most problematic of all was the inability to report upon more than one chief complaint. In many cases patients presented more than one complaint, such as an epileptic patient who had a seizure which caused a laceration on his head. In the paper-based system both complaints would be recorded on the triage form as being equally important. However, in ETRIAGE it was only possible to report upon one complaint. This meant that the triage nurse had to write the second complaint and connected examinations in the small field for free text in the lower right-hand corner of the user interface. When printing the form, the second complaint, which might be essential to the overall treatment, was less obvious when glancing at the form. Lastly, the mandatory fields were problematic. If these were left empty in the ETRIAGE form, the system would not print the form, effectively forcing nurses to enter mandatory information even when this was perceived by the nurses as not directly relevant to the complaint.

Basic Assumptions behind the Design of ETRIAGE

Examining the design and discourse of ETRIAGE provides insights about the problems that have occurred with its use. What makes the cases of THE COORDINATOR and ETRIAGE unique in this matter is that both systems were designed by academics who publish their research connected to their IT-systems, thus providing us with the opportunity to examine how the designers themselves articulate their IT-systems while identifying the discourse of design embedded within the systems. THE COORDINATOR was designed by CSCW researchers, whereas ETRIAGE was designed by academic physicians publishing in academic emergency journals. An analysis of the discourse surrounding ETRIAGE in press releases, journal articles, and other written materials constructed by the academic physicians provides insights about the underlying goals the ETRIAGE system was constructed to meet.

Below we identify the discourse reflected within the writings of the designers about ETRIAGE, a discourse which is embedded within the design and transforms the work practices of the triage nurses in particular ways. Our analysis revealed four basic and interlinked assumptions around which ETRIAGE was built:

(1)   The triage process is objective and can be reduced to a set of rules and protocols;
(2)   Triage work can be understood out of its specified context;
(3)   Nurses do not do their work properly; and
(4)   ETRIAGE is designed to support management.

Each of these assumptions is addressed below:

1. ETRIAGE *is designed upon the assumption that triage is objective and can be reduced to a set of rules and protocols.* ETRIAGE is designed to follow rules and protocols for conducting triage based upon the CTAS standard. The application "requires the user to select from a standardized complaint set, which generates a complaint-specific CTAS-based template displaying all appropriate discriminators to assist the user in assigning the appropriate triage level" (Dong et al., 2006b, p. 503). ETRIAGE structures the interaction with the patients by displaying specific discriminators depending on the chief complaint, while calculating the CTAS level of particular patients on the basis of the input from the triage nurse. The basic assumption behind this design is that it is possible to produce a standardized complaint set and a number of CTAS-based complaint templates. Designing such an application requires that the designers believe that the standards can be applied in such a concrete way as to warrant inclusion in the user interface in a manner that stipulates specific work practices.

The discourse of ETRIAGE reflects an awareness of the existence of situations in which the automatically generated triage scores may differ from the clinical judgment of the triage nurse. In this way the important distinction between protocols and clinical judgment in triage work is acknowledged by the designers. The problem is 'solved' within ETRIAGE by "not only permit[ting] but also *encourage[ing]* overrides when the clinical impression requires it" (Dong et al., 2006b, p. 273, our emphasis). However, "the reason for the override must be recorded *before continuing*" (Dong et al., 2005, p. 503, our emphasis). The need to justify an override and the time required to do so may discourage triage nurses from using the override feature. Indeed some evidence suggests that some nurses disliked the requirement of providing a rationale for use of the override because it made them feel as though they had made an error:

> "Because once you said override it said override in your square that had the big number, so everyone would know you'd overridden it. There was more overriding done in the beginning than later" (Interviewee from Children's Hospital).

It can also be argued that in emergency situations providing a rationale for exercising clinical judgment in favour of a pre-programmed algorithm can disrupt the work. The designers suggested that "it is expected that experienced triage staff" have "greater confidence to override the tool" (Dong et al., 2005, p. 505). It might be true that expert triage nurses will have more confidence in overriding the tool, but it is also important to realize that the exercise of professional intuition is often an automatic and unconscious process. It may be difficult to articulate why such a practice differed from rules and protocols (Dreyfus, 1988; Dreyfus and Dreyfus, 1986) because providing a rational argument for professional intuition may not be possible. Although rules may guide the assignment of triage scores, at times – and for a variety of reasons – other factors captured by tacit professional intuition are taken into account by expert triage nurses. This suggests that the assumption that triage is objective and can be reduced to a set of rules and protocols may itself unnecessarily constrain triage nurses. There are important aspects of triage which are not objective and thus cannot be argued by referring to rules and protocols.

2. ETRIAGE *reflects the assumption that triage work can be understood out of context.* In the literature various 'tests' of the ETRIAGE application are reported (e.g., Bullard et al., 2003; Dong et al., 2004). However, the design of all of these studies reflects the authors' assumptions that triage work can be understood out of context. For example, in one study the use of ETRIAGE by a research nurse is compared to traditional triage conducted by a duty nurse within an ED (Dong et al., 2005). In this study, the two nurses triaged the same 722 patients in real-time, and later the triage data of 100 of these patients were given to an expert panel for assessments. This study reported that the agreement between the research nurse and the expert panel was higher than the agreement between the duty nurse and the expert panel (Dong et al., 2005). On this basis they conclude that triage nurses using ETRIAGE are in better agreement with a consensus standard than with nurses using 'memory-based triage.' In this study the authors also report that the major difference between the duty and research nurse assessments related to the assignment of CTAS level 2. The duty nurse only selected the sickest patients for CTAS 2 and assigned other high-risk yet stable patients to CTAS 3. The authors suggest that this difference between the duty and research nurse might be due to triage drift – "the behavior by triage nurses of subjectively 'down' or 'up' stratifying patients based on the current state of the ED environment" (Dong et al., 2005, p. 504).

The discourse of ETRIAGE views triage drift as something that should be mitigated. Dong et al. (2005, p. 502) argue that "triage decision support tools can mitigate this drift, which has administrative implications for EDs." However, it is important to remember that "rates by triage level are not objectives or standards," but rather the score is "a maker of illness severity and a 'sentinel event' that will reveal differences in triage standards between hospitals and highlight 'triage drift' over time" (Jiménez et al., 2003, p. 9). Triage drift is about triaging according to the *context*; it is about adjusting the rules and protocols to the particular situation at a specific point in time. The importance of context within triage work is embedded within the very definition of triage as a system to ration limited medical resources when the number of injured needing care exceeds the resources available to perform care so as to treat those patients most in need of treatment who are able to benefit first. This means that triage nurses always have to take the limited medical resources available, the context, into account when triaging. The importance of the context in assigning scores is further supported by empirical observations of the work practices in triage work where, in some instances, scores inconsistent with the CTAS are deliberately recorded and altered as a means of improving flow through the facility by insuring that staff on one side are not sitting idle while staff on the other side are over-extended (Balka, 2006).

One must assume that triage can be evaluated independently of the context, when triage work is evaluated by applying a 'gold standard' produced by an expert panel reviewing textual data without any connection to the actual context in which the triage was conducted (or even meeting with the patients face to face) as a measurement for whether the ETRIAGE application provided 'better assessment' than traditional triage. When securing funding for the unit is based upon documentation of patient loads in relation to levels of acuity (as measured through CTAS scores), triage drift might have serious consequences for the ward. However, the main purpose of triage work must be kept in mind when evaluating triage practices – namely, that triage prioritizes patients accordantly to existing severity of complaint and availability of resources. From this perspective, triage drift should be viewed as an essential workaround that helps maintain a functional ED.

3. ETRIAGE *reflects the assumption that nurses do not do their work properly.* This assumption follows from the above assumptions because discourse surrounding the use of ETRIAGE suggests that triage work is fundamentally objective and can therefore be reduced to a set of rules and protocols, and when nurses 'adjust' the rules according to the particular context (triage drift), they are not doing their job properly. This assumption about nurses' work is articulated as the problem with 'traditional triage methods' and a 'reliance on memory' which 'often is flawed' by 'lack of time and ability to recall the guidelines' (Dong et al., 2006a, p. 269; Dong et al., 2005, p. 502). In busy and crowded emergency rooms it cannot be 'expected' that nurses can 'accurately recall the entire' CTAS guidelines 'from memory,' a result of which is 'subjectivity and inconsistency in the triage process' (Dong et al., 2006b; Dong et al., 2005) as well as 'inappropriate assignment of lower or higher' scores (Smith, 2005). While "memory and experience are invaluable", using "ETRIAGE takes the guess work out of the equation" (Smith, 2005, p. 1). The discourse of ETRIAGE reflects a questioning of the nurses' qualifications for conducting triage work. Dong et al. (2005) argue that the length (eleven pages) of the original document defining the characteristics of CTAS is too long for nurses to read and remember. However, one could argue that triage work is much more complicated than what can be summarized in eleven pages. ETRIAGE was built to control nurses' work.

4. ETRIAGE *is designed to support management.* The goal of ETRIAGE is to enable the possibility for comparison between EDs across Canada.

"One major benefit is that we are able to improve triage reliability between RNs', added Dr Michael Bullard, a professor of emergency medicine at the U of A and one of the developers of eTriage. 'We are now better able to compare apples to apples when we look at the types of complaints and levels of acuity among patients in our emergency departments'" (Smith, 2005, p. 1).

In other words, this need for comparison is linked directly to the challenge of overcrowding in EDs. It is claimed that the solution of overcrowding requires standardized data collection to resolve 'the serious barriers' to meaningful comparison between EDs across the country (Rowe, Bond, Ospina, Blitz, Schull et al., 2006). It is also argued that from a quality-improvement perspective ETRIAGE will "allow monitoring of CTAS guidelines" and that CTAS has demonstrated the ability "to predict ED resources utilization" (Dong et al., 2005, p. 505-506). In this way the discourse about ETRIAGE has long been dominated by administrative and managerial agendas comprising the surveillance of nurses' work and control of economic resources. Evidence of the managerial needs that ETRIAGE data help fill can be seen in attempts to assign costs to the treatment of patients of different acuity levels:

"Compared with CTAS 3, the odds ratios for specialist consultation, CT scan, and admission were significantly higher in CTAS 1 and CTAS 2, and lower in CTAS 4 and 5 ($p<0.001$). Compared with CTAS 2-5 combined, the odds ratio for death in CTAS 1 was 664.18 ($p<0.001$). The length of stay also demonstrated significant correlation with CTAS score ($p<0.001$). Cost also correlated significantly with CTAS scores (median cost for CTAS1=\$2,690CAD, CTAS2=\$433CAD, CTAS3=\$288CAD, CTAS4=\$164CAD, and CTAS5=\$139CAD, $p<0.001$). Conclusion: eTriage demonstrates excellent predictive validity for resource utilization, patient acuity and hospital cost" (Dong et al., 2006a, p. 308).

Thus, while the ETRIAGE system may be sold as a product that will support nurses' triage work, it was designed to support administrative and managerial agendas, also referred to as the secondary purpose of health care. We are not against data collection and comparison, but rather point to the fact that if the secondary purpose is blatantly embedded within the design of the electronic systems, such systems can adversely affect the primary work of EDs: providing healthcare for sick patients. By embedding rules for the assignment of CTAS scores into software, the categorizations transform the work practices, at times to the extent of disrupting staff from utilizing workarounds and using their professional intuition enacting triage drift. Thus, while designed to enable the administrative agenda, ETRIAGE had the unintended consequence of constraining triage work practices.

Managerial Agendas of Control

Implementing the CTAS protocol into the embedded workflows of the electronic triage system carries with it an agenda of surveillance and control of nurses' work. Using ETRIAGE altered workflows and dictated what triage nurses should do, even, at times, distracting experienced nurses from exercising their situational expertise in managing patient flow enacting triage drift. The electronic triage system for some led to a mechanical approach to triage interviews, which disturbed triage practices. Consequently, some experienced triage nurses refused to use the system during busy times, returning to paper triage because it was faster. However, although expert triage nurses often experienced ETRIAGE as constraining, nurses with less experience in triaging did not resist using the system in the same ways. Novice triage nurses[5] often appreciated the decision support provided by the system as they went about their triage assessment because they were still in a learning situation in which their decisions were based or partly based upon context-free or situational elements. However, when novice triage nurses apply ETRIAGE there is a risk that they tend to rely upon the system instead of their professional intuition. This was evident with a triage nurse who was trained using ETRIAGE and had difficulties triaging without it.

ETRIAGE can also be used by management to regulate behavior. By requiring that in cases of triage drift the initially input CTAS scores be explicitly overridden and justified, ETRIAGE assumes the role of an all-knowing instructor monitoring triage nurses' situated behavior. For example, with ETRIAGE it is possible to produce reports about how fast nurses triage over time – each nurse can see their personal average triage time (e.g., 6 ½ or 4 ½ minutes). Measuring average time does not reflect any information about either the quality of triaging or the context (e.g., number of interruptions the triage nurse experienced), but it can be used to regulate the time an individual nurse spends on task.

Before ETRIAGE it was a natural part of the work for triage nurses to adjust their work according to the emergent situations during their shifts by enacting triage drift. In high volume times triage nurses are continually interrupted and require mechanisms for stalling some patients while triaging new patients. Triage nurses would normally assign a patient with a bone fracture a higher level in situations where the child also had diabetes so that the diabetic child would not miss a meal. Such triage drifts were an established part of the paper-based triage practice and often undertaken for medically sound reasons. Although ETRIAGE allowed such workarounds, the need to justify those was time consuming and intimidating for some nurses, thereby effectively discouraging nurses from undertaking workarounds for non-medical reasons such as smoothing workflow. However, professional intuition is an aspect of work that is often invisible, which means that you cannot apply rules and protocols and make a rational argument for its exercise; one cannot justify professional intuition (Dreyfus, 1988; Dreyfus and Dreyfus, 1986). In this way the new design artefact (electronic triage system) did not reflect the important flexibility embedded within the former design (paper-based forms). Having formalized the entries in the IT-system the designers inadvertently undermine the flexible and contingent character of the system (Heath et al., 2000).

Designing applications tightly coupled with a classification system external to the immediate work environment and making the system mandatory narrowed the space for conducting workarounds. The ETRIAGE application thereby became an

---

[5] It is important to note that a novice triage nurse is not a novice nurse - quite to the contrary. To become a triage nurse one is first educated as a nurse, typically followed by a numbers of years working as a nurse in various departments within hospitals. Then the nurse will be working within the emergency department for at least a year before starting the training to become a triage nurse.

ordering device (Suchman, 1994). So when the designers of the ETRIAGE argue that by applying their application triage practices will not be changed (triage time will be the same as with traditional triage) and that ETRIAGE would only provide an additional feature, namely allowing a real-life population of a database without any increase of staff requirements (Bullard et al., 2003), it was not acknowledged that the application *would transform* the work of triage nurses in fundamental ways. It was acknowledged that 'some information' might get lost, but this was seen as a price worth paying in the interest of solving problems perceived to be greater.

"(...) standardized presenting complaints enable the establishment of searchable databases for research and administrative purpose. Taking this approach means that triage nurses will have to 'translate' an infinite range of actual patient descriptors into a limited number of standard complaints. Inevitably, some information will be lost in the process (e.g. 'I have gout' becomes 'extremity pain'). This is necessary to allow meaningful information capture and subsequent data analysis, but it may initially cause discomfort among nurses who are specifically trained to be scribes rather than translators of patient information" (Grafstein et al., 2006, p. 11).

By embedding the CTAS protocol within the decision support environment, ETRIAGE was seen as a remedy for perceived flaws and inadequacies in triage practice. Similarly, speech act theory, in the context of THE COORDINATOR, offered a remedy to perceived flaws and inadequacies of communication flows (Suchman, 1994). ETRIAGE promised management control of the complex triage work by mitigating triage drift and taking the "guess work out of the equation" (Smith, 2005, p. 1). Thus by inscribing formal representations of triage practice into the design of a technical application, the designers of ETRIAGE bring the debate about who controls nurses' work in to focus. As Suchman (1994, p. 188) formulates it: "categorization devices are devices of social control involving contest between others' claims to the territories inhabited by persons or activities and their own, internally administered forms of organization." The designers of ETRIAGE are academic physicians claiming the territory of triage. As one nurse articulated it: 'ETRIAGE is designed by doctors but used by nurses.' Implementing ETRIAGE management replaces professional intuition enacting triage drift with a scheme of standardized CTAS categories, administrated through ETRIAGE in a manner that narrow the space for workarounds helping smooth the flow of patients through the ED. Hence, just as THE COORDINATOR "promises to tame and domesticate, to render rational and controllable the densely structured, heterogeneous texture of organizational life" (Suchman, 1994, p. 185), ETRIAGE offered the promise of domestication and taming. Consciously or not, technologies present particular ways of building order and structure into the world (Winner, 1986). They impose a structure that influences how people are going to work and communicate. While THE COORDINATOR is inherently a collaborative tool built upon a constraining and idealized model of communication, ETRIAGE is inherently an individual tool built upon a constraining and idealized model of triaging as an individual activity conducted by an individual triage nurse based upon objective criteria. However, in reality triage practice in EDs comprises highly complex collaborative activities between various emergency staff (nurses, clerks, and paramedics) managed through the use of coordinative artefacts. In this way both applications constrain human actions due to the embedded model of work. In addition, previous studies of IT in health have also identified similar constraints of the embedded model of work on nurses' work. For example, a medical index for nurses screening and provisional diagnostic work did not reflect the collaborative nature of nurses' decision making (Heath et al., 2003). Another example is the hierarchical structure of an index for medical emergency assistance, which was found to constrain the collaborative decision making of nurses in acute medical communication centers by supporting a formal model of individual decision making (Tjora, 2000).

Investigating technology requires identifying the social structures required by or compatible with the workings of a given application. It also requires revealing in which ways the embedded choices about the technology have important consequences for the form and quality of human associations (Winner, 1986). The structure imposed upon EDs by the application ETRIAGE is strongly compatible with the political agenda of comparison, standardization, and economic funding of EDs. The consequences of such comparisons are that they can reduce the professional autonomy of the nurses. In this way ETRIAGE can be seen as a device by which management establishes patterns of power and authority in the setting of EDs. Use of ETRIAGE may have ensured that the ED better met the CTAS guidelines. But, because ETRIAGE actually increased triage times, it may not result in fewer Dorothy-Madden incidents.

Conclusion

Here we have shown that using externally imposed categories as a basis for system design heavily impacts work practices, in this case, the work of triage nurses. We have argued that such imposed categorizations of nurses' work, when encoded into a technical application, brings a risk of control and surveillance which, in turn, may lead expert nurses to resist using the software by regularly abandoning the system. Moreover, we have shed light on the political discourse concerning electronic triage systems within emergency departments in Canada and revealed how this discourse may actually have hindered the work practices of triage nurses and contributed to the problem of overcrowding instead of solving it. We have argued that designing electronic systems for triage work by applying a classification scheme based upon an idealized application of CTAS scores (as opposed to the assignment of CTAS scores in situ) carries a risk of constraining the practical actions of triage nurses, thus decreasing their ability to act on the basis of their tacit knowledge and professional intuition enacting triage drift.

We acknowledge the need to collect data for comparison and that such comparisons call for some degree of standardization. However, we argue that externally imposed categorizations may implicitly standardize human interaction and carry an agenda of control and surveillance that is likely to meet with resistance. Uncritical reinvention of work practices through standardization may take away the professional discretion and skills of triage nurses and seriously constrain triage nursing practice. Alternatively, we propose that new designs of electronic triage systems pay equal attention both to the work practices of the emergency department staff insuring that the important flexibility of former practices is preserved in new designs as well as to the agenda of data collection. We believe that these two sometimes conflicting agendas of the primary and secondary purpose of health care can co-exist within an application; however, it is not a simple task to design such an application, and currently the lack of informed knowledge of triage practices seriously constrains this development. Thus, there is an immediate need for workplace studies within emergency departments portraying the collaborative nature of triage work practices while recognizing the flexibility of existing work practices in order to ensure that essential aspects of work are preserved within new designs of technologies.

Acknowledgments

This study is a part of the research project ACTION for Health, funded by the Social Sciences and Humanities Research Council of Canada, Grant #512-2003-1017, titled 'The role of technology in the production, consumption and use of health information: Implications for policy and practice' with contributions from Simon Fraser University and Vancouver General Hospital.

References

Balka, E. (2006): 'Sorting, Sending and Allocating: Indicators as a Secondary Ordering System in Hospital Triage Work', in *Workshop on Ordering Systems* IT-University of Copenhagen, 2006.

Balka, E. and Whitehouse, S. (2007): 'Whose Work Practice? Situating an Electronic Triage System within a Complex System', In J. Aarts (ed.): *Socio-technical Approaches to Health Informatics. Studies in Health Technology and Informatics*, IOS Press, Amsterdam, Netherlands, 2007.

Bond, K., Ospina, M., Blitz, S., Friesen, C., Innes, G., Yoon, P., Curry, G., Holroyd, B., and Rowe, B. (2006): *Interventions to Reduce Overcrowding in Emergency Departments [Technology report 67.4]*, Canadian Agency for Drugs and Technologies in Health, Ottawa: Canada.

Bowker, G. C. and Star, S. L. (2002): *Sorting Things Out: Classification and Its Consequences*, The MIT Press, Cambridge.

Bullard, M., Meuer, D., Pratt, S., Holroyd, B., and Rowe, B. (2003): 'Evaluation of Triage Nurse Satisfaction with Training and Use of an Electronic Triage', in *2003: SAEM Annual Meeting*, 2003. p. 538.

Dong, S., Bullard, M., Meuer, D., Blitz, S., Colman, I., and Rowe, B. (2004): 'Emergency Department Triage: Evaluating the validity of a Computerized Triage Tool', *Canadian Journal of Emergency Medicine (CJEM)*, vol. 6, no. 3, 2004, p. 209.

Dong, S., Bullard, M., Meuer, D., Blitz, S., Ohinmaa, A., Holroyd, B., and Rowe, B. (2006a): 'Predictive Validity of a Computerized Emergency Triage Tool', *Academic Emergency Medicine*, vol. 13, no. 5, 2006a, p. 307.

Dong, S., Bullard, M., Meuer, D., Blitz, S., Ohinmaa, A., Holroyd, B., and Rowe, B. (2006b): 'Reliability of Computerized Emergency Triage', *Academic Emergency Medicine*, vol. 13, no. 3, 2006b, pp. 269-275.

Dong, S., Bullard, M., Meuer, D., Colman, I., Blitz, S., Holroyd, B., and Rowe, B. (2005): 'Emergency Triage: Comparing a Novel Computer Triage Program with Standard Triage', *Academic Emergency Medicine*, vol. 12, 2005, pp. 502-507.

Dreyfus, H. (1988): 'The Socratic and Platonic Basis of Cognitivism', *AI & Society*, vol. 2, 1988, pp. 99-112.

Dreyfus, H. and Dreyfus, S. (1986): *Mind over Machine: The Power of Human Intuition and Expertise in the Era of the Computer*, The Free Press: A division of Macmillian, Inc., New York.

Eggertson, L. (2004): 'ED Problems results of bed shortages, doctors contend', *Canadian Medical Association Journal (CMAJ)*, vol. 170, no. 11, May 25th 2004, pp. 1653-1654.

EmergencyCareTaskForce. (2004): *Emergency Care Task Force: Report to the Honourable David Chomiak, Minister of Health, Provice of Manitoba*, Winnipeg Regional Health Authority http://www.wrha.mb.ca/media/news/files/ECTF_July2004.pdf.

Flores, F., Graves, M., Hartfield, B., and Winograd, T. (1988): 'Computer Systems and the Design of Organizational Interaction', *ACM Transactions on Office Information Systems*, vol. 6, no. 2, April 1988, pp. 153-172.

Goorman, E. and Berg, M. (2000): 'Modelling Nursing Activities: Electronic Patient Records and their Discontents', *Nursing Inquiry*, vol. 7, no. 1, 2000, pp. 3-9.

Grafstein, E., Unger, B., Bullard, M., and Innes, G. (2006): 'Canadian Emergency Department Information System (CEDIS), Presenting Complaint List (Version 1.0)', *Canadian Journal of Emergency Medicine (CJEM)*, vol. 5, no. 1, 2006, pp. 1-13.

Heath, C., Knoblauch, H., and Luff, P. (2000): 'Technology and Social Interaction: The Emergence of 'Workplace Studies'', *British Journal of Sociology*, vol. 51, no. 2, June 2000, pp. 299-320.

Heath, C., Luff, P., and Svensson, M. S. (2003): 'Technology and Medical Practice', *Sociology of Health & Illness*, vol. 25, 2003, pp. 75-96.

Innes, G., Murray, M., and Grafstein, E. (2001): 'A Consensus-based Process to define Standard National Dats Elements for a Canadian Emergency Department Information Systems', *Canadian Journal of Emergency Medicine (CJEM)*, vol. 3, no. 4, October 2001.

Jiménez, J. G., Murray, M., Beveridge, R., Pons, J. P., Cortés, E. A., Garrigós, J. B. F., and Ferré, M. B. (2003): 'Implementation of the Canadian Emergency Department Triage and Acuity Scale (CTAS) in the Principality of Andorra: Can triage parameters serve as emergency department quality indicators?' *Canadian Journal of Emergency Medicine (CJEM)*, vol. 5, no. 5, 2003, pp. 315-322.

Murray, M. J. (2003): 'The Canadian Triage and Acuity Scale: A Canadian perspective on emergency department triage', *Emergency Medicine - System Management Series*, vol. 15, 2003, pp. 6-10.

News. (2003): 'Emergency Rooms: Winnipeg ERs urged to implement more staff and computer systems', Retrieved 25th of January, 2007, Canadian Healthcare Technology, from http://www.canhealth.com/News061.html.

Ospina, M., Bond, K., Schull, M., Innes, G., Blitz, S., Friesen, C., and Rowe, B. (2006): *Technology Report: Measuring Overcrowding in Emergency Departments - a call for standardization [Technology report no 67.1]*, Canadian Agency for Drugs and Technologica in Health, Ottawa: Canada.

Robinson, M. (1991): 'Double-level Language and Co-operative Working', *AI & Society*, vol. 5, 1991, pp. 34-60.

Rowe, B., Bond, K., Ospina, M., Blitz, S., Afilalo, M., Campbell, S., and Schull, M. (2006): *Frequency, Determinants, and Impact of Overcrowding in Emergency Departments in Canada: A National survey of Emergency Department Directors [Technology report 67.3]*, Canadian Agency for Drugs and Technologies in Health, Ottawa: Canada.

Rowe, B., Bond, K., Ospina, M., Blitz, S., Schull, M., Sinclair, D., and Bullard, M. (2006): *Data Collection on Patients in Emergency Departments in Canada [Technology report no 67.2]*, Canadian Agency for Drugs and Technologies in Health, Ottawa: Canada.

Schmidt, K. and Bannon, L. (1992): 'Taking CSCW Seriously: Supporting Articulation Work', *Computer Supported Cooperative Work (CSCW): An International Journal*, vol. 1, no. 1-2, 1992, pp. 7-40.

Searle, J. R. (1979): 'A Taxonomy of Illocutionary Acts', In *Expression and Meaning: Studies in the Theory of Speech Acts*, Cambridge University Press, Cambridge, 1979, pp. 1-29.

Smith, R. (2005): 'eTriage brings order to emergency departments', Retrieved 27th of January, 2007, ExpressNews, from http://www.expressnews.ualberta.ca/article.cfm?id=6514.

Star, S. L. and Strauss, A. (1999): 'Layers of Silence, Arenas of Voice: The Ecology of Visible and Invisible Work', *Computer Supported Cooperative Work (CSCW): An International Journal*, vol. 8, 1999, pp. 9-30.

Suchman, L. (1987): *Plans and Situated Actions. The Problem of Human Machine Communication*, Cambridge University Press, Cambridge.

Suchman, L. (1994): 'Do Categories Have Politics? The language/action perspective reconsidered', *Computer Supported Cooperative Work (CSCW): An International Journal*, vol. 2, 1994, pp. 177-190.

Timmons, S. (2003): 'A Failed Panopticon: Surveillance of Nursing Practice via New Technology', *New Technology, Work and Employment*, vol. 18, no. 2, 2003, pp. 143-153.

Tjora, A. (2000): 'The Technological Mediation of the Nursing-Medical Boundary', *Sociology of Health & Illness*, vol. 22, no. 6, 2000, pp. 721-741.

Winner, L. (1986): 'Do Artifacts have Politics?' In L. Winner (ed.): *The Whale and The Reactor: A Search for Limites in an age of High Technology*, University of Chicaga Press, Chicago, 1986, pp. 28-40.

Winograd, T. and Flores, F. (1986): *Understanding Computers and Cognition: A new foundation to system design*, Ablex Publishing Corp, Norwood, NU, USA.

L. Bannon, I. Wagner, C. Gutwin, R. Harper, and K. Schmidt (eds.).
ECSCW'07: Proceedings of the Tenth European Conference on Computer Supported Cooperative Work, 24-28 September 2007, Limerick, Ireland
© Springer 2007

How-To Pages: Informal Systems of Expertise Sharing

Cristen Torrey[1], David W. McDonald[2], Bill N. Schilit,[3] and Sara Bly[4]

[1]Human Computer Interaction Institute, Carnegie Mellon University
ctorrey@cs.cmu.edu

[2]Information School, University of Washington
dwmc@u.washington.edu

[3]Google Research
schilit@google.com

[4]Sara Bly Consulting
sara@sarably.com

Abstract. The How-To has recently emerged as a genre of online content that describes how something is done. This study focuses on computer and electronics hobbyists and their use of How-Tos—how hobbyists use existing knowledge to solve technical challenges, how they document their new knowledge for one another, and how they exchange help and feedback. Our analysis describes How-To knowledge sharing as a fully decentralized expertise-location system in which the How-To functions as both a broadcast of the author's expertise and a personal portfolio.

Introduction

Internet technologies have the potential to facilitate knowledge sharing among individuals around the world on every conceivable topic—if experts are able and willing to document their knowledge. Research suggests this is not a straightforward proposition. Experts may not be able to fully articulate what they know (Spender, 1996; Leonard and Sensiper, 1998). Or they may be unwilling to reveal the valuable knowledge they created (Hinds and Pfeffer, 2003). Despite the obstacles, an increasingly popular form of procedural knowledge sharing—known as the How-To—has emerged.

A How-To refers to online content that describes how something is done. How-Tos, largely written by volunteers, explain how to install water heaters, how to knit socks, how to pack a suitcase, and on and on. We were intrigued, in particular, by the use of the How-To among computer and electronics hobbyists. These hobbyists generate detailed, step-by-step descriptions of their creative and often time-consuming activities. As just one example, a lengthy How-To describes the process of taking a Guitar Hero video game controller apart and reassembling it inside a full-size electric guitar[1]. (Figure 1 details one step in this process.) The authors of this How-To estimate that the project took them seventy-five hours to complete, and they introduce the How-To by explaining, "it occurred to us that you might enjoy making one of your own."

> You'll notice that in some pictures we used a thicker wire in the neck. Originally we thought that this thicker wire would be easier to control, but we later discovered that it lacked the flexibility necessary to fit in the main guitar body cavity. So, we replaced it with a piece of nicely-bundled cat-5 networking cable.
>
> Regardless, you can see here that the GH controller's wiring scheme is quite simple: one side of the switches shares a common ground while an individual wire runs from each of the other sides, comprising six wires in total.

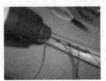

Figure 1. How-To: Build Your Own Custom Full-Sized Wireless Guitar Hero Controller

A knowledge contribution like this is all the more surprising given that computer and electronics hobbyists describe the manipulation of physical objects, which previous research has revealed to be especially difficult in text alone (Pipek and Wulf, 2003). Despite the challenges, hobbyists and their How-Tos appear to be thriving. As far as we are aware, this research is the first to describe How-To knowledge sharing. In this work, we characterize the How-To as a class of online content, and through our study of computer and electronics hobbyists, we provide an initial description of its use and its relationship to other knowledge management practices.

---

1   http://toolmonger.com/2006/12/05/how-to-build-your-own-custom-full-sized-wireless-guitar-hero-controller/

The How-To

The How-To has become a common format for procedural knowledge sharing. It is a class of online content similar to the FAQ (Halverson et. al., 2004) or the personal homepage. How-Tos can be found online for software usage and modification, hardware and electronics, home improvement, knitting, sewing, woodworking, and many other activities. Numerous websites have attempted to consolidate How-To knowledge into standardized repositories[2], but How-Tos continue to be published and distributed in diverse ways.

How-Tos are characterized by a sequential description of procedural information. Some How-Tos relate the chronological story of the author's experience, complete with descriptions of the author's mistakes and workarounds. The authors of the Guitar Hero project documented the story of their process with pictures, including successes and frustrations (see Figure 1). In contrast, other How-Tos are written more like recipes, with a list of the necessary tools and straightforward step-by-step instructions for tested task completion (see Figure 2).

Plug in USB power, your computer should recognize it as a USB to serial converter. Drivers are available from FTDI if they don't come with your OS (most modern ones do)

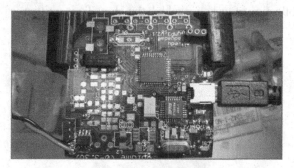

Use the serial driver and tinybld16 (or, if you have decided on a different bootloader, the proper software) to upload the current MintyMp3 firmware. Turn Minty off and on, and use a terminal program (at 1152Kbps) to make sure Minty firmware is loaded. It should at least print out `"Minty MP3! v2 3/25/2004"` or something similar

Figure 2. How-To: MintyMP3 Flashing the Firmware

Computer & Electronics Hobbyists

Hobbyists work on projects they enjoy. There is no company or professional society which structures their work or organizes their contributions, and yet content

---

[2] For example, http://www.instructables.com; http://www.howtopedia.org; http://www.wikihow.com; http://www.howtoforge.com

around electronics and computer projects is growing rapidly. The current proliferation of hobbyist-created online content is supported by a related growth in commercial resources like magazines, books, parts, and kits. A successful United States print publication, *MAKE* magazine, gives detailed instructions for all kinds of do-it-yourself technology. In a recent issue, for example, readers learned how to make biodiesel fuel and how to create ringtones for their cell phones from songs in their music collection. Fairs and conferences give hobbyists the opportunity to display and discuss their work with others. Last year's Maker Faire in San Mateo, California had 20,000 attendees (Goldfayn, 2007). Tools, platforms, and other resources are becoming available as well; an increasing number of hobbyist kits are available for experimenting with technologies like RFID and sensor networks.

MAKE magazine and its extended family of blogs, forums, kits, and fairs refer to hobbyists as *makers* though elsewhere they may be referred to as *enthusiasts*, *hackers*, or *modders*. In this paper, we do not differentiate extensively between these; we refer to anyone building or modifying electronics or computer equipment as a *hobbyist*. When we discuss a hobbyist's work, we use the term *project* because it is the most common way hobbyists refer to their work. Often, a link on a hobbyist's home page collects a set of How-Tos under the header, Projects. A project is the collection of tasks for which the How-To is written.

Figure 3. How-To: Xbox 360 WaterCooling Project

Projects have varying objectives. A *mod* is a modification to an existing product. For example, not long after the Xbox 360 became available, video game enthusiasts found that the device became hot when used for a long time. How-Tos for adding a water-cooling system to the Xbox 360 began popping up in forums and on a variety of websites. The project pictured in Figure 3 is one example[3]. In contrast, other projects are built completely from component parts. Frequently, a hobbyist will mimic the functionality of a commercial product because the product can be built more inexpensively than it can be bought, although building it

---

3   http://www.water-cooling.com/360/1

often requires specialized skills. For example, several hobbyists have built their own versions of the expensive Segway scooter with off-the-shelf parts and open source software code. The MintyMP3 project, introduced in Figure 2, is built from off-the-shelf parts and an Altoids tin[4] (see Figure 4). Another subset of projects combines off-the-shelf parts, and possibly commercial products as well, to create a new product with functionality that is not available to the consumer. Home automation projects, for example, may include lighting, climate, and audio control specifically customized to the hobbyist's needs.

Figure 4. How-To: MintyMP3 Completed

Communicating how something is done can be difficult, particularly when describing how physical objects are manipulated. Computer and electronics hobbyists adopt emerging technologies, from streaming video to 3D modeling software, to improve their ability to communicate process knowledge. Hobbyists link to podcasts, videos hosted on YouTube, 3D models created in Google SketchUp, circuit diagrams, schematics, and usually lots and lots of pictures. The schematic in Figure 5 was posted in a How-To for a one-handed Xbox controller the author designed for a user with a disability[5]. In the How-To, the author describes his design process, makes the schematic available, and specifically asks other hobbyists to develop the idea further. As sophisticated users, hobbyists are in the unique position of making use of a range of existing technologies or, if the solution does not yet exist, building the solution themselves. In observing the online behavior of electronics and computer hobbyists, we are observing a group that feels very comfortable on the Internet and with Internet communication tools.

---

4   http://www.ladyada.net/make/minty/fabrication.html

5   http://benheck.com/Games/Xbox360/controls/1hand/singlehandcontroller.htm

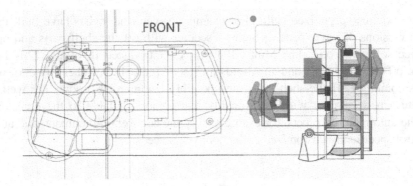

Figure 5. Schematic for Single-Handed Xbox Controller

Method

In order to observe the activities of hobbyists from their viewpoints and in their own words, we invited hobbyists to participate in individual semi-structured interviews. Our first objective in these interviews was to get a sense for what their work was like—how a project got started, completed, and written up as a How-To—paying particular attention to the practices and tools they use. Our second objective was to explore the values that motivate these practices, as well as choices of tools. In our analysis, we used our participants', as well as other hobbyists' project documentation as data. In particular, we contextualized participant interviews with a descriptive analysis of participants' How-Tos, and any public communication about the project posted to relevant blogs and forums.

Interviews were conducted over instant messenger or the telephone, whichever participants preferred. The interviews lasted between one and two hours. We conducted eleven interviews over instant messenger and one interview over the phone. The interview conducted over the phone was transcribed for analysis. Our experience with interviewing over instant messenger was similar to that described by Voida et. al. (2004). Frequently, participants would take time responding to our questions. We received some rather reflective responses as a result, but we could potentially be disadvantaged by not being able to observe participants' immediate, perhaps less censored, reactions.

The interviews were focused around a specific project the participant had recently completed and documented. We began by discussing how the project got started and whether the participant had sought help while working on the project. We asked participants who worked primarily alone if they had ever collaborated on a project before or if they wanted to collaborate with others in the future. In following questions, we explored how and why they chose to document their projects. We asked hobbyists who published their How-Tos on their personal websites whether they had considered publishing to a forum or a wiki. We then asked participants about any responses they might have received to their project documentation and how they felt about those responses. The interview concluded by asking participants who they thought was reading their documentation and how they felt about their work being used or copied by others.

Participants

We solicited hobbyists based on posts to popular blogs, such as hackaday, hackedgadgets, and the blog associated with *MAKE* magazine[6]. We used the project selections of blog editors as our starting point for recruitment in order to locate projects judged to be relevant and useful by hobbyists themselves. Editors of these blogs comment on and link to How-Tos published online by other hobbyists. Often editors will summarize a project and provide a link to the documentation. Readers can interact by adding comments to posts within the blog. Using the hobbyists' documentation, we contacted them directly using any contact information the hobbyist provided. We focused on recent project posts because we believed it would be easier for hobbyists to give specific details about projects that were recently completed.

ID	Gender	Age	Location	Occupation	Sample Projects
A	Male	18	USA	Student	Headphones, Car Stereo
B	Male	27	USA	Student	Video Camera Accessory
C	Male	32	Netherlands	Engineer (Telecom)	Digital TV Display
D	Male	23	Canada	Software (Finance)	Xbox, Microcontroller
E	Male	26	USA	Student	Radio, Xbox
F	Male	20	USA	Student	Robotics, Home Automation
G	Male	24	Denmark	Student	DVD Player, Digital Cable
H	Male	33	USA	Software (Telecom)	Camera Accessories
I	Male	35	UK	Software (Finance)	Radio, Clock, iPod
J	Male	28	USA	Software (Self-employed)	Digital Cable Box, Cell Phone
K	Male	25	USA	Software (University)	Home Audio Network
L	Male	24	USA	Engineer (Biotech)	Clock, Lighting

Table I. Background Information about Interview Participants

Table I summarizes basic information about our participants. Eight participants who accepted our invitation live in the United States; the remaining four participants live in Canada, Denmark, the Netherlands, and the United Kingdom. We

---

6   http://www.hackaday.com; http://www.hackedgadgets.com; http://www.makezine.com/blog

encountered a very limited number of How-Tos written by female hobbyists; consequently, all twelve of our participants were male. They ranged in age from late teens to mid-thirties. Our participants were involved in a diverse selection of projects with a range of different devices and technologies[7].

Findings

The activities of hobbyists include the retrieval of knowledge, as hobbyists work through problems, and the creation of knowledge, as hobbyists document their solutions. The general structure of our interview accounted for building a project and writing the How-To, but it quickly became clear that the How-To was not the only mechanism for hobbyists' interaction. We found that as hobbyists' retrieve knowledge from websites or other How-Tos they often engage in conversation with other hobbyists. Similarly when a How-To is published, hobbyists participate actively in public and private conversations with others about the completed work. Following Huysman and de Wit (2003), we refer to this activity as knowledge exchange. Knowledge exchange occurs directly between individuals without the mediation of the How-To or some other form of documentation. In our findings, we refer to knowledge exchange, retrieval and creation as specific instances of knowledge sharing behavior.

The presentation follows the lifecycle of a project by addressing hobbyists' goals: building their projects, documenting their stories, and broadcasting their contributions. Our use of the terms, *project*, *story*, and *contribution*, is meant to signify how the nature of the work is transformed by each step in a knowledge sharing process. The project is a challenge the hobbyist has accepted. When that challenge is met, the hobbyist tells the story with words and pictures, and the story becomes a part of the hobbyist's portfolio. Finally, that story becomes a contribution when it is recognized by and becomes a resource for other hobbyists. As hobbyists pursue each goal in turn, they may be engaged in knowledge retrieval, knowledge creation, knowledge exchange, or some combination. In the following, we describe these practices in detail, as well as the technological tools and the motivations for using these tools.

Building their Projects

Before a hobbyist can invest their time and effort in a project, there must be inspiration. Our interviews revealed a number of different ways that a project might

---

[7]   By design, hobbyists' projects are quite unique. As such, we will not describe the projects of our participants in great detail as that would indirectly identify them to anyone willing to do a quick internet search. When we describe projects in detail in this paper, we are using comparable examples and not describing the projects of our participants.

get started. Ideas for projects can be sparked by problems the hobbyist faces, such as a commercial product that did not come with a remote control.

> most of the stories we come up with are a result of figuring out a solution to a problem that we were personally wanting solved — Participant J

A hobbyist may focus on a particular device, like a radio, that they would like to learn more about. The functionality of commercialized products is also a potential starting point for hobbyists who then add functionality or build the product cheaper than it can be bought. One participant started his project "because they just don't make what you want." Several participants subscribe to RSS (Really Simple Syndication) feeds of their favorite blogs to stay informed of new project documentation, new commercial products, and news about technology. Participants freely acknowledge their use of ideas they had first seen in other people's projects.

> I generally read those sites and often get ideas from seeing how other people have used technology in interesting ways — Participant F

Several participants' projects were inspired by knowledge about what others were doing. Two of our participants' projects were derivations of someone else's work; each was an attempted improvement on the particular implementation of another hobbyist. Other participants used the work of others more generally to inform their own work on projects with very different goals.

Discovering information via blogs is often a passive retrieval strategy. Our participants were often not specifically looking for the information that inspired them. As a project idea is formed, participants use more active retrieval strategies. Some of the projects described in the interviews were clever but fairly straightforward ideas that were implemented quickly and did not involve a lot of research. Other projects were more difficult, and participants were clear about their desire to reuse information if it was available in order to focus their energies on making something new. Participants reported searching forum archives, manufacturer documentation, Wikipedia, and anything they could find on the Internet. One participant said he was "always reading online," usually project documentation written by other hobbyists that he found by searching the web. Another participant referred to the Internet as a "vast brain-trust" and a "massive card catalog." This participant was not intimidated by the overwhelming amount of information his language implies and spoke optimistically about how great it was to be able to find just the information he was seeking.

> i'd be a lot different if it weren't for PCs and the internet it's like an endless library someone will say "i wish i knew what that means…" and i'll promptly suggest we look it up online which seems so foreign to some, but to me it's 2nd nature … i've learned volumes more online under my own curiosity than i ever did in school — Participant E

Participants spoke positively about searching for information with Google. After mentioning help received from a colleague, another participant said, "and of course : google is my friend too."

Google is not the sole method of information seeking that these participants use. In addition to knowledge retrieval, our participants sought out interactions that are better described as knowledge exchange. Half the participants routinely connect to communities of other hobbyists, either face-to-face or online. Some participants identified face-to-face contacts as the source of their support and advice when they were trying to solve a problem for a project. This was often true for participants working within a university environment where a like-minded community had formed, such as within an engineering program. Two participants specifically implemented community features on their personal websites so that friends, as well as visitors, could interact around their website content.

Other participants had ongoing relationships within an online forum or newsgroup that they used for targeted technical advice. Online hobbyist forums are organized with varying degrees of scope. Forums exist for people working on specific devices like a TIVO, a general category of interest like digital audio, or even a more general domain like electronics. Regardless of the specificity of the community's interests, interview participants spoke about being active in online forums where they felt comfortable among the other people.

> It is a mature place where you don't have to worry about being called a 'newb' when you ask a question and people always try their best to help you out. — Participant A

When asked about getting help, participants talked about their connections with other people, either face-to-face or online.

> we are a group of 4-5 "die-hards" that are really good and interested in microcontroller matters. I talk to them a lot and am very thankful knowing them — Participant G

Participants acknowledged the value of support from other hobbyists, referring to their community members affectionately with terms such as "geeks," "freaks like me," and "die-hards."

Participants utilize knowledge from a variety of sources when building a project. They retrieve knowledge with active strategies, such as a Google search, and with passive strategies, such as staying aware of RSS feeds from technology blogs. At times, our participants were working on problems where existing knowledge was not sufficient. In these cases, they sought help via knowledge exchange from personal contacts, both face-to-face and in online communities.

Documenting their Stories

Projects are rarely documented if they are unsuccessful so, of course, not every project that a hobbyist begins will be documented. Participants gave a range of different reasons when asked why they decided to write a How-To. Some participants spoke specifically about the reaction they hoped it would generate.

> I knew the Internet community would be interested and drive traffic to my site — Participant J

Other participants felt that given the way they had benefited from the knowledge of others, giving back was the appropriate thing to do.

> Once the project was ready for the public I only felt it normal to share what I had created. — Participant C

Some participants took occasional pictures at various stages of the project, but most of the documentation effort is done after the project is complete. Hobbyists described a translation step between the work itself and the activities that follow in the online domain. Participants created digital artifacts, often after the project was completed, including schematic drawings, pictures, and videos in order to capture their process as a How-To. Roughly half of the participants' personal websites were formatted in the style of a blog, using dated entries that could be filtered by keyword. These websites offered communication features like comments, forums, and chat rooms where readers could interact with the site owner and one another. The rest of the websites used a more traditional homepage style with a "Projects" link that consolidated the How-To information.

Nearly all participants posted their How-To to their personal website, which was rarely dedicated exclusively to the hobbyists' projects. These personal websites contain photos, personal news, and other links of interest to the owner.

> I think nowadays it's pretty easy for anyone who wishes to put their work online to do so. ... there are a lot of free tools available for writing docs (openoffice), making diagrams (dia), drawings (the gimp) and so forth. — Participant D

Participants benefit from collecting their project history in a single place. They say the site becomes a reference that they return to when they want to remember what they have done, and it represents the scope of their abilities to new visitors.

> I like saving things. It is kind of like an online blog for me and if someone is looking to do the same thing then it is already done and they can do it easier. — Participant A

Participants see their personal website as one of their projects and appreciate the control they have over every aspect of the layout.

> Im not so into the whole blog/wiki craze ... I like full control of my code, design, etc. plus the content isn't that dynamic — Participant F

Participants also feel that publishing to a personal website makes their project easier for Google to crawl, consequently making it easier for everyone to find.

> The forums are quite niche audiences. If I put it on my website, it receives a MUCH larger audience. Often someone might see something which grabs their attention, and then get interested in that particular aspect of the hobby themselves. And also, the largest proportion of my website visitors come via google searches. Which means they wouldn't find it in a forum. — Participant I

As a place to publish their documentation, forums were seen as more dynamic and more information dense.

> I feel like, things get lost in forums — a lot of noise. And if I have something worth saying, usually it's a lot and I don't like trying to fight the noise. I'm usually making something that fills a hole in the internet and if I'm the only thing filling that hole, it'll show up in Google. — Participant B

This participant gives Google an active role in facilitating the discovery of project websites, and that role upholds the values of a meritocracy. The likelihood that one's project may be found by Google is perceived to be related to the project's uniqueness and usefulness to others.

The How-To is often written as a story of the project, including how it began, the choices that arose, and how the project has been used since its creation. Consider the following excerpt from the Guitar Hero Controller How-To, which describes a challenge and the subsequent workaround.

> At this point we ran into (incredibly) our first major snafu. There was absolutely no place for four AA batteries in here—and of course, you wouldn't want to disassemble it to change them. A quick trip to Batteries Plus netted us a custom-made rechargeable pack made from six 2/3A-sized NiMH batteries. They fit along the top side of the main cavity. The remaining pickup bumps into them, however, so we removed the pickup from the cover, cut out the shiny poles, and hot-glued them back into the cover to make a "fake pickup." — How-To Build Your Own Custom Full-Sized Wireless Guitar Hero Controller

Every participant's documentation included pictures, sometimes annotated to draw attention to a specific part of the photograph. Many of the participants used schematic diagrams to illustrate interaction between components or the details in a circuit. About half of these diagrams are hand drawn and scanned, while the other half are created with a software application. Half of the participants used video, hosted specifically on YouTube, to demonstrate the functionality of their projects. Documentation frequently cites specific people who helped with the project and references that the hobbyist used to complete the project. The overwhelming assertion of participants was that content created by other people was always free to make use of but should be referenced with a link to the referring webpage. In practice, participants did not reference every possible piece of related information. The number of links associated with a project's documentation was never more than five.

In documenting their How-To story, participants create knowledge for others to use. The information provided is sequentially structured but varies in a number of ways. Participants take a range of tones to describe their process, some more factual and others more humorous, and use varying levels of detail. Although most How-Tos are published on a personal website, there is a great deal of variation in format, including the use of video, modeling, and diagramming technologies.

Broadcasting their Contributions

Once the documentation is online, hobbyists want others to see it. An advantage of publishing to a forum is the built-in audience, but when hobbyists use personal websites, they have to create an audience for their work. Several participants were quite attentive to their website traffic, and their "critical mass" gave them confidence that their new content would be found by others.

> I guess I just have critical mass that I don't need to get rediscovered each time. — Participant B

Those who had not established a reputation for their website were explicitly interested in creating one and those pursuing undergraduate degrees believed their websites would represent them favorably to potential employers after graduation.

A quick way to create an audience is to have your project linked from any high-traffic website. In fact, a few participants added "digg this" links to their project webpages. Digg.com is an online community that votes on newsworthy links. One participant whose website averages 40 visitors a day had one of his projects voted to Digg's front page and received 12,000 visitors the next day. We spoke to several participants who had just documented their first project. These participants sent email to several popular blogs when they published their How-To, hoping that their project would be highlighted by one of the blog editors. One participant spoke of being recognized in this way as his "breakthrough."

> You should know that before I got the hack posted, my site was completely unknown. So it was kind of my "breakthrough" ...i couldn't get my hands down when I saw the post on hackaday ... we all like to show off, don't we :) I think it's the global attention and that you display to everybody that you can actually do stuff — Participant G

Other participants agreed that the recognition by blog editors was a validating experience.

> Every day I checked hackedgadgets to see what clever projects people have come up with. Then one day I find my own project over there. That makes me kind of proud. — Participant C

Being linked to by other websites increases a hobbyist's website traffic significantly and identifies the hobbyist as a contributor.

> (someone likened being mentioned on Make is like being "geek Playmate of the Month"). — Participant E

Some participants send a "tip" to the blog editor every time they post a new project, but others establish a reputation they rely on to make their subsequent work visible to others.

We used Google's advanced search to discover the approximate number of websites linking to our participants' websites. Roughly half the participants were linked from more than fifty other websites; the other half were linked by less than ten other websites, if any. In the project documentation cycle, links are used to signify reference material and are rarely used as lists of friends or contacts; this is distinctly different from the way "blogrolls" are used by blog authors. But links from other websites are not the only way to perceive that one's documentation has an audience. Other communication channels are used to send appreciative comments and feedback from readers.

Being recognized as a contributor can expose the hobbyist to a considerable amount of feedback. Feedback comes directly via email or through the comments feature of a referring blog. This feedback is another form of knowledge exchange, and this interaction is sought out by our participants. Many of our participants were vigilant about keeping track of the referring pages when new visitors came to their website and reading all the comments their project received on any referring blog or forum. A few participants implemented a forum or commenting features on their website to encourage discussion of their projects; these participants actively moderated these conversations.

> if it is not a personal attack I will respond on the site so that it's archived for people to make their own minds up If it's just cursing or some such I delete the comment and do not bother to respond — Participant H

Receiving and responding to feedback is a valued part of the experience, despite the negative feedback our participants reported receiving from readers. Participants, in some cases, attempted to defend or explain themselves when criticized, but none of the participants felt it was a reason to avoid publishing their How-Tos in the future. This feedback is relatively anonymous and participants felt comfortable deciding "the guy obviously doesn't know what he was talking about" when a reader had been critical. Another participant said, "I just laugh at them."

In addition to the public knowledge exchange on the blogs, hobbyists often receive numerous emails. Participants said they were less likely to receive negative feedback over email and more likely to receive questions about technical details. Participants were happy to offer help, in some cases developing friendships with these email contacts and encouraging them to publish their own documentation.

> I had one guy who saw my thing on Make, and then he had something that he wanted to make, and he sent me a message and said, "Oh man. I love your thing that I saw, and that makes me want to put my own thing up there." ... and then he submitted to Make and then the next day, it was on. His thing was on there, so that was kind of fun. I talk to him every once in awhile too. — Participant L

One of the most satisfying outcomes of emails for participants was the news that someone else had built their project and personalized or made improvements to it. One participant collected pictures of alternative implementations of his project and published the collection of photos on a separate page on his website.

> Since part of my enjoyment comes from other people getting inspired. It's flattering if someone builds one of my projects. — Participant I

While the number of comments on forums and blogs peaks and then tapers off, participants report receiving and responding to email for some time, in one case years after the How-To was published.

For hobbyists, broadcasting their contribution is critical if they want to participate in knowledge exchange about their completed work. Our participants sought feedback from other hobbyists by sending their How-Tos to blog editors, but they were also proud of helping other hobbyists over email. Hobbyists broadcast their contribution in order to participate in knowledge exchange, the sort of exchange they participated in while the project was being built.

Discussion

As a class of online content, our research characterizes the How-To as a flexible format; we observed a variety of approaches to the implementation of How-Tos.

We have already commented that documenting procedural knowledge in text-based media is a challenge, as previously identified by Pipek and Wulf (2003). Hobbyists rise to this challenge by leveraging a variety of media. A mix of photos, video, drawings, and text are arranged to create a presentation of the hobbyist's process. This sophisticated use of multimedia is only beginning to show up in studies of organizational knowledge management (Grudin, 2006) but is clearly worthy of further investigation.

In addition to the form of the How-To, our research explored the practices surrounding its use. Among our sample of computer and electronics hobbyists, the creation of a How-To is one phase of their knowledge sharing activities. While hobbyists' physical work is largely accomplished alone, social interaction is interleaved throughout. We observed an informal system of knowledge sharing that makes use of multiple communication technologies to connect to different communities. Blogs provide awareness of what other hobbyists are doing. So when a hobbyist's How-To is linked by a blog, the hobbyist's contribution is broadcast and reputation is strengthened. Hobbyists use search engines to directly seek out other hobbyists' How-Tos and may communicate with their authors over email. In the same fashion, hobbyists respond to email they receive regarding their own How-Tos. Finally, hobbyists participate in forums and newsgroups, as well as face-to-face communities; these contacts are valuable resources when hobbyists encounter particularly difficult problems. Our participants had very few complaints about the tools they used or about the How-To sharing process. This evolving, interdependent system of communication tools is acceptable, even satisfying, for our participants.

On the surface, the informal system of How-To sharing we have described bears little resemblance to traditional knowledge management applications, an issue of longstanding interest in the CSCW community. Previous research has focused largely on organizational settings while, of course, How-To sharing exists in a broad, decentralized system of volunteers. Knowledge management tools are frequently an attempt to consolidate knowledge content; as such, they often take the shape of a single application. As we have described it, How-To sharing occurs within and across a collection of communication tools without any centralized control. While acknowledging these important differences, we propose that How-To sharing can be usefully described as an expertise-location system; a hobbyist's collection of How-Tos functions much like a user profile in an expertise-location system.

Early knowledge management systems were repositories for documents or other knowledge content. Expertise-location systems build on this work by connecting people to one another in order to leverage social interactions as a mode of knowledge transfer. An expertise-location system recommends an appropriate person to contact for help in a given area (e.g., Streeter and Lochbaum, 1988; McDonald and Ackerman, 1998; Reichling and Veith, 2005; Pipek and Wulf,

2003). While an expertise-location system uses profiles to match individuals, the hobbyists we observed make use of other hobbyists' How-Tos. The How-To documentation of various projects is an advertisement for hobbyists' areas of expertise. Other hobbyists then use available contact information to seek out this expertise through direct communication.

The combination of explicit knowledge representation in the How-To and the surrounding communications is mirrored in previous systems like the Answer Garden (Ackerman, 1994; Ackerman and McDonald, 1996). In both the Answer Garden and How-To sharing, experts document knowledge for reuse but engage in further communications when necessary. The Answer Garden allows users to communicate with experts directly through the system. In the context of How-To sharing, our participants communicated through both public and private communication channels. A discussion on a public forum, blog, or personal website is archived indefinitely, so the conversation is available for later readers. Private channels like email were also used, frequently by novice hobbyists. These newcomers to the community may prefer to keep their communications private while they gain experience.

In the remainder of the discussion, we continue to explore How-To sharing as an informal instance of an expertise-location system. First, we discuss how our participants met the primary challenge of finding the right expert using a combination of active and passive strategies. Second, we discuss another challenge for expertise-location systems, motivating the experts. We highlight the unique qualities of the How-To, as both a hobbyist's portfolio and personal history, that appear to motivate participation by experts.

Encountering and Searching for How-Tos

Our study of hobbyists' practices illustrates the importance of a diversity of tools. We observed computer and electronics hobbyists adopting a diverse set of technologies to leverage the unique capabilities of each tool. Similar to the findings of McDonald and Ackerman (1998), we found that our participants balance purposeful expertise seeking strategies with a general awareness of their environment. In addition to strategically using Google to search for How-Tos, our participants engage in more passive ways of encountering How-To information.

RSS (Real Simple Syndication) is a rather rudimentary event notification technology that polls a web server to see if there is something new. Our participants scan RSS feeds from blogs and other hobbyists' websites for headlines that interest them. By staying aware of what other hobbyists are doing, they gather information before they even recognize the need for it. The way event notification is adopted and used in organizations has been relevant to CSCW (Fitzpatrick et al., 1999). However, the implications of event notification technologies for identifying expertise have not specifically been addressed. In this case, we saw that RSS provides hobbyists with general technology-related information, as well as introduces them to other hobbyists' activities.

Hacking-related blogs are a primary source of our participants' RSS feeds. On these blogs, an editor highlights specific projects by commenting on a project and linking to the project website. These blog editors fulfill an important role in the system because they become gatekeepers to a much larger collection of projects a hobbyist might not otherwise encounter. The role of the information gatekeeper has been recognized in a number of knowledge sharing systems (e.g. Paepcke, 1996; Erlich and Cash, 1994; McDonald and Ackerman, 1998). In addition to mediating information for hobbyists, the opinions of blog editors are a central way of validating hobbyists' contributions. Hobbyists admire the hacks posted to these blogs and want to be similarly acknowledged and admired; they want to be a part of that blog's community.

How-Tos as Portfolio and Personal History

Participants clearly understand that the online representation of their project is a representation of who they are and what they know—a presentation of self. This finding is similar to system deployment and adoption studies where organizational participants were required to create their own expertise profiles (e.g., Streeter and Lochbaum, 1988; Maybury, D'Amore and House, 2003). But unlike some organizational settings where individuals may resist the time and effort necessary to maintain a profile, hobbyists create and maintain project documentation as a contribution to the broader community and as an artifact that benefits them personally.

Participants talk about their collection of How-Tos as a portfolio. Students, in particular, mentioned the benefit of displaying one's prior work to potential employers. So while participants believe other hobbyists can infer their expertise from their How-Tos, they are also aware of their visibility to the larger population. This visibility has benefits, including the benefit of presenting oneself well to potential employers.

Participants believe their portfolio of work will help other hobbyists and will reflect well on them to potential employers, but they do not disregard the direct benefit they receive from documenting their work. Participants talked about their How-Tos as diaries, as references for the future when they could no longer remember their process, and as a history of their interactions with others. Participants post FAQs and pictures of other hobbyists' implementations of their projects. The How-To is often coupled to its reaction from the larger community and serves as a record of the influence of that project.

Given the motivations of these hobbyists, it comes as no surprise that nearly all of our participants created their websites from scratch. They have specific needs in representing their portfolio to others and in recording their activities for themselves. As such, their website became a project in and of itself; hobbyists' websites are personal expressions. Some participants said they found it motivating to create their own online space. Once it was created, it motivated them to continue doing the difficult work of documenting their How-Tos.

Implications of How-To Sharing

These results have important implications for expertise-location systems. These results reinforce the importance of fostering person-to-person expertise exchange, like that in Answer Garden (Ackerman, 1994; Ackerman and McDonald, 1996; Pipek and Wulf 2003) and the Expertise Recommender (McDonald and Ackerman, 2000; McDonald, 2003). It is rare for a hobbyist to develop a project without some form of individual interaction with another person, even if the physical work was largely solo.

Expertise-location systems need to support awareness as well as purposeful search for others' expertise. We propose that readers of How-Tos can make inferences about the author's expertise. This proposal should be tested in future work, but it remains an interesting possibility for the maintenance of expertise profiles. Rather than asking people to make their skills and areas of expertise explicit, perhaps expertise can be inferred from a portfolio-style profile. Diverse sources of work and work by-products might be used to create the representation of an individual's expertise.

As younger generations of workers join organizations, generations of workers who grew up with MySpace, Friendster or one of the many other profile-based social networking sites, we may find less reluctance to maintain professional online representation. We see these portfolios as distinctly different from an explicitly articulated profile; one where the individual maintains control and which represents work, perhaps from more than one organization, of which the individual is proud. The creation of a portfolio is motivating because it becomes a resource for the worker as well as for the greater community.

Conclusion

This research explored the collaborative aspects of procedural knowledge sharing by computer and electronics hobbyists through the lens of the How-To. Rather than focusing our inquiry on a single website, or a single communication technology, we investigated the knowledge sharing activities of hobbyists. Our participants work from different parts of the world with a range of different devices and technologies, and there is no central organization that codifies their behavior. Our participants created diverse examples of How-To content, yet the practices surrounding the How-To, knowledge retrieval, knowledge creation, and knowledge exchange, were surprisingly similar.

By investigating the knowledge sharing activities involved in building a project, documenting a story, and broadcasting a contribution, we observed a system of knowledge sharing comparable to previous research in expertise location. In its creation, the How-To is a record of its author's activities and expertise. In its publication, the How-To is a way to share this expertise and connect with other hobbyists. The unique qualities of How-To sharing present opportunities for the development of knowledge sharing systems in the emerging technological landscape.

Acknowledgements

This research was initiated with the support of a summer internship with Intel Corporation and was continued with the support of National Science Foundation grants IIS-0121426 and IIS-0624275. We would like to thank Jeremy Goecks, Laura Dabbish, Sara Kiesler, and Susan Fussell for their thoughtful comments on this work.

References

Ackerman, M. S. (1994): 'Augmenting the Organizational Memory: A Field Study of Answer Garden', in *Proceedings of the 1994 ACM Conference on Computer-Supported Cooperative Work* (CSCW '94), pp. 243-252.

Ackerman, M. S. and McDonald, D. W. (1996): 'Answer Garden 2: Merging Organizational Memory with Collaborative Help', in *Proceedings of the 1996 ACM Conference on Computer Supported Cooperative Work* (CSCW'96), pp. 97-105.

Ehrlich, K. and Cash, D. (1994): 'Turning Information into Knowledge: Information Finding as a Collaborative Activity', in *Proceedings of Digital Libraries '94*, pp. 119-125.

Fitzpatrick, G., Mansfield, T., Kaplan, S., Arnold, D., Phelps, T., and Segal, B. (1999): 'Augmenting the everyday world with Elvin', in *Proceedings of the 6th European Conference on Computer Supported Cooperative Work* (ECSCW '99), pp. 431-450.

Goldfayn, A.L. (2007): 'Make something: Magazine bucks trend by building devoted audience', *Chicago Tribune*, February 5, 2007.

Grudin, J. (2006): 'Enterprise Knowledge Management and Emerging Technologies', in *Proceedings of the 39th Hawaii International Conference on System Sciences*, (HICSS '06).

Halverson, C., Erickson, T. and Ackerman, M. (2004): 'Behind the Help Desk: Evolution of a Knowledge Management System in a Large Organization', in *Proceedings of the ACM Conference on Computer Supported Cooperative Work* (CSCW '04), Chicago, IL, pp. 304-313.

Hinds, P.J. and Pfeffer, J. (2003): 'Why Organizations Don't "Know What They Know": Cognitive and Motivational Factors Affecting the Transfer of Expertise', in M. Ackerman, V. Pipek, and V. Wulf (eds.): *Sharing Expertise: Beyond Knowledge* Management, MIT Press, Cambridge, 2003, pp. 111-136.

Huysman, M.H. and de Wit, D. (2003): 'A Critical Evaluation of Knowledge Management Practice', in M. Ackerman, V. Pipek, and V. Wulf (eds.): *Sharing Expertise: Beyond Knowledge Management*, MIT Press, Cambridge, 2003, pp. 111-136.

Leonard, D. and Sensiper, S. (1998): 'The Role of Tacit Knowledge in Group Innovation', *California Management Review*, vol. 40, no. 3, pp. 112-132.

Maybury, M., D'Amore, R. and House, D. (2003): 'Automated Discovery and Mapping of Expertise', in M. Ackerman, V. Pipek, and V. Wulf (eds.): *Sharing Expertise: Beyond Knowledge Management*, MIT Press, Cambridge, 2003, 359-382.

McDonald, D. W. and Ackerman, M. S. (1998): 'Just Talk to Me: A Field Study of Expertise Location', in *Proceedings of the 1998 ACM Conference on Computer-Supported Cooperative Work* (CSCW '98), pp. 315-324.

McDonald, D. W. and Ackerman, M. S. (2000): 'Expertise Recommender: A Flexible Recommendation System and Architecture', in *Proceedings of the 2000 ACM Conference on Computer-Supported Cooperative Work* (CSCW '00), pp. 231-240.

McDonald, D. W. (2003): 'Recommending Collaboration with Social Networks: A Comparative Evaluation', in *Proceedings of the 2003 ACM Conference on Human Factors in Computing System* (CHI '03), pp. 593-600.

Paepcke, A. (1996): 'Information Needs in Technical Work Settings and Their Implications for the Design of Computer Tools', *Computer Supported Cooperative Work: The Journal of Collaborative Computing*, vol. 5, pp. 63-92.

Pipek, V. and Wulf, V. (2003): 'Pruning the Answer Garden: Knowledge Sharing in Maintenance Engineering', in *Proceedings of the 8th European Conference on Computer Supported Cooperative Work* (ECSCW '03), pp. 1-20.

Reichling, T. and Veith, M. (2005): 'Expertise Sharing in a Heterogeneous Organizational Environment', in *Proceedings of The 9th European Conference on Computer-Supported Cooperative Work*, (ECSCW '05), pp. 325-345.

Spender, J.C. (1996): 'Competitive Advantage from Tacit Knowledge? Unpacking the Concept and its Strategic Implications', in B. Mosingeon and A. Edmonson, (eds.): *Organizational Learning and Competitive Advantage*, Sage Publications, London, 1996, pp. 56-73.

Streeter, L. A. and Lochbaum, K. E. (1988): 'Who Knows: A System Based on Automatic Representation of Semantic Structure', in *Proceedings of RIAO '88*, pp. 380-388.

Voida, A., Mynatt, E.D., Erickson, T., and Kellogg, W.A. (2004): 'Interviewing over instant messaging', in *extended abstracts of the ACM SIGCHI Conference on Human Factors in Computing Systems* (CHI '04). Vienna, Austria, pp. 1344-1347.

L. Bannon, I. Wagner, C. Gutwin, R. Harper, and K. Schmidt (eds.).
ECSCW'07: Proceedings of the Tenth European Conference on Computer Supported Cooperative Work, 24-28 September 2007, Limerick, Ireland
© Springer 2007

Seeing Ethnographically:
Teaching ethnography as part of CSCW

Barry Brown[1], Johan Lundin[2], Mattias Rost[4], Gustav Lymer[3], Lars Erik Holmquist[4]

[1]Department of Communications, University of California San Diego; [2]IT University Göteborg; [3]Göteborg University; [4]FAL Lab, Viktoria Institute

Barry.at.brown@acm.org

Abstract. While ethnography is an established part of CSCW research, teaching and learning ethnography presents unique and distinct challenges. This paper discusses a study of fieldwork and analysis amongst a group of students learning ethnography as part of a CSCW & design course. Studying the students' practices we explore fieldwork as a learning experience, both learning about fieldsites as well as learning the practices of ethnography. During their fieldwork and analysis the students used a wiki to collaborate, sharing their field and analytic notes. From this we draw lessons for how ethnography can be taught as a collaborative analytic process and discuss extensions to the wiki to better support its use for collaborating around fieldnotes. In closing we reflect upon the role of learning ethnography as a practical hands on – rather than theoretical – pursuit.

Introduction

Ethnographic fieldwork has made a number of distinct contributions to CSCW. Through the in-depth examination of settings, findings have been drawn with implications not only for design, but also more broadly for how technology fits and conflicts with everyday work and leisure. Ethnographic work within CSCW has featured a distinctive focus when compared to traditional anthropological or sociological ethnography, in particular engaging analytic positions that encourage the close attention to the details of activity (Anderson 1994;Button 2000;Harper 2000). Alongside this academic contribution, design ethnography has become an established part of HCI education. HCI textbooks frequently present ethnography alongside other methods for evaluating and inspiring technology development. Design education has also taken ethnography to heart – paralleling the way in which design firms such as IDEO have adopted forms of ethnography as part of their consulting toolkit (Wasson 2000).

Yet teaching ethnography as part of design or technical programs presents significant challenges. As a method, ethnography rests considerably on craft and analytic know-how that comes from engaged practice. It is a common observation of methods books that ethnography cannot be learnt from books alone. Moreover, ethnography itself involves learning anew about whatever setting one is studying. Teaching ethnography involves both what ethnography might be and also how to learn and understand the specifics of the setting under study. In this paper we examine these practices of teaching and learning ethnography. We examine how ethnography is learnt and conducted as a practical enterprise, how that might be technically supported, and how it might be better taught. For six years ethnographic methods have taught as part of an IT masters program. As part of this course students conduct two weeks of 'quick and dirty' fieldwork, followed by 3 weeks analyzing their data, writing up and presenting their findings to industrial clients. This fieldwork is then used to design and develop prototype systems. Conducting over 75 days in total of fieldwork, studying the students' work provided a valuable forum to study how ethnography is conducted: both as a way of learning about a setting and as a practice to be learned in itself.

In turn, we discuss tools that can be used to support teaching ethnography. As part of this course we experimented with using wikis (an easily editable website) to support sharing and collaboration around fieldnotes. While having received only passing attention within CSCW (Guzdial and Rick 2000), wiki's are an increasingly popular and widespread collaborative technology. For the students the wiki acted as an 'available anywhere' repository of fieldnotes that had in previous years been private. We discuss two lightweight extensions to the wiki developed to better support their use for collecting fieldnotes and discussion around the fieldnotes.

The paper starts with a brief background to fieldwork as used in the design of collaborative systems, as well as a review of discussions of teaching ethnography, and the specific issues that concern teaching design ethnography. Moving onto studying the students we focus first on the practices of ethnography, giving a broad overview, through the students experiences, of how ethnography is conducted. The second section focuses specifically on the collection of fieldnotes and the use of the wiki to support both co-present and distant collaboration. In the third section we address the students experiences learning fieldwork, describing their learning as a process of 'coming to see ethnographically'. In particular, we focus on the crucible of ethnography – analytic work, and engaging students with moving from procedural understandings to an analytic understanding of ethnography.

Ethnography in CSCW

The distinctive nature of fieldwork for design has accumulated considerable commentary as CSCW has developed (Anderson 1994; Harper 2000; Luff, et al. 2001; Sharrock and Hughes 2001). Indeed, there is a not inconsiderable debate about what ethnography actually is, with a range of views on how wide or narrow to define ethnographic practice. As Harper comments, many sociologists use ethnography as a 'catch-all phrase for a range of different things, just as long as they involve field work of some sort' (Harper 2000). Others would restrict the definition - Button in particular criticises 'scenic fieldwork' where fieldwork only 're-cords what is to be seen' (Button 2000). Whilst located in computer science departments or research labs, design ethnography has not escaped the systemic disputes of the social sciences (Sharrock and Hughes 2001).

One key challenge of ethnography within CSCW is to connect with design – with commentary ranging from the prescriptive (Beyer and Holtzblatt 1997) to the reflective (Anderson 1994). Dourish (2006) argues that the significance of ethnographic work is frequently not in how it can influence specific interventions, but more broadly for how it can support understanding and reflection on technological practice. For example, Bowers *et al's* (Bowers, et al. 1995) discussion of the flow of work in a printing firm is a valuable counterpoint to technologists conceptions of workflow. The value of ethnography here is broader than implications for a specific technology rich though that contribution can be.

A contrasting criticism is that the brevity of CSCW's design ethnographies can seem a deficiency when compared to the longer studies of anthropology or sociology. However, this would be to misunderstand the design ethnographer's job. Design ethnographies do not fail if they do not give an account that will equip an outsider to do that particular job, or even if they do not capture all the essential features of a lifeworld. The orientation of this work instead is to what essential practices have an impact on technological interventions and understanding. This is not simply a documentation of practices, but an understanding of why features and activity are arranged in such and such a way, the resources that are used to do what is done. This is not to downplay the value of time in the field when ethnographers have goals beyond specific designs or validating fieldwork to others (Harper 2000).

Yet while the conceptual or theoretical positions of ethnography have thus scarcely ever escaped debate, discussions of the concrete practical trade of ethnographic study, and the teaching of those skills to others, are more lacking within CSCW. Method textbooks provide valuable introductions to fieldwork and the skills of fieldwork, although in a pedagogical role there is less space for reflection on teaching itself (Crabtree 2003; Randall et al 2007).

Indeed, within CSCW teaching as an activity has been somewhat neglected. The impact of CSCW has been not only in its academic research impact, but in the skills it has passed onto non-researchers and those skills carried into distinct workplaces. Indeed, this in some contrast to HCI and Information Sciences, where teaching have played a more prominent role. While textbooks and the like can summarise what is to be learnt, teaching CSCW involves imparting a distinctive attitude– in particular a sensitivity to workplace co-ordination – and no more so than with teaching design ethnography. Ethnography is specifically challenging to teach since it combines a complex of theoretical, analytic, observational and organisational skills. In Weinberg and Stephens' paper on teaching ethnography as part of computer science (Weinberg and Stephens 2002), they discuss how the challenges of teaching ethnography invite reflection onto the practice of professional ethnography itself. Studying the teaching of ethnography is not only an opportunity to examine pedagogy but to look afresh at ethnography itself. Outside CSCW there has been more extensive discussion of how to teach ethnography, with an emphasis on the importance of practical engagement with the activity as opposed to learning through conventional lecture format. Trujillo (1999) discusses going as far as to write and submit academic papers in a research team with his students, embedding their practices of fieldwork analysis and writing into his own professional academic practice. Sotrin (1999) in contrast focuses on the analytic purposes of ethnography – and how students struggle with 'bracketing the familiar' of their commensense assumptions.

Technical support for teaching ethnography is one approach that we have explored here. Systems for tagging data such as HyperResearch and ATLAS-TI have gained some use amongst ethnographers. However, for many these tools remain controversial, in part because of the analytic orientation they encourage, and connections with approaches such as grounded theory and strip analysis (Coffey, et al. 1996). More radically some authors have experimented with using the web to present multimedia accounts of fieldwork and more multi-voiced accounts (Kersenboom 1995), echoing work on the 'designers notepad' that supported richer descriptions of fieldwork as part of the design process (Sommerville 1993). Much ethnographic data itself, of course, is also increasingly collected online from emails, blogs, websites and the like. For the project discussed here we explored the use of wikis as a tool to support students learning ethnography (the focus of (Lymer, et al. 2007)). Wikis are websites which support the editing of pages through the addition of an 'edit' button on each page. Wikis have been particularly successful in the classroom (Da Lio, et al. 2005). The CoWeb (Guzdial and Rick 2000) system, for example, supported co-present learning amongst groups of architecture students, who used the wiki website to share their coursework. Wikis suited our purposes not only because of their simplicity, but also for how they could potentially open up the process of writing and reviewing fieldnotes, a practice we discuss in our results section.

Studying the studies

A core part of teaching in the Scandinavian informatics tradition has been to focus attention on users and those that are affected by technology. Over the last five years at the IT University, Göteborg a class in fieldwork has been taught to masters IT students in an attempt to engage the students with a richer sense of the work settings that they design for. To better understand teaching ethnographic practice, how students could learn fieldwork skills, and how to support collaboration, for one class we collected data on the students' experiences of one class. Nineteen students were divided into five project groups each, and engaged fulltime in two weeks of fieldwork, followed by four weeks of analysis and finally writing a report on their findings. All of the groups worked with clients who wanted to study and explore the possibility of supporting a specific practice with mobile technology. The students had been taught basic ethnographic theory and fieldwork techniques, and were familiarisation with methods through conducting a one day study. They students had also been required to take part in reading seminars, focusing on fieldwork papers from CSCW.

In approaching the students work we were conscious that while this was a opportunity to study concentrated fieldwork, the students were not experienced fieldworkers. As Forsythe points out, ethnography is a complex trade (Forsythe 1999) (although this point is frequently laboured). Moreover, as we discuss below the 'students problem' – learning a skill (and passing the course) was subtly different from that of simply producing a publishable field study. Yet the students dealt with many of the same problems – concrete and conceptual - we ourselves experienced in our own fieldwork. Indeed, the students talked about, and displayed through their learning, aspects that would perhaps have been hidden if we studied experienced fieldworkers, or reflected on our own practices (Ten Have 2003). The friction between the advisors, the students and ourselves was revealing of ethnographic practice (and our own failings and analytic purposes). Our view of the students experiences, as well as the lessons we drew for design, are therefore seen through the prism of our own fieldwork experiences.

The groups studied a wide range of different sites and arranged their own access. Group one studied learning support amongst school children, investigating a local science discovery centre. The second group explored ideas of supporting the mobile repair of trucks, studying repair workshops for trucks, planes and buses. Group three investigated the use of paper within journalism and advertising, studying a newspaper and a photo bureau. Group four looked at how facility management work takes place studying an office building where an external company provided the facility support, and lastly, the final group focused on messenger firms that made daily deliveries by truck and car.

The main bulk of the students' learning of the practices of ethnography took place in and through the actual carrying out of fieldwork. This means that the content of the course was made visible to the students in the form of real problems, "owned" by the students themselves, rather than as intellectual problems posed as school assignments. For example, facing the awkwardness of observing school kids at a science centre required the students to find ways of dealing with the situation then and there. The students met the problems of ethnographic fieldwork in much the same ways as would a "real" ethnographer. These problems were intended as the main stimulus and focus of student activity; and thus the approach taken was student centred rather than textbook centred (Charlin, et al. 1998).

Figure 1. Two fieldnotes from the wiki

Alongside the students' fieldwork we conducted our own fieldwork *on* the groups' fieldwork. This involved video taping supervisory meetings with the students (ten supervisory meetings in total), video taping three of the students own analysis sessions, and interviewing eight of the students about their experiences in the field. While it was difficult to follow the students conducting their fieldwork, due to access issues, we did video record two days from the group who were studying a local science centre.

The use of the wiki amongst the students also provided a valuable source of log data on their sharing of fieldnotes. The original aim of the wiki (figure 1) was to allow the students to share their fieldnotes within their fieldwork group. We used the open source 'TikiWiki' (http://tikiwiki.org/) software, one of the most popular free Wiki systems available. Tikiwiki has many of the features of more advance groupware systems such as support for forums, blogs, and even workflow integration. Its ability to password protect pages of the wiki allowed us to support the privacy of fieldnotes amongst the class. We specifically asked the students when gaining access to their field site to specifically ask for permission to share their fieldnotes with advisors and classmates. All groups obtained permission, except one group where the notes were confidential. For all the other groups fieldnotes were left open, editable to ourselves, the respective clients, and the whole of the class. The students were given accounts on a wiki, alongside a demo in class, and were asked to enter all their typed fieldnotes into the wiki as the fieldwork progressed. In total over 109 fieldnotes and analytic notes were entered into the system (6 per student), distributed over 86 separate pages in the wiki. For the final grade of the ethnographic part of the course the students were simply evaluated in terms of 'pass' or 'fail' –all the students successfully passed this part of the course. While none of the authors were involved in the grading or evaluation of the students work, the second author was involved in a supervisory role discussing with the students their results and fieldwork. The other authors also engaged in helping the students during analysis sessions.

Results

The first section 'doing ethnography' gives an overview of the ethnographic process, discussing the different stages involved in ethnography. In particular, we highlight the importance of the transformation of data, over than simply capturing data. In the second section 'writing ethnography' we discuss how fieldnotes were collected and shared using the wiki. Lastly, in 'seeing ethnographically', we discuss the students experiences of 'learning ethnography' as a double learning process about both about the setting they were studying, and the practices of ethnography themselves.

Doing ethnography

While the practices of ethnography will be familiar to many readers, from experience or knowledge of methods, it is worth reflecting on what is involved in ethnography while discussing how the student ethnographers faired. We would argue that much of the social interactional processes of ethnography are glossed by designations such as "getting in", "getting on" and "getting out" (Buchanan, et al. 1988). In particular, while the competencies involved in (for example) impression management are frequently identified in the literature, they are seldom examined in depth as practical mundane activity (Bell, 2004).

Reflecting on the skills of our student ethnographers, we can characterise their ethnography very broadly into five different stages where different activities dominate. In the *organisation* phase access to the setting is obtained, and the fieldwork organised. Setbacks and contingencies can mean that organisation can be conducted *ad hoc* as a project progresses. A common piece of advice from fieldwork manuals is to use one's own connections to gain access: an approach followed by the mobile workshop group, who had a member who had originally worked as a mechanic helping them to gain access to his old workshop. More broadly (to our surprise) the groups found little difficulty gaining access - perhaps in part because of their ability to describe their involvement as a 'student project'.

Observation and participation involves making observations and interviews in the setting, alongside participation and prolonged study. Fieldnotes are taken de-

scribing the setting, as well as photographs, video and audio recordings. The prolonged observation that is key in fieldwork is not an activity that many of us normally do, and it can seem a disturbing and even rude activity. Yet observation is a
prevalent part of our everyday lives - we observe what people do when we cross
the road or queue in a shop. So many of the mundane practices of observation are
those that we know and use as part of our everyday lives. Indeed, even prolonged
observation is not that unusual, a newcomer to a job might 'shadow' the employee he is replacing.

The way in which the groups carried out their fieldwork adjusted to the possibilities of the different field sites. With the first group looking at learning, they
wanted a high concentration of children engaging in learning. They arranged access to a local science centre, where they followed classes around the centre. Alternatively, the group working with truck repairs visited a number of different
workshops on what they called 'educational' visits. This involved observations of
groups of workers at different workshops, and trailing mechanics as they went out
in the field and worked on repairs.

Central to observation during fieldwork is taking notes. While it might seem a
trivial point the form factor of a notebook can have subtle effects on note taking
and observation. The students spent considerable time discussing what *type* of
notebook to take. The physical appearance of a paper notebook (and in particular
its size) contributes to the 'strangeness' of fieldwork. The format of the notebook
also impacts what notes can be taken – a smaller notebook makes it harder to
write down long notes, but is more suitable for quickly jotting down short notes.
Since note taking has to be done during ongoing activity the ability to take notes
quickly is essential.

In the *transformation* phase the experiences of fieldwork are transformed into
materials that are more suitable for analysis. The classic example is the typing up
of fieldnotes at the end of each day - where observations are enriched for the record, brief notes taken at the time transformed into longer descriptions augmented
with further observations. Transformation can take on other forms such as selecting sections of video, transcribing audio, typing up handwritten notes, making
diagrams from photographs etc. Even though this frequently involves the mundane work of transcribing or typing up, it is a crucial stage in many ways. It is not
just that the fieldworker is immersing themselves in the data: transformation starts
the process of analysis as data is extracted or enriched through rewriting and representation. As one student commented about continually rewriting their fieldnotes:

> When I walked with them I tried to write down quick keywords. And then, when I got some
> time, maybe when we were in the office, I sat down and then wrote what I had seen. But it was
> kind of sloppy notes, it was difficult to read what I wrote myself. So every night afterwards I
> wrote out my notes. Then I wrote them in on the computer, and so on.

Analysis can take many different forms based on the orientation of the fieldworker. While the distinctiveness of *fieldwork* makes it perhaps the easiest part to

describe and discuss (and in discussions of methods it can often dominate) analysis is the crucible of ethnographic work. Analysis involves taking a stance on those observed and how they engage with the world. In CSCW, and in ethnomethodologically influenced ethnographies such as ours, a key question is *how someone can do what they do.*

In concrete terms during analysis there was much reading, rewriting, discussion, drawing and reorganisation in the students analysis. Much of the students work was simply extracting, re-representing comparison and re-reading:

> After the fieldstudy we wrote everything out and then everyone read the same and marked out those things that we considered relevant... It turned out to be something like 80 or 90 pages.

Broadly the students looked for themes that they could extract from the fieldwork – 'what might be interesting' - drawing as much on the experiences of the fieldwork as the notes themselves. One challenge here was that different fieldworkers had looked at different settings. As one student remarks in an analysis session:

> A: You know we have so many different settings, we got the airport, we got the boat testing central, or boat motor test [...]
>
> M: Well in that case we might be able to find some common patterns at least [..] Or deviant patterns which also would be interesting

For ourselves as analysts studying the students was challenging in that it highlighted our own analytic perspectives, perspectives not always shared by the students. This came to the fore in analysis sessions – the students generally tried to downplay the detail of their own observations, in favour of explanations based around psychology or managerial logic. Students would produce elaborate descriptions of the motivations or desires of those they had observed – projecting needs and cognition onto those they were studying which we argued they had few resources to confirm. Rather than addressing how those being studied did what they did, these explanations addressed more why they acted as they did. In turn, *managerialist descriptions* came from interviews with management in the studied organisations. In this form of analysis the students repeated management descriptions of problems and practices, at times in direct contradiction to what their own observations showed.

Lastly, in *writing up* the analysis is written into the final report on the fieldwork. The development of this text often takes place in parallel with the analysis, in that through writing about the data fieldworkers come to new understandings of what is in the data. Writing up thus draws upon transformed documents written in the field, and text produced by the analysis. Within anthropology the writing up phases of fieldwork continues to gain much analytic focus – the ethnographic text, and the presentation of the ethnographer and those studied has initiated much debate (Katz 2000). This has been less of an issue in CSCW, where questions of the writing up phase have mainly engaged with the specific *design* colour of CSCW: fieldwork may end up being presented to designers, and results worked through with designers to connect findings with those concerns. This can involve the ethnographer working as some sort of proxy for the user, or alternatively as a designer themselves. As we have mentioned, the nature of this interface is a recurring theme within CSCW and related fields. In the final reports it was clear that all the groups engaged in original ways with their fieldwork. One group's client, the mobile truck repair group, set the group the task of designing support for the repair of trucks at the side of the road rather than in a workshop. However, the groups' fieldwork questioned the need for this, and with the client's agreement they instead built a system that supported deciding *when* to repair a truck outside the workshop.

While we have set out ethnography and the students work in terms of a set of stages, they are more schematic holders for the practices of ethnography. In common with many other complex endeavours these activities span across different stages, and need not follow each other in a linear pattern. After all, ethnography is by its very nature a *discovering practice* – one does not know the end result until one gets there. It is a commonplace observation in the methods literature and confessional ethnographic accounts (Van Maanen 1988) that the retrospective accounts given in methods descriptions have only a schematic similarity to research as a prospective concern.

Writing ethnography

Fieldnotes are a central part of ethnographic practice, and have attracted attention in themselves with a number of volumes discussing how and what fieldnotes might be (Emerson, et al. 1995). Alongside their analytic and ethnographic work, the groups made heavy use of fieldnotes to discuss the settings. However, as we have remarked above, these fieldnotes were also shared amongst the class through a wiki. As experienced fieldworkers we had our own sensitivities to sharing fieldnotes, particularly in a system where the access to the fieldnotes was deliberately open. However, *all* the students typed up all their fieldnotes and put them online. At its peak, students were reading an average of 26 pages a week each, dropping to 7 in the week before they submitted their reports. Each student also entered an average of 6, usually lengthy, fieldnotes into the wiki. A number of students also collected photographs from the fieldsites, annotated those photographs, and interested them into the text. The flexibility in which photographs could be inserted into text supported reference to specific aspects of the photographs in the fieldnotes. The elaborate nature of the fieldnotes created by some of the students – with mixes of scanned documents, photos and text – suggests that the notes were not just produced for the author, but for other readers. The history of classroom wiki systems contains many failed systems (Guzdial and Rick 2000) and one could imagine a sensitivity to sharing fieldnotes preventing use of the system. As we had not set submitting fieldnotes as a requirement for the course, this comprehensive entering of data was noteworthy.

As described by (Scribner and Cole 1981), transforming the practices and technologies surrounding writing can have general consequences for how participants relate to text, and for the skills and competencies that are engaged with and learned. Although Scribner & Cole refer to more large-scale differences in literacy practices, a change as local and small scale as the introduction of a wiki – and the associated practices of writing that change along with it – could nevertheless have consequences that go beyond the mere organisation of textual work. With the students, one function of the wiki that became apparent was the way in which it supported and encouraged students' orientations towards relevant practices and competencies involved in fieldwork.

That is to say, the sharing of fieldnotes provided awareness amongst the students and advisors of each others' 'hidden work'. Fieldwork was mostly conducted individually. In the interviews the students talked about reading each others fieldnotes to get a sense of 'what a fieldnote was'. This was confirmed by the website logs which showed students reading each others' fieldnotes. Putting field notes into the wiki thus made individual member's production and work visible, both to other group-members and to the advisors. This also made non-use of the wiki visible and publicly accountable. The edit history on particular pages also made visible when others edited fieldnotes, and we noted that fieldnotes on the whole remained single authored, with little collaborative editing of notes.

The availability of fieldnotes was particularly valuable for supervisory meetings. Beginning each session with knowledge of students' work proved beneficial, as teachers knew what students were doing even in the absence of any submitted texts. Analytic notes posted by students would show, for example, how groups had analyzed their fieldnotes, the analytic concepts they had in play. For the instructors they could then respond to the students' choices of categories and strategies, seeing them for the ways in which they differently measured up to the sought after brand of design-oriented fieldwork. This instructive function of the open access to fieldnotes hinged on the responsive nature of teaching; teachers and students, that is, "interpret each others' actions and make, what seems to them, relevant responses" (Dyson 1999, p144). Just as students had access to disciplinary knowledge through the supervisors' instructions, the supervisors gained access to a context in which to formulate instructions through students' actions. The teacher could respond directly to students' own products, counter students' formulations of their own work, seeing in their notes qualities that they themselves had not the ability yet to see.

The effects of having an open collection of fieldnotes also supported students reading each others' fieldnotes and bringing their own notes into alignment with each other. One practice that spread from group to group, for example, was putting times to the left of each paragraph in the wiki, time-stamping different observations. A number of students also used 'smileys' and other email shortcuts, styles that they later went back and deleted as they found that others took a more serious tone in their notes. The shared fieldnotes also supported a 'ratchet effect' increasing the expressiveness of the students' fieldnotes. The students could learn from each others' fieldnotes what sort of things could constitute an observation. As with any practice is not simply one of coming into alignment with other students. The teachers endeavoured to review and comment on notes so as to guide the students so as to examine the better quality fieldnotes, and to emulate the best observational practices, rather than simply come to some average.

At times, though, less desirable practices spread between fieldnotes because of their perceived suitability – e.g. colour coding of fieldnotes according to importance featured in groups of students' notes. Moreover, the wiki proved less flexible in allowing teachers to comment on notes. As the only way to comment on fieldnotes was through editing the fieldnote itself, the supervisors felt it inappropriate to directly comment or edit the fieldnotes and instead commented on fieldnotes in the supervision meetings. As the teachers read all the fieldnotes this was perhaps a missed opportunity.

The fieldnotes in the wiki displayed a feature distinct from publicly available Internet wikis. The fieldnotes were not written as objective records of the fieldwork (if ever such a thing was possible). Rather, they were fieldnotes that made sense to their likely readers – predominantly the author of the fieldnote, but also the group of students collaborating in studying that particular fieldsite. Many of the details, jargon, names and such like would make sense to those involved in the fieldsite, but to ourselves and the advisors were much more opaque. The fieldnotes were written for situated reading. Unlike wiki pages written for 'anyone likely to read them' (for example wiki pages publicly available on the internet) these pages were written with a great deal of knowledge about their audience. In this aspect the fieldnotes have many similarities to other forms of record keeping studied within CSCW, in particular medical notes (Heath and Luff 1996). For example, the notes of the group studying the science center assume knowledge of the different exhibits, and how they were used:

> He walks over to the mobilia exhibition and clicks on the beard and glasses for half a minute. He seems bored. He walks into the color room and stays there for a minute or so. He comes out and watches a couple of girls and a guide while they play around with the nail rug.

This presented the 'outsiders problem' for ourselves as researchers using the fieldnotes. Often we could not understand fieldnotes, and without access to the situation in which they were produced (e.g. the exhibits) the fieldnotes were little help in understanding the fieldsite. The fieldnotes did not therefore stand as an objective resource for understanding the fieldwork, they were instead collaborative resources embedded in the conduct of group fieldwork.

A last point we will draw out about the use of fieldnotes concerns the use of the wiki as a co-present resource in the students interactions. As mentioned in the introduction to this paper, recently wikis have gained attention for their use as a distributed collaborative tool. Yet the students were co-present in the same university setting, and could easily meet to discuss their fieldwork, their use of the wiki and their fieldnotes. In these meetings the wiki pages were used as a physical resource to be drawn upon. The students printed out a large number of the pages of the wiki, and these would be distributed as they talked about their fieldwork.

Figure 2. Students in an analysis meeting sharing and talking around viewed wiki pages on their laptops and printed out.

Moreover, since the wiki pages were available online and all the students had laptops (rented to them as part of the program), the students would open specific wiki entries on their laptops as reference in conversation. This occurred particularly during analysis and writing fieldnotes would be 'talked up', read by the author and explained in the meeting and the relevance established for the writing and analysis. Since the wiki pages were commonly available, the student would talk around fieldwork notes read in common on their own laptops. While this sort of discussion could quickly and effectively sort out and ground discussion it left no traces in the wiki. As time went on this meant that the fieldnotes become less relevant since they did not contain discussions that worked up the fieldnotes' relevance. However, the students did keep notes from their meetings that they typed into the wiki as analytic notes. This meant that in the wiki alongside the fieldnotes the analysis process was partial documented.

Seeing ethnographically

With this schematic description of the students practices in place we can now engage more closely with the learning experiences of the students – in particular how they came to develop an ethnographic sense of what might be an interesting finding. As we have mentioned, we do not wish to overplay the similarities between the students work and the work of professional ethnographers. Indeed the students 'problem' in studying and conducting ethnography was subtly different from that of professional ethnographers. First, the students had to study the setting itself, and learn from those in the setting what was involved in doing that particular job. This was not simply learning about a site or simply collecting facts from the field: the students had to learn 'knowing-in-action' - the knowing inherent in competent and valid action in the setting. Second, the students were also learning the specific practices of fieldwork and ethnography. Since the students were conducting fieldwork as part of a course, there was a concern for producing the 'right' ethnography – not simply decoding ethnography as some sort of abstract process, but as what they could do to get them successfully through their course.

The skills of learning about a setting and the nature of that setting are interconnected. Ethnography is not the same in different arenas: an ethnographer must adjust their methods to each setting and in a sense learn the skills of ethnography afresh. An ethnographer does not observe in exactly the same way, or the exact same order every time. That ethnography cannot be learnt from a book is therefore not a mysterious but a very practical point: only by engaging in the adaptation of methods to a setting – and at times failing to understand a practice– can one come to learn what is involved in an ethnographic study.

The first part of the student's problem was to recognise, in the field, what might be something of interest for the research. We would liken the process of learning ethnography to that of 'learning to see'. In Goodwin's studies of professional vision (Goodwin 1994) he explores how it is that the work of professionals is often organised around their ability to see aspects of the world that we cannot normally see. Goodwin takes vision and rather than treat it as a cognitive ability of particular individuals, documents it as a socially organised professional practice. So, for example, in his study of archaeologists he showed how they can see colour differences in a sample of soil as suggestive of a particular historical artefact. While an uneducated observer may only see numbers on a computer screen, a professional oceanographer may see these as a 'nice' feature of a particular flow of seawater. Seeing for scientists and archaeologists is something that is learnt through instructed seeing – through the highlighting of signs and objects in fields – moving from figure to ground.

The work of the students in learning ethnography was in many ways learning to 'see ethnographically'. The students had to find, from each confusing fieldsite what was a 'feature' – what was something that could be discussed. To make this problem more complex, the students not only had to understand what might be an interesting feature, but had to do this through the participants point of view – how did they themselves organise their seeing, rather than (say) taking the descriptions given by their managers. This involved recognising what the objects and people did, and what relevance those people and objects had. For example, for the group studying truck repairs, they had to learn to see the different urgencies of different truck breakdowns, how truck repairs were scheduled, and the importance of that schedule in providing a good service.

In analysis meetings relevant categories would be highlighted by the supervisors from relevant 'features' in the data. Yet the students still struggled in understanding what aspects these 'features' had in common, and why those features had been chosen as of interest. It was only when the students later came to analysis that the relevance of particular findings were shown. In this way the students struggled with the documentary method of interpretation (Goodwin 1994). The highlighting of a feature in a field site goes on to highlight that feature and contrast it with other less interesting parts of the fieldwork. That in turn sets up a context of relevance – other parts of the fieldwork can be seen in relation to that feature and the parts can be seen to illustrate the original.

Another example: in one meeting the students discussed how the delivery drivers they were studying arranged and re-arranged the route they took when delivering packages. Often a new urgent package would come into the depot during the day, and the drivers had to go back to the depot to collect and then deliver that package. To deal with this the drivers would call up other drivers, even from competitor companies, and ask them to deliver their existing packages while they went back to the depot. On hearing this during an analysis session the advisor marked this out as a 'feature' – and described it as an example of 'cooperation within the profession'. He then urged the students to look at other examples of the drivers cooperating across companies. This feature structured the domain of scrutiny – it became one of 'driver collaboration', and other features could be picked out from the study with reference to 'driver collaboration'.

Alongside being able to 'see' features in the data, the students needed to be able to render those features in ways of interest. Goodwin points out the importance of graphical representations as ways of structuring, recording and communicating the features that are part of professional work. In the case of the students the problem was not so much graphically as textually rendering what they found in ways that were of interest. The first fieldnotes they produced were merely descriptions that missed out much of the interaction and details of the work. They produced maps of where things were, descriptions of what was done where - descriptions which focused on *what* people did rather than *how* they did their work (in contrast to (Katz 2000)).

This all said, we would not want to describe the students' emerging analytic skills as simply those of identifying and rendering 'interesting' observations. The development of seeing ethnographically, as we have put it, involves a growing sensibility in the observer - seeing not only that those events are interesting but that they cut with the problems of those involved in making sense of and acting in that social world. This in part involves drawing on an analytic approach, our own draws heavily on ethnomethodology, so as such we encouraged the students to draw on familiar analytic tropes, such as the procedural nature of work tasks or the importance of everyday routines. Yet we also wanted the students to move beyond cookie cutter analysis to creatively engage with what they saw - to generate understandings that came not from simply parroting theory but rather to form insights into the seen yet frequently unnoticed. Ethnomethodology is distinctive here in its focus on the description of practical action. This is not to say that the students could not have made work out of other analytic approaches, but our attempt to sensitising them alongside their short training in ethnomethodology, meant that they especially focused on these ordinary workplace methods.

Yet in common with teaching other complex activities that rely upon insight, the crux of the matter for analysis is not to rely upon the theoretical, but to move and differentiate with what each individual setting demands and teaches. We sought to tutor the students moving from the procedural to the insightful. That involves, drawing on Randall et al (2007), an ethnographic design sensibility where in a particular case one can engage with what is happening, but also turn in a manner that makes design possible - that can start the process of creative engagement with particular members' problems, or inventing new forms of using technology and working. In this sense their work was interdisciplinary, but this would somewhat over academicaise their practices – rather their problems were uncovering 'whats and hows' that had relevance for later design. The problem of design relevance then was one that needed to be managed in each analytic moment - moving from 'interesting observations' to analytic finding.

It was in this work that the students developing professional competence could be seen by ourselves and the teachers in their ability to see and talk about our discipline's workaday objects – in this case interesting ethnographic findings. While we have referred to Goodwin focus on vision *per se*, the instructive practices he describes more broadly – what he calls "the interactive organisation of apprenticeship" (Goodwin 2007, p57) – demonstrate how interaction can be pedagogically by virtue of developing shared orientations to common "domains of scrutiny". So while it may seem unusual to summarise the ethnographic skills of our students in terms of 'seeing' this focuses our own analytic attention on this first important analytic steps. Of course, these *seeings* are only the start of analytic work, yet this crucial skill crystallised the many different skills the students needed to learn and engage with.

Discussion

Documenting this course and the students work gives us an opportunity to reflect on aspects of teaching ethnographic work. One distinctive aspect of the course we studied was the almost luxurious time given to the students to learn ethnography. Perhaps more distinctive, however, was the focus on letting students conduct ethnography 'all the way through' - going into the field, engaging with a domain of practice, interacting with more experienced fieldworkers, and writing this up as a report. In the field (as well as in analysis) the students needed to work out themselves how to proceed. Indeed, even the advisors and ourselves needed to learn each different, and new, setting and how it could be approached. This gave students not only an opportunity to learn methods but also a sense of why ethnography is the way it is, and the complexities (and value) of practices that can be uncovered. The shared nature of the fieldwork experiences – supported by the shared wiki and analysis sessions – opened up the experiences for reflection by both students and teachers. Since the teachers could see the fieldnotes as they were entered, they could comment and observe, crucially making their observations relevant to where the students were now, not just where the teachers intended to take the class. This also supported interaction and input between students. However this seldom took the role of direct interventions in each others work; rather it was a 'ratchet' effect of students exploring and seeing others practice and attempting to emulate this in their own work. As we mentioned however this could cause problems if unhelpful practices were duplicated.

In terms of concrete lessons for the teaching of ethnography we make three points. First, ethnographic courses should include as much as possible, a focus as much as possible on practical ethnographic and analytic skills. While it is certainly easier for those teaching courses to rely upon the conventional lecture format (of which we have been guilty ourselves), much of the essence of ethnography can be lost. As we have documented, with support students can engage with settings and learn practical and analytic skills. Second, we would argue for the value of an open resource of fieldnotes and analytic notes. In our case the wiki supported a range of rich interactions around fieldnotes that helped support the learning process and allowed better support by supervisors. Lastly, we would suggest that the teaching of ethnographic practices is conducted over sufficient time to support a supervised iterative engagement with the setting. Obviously, it would be impractical for many courses to have as lengthy a ethnographic component as this case, yet having an iterative engagement over time is important to allow students to make mistakes, return to their material, and be supervised during this process.

Perhaps most important of all, the study underlines the value of teaching ethnography as part of CSCW. While the students did not become expert ethnographers in two months, they gained a much deeper understanding of how to engage with understanding a setting, before coming to think about design. This is perhaps the most important student outcome and a core lesson of CSCW – the connected nature of the technical and the social. We have discussed this in terms of students 'coming to see' ethnographically. The joint analysis sessions that were run with the students were most valuable for this, in that the students and advisors shared the work of going through the data trying to understand what might be interesting about the practice under study. The students' final reports demonstrated a subtlety of understanding about how work is engaged with and carried out in the different settings under study something missing from the initial fieldnotes. Perhaps more important than the method *per se*, the course engaged the students with understanding the complexities of work practice: a valuable input into their future technical careers. This we saw as the real contribution of our teaching: how our students began to see what ethnography might be and how they might systematically understand others' lifeworld, and design taking that into account.

Although we have focused in this paper on the teaching experience around ethnography, we have explored how to better support technically the students collaboration around fieldnotes and wiki entries. The wiki provided considerable support for co-present interactions around fieldnotes. However, there is currently little support for commenting and annotating pages. This meant that for teachers (and at times even for the groups themselves) it was not easy to comment on fieldnotes apart from actually editing the notes. We have recently added this ability within our wiki to produce a more multi-layered text by attaching notes to areas in the wiki text commentary can be added to fieldnotes, or any wiki pages, without editing the pages themselves. This also supports a form of 'anchored chat', in that conversations can take place around fieldnotes in the notes.

Figure 3. Screenshots from the extensions to the wiki. The text notes allows annotations to be made to the text, while the awareness tool provides an overview of who has edited the wiki and when.

Second, we wanted to address the need for better awareness of the group's activity – a common problem addressed by awareness displays. From the study we could see that reading and noticing others fieldnotes allowed for self-assessment of progress with students comparing their progress to the class. To support this we have designed an awareness display that shows who has edited what allowing editors to compare their own level of contribution to others.

Conclusions

The focus of this paper has been on a practice well known to CSCW practitioners. Through studying the attempts of a class coming to learn those practices, we have attempted to cast new light on what is involved in fieldwork, both the mundane practices of organisation, note taking, observation, and analysis, but also the analytic skill of 'coming to see'. We have explored at length one class, using their experiences to both describe ethnographic practice, but also how ethnography can be taught as part of CSCW classes.

Teaching any practice is an opportunity to reflect upon that practice and its conduct. A secondary theme of this paper has been to explicate some mundane practices of ethnography, and to invite reflection on the distinctive practices of ethnography as part of CSCW. In particular, the experiences here with sharing fieldnotes are suggestive broadly of how better to support the collaborative practices of design ethnography. We in turn also offer this as a contribution to ongoing debates concerning the status of design ethnography – emphasising the grounded and methodical practices of insight that ethnography feature. In closing, ethnography is a complex professional practice of which collaboration is a key part. In this paper we have explored how ethnography is not only a key part of CSCW – as a core method and approach – but as a potential site for enhancing the teaching of CSCW, and engaging future practitioners and academics with the nature of work practice and design.

Acknowledgements

The work discussed in this paper was supported by the Wallenberg Global Learning Network II. The authors would also like to thank the students who took part, Alexandra Weilenmann for her help and insights during the project, and Eric Laurier for comments on an earlier draft.

References

Anderson, R. J. (1994): Representations and requirements: The value of ethnography in system design. *Human-computer interaction*, Vol. 9, pp. 151-182.
Bell, E. (2004): The negotiation of a working role in organisational ethnography. *International Journal of Social Research Methodology*, Vol. 2, no. 1, pp. 17-37.
Beyer, H. and K. Holtzblatt (1997): *Contextual Design : A Customer-Centered Approach to Systems Designs*. Morgan Kaufmann Publishers.
Bowers, J., G. Button and W. Sharrock (1995): Workflow from within and without. In: *Proceedings of ECSCW '95. Stockholm, Sweden*: Kluwer Academic Publishers.
Buchanan, D., D. Boddy and J. McCalman (1988): Getting in, getting on and getting back. In: *Doing research in organisations*. Routledge.
Button, G. (2000): The Ethnographic Tradition and Design. *Design Studies*, Vol. 4, no. 21, pp. 319-332.
Charlin, B., K. Mann and P. Hansen (1998): The many facets of problem based learning: A framework for understanding and comparison. *Medical teacher*, Vol. 20, no. 4, pp. 323-330.
Coffey, A., B. Holbrook and P. Atkinson (1996): Qualitative Data Analysis: Technologies and Representations. *Sociological Research Online*, Vol. 1, no. 1.
Crabtree, A. (2003): *Designing Collaborative Systems: A Practical Guide to Ethnography*. Heidlberg: Springer.
Da Lio, E., L. Fraboni and T. Leo (2005): TWiki-based facilitation in a academic community of practice. In: *Proceedings symposium on Wiki technology*. ACM Press, pp. 85-111.
Dourish, P. (2006): Implications for Design. In: *Proceedings of CHI 2006*. ACM Press.
Dyson, A. (1999): Transforming transfer: Unruly children, contrary texts, and the persistence of the pedagogical order. *Review of Research in Education*, Vol. 24, pp. 143-171.

Emerson, R. M., R. I. Fretz and L. L. Shaw (1995): *Writing ethnographic fieldnotes*. Chicago University Press.

Forsythe, D. (1999): "It's just a matter of common sense": ethnography as invisible work. *Computer supported collaborative work*, Vol. 8, no. 1-2, pp. 127-145.

Goodwin, C. (1994): Professional Vision. *American Anthropologist*, Vol. 96, no. 3, pp. 606-633.

Goodwin, C. (2007): Participation, stance and affect in the organisations of activities. *Discourse and Society*, Vol. 18, no. 1, pp. 15-73.

Guzdial, M. and J. Rick (2000): Recognizing and Supporting Roles in CSCW. In: *Proceedings of CSCW 2000*. ACM Press, pp. 261-268.

Harper, R. H. R. (2000): The Organisation in Ethnography: A Discussion of Ethnographic Fieldwork Programs in CSCW. *Comput. Supported Coop. Work*, Vol. 9, no. 2, pp. 239-264.

Have, P. T. (2003): Teaching students observational methods: visual studies and visual analysis. *Visual Studies*, Vol. 18, no. 1, pp. 29-35.

Heath, C. and P. Luff (1996): Documents and professional practice: bad organisational reasons for good clinical records. In: *Proceedings of CSCW'96*. ACM, pp. 354-363.

Katz, J. (2000): From How to Why: On Luminous Description and Causal Inference in Ethnography. *Ethnography*, Vol. 2, no. 4, pp. 443-473.

Kersenboom, S. (1995): *Word, Sound Image: The Life of the Tamil Text*. Oxford: Berg.

Luff, P., J. Hindmarsh and C. Heath (eds.) (2001): *Workplace studies: recovering work practice and informing system design*. Cambridge University Press, Cambridge, UK.

Lymer, G., J. Lundin, B. Brown, M. Rost and L. E. Holmquist (2007): Web based platforms in co-located practice – The use of a wiki as support for learning and instruction. In: *Proceedings of CSCL 2007*. Lawrence Erlbaum Associates, In Press.

Maanen, J. V. (1988): *Tales from the field: on writing ethnography*. Chicago: University of Chicago Press.

Randall, D., R. Harper and M. Rouncefield (2007): *Fieldwork for Design: Theory and Practice*. London: Springer.

Scribner, S. and M. Cole (1981): *The psychology of literacy*. Harvard University Press.

Sharrock, W. and J. A. Hughes (2001): Ethnography in the workplace: Remarks on its theoretical bases. *Team Ethno*, Vol. 1, no. 1.

Sommerville, I. (1993): Integrating ethnography into the requirements engineering process. In: *Proceedings of the international symposium on requirements engineering*. Los Alamitos, Calif.: IEEE CS Press.

Sotirin, P. (1999): Bringing the outside in: ethnography in/beyond the classroom. In: *Proceedings of the annual meeting of the national communication association*.

Trujillo, N. (1999): Teaching ethnography in the twenty-fifth century using collaborative learning. *Journal of contemporary ethnography*, Vol. 28, no. 6, pp. 705-719.

Wasson, C. (2000): Ethnography in the field of design. *Human Organisation*, Vol. 59, no. 4, pp. 377-388.

Weinberg, J. and M. Stephens (2002): Participatory design in a human computer interaction course: teaching ethnography methods to computer scientists. In: *Proceedings of SIGCSE 02*. ACM Press, pp. 237-247.

L. Bannon, I. Wagner, C. Gutwin, R. Harper, and K. Schmidt (eds.).
ECSCW'07: Proceedings of the Tenth European Conference on Computer Supported Cooperative
Work, 24-28 September 2007, Limerick, Ireland
© Springer 2007

Cues to Common Knowledge

N. Bryan-Kinns, P. G. T. Healey, D. Papworth, and A. Vaduuva
IMC Group, Department of Computer Science, Queen Mary, University of
London
Mile End, London. E1 4NS
nickbk@dcs.qmul.ac.uk

Abstract. We show that asynchronous collaboration can be made more effective by providing cues to common knowledge. We demonstrate this by empirically comparing two
user interfaces used to support collaborative work. Our position is that effective collaboration is characterized by more co-ordinated and speculative interaction, and that cues to
common knowledge help participants develop common ground for interaction. We also
suggest that more effective collaboration is indicated by increased reliance on expectations of others' knowledge which is characterized by implicit references to shared documents and ideas.

Introduction

Collaboration; the stuff that happens between people when they work together.
But how do we understand collaborative activity and design for it? There is a
plethora of research on understanding collaboration from approaches which de-
compose the cognitive structures of collaboration (Johnson and Hyde, 2003) to
task-agnostic work which focuses on the nature of the communicative media utilized in collaboration (Watts and Monk, 1998). We can analyze collaborative activities as distributed cognitive systems (Hutchins and Klausen, 1996) and use this
to understand how information is shared and transformed in the system. We could
think of collaborative activities as activity systems transforming objects in a work
context (Issroff and Scanlon, 2002) in order to understand the conflicts inherent
within a system. The content of communication could be analyzed (Olsen et al.,
1993) to tell us whether we focus more on the technological issues than the actual
work we are attempting to undertake. All these approaches, and more, shed light

on the nature of our interaction with other, and with the systems we use to support us. They can be used to direct our design decisions, and to allow us to evaluate the systems we build. For instance, a range of key attributes of systems that support us in collaborating with others who are not in the same space have been developed over the last twenty years or so. These emphasize the importance of features such as shared and consistent representations (Robertson, 1997), and awareness mechanisms (Dourish and Bellotti, 1992; Gutwin and Greenberg, 2002). By designing representations which are shared and consistent between remote spaces we reflect the nature of co-located collaboration where we share the same aural, and to some extent visual space. Similarly, awareness mechanisms attempt to support ongoing awareness of others' activities even when we are not co-located. Such awareness helps to co-ordinate the collaborative activity and, in remote collaboration, is typically supported through representations of the current activity of others, and indicators of past contributions. Such representations are central not only to work oriented collaboration, but also to support creative collaborations (Bryan-Kinns and Healey, 2007). Gutwin and Greenberg's approach focuses on real-time aspects of workspace awareness, in particular, the who, what, and where questions. For instance, who is present in the shared workspace at the moment, what are they doing, and where are they looking at the moment. Designing user interfaces that allow participants to answer these questions gives collaborators an awareness of what is going on in the group on a moment by moment basis. However, our understanding of group work is not just informed by what is going on at one moment, but also by what has happened in the past. In particular, we rely on presumptions about who knows what about what has gone on, and beliefs about what we think other people know about what we know (cf. Clark, 1996). The question then becomes one of how to support the development and sustenance of *common knowledge* in collaborations – the set of beliefs individuals have about others and their beliefs – that enables communication and collaboration to progress without continuous affirmation and reaffirmation of understanding.

Shared Information or Common Knowledge?

The distinction between information that is shared and information that is mutually-known to be shared is illustrated by the Conway paradox (see Barwise, 1989). Consider two people, Ann and Bob, playing cards. Each has an ace. They each know, amongst other things, that 'at least one of us has an ace'. This is shared information in the sense that they both know the same thing. Now, if another person, Claire say, asks them "Do you know anything about other's cards?" they will answer "no". Moreover, they will still answer "no" if Claire asks the same question a second or third time.

Consider what happens if Claire now tells Ann and Bob that "at least one of you has an ace". What was shared -but independently known- information is now mutually-known i.e., Ann and Bob both know that the other knows that "at least one of you has an ace". From each individual's point of view very little has changed. Claire has only told them something they each already knew. If Claire now asks, as before, "Do you know anything about other's cards?" they will again answer "no". However, this initial response now has the effect of indicating to them the additional information that each of them has an ace. They each now know that the other's "no" entails that the other has an ace (since, if they didn't they would be able to answer "yes" to the first question).

One of the difficulties in modeling common knowledge is that it involves this problematic form of self-reference - my knowledge of your knowledge involves your knowledge of my knowledge and so on. Clark and Marshall (1981) adopted what is known as the shared environment response to this problem. Instead of securing 'full' common knowledge we use the cues available to us as a basis on which common knowledge could reasonably be assumed. The simplest ground for such mutual-belief is physical co-presence. If I can see a cup between us, and I can see that you can see it too, then we can (defeasibly) assume that we both know there is a cup between us. Likewise if someone says "at least one of you has an ace" to us we can, all things being equal, assume that we mutually-believe that that at least one of us has an ace.

The grounding model, developed by Clark and co-workers (e.g. Clark, 1996) explores the processes through which people provide one-another with evidence for establishing the layers of mutual-beliefs about common knowledge that are necessary for effective communication. Various levels can be distinguished. For example, we might both know that something was said but not what was said. Or we might both know what was said but not what it meant. For example, Clark and Brennan (1991) defined four distinct states of grounding with respect to an utterance:

State 0: B didn't notice that A uttered any u.

State 1: B noticed that A uttered some u (but wasn't in state 2).

State 2: B correctly heard u (but wasn't in state 3).

State 3: B understood what A meant by u.

The central focus of the grounding model is understanding how people manipulate the shared environment to achieve these different levels of mutual belief (Clark, 1996). In most of these analyses the focus is on synchronous conversational interactions where people can provide each other with particularly direct forms of linguistic and paralinguistic evidence that they understand each other. There are difficulties in directly applying notions of common ground to the design and evaluation of synchronous collaboration (Koschmann and LeBaron, 2003), but we believe that it can nonetheless be used in a productive way in design.

Brennan (1998) exploited the grounding model to design system feedback that provides cues to the current level of grounding that has been reached with respect to the user's goals. Healey and Bryan-Kinns (2000) extended this approach to modeling the role of artifacts in supporting common-knowledge in asynchronous collaboration.

In this paper we report on an experimental exploration of the impact, on collaboration, of cues that are designed to help people maintain mutual-beliefs about the current state of that collaboration. We start our journey with a description of the experiment itself. We then move on to hear the results of our experiment and draw these into discussion. Our journey ends with the conclusion in which we set out the plans for further explorations in the domain of support for remote collaboration.

The Experiment

In order to investigate the effects of providing cues to grounding state on the effectiveness of collaboration in a shared workspace we distinguish three classes of cues that could be simply graphically represented in a computer based interface:

- *First Order*: Cues to the activities of an individual in an environment. For example; icons indicating whether an email has been read, forwarded or replied to.
- *Second Order*: Cues to the activities of others in an environment. For example, the read receipt indication that someone has received and opened an email.
- *Third Order*: Cues that support mutual-beliefs about people's activities in an environment. For example, a conversation about an email that everyone received.

Hypothesis

If the maintenance of mutual-beliefs about the current state of a joint activity plays an important role in collaboration then, we predict, third order cues should have a positive impact on it. In particular we would predict that increased support for mutual-belief should lead to:

- *Less conservative contributions* – more activity related communication, and more discussion than in ineffective collaboration. For us, communication in effective collaboration focuses on the activity at hand, rather than the technological or co-ordination problems that need to be resolved in order to collaborate.
- *Co-ordinated use of artifacts* – participants share ownership of artifacts and manipulate each others' artifacts. This moves beyond reading others' contributions as it entails explicitly adding to, or referring to, each others' contributions. Such activity relies on a shared understanding of the public events that have occurred so far, and an understanding of what is important to the current state of the joint activity, and an understanding of what is

meant by the content of the artifacts. All of these rely on the existence of common ground between participants.

- *Less reliance on explicit references to artifacts* – rather than referring to artifacts explicitly, there is an increased reliance on assumptions about common knowledge i.e. assumptions about others' knowledge of the existence of artifacts in the workspace, their content, and their meaning.

Materials

For this experiment two versions of a shared workspace application were developed: Npathy and Mpathy. They were designed to be functionally equivalent, and to differ in the cues they provide about the pattern and state of communication, or grounding, amongst the users of the shared workspace as follows:

- Npathy: 1st and 2nd order cues
- Mpathy: 1st, 2nd, and 3rd order cues

The shared workspaces Npathy and Mpathy were developed in Mushroom (Kindberg et al., 1996) – a CSCW architecture that supports the development of applications for collaborative work based around a notion of shared workspaces. In Mushroom shared objects embody both client and server functionality and are replicated in a 'persistence' domain. In the experimental setting, the Npathy and Mpathy workspaces were individual clients per subject, which had a view onto the relevant part of the persistence domain for their subject group's data. Two user manuals were produced, one for each version of the system.

Npathy

The Npathy workspace provides a title bar at the top, a shared workspace area for documents, a command bar at the bottom and a list of users (referred to as the user menu) on the left hand side as illustrated in figures 1a and 1b. The user menu consists of a strip of icons of other workspace users with their name and, where available, a thumbnail picture of them. These icons change colour to indicate who is currently active in the workspace during a given session. Documents are immutable[1] and represented by different icons according to their type (memo, test, image, document). Each document also has three text fields displayed below the icon showing creation date, author and subject. Small icons were also added to documents as iconic 'superscripts' to indicate if a document has an attachment or

---

[1] The Npathy and Mpathy applications were actually versions of an application developed for the support of Diabetic patient care (Kindberg et al., 1999). A key design constraint inherited from the medical application domain was that the body of a medical record or other document should not be altered once introduced into the workspace. Nonetheless, effective support for collaboration requires that comments and notes can be made on each document. In Npathy and Mpathy these functions were supported by functions for adding marginal notes or annotations to the existing documents or creating a new document that cross referenced another through an attachment mechanism.

annotation. Because annotations could be added at any point, colour was used (red) to signal if they were new.

Although all workspace users share the same set of documents and people, their view of the workspace varies. Firstly, Npathy allows individual users to arrange documents in the workspace according to their preferences by dragging the document icons across the workspace (all documents are always visible in the workspace). They can also choose to rearrange the order of the icons on the user menu. In addition, each user receives information about their pattern of activity in the workspace. A tick icon is added to each document in the workspace that the user has read during a current or previous session. Furthermore, where the author of a document has elected to deny a user access to that document this is indicated to them through a padlock icon attached to the document.

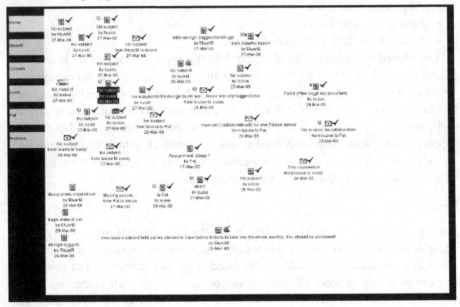

Figure 1a: Screenshot of Npathy

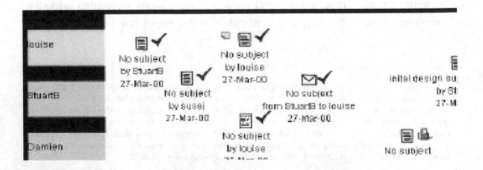

Figure 1b: Detail of Npathy

Mpathy

The Mpathy application reproduces all the document information available in Npathy and additionally provides extra cues about the pattern of collaborative activity with respect to the workspace. As illustrated in figure 2, Mpathy adopted a more structured approach to the representation of the document workspace. Instead of allowing users to individually determine the position of documents we adopted a time based matrix representation which reflects the model developed in Healey and Bryan-Kinns (2000) - in Mpathy, a timeline is associated with each user. As each user contributes new documents they are ordered along the timeline according to the dates on which they were introduced into the workspace.

The document workspace in Mpathy provides all users with information about the level of grounding within the group for each document or artifact. Firstly, while Npathy only shows if a user themselves has read a document, Mpathy also shows whether each other member of the workspace has read the document by displaying ticks on the corresponding part of their timeline. For instance, in figure 2, both *C Day* and the *Cardiothoracist* have read the *Referral letter* sent by the *Cardiologist* on *11 Jun 1998*. Secondly, while Npathy only shows a user if they are denied access to a document, Mpathy also shows all other users' level of access to a document. For example, in figure 2 we see that the *Optician* does not have access to any of the documents displayed. Thirdly, in Npathy, the intended recipient of a memo can only be determined by reading the memo whereas in Mpathy the intended recipient of a memo is directly indicated to all users. For example, the recipient of the *Referral letter* sent by the *Cardiologist* on *11 Jun 1998* is illustrated by the grey arrow pointing to *C Day* in figure 2.

Aside from the addition of cues to grounding the other major difference between Mpathy and Npathy is that in Npathy all document icons are visible to the user, whereas in Mpathy users have to scroll to find document icons. This difference, and its possible impact on user behaviour, is returned to in the discussion section.

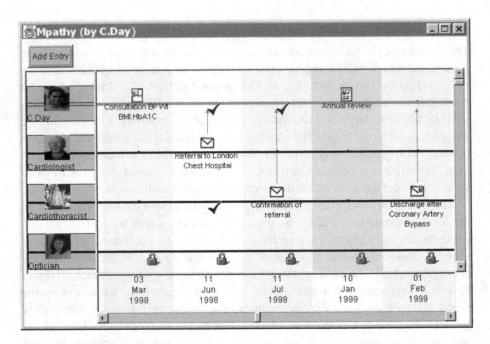

Figure 2: Mpathy user interface

Subjects

Thirty subjects were recruited from an MSc. class in Computer Supported Co-operative Work. They carried out the evaluation as part of a coursework. They were randomly assigned into 10 groups (5 for Mpathy, and 5 for Npathy) of 3 with a single workspace per group. In order to introduce some role asymmetries and promote subjects' use of access control on documents all groups also included three of the authors. One author was present to provide user help, another provided technical support in the event of crashes or bugs and the third set and marked the assignment.

Procedure

User manuals for Mpathy and Npathy were distributed to all the subjects. Subjects were instructed that they should collaborate, using the workspace, to produce 3 documents:

- A list of design problems ranked according to their severity.
- A list of design suggestions ranked according to their potential to improve the effectiveness of the workspace.
- A list of 'bugs' ranked according to their severity.

It was emphasized that as far as possible all assignment related collaboration should take place in the workspace. Subjects were informed that the assessment of the coursework would be based only on the documents in the workspace, and the amount of activity in the workspace. They were given 14 days to complete the assignment.

Experimental Design

The experiment was carried out with a between subjects factors of user interface (Mpathy/ Npathy). We assumed that each individual in the experiment provides independent data which constrains the dependent measures we can use. The dependent measures derived from our characterization of effective collaboration outlined at the start of this section were:

- *Number of contributions* (documents and annotations). Increased contribution of documents indicates to us an increased amount of co-ordination between participants and an increase in the willingness to communicate.
- *Average size of documents*. In terms of efficiency of collaboration, the size of the documents is related to the number of contributions. A small number of long contributions indicates a conservative attitude to collaboration which is less co-ordinated than situations in which there are a large number of short contributions. With large numbers of short contributions participants indicate a willingness to interact with others and to share the work space. Moreover, they rely on the user interface and shared knowledge to help them navigate the shared documents. Anecdotally we suggest that large numbers of small documents makes the collaboration more akin to conversation than email or letter writing.
- *Number of times documents were read*. Unlike the number of contributions, we argue that increases in the number of times documents are re-read indicates less efficient collaboration. For us, increased document reading would indicate reduced knowledge about the content of each document is i.e. people repeatedly read documents to remind themselves of the content. When people increasingly read others' documents it indicates a willingness to collaborate, but also a lack of shared knowledge about the content of the shared documents.
- *Number of cross-references between documents*. Creating cross-references between documents implies an understanding of the content of both documents that are linked. Where the documents are created by different people this indicates effective collaboration which relies on common knowledge about the content of both documents.

In addition, dependent measures of the topics of textual content of the documents were developed drawing on previous analyses of shared document creation and editing (Olson et al., 1993). We developed three categories of document content topic:

(1) *References to other documents* – where subjects refer to the content of other documents or previous discussion. This is divided into whether subjects referred to documents *explicitly* e.g. *"part of my 'discussion' suggestion in my 27/03/2000 document"*, or *implicitly* e.g. *"I agree with most of what J. said"*. From our position, implicit references indicate more effective communication as there is more reliance on assumptions about others' knowledge of the content and meaning of documents i.e. there is more shared knowledge about the public events so far.

(2) *Requests for action* – where subjects request action from others e.g. *"I suggest we all put onto the workspace our ideas and then take it from there"*. High numbers of requests for action indicate to us uncoordinated activity where subjects have to explicitly co-ordinate their action rather than relying on assumptions about shared goals and plans.

(3) *System related issues* – where subjects discuss technical difficulties with the system or test out its features e.g. *"just testing out the memo feature"*. A high proportion of system related discussion would indicate that the design of the interface is interfering with the interaction. This is essentially a group measure, and not related to the provision of cues to common knowledge per se, but provides us with an indication of whether there are system related issues confounding our results.

Results

One group from the Mpathy condition failed to carry out the assignment and they were dropped from the analysis. A criterion level of 0.05 was adopted for all statistical tests. To preserve statistical power we analyse throughout by individual rather than group. A statistical issue that arises here is whether it is appropriate to treat the observations as independent. For measures such as number of 'read' accesses to a document the assumption that the individual is the unit of analysis seems appropriate. However, for a measure like frequency of requests for action it is unclear. The fact that a group contains one particularly active participant who makes a lot of requests might increase the activity of each other participant in that group. Although these are logically and causally independent –nothing about my making a request directly entails that you will make a request (although it might directly cause you to make an answer)- they might nonetheless be correlated. This is an issue for any analysis of human-human interaction in which the presumption is that one person's activities (utterances, gestures, etc.) will affect those of others. Fully addressing this problem would require a much larger sample size. The main risk for present purposes is an increase in Type I errors or 'false positives' in the results reported below. However, as it happens the measures most likely to be affected by this problem show no reliable difference (see Table 1).

Logs of activity on the system were collected for a 45 hour period prior to the deadline. This period was chosen both because the subjects would have become more experienced with using the system by this point and the approaching deadline meant that higher levels of activity would occur. The global statistics for this period show that there were a total of 2000 object accesses of which 57% were Read accesses, 34% Modifications and 8% Creations.

The number of documents or annotations created by each individual in the two conditions was calculated. This was entered into a one-way analysis of variance with application type (MPathy vs. Npathy) as a single between subjects factor. This showed a reliable main effect of interface ($F(1,25)=6.01$, $p=0.02$) with subjects in using the Npathy workspace making an average of 5.1 contributions each and subjects using the Mpathy workspace contributing an average of 11.1 documents each.

The number of times each individual made a read access to any document in the workspace was calculated. This was analyzed in an analysis of variance with workspace type as a between subjects factor. This showed no reliable difference in average number of read accesses for users of Mpathy (59%) or Npathy (57%) ($F(1,25)=2.47$, $p=0.12$)

The average size of documents (number of lines of text in the document) created by participants in the two conditions was calculated. The showed no reliable difference in average size of documents for participants of Mpathy (6.88) or Npathy (8.61) ($F(1,25)=0.89$, $p=0.37$).

The average number of cross-references made between documents was calculated which showed no reliable difference between Mpathy (4) and Npathy (1.2) ($F(1,25)=4.26$, $p=0.07$).

Table 1 and figure 3 illustrate the results of analyses of document content topics in terms of the previously detailed categories: (1) References to other documents (Explicit or Implicit), (2) Requests for action, and (3) System related topics. Table 1 shows the average number of occurrences of each topic followed by the percentage of the overall identified topics. Figure 3 shows the average occurrences of topics as a percentage of overall topics identified, and the variance of occurrences between groups. None of these showed a significant difference in document content between Npathy and Mpathy.

Condition	Explicit	Implicit	Request	System
Npathy	64 (41%)	15 (11%)	34 (21%)	43 (27%)
Mpathy	52 (34%)	20 (13%)	37 (22%)	33 (31%)

Table 1: Average numbers of topics of document content per condition

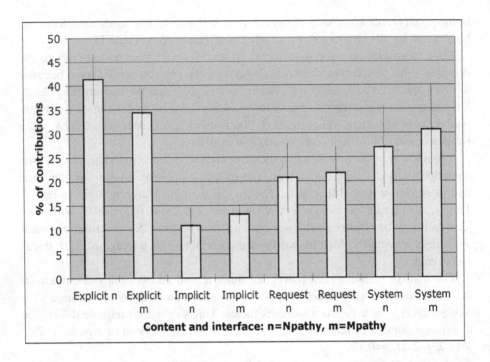

Figure 3: Average percentage and variance of topics of contributions in different conditions

Discussion

This paper examines the effect of cues to common knowledge on the effective-ness of collaboration. We compared one user interface which provided 3 levels of cues about shared information to one which only provided 2 levels. Consistent with our expectations, we found that the groups who were provided with an extra level of cues to common knowledge did indeed collaborate more effectively as characterised by increased contributions, increased co-ordinated use of docu-ments, and relatively more implicit references to common knowledge. These indi-cators are discussed in the following paragraphs, but, given the nature of the two user interfaces examined, caution must be exercised before making assumptions about the critical differences between the two user interfaces. We designed the interfaces to provide different cues to possible grounding with reference to arti-facts, in doing so, we necessarily created interfaces which were different in sev-eral respects, not just which cues to grounding were visible. For instance, partici-pants could see all document icons in Npathy, but not Mpathy, participants could exercise control over where icons were placed in Npathy compared to Mpathy, and Mpathy made time a prominent aspect of the interface. We discuss these differences later in this section and argue that whilst any of these could have caused the differences we found, the overall results are consistent with our expectations that providing cues to common knowledge increases the effectiveness of collaboration.

Before launching into a discussion of the results, we would like to highlight that we found that both groups of participants performed the same amount of reading of documents, as indicated by there being no significant difference between the average number of read accesses by participants ($F(1,25) =2.47$, $p=0.12$). This indicates that although Npathy users contributed fewer documents, they had to read each document more often which may be because it either contained several points of information (which may have been kept in individual documents in Mpathy), or it was harder to identify which documents were pertinent. Our analysis of the size of documents indicates that there were probably not more points per document in Npathy as the documents were, on average, similar in size to those in Mpathy. Either way, it points to more inefficient collaboration in Npathy users as documents have to be read each document more often than in Mpathy.

More contributions

In the experiment Mpathy users contributed almost twice as many documents as Npathy users (Mpathy average: 11.1 contributions, Npathy average: 5.1 contributions), ($F(1,25) =6.01$, $p=0.02$). This, coupled with the similarity in the average size of documents between Mpathy and Npathy, and the lack of any significant difference between the topics of communication indicates that collaboration was more efficient in that participants were more able to contribute. The task set to the participants was to evaluate the system and produce a list of bugs as a group. This group activity requires discussion in order to develop the shared list of bugs, and discussion necessarily involves communication. The increased number of contributions in Mpathy is an indication that providing cues to common knowledge supports greater communication and so greater discussion.

More co-ordinated use of documents

Not only were there more documents created in Mpathy than Npathy, but participants also annotated more documents (Mpathy 37% documents annotated, Npathy 11% documents annotated). Moreover, anecdotally there were (non-significantly) more cross-references made between documents in Mpathy (average per group: 4) than Npathy (average: 1.2). We suggest that just by providing more cues to common knowledge, participants became more engaged with the artifacts in the collaborative environment. We interpret this as more focused use of the information – in commenting on a point, participants annotated the document itself rather than creating a new document and explicitly referring to the point. Again, there were less contributions in Npathy anyway, so the increased annotation in Mpathy indicates that the overall level of engagement with the material is higher when cues to common knowledge are provided.

Explicit references to documents

Although not significant, there are indications that explicit references to documents were more likely in Npathy (41%) than in Mpathy (34%). This indicates to us that the level of common knowledge established during the collaboration was greater for participants using Mpathy than those using Npathy as they did not have to rely on explicitly referring to documents during discussions (which, as discussed previously, there were more of). Assumptions about common knowledge are key to the success and efficiency of collaboration. The key point here is that by providing 3rd order cues to common knowledge about who has read and annotated documents, the assumed common knowledge about the activity is increased i.e. there is greater understanding of what has happened in the group. Speculatively, the slight increase in implicit references to document content in Mpathy (13%) compared to Npathy (11%) weakly supports our position that participants were relying on assumptions about common knowledge.

The timeline in Mpathy

Mpathy has a time based user interface, whereas Npathy's interface is based on a desktop metaphor. This distinction was introduced to allow cues to common knowledge to be shown in Mpathy – each participant has their own timeline on which their actions are represented relative to other participants' actions so providing a representation of the public events so far in chronological order. We argue that the improved collaboration we observed with users of Mpathy is not a product of the explicit representation of time in the interface, but rather a product of the representation of participants' activities (cues to common knowledge). This is because compared to Npathy's desktop interface, the timeline is extremely restrictive in the following ways which may negatively affect user performance:

- The length of the work (14 days) meant that a lot of objects (documents, memos, and annotations) were produced (average: 41.5). Users of the timeline interface would have to perform substantial scrolling to see all the documents produced as a typical window could only show about 10 documents at a time). Moreover, the cognitive load placed on users as they scroll to find documents whilst remembering where other documents is much higher than in the desktop interface of Npathy where all documents can be seen on one screen.
- The ordering of the documents in the timeline is not under user control, and it is not possible to move documents. Documents are ordered strictly by time in Mpathy's interface, whereas users may group the documents as they

see fit in Npathy. It could be argued that this violates basic HCI guidelines such as supporting user control. This may also account for the slightly larger proportion of topics concerning the System functionality with Mpathy – users may have been confused to some extent when trying to impose an ordering or grouping on the documents e.g. *"just testing to see if the system permits me to change the date"*. However, regardless of the usability of the timeline interface, it remains the case that Mpathy encouraged more collaboration than a conventional desktop metaphor primarily because of the third order cues to common knowledge embodied in the interface.

Considerations

This study focused on a very particular form of collaboration: asynchronous collaboration involving discussion and development of a single joint artifact. Whilst we believe that the notion of grounding, and the importance of providing cues to common knowledge is fundamental to understanding and supporting collaboration, we believe that other forms of collaboration need to be assessed in other domains e.g. synchronous negotiation activities as discussed by Clark (1996).

As discussed previously, the means of providing 3rd order cues to common knowledge was the timeline representation. This design allowed us to lay out all the events over time and show who had read contributions, but may have had some usability issues. In order to further strengthen our claims we need to assess other means of providing such cues as the effectiveness of such representations may vary with the nature of the collaboration. For instance, there may be novel ways to augment a more conventional desktop metaphor with indicators of who has read and accessed documents using 3 dimensional representations of the state of collaborative activity.

In the course of this study we collected a rich set of data which has much potential for further analysis. For example, we could analyze whether there is a difference in the amount of breakdown and repair that occurs in the two systems. We would expect that there would be more breakdowns in Npathy than Mpathy due to the lack of common knowledge about the collaboration, and so increased likelihood of misunderstandings occurring. We might also attempt to assess whether document names are used more effectively in one interface than another. Although the analysis of topics of document content did not show any significant results in this study we believe that such analyzes could yield useful results in future studies, especially if more communication channels are made available to participants.

Conclusion

This paper set out to show that asynchronous collaboration benefits from extra cues to common knowledge. We argued that such cues increase participants ability to contribute and promotes more focused use of information within the collaborative environment. Such findings should be of great interest to designers and developers of collaborative support systems as well as people interested in the nature of collaboration. We intend to further our research by studying asynchronous collaboration in a wider range of domains, by developing more detailed explanations of the nature of collaboration, and by iteratively informing and refining the design of collaboration support.

Acknowledgments

This work is supported by EPSRC grant Engaging Collaborations GR/S81414/01, and previous work on the Mushroom project funded by EPSRC grants GR/L14602 (1996-97) and GR/L64300 (1998-2000).

References

Barwise. J. (1989): *The Situation in Logic*, CSLI Lecture Notes Number 17, Center for the Study of Language and Information, Stanford, CA, USA.

Brennan, S. (1998): 'The Grounding Problem in Conversations with and Through Computers', in S. R. Fussell, and R. J. Kreuz (eds.): *Social and cognitive approaches to interpersonal communication*. Mahwah: Lawrence Erlbaum Associates, 1998, pp. 201-225.

Bryan-Kinns, N., Healey, P. G. T., and Leach, J. (2007): 'Exploring Mutual Engagement in Creative Collaborations', in *Proceedings of Creativity and Cognition*, Washington DC, USA, 2007, pp. 223-232.

Clark, H. H. (1996): *Using Language*, Cambridge University Press.

Clark, H.H. and Brennan, S.E. (1991): 'Grounding in Communication', in L. B. Resnick, J. Levine, and S. D. Behrend (eds.): *Perspectives on Socially Shared Cognition*, Washington DC.: American Psychological Association, 1991, pp. 127-149.

Clark, H. H. and Marshall, C. R. (1981): 'Definite reference and mutual knowledge', in A. K. Joshi, B. Webber, and I. Sag (eds.), *Elements of discourse understanding*, Cambridge: Cambridge University Press, 1981, pp. 10-63.

Dourish, P. and Bellotti, V. (1992): 'Awareness and Coordination in Shared Workspaces', in *Proceedings of ACM Conference on Computer-Supported Cooperative Work (CSCW'92)*, Toronto, Canada, 1992, pp. 107-114.

Gutwin, C. and Greenberg, S. (2002): 'A Descriptive Framework of Workspace Awareness for Real-Time Groupware', *Computer Supported Cooperative Work*, vol. 11, pp. 411-446.

Healey, P. G. T. and Bryan-Kinns, N. (2000): 'Analysing Asynchronous Collaboration', in *Proceedings of HCI 2000*, Sunderland, UK, 2000, pp. 239-254.

Hutchins, E. and Klausen, T. (1996): 'Distributed Cognition in an Airline Cockpit', in D. Middleton and Y. Engeström (eds.): *Communication and Cognition at Work*, Cambridge: Cambridge University Press, 1996, pp. 15-34.

Issroff, K. and Scanlon, E. (2002): 'Using technology in Higher Education: an Activity Theory perspective', *Journal of Computer Assisted Learning*, vol. 18, 2002, pp. 77-83.

Johnson, H. and Hyde, J. (2003): 'Towards Modeling Individual and Collaborative Construction of Jigsaws Using Task Knowledge Structures (TKS)', *ACM Transactions on CHI, vol. 10, no. 4*, December 2003, pp 339–387.

Kindberg, T., Coulouris, G., Dollimore, J., and Heikkinen, J. (1996): 'Sharing objects over the Internet: the Mushroom approach', in *Proceedings of IEEE Global Internet 96*, London, UK, November 1996, pp. 67-71.

Kindberg, T., Bryan-Kinns, N., and Makwana, R. (1999): 'Supporting the Shared Care of Diabetic Patients', in *Proceedings of ACM GROUP '99*, Phoenix, Arizona, 1999, pp. 91-100.

Koschmann, T. and LeBaron, C. D. (2003): 'Reconsidering Common Ground: Examining Clark's Contribution Theory in the OR', in *Proceedings of ECSCW 2003*, Helsinki, Finland, 2003, pp. 81-98.

Olson, J. S., Olson, G. M., Storrøsten, M., and Carter, M. (1993): 'GroupWork close up: A comparison of the Group Design Process With and Without a Simple Group Editor', *ACM Transactions cm Information Systems*, vol. 11, no. 4, 1993, pp. 321-348.

Robertson, T. (1997): 'Cooperative Work and Lived Cognition: A Taxonomy of Embodied Actions', in *Proceedings of ECSCW 1997*, Lancaster, UK, 1997, pp. 205-220.

Watts, L. A. and Monk, A. F. (1998): 'Reasoning about tasks, activities and technology to support collaboration', *Ergonomics*, vol. 41, no. 11, 1998, pp. 1583-1606.

Index of Authors